THE CONSERVATION ATLAS
OF
TROPICAL FORESTS

THE AMERICAS

Contributors

CELESTE ACEVEDO, Fundación Moisés Bertoni, Asunción, Paraguay

DENIS ADAMS, Natural History Museum, London, UK

MARK ALDRICH, Cambridge, UK

JAVIER ARCE, Fundación Peruana de Conservación de la Naturaleza, Lima, Peru

ROBERTO ARAQUISTAIN, Director Forestal SFN-IRENA, Managua, Nicaragua

STEVE BASS, IIED, London, UK

NEIL BIRD, Belize Forest Planning and Management Project, Belmopan, Belize

RICHARD O. BIERREGAARD, JR., Smithsonian Institution, Washington, USA

TIM BOYLE, CIFOR, Bogor, Indonesia

ROBERT BROWN, Georgetown, Guyana

GERARDO BUDOWSKI, San José, Costa Rica

LISA BURLEY, IUCN-South America, Quito, Ecuador

JOHN BURTON, Programme for Belize, Saxmundham, Suffolk, UK

JORGE CASTIGLIONE, ORCA, San José, Costa Rica

GUILLERMO CASTILLEJA, WWF-US, Washington, USA

LUIS H. ELIZONDA CASTILLO, INBio, San José, Costa Rica

BRUCE CABARLE, WRI, Washington, USA

DAN CHALMERS, Taverham, Norfolk, UK

GRAHAM CHAPLIN, CONSEFORH, Siguatepeque, Honduras

ROB CLAY, BirdLife International, Cambridge, UK

DAVID CLEARY, Centre of Latin American Studies, Cambridge University, Cambridge, UK

MARCUS COLCHESTER, World Rainforest Movement, Oxford, UK

NIGEL COLLAR, BirdLife International, Cambridge, UK

JIM CRISP, President, Monteverde Conservation League, Costa Rica

MIKE CROSBY, BirdLife International, Cambridge, UK

STEPHEN DAVIS, Kew, Surrey, UK

ALONSO MATAMOROS DELGADO, San José, Costa Rica

MARK DILLENBECK, IUCN-US, Washington, USA

CHARLES DOUMENGE, IUCN, Gland, Switzerland

MARC DOUROJEANNI, Inter American Development Bank, Washington, USA

GILES D'SOUZA, TREES, EC-Joint Research Center, Ispra, Italy

RODRIGO DUNO, BIOMA representative, Reading, UK

MARIA JOSÉ DURAN, Fundación Pro-Sierra Nevada de Sante Marta, Colombia

MICHAEL EDEN, Royal Holloway and Bedford College, London, UK

SUSAN EGGEN-MCINTOSH, USDA/Southern Forest Experiment Station, New Orleans, USA

DAVID EVANS, USDA/Southern Forest Experiment Station, New Orleans, USA

PHILIP FEARNSIDE, INPA, Manaus, Brazil

JULIO FIGUEROA COLON, International Institute of Tropical Forestry, Rio Piedras, Puerto Rico

JENNIFER FOX, CDC-Paraguay, Asunción, Paraguay

WILFREDO FRANCO, Centro Amazónico de Investigaciones Ambientales Alexander von Humboldt, SADA-AMAZONAS, Caracas, Venezuela

RAUL GAUTO, Fundación Moisés Bertoni, Asunción, Paraguay

THE late ALWYN GENTRY, Missouri Botanical Garden, St Louis, Missouri, USA

FERNANDO GHERSI, IUCN, Gland, Switzerland

MARIANO GIMENEZ-DIXON, IUCN, Gland, Switzerland

JUAN CARLOS GODOY, IUCN, Guatemala City, Guatemala

JEAN-JACQUES DE GRANVILLE, ORSTOM, Cayenne, French Guiana

N.R. DE GRAFF, Wageningen Agricultural University, Wageningen, The Netherlands

DAVID GRAY, Belize Forest Planning and Management Project, Belmopan, Belize

CHARLES HALL, Syracuse University, Syracuse, USA

PAT HALPIN, University of Virginia, Charlottesville, USA

SYLVIA HARCOURT CARRASCO, Charles Darwin Foundation, Quito, Ecuador

JERRY HARRISON, WCMC, Cambridge, UK

GARY HARTSHORN, WWF-US, Washington, USA

ALAN HAMILTON, WWF-UK, Godalming, UK

JOHN HEMMING, Royal Geographical Society, London, UK

JORGE HERNANDEZ, INDERENA, Bogotá, Colombia

OLGA HERRERA-MACBRYDE, Smithsonian Institution, Washington, USA

HENRY HOOGHIEMSTRA, Hugo de Vries Laboratory, University of Amsterdam, Amsterdam, The Netherlands

DIETER HOENER, Servicio Alemán, Santo Domingo, Dominican Republic

STEVEN HUGH-JONES, Cambridge University, Cambridge, UK

OTTO HUBER, Fundacion Instituto Botánico de Venezuela, Caracas, Venezuela

SUSAN IREMONGER, The Nature Conservancy, Arlington, USA

MARTIN JENKINS, Cambridge, UK

M. JOHNSTON, GAHEF, Georgetown, Guyana

W.B.J. JONKERS, Wageningen Agricultural University, Wageningen, The Netherlands

CHARLES KENNY-JORDON, Desarollo Forestal Participativo en los Andes, FAO, Quito

BRYAN KERR, Commonwealth Secretariat, London, UK

BRUCE KING, Land Information Centre, Belmopan, Belize

ERIK M. LAMMERTS VAN BUEREN, The Tropenbos Foundation, Wageningen, The Netherlands

ADRIAN LONG, BirdLife International, Cambridge, UK

JAMES LOWEN, BirdLife International, Cambridge, UK

MARIA MARCONI, CDC-Bolivia, La Paz, Bolivia

JEFF MCNEELY, IUCN, Gland, Switzerland

CRAIG MCFARLAND, President, Charles Darwin Foundation, Moscow, USA

JAIME MELO P., Universidad Nacional Agraria - La Molina, Lima, Peru

DOUG MUCHONEY, The Nature Conservancy, Arlington, USA

JULIO RUIZ MURRIETA, IUCN, Gland, Switzerland

CHARLES C. MUELLER, University of Illinois, Urbana, Illinois, USA

LISA NAUGHTON, Program for Studies in Tropical Conservation, Florida University, Gainesville, USA

JEREMY NARBY, Moudon, Switzerland

NAMIKO NAGASHIRO, CDC-Bolivia, La Paz, Bolivia

JOSÉ PEDRO DE OLIVEIRA COSTA, IUCN, Sao Paulo, Brasil

JOSE OTTENWALDER, Florida Museum of Natural History, Gainesville, USA

GRACIELA PALACIOS S., ANCON, Panama City, Panama

HELIODORO SANCHEZ PAEZ, INDERENA, Bogotá, Colombia

JOHN PALMER, Oxford, UK

SILVIA PARDI, BIOMA, Caracas, Venezuela

PAUL PARYSKI, UNDP, Port-au-Prince, Haiti

A.M. POLAK, University of Utrecht, Utrecht, The Netherlands

ERNESTO PONCE, CONSEFORH, Siguatepeque, Honduras

GHILLEAN PRANCE, Royal Botanic Gardens, Kew, Surrey, UK

MAARIT PUHAKKA, Department of Biology, University of Turku, Turku, Finland

ROSARIO ORTIZ QUIJANO, Fundacion Pro-Sierra Nevada de Sante Marta, Colombia

C.R. QUIROA, IUCN, Guatemala City, Guatemala

ERNESTO RAEZ LUNA, Program for Studies in Tropical Conservation, Florida University, Gainesville, USA

KENT H. REDFORD, Program for Studies in Tropical Conservation, Florida University, Gainesville, USA

HENK REMME, Desarollo Forestal Participativa en los Andes, FAO, Quito, Ecuador

JOSE FLORES RODAS, ORCA, San José, Costa Rica

JOSÉ CARLOS RODRIGUEZ GRAU, BIOMA, Caracas, Venezuela

ALDEMARO ROMERO, BIOMA, Caracas, Venezuela

KALLE RUOKOLAINEN, Department of Biology, University of Turku, Turku, Finland

MARCOS SANJURJO, Fundación Moisés Bertoni, Asunción, Paraguay

DANIEL SABATIER, Sauve, France

ANDREAS SCHUBERT, Servicio Alemán, Santo Domingo, Dominican Republic

F.N SCATENA, International Institute of Tropical Forestry, Rio Piedras, Puerto Rico

CHARLES SECRETT, FoE, London, UK

CHRIS SHARPE, Protected Areas Data Unit, WCMC, Cambridge, UK

NIGEL SIZER, World Resources Institute, Washington, USA

CLAUDIA SOBREVILA, The Nature Conservancy, Arlington, USA

CLAIRE SORENSON, USAID, Washington, USA

JAMES SOLOMON, Missouri Botanical Garden, St Louis, Missouri, USA

ALISON STATTERSFIELD, BirdLife International, Cambridge, UK

BOB STYLES, Department of Plant Sciences, University of Oxford, Oxford, UK

LUIS SUAREZ, EcoCiencia/WCI-NYZS, Quito, Ecuador

GUSTAVO SUAREZ DE FREITAS C., Fundación Peruana de Conservación de la Naturaleza, Lima, Peru

BYRON SWIFT, IUCN-US, Washington, USA

PAOLA SYLVA, Directora Area de Investigación, Centro de Educación y Promocion Popular, Ecuador

ED TANNER, The Botany School, University of Cambridge, Cambridge, UK

JIM THORSELL, IUCN, Gland, Switzerland

HERNAN TORRES, Corporación, Nacional Forestal, Chile

CARLOS CASTAÑO URIBE, INDERENA, Bogotá, Colombia

THOMAS VAN DER HAMMEN, Hugo de Vries Laboratory, University of Amsterdam, Amsterdam, The Netherlands

VIRGINIA VASQUEZ, Belize Audubon Society, Belize City, Belize

W. VEENING, European Working Group in Amazonia, Amsterdam, The Netherlands

JANE VILLA-LOBOS, Smithsonian Institution, Washington, USA

FRANK WADSWORTH, Southern Forest Experiment Station, Rio Piedras, Puerto Rico

P.L. WEAVER, International Institute of Tropical Forestry, Rio Piedras, Puerto Rico

MARGA WERKHOVEN, National Herbarium of Suriname, Paramaribo, Suriname

DAVID WEGE, BirdLife International, Cambridge, UK

PADRAIG WHELAN, Investigator, Chales Darwin Research Station, Galapagos, Ecuador

CHARLES WOODS, Florida Museum of Natural History, Gainesville, USA

THE CONSERVATION ATLAS OF TROPICAL FORESTS

THE AMERICAS

Editors

CAROLINE S. HARCOURT

World Conservation Monitoring Centre, Cambridge, UK

JEFFREY A. SAYER

IUCN — The World Conservation Union, Gland, Switzerland
Center for International Forestry Research, Bogor, Indonesia

Map Editor and Editorial Assistant: Clare Billington

World Conservation Monitoring Centre, Cambridge, UK

Simon & Schuster

New York • London • Toronto • Sydney • Tokyo • Singapore

ACKNOWLEDGEMENTS

This Atlas was produced under the Forest Conservation Programme of IUCN, The World Conservation Union. IUCN's work in tropical forests receives financial support from the government of Sweden. Most of the research and editing and the map preparation was done at the World Conservation Monitoring Centre (WCMC), which is supported by IUCN, The World Wide Fund for Nature (WWF) and the United Nations Environment Programme (UNEP); the Centre is also part of UNEP's Global Environment Monitoring System, towards which this Atlas is a contribution.

IUCN is especially indebted to The British Petroleum Company p.l.c. for the original idea for the Atlas and for the generous funding which enabled the research for the project to be undertaken.

Thanks also go to Sun Microsystems Inc. and IBM, for computer donations which were used for running the Geographic Information System (GIS) at WCMC needed to compile the maps, and to the Environmental Systems Research Institute (ESRI) of California, who donated the ARC/INFO software for the project. Petroconsultants Ltd of Cambridge kindly made available 'MundoCart', a world digital mapping database which proved invaluable in the preparation of this Atlas.

Thanks are due to the many authors and contributors to this Atlas, both those listed in this publication and the many unnamed people whose work is essential for the production of a book such as this.

The editors would also like to thank all their colleagues at WCMC, IUCN and CIFOR without whose work this project would not have been possible. Particular thanks are due to the following staff at WCMC: Corinna Ravilious, Simon Blyth, Gillian Bunting, Mary Edwards and Jonathan Rhind for help with the maps and Barbara Brown, Brian Groombridge, Martin Jenkins, Richard Luxmoore, Jim Paine and Chris Sharpe for much appreciated, varied assistance. At IUCN, invaluable help was provided by Jill Blockhus and Ursula Senn.

Copyright © IUCN 1996

Macmillan Library Reference USA
Simon & Schuster Macmillan
866 Third Avenue
New York, NY 10022

Printed in Singapore

Printing number
1 2 3 4 5 6 7 8 9 10

Library of Congress Cataloging-in-Publication Data
The conservation atlas of tropical forests: the Americas/the World Conservation Union;
editors Caroline S. Harcourt, Jeffrey A. Sayer; map editor Clare Billington.
p. cm.
"Copyright IUCN" – Verso t.p.
Includes bibliographical references, glossary and index.
Contents: The issues – Country studies.
ISBN 0-13-340886-8 (lib. bdg.)
1. Rain forests – America – Maps. 2.Man – Influence on nature – America – Maps.
3. Conservation of natural resources – America – Maps.
I. Harcourt, Caroline. II. International Union for Conservation of
Nature and Natural Resources.
G1101.K3C6 1995   333.75'16'0728022 --dc20

This paper meets the requirements of ANSI/NISO Z39.48-1992 (Permanence of Paper).

ISBN 0-13-340886-8

Acknowledgement of Sources
The sources of the country maps are given at the end of each chapter.
The sources of the illustrations and sketch maps are given in footnotes and captions.
The designations of geographical entities in this book, and the presentation of the
material, do not imply the expression of any opinion whatsoever on the part of WCMC
or other participating organisations concerning the legal status of any country, territory,
or area, or of its authorities, or concerning the delimitation of its frontiers or boundaries.
The views of the authors expressed in this publication do not necessarily reflect those of
WCMC or other participating organisations. Printed and bound in Singapore.

Contents

Foreword

The threats to the rainforests of tropical America have been at the centre of international environmental concerns now for a couple of decades. Yet the material in this up-to-date and authoritative atlas highlights the continuing extent of scientific uncertainty over the critical issues that will determine the future use and conservation of the forests. We learn that the forests were radically different under the drier climates that prevailed as recently as 10,000 years ago, and that human populations have had a major impact on the forests since much earlier. We learn too that the population of Amazonia may have been higher when the first Spanish explorers arrived, than in the middle of the 20th Century. The present biological diversity of the forests has evolved in an environment constantly subject to modification due to human activities and changes in climate. And today, the ability of the forests and their biodiversity to resist the activities of extractivists (or even selective loggers) remains unclear.

This atlas will not finally lay to rest the controversy over the rate at which tropical American forests are being attacked. Uncertainty will persist. In spite of the sophistication of modern remote sensing technology there are still major discrepancies between estimates of forest area and rates of loss derived from different sources. Much of this uncertainty stems from a tendency to over-simplify the processes going on in the forests. In most situations we are not dealing with an abrupt change from forest to non-forest. We are dealing with a gradual insidious degradation resulting from abusive harvesting of some of the forest components, or — more frequently — from the progressive expansion of low-intensity agriculture. It is relatively easy to measure the areas from which the forest has disappeared completely; it is much more difficult to measure the impact of gradual deterioration on species-poor or scrubland situations. It is reassuring to see that much of the forest in the heart of Amazonia is still intact; it is alarming to see the extent to which the forests on the periphery of the region have been devastated. The implications for the conservation of biodiversity and ecological functions are far more complex than might be implied by the popular vision of an across-the-board loss of so many football fields a day.

If understanding of the biophysical processes in the forests is limited, that of the social and economic issues is even more problematic. Much more work clearly needs to be done if governments are to understand properly the impacts of their macro-economic policies on their forests. Is economic growth good for the forests or bad? As timber resources in Asia and Africa decline, will the industry turn to South America? Is this a potential threat to the forests or is it an opportunity to conserve them as an economically valuable resource? Will the development of major food exporting industries in the region generate the wealth which will pay to conserve the forests or will it lead to further fragmentation and degradation?

Not all is uncertain or unsettling. Certain facts which emerge from this book give grounds for optimism. The population of South America will stabilise sooner — and at a lower density — than the populations of Africa and tropical Asia. There will be far more land per capita when this equilibrium is reached than there will be in the other regions. The level of concern for forest conservation issues in the region is high and growing fast. This is manifest, for example, in the rapidly growing number of members of IUCN — The World Conservation Union in the region and in the intensity and quality of their contributions to the Union's work. There is room in the Americas for both economic development and large scale conservation of natural habitats. The value of these natural areas, particularly the forests, is increasingly recognised by the international community. If appropriate financial mechanisms can be refined, we may not be too far from the days when the world can begin to make equitable payment for the benefits that we all derive from tropical forests.

The United Nations Commission on Sustainable Development has assumed some responsibility for — and resumed its deliberations on — the future of our forests. I trust that this will yield some progress in making the world's attempts to conserve forests more cohesive and effective and that the facts and analysis in this atlas will contribute to the process.

DAVID MCDOWELL
Director General
IUCN — The World Conservation Union

PART I

1 Introduction

The countries covered in this Atlas — those in the Caribbean, Central America (including Mexico) and South America — hold over half of the world's tropical forests; they have considerably more forest than either Africa or Asia and the Pacific. Nevertheless, this rather favourable general picture requires qualification. Although very large areas of the forest in the Amazon and Orinoco basins have been little changed during the present century, there are regions on the southern and eastern borders of Amazonia, on the Pacific coasts of Ecuador and Colombia and many locations in Central America and the Caribbean that have suffered devastating deforestation in recent decades, whilst the Atlantic coastal forest in Brazil was already depleted well before the beginning of this century.

The area of forest cleared each year in The Americas is also considerably higher than in Africa or Asia and the Pacific, although the annual percentage cleared in the Americas is exceeded by that in Asia. The causes of deforestation are many and varied, although, in contrast to the situation in Africa and Asia, the overriding direct cause in recent years has been the extension of the agricultural frontier for large-scale farming and ranching operations. These and other problems are discussed in more detail in Chapters 2–9, while separate analyses for each country are provided in Chapters 10–33.

Forest Cover in Latin America and the Caribbean as Estimated by FAO

FAO has recently updated estimates of forest cover in all countries in the tropical region and published them in a report entitled *Forest resources assessment 1990: Tropical countries* (FAO, 1993). However, unlike in the publication used in the earlier two volumes of this series of Atlases (*An Interim Report on the State of Forest Resources in the Developing Countries –* FAO, 1988) which gave estimates for forest cover in 1980, the forests are not divided into open and closed broadleaved forests, nor are figures given for conifer or bamboo forests. The estimates given by FAO (1993) are for all forests with a canopy cover of more than 10 per cent within six different ecofloristic zones (Table 1.1). FAO (1993), however, give no detailed descriptions of the different forest formations or of the zones in which they occur. In this Atlas, as for the other two, the intention is to map closed formations only. For this reason, the FAO estimate of forest area given at the head of each chapter includes the areas of forests within only the tropical rain forest zone, the moist deciduous forest zone and the hill and montane zone of Table 1.1. The much drier and apparently more open formations in the other categories given by FAO have been excluded.

The countries that FAO includes in each region and the areas

of forest that occur within them are listed in Table 1.1. These countries are the same as those covered in this Atlas, except that the Bahamas has not been included here as it is outside the tropics. The regional grouping of the countries is, however, different. The Guianas are included in South America in this Atlas, whereas FAO includes them with the Caribbean countries.

Including all forests with a canopy cover of 10 per cent or more, it is estimated by FAO (1993) that, as of 1990, forest cover in Latin America and the Caribbean is 918 million ha (9,181,160 sq. km in Table 1.1) or 52 per cent of the total tropical forest area. Of this, the vast majority (8,029,040 sq. km or 87.5 per cent) is in South America, with 70 per cent of that in Brazil, while only 471,150 sq. km or 5.1 per cent is in the Caribbean and 680,970 sq. km or 7.4 per cent is in Central America. Calculating the area of forest within the three ecofloristic zones considered here gives a figure of 8,700,000 sq. km of forest in Latin America and the Caribbean (Table 7 in FAO, 1993).

Although estimates for closed broadleaved forests are given in FAO's *Forest resources assessment 1990: Tropical countries*, those in Latin America and the Caribbean are referred to in this publication only in Table 5c, entitled "state of logging 1990". Here it is indicated that this forest type covers 6,683,670 sq. km in Latin America and the Caribbean. However, some countries (El Salvador, Antigua/Barbuda, Dominica, Grenada, St. Kitts/Nevis, St Lucia, St Vincent and Puerto Rico) have been omitted from the list and it is unclear whether this is because they are considered to have no closed broadleaved forest or because no logging takes place in them. The estimates of closed broadleaved forest cover from Table 5c (FAO, 1993) are given here in Table 1.2.

FAO (1993) gives estimates for annual deforestation in the tropics between the years of 1981 and 1990. In Latin America and the Caribbean as a whole, average annual deforestation during the last decade (1981–1990) in all formations was 74,000 sq. km (0.8 per cent). Almost 50 per cent of this occurred in Brazil. It should be noted, that the figure given for annual deforestation at the head of each country chapter excludes clearing in the dry formations.

FAO's Estimates of Forest Cover in Africa and Asia and the Pacific

It seems appropriate in this final volume in the series *The Conservation Atlas of Tropical Forests*, to give a brief account of the recent FAO (1993) statistics for forest area in the regions covered in the earlier volumes (Collins *et al.*, 1991, Sayer *et al.*, 1992) as a comparison with those given here for Latin America and the Caribbean.

Table 1.1   Area of forest formations in Latin America and the Caribbean in 1990 as reported by FAO

FOREST FORMATION

Country	Total forest (sq. km)	Tropical rain forest zone (sq. km)	Moist deciduous forest zone (sq. km)	Dry deciduous forest zone (sq. km)	Very dry forest zone (sq. km)	Desert zone (cold/hot) (sq. km)	Hill and montane (sq. km)
Costa Rica	14,280	6,250	0	0	0	0	8,020
El Salvador	1,230	330	120	0	0	0	790
Guatemala	42,250	25,420	16,150	0	0	0	690
Honduras	46,050	12,860	4,370	0	0	0	28,820
Mexico	485,860	24,410	111,100	15,900	7,590	14,240	312,610
Nicaragua	60,130	37,120	3,480	0	0	0	19,530
Panama	31,170	18,020	670	0	0	0	12,490
CENTRAL AMERICA	680,970	124,400	135,880	15,900	7,590	14,240	382,940
Antigua/Barbuda	100	0	100	0	0	0	0
Bahamas	1,860	0	1,240	470	50	40	60
Belize	19,960	19,570	390	0	0	0	160
Cuba	17,150	1,140	12,470	20	0	0	3,520
Dominica	440	440	0	0	0	0	0
Dominican Rep.	10,770	3,410	2,730	0	0	0	4,630
French Guyana	79,970	79,930	30	0	0	0	0
Grenada	60	0	60	0	0	0	0
Guadeloupe	930	930	0	0	0	0	0
Guyana	184,160	133,370	31,670	0	0	0	19,120
Haiti	230	50	90	0	0	0	100
Jamaica	2,390	1,220	1,130	0	0	0	30
Martinique	430	430	0	0	0	0	0
Puerto Rico	3,210	490	1,510	0	0	0	1,210
St Kitts/Nevis	130	0	130	0	0	0	0
St Lucia	50	50	0	0	0	0	0
St Vincent	110	100	0	0	0	0	0
Surinam	147,680	114,400	33,280	0	0	0	0
Trinidad/Tobago	1,550	1,550	0	0	0	0	0
CARIBBEAN	471,150	357,070	84,830	490	50	40	28,670
Bolivia	493,170	0	355,820	73,460	0	40	63,850
Brazil	5,611,070	2,915,970	1,970,820	288,630	0	0	435,650
Colombia	540,640	474,550	41,010	180	0	0	24,900
Ecuador	119,620	71,500	16,690	440	0	0	31,000
Paraguay	128,590	0	60,370	67,940	0	0	270
Peru	679,060	403,580	122,990	190	2,690	1,840	147,770
Venezuela	456,910	196,020	154,650	2,220	120	0	103,900
SOUTH AMERICA	8,029,040	4,061,620	2,722,350	433,040	2,820	1,880	807,340
Total	9,181,160	4,543,090	2,943,060	449,440	10,450	16,160	1,218,950

Numbers may not tally due to rounding – these figures are taken directly from Table 7c in FAO (1993) but have been converted from ha to sq. km.
(*Source:* FAO 1993)

Total forest cover in Africa as of 1990 is 5,280,000 sq. km (30 per cent of the world's total) and in Asia and the Pacific there are 3,110,000 sq. km (18 per cent). Considering only the three zones covered in the country chapters of this Atlas, the cover in Africa is 3,730,000 sq. km and that in Asia and the Pacific is 2,660,000 sq. km. The figures given for closed broadleaved forests in the *state of logging* tables in FAO 1993 (Tables 5a and 5b respectively) are 2,046,030 sq. km for Africa and 2,342,310 sq. km for Asia and the Pacific.

Average annual deforestation in all formations during the last decade (1981–1990) is estimated to be 41,000 sq. km (0.7 per cent) in Africa and 39,000 sq. km (1.2 per cent) in Asia and the Pacific.

Geographic Boundaries
The Atlas includes all countries within South and Central America and the Caribbean lying entirely or mostly between the tropics of Capricorn and Cancer. For example, Mexico is included as at least half of its area is south of the Tropic of Cancer, but Argentina and Chile are excluded as only a tiny proportion of these countries lies within the tropics. Obviously these lines are totally arbitrary as far as changes in the floristic composition and structure of the forest go, but as noted above, all but one of the countries included by FAO in its recent project to assess forest cover in tropical countries (FAO, 1993) have been covered here.

Forests of the Region

The forests covered in this Atlas stretch from Mexico in the north, down through the isthmus of Central America, to the Pacific countries of Colombia, Ecuador and Peru; across to Venezuela, Guyana, French Guiana and Surinam; through the huge Amazon forest and into others in Brazil; and onto the landlocked countries of Bolivia and Paraguay. Also covered are the tropical forests throughout the islands of the Caribbean. The area covered is vast, comprising 32 countries, with a very varied relief and climate. This has resulted in a great diversity of forest types and a wide array of species of both flora and fauna.

The forest types of Central and South America and the Caribbean vary from rain forest, occurring where there is no or virtually no dry season, such as in southeastern Colombia, to arid vegetation types where there is a very strong dry season, such as the caatinga of northeastern Brazil and the thorn scrub of northern Venezuela (Haffer, 1987).

Relief and Climate

The Amazon Basin lies at less than 200 m above sea-level and flat, or gently rolling lowlands stretch from the eastern slopes of the Andes to the Atlantic coast. In contrast, the Andean Range tracks down the western side of the southern continent reaching more than 6500 m above sea-level in Peru and Bolivia. In northern Ecuador, the Andes split in two (the Cordillera Occidental and Cordillera Central). A third Cordillera (Oriental) emerges in the east, in northeastern Colombia, running through northern Venezuela along the coast of the Caribbean to Trinidad. The llanos lowlands of eastern Colombia and Venezuela are separated from the Amazonian lowlands by the Guiana Shield which extends from the middle of the Guianas and southern Venezuela into southeastern Colombia (Haffer, 1987 — see Figure 1.1). Central America comprises a central backbone of mountains with lowlands along the Pacific and Caribbean coasts. The Caribbean islands are a mixture of continental, high volcanic and low limestone islands. The first two categories have varied and often steep topography, though all below 3200 m; the last, which have little rainforest, are flat and generally arid.

Climate is also varied. Western Amazonia from the Andes to the lower Rio Negro, and the Pacific lowlands of Colombia have a warm, perhumid climate with two seasons of marginally reduced rainfall. Easterly trade winds carry moisture from the Atlantic Ocean and transfer it to the eastern slopes of the mountains from Mexico, through northern South America, to Brazil. A humid climate extends from northwestern Colombia along the Caribbean slope of Central America north to southern Mexico. The Pacific slope of Central America is mostly dry. A reduced annual precipitation and a definite dry season are characteristic of the seasonal climate found in northern and central South America surrounding humid Amazonia. A dry tropical climate is found in the Caribbean lowlands of northern Venezuela and in northeastern Brazil; the narrow Pacific coastal lowlands from southwestern Ecuador south are also arid. The Caribbean islands have an oceanic climate, heavily influenced by the moisture-laden trade winds. They are within the hurricane belt, which has a significant influence on the structure of the forests.

A number of different soil types occur under Neotropical forests — each helping to support a distinct and recognizable type of vegetation. For further information see chapters in Whitmore and Prance (1987).

Table 1.2 Area of Closed Broadleaved Forest in Latin America and the Caribbean as estimated by FAO

Country	Closed Broadleaved Forest (Area sq. km)
Costa Rica	13,010
Guatemala	39,460
Honduras	24,060
Mexico	81,770
Nicaragua	47,380
Panama	31,170
CENTRAL AMERICA	236,850
Belize	18,680
Cuba	17,150
Dominican Rep.	8,540
French Guyana	79,250
Guadeloupe	930
Guyana	181,950
Haiti	180
Jamaica	2,390
Martinique	430
Surinam	146,050
Trinidad/Tobago	1,550
CARIBBEAN	457,090
Bolivia	407,850
Brazil	3,871,210
Colombia	497,930
Ecuador	117,710
Paraguay	26,490
Peru	662,820
Venezuela	405,730
TROPICAL S. AMERICA	5,989,740
Total	6,683,670

Numbers may not tally due to rounding – these figures are taken directly from Table 5c in FAO (1993), but have been converted from ha to sq. km.
(*Source:* FAO 1993)

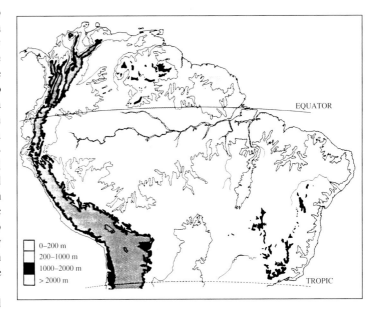

Figure 1.1 General relief map of tropical South America

(*Source:* Haffer, 1987)

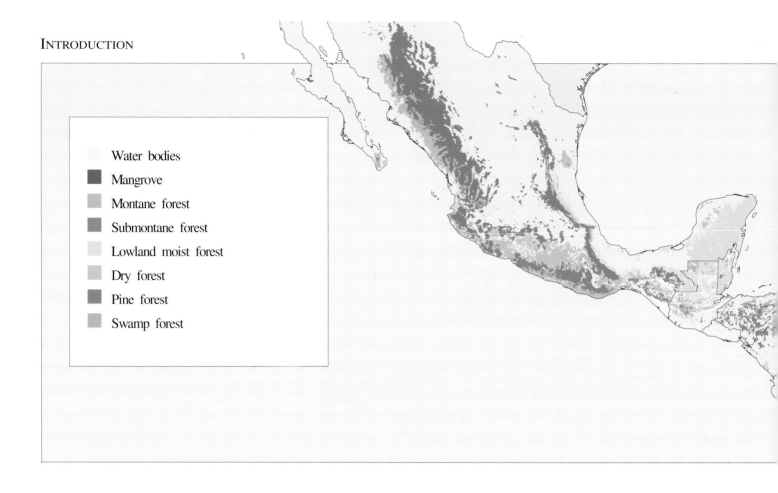

Figure 1.2 Extent of the forests shown in this Atlas, compiled from the country maps

Forest Cover

The closed forest formations that are discussed in the following country chapters comprise the lowland moist forests of the Amazon Basin, the Guianas, the Colombian Choco, the Brazilian Atlantic coastal forests and the Caribbean slope of Central America; the submontane and montane moist forests of the Andes, southern Venezuela and Central America; the extensive pine forests of Mexico, Guatemala, Honduras, Nicaragua and the Araucaria forests of southeastern Brazil; and the dry, mostly deciduous formations found along the Pacific coast, in central and southwestern Brazil, central and northern Venezuela and throughout Central America (mostly along the Pacific slope). Note that, although the very dry forests such as thorn scrub, caatinga, cerrado and chaco are found throughout the area within this study, these open formations are not mapped and are only touched on briefly within the country chapters. Moist and dry forest cover are also mapped for Cuba, Jamaica and Trinidad and overviews given for the Lesser Antilles and other Caribbean countries where no map data are available.

The extent of the forests illustrated in this Atlas are shown on Figure 1.2. This regional compilation comprises an amalgamation of the country maps shown in Chapters 10–33 and provides a regional overview of the forest remaining in the Americas.

Forest Classification

This Atlas, along with the other two in the series, attempts to achieve a synoptic view by combining the numerous forest formations depicted on country maps into broader classifications. In addition to the forest types in the previous two Atlases, submontane forests, seasonally dry forests and pine forests have

been mapped here because of their ecological importance.

The broad categories depicted in this Atlas are suited to the sub-regional working scales of 1:3 million mostly used here — this is not the place in which to find a detailed delimitation of the vast number of different forest formations, nor of their floristic composition. It must also be emphasised that although it is convenient for comparison to divide the forest types into major groups, the exact boundaries are somewhat arbitrary. In reality, natural vegetation types are rarely sharply bounded and transitional formations are frequent.

With the previous Atlases it was possible to relate forest cover to potential vegetation types, enabling the harmonisation of forest types into the broad classification. It has not been possible to take this approach here, as a potential classification relevant to South America, Central America and the Caribbean has not been obtained. It has, therefore, been more difficult to reconcile the different and complex forest categories used in the various national source maps and to compare and contrast across boundaries in the whole of the Americas.

To help with categorisation in South America, reference has been made to the Unesco classification (Unesco, 1981), which is based on mean annual rainfall, mean monthly temperature and mean annual number of dry months, dividing the continent into some twenty distinct climatic zones. For Central America, the Holdridge Life Zone System (Holdridge, 1967), a forest classification based on rainfall, temperature and altitude, has been applied to those countries, namely Costa Rica and Panama, where forest type information was unavailable or inadequate. In Central America, where montane forests were not demarcated in the source data, they were delimited by the 3000' (ca. 1000 m)

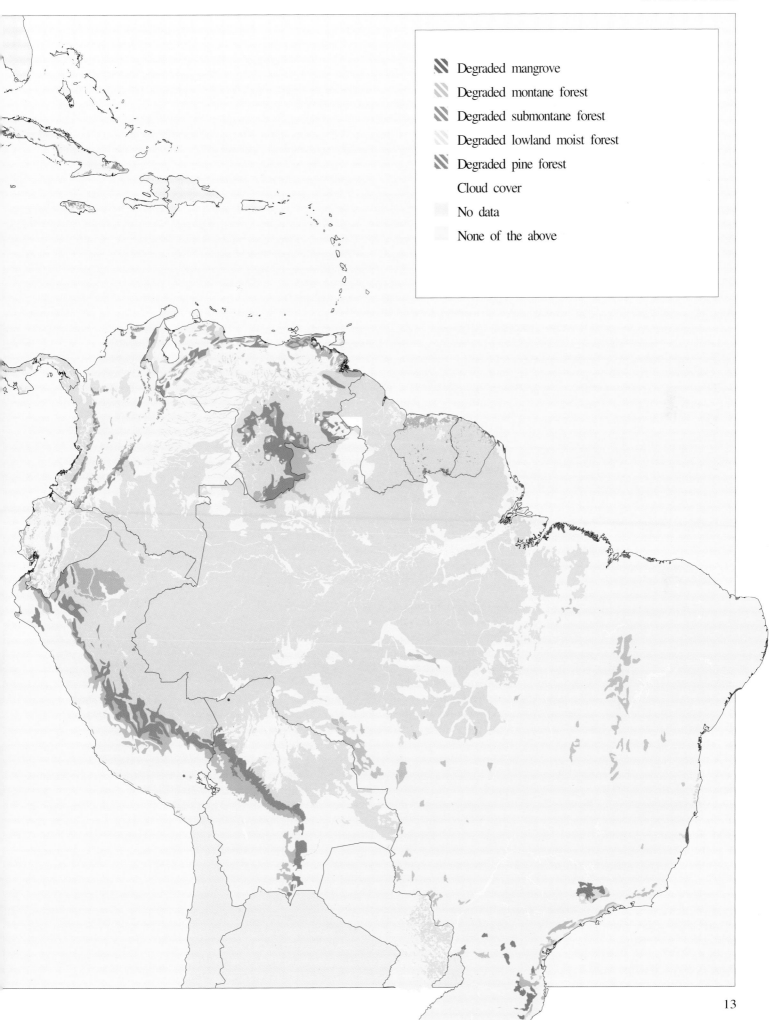

Degraded mangrove

Degraded montane forest

Degraded submontane forest

Degraded lowland moist forest

Degraded pine forest

Cloud cover

No data

None of the above

contour taken from the Digital Chart of the World, which is based on the Defense Mapping Agency Operational Navigation Charts at a scale of 1:1 million.

Although, no overriding potential classification has been rigidly adhered to, the categories attributed in the source maps have, on the whole, been followed meticulously. On only a few occasions has the information on the source maps been modified. For instance, a source map may have indicated that a particular stretch of forest was submontane and yet this has been shown on the Atlas Map as lowland (e.g. see Chapter 25). Where such modifications have been made, it has been on the basis of advice from independent reviewers within country and the sources of the changes are cited in the Map Legends. Indeed, the Map Legends in each country chapter, always give full descriptions of which forest types 'fit into' the broader classification depicted in this Atlas. The reader should also refer to the forest descriptions given in the country chapters.

Table 1.3 shows the major forest formations which have been grouped into the categories shown in this Atlas. The forest types shown on the Atlas Maps are italicised in the table. In some cases, degraded formations have also been shown on the Maps.

Issues which Affect Forests in the Americas

As in the other two Atlases in this series, the first part of this volume deals with subjects that are relevant to the region in general, rather than to particular countries, although several of the chapters concentrate on South America rather than including the Caribbean and Central America. In Chapter 2 the history of the forests in tropical South America is analysed by use of the pollen record. As in Africa, it is evident that there have been considerable changes in forest extent as the climate of the world has altered over time. During dry periods in the Quaternary, the forests were considerably less extensive than they are today. Recent work on the distribution and conservation of plants and birds are covered in Chapters 3 and 4 respectively. These chapters could be particularly valuable and timely in enabling the countries of the region to make informed decisions on the allocation of land for conservation purposes.

The following three chapters are more concerned with human activities within the forests. In Chapter 5, the ways in which the rich diversity of vertebrate fauna in the Neotropics has been affected by people is discussed. This chapter emphasises that the widely held assumption that a good community of trees is necessarily equivalent to a healthy fauna population is fallacious. The number of large forest-living vertebrates killed, even by indigenous hunters, can be enormous, and with modern weapons the numbers rise considerably, so that the forests can be left severely depleted of species. Chapter 6 outlines the history of human colonisation in The Americas and details the pressures imposed on the indigenous people, from as far back as the arrival of Europeans in the region 500 years ago, to the present day. Chapter 7 deals with the affects of the colonisation policies in the Amazonian countries of Brazil, Bolivia, Peru, Ecuador, Colombia and Venezuela. The final conclusion in this chapter is that the colonisation schemes in these countries have caused enormous social and environmental problems and have yielded only modest benefits.

Chapter 8 examines the protected areas in America. The conclusions of this chapter are, in general, quite optimistic. On the whole, the countries of the Americas have fairly extensive protected area systems, new areas are being added and legislation is good. Although the difficult economic conditions means that finance for and, consequently, management of, the areas is often

Table 1.3 Forest types shown on the Maps in this Atlas

DRYLAND MOIST FORESTS
Lowland moist forest
    tropical evergreen rain forest
    tropical semi-evergreen rain forest
    tropical semi-deciduous forest
    tropical humid forest
    tropical perhumid forest
    riverine/gallery forest
    evergreen seasonal forest
    semi-evergreen seasonal forest

Submontane forest
    lower montane moist forest
    lower montane wet forest
    lower montane rain forest

Montane forest
    montane wet forest
    montane rain forest
    cloud forest

DRYLAND DRY FORESTS
Dry forest
    dry deciduous forest
    xerophytic forest
    tropical dry forest
    dry evergreen forest
    dry semi-evergreen forest

Pine forest
    pine and oak forest
    oak and pine forest
    conifer forest

WETLAND MOIST FORESTS
Mangrove forest

Swamp forest
    palm swamp forest
    marsh forest

lacking, the conservation community, in both governmental and non-governmental organisations, is very concerned with the well-being of these areas.

In the concluding chapter on the future of forests in the Americas, it is suggested that, although it may be too late to save the forests in some of the smaller Caribbean and Central American countries, there is room in South America, at least, to conserve the forests and, with productive, sustainable and intensive agricultural practices, still have the expanding economy which is essential for the countries concerned.

We have tried to situate conservation initiatives in their broader political, social and economic context. The generally low demographic pressure, the potential of a vigorous private sector to drag South American economies out of their stagnation of recent decades and the long-awaited emergence of democratic processes in several important countries have all led us to conclude that prospects for the conservation and rational use of forests in the Neotropics are more favourable than prospects in Asia and Africa.

Country Studies

The country chapters in Part II of the Atlas follow the same format as those in the Asian and African volumes in examining the situation in each country in detail. As far as possible, the authors are nationals or long-term residents of the countries concerned. Where local authors could not be found, local perspectives have been reflected in the text by seeking reviewers within the country concerned. Many of the original texts were in Spanish or were written by people whose native language was not English. The editing, after translation, has therefore been a more complex process than for the Asian and African volumes. It is hoped, however, that the spirit of the original authors' contributions have been retained.

Basic statistics are provided at the head of each chapter. In this volume both country and land area are given — the latter excludes bodies of water in the country; these figures are from FAO (1989) — except for Guyana (see Chapter 29) and Surinam (see Chapter 32). It is the land area figure that is used in calculations such as per cent forest cover. Demographic and economic data are from the *1994 World Population Data Sheet* compiled by the Population Reference Bureau in Washington (PRB, 1994) or, in the case of French Guiana, the figures were supplied by PRB from their unpublished data. Forest cover statistics from FAO (1993) are compared with those measured from the Maps shown in this Atlas. However, as explained above, it is not always entirely clear if like is being compared with like as far as the definitions of forest goes. As in the African Atlas (Sayer *et al.*, 1992), for countries where source maps were very old or appeared to be particularly sketchy, statistics have not been derived from the Maps shown here as these would probably be misleading. Figures for annual deforestation are from FAO (1993), calculated for forest in the tropical rain forest, moist deciduous and hill and montane zones only. Forest product information is from the 1994 *FAO Yearbook: Forest Products* (FAO, 1994) and includes the following:

Industrial roundwood this is wood in the rough, i.e. in its natural state as felled or otherwise harvested. It includes wood removed from the outside, as well as inside, forests. The commodities included are sawlogs and veneer logs, pulpwood, other industrial roundwood and, in the case of trade, chips and particles and wood residues. The statistics include recorded volumes as well as estimated unrecorded volumes.

Fuelwood and charcoal both coniferous and non-coniferous wood are included.

Processed wood the figures given are aggregates of the figures in FAO (1994) for sawnwood and wood-based panels. The sawnwood may be planed or unplaned and it generally exceeds 5 mm in thickness. The wood-based panels include veneer sheets, plywood, particle board and fibreboard.

In cases where countries have not reported to FAO, the information supplied in the Yearbook has been taken from national yearbooks, from reports, from unofficial publications or has been estimated by FAO (FAO, 1994).

As in the other volumes, most chapters follow a standard format with a preliminary overview and an introduction giving general geographical, climatic, population and economic details; followed by a brief botanical description of the major forest formations. The following section reports on the management of the forests, and on the extent of forest in the country. As there are frequently discrepancies between the estimates of remaining forest given in the various sources used, an attempt is made to resolve the differences. They are frequently due to the use of different definitions of the term forest or to changes over time. Similar problems occur in the section on deforestation within the country. Number of vertebrate species and information on some of the threatened ones are generally given next, followed by information on the conservation areas within the country and, finally, reports of some initiatives to protect the forests and fauna are included.

Maps

Cartographic data for all the eighteen countries in Central and South America that are covered in this Atlas have been located. However, for the fourteen Caribbean countries included here, maps showing forest cover were found for only three. These country maps accompany the country texts, which explain in more detail the floristics of the forest types which have been harmonised into the broad forest classes shown on the maps. It is important that the maps are referred to in conjunction with the explanatory Map Legends which have been compiled for each map and are located at the end of each chapter. These legends explain the sources, date, scales etc. of the source data and how

Forests of the Península de Paria National Park — one of the areas with the highest degree of endemism in Venezuela
Chris Sharpe

the primary data have been harmonised.

The forest data are 'fitted' to country outlines and river systems provided by MundoCart, a digital world topographic database produced by Petroconsultants Ltd, compiled from The Defence Mapping Agency's 1: 1 million Operational Navigation Charts. Figures for the areas of different forest types have been derived from these Maps using a Geographic Information System (GIS). Boundary data for conservation areas within IUCN's categories I-IV have been digitally overlain onto the Maps. Where boundary data were not available, the protected areas have been located by a centre point derived from latitude and longitude information held within the WCMC protected areas tabular database.

The designation of the geographical entities in this Atlas do not imply the expression of any opinion on the part of WCMC, IUCN, or any sponsoring organisation concerning the legal status or the delimitation of borders of any country depicted.

Availability of Data

The spatial data recorded in this volume are maintained at the World Conservation Monitoring Centre, Cambridge, U.K on the Biodiversity Map Library, a GIS designed to house and analyse biodiversity information. These data are available in digital or hard copy form for those interested. It is essential that these data are updated and WCMC would appreciate any comments on or updates of the datasets. The Centre will be pleased to collaborate with organisations wishing to use the data in the interest of nature conservation.

References

Collins, N.M., Sayer, J.A. and Whitmore, T. (1991). *The Conservation Atlas of Tropical Forests: Asia.* Macmillan, London.

FAO (1988) *An Interim Report on the State of Forest Resources in the Developing Countries.* FAO, Rome, Italy.

FAO (1989). *FAO Production Yearbook Volume 42.* FAO, Rome, Italy.

FAO (1993). *Forest resources assessment 1990: Tropical countries.* FAO Forestry Paper 112. FAO, Rome, Italy.

FAO (1994). F*AO Yearbook: Forest Products 1981–1992.* FAO Forestry Series No. 27, FAO Statistics Series No. 116. Food and Agriculture Organisation of the United Nations, Rome, Italy

Haffer, J. (1987). Quaternary history of tropical Africa. In: *Biogeography and Quaternary History in Tropical America.* Whitmore, T.C. and Prance, G.T. (eds). Clarendon Press, Oxford. Pp 1–18.

Holdridge, L.R. (1967). *Life Zone Ecology.* Tropical Science Centre. San José, Costa Rica

PRB (1994). *1994 World Population Datasheet.* Population Reference Bureau Inc., Washington, D.C., U.S.A.

Sayer, J.A., Harcourt, C.S. and Collins, N.M. (1992). *The Conservation Atlas of Tropical Forests: Africa.* Macmillan, London. Pp. 1–288.

Unesco (1981). *Vegetation map of South America: Explanatory notes.* Unesco, Paris. Pp. 1–189

Whitmore, T.C. and Prance, G.T. (eds) (1987). *Biogeography and Quaternary History in Tropical America.* Clarendon Press, Oxford. 214 pp.

Authors: Caroline Harcourt and Clare Billington, WCMC, Cambridge and Jeff Sayer, IUCN, with contributions from Martin Jenkins, Cambridge.

2 The History of the Forests and Climate of Tropical South America

Introduction

The tropical forests of South America have a complex and dynamic history and many of the changes that have taken place over time can be deduced by a study of the pollen record. The history of South America's upper montane forests, in particular, is well documented by pollen records. The extremely long pollen records from the former lake of Bogota are particularly important, revealing a wealth of information on the development of the Andean forests during the Late Tertiary and Quaternary. The latter period covers the last 2.5 million years or so, and is characterized by the repeated occurrence of ice ages at high latitudes. The pollen records of Bogota show that the Andean forests during the late Pliocene were of a markedly different composition from those that occur in the area today. They show correlations with glacial advances and retreats in the polar regions (see, for example, Van der Hammen and González, 1960; Hooghiemstra, 1984, 1989).

Pollen records covering the past 15,000 years have been obtained from between 2500 m and 4200 m elevation in the Eastern and Central Cordilleras of Colombia (e.g. Melief, 1985; Salomons, 1986; Kuhry, 1988) and the Venezuelan Cordillera (e.g. Salgado-Labouriau et al., 1977). These records show details of the environmental changes of the upper montane forests and their relation to climatic change.

In contrast, the history of the lower montane forest belt, extending from about 1000 m to 2300 m elevation, and the warm tropical lowland forest belt, extending from sea level to around 1000 m in elevation, is considerably less well documented. Suitable locations to study the history of these two forest types, which are recorded in the pollen in peat bogs and accumulated sediments on lake bottoms, are less easy to find. An additional problem in palynological studies at lower elevations is caused by the very rich vegetation: the variety of fossilized pollen grains and fern spores encountered is so high that it is more difficult to deduce past vegetation types.

Important studies of the biogeography and Quaternary history of South American forests include those by Fittkau et al. (1968–1969), Van der Hammen (1974), Livingstone and Van der Hammen (1978), Vuillemier and Monasterio (1986) and Whitmore and Prance (1987). Good reviews of research on the natural resources of Neotropical forests include those by

Meggers et al. (1973), Unesco (1978), Prance (1982a), Lieth and Werger (1989) and Gentry (1990).

Quaternary History of Andean Forests

Knowledge of the history of the Andean forests during the Quaternary is based mainly on the long pollen records from Lake Bogota. These are representative of that part of the northern Andes that lies within the tropical zone. The foothills in this part of the Andes now have a warm tropical climate, but the upland regions have a cool to cold climate and at the highest levels there is perpetual snow.

Large diurnal temperature fluctuations are characteristic of tropical mountain ranges. Temperatures do not vary seasonally to any great extent and, given sufficient humidity, most plants are evergreen. This includes the trees near the upper forest limit.

The altitudinal vegetation zones of the Eastern Cordillera of Colombia provide a good example of the general situation in the tropical Andes north of the equator (Figure 2.1). The Eastern Cordillera of the northern Andes rises up from the tropical lowlands, where rain forests, savannas, or xerophytic vegetation types dominate. To the northeast of this Cordillera lies the savanna area of the Llanos Orientalis and the Orinoco, and to the south east lies the rain forest. West of the Cordillera is the Magdalena valley, the northern part of which supports rain forest, while in the southern part, tropical xerophytic vegetation or dry forest is found. In the Eastern Cordillera the warm tropical vegetation belt extends from the lowlands to around 1000 m. At about this elevation several 'tropical' taxa, such as most Bombacaceae, disappear. Several other taxa are restricted in their occurrence to this belt or to a part of it (e.g. *Byrsonima*, *Iriartea*, *Mauritia* and *Spathiphyllum*).

The next altitudinal zone is that of the sub-andean forest from approximately 1000 m to 2300 m. Genera such as *Acalypha*, *Alchornea* and *Cecropia* are of frequent occurrence in this zone and do not extend beyond its upper limit. The same holds for many Palmae, *Hyeronima*, *Ficus* and Malpighiaceae. From about 2300 to 3200–3500 m elevation lies the Andean forest belt, in which species of *Weinmannia* and *Quercus* dominate (Figure 2.2). *Alnus*, *Clusia*, *Hedyosmum Ilex*, *Juglans*, *Myrica*, *Podocarpus*, *Rapanea* and *Styloceras* are frequently represented,

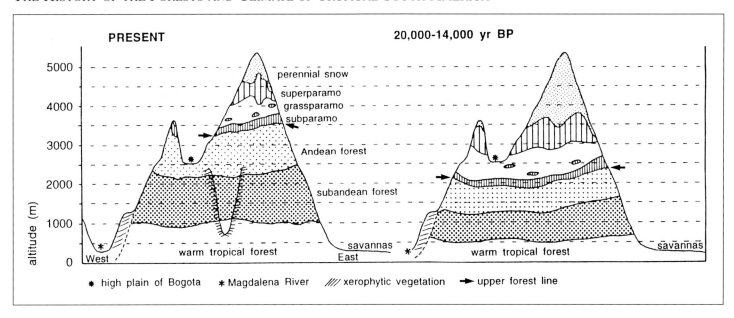

Figure 2.1 Schematic presentation of the zonation of the main vegetation belts in the Colombian Andes during present-day conditions (interglacial) and during ice age (glacial) conditions about 18,000 years ago. *(Source:* After Van der Hammen, 1974)

although most of these genera are not restricted in their distribution to this belt.

The next vegetation zone, extending from approximately 3200 to 3500 m elevation, is the irregular belt of high Andean dwarf forest and shrub formations, and the sub-paramo. The forest trees of the genera *Weinmannia* and *Quercus* are absent and the most common woody taxa belong to the Compositae, *Ericaceae, Aragoa, Escallonia, Hypericum* and *Polylepis.* Above this, the paramo extends from about 3500 m up to 4000-4200 m elevation. Apart from grasses, the most characteristic elements of the paramo are stem-rosette plants of the genus *Espeletia,* and a number of herbs, such as *Bartsia, Gentiana, Geranium, Halenia, Paepalanthus, Plantago, Ranunculus* and *Valeriana.* The super-paramo belt extends upwards from 4000-4200 m to the snow-covered zone.

In order to make the pollen diagrams more easily understood, they are presented here as cumulative diagrams. They show the variation with time of the percentages of the major ecological groups of pollen: subandean forest elements, Andean forest elements, subparamo elements and paramo elements. It will be clear that for correct interpretations one must take into account the relationships between vegetation and pollen rain, and the altitudinal ranges and ecologies of the individual taxa present.

The Andes have been subjected to great geological uplift over the last few million years. This uplift has created new environments at high elevations in tropical South America. Resulting vegetation changes are recorded in pollen records (Van der Hammen *et al.,* 1973). Open Andean vegetation developed, while the forest taxa adapted gradually to colder conditions. During this Pliocene-Quaternary period of adaptation, the sub-andean forest belt became wider and reached its present day altitudinal ranges. New elements arrived successively in these Andean forests: *Hedyosmun* and *Rapanea* approximately 4 million years ago, *Myrica* about 3.5 million years ago, *Alnus* (alder) 1 million years ago and *Quercus* (oak) around 0.3 million years ago.

The pollen record of Funza, of which Figure 2.2 shows the upper 220 m, demonstrates with amazing detail the immigration of *Alnus* at a core depth of 257 m and presents direct biogeo-

graphical evidence of the immigration of important floral elements (Hooghiemstra, 1984, 1989). *Alnus* is a northern hemisphere genus that apparently reached Colombia only after the Panamanian isthmus had formed some 5 million years ago (Keigwin, 1978). Much later, around 300,000 years ago, *Quercus* also arrived via the Panama landbridge, and colonised the area of Bogota. The difference in the time of arrival can probably be explained by the pioneer qualities of *Alnus,* which disperses more rapidly than *Quercus,* a species of mature forest. The relative frequency of *Vallea* and *Weinmannia* also changed markedly during this period. *Vallea* was abundant in the Andean forests up to about one million years ago and then decreased; after this time it was replaced by *Weinmannia* as a major element of the Andean forest belt (Hooghiemstra, 1984, 1989). It is likely that *Quercus* is still invading the original Lauraceae forests and that it will eventually become a more significant component of the flora if present day environmental conditions persist.

The composition of the Andean forest belt obviously changed considerably during the Late Pliocene and Quaternary as a result of immigration and evolutionary adaptation. During the Quaternary periods of glacial advance in northern Europe and northern America, temperatures in the tropical areas were reduced, resulting in a lowering of the position of the altitudinal forest belts (Figure 2.1). During the warmest phases of interglacials, the present-day upper forest line (c. 3200-3500 m altitude) may have reached 3400-3600 m, and locally even 4000 m. In contrast, during the coldest phases of the glacials it may have descended to around 2000-1800 m. The Funza pollen record (Figure 2.2) clearly shows the shifting upper forest line following the changes in temperature during the ice ages. The former lake of Bogota was alternately situated in the Andean forest belt, the sub-paramo and paramo belt.

Climatic and Forest Changes During the Past 30,000 Years
The last 30,000 years of the forest history in the northern tropical Andes is known from many pollen records: the 12 m long pollen record of Laguna de Fuquene in Colombia (Van Geel and Van der Hammen, 1973) is presented here (Figure 2.3). It shows

Figure 2.2 Pollen diagram of the long pollen record Funza I from the high plain of Bogota (Eastern Cordillera, Colombia, 2550 m elevation) showing the vegetational history of the last one million years or thereabouts.

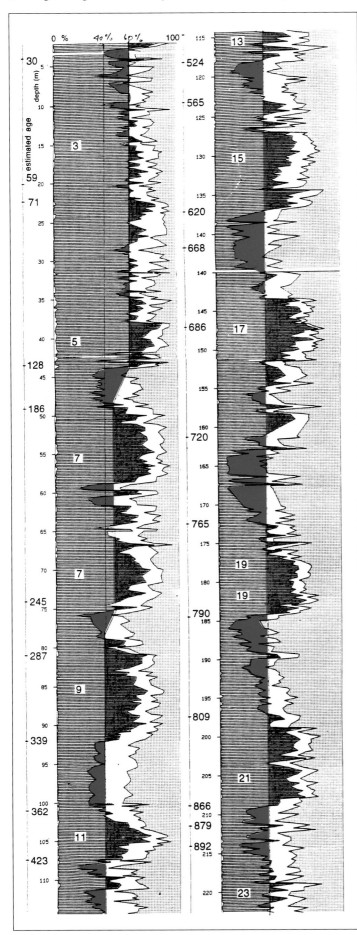

Core depth (in metres) and age (in thousands of years) are indicated at the left hand side of the diagram. For convenience, stage numbers (3 through 23) from the well known deep-sea oxygen isotope stratigraphy, are indicated in the diagram. From left to right the downcore representation of the following vegetation belts is shown: sub-andean forest, Andean forest, sub-paramo, and paramo.

The graph of downcore changes of the percentage of total arboreal pollen (AP) shows oscillations that, in fact, represent vertical shifts of the upper forest line over the mountain slopes. Red coloured intervals have an upper forest line from 2550 to 3500 m elevation and represent periods with a warm climate (interglacials). Blue coloured intervals have an upper forest line from 1800 to 2550 m elevation and represent periods with a cold climate (glacials). The inferred changes in mean annual temperature, at the elevation of Bogota, are from about 6° to 15°C. The level of AP, on which the boundary between interglacial and glacial periods is based, shift around 45 m and 77 m core depth: these shifts are approximations to account for distinct changes in the composition of the Andean forest belt at those levels. The former lake of Bogota desiccated c. 27,000 years ago, some 9000 years before the last ice age reached its coldest conditions (compare Figure 2.1), causing a hiatus in the pollen record. The samples at the top of the record are of Holocene age.

(*Source:* after Hooghiemstra, 1984; Andriessen *et al.*, 1993)

very high percentages of *Polylepis* in the period from around 30,000–25,000 years ago. Taking into account its recent relative pollen production, there can be no doubt that a very broad and extensive *Polylepis* dwarf-forest zone was dominant on the high plains near the tree line at 2550 m. Such an extreme dominance of this species is not known from anywhere in the Andes today, and suggests that special conditions of climate and/or soil occurred at that time.

The period before 25,000 BP was characterized by cold and humid conditions, with a maximum extension of the glaciers, a higher tree-line and higher lake levels. Around 21,000 BP the *Polylepis* forest had largely been displaced by open paramo. At the same time the lake level fell markedly. This period, with an extremely cold and dry climate, lasted until c. 14,000–13,000 BP, that is until the period of maximum glacial retreat at high latitudes. At this time, forest colonised the area again, replacing the paramo during the periods of minor glacial retreat. The abundance of the shrubby pioneer species *Dodonaea*, which grows on eroded soils, is characteristic of this period. This taxon almost disappeared in the Holocene, and reappeared only during recent periods of human disturbance.

Between the Guantiva glacial retreat, that lasted from about 12,400 to 10,900 BP, and the beginning of the Holocene there was another cold interval, called the El Abra stadial (between 4 and 5 m in Figure 2.3), which began at around 10,900 BP. This brief temperature depression is known from several Colombian pollen records. The Holocene represented a return to full interglacial conditions. Forests, dominated by *Weinmannia* and *Quercus*, invaded the area and sub-andean forest elements reached Laguna de Fuquene, indicating that mean annual temperatures must have been somewhat higher than present day values. In several pollen records, a cooling of the climate is also evident about 3000 BP.

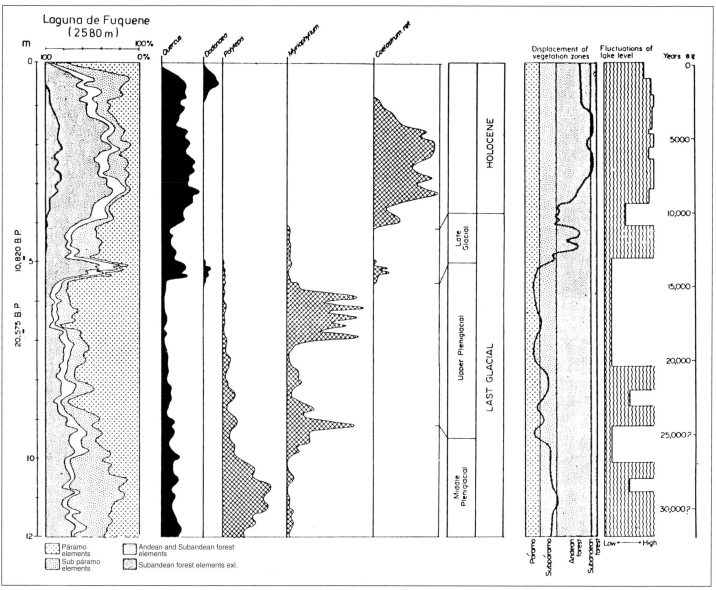

Figure 2.3   Pollen record from Laguna de Fuquene (Eastern Cordillera, Colombia, 2580 m elevation) showing the vegetational and climatic history of the last c. 30,000 years. At the left hand side, a summary diagram shows the downcore contribution of the four main vegetation belts. Records of selected pollen taxa are shown. At the right hand side the chronostratigraphy, vertical displacement of vegetation belts, and estimated fluctuations of the lake level, are indicated.

Source: After Van Geel and Van der Hammen (1973)

Forest History of the Amazon Basin

During the wet season, broad belts along the Amazon River and its tributaries become inundated (see Box). The várzea forest that occurs in these belts is adapted to flooding of up to several months duration. The almost permanently inundated sites, such as oxbow lakes and deep backswamps, may support 'floating meadow' vegetation near the shores where the water is rather shallow. The meadows may become more extensive when the mean annual water levels are lower (Van der Hammen, 1986). These more or less permanently flooded sites have vegetation similar to that in the swamps of the Colombian lower Magdalena valley.

Analysis of the sediments in Amazonian lakes show that there have been periods of extensive spreading of the 'floating meadows', and all evidence points to coincidence with periods of low water levels. In the sediments of the Amazon valley itself, there are also considerable increases in grass pollen. These are often associated with an abundance of *Cecropia*, a pioneer tree which colonises thicker or 'stranded' patches of

'floating meadows'. Again, there are striking similarities with developments in the lower Magdalena valley. The knowledge of the sequence of relatively dry and wet periods in the Amazon Basin during the last 10,000 years or so is based mainly on work by Absy (1979, 1982), Absy *et al.* (1991), Urrego (in press), Van der Hammen *et al.* (1992), Van der Hammen and Absy (1994) and Van der Hammen and Cleef (1992). These Holocene changes of river levels are certainly caused by changes of rainfall, and may very well be linked to El Niño events (Dueñas, 1992; Van der Hammen and Cleef, 1992).

These recent changes in the vegetation cover and in precipitation are trivial when compared with the changes that are believed to have occurred in the Amazon Basin at earlier times. The very dry periods that are thought to have occurred during the Quaternary must have had far-reaching effects on the extent of the Amazonian forests. These dry periods are believed by some biogeographers to account for centres of endemism in, for example, birds, lizards, butterflies and woody angiosperms (Haffer, 1969, 1977; Vanzolini and Williams, 1970; Vanzolini,

WESTERN AMAZONIAN FLOODPLAINS, A VARIABLE AND DYNAMIC ENVIRONMENT

Extensive areas of Western Amazonia are annually flooded by rivers. It has, for example, been estimated that river floodplains cover 12 per cent of Amazonian Peru (Salo *et al.*, 1986). The width of the floodplains along the major river courses varies a lot, from a few hundred meters up to scores of kilometres. The largest floodplains are found in areas that are subsiding because of tectonic movements related to the uplift of the Andean mountains. These sinking areas form the basins of the Madre de Dios, Ucayali, Acre and Pastaza-Marañon Rivers (Räsänen *et al.*, 1987).

The rivers that erode the slopes of the Andes carry large quantities of sediments. When they enter the flat Amazonian lowlands, especially the basin areas, the velocity of the water slows down and a considerable amount of the sediment load is deposited. The result is that relatively loose and fine-grained fluvial sediments accumulate in the lowland areas. These easily erodible sediments and the flat terrain allow the rivers to move around freely in search of the least resistant routes.

Erosion and sediment deposition along a meandering river channel results in lateral migration of the channel. The movement can be very rapid; a maximum annual migration rate of 160 meters has been reported from the Ucayali river in Peru (Kalliola *et al.*, 1992). However, the actively growing phase of any one meander lasts for only relatively short periods of time. When the loop grows rounder, its neck gets thinner, until the river ultimately breaks through and a new cut is formed. The abandoned loop becomes an oxbow lake. These are a conspicuous component of active floodplains. The processes of river meandering and annual flooding also form characteristic sequences of relatively higher ridges and lower swales parallel to the river.

The rate of channel migration varies significantly both in time and place. The straighter parts of a river are generally fairly stable, but the migration is very fast in the apices of meander loops. The erosion rates vary also between different river types. Suspension-rich white water rivers originating from the Andes are more active compared to stable black water rivers that drain only lowland areas.

The very rapidly changing geomorphology of the floodplains has a pronounced influence on the vegetation. Old forest is destroyed at the eroding bank, while primary succession takes place at the advancing beaches. When the point-bars are exposed after the annual flood, their higher parts become rapidly vegetated by pioneer species. During the subsequent years, the annual pioneer species are replaced by stronger competitors, and a series of belts of vegetation in different stages of succession is formed from the point-bar towards the meander neck.

The first successional stages are usually rather poor in species. Young point-bar beaches are colonized patchily by herbs and seedlings of woody riparian plants. Many of the herbs, such as *Ipomoea* spp., *Fimbristylis* spp., *Ludwigia* spp. and *Panicum* spp., are also found as weeds in nearby cultivated areas. Somewhat older vegetation is typically formed by almost monospecific stands of first *Tessaria integrifolia* or *Gynerium sagittatum* and later by *Cecropia* spp.. Thereafter the vegetation gets more diverse in species and structure. The first dominant trees are *Cedrela odorata* and *Ficus insipida*, but in older forests it is no longer possible to distinguish clear zonation (Salo *et al.*, 1986; Kalliola *et al.*, 1987; Kalliola *et al.*, 1991). The boundary between older and younger vegetation disappears partly because the relative age differences get smaller and partly because tree senescence and regeneration in gaps blur the pattern. Also the river activity itself can break the regularly sequential vegetation structure by erosion and by depositing sediment.

The above sequences of vegetation succession create the basic level of heterogeneity of floodplain vegetation. Further elements of mosaicism in floodplains are formed by different vegetation patches in oxbow lakes and backswamps. Oxbow lakes are slowly filled by fine sediments brought in by the floods, and by debris from the surrounding vegetation that accumulates in the lake bottom. First, the lake is covered by floating plants such as *Eichhornia crassipes* and *Pistia stratiotes*. The giant water lily *Victoria amazonica* often occurs. Later come floating grasses that are nevertheless rooted in the soil. After those come stages of continuous herbaceous vegetation and scattered woody vegetation dominated by only a few species — *Pseudobombax munguba* is one of the most important ones. Eventually more species rich and complex forest finally conquers the former lake. Backswamps are found further from the actual river channel, close to the margin of the floodplain. These areas are always poorly drained and typically the vegetation is characterised by extensive and almost pure stands of the palm *Mauritia flexuosa*.

Sometimes tectonically induced tilting of the ground can force a long stretch of a river channel abruptly to change its location and abandon its old course. In the formerly active channel area vegetation succession begins to advance more peacefully. In contrast, the new channel area is exposed to drastic changes (Kalliola *et al.*, 1991). Entirely new areas become susceptible to the effects of river processes such as floods and erosion, and in many places the vegetation will experience a regressive succession: the forest declines and herbaceous vegetation expands as a result of increasing water levels. Even previously unflooded forests may become flooded.

Perhaps the most outstanding consequence of river activity is the splitting of the floodplain environment into a mosaic of habitats different in relief, flood intensity, age and soil properties. It is also important to realize that the structure of the mosaic is continuously changing and the direction of the change is not readily predictable. A floodplain forest can be eroded away by the river or regressive succession can turn the forest into a grassland, or a backswamp appears, or perhaps even the whole area remains outside the flood zone and a new patch of terra-firme forest is formed.

The unpredictability of the floodplain environment extends to the distribution patterns of species. For example, an exceptionally strong flood can wipe out species that otherwise would be common at a site, or a certain kind or habitat can emerge so far away from other similar patches that not all species typical of the conditions are able to colonise the area.

The understanding of river dynamics may give clues to understanding unflooded terrain. Most of the surface sediments in western Amazonia are deposited in fluvial environments, and there are many signs of ancient river activity in the soils of terra-firme forests.

Source: Kalle Ruokolainen and Maarit Puhakka.

1973; Simpson and Haffer, 1978; Prance, 1978, 1982b).

The refuge theory, expounded clearly by Haffer in 1969, postulates that vegetational changes following climatic changes cause the fragmentation of species ranges and their isolation in ecological refuges (Figure 2.4). In these refuges, species populations may (a) become extinct, (b) survive unchanged, or (c) differentiate at subspecies or species level. The theory has been much debated (e.g. Colinvaux, 1979, 1987) and several other theories to explain centres of diversity and of endemism have been put forward. These alternative theories include river dynamics, temperature changes and contemporary ecological differences between areas (Colinvaux et al., 1985; Salo et al., 1986). Whatever the cause, the palynological evidence now available shows that savannas used to be present in areas that are today covered with tropical forest. The pollen records from Rondonia and Carajas illustrate this particularly well.

The pollen record from Rondonia (Figure 2.5) shows the replacement of the Amazonian forest by grass-savanna (Van der Hammen, 1972; Absy and Van der Hammen, 1976). Two fractions of two samples from the Katira section were recently dated (Van der Hammen and Absy, 1994). This part of the Amazon Basin, under today's natural conditions, is completely covered with dense tropical rain forest (annual rainfall around 2500 mm), and the nearest patches of more open natural vegetation are found at least 150-200 km to the south. The savanna periods of Rondonia are dated at 42,500+/-2500 years BP and 18,500 +/-150 years BP. The geological context suggests that the dates correspond to two savanna periods, separated by a wetter forest period. The last savanna period, at and after 18,500 BP, was associated with thick colluvial deposits in the valley and was probably the drier period. We have no data from Rondonia as to when the rain forest invaded the area again, but, based on data from other places, this probably happened at the beginning of the Holocene.

The pollen record from Carajas, Brazil (Figure 2.6) came from the southern Serra do Carajas on a narrow plateau at 700–800 m elevation (Absy et al., 1991). This region is situated in a NW-SE oriented corridor inside the Amazon Basin where the annual precipitation (1500–2000 mm) is lower than in adjacent regions (2000–3000 mm). In the rain forest surrounding the plateau, relative seasonal dryness is reflected by the occurrence of patches of deciduous trees. The pollen record presented (Figure 2.6) is from a core drilled in the centre of a former lake, situated on the plateau. The bulk of the present pollen supply to the lake originates from the surrounding rain forest. The eight pollen zones recognised correlate strongly with the lithological sequence: in the sandy layers, pollen from savanna species dominates (pollen zones Al, B and D), whereas forest species are dominant in pollen zones from organic-rich sediments. The last organic-rich deposition of Holocene age shows marked differences from its Pleistocene equivalents. The extension of savanna around 6000 BP (pollen zone E2) represents a different type of savanna vegetation. The abundant charcoal fragments suggest that fire must have played an important role in the spread of savanna at this time. The final increase of rain forest around 3000 BP (pollen zone E3) is reflected in the occurrence of pollen from pioneer species.

The overall pollen record shows clear vegetational and climatic change over the last 60,000 years. Dry periods occurred around 60,000 BP, shortly before 40,000 BP and during 21,000–11,000 years BP. The drying of the lake after 22,000 BP and before 12,500 BP, its reappearance slightly before 12,500 BP and the subsequent rise of the water level during the Late

Glacial are events which have also been described for tropical African lakes (Livingstone and Van der Hammen, 1978; Servant and Servant-Vildary, 1980; Maley, 1987; Street and Grove, 1979).

During the dry periods of the Quaternary, pollen representing forest elements is less frequent and sometimes absent. Hence it seems very likely that the forest disappeared, not only from the plateau, but also from the surroundings of the plateau. The driest parts of the dry Quaternary periods are not represented because sediment no longer accumulated in the lake. Considering the present distribution of Amazonian forest, the

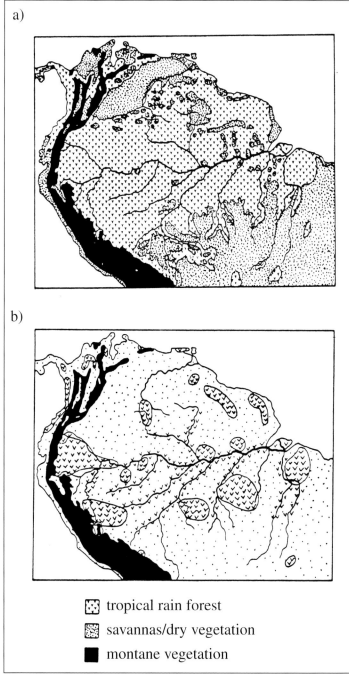

a)

b)

▨ tropical rain forest

▨ savannas/dry vegetation

■ montane vegetation

Figure 2.4 Maps of tropical South America, with present distribution of major vegetation types (a), and with a tentative reconstruction of the situation during the driest phases of glacial periods, with forest refuges (b).

Source: Adapted from Van der Hammen (1979); after Haffer (1977), Prance (1973) and Huber (1974)

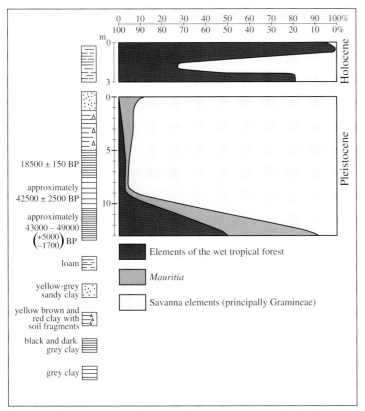

Figure 2.5   Pollen records from Capoeira (top) and Katira (bottom) (Rondonia, Brazil, latitude 4°S; longitude 6°W) in the Amazon Basin. The diagram reflects a dramatic change from dense tropical forest towards grass-savanna and vice versa.

Source: After Absy and Van der Hammen (1976)

type of change registered at the end of the dry periods would mean a lowering of at least 500 mm in the annual precipitation (from 2000–1500 mm to 1500–1000 mm) in the drier Amazonian corridor and eventually the fragmentation of the Amazon rain forest area into two large parts.

Van der Hammen and Absy (1994) have mapped the potential distribution of rain forest in the Amazon Basin at an annual precipitation of 500 mm (Figure 2.7b) and 1000 mm (Figure 2.7c) lower than at present (Figure 2.7a). As illustrated in Figure 2.7c, the sites of Katira and Carajas, which experienced savanna conditions some 20,000 years BP, would have been located in savanna vegetation. Interestingly, the same figure suggests that Georgetown would also have experienced savanna conditions with precipitation reduced by 1000 mm. This conclusion is supported by pollen records (Van der Hammen, 1963). These data show that considerable areas of tropical forest were once replaced by savanna and savanna woodland or cerrado types of vegetation. It is highly probable, therefore, that the Amazonian forest was, at times, reduced to a number of larger and smaller fragments that could be called forest refuges.

Prehistoric Man and Forests
People may have entered South America as early, or earlier than 30,000 years ago, but good evidence of their presence exists from about 15,000 years BP onward. It seems probable that there have always been some people adapted to forest-life, but many of the cultural remains from the period of the last glacial advance are from groups adapted to more open environments. During the past 15,000 years, people have produced some finely worked stone artifacts, which suggest that they were hunting large mammals. Humans will also have used the other resources

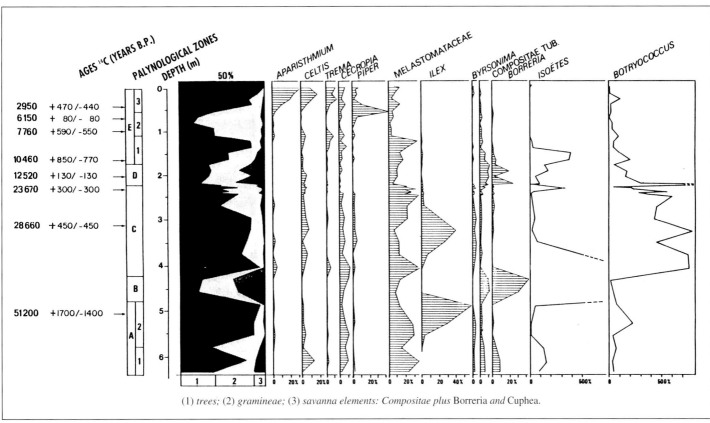

(1) *trees;* (2) *gramineae;* (3) *savanna elements: Compositae plus* Borreria *and* Cuphea.

Figure 2.6   Simplified pollen record and radiocarbon dates of a 6.5 m long core from a swamp area in the Serra do Carajas (Brazil, lat. 6°20'S; long. 50°25'W; 700–800 m asl). The downcore changing representation of trees, savanna elements and grasses reflects a sequence of open and forested environments near Carajas during the last c. 50,000 years.

Source: After Absy *et al.* (1991)

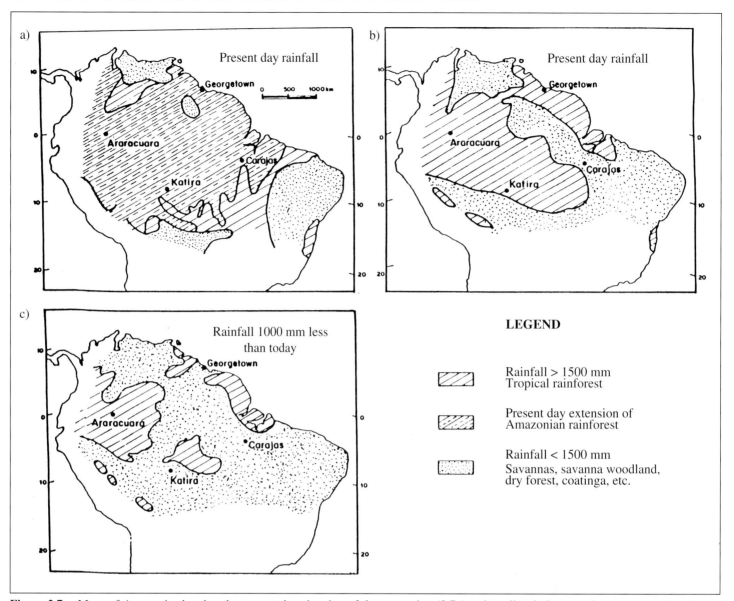

Figure 2.7 Maps of Amazonia showing the present-day situation of the vegetation (2.7a) and predicted changes of major vegetation formations when average rainfall is 500 (2.7b) and 1000 mm (2.7c) lower than at present. The sites of Carajas and Katira, under savanna type vegetation some 20,000 years ago, are indicated. The site of Georgetown also experienced savanna conditions during the last glacial advance.

Source: After Van der Hammen and Absy (1994)

that the savannas and patches of trees in the South American cerrados offered. It seems certain that the wooded areas were altered by burning from very early on.

It is known that from as long ago as the Late Glacial, people were adapted to the upper montane forest-paramo boundary. This offered very diverse resources: small animals, fruits, etc. (Van der Hammen and Correal Urrego, 1978). At that time there were also people living in the western Amazon (A. Rooseveld, unpublished data) who made stone points and apparently used the broad spectrum of fruit and seed resources which the forest offered.

When the upper limit of the forest rose at the beginning of the Holocene and open or semi-open vegetation types were greatly reduced, people seemed to adapt to forest-life and to using the numerous resources that the forest offers (roots, fruits,

nuts, meat, fish etc.). This happened both in the Andes and Amazonia. The effect these people had on the forest may not have been very great, but it seems to have led to an increased frequency of useful trees and palms in both montane forests and the tropical lowlands.

The impact of man on the forest increased with the beginning of horticulture and agriculture; in some areas, this occurred as far back as 8000 years ago. During the few thousand years before the Spanish conquest (at around 1500 AD) the impact of flourishing Indian cultures on the forest vegetation was considerable. However, the action of humans became really destructive only after the conquest and has increased during the last few decades to culminate in today's unprecedented rates of forest clearance.

References

Absy, M.L. (1979). *A Palynological Study of Holocene Sediments in the Amazon Basin.* PhD thesis, University of Amsterdam: 104 pp.

Absy, M.L. (1982). Quaternary palynological studies in the Amazon Basin. In: *Biological Diversification in the Tropics.* Prance, G.T. (ed.). Columbia University Press, New York. Pp. 67–73.

Absy, M.L. and Van der Hammen, T. (1976). Some paleoecological data from Rondonia, southern part of the Amazon Basin. *Acta Amazonica* 6(3): 293–299.

Absy, M.L., Cleef, A.M., Fournier, M., Martin, L., Servant, M., Sfeddine, A., Ferreira da Silva, M.F., Soubies, F., Suguio, K., Turcq, B. and Van der Hammen, T. (1991). Mise en evidence de quatre phases d'ouvertures de la forêt dense dans le sudest de l'Amazonie au cours des 60,000 dernieres annees. *Comptes Rendues Academie de Sciences, Paris* 312, serie II: 673–678.

Andriessen, P.A.M., Helmens, K.F., Hooghiemstra, H., Riezebos, P.A. and Van der Hammen, T. (1993). Absolute chronology of the Pliocene-Quaternary sediment sequence of the Bogota area, Colombia. *Quaternary Science Reviews* 12: 483–501.

Colinvaux, P.A. (1979). The Ice-age Amazon. *Nature* 278: 399–400.

Colinvaux, P.A. (1987). Amazon diversity in the light of the paleoecological record. *Quaternary Science Reviews* 6: 93–114.

Colinvaux, P.A., Miller, M.C., Liu, K-b., Steinitz-Kannan, M. and Frost, I. (1985). Discovery of permanent Amazon lakes and hydraulic disturbance in the upper Amazon Basin. *Nature* 313: 42–45.

Dueñas, H. (1992). The Paleo ENSO record in the lower Magdalena basin, Colombia. In: *Paleo-ENSO Records International Symposium, Lima. Extended abstracts: 81–85.* Ortlieb, L. and Machare, J.(eds). Orstom-Concytec, Lima.

Fittkau, E.J., Illies, J., Klinge, H., Schwabe, G.H. and Sioli, H. (eds) (1968–1969). *Biogeography and Ecology in South America.* Junk, The Hague: 2 Volumes, 946 pp.

Gentry, A.H. (ed.) (1990). *Four Neotropical Rainforests.* Yale University Press, New Haven: 627 pp.

Haffer, J. (1969) Speciation in Amazonian forest birds. *Science* 165: 131–137.

Haffer, J. (1977). Pleistocene speciation in Amazonian birds. *Amazoniana* 6(2): 161–191.

Hooghiemstra, H. (1984). Vegetational and climatic history of the high plain of Bogota, Colombia: a continuous record of the last 3.5 million years. *Dissertaciones Botanicae* 79: 1–368.

Hooghiemstra, H. (1989). Quaternary and Upper-Pliocene glaciations and forest development in the tropical Andes: evidence from a long high-resolution pollen record from the sedimentary basin of Bogota, Colombia. *Palaeogeography Palaeoclimatology Palaeoecology,* 72: 11–26.

Huber, O. (1974). *Le Savane Neotropicali.* Instituto Italo-Latino Americano, Rome. 855pp

Kalliola, R., Salo, J., and Mäkinen, Y. (1987). Regeneracion natural de selvas en la Amazonia Peruama 1: Dinamica fluvial y sucesion riberena. *Memoria del Museo de Historia Natural "Javier Prado"* 19A1-102.

Kalliola, R., Puhakka, M., Salo, J., Tuomisto, H. and Ruokolainen, K. (1991). The dynamics, distribution and classification of swamp vegetation in Peruvian Amazonia. *Ann Bot Fennici* 28: 225–239.

Kalliola, R., Salo, J., Puhakka, M., Rajasilta, M., Häme, T., Neller, R.J., Räsänene, M.E., and Danjoy Arias, W.A. (1992). Upper Amazon channel migration. *Naturwissemchaften* 79: 75–798.

Keigwin, L.D. (1978). Pliocene closing of the Isthmus of Panama, based on biostratigraphic evidence from nearby Pacific Ocean and Caribbean Sea cores. *Geology* 6: 630–634.

Kuhry, P. (1988). Palaeobotanical-palaeoecological studies of tropical high Andean peatbog sections (Cordillera Oriental, Colombia). *Dissertaciones Botanicae* 116: 1–241. J. Cramer, Berlin .

Lieth, H. and Werger, M.J.A. (eds) (1989). *Tropical Rain Forest Ecosystems: Biogeographical and Ecological Studies.* Elsevier, Amsterdam: 713pp.

Livingstone, D.A. and Van der Hammen, T. (1978). Palaeogeography and palaeoclimatology. In: *Unesco, Tropical Forest Ecosystems. A state-knowledge report:* 61–90. Unesco, Paris.

Maley, J. (1987). Fragmentacion de la forêt dense humide africaine et extension des biotopes montagnards au Quaternaire recent: nouvelles donnees polliniques et chronologiques. Implications paleoclimatiques et biogeographiques. *Palaeoecology of Africa* 18: 307–334.

Meggers, B.J., Ayensu, E.S. and Duckworth, W.D. (eds) (1973). *Tropical Forest Ecosystems in Africa and South America: a comparative review.* Smithsonian Institution Press, Washington D.C.: 350 pp.

Melief, A.B.M. (1985). *Late Quaternary Paleoecology of the Parque Nacional Natural los Nevados (Cordillera Central), and Sumapaz (Cordillera Oriental) Areas, Colombia.* PhD thesis, University of Amsterdam: 162 pp.

Prance, G.T. (1973). Phytogeographic support for the theory of Pleistocene forest refuges in the Amazon Basin, based on evidence from distribution patterns Caryocaraceae, Chrysobalanaceae, Diphapetalaceae and Lecythidiaceae. *Acta Amazonica* 3(3): 5–28.

Prance, G.T. (1978). The origin and evolution of the Amazon flora. *Intersciencia* 3(4): 207-222.

Prance, G.T. (ed.) (1982a). *Biological Diversification in the Tropics.* Columbia University Press, New York: 714 pp.

Prance, G.T. (1982b). Forest refuges: evidence from woody angiosperms. In: *Biological Diversification in the Tropics.* Prance, G.T. (ed.). Columbia University Press, New York: pp. 137–157.

Räsänen, M.E., Salo, J.S., and Kalliola, R.J. (1987). Long-term fluvial perturbance in the Western Amazona basin: Regulation by sub-andean tectonics. *Science* 238: 1398–1401.

Salo, J., Kalliola, R., Hakkinen, L., Kukinen, Y., Niemela, P., Phakka, M. and Coley, P.D. (1986). River dynamics and the diversity of Amazon lowland rain forest. *Nature,* 322: 254–258.

Salomons, J.B. (1986). Paleoecology of volcanic soils in the Colombian Central Cordillera (Parque Nacional Natural de los Nevados). *Dissertaciones Botanicae* 95: 1–212. J. Cramer, Berlin.

Salgado-Labouriau, M.L., Schubert, C. and Valastro, S. (1977). Paleoecologic analysis of a Late Quaternary terrace from Mucubaji, Venezuelas Andes. *Journal of Biogeography* 4: 313–325.

Servant, M. and Servant-Vildary, S. (1980). L'environnement quaternaire du bassin du Chad. In: *The Sahara and the Nile.*

Williams, M.A.J. and Faure, H. (eds). Balkema, Rotterdam. Pp. 133–162.

Simpson, B.B. and Haffer, J. (1978). Speciation patterns in the Amazonian forest biota. *Annual Reviews of Ecology and Systematics* 9: 497–518.

Street, F.A. and Grove, A.T. (1979). Global maps of lake-level fluctuations since 30,000 BP. *Quaternary Research* 12: 83–118.

Unesco (1978). Tropical forest ecosystems; a state-of-knowledge report prepared by Unesco/UNEP/FAO. Unesco, Paris: 683 pp.

Urrego, L.E. (in press). A Holocene vegetational succession in the middle Caqueta River valley (Colombian Amazonia). *Colombia Amazonica.*

Van Geel, B. and Van der Hammen, T. (1973). Upper Quaternary vegetational and climatic sequence of the Fuquene area (Eastern Cordillera, Colombia). *Palaeogeography Palaeoclimatology Palaeoecology* 14: 9–92.

Van der Hammen, T. (1963). A palynological study on the Quaternary of British Guiana. *Leidse Geologische Mededelingen* 29: 125–180.

Van der Hammen, T. (1972). Changes in vegetation and climate in the Amazon basin and surrounding areas during the Pleistocene. *Geologie en Mijnbouw* 51: 641–643.

Van der Hammen, T. (1974). The Pleistocene changes of vegetation and climate in tropical South America. *Journal of Biogeography* 1: 3–26.

Van der Hammen, T. (1979). Changes in life conditions on earth during the past one million years. *Kongelige Danske Videnskabernes Selskab, Biologiske Skrifter* 22(6): 22pp.

Van der Hammen, T. (1986). Fluctuaciones Holocenicas del nivel de inundaciones en la cuenca del bajo Magdalena-Cauca-San Jorge (Colombia). *Geologia Norandina* 10: 11–18.

Van der Hammen, T. and González, E. (1960). Upper Pleistocene and Holocene climate and vegetation of the Sabana de Bogota (Colombia). *Leidse Geologische Mededelingen* 25: 261–315.

Van der Hammen, T. and Correal Urrego, G. (1978). Prehistoric man on the Sabana de Bogota: data for an ecological prehistory. *Palaeogeography Palaeoclimatology Palaeoecology* 25: 179–190.

Van der Hammen, T., Werner, J.H. and Van Dommelen, H. (1973). Palynological record of the upheaval of the northern Andes: a study of the Pliocene and Lower Quaternary of the Colombian Eastern Cordillera and the early evolution of its high-Andean biota. *Review of Palaeobotany and Palynology 16; 1–122.*

Van der Hammen, T., Duivenvoorden, J.F., Lips, J.M., Urrego, L.E. and Espejo, N. (1992). Late Quaternary of the middle Caqueta River area (Colombian Amazonia). *Journal of Quaternary Science* 7(1): 45–55.

Van der Hammen, T. and Absy, M.L. (1994). Amazonia during the last glacial. *Palaeogeography Palaeoclimatology Palaeoecology* 109.

Van der Hammen, T. and Cleef, A.M. (1992). Holocene changes of rainfall and river discharge in northern South America and the El Niño phenomenon. *Erdkunde:* 46: 252–256.

Vanzolini, P.E. (1973). Paleoclimates, relief, and species multiplication in equatorial forests. In: *Tropical Forest Ecosystems in Africa and South America: a comparative review.* Meggers, B.J., Ayensu, E.S. and Duckworth, W.D. (eds). Smithsonian Institution Press, Washington D.C. Pp. 255–258.

Vanzolini, P.E. and Williams, E.E. (1970). South American anoles: the geographic differentiation and evolution of the *Anolis chrysolepis* species group (Sauria, Iguanidae). *Arquivos de Zoologia (Sao Paulo)* 19: 1–240.

Vuilleumier, F. and Monasterio, M. (eds) (1986). *High Altitude Tropical Biogeography.* Oxford University Press, Oxford. Pp. 649.

Whitmore, T.C. and Prance, G.T. (eds) (1987). *Biogeography and Quaternary History in Tropical America.* Oxford Monographs on Biogeography, 3. Clarendon Press, Oxford Pp. 214.

Authors: Thomas Van der Hammen and Henry Hooghiemstra,Hugo de Vries Laboratory, Department of Palynology and Paleo/Actuo-Ecology, University of Amsterdam, The Netherlands. With contributions from Michael Eden, Royal Holloway and Bedford College, London; Alan Hamilton, WWF-UK; Tim Boyle, CIFOR, Bogor, Indonesia; and Kalle Ruokolainen and Maarit Puhakka, Department of Biology, University of Turku, Finland.

3 Identifying Areas for Plant Conservation in the Americas

INTRODUCTION

Plants are the basis of most terrestrial ecosystems, and most animals, including humans, are ultimately totally dependent on them as sources of food. They provide humans with a host of other products, such as fuel, fibres, oils, medicines, dyes, tannins and forage crops for domesticated animals. In addition, they provide many valuable ecological services, such as the protection of watersheds, the cycling of nutrients and climate amelioration.

However, plant life throughout the world, and especially in the tropics, is under serious threat as habitats are destroyed or modified. Raven (1987) used island biogeography theory to predict how many species of plants are under threat of extinction worldwide. This theory predicts that if a habitat is reduced to a tenth of its original size, this will lead to the extinction, or near extinction, of half of its species. Raven's assessment is alarming: as many as 60,000 vascular plant species (one in four to one in five of the world's total) could become extinct or their populations seriously reduced by 2050 if present trends continue. Furthermore, Myers (1988) predicted that 17,000 vascular plant species (seven per cent of the Earth's vascular plant species) could become extinct in just 10 critical tropical forest areas (or "hotspots") covering 0.2 per cent of the Earth's land surface. Some of the richest areas he identified were in Latin America.

Recent work has questioned some of these assumptions and attempted to achieve greater precision in predicting extinction rates (e.g. see Whitmore and Sayer, 1992). However there is general agreement that a great loss of plant diversity is occurring and that a considerable amount of this is in the Neotropics.

Plant Diversity and Endemism in the Americas

The Americas (South and Central America and the Caribbean islands) are currently estimated to contain between 90,000 and 100,000 vascular plant species (or between 36–40 per cent of the world's vascular plants) (Gentry, 1993). More than 60,000 vascular plant species (c. 25 per cent of the total world flora) occur in just three South American countries: Colombia, Ecuador and Peru, while Brazil alone has been variously estimated as having between 40,000 and 80,000 vascular plant species.

However, habitats, individual species and genetic variation within species are not evenly distributed in these, or in other areas, of the Americas. Effective conservation of biodiversity therefore requires very careful selection of areas rather than a random selection of sites that are unwanted for other uses. For example, the Brazilian system of the 1970s that required farmers to leave half their property uncut and to develop the other half, thereby creating a chess-board effect, was never likely to be an effective way of conserving the biodiversity of the Amazon forest. Rather, careful consideration needs to be given to the distribution and fragility of the various vegetation types in the region, and to patterns of species diversity and endemism. These factors are considered below.

Vegetation

The maps in this Atlas of necessity show only major forest formations in each country and thereby give an impression of uniformity throughout the region. However, because of the great variation in soil, geology, topography and climate, the Americas are covered by a mosaic of many different forest formations, as well as other vegetation types. The forests vary from the world's wettest in the Chocó of Colombia, where up to 11,770 mm of rain has been recorded in one year (Gentry, 1982a), to the *lomas* in the arid region of western Peru where it never rains and the vegetation is sustained by mist alone. The forests are also found at altitudes varying from sea level up to 3800 m (Prance, 1989) where they meet the alpine vegetation of the paramo and puna just below the snowline of the Andes.

Table 3.1 shows the number of basic vegetation types recognised in some vegetation maps of South America. The two large-scale maps of South America (Hueck and Seibert, 1972; Unesco, 1981) use 88 principal formations, many more than is possible in this Atlas. More recent maps of smaller areas shows that even these are vast over-simplifications of the actual vegetation. For example, Huber and Alarcón (1988) used 150 categories for Venezuela alone.

It is important to recognise that each type of vegetation contains a unique assemblage of species. For example, most of Amazonia is covered by various types of tropical rain forest on different substrates, each substrate giving rise to a different assemblage of species. Furthermore, some forests, such as

Table 3.1 Number of vegetation types identified in various vegetation maps of South America.

Source	Categories	Region
Hueck and Seibert (1972)	88	South America
Unesco (1981)	88	South America
IBGE (1988)	37	Brazil
Projeto RADAM (1975) Folha SB21	36	Brazil 45–60°W; 4–8°S
Huber and Alarcón (1988)	150	Venezuela

várzea (or *tahuampa*), are subject to seasonal flooding, and species composition varies between those forests inundated by nutrient-poor black-water rivers and those which are seasonally inundated by richer white-water rivers.

Some forest formations cover large areas and are likely to be conserved adequately within any plan for conservation. However, other vegetation types are found only in small restricted areas and may be severely at risk. Conservation of these vegetation types requires careful planning to ensure that they are not lost. For example, within Amazonia there are several types of vegetation (Amazon *caatinga*, *campina* and *restinga*) on pure white sand which contain many endemic species, especially in the upper Rio Negro region. Not only will deforestation of these white sand areas result in extinction of locally endemic species, but their clearance also creates a semi-desert of exposed sand over which forest is slow to regenerate. For example, areas cleared by the Guarito culture some 800 years ago still have large bare patches of soil (Prance and Schubart, 1978). Clearly it is preferable to preserve intact forest over white sands. In contrast, the transition forests of south-western Amazonia have few endemic species, low diversity, and are dominated by the multi-use babassu palm (*Orbignya phalerata*) which often occurs in dense single species stands. This is an example of an area which is more appropriate for use and where the conservation of a reasonable sample will ensure the survival of the plant species which it contains.

In the Caribbean islands, the most luxuriant forests are those at low elevations up to about 300 m above sea-level, although truly evergreen, non-seasonal lowland rain forest does not occur on the islands. Each type of climax forest has its own dominant tree species, and floristic composition of the forests differ between each of the major islands. However, as discussed elsewhere in this Atlas (Chapters 10–15), most of the lowland forests have been destroyed.

Bearing in mind that local variations occur, some general comments can be made on diversity and endemism within the main forest types of the Neotropical region.

Moist Forests

Lowland tropical moist forest is the most structurally and taxonomically diverse vegetation type in the region. In general, there is a strong correlation between the amount of rainfall and diversity, with wetter forests being floristically richer than drier types. The richest forests of all are the aseasonal lowland moist and wet forests of upper Amazonia and the Chocó region. These forests hold two "world records" for plant species diversity. For plants with a diameter of more than 2.5 cm in 0.1 ha samples, the world record site is in the Colombian Chocó pluvial forests (258–265 species); for plants with a diameter of more than 10 cm in 1 ha plots the world record is near Iquitos in Peru where there were 300 species of this size in a sample of 606 individual plants (figures from A.H. Gentry in Davis et al. in press).

Amazonian moist forests contain the highest number of *regional* endemics, with an estimated 14,000 endemic species or 76 per cent of the Amazonian flora (Gentry, 1992). Most of these species have wide distributions within Amazonia. In contrast, the "Mata Atlantica" forests of coastal Brazil have a high local endemism, as well as a high regional endemism (73 per cent for the latter).

Estimates of regional endemism for the Chocó region are around 20 per cent. For the northern Andean region as a whole, including the coastal lowlands of western Colombia and Ecuador and adjacent uplands, Gentry (1992) estimated over 8000 endemic species (about 56 per cent of the region's flora). This area is one of the least known areas botanically, and it is likely that there are several thousand more species awaiting discovery. Most of these are likely to be endemic.

Endemism is not always correlated with diversity. Thus, local endemism appears to be concentrated in "cloud forests" along the base of the northern Andes and in adjacent southern Central America, and in the north-western sector of Amazonia where there is a mosaic of sedimentary substrates associated with the Guayana shield (Gentry, 1986). The Andes montane

Mauritia flexuosa (mauritia palm) bearing fruits which are eaten by monkeys and humans. Tambopata Reserve, Peru.

(WWF/Sylvia Yorath)

THE MANAUS WORKSHOP: AREAS OF BIOLOGICAL PRIORITY FOR CONSERVATION IN AMAZONIA

The aim of the workshop, which brought together almost 100 Amazon specialists, was to pool scientific data to indicate areas of maximum biological interest and diversity in order to help and encourage the planning of conservation areas within the Amazon region. Representatives of all nine Amazon countries attended.

The scientists began by working for three days in small specialist groups covering Plant Systematics, Plant Ecology, Mammals, Ornithology, Herpetology, Icthyology, Entomology, Geomorphology and Climate, and Units of Conservation. These first order discussions were intense while participants exchanged their knowledge. At the end of the three days, each of the seven biological groups produced thematic maps, backed by scientific information forms, to justify their selection of priority areas. This was followed by separate meetings of all botanists and zoologists to pool their data and consolidate their chosen areas on two maps; one for plants and one for animals. Although the consolidation process involved a great deal of discussion, the areas selected by the different groups corresponded to a large degree. At the same time, the geomorphologists and climatologists produced their map locating the most fragile soils and ecosystems requiring greatest protection. The Conservation Units Group discussed policy and other important factors for future analysis and planning of preservation, conservation and management of priority areas.

The first step was the fusion of the 104 areas of major biological importance for plants with the areas selected for animals. This resulted in the production of a final map of 94 areas evaluated with a 5–1 scale of priority for conservation (see Figure 3.1). Areas with maximum overlap between the disciplines were given the highest priority.

The final map covered about 60 per cent of the Amazon region, and together with the back-up material will provide a much more logical basis for future conservation planning throughout the Amazon region. It is encouraging that many existing parks and reserves occur within the areas selected as priorities at the workshop. However, the areas selected at the workshop are broad regions, and now it is up to conservation organisations of the nine countries to carry out on-site work to define the exact areas that are suitable for different categories of protection, managed forest, indigenous reserves, national parks, ecological reserves and other conservation areas.

The results of the workshop are a challenge to governments and NGOs of the developed world to mobilise the resources needed for the establishment of the areas selected by the conservation agencies of the Amazon country governments.

Source: G.T. Prance

Figure 3.1 Biological Priorities for Conservation in Amazonia *Source:* Conservation International (1991)

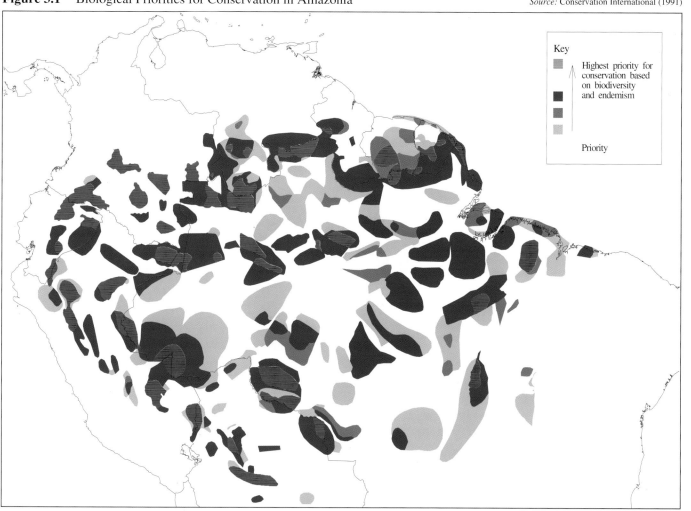

Key

■ Highest priority for conservation based on biodiversity and endemism

Priority

Orchid in Canaima National Park, Venezuela.
(WWF/Chris Elliot)

forests of Peru, Colombia, and Ecuador are particularly rich in local endemics, and what little remains of these forests is under severe threat.

In Central America, the greatest concentrations of endemic species is in high mountains. For example, 70 per cent of the vascular flora of high mountains of Guatemala and Mexico are endemic (D'Arcy, 1977).

Dry Forests
Tropical dry forest is, by some estimations, the most acutely threatened of all Neotropical vegetation types. In Central America the area of strongly seasonal climate which gives rise to dry forest occurs mostly along the Pacific coast in a narrow, but formerly continuous band, from Mexico to the Guanacaste region of north-western Costa Rica. There are also outliers farther south in the Terraba Valley of Costa Rica, the Azuero Peninsula of Panama and around Garachine in the Darién region of Panama. In South America, more extensive dry forests occur in northern Colombia, Venezuela, coastal Ecuador and adjacent Peru, and from north-west Argentina to north-east Brazil. The main area of dry forest is the chaco (encompassing the western half of Paraguay and adjacent regions of Bolivia and Argentina).

While dry forests are not as species-rich as moist forests, they are floristically distinct and contain a high degree of regional endemism. For example, 73 per cent of the flora of the *chaco-cerrado-caatinga* dry areas are regionally endemic. The very dry, open forest types have not been mapped in this Atlas.

Centres of Plant Diversity and Endemism
Several theories have been advanced to explain patterns of diversity and endemism in the Americas and why some areas of rain forest, in particular, have higher degrees of endemism than others. A popular theory is that the forest in South America was reduced to isolated refugia during Pleistocene glacial advances when the climate of the region became drier and cooler. Whether or not they were refugia, the fact that centres of endemism exist for a large number of different organisms (e.g. Haffer, 1969 and Chapter 4 for birds; Brown, 1976, 1982, 1987 for insects; Prance, 1973, 1979, 1982 for plants) has been well established (although there have been suggestions that these apparent centres of richness are merely well-collected areas, see Granville, 1988; Nelson *et al.*, 1990). The existence of centres of endemism certainly makes conservation of these areas of prime importance since their protection would conserve clusters of endemic species.

Other theories to explain speciation in the region focus on the previously more extensive "cloud forests" (Gentry, 1982b, 1989; Gentry and Dodson, 1987), speciation associated with habitat complexity in north-western and north-central Amazonia (Gentry, 1986, 1989; Gentry and Ortiz, 1993), speciation associated with riverine barriers to gene flow in the largest river system of the world (Capparella, 1988; Ducke and Black, 1953), and biogeographical theories focusing on the "Great American Interchange" following the joining of South and Central America approximately 3.1 million BP (Gentry, 1982b; Marshall *et al.*, 1979).

Centres of Crop Plant Diversity
It has long been known that some areas have been of particular importance for the number of crop plants which originated there. They are known as Vavilov Centres after the Russian scientist who first described them. Four are located in the Neotropics (Vavilov, 1951). The Mexican-Central American Centre was the original source of such plants as cotton, amaranth, sweet potato, maize, green peppers and *Phaseolus* beans; the Peru-Ecuador-Bolivia Centre produced the potato, beans, tobacco, papaya, quinoa, tomato and others; the Chilean Centre yielded the strawberry and the Central Brazil-Paraguay Centre was the home of the pineapple, peanut, maté, cashew and cassava amongst others.

The areas where wild relatives of crop plants are likely to occur are of prime importance for conservation. For example, wild species are still contributing considerably to breeding programmes of potato and tomato, adding genes for such properties as disease resistance, sweetness and hardiness. The areas of importance for the contribution of plants of economic value are not confined to the Vavilov Centres. For example, in recent years attention has been drawn to the region of the Brazil-Peru-Colombia frontier, the area inhabited by the Tikuna Indians. Crops which have originated in this area include peach palm

---

CRITERIA FOR CPD SITE SELECTION
The following broad set of criteria have been developed following consultation with a large number of botanists and conservation biologists worldwide.

To be selected as a CPD site, areas have one of the following characteristics:

1. the area is evidently species-rich, even though the number of species present may not be accurately known;

2. the area is known to contain a large number of species endemic to it.

The following characteristics are also considered in the selection:

a) the site contains an important gene pool of plants of value to man, or plants that are potentially useful;

b) the site contains a diverse range of habitat types;

c) the site contains a significant proportion of species adapted to special edaphic conditions;

d) the site is threatened or under imminent threat of large-scale devastation.

Source: WWF/IUCN (1994)

Table 3.2 List of CPD sites in the Caribbean and Central America

Country	Code	Site Name	Country	Code	Site Name
Cuba	Cb3	Cajalbana Tableland and Preluda Mt Region	Mexico	MA11	Apachian-Madrean Region
Jamaica	Cb10	Blue and John Crow Mountains	Mexico	MA12	Central Region of Baja California Peninsula
Jamaica	Cb11	Cockpit Country	Guatemala	MA13	Petén Region and Maya Biosphere Reserve
Mexico	MA1	Lacandon Rain Forest Region	Guatemala	MA14	Sierra de la Minas Region and Biosphere Reserve
Mexico	MA2	Uxpanapa-Chimalapa Region			
Mexico	MA3	Sierra de Juárez, Oaxaca	Honduras	MA15	NE Honduras and Río Plátano Biosphere Reserve
Mexico	MA4	Tehuacán-Cuicatlán Region			
Mexico	MA5	Canyon of the Zopilote Region	Costa Rica	MA16	Braulio Carrillo-La Selva Region
Mexico	MA6	Sierra de Manantlán Region and Biosphere Reserve	Costa Rica Panama	MA17	La Amistad Region
Mexico	MA7	Pacific Lowlands, Jalisco			
Mexico	MA8	Upper Mezquital River Region, Sierra Madre Occidental	Costa Rica	MA18	Osa Peninsula and Corcovado National Park
Mexico	MA9	Gómez Farías Region and El Cielo Biosphere Reserve	Panama	MA19	Cerro Azul and Cerro Jefe (in Chagres National Park)
Mexico	MA10	Cuetras Ciénagas Region	Panama	MA20	Darién Province and Darién National Park

Figure 3.2 Centres of Plant Diversity in Central America and the Caribbean

Source: Davis *et al.* (in press)

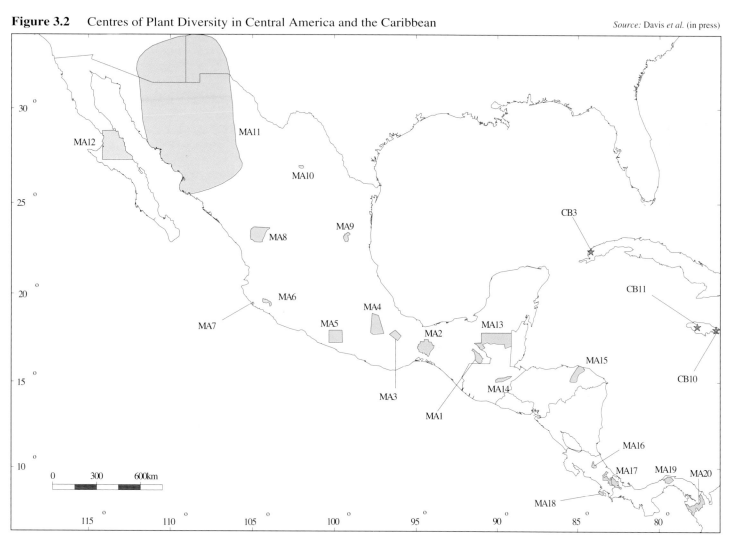

Table 3.3   List of CPD sites in South America*+

Country	Code	Site Name
CARIBBEAN		
Venezuela	SA1	Coastal Cordillera
GUAYANA HIGHLANDS		
Venezuela	SA2	Pantepui Region
AMAZONIA: Northeastern Amazonia-Guyana		
French Guiana	SA3	Saül Region
Brazil	SA4	Transverse Dry Belt[1]
AMAZONIA: Central and Guayanan Amazonia		
Brazil	SA5	Manaus Region
Brazil, Colombia, Venezuela	SA6	Upper Rio Negro Region
Colombia	SA7	Chiribiquete-Araracuara-Cahuinarí
AMAZONIA: Western Amazonia		
Ecuador	SA8	Yasuní NP and Waorani Ethnic Reserve
Peru, Colombia	SA9	Iquitos Region
AMAZONIA: Southwestern Amazonia		
Peru	SA10	Tambopata Region
AMAZONIA: Pre-Andean Amazonia		
Peru	SA11	Lowlands of Manu National Park
MATA ATLANTICA: Northern Region (Rio Grande de Norte to Bahia)		
Brazil	SA12	Atlantic Moist Forest of Southern Bahia
MATA ATLANTICA: Central Region, Espirito Santo to Sao Paulo		
Brazil	SA13	Tabuleiro Forests of Northern Espírito Santo
Brazil	SA14	Cabo Frio Region
Brazil	SA15	Mountain Ranges of Rio de Janeiro
MATA ATLANTICA: Southern Region (Southern São Paulo to Rio Grande do Sul)		
Brazil	SA16	Serra do Japi
Brazil	SA17	Juréia-Itatins Ecological Station
MATA ATLANTICA: Interior: Paraná Basin		
Paraguay	SA18	Mbaracayú Reserve
INTERIOR DRY AND MESIC FORESTS		
Brazil	SA19	Caatinga of Northeastern Brazil[2]
Brazil	SA20	Espinhaço Range Region[1]
Brazil	SA21	Distrito Féderal
Argentina, Paraguay, Brazil, Bolivia	SA22	Gran Chaco
Bolivia	SA23	Southeastern Santa Cruz
Brazil	SA24	Llanos de Mojos Region
(Tropical) ANDEAN: Paramo with Espeletiinae		
Colombia	SA25	Sierra Nevada de Santa Marta
Colombia	SA28	Los Nevados National Park
Colombia	SA29	Central Colombian Massif
Colombia	SA30	Volcanoes of Nariñense Plateau
(Tropical) ANDES: Paramo without Espeletiinae		
Ecuador	SA31	Páramo and Andean Forests of Sangay NP
Ecuador, Peru	SA32	Huancabamba Region
Peru	SA33	Peruvian Puna
(Tropical) ANDEAN: Tucumano-Boliviano Region		
Argentina	SA35	Anconquija Region
(Tropical) ANDEAN: Eastern Slope		
Bolivia	SA36	Madidi-Apolo Region
Peru	SA37	Eastern Slopes of Peruvian Andes
Ecuador	SA38	Gran Sumaco and Upper Napo River Region
PACIFIC COAST		
Colombia	SA39	Chocó Region
Ecuador	SA40	Mesic Forests on the Pacific Coast
Peru	SA41	Cerros de Amotape National Park Region
Peru	SA42	Lomas Formations
Chile	SA43	Lomas Formations of Atacama Desert
SOUTHERN CONE		
Chile	SA44	Mediterranean Region and La Campana NP
Chile	SA45	Temperate Rain Forests
Argentina, Chile	SA46	Patagonia

*   See Note on Table 3.2

+   South America has been divided phytogeographically (see names in bold on this Table) according to the classification developed at the 1991 CPD Workshop in Quito, Ecuador.

[1]   not mapped in this Atlas

[2]   will be mapped in more detail in Davis *et al.* (in press)

Bactris gasipaes, sapota *Quararibea cordata*, abiu *Pouteria caimito*, biribá *Rollinia mucosa*, sachamanga *Grias neuberthii*, uvilla *Pourouma cecropiifolia* and cubiu *Solanum sessiliflorum* (Clement, 1989). These and other fruit make the Tikuna area one of extreme importance for conservation.

Identifying Areas for Conservation

Until recently, the various factors discussed above have not been considered properly in conservation planning in the region, although some conservation plans have taken into account some, but not all, of the factors. For example, a Brazilian plan for the Amazon region, Wetterberg *et al.*, (1976, 1981), used phytogeographic regions (Prance, 1977) and proposed centres of endemism as its main criteria. Highest priority was given to

areas where plant, insect and bird endemism overlapped, and reserves were proposed within each region.

One recent initiative which considered all the various biological factors for planning an effective conservation areas system in Amazonia was a workshop held in Manaus, Brazil, in January 1990 (see Box 1). This brought together almost 100 biologists, physical scientists, ecologists, and conservation planners and resulted in a map indicating 94 areas of top priority for conservation (Figure 3.1).

The WWF/IUCN Centres of Plant Diversity (CPD) Project

The identification of sites of top priority for plant conservation is the objective of the *WWF/IUCN Centres of Plant Diversity* (CPD) project. Started in 1989, CPD is a major international collaborative project, partly funded by ODA and the EC. The results of the project will be published in late 1994, and will provide a global analysis of centres of plant diversity and endemism, indicating those areas which, if protected, would save the majority of wild plant species (WWF/IUCN, 1994).

The CPD concept is related to that of the work by crop geneticists in selecting centres of origin and diversity of crop plants — the so-called Vavilov Centres of Crop Genetic Diversity (Hawkes, 1983) described above. However, the main criteria for selecting CPD sites are those of high plant species diversity and/or endemism, while habitat diversity and the presence of important gene pools of plants are secondary criteria (see Box 2).

A total of 232 sites worldwide meet CPD criteria and will receive detailed treatment in Data Sheets. Other areas of botanical importance, meeting the general criteria for selection as CPD sites, will be included in the CPD publications, but these other sites will not be treated in detail.

In practice, most sites selected in the CPD project have in excess of 1000 vascular plant species, of which at least 10 per cent are endemic to the phytogeographic region in which the site occurs, and often a significant proportion of the total flora is endemic to the chosen site.

The selection of CPD sites for Latin America built upon initiatives such as that of the Manaus workshop for the Amazonian region, and has involved the collaboration of numerous botanists, botanical institutions and conservation organizations throughout the region. The work of coordinating these efforts has been undertaken by Olga Herrera-MacBryde at the Smithsonian Institution for Middle and South America, and by Dennis Adams in London for the Caribbean region, as well as by Stephen Davis and Vernon Heyward in the IUCN Plant Conservation Office. For South America, the work culminated in a workshop held in Quito in June 1991 at which the final selection of CPD sites was made.

Tables 3.2 and 3.3 list the sites selected for detailed Data Sheet treatment for the Americas (Davis *et al.*, in press) and they are mapped on Figures 3.2 and 3.3 respectively. These sites are considered to be the top priorities for plant conservation. Site codes in the lists below correspond to those used on the maps in this Atlas but may vary slightly from those used in the final CPC publication (Davis *et al.*, in press).

Conclusion

Conservation of these sites would not only save many of the plant species that could be in danger of extinction, but could also protect a wide range of other organisms which are depen-

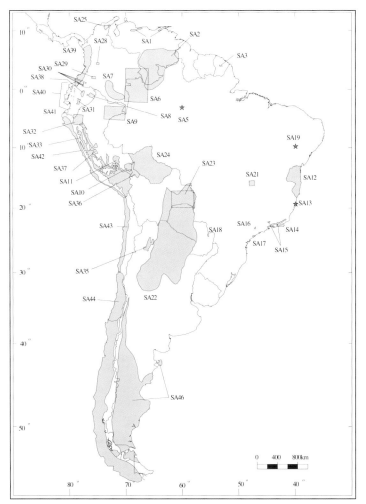

Figure 3.3 Centres of Plant Diversity — South America
Source: Davis *et al.* (in press)

dent upon the habitats that plants and natural vegetation provide. Their conservation may also provide local, regional and national economies with sustainable longterm benefits through, for example, ensuring a continued supply of plant foods and other products, ecological services, such as the prevention of soil erosion, and through attracting tourism.

References

Brown, K.S., Jr. (1976). Geographical patterns of evolution in neotropical Lepidoptera. Systematics and derivation of known and new Heliconiini (Nymphalidae : Nymphalisae). *Journal of Entomology B*. 44: 201–242.

Brown, K.S., Jr. (1982). Paleoecology and regional patterns of evolution in neotropical forest butterflies, pp. 255–308. In: *Biological Diversification in the Tropics*. Prance, G.T. (ed.). Columbia University Press, New York.

Brown, K.S., Jr. (1987). Biogeography and evolution of Neotropical butterflies. Pp. 64–104. In: *Biogeography and Quaternary History in Tropical America*. Whitmore, T.C. and Prance, G.T. (eds). Oxford Monographs on Biogeography 3, Clarendon Press, Oxford.

Capparella, A. (1988). Genetic variation in neotropical birds: Implications for the speciation process. Pp. 1658–1664, 1669–1673. In: *Acta XIX Congress International Ornithology: Volume 2*. Ouellet, H. (ed.), University of Ottowa Press, Canada.

Clement, C.R. (1989). A center of crop genetic diversity in western Amazonia. *Bioscience* 39: 624–630.

Davis, S.D., Heywood, V.H. and Herrera-MacBryde, O. (eds) (in press). *Centres of Plant Diversity: A Guide and Strategy for their Conservation. Volume 3: The Americas*. World Wide Fund for Nature and IUCN — The World Conservation Union.

D'Arcy, W.G. (1977). Endangered landscapes in Panama and

Central America: the threat to plant species. In: *Extinction is Forever*. Prance, G.T. and Elias, T.S. (eds). New York Botanical Garden, New York. Pp. 89–102.

Ducke, A. and Black, G. (1953). Phytogeographical notes on the Brazilian Amazon. *Anais-Academia Brasileira de Ciencias* 25 (1): 1–46.

Gentry, A.H. (1982a). Phytogeographic patterns in northwest South America and Southern Central America as evidence for a Chocó refugium. Pages 112–136. In: *Biological Diversification in the Tropics*. G.T. Prance (ed.), Columbia University Press, New York.

Gentry, A.H. (1982b). Neotropical floristic diversity: phytogeographical connections between Central and South America, Pleistocene fluctuations or an accident of the Andean orogeny. *Annals Missouri Botanical Garden* 69: 557–593.

Gentry, A.H. (1986). Endemism in tropical vs temperate plant communities. In: *Conservation Biology*. Soulé, M. (ed.). Sinauer Press, Sunderland, Massachusetts. Pp. 153–181.

Gentry, A.H. (1989). Speciation in tropical forests. In: *Tropical Botany*. Larsen, K. and Holm-Nielson, L.B. (eds). Academic Press, London. Pp. 113–134.

Gentry, A.H. (1992). Tropical forest biodiversity: distributional patterns and their conservational significance. *Oikos* 63: 19–28.

Gentry, A.H. and Dodson, C. (1987). Contribution of nontrees to species richness of a tropical rain forest. *Biotropica* 19: 149–156.

Gentry, A.H. and Ortiz, R. (1993). Patrones de composicion floristica en la Amazonia Peruana. In: *Amazonia Peruviana — vegetación húmedo tropical en el llano subandino*. Kalliola, R., Puhakka, M and Danjoy, W. (eds). Proyecto Amazonia, Universidad de Turku, Finland/Oficina Nacional de Evaluación de Recursos Naturales, Lima, Peru.

Granville, J.J. de (1988). Phytogeographical characteristics of the Guianan Forests. *Taxon* 37(3): 578–594.

Haffer, J. (1969). Speciation in Amazonian forest birds. *Science* 165: 131–137.

Hawkes, J.G. (1983). *The Diversity of Crop Plants*. Harvard University Press, Cambridge, Massachusetts

Huber, O. and Alarcón, C. (1988). *Mapa de la Vegetación de Venezuela*. MARNR & The Nature Conservancy, Caracas, Venezuela.

Hueck, K. and Seibert, P. (1972). *Vegetationskarte von Sudamerika*. Gustav Fischer Verlag, Stuttgart.

IBGE (1988). *Mapa de Vegetação do Brasil*. Fundação Instituto Brasileiro de Geografia e Estatística, Brasília.

Marshall, L., Butler, R., Drake, R., Curtis, G. and Tedford, R. (1979). Calibration of the great American interchange. *Science* 204: 272–279.

Myers (1988). Threatened biotas: "hotspots" in tropical forests. *Environmentalist* 8: 1–20.

Nelson, B.W., Ferreira, C.A.C., da Silva, M.F. and Kawasak, M.L. (1990). Endemism centres, refugia and botanical collection density in Brazilian Amazonia. *Nature* 345: 714–716.

Prance, G.T. (1973). Phytogeographic support for the theory of Pleistocene forest refuges in the Amazon Basin, based on evidence from distribution patterns in Caryocaraceae, Chrysobalanaceae, Dichapetalaceae and Lecythidaceae. *Acta Amazonica* 3: 5–28.

Prance, G.T. (1977). The phytogeographic subdivision of Amazonia and their influence on the selection of biological reserves. Pp. 195–213. In: *Extinction is Forever*. Prance, G.T. and Elias, T.S. (eds). New York Botanical Garden.

Prance, G.T. (1979). Distribution patterns of lowland neotropical species with relation to history, dispersal and ecology with special reference to Chrysobalanaceae, Caryocaraceae and Lecythidaceae, pp. 59–88. In: *Tropical Botany*. Larsen, K. and Holm-Nielson, L.B. (eds.). Academic Press, London, New York.

Prance, G.T. (1982). Forest refuges: evidence from woody angiosperms. In: *Biological Diversification in the Tropics*. pp. 137–156. G.T. Prance (ed.). Columbia University Press, New York.

Prance, G.T. (1989). American tropical forests. In: *Ecosystems of the World 14B: Tropical Rain Forest Ecosystems, Biogeographical and Ecological Studies*. pp. 99–132. Lieth, H. and Werger, M.J.A. (eds). Elsevier, Oxford.

Prance, G.T. and Schubart, H.O.R. (1978). Notes on the vegetation of Amazonia I. A preliminary note on the origin of the open white sand campinas of the lower Rio Negro. *Brittonia* 30: 60–63.

Projeto RADAM (1975). *Levantamento de recursos naturais: 7*. Ministmrio das Minas e Energia, Rio de Janeiro, Brazil.

Raven, P.H. (1987). The scope of the plant conservation problem world-wide. In: *Botanic Gardens and the World Conservation Strategy*. Bramwell, D., Hamann, O., Heywood, V. and Synge, H. (eds). Academic Press, London. pp. 19–29.

Unesco (1981). Vegetation Map of South America. *Natural Resources Research Publication* 17.

Vavilov, N.I. (1951). The origin, variation, immunity and breeding of cultivated plants. Chronica Botanica, Waltham, Mass.

Wetterberg, G.B., Jorge Pádua, M.T., Castro, C.S. and Vasconcellos, J.M.C. de (1976). *Uma análise de prioridades em conservao de natureza na Amazônia*. PNUD/FAO/IBDF/BRA-45 Serie Tecnica No. 8. 62 pp.

Wetterberg, G.B., Prance, G.T. and Lovejoy, T.E. (1981). Conservation progress in Amazonia: a structural review. *Parks* 6(2): 5–10.

Whitmore, T.C. and Sayer, J.A. (eds) (1992). *Tropical Deforestation and Species Extinction*. Chapman and Hall, London.

WWF/IUCN (1994). *Centres of Plant Diversity: A Guide and Strategy for their Conservation*. World Wide Fund for Nature and IUCN — The World Conservation Union (3 vols).

Authors: Stephen Davis, IUCN Plant Conservation Office, and Ghillean Prance, Royal Botanic Garden Kew, using additional material from accounts written for the forthcoming CPD publication by Denis Adams, London, for the Carribean; the late Alwyn Gentry, Missouri Botanical Garden, for South America; Otto Huber, Caracas, Venezuela and Carlos Villamil, Universidad Nacional del Sur Argentina, for South America; Jane Villa-Lobos and Olga Herrera-MacBryde, both from the Smithsonian Institution, for South and Central America.

4 Establishing Conservation Priorities Using Endemic Birds

INTRODUCTION

The Neotropics are extremely rich in species of wildlife. Taxonomists and biogeographers, faced by the sheer scale of this variety, are still struggling with calculations of the number of possible species to be discovered in the region. Meanwhile, the conservationist is left in pressing need of knowing where this diversity is most concentrated, so that something may be done to secure its future.

This is particularly true as rampant human population growth exploits and exhausts the planet's natural resources at such a speed that many species are lost even before being identified. Wilson's (1988) call for a map of biodiversity recognized the value of identifying the areas for conservation that would ensure the continued survival and evolution of the highest proportion of the world's biota. The question remains how to construct such a map.

One key approach is to analyse and extrapolate from a major group of animals or plants that is both taxonomically well researched and distributionally well understood, for without these two factors any geographic quantification becomes highly unreliable. Birds are the most amenable group. Attempts to consider *richness* in terms of sheer numbers in individual areas are subject to serious biases and inconsistencies in available data. However, allied to the concept of *endemism*, richness becomes a useful criterion.

Knowledge of centres of endemism — areas that hold assemblages of species found nowhere else — is critical to any conservation programme. On the assumption that wider-ranging species are likely to have greater chances of survival, centres of endemism should represent primary targets for conservation; and the richer they are in unique species, the more significant their claim on our attention.

BirdLife International's Biodiversity Project (ICBP, 1992; Crosby, 1994; Stattersfield *et al.*, in prep.) has advanced the analysis of centres of endemism throughout the world, and this chapter places the results of its work in the context of forest conservation in the American tropics. However, it is important to emphasize that birds make many contributions to the diversity of forests other than guiding conservationists to the hotspots. Low density, wide-ranging species, such as raptors, may be essential for the functioning of ecosystems, and these birds can-not be conserved in small forest reserves that are at a great distance from each other (Thiollay, 1985). Indeed the long-term *Forest Biodynamics Project* of the Smithsonian Institution and World Wildlife Fund in the Brazilian Amazon which examines the rates and patterns of species loss from different-sized forest patches uses birds as the key indicators (Lovejoy *et al.*, 1984; Bierregaard and Lovejoy, 1989; Bierregaard, 1990; see Chapter 26). Birds are major dispersers of seeds and pollinators of plants, and thus play a vital role in the spatial heterogeneity and taxonomic diversity of Neotropical forests (Stiles, 1985). Moreover, these forests host not only thousands of resident species, but many Nearctic migrants, whose ecological functions are as important as those of the residents (Rappole, 1991).

Mapping Endemic Bird Areas

The BirdLife Biodiversity Project has collected data on all landbirds which have had, in historical times, a total global breeding range estimated to be below 50,000 sq. km ("restricted-range species"), which is about the size of Costa Rica. The 50,000 sq. km range size criterion is arbitrary, but produces a manageable sample of those species which are most vulnerable to habitat destruction and need some form of protection. The use of this size as the threshold was influenced by the work of Terborgh and Winter (1983), who mapped the distributions of 155 Colombian and Ecuadorian bird species with ranges below 50,000 sq. km. Terborgh and Winter used the bird distributions to locate areas of endemism and advocated the technique as a cost-effective method for designing protected area networks in tropical countries.

Candidate bird lists for BirdLife's project were drawn up by region, using the available literature. For each species, distributional information was collated from published and unpublished sources, the latter obtained mainly from BirdLife International's extensive network of contacts. A database of precisely geo-referenced localities was developed, from which the distribution of each bird could be mapped using a Geographic Information System (see Figure 4.1).

The data-gathering spanned four years, and resulted in more than 50,000 locality records (of which 87 per cent have been assigned coordinates) for 2609 restricted-range species of the

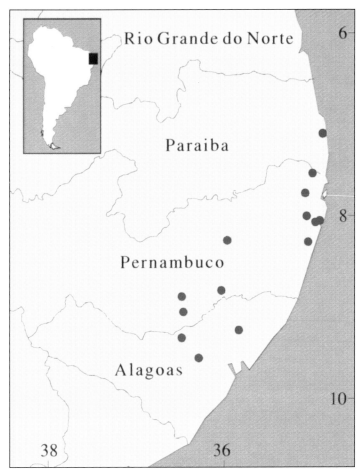

Figure 4.1 Distribution of the seven-coloured tanager *Tangara fastuosa* in the Atlantic forest

world. In addition to these extant species, a total of 59 restricted-range bird species which have become extinct since 1800 were used in the analysis.

The initial aim was to identify areas with concentrations of restricted-range species. Areas which support two or more species that are entirely confined to them were considered of primary importance, and are referred to as Endemic Bird Areas (EBAs). The EBAs were identified by a combination of a multivariate statistical analysis and an investigation of the habitat and altitudinal requirements of the bird species. Simultaneously, patterns of endemism in other life-forms were investigated and shown to be closely congruent with those that emerged from the avian analysis.

Global Patterns

More than one-quarter of all bird species have a breeding range of 50,000 sq. km or less, and these restricted-range species are found in 147 countries out of the world total of 235, that is in more than 62 per cent of all countries. A total of 223 EBAs, all with at least two restricted-range bird species confined to them, have been identified (Long *et al.*, in press). Over 95 per cent of restricted-range birds occur in these areas. The remaining 125 either do not overlap with other restricted-range species, or overlap with only a small portion of their ranges.

The number of restricted-range species in each of the world's EBAs ranges from just two to 67, but the majority of areas (53 per cent) support between two and 10. The number of restricted-range species per unit area also varies considerably, with small island EBAs often containing relatively high numbers of species

and large continental areas sometimes supporting relatively low numbers. Most of the EBAs have a density of less than four restricted-range species per 1000 sq. km.

Trends in the Americas

There are 1046 restricted-range bird species in the Americas, 40 per cent of the global total. South America, with over 700 species, has more restricted-range birds than any other continent; there are 130 in the Caribbean and 205 in Central America. Some countries have exceptionally high numbers of restricted-range species. For example, although Indonesia leads with 411, six of the American countries (Peru, Brazil, Colombia, Ecuador, Venezuela and Mexico) are in the top ten countries for the world, each having over 100 restricted-range species occurring in their territory (Figure 4.2). Other important countries in the Americas are Costa Rica and Panama, which when combined have 171 restricted-range species in their small territories. There are 79 EBAs in the Americas (35 per cent of the global total), and Brazil, Peru, Mexico, Colombia, Ecuador and Argentina are all among the top ten countries in the world in terms of the number of EBAs they each hold.

Forest is the most important habitat for restricted-range birds, and in the Americas tropical humid forests are especially important. Nearly two-thirds of mainland EBAs in South America have some humid forest habitat within them, and 55 per cent are wholly characterized by this vegetation type. Each of the EBAs in the Caribbean have some species using humid forest and in central Mexico half of the EBAs are made up of this habitat.

EBAs in the Caribbean

The Caribbean islands consist of two distinct groups: the Greater Antilles and the Lesser Antilles. The avifaunas of the Greater Antilles show greater similarities to Central and North America than do those of the Lesser Antilles, which are more closely related to South America. Collectively, however, the Caribbean avifauna is quite discrete from that of the mainland

Figure 4.2 Countries with the highest numbers of restricted-range bird species in the Americas

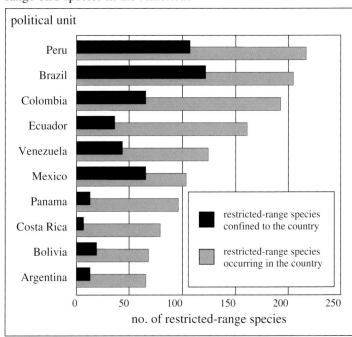

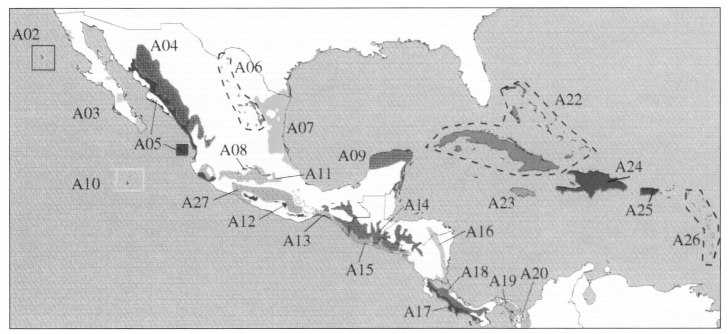

Figure 4.3 The Endemic Bird Areas of Central America and the Caribbean

(Lack, 1976), with just four restricted-range bird species being shared between the islands and continental America. Nearly every island in the Caribbean is included within, or forms, an EBA, with a total of five in the region (Figure 4.3, Table 4.1). Each of the EBAs is characterized in part by humid forest and this is reflected by more than two-thirds of the Caribbean

restricted-range species requiring this habitat.

Notable single-island EBAs are Jamaica and Puerto Rico, both supporting high numbers of restricted-range species (34, 26) in relation to their size (11,000 sq. km, 9000 sq. km). The Eastern Caribbean EBA (A26 on Figure 4.3) incorporates 14 political units and many islands from the Virgin Islands south to

Table 4.1 Endemic Bird Areas of Middle America

Area code and name	Altitude (m)	Habitat[s]°	Size sq. km	r-r species confined	r-r species occurring
A02 Guadalupe Island*	sea level	mixed	280	1	1
A03 Baja California	0–1,000	mixed	24,000	3	3
A04 Sierra Madre Occidental	1,200–3,050	forest	117,000	3	5
A05 North-west Mexican Pacific slope	0–1,000	humid and dry forest, scrub	14,000	7	7
A06 Sierra Madre Oriental	1,800–3,500	forest	9,500	2	2
A07 North-east Mexican Gulf slope	0–1,000	mixed	97,000	4	4
A08 Central Mexican marshes	1,500–2,500	wetland	6,600	1	1
A09 Yucatán Peninsula	0–300	humid and dry forest, scrub	56,900	14	18
A10 Revillagigedo Islands	0–300	scrub, forest	280	5	5
A11 Central Mexican highlands	900–3,500	scrub, forest	57,000	1	9
A12 Sierra Madre del Sur	300–2,000	humid and dry forest, scrub	7,400	4	9
A13 Isthmus de Tehuantepec	0–1,000	scrub, dry forest	7,100	2	4
A14 North Mesoamerican highlands	600–3,000	humid forest	102,000	18	18
A15 North Mesoamerican Pacific slope	0–1,050	humid and dry forest, scrub	28,000	3	4
A16 Central American Caribbean slope	0–1,200	humid forest	43,000	7	12
A17 Southern Central American Pacific slope	0–1,500	humid forest	22,000	13	16
A18 Costa Rica and Panama highlands	600–3,350	humid forest	28,000	49	52
A19 Darién and Uraba lowlands	0–1,000	humid forest	41,000	5	15
A20 East Panama and Darién lowlands	600–1,600	humid forest	1,700	12	16
A21 Cocos Island	sea level	humid forest, dry forest, scrub	37	3	3
A22 Cuba and the Bahama Islands	0–2,000	humid forest, dry forest, scrub	93,000	19	24
A23 Jamaica	0–2,200	humid forest, dry forest, scrub	11,000	27	35
A24 Hispaniola	0–3,000	humid forest, dry forest, scrub	76,000	23	35
A25 Puerto Rico	0–1,200	humid forest, dry forest, mixed	9,000	10	25
A26 Eastern Caribbean	0–1,200	humid forest, dry forest, scrub	6,600	25	39
A27 Balsas Drainage	0–1,500	humid forest, dry forest, scrub			
			64,000	11	13

° the most important habitat of the EBA is given first.

r-r = restircted range.

* Guadalupe Island is an EBA because it had one restricted-range species that is now extinct, as well as its one extant restricted range species.

The St. Lucia Amazon Amazona versicolor, *endemic to St. Lucia: one of the most threatened birds in the world.*

(WWF/Paul Wachtel)

Grenada. Several of the islands support their own single-island endemics, indeed St Lucia (620 sq. km) has four species unique to it. However, many more restricted-range species are shared with nearby islands, thus making the whole of the Eastern Caribbean one EBA.

Patterns of endemism for other life-forms in the Caribbean are relatively well documented and show congruence with the bird distributions. A general trend for reptiles and amphibians is the occurrence of a large number of single-island or island-group endemic species on the four Greater Antillean islands of Cuba, Jamaica, Hispaniola and Puerto Rico. The Lesser Antilles have relatively fewer single-island endemic species, but a large element of the herpetofauna is endemic to the Lesser Antilles as a whole, mirroring the Eastern Caribbean EBA. Similar patterns were shown in the Caribbean mammal fauna in historic times (Woods, 1989), but many of these species are now extinct. The described patterns of endemism in insects for the Caribbean as shown by Liebherr (1988) indicate congruence with the bird and other life-forms. In the Greater Antilles there a high numbers of single-island endemic plants, with for instance 3000 endemic species on Cuba and 1800 species on Hispaniola (Davis *et al.*, 1986).

EBAs In Central America

There are 26 EBAs in this region with three (Guadalupe, Socorro and Cocos) being islands and the rest located on the mainland (Figure 4.3, Table 4.1). Central America (including Mexico) forms a land-bridge between North and South America, but despite having avifaunal relationships with both continents it shares few restricted-range species with either. The topography of the region is complex with a series of mountain chains passing through it, effectively separating the Pacific lowlands from the Atlantic or Caribbean lowlands. EBAs are situated in the lowlands on both of these slopes (such as the Northern Central American Pacific slope – A15) and in the higher mountainous areas (such as the Costa Rican and Panamanian highlands – A18).

Most of the EBAs from south of the Isthmus of Tehuantepec in southern Mexico to Panama are humid forest areas, but north of the isthmus several are located in other vegetation types. For instance, there are a few EBAs that consist of temperate habitat, especially of pine-oak forest (Sierra Madre Occidental – A04 and Central Mexican highlands – A11); a number occur in the coastal plains and interior plateaus in which the habitat is typically tropical deciduous in nature (North-west Pacific slope – A05 and Northeast Mexican Gulf slope – A07); and some EBAs, especially the submontane and montane forests of the region, such as the Sierra Madre del Sur (A12), show both tropical and temperate elements in the flora.

The majority of EBAs in Central America contain less than 10 restricted-range species, but a number of the humid forest EBAs have more (e.g. A14 has 18; A27 has 14), and the Costa Rican and Panamanian highlands EBA (A18), with 52 species, has one of the highest number in the world although the mountain range is only 30,000 sq. km in size.

Patterns of endemism for other life-forms in Central America are overall less well documented than for birds, but valuable comparisons between taxa can be drawn for some parts of the region. There are striking similarities between areas of endemism in the herpetofauna (Duellman, 1966; Savage, 1966, 1982) and the forest EBAs of southern Central America (EBAs A09 and A13 to A19). Studies of heliconiine and ithominiine butterflies in southern Central America (Brown, 1987) and recent work on the lepidopteran fauna of Costa Rica (Thomas, 1991) suggest similar congruence with these forest EBAs.

High levels of endemism in the flora of Central America have been noted for Mexico (Rzedowski, 1978) and for Costa Rica and Panama, where the level of national endemism is expected to exceed 20 per cent of the total flora (Gentry, 1986). The boundaries of these areas of endemism are not yet well defined, but certain habitats such as the mesophyllous evergreen forests (cloud forests) are noted as holding particularly high numbers of endemic plants (Breedlove, 1981).

EBAs in South America

South America has a higher diversity of birds than any other continent, with almost 3000 landbird species; and its 52 EBAs are more than occur in any other biogeographic region (Figure 4.4). The tropical lowland and montane humid forests hold the greatest proportion of the continent's EBAs (Table 4.2). There are many humid forest EBAs along both slopes of the Andes, in the Amazon basin and in the Atlantic coastal forests.

The Andes run from north to south along the entire length of the western part of the continent, forming a barrier to the dispersal of lowland and submontane animals and plants on either side. This has led to the development of a series of EBAs run-

Table 4.2 Endemic Bird Areas of South America

Area code and name	Altitude (m)	Habitat[s]°	Size sq. km	r-r species confined	r-r species occurring
B01 Guianas	0–1,100	humid forest	62,000	4	6
B02 Tepuís	500–2,800	humid forest	56,000	35	41
B03 Cordillera de Caripe and Paria Peninsula	700–2,500	humid forest	4,500	5	14
B04 Cordillera de la Costa Central, Venezuela	750–2,400	humid forest	6,800	5	19
B05 North and Central Venezuelan lowlands	0–1,100	savanna, mixed	65,000	2	2
B06 Cordillera de Mérida	750–4,000	humid forest	17,000	11	29
B07 Caribbean dry zone of Colombia and Venezuela	0–600	scrub, dry forest	53,000	10	12
B08 Santa Maria Mountains	750–4,600	humid forest	4,000	15	22
B09 Nechí lowlands	0–1,500	humid forest, scrub	33,000	3	13
B10 East Andes of Colombia	900–5,200	humid forest, wetland	70,000	12	32
B11 Upper Río Negro and Orinoco white sand forests	100–500	humid forest	32,000	11	13
B12 Subtropical Inter-Andean Colombia	1,200–2,500	humid forest	46,000	5	17
B13 Dry Inter-Andean valleys, Colombia	200–1,700	dry forest, scrub	17,000	4	4
B14 Chocó and Pacific slope Andes	0–1,200	humid forest	96,000	52	62
B16 Galapagos Islands	0–1,300	scrub, forest	8,000	23	23
B17 North Central Andean forests	1,500–3,500	humid forest	29,000	4	8
B18 Eastern Andes of Ecuador and northern Peru	400–2,000	humid forest	24,000	11	15
B19 Napo and upper Amazon lowlands	100–600	humid forest	195,000	10	10
B20 Tumbesian Western Ecuador and Peru	0–2,000	dry and humid forest, scrub	101,000	45	55
B21 South Central Andean forests	1,500–3,200	humid forest	11,000	5	8
B22 Marañón valley	200–2,400	forest, scrub	11,000	11	22
B24 Sub-Andean ridgetop forests	1,000–2,450	humid forest	2,500	6	7
B25 Northeast Peruvian cordilleras	1,900–3,700	humid forest	32,000	19	24
B27 The High Peruvian Andes	1,800–4,300	scrub, humid forest	86,000	21	30
B28 Junin puna	3,700–5,000	wetland, grassland	11,000	4	5
B29 Eastern Andean foothills of Peru	700–1,600	humid forest	25,000	5	11
B30 South-east Peruvian lowlands	100–400	humid forest	174,000	14	15
B32 South Peruvian and north Chilean Pacific slope	0–3,000	scrub, mixed	79,000	9	12
B33 Upper Bolivian yungas	1,800–3,700	humid forest	24,000	14	18
B34 Lower Bolivian yungas	700–2,400	humid forest	35,000	10	17
B35 Bolivian Andes	1,400–4,600	scrub, humid forest	38,000	11	17
B36 East Bolivian lowlands	200–750	humid forest, grassland	169,000	3	3
B37 North Argentine Andes	2,000–4,000	scrub, mixed	23,000	3	5
B39 Argentine cordilleras	1,600–2,900	scrub, mixed	7,200	3	3
B40 Juan Fernández Islands	0–1,350	forest, scrub	180	3	3
B41 Central Chile	0–1,600	humid forest, scrub	106,000	6	7
B42 Tierra del Fuego and the Falklands	0–1,200	grassland, wetland	126,000	9	9
B43 Central Amazonian Brazil	0–300	humid forest	275,000	11	11
B45 Fernando de Noronha	0–60	forest, scrub	26	2	2
B46 North-east Brazilian caatinga	0–900	dry forest, scrub	651,000	5	5
B47 Alagoan Atlantic slope	0–1,000	humid forest	23,000	10	14
B48 Bahian deciduous forests	250–900	dry forest	12,000	2	2
B49 Minas Gerais deciduous forsts	300–500	dry forest	33,000	2	2
B50 Serra do Espinaço	700–1,600	grassland, scrub	87,000	5	5
B52 South-east Brazilian lowland to foothills	0–1,500	humid forest	216,000	53	60
B53 South-east Brazilian mountains	500–2,200+	humid forest	25,000	19	20
B54 South-east Brazilian *Araucaria* forest	0–1,000+	forest	153,000	4	4
B55 Entre Ríos wet grasslands	0–200	wetland	76,000	3	3
B56 Upper Río Branco	0–100	humid forest	12,000	2	2
B57 Boliviano-Tucuman Yungas	800–3,000	humid forest	31,000	8	9
B58 Valdivian Nothofagus and *Araucaria* forests of Central Chile and Argentina	0–3,000	humid forest	276,000	4	5
B60 Central Andean paramo	2,000–5,000	scrub, grassland	30,000	9	10

° the most important habitat of the EBA is given first.
r-r = restircted range.

Figure 4.4 The Endemic Bird Areas of South America

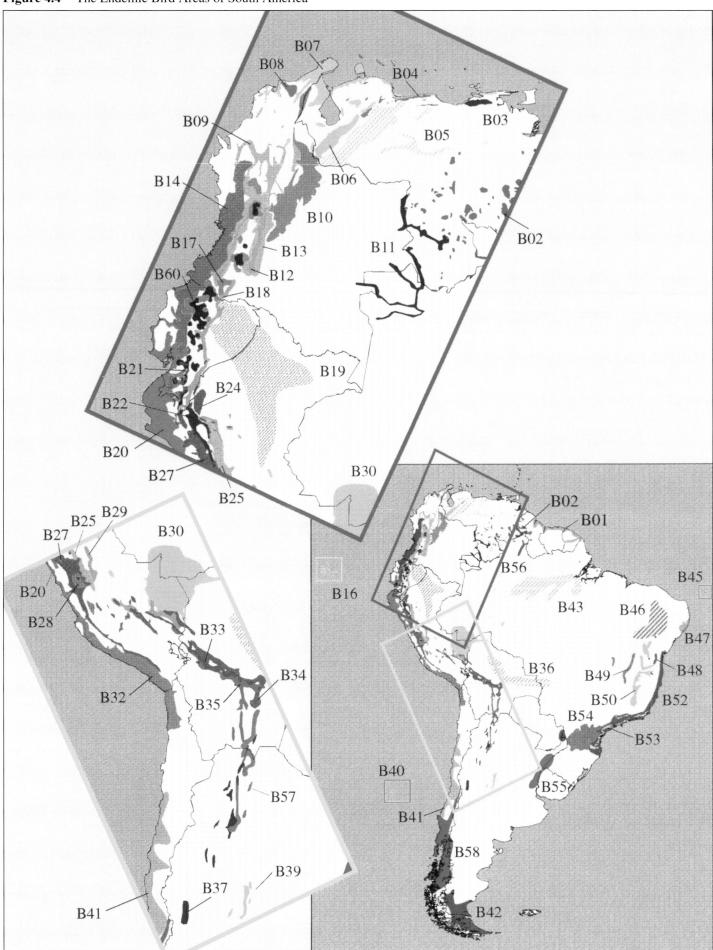

WHERE THE AMAZON BASIN MEETS THE ANDES

The South-east Peruvian lowlands EBA (B30) is a vast area (c.155,000 sq. km) in south-east Peru and westernmost Brazil, primarily between 200 and 500 m in elevation, cloaked in almost pristine lowland wet forest. The limits of the area are poorly defined (due in part to the lack of available information on the species endemic to the area), but it appears to be characterized by exceptionally high rainfall and bounded by the lower-lying Amazon basin to the east and the Andean foothills to the south-west. This EBA has a relatively large number of species (14) confined to it (see Table).

The restricted-range bird species of the south-east Peruvian lowlands EBA (B30)

Latin name	English name	Status
Pyrrhura rupicola	Black-capped parakeet	
Brachygalba albogularis	White-throated jacamar	
Galbalcyrhynchus purusianus	Chestnut jacamar	
Malacoptila semicincta	Semicollared puffbird	
Eubucco tucinkae	Scarlet-hooded barbet	T
Foricarius rufifrons	Rufous-fronted antthrush	T
Grallaria eludens	Elusive antpitta	N
Myrmeciza goeldi	Goeldi's antbird	
Percnostola lophotes	White-lined pitta	
Conioptilon mcilhennyi	Black-faced cotinga	
Lophotriccus eulophotes	Long-crested pygmy tyrant	
Poecilotriccus albifacies	White-cheeked tody tyrant	N
Todirostrum pulchellum	Black-backed tody-flycatcher	
Cacicus koepckeae	Selva cacique	T

T – Threatened, as listed by Collar *et al.* (1992)
N – Near-threatened, as listed by Collar *et al.* (1992)

Probably most importantly, however, this area has the highest diversity of birds in any area of the world. The extraordinary diversity of the avifauna (which has characteristics of both western Amazonia and the eastern Andes) is demonstrated by the occurrence of over 500 species of bird at Tambopata Natural Wildlife Refuge (55 sq. km) and in a similar sized area around Cocha Cashu Biological Station (within the Manu National Park and Biosphere Reserve), where 15,000 sq. km are thought to harbour over 1000 bird species. This remarkable biodiversity extends to all other life-forms, with 153 species of tree recorded from 1 ha of forest at Tambopata (Parker, 1982), and more than 90 species of mammals, 130 species of amphibians and reptiles and 1100 species of butterflies recorded from the two reserve areas (Terborgh *et al.*, 1984; Erwin and Rios, 1986).

It appears that for various reasons, including exceptionally high rainfall and constant renewal of nutrients from the Andean foothills, the diversity (and endemicity) of species is greater along the pre-Andean headwater regions of the Amazon than in the vast central lowlands: the diversity of birds at least falls steadily as one travels east (Collar, 1990). For these reasons, it is clear that for the conservation of species diversity the highest priorities lie not in the vast central lowlands of Amazonia, but rather in the areas around the southwestern fringes of the basin. However, this does not diminish the critical importance of the forested Amazon basin, as this is clearly the source of rainfall for all of the fringing headwater regions of the Amazon.

ning from north to south along the Pacific lowlands to the west of the Andes (such as the Chocó and Pacific slope Andes – B14). There are also EBAs along the central spine of the Andes (such as North Central Andean forests of Colombia and Ecuador – B17), in some of the larger Andean intermontane valleys (such as the Marañon valley – B22), on mountain ranges which run parallel to, but separate from, the main range (such as the Sub-Andean ridgetop forests of Ecuador and Peru – B24) and on isolated massifs (such as the Santa Marta Mountains – B08). In some parts of the Andes, for example in Peru and Bolivia, the distribution of bird species is very complex due to the varied topography and climatic patterns causing a mosaic of different habitat types.

There are relatively few EBAs in the Amazon basin compared to the Andes, because most Amazonian species are more widely distributed than the 50,000 sq. km range criterion. In addition, the distributions of many Amazonian birds are incompletely known, so the boundaries and areas of the EBAs have been only approximately defined. The high rainfall zone where the Amazonian rain forests meet the Andean foothills has the highest avian diversity of any region of the world (Ridgely and Tudor, 1989); half of the Amazonian EBAs are in this region, and there are several more in the lower parts of the adjacent foothills (see Box 1 for more information on an EBA located in this region).

An important concentration of five EBAs is located in the humid tropical Atlantic coastal forests that stretch the length of eastern Brazil (from Alagoas to Rio Grande do Sul), eastern Paraguay and across to Misiones in north-eastern Argentina. This region includes lowland rain forests and a variety of sub-

montane and montane forest types that are isolated from the rain forests of the Amazon basin by a relatively arid zone (*caatinga*, *cerrado* and *chaco*). Although some species are shared with the Amazon rain forests, there is a high level of endemism throughout the Atlantic forests. The patterns in the distributions of restricted-range species in this region are complex, and the precise delineation of EBAs is made more difficult by the extremely high levels of forest loss to which the region has been subjected since 1500.

Congruence between EBAs and areas of endemism for other life-forms is marked in some parts of South America, but more studies that use constant criteria are needed for comparing distribution and areas of endemism for different groups (Thirgood and Heath, 1994). Studies in the higher Andes are poorly documented, but the EBAs, particularly in the northern Andes, are well matched by the distribution of the endemic herpetofauna (Duellman, 1979). The flora of the eastern slopes of the Andes has been identified by Myers (1988) as a global floristic "hotspot".

Endemism occurs at a variety of different scales, especially in plants (Gentry, 1992), so that a single EBA may represent several areas of, for instance, floral endemism. This is the case in the humid forests of the Darien Highlands (A20), which comprise several isolated peaks, each with their own endemic flora (Gentry, 1986). However, nowhere is this factor of scale more apparent than in the wet tropical forests of the Pacific lowlands and foothills of western Colombia and western Ecuador. It was in this region that Gentry (1986) reported the high levels of endemism on the Centinela ridgetop, an area only about 1 km wide and 20 km long (and now destroyed). This small area supported 38 plant species that were known nowhere else on earth, including 25 per cent (six species) of the world's representatives of one genus (*Gasteranthus*).

Forero and Gentry (1988) estimate that the Choco department in Colombia (which covers the main range of EBA B14) alone holds at least 10,000 plant species, of which no fewer than a quarter are endemic. Studies of the Chocoan fauna are limited, but the high levels of endemism in the birds, also noted by Terborgh and Winter (1983), are seemingly matched in the reptiles and amphibians (Lynch, 1979) and butterflies (Brown, 1982). Similarly high levels of endemism have also been noted in the flora of the wet and dry forests below 900 m in western Ecuador (Dodson and Gentry, 1991), these forests being concordant with EBAs B14 and B20 respectively.

A large proportion of biogeographical studies have concentrated on the lowlands of Amazonia, where patterns of endemism have been presented for birds (Haffer, 1987), lizards of the genus *Anolis* (Vanzolini and Williams, 1970), heliconiine and ithominiine butterflies (Brown, 1987), and trees of the families Bignoniaceae and Chrysobalanaceae (Prance, 1987). A workshop in 1990 attempted to gather leading Amazonian experts to prioritize areas within the Amazon basin using faunal and floral distributions (Collar, 1990). The results have been published recently as a map (see Chapter 26). However, Nelson *et al.* (1990) have pointed out the dangers of using such approaches: in some areas apparent species richness may well be merely a reflection of collecting density rather than a real phenomena. No such difficulties attend the Atlantic coastal forests of Brazil, however, with high degrees of endemism of plant and animal

Figure 4.5 The distribution of threatened humid forest bird species in South America

Number of species

- 1 to 4
- 5 to 9
- 10 to 14
- 15 to 24

Table 4.3 Habitat breakdown of threatened and threatened restricted-range bird species in the Americas

Habitat	Threatened Species	
	Total	*Restricted-range*
Humid forest	203	178
Dry forest	54	46
Savanna & Gallery forest	31	22
Grassland	64	41
Wetland	27	16
Riverine	4	1
Coastal	18	7
Marine	9	
Unknown	4	3

N.B. The number of threatened species in the total column adds up to more than the total number of threatened species in the Americas as some species have been assigned to more than one habitat.

species (Jackson, 1978; Mori *et al.*, 1981; Brown, 1982; Duellman, 1982; da Fonseca, 1985; Mittermeier, 1987).

Threats to Humid Forests as Indicated by Birds

Nearly 55% (180 species) of the threatened birds of the Americas are confined to humid forest. Figure 4.5 shows the distribution of these species within South America. The Atlantic coastal forests of Brazil and eastern Paraguay immediately stand out as of critical importance, with between 15 and 24 threatened species in some of the 1 degree grid cells covering the Brazilian states of Bahia, Espírito Santo, Rio de Janeiro, Minas Gerais and São Paulo. Also highlighted are the northern Andes (and adjacent lowlands), and in particular the central East Andes, Central and West Andes of Colombia, the northern Ecuadorian Andes, the Pacific slope of Colombia and Ecuador (the Chocó), the Andes of southern Ecuador and northern Peru, and the central Peruvian Andes. In comparison to all other habitat types, the humid forests support between two and four times as many threatened species, and their importance cannot be over-emphasized.

A large number of restricted-range species are threatened (761, e.g. 29 per cent of all such birds) and these species total 77 per cent of all the world's threatened birds. In the Americas, 79 per cent (259 species) of the region's 328 threatened species, as listed by Collar *et al.* (1992), also have restricted ranges. The major cause of threat to restricted-range birds is habitat destruction, affecting 78 per cent of all birds at risk in the Americas. This figure has particular relevance to the humid forests of the region. As Table 4.3 shows, the principal habitat of threatened species and those that are of restricted range is humid forest. If deforestation continues at the present high rate it is likely that many more species, especially those with restricted ranges, will become globally threatened.

EBAs vary in the percentage of their restricted-range birds which are threatened. In the Americas, most EBAs (72 per cent) have one or more threatened restricted-range species, but some have much higher proportions of threatened species, clearly marking them as priorities for conservation action (see Box 2). A preliminary evaluation of the world's EBAs has been made on the basis of biological importance and threat (ICBP, 1992). Biological importance was based on richness in restricted-range species in relation to what would be expected for the area of each EBA. Modifications were allowed for taxonomic uniqueness of the species involved and the importance for other floral

SOME THREATENED EBAS

Some EBAs are more threatened than others and need conservation measures now if extinctions are to be averted. The Paria Peninsula and the Cordillera de Caripe EBA (B03) and the Alagoan Atlantic slope forest EBA (B47) illustrate how some EBAs contain significant numbers of restricted-range species that are also threatened, largely through habitat destruction.

EBA B03 is a highly threatened area of endemism in northern Venezuela. It covers only 4000 sq. km or thereabouts, consisting of two disjunct mountain ranges: the low-lying and coastal mountains (highest peaks 1300 m) of the Paria Peninsula, and the Cordillera de Caripe (highest peaks 2,600 m) located further inland to the south-west.

The EBA is rich in restricted-range species, with 13 occurring including five endemics (see Table). All of the species are found in the humid forests of these mountains. The five endemic species are listed as threatened and are currently known from only a handful of localities within the two mountain ranges. Indeed, *Hylonympha macrocerca* and *Myioborus pariae* are restricted to the Paria Peninsula mountains and *Basileuterus griseiceps* is confined to the Cordillera de Caripe. A sixth restricted-range species, *Campylopterus ensipennis*, is also considered threatened, but extends onto the island of Tobago.

The restricted-range bird species of the Paria Peninsular and Cordillera de Caripe (B03)

Species	English name	Status	Other EBAs
Nannopsittaca panychlora	Tepui Parrotlet		B02
Campylopterus ensipennis	White-tailed Sabrewing	T	
Chlorostilbon alice	Green-tailed Emerald		B04
Hylonympha macrocerca	Scissor-tailed Hummingbird	T	
Pharomachrus fulgidus	White-tipped Quetzal		B04, B08
Aulacorhynchus sulcatus	Groove-billed Toucanet		B04
Premnoplex tatei	White-throated Barbtail	T	
Syndactyla guttulata	Guttulated Foliage-gleaner		B04
Pipreola formosa	Handsome Fruiteater		B04
Diglossa venezuelensis	Venezuelan Flowerpiercer	T	
Thlypopsis fulviceps	Fulvous-headed Tanager		B04, B06, B10
Basileuterus griseiceps	Grey-headed Warbler	T	
Myioborus pariae	Yellow-faced Redstart	T	

T – Threatened, as listed by Collar *et al.* (1992).
N – Near-threatened, as listed by Collar *et al.* (1992).

The area is a priority site for conservation action because of extensive forest clearance (Wege and Long, 1994). Conservation is needed at more than one site in the EBA as there is no single locality that holds all the threatened species. Particularly important sites are Cerro Humo in the central Paria Peninsula and Cerro Negro in the Cordillera de Caripe (Long, 1993). Both are located in protected areas, Cerro Humo in the Paria Peninsula National Park and Cerro Negro in the El Guacharo National Park, but habitat destruction in the area is still proceeding at an alarming rate.

The Atlantic coastal forests of Brazil hold as many as 17 per cent of the threatened bird species of the Americas. The region has suffered extensive deforestation, having been one of the first parts of South America to be colonized by Europeans. It is estimated that only 2–5 per cent of the original forest cover remains in the region (Oliver and Santos, 1991).

The northernmost stands of the Atlantic coastal forest in Alagoas state, form a particularly important EBA (B47). In the lowland humid forests and hill forests of this narrow coastal slope there exist a concentration of threatened restricted-range species, several of which are on the verge of extinction. The area holds 14 restricted-range species (see Table), of which nine are confined to this part of the Atlantic coastal forests and 12 are listed as threatened (Collar *et al.*, 1992). The Alagoas curasow *Mitu mitu* is thought to be extinct in the wild as a result of hunting and clearance of the few patches of lowland forest that still existed in the 1970s. Two of the threatened species (*Philydor novaesi* and *Myrmotherula snowi*) are now known from only 15 sq. km of hill forest at Murici. This forest is important for another 11 threatened species including nine of the restricted-range birds and additionally *Carpornis melanocephalus* and *Carduellis yarrellii*.

The restricted-range bird species of the Alagoan Atlantic coastal forests EBA (B47)

Latin name	English name	Status	Other EBAs
Mitu mitu	Alagoas Curassow	T	
Amazona rhodocorytha	Red-browed Parrot	T	B51, B52
Touit surda	Golden-tailed Parrotlet	T	B51, B52
Picumnus fulvescens	Tawny Piculet	N	
Philydor novaesi	Alagoas foliage-gleaner	T	
Synallaxis infuscata	Pinto's Spinetail	T	
Hylopezus ochroleucus	White-browed Antpitta	N	
Myrmeciza ruficauda	Scalloped Antbird	T	B51
Myrmotherula snowi	Alagoas Antwren	N	B52
Terenura sicki	Orange-bellied Antwren	T	
Iodopleura pipra	Buff-throated Purpletuft	T	B52
Xipholena atropurpurea	White-winged Cotinga	T	B51
Hemitriccus mirandae	Buff-breasted Tody-tyrant	T	
Phylloscartes ceciliae	Alagoas Tyrannulet	T	
Tangara fastuosa	Seven-coloured Tanager	T	
Curaeus forbesi	Forbes' Blackbird	T	

T – Threatened, as listed by Collar *et al.* (1992).
N – Near-threatened, as listed by Collar *et al.* (1992).

and faunal groups where this was known. Threat was evaluated on the proportions of restricted-range species which are considered threatened by Collar and Andrew (1988) and Collar *et al.* (1992) and on the proportion of land cover which has no protected status. The EBAs were categorized into those of critical, urgent and high importance for conservation action.

Within the Americas, 22 of the 81 EBAs fell into the highest category (critically important). Of these, 17 are composed, at least in part, of humid tropical forests. There were only two EBAs classified under this category in Central America, the South Central American slope (A17) being the only humid forest area. In the Caribbean four of the five EBAs (Cuba and the Bahamas – A22, Hispaniola – A24, Puerto Rico – A25, and the Eastern Caribbean – A26) were ranked as critically important.

The Tangara fastuosa, *seven-coloured tanager, is threatened and restricted to the Atlantic coastal forest of north-east Brazil.*
(Painting by Peter Hayman and reproduced with permission of the Rare Bird Club)

In South America, 10 of the 15 EBAs that ranked as critically important are humid forest areas (Table 4.4).

Conclusions

Identifying key sites is crucially important for the conservation of biological diversity, and it is clear that a very high proportion of such areas in the tropical Americas are forested. Information relating to other elements (such as wide-ranging, low-density raptors, pollinators and seed dispersers, and migratory birds) and to the distribution and ecology of other life-forms must clearly continue to refine and extend the number and type of forest areas to be targeted. Although, BirdLife International is in the process of making further additions and adjustments (Stattersfield *et al.*, in prep.; Wege and Long, 1995), its Biodiversity Project and associated analysis of threatened species have laid the foundation for work to begin in the field on improving the conservation status of many key areas.

Table 4.4 Humid forest EBAs in South America that are ranked as of critical importance globally

Endemic Bird Area	EBA code	Humid forest type
Cordillera de Caripe & Paria Peninsula	B03	lowland/montane
Choco	B14	lowland
Western Andes of Colombia and Ecuador	B15	lowland/montane
East Peruvian cordilleras	B25	montane
South-east Peruvian lowlands	B30	lowland
Lower Bolivian yungas	B34	lowland
Alagoan Atlantic slope	B47	lowland
Bahian & Espirito Santo Atlantic slope	B51	lowland
South-east Brazilian lowland to foothills	B52	lowland
South-east Brazilian montains	B53	montane

References

Bierregaard, R.O. (1990). Avian communities in the understorey of Amazonian forest fragments. In: *Biogeography and Ecology of Forest Bird Communities*. Pp.333–343. Keast, A. (ed.). SPB Academic Publishing, The Hague.

Bierregaard, R.O. and Lovejoy, T.E. (1989). Effects of forest fragmentation on Amazonian understorey bird communities. *Acta Amazonica* 19: 215–241.

Breedlove, D.E. (1981). *Introduction to the Flora of Chiapas*. Part 1. California Academy of Sciences, San Francisco, U.S.A.

Brown, K.S. Jr. (1982). Paleoecology and regional patterns of evolution in neotropical forest butterflies. In: *Biological Diversification in the Tropics*. Pp. 255–308. Prance, G.T. (ed.). Columbia University Press, New York.

Brown, K.S. Jr. (1987). Biogeography and evolution of neotropical butterflies. In: *Biogeography and Quaternary History in Tropical America*. Pp. 66–104. Whitmore, T.C. and Prance, G.T. (eds). Clarendon Press, Oxford.

Collar, N.J. and Andrew, P. (1988). *Birds to Watch: the ICBP*

World Checklist of Threatened Birds. International Council for Bird Preservation Technical Publication 8. ICBP, Cambridge, U.K.

Collar N.J. (1990). The Amazon as Ark. *World Birdwatch:* 12(1–2): 10–12.

Collar, N.J., Gonzaga, L. P., Krabbe, N., Madroño Nieto, A., Naranjo, L. G., Parker, T. A. and Wege, D. C. (1992). *Threatened Birds of the Americas: the ICBP Red Data Book.* Third edition (part 2). International Council for Bird Preservation, Cambridge, U.K.

Crosby, M.J. (1994). Mapping the distributions of restricted-range birds to identify global conservation priorities. In: *Mapping the Diversity of Nature.* Pp. 145–154. Miller R.I. (ed.). Chapman and Hall, London.

Davis, S.D., Droop, S.J.M., Gregerson, P., Henson, L., Leon, C.J., Villa-Lobos, J.L., Synge, H. and Zantovska, J. (1986). *Plants in Danger: What do we know?* International Union for Conservation of Nature and Natural Resources, Gland, Switzerland and Cambridge, U.K.

Dodson, C.H. and Gentry, A.H. (1991). Biological extinction in western Ecuador. *Annals Missouri Botanical Garden* 78: 273–295.

Duellman, W.E. (1966). The Central American herpetofauna: an ecological perspective. *Copeia* 1966: 700–719.

Duellman, W.E. (1979). The herpetofauna of the Andes: patterns of distribution, origin, differentiation and present communities. In: *The South American Herpetofauna: its origin, evolution, and dispersal.* Pp. 371–459. Duellman, W.E. (ed.). University of Kansas Museum of Natural History (Monograph 7).

Duellman, W.E. (1982). Quaternary climatic-ecological fluctuations in the lowland tropics: frogs and forests. In: *Biological Diversification in the Tropics.* Pp. 389–402. Prance, G.T. (ed.). Columbia University Press, New York.

da Fonseca, G.A.B. (1985). Observations on the ecology of the muriqui (*Brachyteles arachnoides* E. Geoffroy 1806): implications for its conservation. *Primate Conservation* 5: 48–52.

Erwin, T.L. and Rios, D.V. (1986). *Zona Reservada de Tambopata: a plan for strengthening science, conservation and community utilization of bioresources in the Tambopata region.* Smithsonian Institution, unpublished report.

Forero, E. and Gentry, A.H. (1988). Neotropical plant distribution patterns with emphasis on north-western South America: a preliminary overview. In: *Proceedings of a Workshop on Neotropical Distribution Patterns.* Pp. 21–37. Vanzolini, P.E. and Heyer, W.R. (eds). Academia Brasileira de Ciências, Rio de Janiero, Brazil.

Gentry, A.H. (1986). Endemism in tropical vs. temperate plant communities. In: *Conservation Biology.* Pp. 153–181. Soulé, M.E. (ed.). Sinauer Press, Sunderland, Massachusettes, U.S.A.

Gentry, A.H. (1992). Tropical forest biodiversity: distributional patterns and their conservational significance. *Oikos* 63(1): 19–28.

Haffer, J. (1987). Biogeography of neotropical birds. In: *Biogeography and Quaternary History in Tropical America.* Pp. 105-150. Whitmore, T.C. and Prance, G.T. (eds). Clarendon Press, Oxford.

ICBP (1992). *Putting Biodiversity on the Map: priority areas for global conservation.* International Council for Bird Preservation, Cambridge, U.K.

Jackson, J.F. (1978). Differentiation in the genera *Enyalius* and *Strobilurus* (Iguanidae): implications for Pleistocene climatic

The forests of Itatiaia National Park hold a wide selection of the restricted-range species of the montane forests of south-east Brazil (Joe Tobias)

changes in eastern Brazil. *Arquivos de Zoologia do Estado de São Paulo.*

Lack, D. (1976). *Island Biology Illustrated by the Land Birds of Jamaica.* Blackwell, London.

Liebherr, J.K. (1988). Biogeographic patterns of West Indian *Platynus* carabid beetles (Coleoptera). In: *Zoogeography of Caribbean Insects.* Pp. 121–152. Liebherr, J.K. (ed.). Cornell University Press, Ithaca, New York.

Long, A.J. (1993). Restricted-range and threatened bird species in tropical montane cloud forest. In: *Tropical Montane Cloud Forests: Proceedings of an International Symposium.* Hamilton, L.S., Juvik, J.O. and Scatena, F.N. (eds). East-West Center, Honolulu, Hawaii, USA.

Long, A.J., Crosby, M.C., Stattersfield, A.J. and Wege, D.C. (in press). Towards a global map of biodiversity: patterns in the distribution of restricted range birds. *Biogeography.*

Lovejoy, T.E, Rankin, J.M., Bierregaard, R.O., Brown, K.S., Emmons, L.H. and Van der Voort, M.E. (1984). Ecosystem decay of Amazon forest remnants. In: *Extinctions.* Pp. 295–326. Nitecki, M.H. (ed.). University of Chicago Press, Chicago, U.S.A.

Lynch, J.D. (1979). The amphibians of the lowland tropical forests. In: *The South American Herpetofauna: its origin, evolution and dispersal.* Duellman, W.E. (ed.). University of Kansas Museum of Natural History, Monograph 7. Pp. 189–215.

Mittermeier, R.A. (1987). Framework for primate conservation in the Neotropical region. In: *Primate Conservation in the Tropical Rainforest.* Pp. 305–320. Marsh, C. and Mittermeier, R.A. (eds). Alan R. Liss, New York.

Mori, S.A., Boom, B.M. and Prance, G.T. (1981). Distribution patterns and conservation of eastern Brazilian coastal forest tree species. *Brittonia* 33(2): 233–245.

Myers, N. (1988). Threatened biotas: "hotspots" in tropical forests. *Environmentalist* 8: 187–208.

Nelson, B.W., Ferreira, C.A.C., da Silva, M.F. and Kawasak, M.L. (1990). Endemism centres, refugia and botanical collection density in Brazilian Amazonia. *Nature* 345: 714–716.

Oliver, W.L.R. and Santos, I.B. (1991). *Threatened Endemic Mammals of the Atlantic Forest Region of South-east Brazil.* Jersey Wildlife Preservation Trust, Special Scientific Report 4.

Parker, T.A. (1982). Observations of some unusual rainforest and marsh birds in southeastern Peru. *Wilson Bulletin* 94: 477–493.

Prance, G.T. (1987). Biogeography of neotropical plants. In: *Biogeography and Quaternary History in Tropical America.* Pp. 46–65. Whitmore, T.C. and Prance, G.T. (eds). Clarendon Press, Oxford.

Ridgely, R.S. and Tudor, G. (1989). *The Birds of South America: the oscine passerines.* Vol 1. Oxford University Press, Oxford and Tokyo.

Rappole, J.H. (1991). Migrant birds in Neotropical forest: a review from a conservation perspective. In: *Conserving Migratory Birds.* Pp. 259–277. Salathé, T. (ed.) International Council for Bird Preservation Technical Publication 12. ICBP, Cambridge, U.K.

Rzedowski J. (1978). *Vegetación de México.* Editorial Limusa, México D. F.

Savage, J.M. (1966). The origins and history of the Central American herpetofauna. *Copeia* 1966: 719–766.

Savage, J.M. (1982). The enigma of the Central American herpetofauna: dispersal or vicariance? *Annals Missouri Botanical Garden* 69: 464–547.

Stattersfield, A.J., Crosby, M.J., Long, A.J., Wege, D.C. and Heath, M.F. (in prep.). *Global Directory of Endemic Bird Areas (EBAs).* BirdLife International, Cambridge, U.K.

Stiles, F.G. (1985). On the role of birds in the dynamics of Neotropical forests. In: *Conservation of Tropical Forest Birds.* Pp.49–59. Diamond, A.W. and Lovejoy, T.E. (eds). International Council for Bird Preservation Technical Publication 4. ICBP, Cambridge, U.K.

Terborgh, J. and Winter, B. (1983). A method for siting parks and reserves with special reference to Colombia and Ecuador. *Biological Conservation* 27: 45–58.

Terborg, J.W., Fitzpatrick, J.W. and Emmons, L. (1984). Annotated checklist of the bird and mammal species of Cocha Cashu Biological Station, Manu National Park, Peru. *Fieldiana Zoology* 21: 1–29.

Thomas, C.D. (1991). Habitat use and geographic ranges of butterflies from the wet lowlands of Costa Rica. *Biological Conservation* 55: 269–281.

Thiollay, J.-M. (1985). Falconiforms of tropical rainforests: a review. In: *Conservation Studies on Raptors.* Pp.155–165. Newton, I. and Chancellor, R.D. (eds). International Council for Bird Preservation Technical Publication 5. ICBP, Cambridge, U.K.

Thirgood, S.J. and Heath, M.F. (1994). Global patterns of endemism and the conservation of biodiversity. In: *Systematics and Conservation Evaluation.* Forey, P.L., Humphries, C.J. and Vane-Wright, R.I. (eds). Systematics Association Special Volume No. 50, pp. 207–227, Clarendon Press, Oxford.

Vanzolini, P.E. and Williams, E.E. (1970). South American anoles: geographic differentiation and evolution of the *Anolis chrysolepis* species group. *Arquivos de Zoologia do Estado de São Paulo* 19: 1–298.

Wege D.C. and Long A.J. (1995). *Key areas for threatened birds in the Neotropics.* BirdLife International (Conservation Series), Cambridge, U.K.

Wilson, E.O. (1988). International conservation: the ultimate goal. *Orion* 7(3): 16–21.

Woods, C. A. (1989). The biogeography of West Indian rodents. In: *Biogeography of the West Indies.* Pp. 741–798. Woods, C.A. (ed.). Sandhill Crane Press, Gainseville.

Author: Adrian Long, BirdLife International, with contributions from Nigel Collar, David Wege, Mike Crosby and Alison Stattersfield of BirdLife International and Mariano Gimenez-Dixon, IUCN, Gland, Switzerland. (BirdLife International is the new name for ICBP, the International Council for Bird Preservation.

5 Forest Wildlife and Its Exploitation by Humans

INTRODUCTION

In this chapter the vast wealth of vertebrates — amphibians, reptiles, fish, birds and mammals — in Neotropical forests is documented and the ways in which these fauna have been affected by human activities are discussed. Attention focuses on the birds and mammals which are the best studied of the groups. In conclusion, the importance of distinguishing between the forest and the fauna when discussing the conservation of tropical biota is noted.

PATTERNS OF DIVERSITY

Amphibians and Reptiles

There are over 1000 species of amphibians recorded from South America and 1100 species of reptiles. The larger species include 36 species of turtles and seven species of crocodilians (Duellman, 1979). Approximately 500 reptile species are found in the Neotropical lowland rain forest area; of these about 300 are endemic to that area (Dixon, 1979).

Within Neotropical countries, Colombia has the greatest number of amphibians (585 species — but see note on Table 5.1) and Mexico the greatest number of reptiles (717 species) (Table 5.1).

The average number of amphibian and reptile species per site, from five Neotropical forest sites, was 143 (range 131–185, see Table 5.2). These local faunas consisted, on average, of two caecilians, two salamanders and 59 anurans for a total of 63 species of amphibians, and four turtles, two crocodilians, 24 lizards, one amphisbaenian and 49 snakes for a total of 80 species of reptiles (Duellman, 1991). Most herpetofaunal assemblages in the Neotropical forests consist of about half diurnal and half nocturnal species; about half of the species are terrestrial and half arboreal (Duellman, 1991).

Fish

The Neotropics have the richest freshwater fish fauna in the world with more than 2400 species already described. Within this region, the Amazon basin has more than 1300 species, making it the richest river basin in the world for fresh water fish (Lowe-McConnell, 1987). Goulding *et al.* (1988) report a total of at least 450 fish species from the blackwaters of the Rio Negro, making this the most diverse tributary river in the world. They further report that communities of fish at single collecting locations are the richest yet recorded for freshwater lakes, rivers or streams anywhere in the world — with over 100 species collected from a 4-8 x 30 m rocky pool from the upper Rio Negro.

Many Amazonian fish species are used by humans. In the Brazilian Amazonian town of Itacoatiara a total of at least 86 species in 56 genera and 18 families are known to be consumed (Smith, 1981a). In the markets of Manaus, 64 fish species were recorded, though only a few species account for the majority of the catch (Lowe-McConnell, 1987).

Birds

The Neotropics are also extremely rich in forest birds — of the 3300 Neotropical avian species, 1300 are forest species. This compares with 800 forest bird species for Southeast Asia and 400 for Africa (Karr, 1989). The explanations for the high diversity of Neotropical forest avifauna vary depending on the geographical scale considered. Climatic conditions, geographic position, extent of forest area and differences in habitat types all influence diversity at the broadest scale. At a regional scale, the extent of forest cover and the history of forest distribution affect patterns of diversity (Karr, 1989).

The avifauna of the Neotropics is characterized by having numerous families, most with a relatively small number of species (Diamond, 1985). Moreover, as compared to the Old World tropics, Latin American forests are extraordinarily rich in raptors and woodpeckers (Picidae) (Karr, 1989). They also have an exceptionally diverse radiation of parrots (Psittacidae) and trogons (Trogonidae). Amongst the passerines, the suboscines dominate in the Neotropics. They include two major groups in South America: tyrant-flycatchers (Tyrannidae), cotingas (Cotingidae) and manakins (Pipridae) in one group and wood-creepers (Dendrocolaptidae), ovenbirds (Furnariidae), antbirds (Formicariidae) and tapaculos (Rhinocryptidae) in the other. The suboscines may be classified as a New World group as only three small families occur in the Old World tropics: the broadbills — Eurylaimidae, pittas — Pittidae and false sunbirds — Philepittidae (Stiles, 1983).

New World forests hold several endemic groups, including: tinamous (Tinamidae), trumpeters (Psophiidae), puffbirds (Bucconidae), motmots (Momotidae), jacamars (Galbulidae), oilbirds (Steatornithidae), potoos (Nyctibiidae) and ovenbirds (Karr, 1989; Stiles, 1983; Keast, 1985). In the Neotropics, as in the other tropical regions, only four to 12 per cent of bird species are temperate-tropical migrants (Karr, 1989).

Avian diversity at any given site depends on the extent of the forest cover, local habitat heterogeneity, the history of forest distribution and the nature of human activities. As a result, the distribution of bird species is patchy. This patchiness is of great concern to conservationists. It has given rise to an extensive literature on centres of endemism (see Chapter 4) and sites of high

Table 5.1   The ten countries within this Atlas with the highest numbers of mammals, birds, reptiles and amphibians.

Mammals		Birds		Reptiles		Amphibians	
Mexico	449	Colombia	1,721	Mexico	717	Colombia*	585
Brazil	428	Peru	1,701	Colombia	590	Brazil	516
Peru	359	Brazil	1,622	Brazil	467	Ecuador	402
Colombia	359	Ecuador	1,500	Ecuador	379	Mexico	284
Ecuador	324	Venezuela	1,325	Peru	298	Peru	241
Venezuela	323	Bolivia	1,274	Venezuela	246	Venezuela	183
Bolivia	316	Mexico	961	Guatemala	231	Panama	164
Costa Rica	228	Panama	929	Panama	226	Costa Rica	160
Panama	218	Costa Rica	850	Costa Rica	215	Bolivia	112
Guyana	193	Paraguay	650	Bolivia	208	Surinam	95

*   This estimate, see Chapter 26 for source, is considerably higher than that suggested by other sources.

Sources: As in the relevant chapters within this Atlas or WCMC (1992)

species richness. The theoretical explanation for these centres is much debated, but their existence is not generally disputed. However, the work of Nelson *et al.* (1990) has drawn attention to the influence of collecting intensity on apparent distribution of species diversity.

The highest bird diversity so far recorded occurs in the forests of the western Amazon. At one site in Manu National Park, Peru, Terborgh and colleagues identified over 550 species of birds (Karr *et al.*, 1990; Terborgh *et al.*, 1990; Table 5.2). As one ascends the mountains from the Amazonian lowlands, species richness declines, although some authors suggest that there is a peak in avian species richness in the wettest cloud forests lying between 600 and 1400 meters (Terborgh in Stiles, 1985). Avian diversity is highest in Colombia with 1721 species, followed closely by Peru with 1701 (Table 5.1).

The avifauna of Central America is less rich than that in South America, but is still well above the levels of diversity for tropical forests of other continents.

Mammals

Mexico, Central America and South America have about 1116 species of mammals in 294 genera and 11 orders (not including Cetacea) (Baker, 1991). Within this region, as elsewhere in the world, tropical rain forests are the richest ecosystems for mammals — a typical lowland rain forest can contain over 120

Table 5.2   Vertebrate diversity at selected sites in the Neotropics

TAXON	SITES				
	1	2	3	4	5
Amphibians	93	48	52	44*	77
Reptiles	92	86	81	89*	54
Birds	nd	410	444	351	554
Mammals (non-flying)	nd	50	39	51*	70
Mammals (bats)	nd	63	nd	nd	nd

Sites: 1 – Santa Cecilia, eastern Ecuador
2 – La Selva Biological Station, Costa Rica
3 – Barro Colorado Island and adjacent mainland, Panama
4 – Manaus, Brazil or (*) the study area for the Minimum Critical Size of Ecosystems Project 80 km north of Manaus
5 – Cocha Cashu field station in Manu National Park, Peru

Source: Gentry (1990)

species of mammals. However, bird species diversity always greatly exceeds that of mammals, sometimes by up to a factor of five (Bourliére, 1989).

The numbers of families, genera and species of mammals inhabiting Africa and the Neotropical region are very similar. For instance, rodents and primates are equally diverse in tropical Africa and tropical America. Ungulates are, however, considerably more diverse in Africa (Bourliére, 1973). The Neotropics are, nevertheless, slightly richer. This is due, in particular, to the higher diversity of bats found there. In some areas of the Neotropics, the number of bat species may equal or, in some cases, even exceed that of all other mammal species combined. Bats are, however, very sensitive to changes in temperature and humidity; at altitudes above 1000 m the number of species can decline by half (Eisenberg, 1990).

Costa Rica has 228 known mammal species (Table 5.1) with 113 species recorded from La Selva rain forest (Wilson, 1990). While in South America, Peru has 361 known mammalian species (Table 5.1) with single rain forest locations possessing about 122 species (Patton *et al.*, 1982). This well documented increase in mammal species richness is mainly attributable to a rise in the number of bat species as the equator is approached (Willig and Sandlin, 1991).

The Neotropical mammal fauna can be divided into three major components according to their evolutionary origin and their time of arrival in the region. The original fauna consisted of the Marsupialia and Xenarthra. The early invaders of South America are the New World Primates, caviomorph rodents (guinea pigs *Cavia* spp., capybaras *Hydrochaeris hydrochaeris* and their allies) and Procyonid carnivores (racoons and their allies); while the more recent invaders are Perissodactyla, Artiodactyla, non-caviomorph rodents and non-procyonid carnivores. Members of all three groups, found in ten orders (with Sirenia excluded), now occur together in the forested habitats of the Neotropics (Eisenberg, 1989).

Emmons (1990) recognises four main biogeographical regions for Neotropical rain forest mammals: 1) Central America and the Pacific forests of Colombia, Ecuador and northern Peru; 2) the Amazon Basin; 3) the Brazilian Atlantic coastal rain forests; and 4) the Caribbean coastal rain forests of Colombia and Venezuela. The most species rich of these is the Amazon, though it has few endemics. In contrast, the Atlantic coastal rain forests, with a mammal fauna very different from the Amazon, have many endemic species and genera of mammals.

MANU BIOSPHERE RESERVE: A CASE STUDY OF SUBSISTENCE HUNTERS AND WILDLIFE CONSERVATION

Manu National Park, in Southeastern Peru, with an area of 15,328 sq. km, is the largest national park in Western Amazonia and one of the largest in the world. Starting in the Andean highlands, the park protects the whole basin of the Manu River. The park was created in 1973. In 1976, it and the adjacent lowlands outside its eastern boundary were declared a Biosphere Reserve. The eastern lowlands area is inhabited by Indians and colonists in constant contact with the national society. The Park itself is inhabited by at least three native ethnic groups, of which the Matsigenka is the most numerous, numbering several hundred persons spread along the middle and upper Manu River (Vasquez and Barrena, 1990).

In order to assess the impact of indigenous subsistence hunting on Manu's wildlife, a group of ecologists (funded by Wildlife Conservation International and the Jessie Smith Noyes Foundation) made counts of game animals along hunting trails in the forest surrounding two Indian villages during 1989 and 1990. The first village, Yomuibato, located on the Andean foothills, is the largest Matsigenka settlement inside Manu National Park (one hundred people). All hunting in Yomuibato is for subsistence and is with bow and arrow. Diamante, the second village, just outside the Biosphere Reserve, is a Piro Indian community of about two hundred individuals. Diamante is as old as Yomuibato (about ten years), but established in an area with greater outside contact. Diamante hunters prefer to use shotguns, and their hunting is mainly for subsistence. Villagers in both communities also fish, gather and practice slash-and-burn shifting cultivation (Alvard and Kaplan, in press).

A comparison between these hunted sites and ecologically similar unhunted forest suggests a 70–90 per cent reduction in the densities of large primates and a 50–80 per cent decrease in cracid (guans and curassows) densities in the forest around the villages. However, in Yomuibato, the more traditional settlement, spider monkeys *Ateles paniscus*, razor-billed curassows *Mitu tuberosa* and white-winged trumpeters *Psophia leucoptera*, all species vulnerable to hunting, can be found within one kilometre of the village. In contrast, they had completely disappeared within a 3 km radius of Diamante and were severely reduced within 8 km, about the average distance of a one-day hunting trip (Mitchell and Raez-Luna, 1990).

The administration policy of Manu Park was based on the assumption that as long as the Indian populations kept their traditional, subsistence, low-technology lifestyle, they would not represent a threat to the park's wildlife. In order to accomplish this, all trade of forest items and the use of firearms were banned, contact between natives and outsiders was kept to a minimum and visits outside the park by Indians were discouraged.

From the point of view of pure wildlife conservation, these policies have yielded results — at least in the short-term. The forest surrounding Yomuibato supports a diminished, but apparently healthy, bird and mammal fauna, in striking contrast to forest near Diamante and even smaller communities outside the park. On the other hand, the isolation policy has resulted in severe conflict between the Indians and the Park administration. Greater economic independence, and participation in the park's administrative decisions are being actively lobbied for by the Indians.

While the right to self-determination on the part of the indigenous peoples of Manu is unquestionable, the severe effects of human cultural, technological and demographic change on the conservation of the forest wildlife is equally clear (see also Bodmer *et al.*, 1994). What is necessary now are: 1) policies which involve participation by local peoples; and 2) research on alternatives to game as a source of protein.

Exploitation of Neotropical Forest Vertebrates by Humans

Humans have exploited the tremendous diversity of terrestrial vertebrates in Neotropical forests ever since they arrived on the continent. This exploitation has been both indirect and direct (Redford, 1992).

Habitat destruction has been a major indirect cause of faunal loss. A less-often considered process involves the destruction of critical habitat outside that being considered, therefore extirpating a species from what would seem to be ideal habitat — examples of this include beach nesting turtles which can be eliminated from an entire watershed if a nesting beach is destroyed, or white-lipped peccary *Tayassu pecari* which appear to move through very large areas and appear to be eliminated from a piece of forest by the construction of an agricultural colony that blocks a traditional peccary transit path.

People have indirectly effected the fauna in many other ways. One of the most important is probably the effect of forest-extraction activities by humans. For example, logging can remove fruit-bearing trees and destroy nesting and other habitats. Extraction by humans, of either forest fruits or minor forest products, may result in changes in the availability of resources to the vertebrate forest fauna. Subsistence or commercial hunting and fishing may remove potential prey from tropical forests, thereby affecting predators, scavengers, and the animals that depend on them (Thiollay, 1984). For example, Emmons (1987) has pointed out that every major prey species of the jaguar *Panthera onca* is intensively hunted by humans.

"Modern" human activities also have major impacts on the fauna. These include the effects of mercury and sediment contamination on fish, the effects of smoke on plants and animals, including pollinators, the effect of gold mining on beach and riparian forests and the increase of edge habitat and its effects within the forest.

These indirect effects of human activity on the Neotropical fauna have largely arisen during recent decades. In contrast, the direct exploitation of animals, has a very long history in Neotropical forests. Animals have been and continue to be hunted for a multitude of purposes: they are killed for food, for skins, leather and other non-edible products; live animals are collected for pets, zoos and the biomedical trade; they are exploited for sport hunting or tourism; and they are used as a source of domesticated animals (Redford and Robinson, 1991). In this account we will focus on the first two of these categories, which are by far the most significant.

Hunting of animals for food has been going on as long as humans have occupied Neotropical forests. This hunting has

THE MILITARY AND FOREST WILDLIFE CONSERVATION — THE CASE OF ECUADOR

The traditional strategy of relying entirely on a state agency to protect forests within national parks has proven unrealistic in developing countries. Conservationists now reach out to local communities, non-governmental organizations and even the private sector to improve forest management in and around parks and reserves. These innovative efforts have overlooked what may be a key institution for conservation: the military (but see McNeely *et al.*, 1990).

Military forces hold substantial political, social and economic power throughout most of Latin America. During the development history of the Brazilian Amazon, military dominance has accelerated deforestation and debilitated indigenous resource management systems (Hecht and Cockburn, 1990). Today military influence continues to be particularly intense at development frontiers where forests of rich biodiversity remain. To ignore the military in such areas is to disregard a very real political force. Conservationists must work with the military so as to check their environmentally destructive actions, but use their authority to strengthen forest protection.

The Armed Forces of Ecuador has recently initiated activities with a potentially positive role in protecting the country's endangered natural patrimony. Throughout 1991, the Santa Cecilia Battalion (Sucumbios Province) confiscated illegal timber coming from the upper reaches of the Aguarico and San Miguel Rivers. Illegal wildlife and wildlife products were seized as well. Those animals judged to be healthy were released. Meanwhile, pelts, skins and feathers were burned at roll-call in order to demonstrate the commitment of Commander Lt. Col. Hernández to halt the illegal wildlife trade. The Battalion also actively protected a 8 sq. km natural forest relic adjacent to their training grounds. Elsewhere in the Ecuadorian Amazon, army battalions participated in the 1990 National Campaign Against Wildlife Trafficking, sponsored by a group of national NGOs. In Ecuador's Sierran provinces, conscripts have worked to reforest over 100 sq. km of steeply eroded hillsides. In 1992, the National Forest Department requested assistance from the Armed Forces to control arson in the Pichincha Forest Reserve overlooking Quito.

Unfortunately, these are isolated deeds within a national context of economic activities such as mining, oil production and road construction that threaten Ecuador's forests. Moreover, Ecuadorian conservation NGOs as well as residents of Amazonian provinces report that the Armed Forces actively participate in the illegal domestic wildlife trade. Indeed, in many Amazonian battalions, soldiers openly carry macaws, tamarins and even ocelots. Hunting and fishing with dynamite are common leisure activities for soldiers, often in "protected areas" such as Yasuni National Park.

The Armed Forces of Ecuador demonstrate the potential for both positive conservation action and environmental destruction. For conservationists to ignore the powerful impact of this institution on forest resources is unrealistic. This is particularly true for national parks in the Ecuadorian Amazon, where park guards are unarmed, weak in authority, and, on average, each responsible for protecting over 1000 sq. km from illegal activities (Cabarle, 1989).

The potential consequences of including the military in conservation programs will vary dramatically between countries. In war-torn areas or where military forces flagrantly abuse human rights, the result would likely be disastrous. The following specific factors merit attention in evaluating the role of the military in forest conservation in tropical South America:

1) The military is often the central authority at Amazonian frontiers, where much of the remaining biodiversity is found.

2) Relative to other state agencies the military has superior logistical capacity and access to information on physical resources (potentially useful for park protection and monitoring).

3) Certain conservation issues require enforcement beyond the capacity of a park service, particularly the illegal wildlife trade. Unfortunately, the military is currently more likely to participate in wildlife trafficking than to control it, as is the case presently in Ecuador, Peru and Colombia.

Based on experiences working with the military in Ecuador, conservationists are advised to proceed cautiously, but proceed. The military is capable of operating quickly on a big scale; thus the potential for rapid results is high. A logical first step is to promote environmental education for military officers, and familiarise them with existing laws designed to protect national forests and wildlife.

---

been for both subsistence and commercial purposes. In Latin America, game is a vital protein source to many groups living outside urban areas. As a general rule, wildlife is most important to Indian groups, of somewhat lesser importance to settlers of European descent who have lived for decades in tropical forest areas and of least importance to recently arrived colonists. Indians have a stronger hunting tradition, they possess fewer domestic animals and have less access to packaged meat. Hunters generally take more mammals than birds and more birds than reptiles (Redford and Robinson, 1987).

There are, throughout Amazonia and Latin America, certain mammal and bird species which are by far and away the most commonly killed game animals. The mammals include monkeys, peccaries, deer, armadillos and large rodents like paca and capybara, while the birds include the guans and curassows, toucans, trumpeters and macaws. Figures 5.1 and 5.2 compare the importance of different mammal and bird species to Indian and colonist groups (Redford, 1992).

The number of animals taken by subsistence hunters can be very large. Over a period of less than a year, the 230 inhabitants of three Waorani villages in Ecuador killed 3165 mammals, birds, and reptiles. This total included 562 woolly monkeys *Lagothrix lagothricha*, 313 Cuvier's toucans *Ramphastos cuvieri* and 152 white-lipped peccaries. Certainly not all subsistence hunters hunt at this intensity; but by using average kill rates, it is possible to estimate the number of mammals killed in one year by the rural population of Amazonian Brazil. In 1980, there were an estimated 2,847,000 people living outside cities in an area of 3,581,180 sq. km. This number of consumers, multiplied by the annual per capita consumption values of each mammalian family, derived from studies of colonist hunting (Redford and Robinson, 1987), gives a figure of 14 million indi-

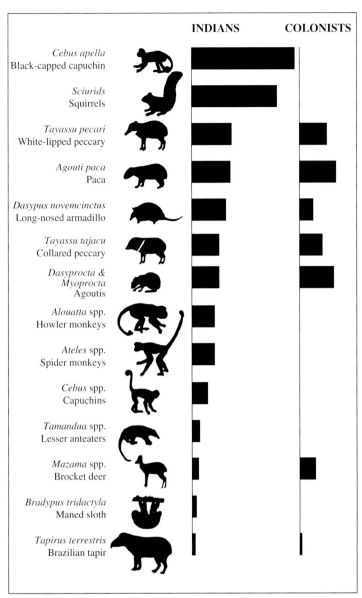

Figure 5.1 The importance of mammals to contemporary Indian and colonist hunters. Only those species that were found in at least five Indian studies and three colonist studies are included. Bars denote the number of individuals of that taxon killed per hunter per year. To give an idea of scale, there were approximately 2.5 individual *Cebus apella* killed annually by each Indian hunter and approximately 0.05 *Tapirus terrestris*. Data from Redford and Robinson (1987). *Source:* Redford (1992)

Although no longer available on the scale once observed, game is still readily obtained in many local markets. Castro *et al.* (1975–1976) reported the meat of 24 species of wildlife for sale, including six species of primates, in the markets of Iquitos, Peru. They estimate that 11,000 primates were sold annually in this market and that the inhabitants of the Peruvian department of Loreto, which includes Iquitos, kill 370,000 monkeys annually for consumption and sale.

In addition to meat, there has been extensive exploitation of fauna for non-edible products — especially leather and skins. Most of the recent market for leather has been for luxury items such as purses, gloves and expensive shoes and has concentrated on peccaries, capybara and various species of reptiles. The most important wildlife in the leather industry at the present time are the reptiles, principally the crocodilians. During the peak of the trade in the 1950's and 1960's, five to 10 million crocodilian skins were traded worldwide each year. The extent of the market is staggering: for example, in Venezuela during 1930 and 1931, 3000 – 4000 caiman skins were being sold daily, and between 1951 and 1980, Colombia legally exported 11,649,655 *Caiman sclerops* skins.

The trade in skins from Neotropical forests has focused on only a relatively few species: giant otter *Pteronura brasiliensis*, river otter *Lutra longicaudis*, jaguar and "ocelot" (*Felis pardalis* and much smaller numbers of *F. wiedii* and *F. tigrina*). Between 1960 and 1969, 23,900 giant otter skins were exported from the Peruvian and Brazilian Amazon (Smith, 1981b). In the 20 years beginning in 1946, 22,644 giant otter skins, 90,574 river otter

Figure 5.2 The importance of birds to contemporary Indian and colonist hunters. Only those species that were found in at least five Indian studies and two colonist studies are included. Bars denote the number of individuals of that taxon killed per hunter per year. To give an idea of scale, there were approximately 0.9 individual *Penelope* spp. killed annually by each Indian hunter and approximately 0.09 *Ara* spp. Data from Redford and Robinson (1987).

Source: Redford (1992)

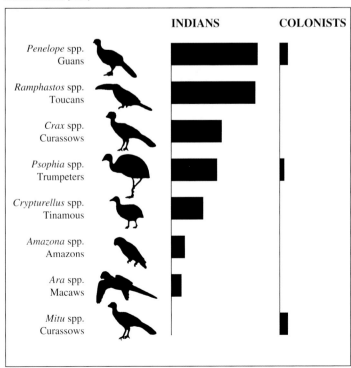

vidual mammals killed each year. This figure indicates the extent of subsistence hunting. Adding birds and reptiles, the number of game animals killed each year in Amazonian Brazil probably reaches 19 million individual animals.

In addition to this subsistence hunting, there has been extensive commercial exploitation of wildlife in Neotropical forests. Trade in wildlife did not assume major proportions until the Europeans arrived and, as early as the 17th century, began the commercial harvesting of manatees *Trichechus* spp. Giant river turtles *Podocnemis expansa* and their eggs were extensively exploited for commercial purposes. In the Amazon basin, the eggs of this turtle were so abundant that an industry developed to process them. Oil from the eggs was used for cooking and lighting and by the 18th century a royal decree controlled the lucrative harvest in Brazil (Smith, 1974).

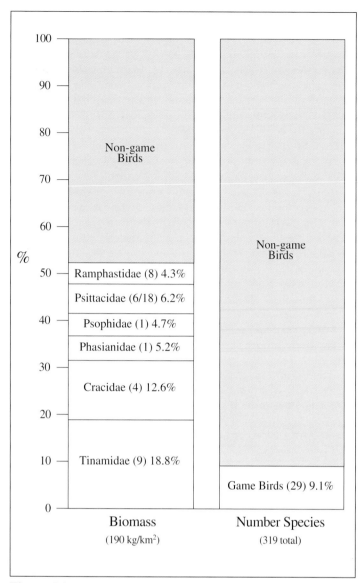

Figure 5.3 Avian diversity in Amazonian Peru. Figures in parentheses are numbers of species in each taxon.

Source: Terborgh *et al.* (1990)

skins, 12,704 jaguar skins and 138,102 ocelot skins were exported from the Amazon river port of Iquitos in Peru (Grimwood, 1968).

Faunal Exploitation and Forest Ecology

The Neotropical forest mammal, bird, reptile and fish species most affected by human activities are not a random subset of all possible species in terms of size or food habits. They are almost always the largest members of their group, and usually the largest ones in the forest. The only exception to this pattern are the large raptorial birds, which are not directly affected by human activities (Redford, 1992). Amongst the mammals, the large ungulates, primates, manatees and rodents are killed for meat and the large carnivores (felids and otters) are killed for their skins. Of the birds, the currasows (Cracidae), tinamous (Tinamidae), trumpeters (Psophiidae) and, less frequently, wading birds are killed for their meat. The large reptiles — caiman, boas, turtles — are killed for their meat and hides. The largest fish are always principal targets for fishermen.

The large-bodied species make up a significant part of the biomass of unhunted communities of Neotropical vertebrates.

At Cocha Cashu in the Peruvian Amazon there are a total of 319 species of birds recorded. At this unhunted site, the tinamous, wood quails (Phasianidae) guans and currasows (both in Cracidae) and trumpeters, a total of only 15 species, make up over 40 per cent of the avian biomass (Figure 5.3). At the same site, there are 67 recorded species of non-flying mammals. The deer and peccaries, tapir, large rodents and large primates, 12 species in total, make up over 75 per cent of the biomass (Janson and Emmons, 1990; Terborgh *et al.*, 1990). All of these species are major game animals (Figure 5.4).

One of the results of this relationship between large size and preferred game status is the dramatic effect of hunting on density. In a comparison of large primate biomass in hunted and unhunted sites, Peres (1990) showed that in unhunted areas monkeys over 4 kg contributed 64.1 per cent to the primate biomass compared to 16.2 per cent in hunted sites.

The conclusions are clear: 1) many of the largest mammals and birds in Neotropical forests are hunted; 2) these large animals make up a very large proportion of the biomass in situations where hunting does not occur; 3) densities, and therefore biomass contribution, of these species are greatly decreased under both moderate and heavy hunting pressure (Redford, 1992).

Figure 5.4 Diversity of non-flying mammals in Amazonian Peru. Figures in parentheses are numbers of species in each taxon.

Source: Redford (1992)

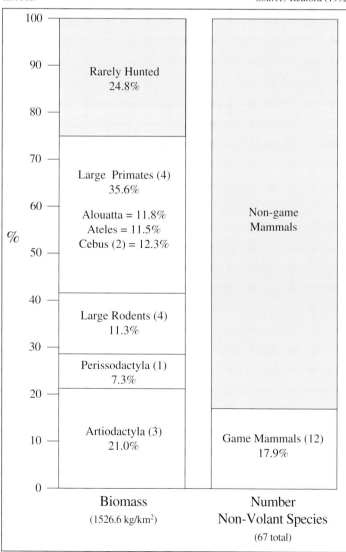

MANAGEMENT OF NEOTROPICAL FOREST ANIMALS: GREEN IGUANAS AND WILD MACAWS

One way to alleviate the pressure on wildlife, and yet meet the food and cash requirements of local peoples, is the raising in the household of small domestic animals, such as poultry and pigs. A frequently proposed alternative is the raising/management of native species, which are better adapted to local conditions than conventional domestic species. Native animals are close to the everyday experience of indigenous people; hunters often possess detailed knowledge of wild species and pets from the forest are a common sight in both Indian and mestizo villages throughout the Neotropics. Two ongoing promising efforts in forest wildlife management involve green iguanas (*Iguana iguana*) and macaws (*Ara* sp.).

Throughout Central America, green iguanas are an appreciated game animal, but hunting and habitat destruction are contributing to declines of their populations. The Iguana Management Project (IMP) in Panama is a joint venture of the Smithsonian Institution and the Panamanian Pro-Iguana Verde Foundation. The IMP focuses on developing captive breeding techniques for the green iguana, in order to restore the species populations in the wild and enhance its sustainable use by local peoples (Werner, 1991).

After several years, the project has collected a very detailed data set on iguana reproductive ecology. Careful handling of captive individuals, allows reproductive output, clutch size and survival of young to be maximized. It is estimated that 60 per cent of the released individuals survive. In addition, in an effort to restore and increase the iguana's habitat, the project stimulates planting of native trees by locals.

Although IMP reports successful trends in the captive breeding and release to the wild of green iguanas, the project's labour intensive approach means it is not yet competitive with the exploitation of wild iguanas. Nevertheless, the high national esteem of iguana meat and decreasing costs in the captive rearing system could yield acceptable benefit/cost ratios from IMP in the near future.

Another rather different approach to wildlife management is illustrated by projects working on wild macaws (Beissinger and Bucher, 1991; 1992). Throughout Amazonia, macaws are eagerly sought for the pet trade and for food. These factors, together with habitat destruction, have resulted in a severe decline of wild macaw populations and an increase in their market prices.

A group of North American and Peruvian scientists, funded by Wildlife Conservation International, is working on macaw ecology in Southeastern Peru (Munn *et al.*, 1991). In this region, availability of nesting sites limits macaw populations. The natural rarity of suitable nesting sites (holes in palms and big trees) has been exacerbated by the practice of tree-felling to collect the chicks for the pet trade. This has limited reproduction for an important fraction of adult pairs every breeding season. The homeless adults become an annoying bother for the breeding pairs, which is a factor in chick mortality, resulting in further decreases in the populations' reproductive success.

Artificial nest sites built with local materials, mimicking natural holes in palm trunks, were readily accepted by wild macaws. Artificial nests have been used before, for instance in the recovery of the Puerto Rican parrot *Amazona vittata* (Synder *et al.*, 1987). The technique is simple, and can be adapted to low-budget conditions. Artificial nests can contribute to the recovery of wild populations, allow less destructive pet collection (indeed, of chicks that would not have lived otherwise) and can be used as a tourist attraction.

The management of forest animals faces extraordinary difficulties due to the normal low densities of populations and low rates of growth and reproduction of many of the species. This is particularly true for big to medium-sized mammals, a group much sought after by hunters. Also, the money and labour cost of management and uncertainty of benefits, can decrease the acceptance of wildlife management projects by local peoples. However, in the case of captive iguanas in Panama and wild macaws in Peru, as well as in the case of ox-bow lakes where caimans and fish can be reared, management practices performed within natural or artificial enclosures offer an appealing alternative to hunting of wild animals. Most likely, successful wildlife management efforts in the Neotropical rain forest will be part of integrated approaches, combining clearly-stated goals with ecological knowledge and a sound assessment of local needs and socio-economic conditions.

What *IS* a Forest?: The Flora vs The Fauna

Much of the world's concern about the loss of biodiversity has been focused on tropical forests. Tall trees have tended to be used as a symbol for the complete set of animal and plant species found in tropical forests. This set of plant species is being used by conservation biologists, park planners and others as an indication of the health of the entire tropical forest biota, a shorthand indicating conservation-worth (Redford, 1992).

Conservation programmers must recognise that confusing forest plants with the forest fauna is a dangerous practice. What is a forest to a forester, an ethnobotanist or a casual tourist, is not necessarily a forest which contains ecologically functional populations of vertebrate species. Many areas of Neotropical forest have been emptied of their vertebrate fauna as a result of human actions. Data from botanical, archaeological and anthropological studies in many parts of the world, including the Neotropics, have shown that humans have had widespread impacts on fauna and flora. Indeed, Balée (1989: 14) has recently suggested that at least 11.8 per cent of the *terra firme* forests of the Brazilian Amazon, almost 400,000 sq. km, *"exhibit the continuing effects of past human interference"*.

In other words, the commonly held assumption that a good community of trees is always equivalent to a healthy population of vertebrates is fallacious. There are some species of vertebrates which appear to be very sensitive to even low levels of human activity, such as rubber tapping. Species that either leave or are extirpated from these lightly affected forested areas include woolly monkeys and some forest birds of prey. Many other large vertebrate species have been severely affected by hunting and indirect habitat destruction. In consequence, they are present at such low densities that they can be considered ecologically extinct — no longer interacting with other species in the system at ecologically significant levels. Such species include the most important predators, large-seed dispersers and seed predators in the Neotropical forests (Janson and Emmons,

WHO OWNS THE WILD ANIMALS?

Rules governing wildlife ownership in human society date back to the earliest human societies. Wildlife managers today serve a broader agenda: to protect wildlife for ecological and aesthetic, as well as material, purposes for present and future human populations. The non-utilitarian goals require a transformation in how wildlife ownership is defined. First, when wildlife is protected for non-utilitarian purposes it becomes difficult to identify exactly who benefits from a species' survival. Second, wildlife habitat transcends political boundaries. Therefore the domain of a single government is an insufficient context for defining ownership and management responsibility for many wildlife species. In other words, the customary set of property rights constructed for protecting a community's hunting reserve does not suffice today for protecting, for instance, a given species of migratory warbler and its habitat.

Property is the basic institution by which society guarantees future income flow from a resource. Property rights link *"not merely a person to an object, but rather a person to an object against other persons"* (Bromley, 1989:202). The three conventional types of property are: 1) state, 2) private and 3) common. Economic theory would argue that efficient resource management depends on the correct match of type of property with type of resource.

Assigning an optimal property type to wildlife is difficult due to its elusive status as a resource. To define a resource as property one must be able to attribute a concrete value to it and to distinguish between its users and non-users. In the context of wildlife these requisite specifications present problems, particularly for non-game species. First, it is difficult to assign an exact ecological value to most species, let alone an economic value. Second, the ecological and aesthetic services of wildlife are not confined to a certain user group but instead provide diffuse benefits to non-users over the long term.

Neotropical wildlife is held in various property forms, with different consequences for its conservation (Lyster, 1985). The most conventional arrangement in Latin America is the designation of wildlife as state property. Typically the state establishes national parks or reserves in which to conserve this property for long-term public welfare. Due to their status as public domain, national parks can be established at a larger scale than most private or communal landholdings. This is important for the survival of species requiring several hundred square kilometres of forest. Unfortunately, throughout Latin America, state agencies have found it difficult to protect wildlife in these areas.

In response to the failure of the state to protect wildlife, many people propose private ownership as an effective alternative for managing species. They argue that in Latin America, private property receives maximum legal and political support, allowing for strict protection of wildlife from over-exploitation by non-owners. Nonetheless, private landholdings may prove inadequate in size for the long term conservation of many species. Furthermore, private owners may ultimately choose to respond to market forces and disregard the public good by overharvesting wildlife or converting areas of natural habitat.

Common property is a third property arrangement that is similar to private property as it is based on the exclusion of non-owners. Communal ownership of game species is widespread among subsistence hunting societies who have developed long-term management techniques such as the rotation of hunting areas within forested regions (Vickers, 1991). These common property regimes are optimal for meeting the immediate resource needs of a local community. In the development context, however, these systems collapse under conditions of rapid population growth, colonization, technology change and market penetration (Chicchón, 1992). The breakdown of common property systems eliminates putative regulations on individual use of wildlife, leading to a situation of open access (Hardin, 1968). This condition of undefined property rights seriously threatens wildlife survival because without clear property rights, no one will invest in securing future benefits from a resource.

No single property form is universally appropriate for wildlife management; rather conservationists must establish property rights appropriate to each context. Moreover, the management of wildlife as a global commons challenges our traditional definitions of property and forces us to consider alternative property arrangements linking local managers to the international community. New forms of defining wildlife ownership are indeed already evolving in the form of international treaties which restrict the trade of certain species. Programmes designed to harvest Neotropical wildlife sustainably are being tested which involve a combination of property forms (see Box "3"). As wildlife becomes ever more scarce, its ownership will become increasingly important. Assigning the appropriate property rights to wildlife is alone insufficient to guarantee its survival. It is, however, a necessary first step in establishing the good stewardship of any resource.

1991). It is these large animals that provide what Terborgh (1988) has referred to as a *"stabilizing function"*. Animals like black caiman *Melanosuchus niger*, jaguars and harpy eagles *Harpia harpyja* help maintain the incredible diversity of tropical forests through *"indirect effects,"* a term referring to *"the propagation of perturbations through one or more trophic levels in an ecosystem, so that consequences are felt in organisms that may seem far removed, both ecologically and taxonomically, from the subjects of the perturbation."*

The effect of hunting on large animals is not just of concern to those interested in biodiversity conservation and tropical ecology. Wild animals provide an important source of nutrition for millions of Neotropical forest dwelling humans — a subsidy from nature without which many other activities, such as rubber tapping, would not take place. Animals are also important as pollinators and dispersers of economically important plant species, as regulators of pest populations and for a myriad of other reasons.

The bird, mammal and reptile species of Neotropical forests represent an enormous variety of species, adaptations and beauties. They have values intrinsic to themselves as well as values to local and global humanity. Until these values are recognized as independent from that of the tropical flora, their survival will continue to be threatened.

References

Alvard, M., and Kaplan, H. (1991). Procurement technology and prey mortality among indigenous Neotropical hunters. In: *Human Predators and Prey Mortality*, pp. 79–104. Stiner, M.C. (ed.). Westview Press, Boulder.

Baker, R.H. (1991). The classification of Neotropical mammals — A historical resume. In: *Latin American Mammalogy*, pp. 7–32. Mares, M.A. and Schmidley, D.J. (eds). University of Oklahoma Press, Norman.

Balée, W. (1989). The culture of Amazonian forests. In: *Resource Management in Amazonia: Indigenous and Folk Strategies*, pp. 1–21. Posey, D.A. and Balée, W. (eds). Advances in Economic Botany vol. 7.

Beissinger, S.R. and Bucher, E.H. (1991). Sustainable harvest of parrots for conservation. In: *New World Parrots in Crisis: Solutions from Conservation Biology*, pp. 73–115. Beissinger, S.R. and Snyder, N.F.R. (eds). Smithsonian Institution Press, Washington, D.C.

Beissinger, S.R. and Bucher, E.H. (1992). Can parrots be conserved through sustainable harvesting? *BioScience* 42(3): 164–173.

Bodmer, R.E., Fang, T.G., Moya, L and Gill, R. (1994). Managing wildlife to conserve Amazonian forests: population biology and economic considerations of game hunting. *Biological Conservation* 67: 29–35.

Bourliére, F. (1973). The comparative ecology of rain forest mammals in Africa and tropical America: some introductory remarks. In: *Tropical Forest Ecosystems in Africa and South America: A Comparative Review*, pp. 279–292. Meggers, B.J., Ayensu, E.S. and Duckworth, W.D. (eds). Smithsonian Institution Press, Washington D.C.

Bourliére, F. (1989). Mammalian species richness in tropical rainforests. In: *Vertebrates in Complex Tropical Systems*, pp. 152–168. Harmelin-Vivien, M.L. and Bourliere, F. (eds). Springer Verlag.

Bromley, D.W. (1989). *Economic Interests and Institutions: The Conceptual Foundations of Public Policy*. Basil Blackwell, New York.

Cabarle, B.J., Crespi, M., Dodson, C./H., Luzuriaga, C., Rose, D. and Shores, J.N. (1989). *An Assessment of Biological Diversity and Tropical Forests for Ecuador*. USAID/Ecuador Document published by World Resources Institute, Washington, D.C.

Castro, N., Revilla, J. and Neville, M. (1975–1976). Carne de monte como una fuente de proteínas en Iquitos, con referencia especial a monos. *Revista Forestal del Peru* 6: 19–32.

Chicchón, A. (1992). *Chimane Resource Use and Market Involvement in the Beni Biosphere Reserve*, Bolivia. Unpublished Ph.D. Dissertation, University of Florida, Gainesville.

Diamond, A.W. (1985). The selection of critical areas and current conservation efforts in tropical forest birds. In: *Conservation of Tropical Forest Birds*, pp. 33–49. Diamond, A.W. and Lovejoy, T.E. (eds). ICBP Technical Publication No. 4, Cambridge, England.

Dixon, J.R. (1979). Origin and distribution of reptiles in lowland tropical rainforests of South America. In: *The South American Herpetofauna: Its Origin, Evolution, and Dispersal*, pp. 217–240. Duellman, W.E. (ed.). Monograph of the Museum of Natural History, University of Kansas, Lawrence, Kansas.

Duellman, W.E. (1979). The South American herpetofauna: A panoramic view. In: *The South American Herpetofauna: Its Origin, Evolution, and Dispersal*, pp. 1–28. Duellman, W.E. (ed.). Monograph of the Museum of Natural History, University of Kansas, Lawrence, Kansas.

Duellman, W.E. (1991). Herpetofaunas in Neotropical rainforests: comparative composition, history, and resource use. In: *Four Neotropical Rainforests*, pp. 455–508. Gentry, A.H. (ed.). Yale University Press. New Haven.

Eisenberg, J.F. (1989). *Mammals of the Neotropics. The Northern Neotropics*. University of Chicago Press, Chicago.

Eisenberg, J.F. (1990). Neotropical mammal communities. In: *Four Neotropical Rainforests*, pp. 358–370. Gentry, A.H. (ed.). Yale University Press. New Haven.

Emmons, L.H. (1987). Comparative feeding ecology of felids in a Neotropical rainforest. *Behavioral Ecology and Sociobiology* 20: 271–283.

Emmons, L.H. (1990). *Neotropical Rainforest Mammals. A Field Guide*. University of Chicago Press, Chicago.

Gentry, A.H. (ed.) (1990). *Four Neotropical Rainforests*. Yale University Press, New Haven.

Goulding, M., Leal Carvalho, M. and Ferreira, E.G. (1988). *Rio Negro. Rich Life in Poor Water*. SPB Academic Publishing bv, The Hague.

Grimwood, I.R. (1968). *Notes on the Distribution and Status of*

Trade in skins from the Neotropics has focussed on relatively few species; the ocelot being one of them.   (Kent Redford)

some Peruvian Mammals. American Committee for International Wild Life Protection, Bronx, New York.

Hardin, G. (1968). The Tragedy of the Commons. *Science* 162:1243–1248.

Hecht, S. and Cockburn, A. (1990). *The Fate of the Forest; Developers, Destroyers and Defenders of the Amazon.* Harper Perennial Press, New York.

Janson, C.H. and Emmons, L.H. (1990). Ecological structure of the nonflying mammal community at Cocha Cashu Biological Station, Manu National Park, Peru. In: *Four Neotropical Rainforests*, pp. 314–338. Gentry, A.H. (ed.). Yale University Press. New Haven.

Karr, J.R. (1989). Birds. In: *Ecosystems of the World*, vol. 14B. Leith, H. and Werger, M.J.A. (eds). Elsevier Press, Elsevier, New York.

Karr, J.R., Robinson, S., Blake, J.G. and Bierregaard, Jr., R.O. (1990). Birds of Four Neotropical Forests. In: *Four Neotropical Rainforests*, pp. 237–269. Gentry, A.H. (ed.). Yale University Press. New Haven.

Keast, A. (1985). Tropical Rainforest Avifaunas: an Introductory Conspectus. In: *Conservation of Tropical Forest Birds*, pp. 3–33. Diamond, A.W. and Lovejoy, T.E. (eds). ICBP Technical Publication No. 4, Cambridge, England.

Lowe-McConnell, R.H. (1987). *Ecological Studies in Tropical Fish Communities.* Cambridge University Press, New York.

Lyster, S. (1985). *International Wildlife Law.* Grotius Publications Ltd, Cambridge, England.

McNeely, J.A., Miller, K.R., Reid, W.V., Mittermeier, R.A. and Werner, T.B. (1990). *Conserving the World's Biological Diversity.* IUCN, Gland, Switzerland.

Mitchell, C.L., and Raez-Luna, E.F. (1990). *The Effects of Hunting by Indigenous People on Prey Densities in the Manu Biosphere Reserve, Peru.* Paper presented at the Workshop on Protected Areas and Parks of the 'Reunion Internacional Experiencias para el Desarrollo Sostenido de la Amazonia', Lima, Peru.

Munn, C.A., Blanco D.S., Nycander M.E, and Ricalde, D.R. (1991). Prospects for sustainable use of large macaws in Southeastern Peru. In: *Proceedings of the First Mesoamerican Workshop on the Conservation of Macaws.* Clinton-Eitniear, J. (ed.). Center for the Study of Tropical Birds, San Antonio, Texas.

Patton, J.L., Berlin, B. and Berlin, E.A. (1982). Aboriginal perspectives of a mammal community in Amazonian Peru: knowledge and utilization patterns among the Aguaruna Jivaro. In: *Mammalian Biology in South America*, pp. 111–128. Mares, M.A. and Genoways, H.H. (eds). Volume 6 (Bats) Special Publication series. Pymatuning Laboratory of Ecology University of Pittsburg.

Peres, C.A. (1990). Effects of hunting on western Amazonian primate communities. *Biological Conservation* 54: 47–59.

Redford, K.H. (1992). The empty forest. *BioScience* 42: 412–422.

Redford, K.H. and Robinson, J.G. (1987). The game of choice. Patterns of Indian and colonist hunting in the Neotropics. *American Anthropologist* 89: 650–667.

Redford, K.H. and Robinson, J.G. (1991). Subsistence and commercial uses of wildlife in Latin America. In: *Neotropical Wildlife Use and Conservation*, pp. 6–23. Robinson, J.G. and Redford, K.H. (eds). University of Chicago Press, Chicago.

Smith, N.J.H. (1974). Destructive exploitation of the South American river turtle. *Association of Pacific Coast Geographers* 36: 85–102.

Smith, N.J.H. (1981a). *Man, Fishes, and the Amazon.* Columbia University Press. New York.

Smith, N.J.H. (1981b). Caimans, capybara, otters, manatees, and man in Amazonia. *Biological Conservation* 19: 177–187.

Snyder, N.F.R., Wiley, J.W. and Kepler, C.B. (1987). *The Parrots of Luquillo: The Biology and Conservation of the Puerto Rican Parrot.* Western Foundation for Vertebrate Zoology, Los Angeles, California.

Stiles, F.G. (1983). Birds In: *Costa Rican Natural History.* Janzen, D.H. (ed.). The University of Chicago Press, Chicago, Illinois

Stiles, G.F. (1985). On the role of birds in the dynamics of Neotropical forests. In: *Conservation of Tropical Forest Birds*, pp. 49–63. Diamond, A.W. and Lovejoy, T.E. (eds). ICBP Technical Publication No. 4, Cambridge, England.

Terborgh, J. (1988). The big things that run the world - a sequel to E. O. Wilson. *Conservation Biology* 2: 402–403.

Terborgh, J., Emmons, L.H. and Freese, C. (1986). La faune silvestre de la Amazonía: el despilfarro de un recurso renovable. *Boletín de Lima (Perú)* 46: 77–85.

Terborgh, J., Robinson, S., Parker III, T.A., Munn, C.A. and Pierpont, N. (1990). Structure and organization of an Amazonian forest bird community. *Ecological Monographs* 60(2): 213–238.

Thiollay, J. (1984). Raptor community structure of a primary rain forest in French Guiana and effect of human hunting pressure. *Raptor Research* 18: 117–122.

Vasquez, P.G. and Barrena, V.M. (1990). *Diseño de una Metodología para el Monitoreo del Impacto de las Actividades Humanas en Areas Protegidas de la Amazonia Peruana.* Conservation Data Center, Peru and European Economic Community, Lima, Peru.

Vickers, W.T. (1991). Hunting yields and game composition over ten years in an Amazon Indian territory. In: *Neotropical Wildlife Use and Conservation.* Robinson, J.G. and Redford, K.H. (eds). University of Chicago Press, Chicago.

Werner, D.I. (1991). The rational use of green iguanas. In: *Neotropical Wildlife Use and Conservation*, pp. 181–201. Robinson, J.G. and Redford, K.H. (eds). The University of Chicago Press, Chicago.

Willig, M.R. and Sandlin, E.A. (1991). Gradients of species diversity and species turnover in New World bats: A comparison of quadrat and band methodologies. In: *Latin American Mammalogy*, pp. 81–96. Mares, M.A. and Schmidley, D.J. (eds). University of Oklahoma Press, Norman, Oklahoma.

WCMC (1992). *Global Biodiversity: Status of the Earth's Living Resources.* Chapman and Hall, London xx + 594 pp.

Wilson, D.E. (1990). Mammals of La Selva, Costa Rica. In: *Four Neotropical Rainforests*, pp. 273–286. Gentry, A.H. (ed.). Yale University Press. New Haven.

Authors: Kent H. Redford, Lisa Naughton and Ernesto Raez-Luna, all at Program for Studies in Tropical Conservation, Florida University, Gainesville with contributions from Mariano Gimenez-Dixon, IUCN, Switzerland and Nigel Sizer, WRI

6 Forest Peoples

Origins

Archaeologists are uncertain how long ago human beings arrived in the New World. It is thought that they might have first crossed the Bering Strait — periodically a landbridge — as long as 45,000 years ago. What is clear, though, is that various Indian peoples have been living in the forests of Central and South America for thousands of years.

Hunting, fishing and gathering was the main way of life of the early migrants and remains important for most lowland forest dwellers today. Yet, the Neotropics also saw the very early domestication of crops. Maize, beans and squashes, New World yams and cocoyams, cassava and chillies were some of the most important, all well suited to the region's moist climate and poor forest soils.

Where environmental and social conditions were favourable, such as along the silt-laden banks of the rivers draining the Andes and on the lime-rich soils of the Yucatan, dense populations built up, allowing civilisations to flourish and fade long before Europeans first set about colonising the continent.

Best known of these forest cultures was the Mayan civilisation of the Yucatan, which had endured for several hundred years and had already passed its peak by the time that Spanish conquistadors arrived (Stephen and Wearne, 1984). Yet even in decline, the population density of the Mayans awed the Spaniards. As Bishop Bartolome de Las Casas, who spoke out against the excesses of the conquistadors, noted *"all that has been discovered up to the year forty-nine (1549) is full of people, like a hive of bees, so that it seems that God had placed all, or the greater part of, the human race in these countries."*

Recent archaeological research has revealed highly complex civilisations along the Orinoco and Amazon, especially on Marajó island at the great river's mouth. These were based on fishing and turtle farming, as well as on maize, manioc and bean cultivation on periodically flooded banks and islets (Roosevelt, 1980). When the first Spaniards descended the Amazon in the 16th century, they saw Indian settlements all along the banks of the river, from the area of the Omagua people on the present Peruvian border right down to the river's mouth.

The fertile Amazon floodplains were densely settled and large numbers of people migrated outwards from them into the less fertile hinterlands to north and south. Here, along the nutrient-poor black water rivers and on the sandy soils in the boundless forests of the Guyanan and Brazilian shields, the Indians adopted much more dispersed residence patterns, dependent on hunting, gathering and shifting cultivation. Yet they were far from isolated. Intricate trading networks linked the communities along the different river systems over thousands of miles. These trade and cultural exchanges reached up into the densely populated Andean highlands and across the Caribbean to Florida.

Sustainable Livelihoods

The Indians' long familiarity with their environment has given them a profound understanding of the possibilities and limits of the forests. As ethnobiologists are now beginning to appreciate, Indian lore regarding plants and animals, soils and waters, climate and seasons is both rich and detailed and provides the basis for complex systems of resource use and management (Posey, 1983; Clay, 1988). Some Indian groups make use of literally hundreds of plant species as medicines, potions, poisons, drugs and charms. Plants are used as dyes, paints, resins, basts, curares, ropes, clubs, bows and arrows, baskets, bark cloth, hammocks, huts and canoes, and for a thousand other purposes. The Indians' subtle understanding of animal behaviour allows them to interpret spoor and animal calls to maximise their efficiency as hunters (Colchester, 1982a). Yet, the forests are much more to the Indians than natural resources, they also provide them with the symbols by which they order their social and intellectual universe (Nelson, 1977; Lizot, 1986).

Some scientists have postulated that these symbolic schemes provide Amazonian Indian shamans with the means directly to regulate human behaviour and their interactions with nature (Reichel-Dolmatoff, 1976). Hunting taboos, sexual mores and religious festivals may ensure that human numbers and practices do not lead to over-exploitation of the environment. It is, however, difficult to establish this scientifically, but what is clear is that the combination of practical lore and Indian social and political processes act efficiently, if indirectly, to moderate pressure on the environment. In the resource-poor interfluves of the Amazon basin, villages are small, dispersed and mobile, reflecting a political system in which power is diffuse and rights and obligations are focused on small kin groups. Mobility, warfare, trekking and an identity with a general territory rather than ties to small plots of land combine to ensure that depleted areas can be left to recover naturally (Colchester, 1981 and see Box 1).

Social and technological change upsets this subtle balance between the Indians and their environment. The Indians' rising demand for manufactured goods obliges them to produce a surplus for exchange. New technologies bring more destructive impacts and increase the range over which supplies can be collected. Mission schools, dispensaries, air-strips and trading posts, as well as new machines to process crops and forest products, restrict the mobility of Indian communities. The result is local environmental depletion; making a living becomes harder work and whilst dependence on new technologies may increase, nutritional standards fall (Colchester, 1981, 1982b and see Figures 6.1 and 6.2).

WE RESPECT THE FOREST

'We Indians were born, work, live and die in the basin of the Madre de Dios river of Peru. It is our land — the only thing we have, with its plants, animals and small farms: an environment we understand and use well. We are not like those from outside who want to clear everything away, destroying the richness and leaving the forest ruined forever. We respect the forest, we make it produce for us.

Many people ask why we want so much land. They think we do not work all of it. But we work it differently from them, conserving it so that it will continue to produce for our children and our grandchildren. Although some people want to take it from us, they destroy and abandon it, moving on elsewhere. But we cannot do that: we were born in our woodlands. Without them we will die.'

Statement by the Amarakaeri of eastern Peru (Moody, 1988).

Table 6.1 Estimated numbers of Indians in tropical forests in 1492

Area	People
Caribbean	6 million
Mesoamerica	14 million
Lowland South America*	10 million
Total	30 million

* including the Pacific coast

Source: Estimates are derived from: Wilbert, 1972; Denevan, 1976; Hemming, 1978; Fried *et al.*, 1983; Coppens, 1983–89 and other documents in Survival International's archives. It must, however, be noted that there is considerable debate about these numbers.

Conquest and Enslavement

Unfortunately other pressures from outside pose a far greater threat to the survival of Indian communities and their forests than intensifying trade (Bodley, 1982). For if Europeans have praised the Indians for their natural honesty, they have equally coveted their lands and resources.

The pattern was set right from first contact. As Christopher Columbus noted of the Arawak peoples who predominated in the Caribbean: *'they love their neighbours as themselves and their way of speaking is the sweetest in the world, always gentle and smiling . . . They are so affectionate and have so little greed and are in all ways so amenable, that there is in my opinion no better people and no better land in all the world'. In almost the same breath he reported to the Spanish crown they should be good servants and intelligent . . . should your Highness command it, all the inhabitants could be taken to Castile or held as slaves on the island, for with fifty men we could subjugate them all and make them do whatever we wish* (Cohen, 1969).

So it was to be. After some fierce wars of conquest, which endured for several decades in Central America, the Indians were enslaved or made to work for their new masters. The Europeans and their African slaves also brought new diseases to the continent. Literally millions of Indians perished as epidemics of smallpox, viral infections and tuberculosis swept through the interior. In Mesoamerica as a whole, the Indian population declined from 14 million to two million between 1524 and 1600 (Fried *et al.*, 1983). In the Caribbean, the Indian peoples declined to almost nothing, today being limited to small communities on the islands of Roatan, Dominica and Trinidad (Wilbert, 1972).

The fatal vulnerability of the Indians to Old World diseases remains a problem to this day. In isolated areas, a single epidemic of an infection like measles has been known to kill off up to 30 per cent of a village, while repeated epidemics have led to extinctions of whole peoples (Colchester, 1984).

The initial aim of the colonists was to seize gold and silver. Early successes in Mesoamerica and in the Andes led to fantastic expeditions to the headwaters of some of the main rivers of Amazonia in search of fictional Indian kingdoms with fabulous wealth. These dreams were turned to more practical ends as the new colonies were developed to produce sugar, dyes and cotton for the metropolitan centres in Europe. Indian labour was in sharp demand and force had to be used to prise the Indians from their self-sufficient communities. Slaving expeditions to provide labour for the sugar plantations and mills of Brazil's northeast coast led to the first main assault on the Amazon. Rowed painfully upstream by Indian slaves, whole Indian communities were captured and taken back down to the coast by the Portuguese.

By 1650, the Vice General of the Portuguese colony of Maranhao at the mouth of the Amazon claimed that almost two million Indians had been killed, destroyed *'in their violent labour, exhausting discoveries and unjust wars'*. By the turn of the century, the lower Amazonian rivers were almost completely depopulated and the slaving expeditions were forced to travel far up the Amazon and its tributaries to secure more workers (Hemming, 1978). Eventually, the plantations of the Caribbean and South America were supplied with African slaves, groups of whom would periodically escape into the forests, some managing to re-establish viable Afro-Amerindian societies, the so-called 'Bush Negroes' of Surinam and French Guiana.

Despite the almost total annihilation of the Indians of the lower Amazon and Caribbean and the subjugation of the Indians of central America, other Indian societies of lowland South America and the Atlantic coast of Mesoamerica survived the era of conquest as autonomous societies (Nietschmann, 1973; CEDI/PETI, 1990).

Figure 6.1 The traditional system of resource use. In this system, the negative feedback cycle prevents excessive long-term use of the environment. *Source:* Colchester (1981)

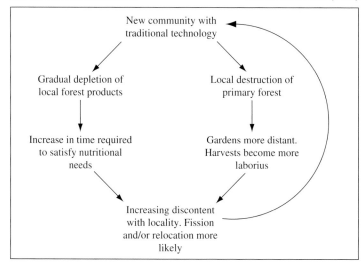

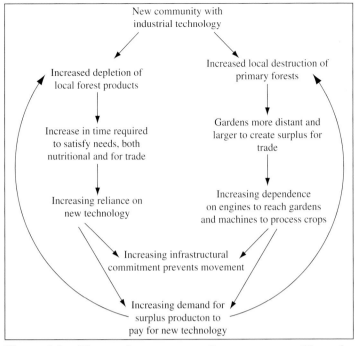

Figure 6.2 The modern system of resource use. Here the positive feedback cycle exaggerates the speed of environmental destruction and this leads to increasing dependence on the outside world.

Source: Colchester (1981)

Supplying the Market

Authority for the Indians in the Spanish and Portuguese colonies was shared between the Church and the landlords. In frontier zones where the colonial economies barely penetrated, the Church was often entrusted with full control of the Indians. Where possible, the Indians were forced to relocate from their dispersed homesteads and villages to *reducciones* — large settlements supervised by the missions. Relations between the Indians and the Church were far from easy, yet the stern paternalism was often preferable to the uncontrolled exploitation of the landowners.

For the vast majority of the Indians, colonial rule denied them any firm rights to their traditional lands. A small number of communities were able to secure colonial titles but for the rest their best security lay either in isolation or with the missions whose fiefdoms acted as a buffer to land annexation. Independence of American nations from colonial rule in the early nineteenth century brought no improvement. On the contrary, new export crops, such as coffee, cardamom and bananas, liberated markets and new forms of transport and refrigeration, all intensified the pressure on Indians in upland and coastal forests alike. In Central America, great swathes of forested Indian land on both coasts were taken over by plantations and ranches, while coffee estates expanded up the mountains forcing the Indians to clear tiny plots for their maize fields right up to the tree line (Plant, 1978; Annis, 1987).

The main trading opportunity offered by Amazonia was the region's rubber, which, after the discovery of the process of vulcanisation, found many applications in the industrial world. The result was a prodigious economic boom which made cities such as Manaus and Iquitos into important trade centres. For the first time colonists migrated en masse into Amazonia (Hemming, 1987).

The traders' wealth was based almost entirely on the manual labour of the Indians. They alone knew where the rubber trees were, scattered throughout the immense forest. Rubber barons used the most extreme means to force the Indians to work for them leading to the violent deaths of hundreds of thousands of people. A detailed exposé of these excesses found, in the Putumayo region alone, that *'in the course of the last 12 years (1900–1912), the number of Indians killed either by starvation — often deliberately brought about by the destruction of crops throughout entire regions, or inflicted as a death penalty on individuals who were unable to fill their rubber quota — or by deliberate murder by gunfire, burning, decapitation or flagellation and accompanied by a variety of atrocious tortures, in order to extract a total of four thousand tons of rubber, cannot be lower than thirty thousand, and might possibly be vastly higher'* (Taussig, 1987:20). In Brazil, from 1900 onwards, fifty-nine tribes were exterminated in the course of the activities related to rubber extraction (Davis, 1977).

With the advent of Asian rubber plantations by 1915, the price of Amazonian rubber collapsed. Economic recession followed as suddenly as the boom had come and outside interest in the Amazon waned for half a century, providing the Indians with a brief respite.

In 1910, the great Indianist and explorer Cândido Rondon led a new Indian Protection Service (SPI) in Brazil. This Service aimed to protect Indian lives, lands and cultures and also to reduce the attentions of Christian missionaries. It flourished in its early years but was starved of resources until a revival in the 1950s, when the Villas Boas brothers were creating the first Indian park on the upper Xingu River. The SPI collapsed amid scandals in 1967 and was replaced by the National Indian Foundation (FUNAI), which has had a chequered history. However, over a hundred Brazilian indian tribes now have relative security of tenure of over 200,000 sq. km of their land thanks to the work of some officials of the SPI and FUNAI and some missionaries.

Imposed Development

The present century has witnessed an exponential increase in forest loss as Indian territories have been expropriated to make way for development. In Central America, the upland forests have been squeezed by the double pressure of expanding cash cropping regimes and mechanization. Large areas of hill forest have been directly cleared for crops such as coffee and cardamom, while much more has been cut down by peasant farmers forced off the more fertile valley lands by the expansion of the large estates, the owners of which want the Indians' lands but no longer require their labour. The growing concentration of land in the hands of agribusinesses remains the main threat to Central America's forests and is leading to an accelerating migration of landless peasants, mainly of Indian descent, into the lowland forests (Utting, 1991).

Yet, even in the lowlands, the inequities of land holdings replicate themselves. Since Indians and peasants lack clear title to their lands, cleared areas are readily taken over by the rich and powerful to create new estates, mainly for cattle (see Box 2). Indian protests and demands for land security and agrarian reform have led to repression and massacres. In Guatemala, this process culminated in a civil war in which just to be Indian was to be identified as a target for counter-insurgency. In all some 100,000 people were killed and 40,000 'disappeared' in the turmoil of the early 1980s, while some 400 Indian villages were destroyed and at least 1,000,000 peasants displaced as internal refugees. According to official figures some 200,000 Guatemalans fled the country during these years and nearly 46,000 have still to return (Colchester and Lohmann, 1992).

THE SIERRA DE LAS MINAS BIOSPHERE RESERVE

The Sierra de las Minas in eastern Guatemala harbours a rich forest system with a very wide range of Central American fauna. It is considered to have the highest diversity of tropical pine species in the world. A 2,360 sq. km area of the range was legally designated a biosphere reserve in 1990.

The problems confronting the area are typical of the Central American dilemma. Over the past half century, the northern flanks of the Sierra have been settled by tens of thousands of K'ekchi Indians who have been displaced from the more fertile lowlands by logging, ranching and cardamom cultivation. The poor soils on the steep mountain slopes make stable agriculture almost impossible, implying a progressive degradation of the environment as the Indians are obliged to clear new areas, once their old plots become exhausted. At the same time, two thirds of the area have been secured as private property by largely absentee landlords, most of whom plan to sell the area's timber to pulp and sawmills in the Motagua valley to the south and turn the hills over to cattle.

The Guatemalan Foundation promoting the Reserve recognises that it cannot be made viable without buying up the privately owned lands of the rich and acquiring other areas of fertile valley land outside the reserve, or in the 'Buffer Zone' of the biosphere reserve, to resettle the Indians. The problems in this area demonstrate with startling clarity the fact that, in Central America, the conservation of natural resources is inextricably linked to the need for a redistribution of land.

The political obstacles to such an approach have also been made clear. Predictably, the landowner lobby has mounted an advertising campaign in national newspapers to vehemently denounce the conservation plan as an assault on private property. All those who advocate providing alternative lands to the Indians have been labelled as 'communists' (Colchester and Lohmann, 1992).

In Amazonia, pressure to annex Indian lands is much more recent, commencing on a large-scale in the 1970s with the construction of the TransAmazonica highway (Brooks *et al.*, 1973). In the early 1980s, World Bank-funded projects in Mato Grosso and Rondonia led to widescale colonisation of Indian lands with whole communities being all but wiped out by epidemics (Johnson *et al.*, 1989; Survival International France, 1990). Many of the migrants to Rondonia were peasants displaced by agribusiness from the south Brazilian states such as Santa Catarina and Rio Grande do Sul. At the same time, in the states of Para and Maranhao, the Grande Carajas regional development programme, brought catastrophic health and cultural problems to the Indians of the region (Treece, 1987). The extensive networks of roads also fostered a frenzy of land speculation (Branford and Glock, 1985; Hecht and Cockburn, 1989), so that the southern and south-eastern sections of the Amazonian forest, which thirty years ago were barely subject to land claims, are now a chequer-board of often overlapping indigenous reserves, individual land titles, logging concessions and mining claims (CEDI, 1985; CEDI/CONAGE, 1988).

The pattern has been repeated in neighbouring countries. In Colombia, the Caqueta was for a time promoted as a colonisation zone and in Ecuador, extensive oil prospecting has opened Indian territories to settlement by landless poor from the highlands (Hicks *et al.*, 1990). Planned colonisation, often along logging roads, has occurred too in Peru and Bolivia (Leonel, 1992), while landless Brazilian peasants displaced by mechanised soya cultivation in Parana and Mato Grosso do Sul streamed into the forested lands of the Mbya Indians of eastern Paraguay. In the north of Brazil, poverty-stricken migrants have invaded Indian lands to work as gold-prospectors, many overrunning the frontiers onto Indian territories in Venezuela and Guyana. In the conflicts and outcries which have ensued local politicians have condemned the Indians as 'obstacles to progress' and charged their supporters as agents for foreign interests (Burger, 1987)

Past attempts to exploit Amazonia to supply markets in the densely settled coastal and mountainous parts of the Amazon countries has been characterized by Emilio Moran as *'growth without development'*. It represents the antithesis of the indigenous peoples' approach, which starts with subsistence and social requirements and draws on a long experience of local environments (Moran, 1983; Monbiot, 1991).

However, conservation efforts have until recently been hardly more considerate of Indian rights. In most Latin American countries national parks are state-owned lands and legislation outlaws residence, hunting, fishing or the cutting of vegetation, thus rendering Indian systems of land-use illegal (Clad, 1984). As one Yaruro spokeswoman from Venezuela complains of a Park established on her peoples' territory *'we are prohibited from moving to our hunting grounds and to the areas where we seasonally collect wild fruits. It is like being told that you cannot go to the kitchen or the bathroom in your own house. We demand title to our lands. Caramba! We are not children.'*

Fighting Back

The Indians have resisted these impositions ever since first contact (Gray, 1987). War and rebellion were a regular feature of the early years of the conquest and Indians still resort to armed resistance when other means fail. Until recently in Brazil, it has been relatively commonplace for Indians, denied effective protection or the means to represent themselves in courts and local government, to take up arms to defend their lands from invasions by settlers, loggers and ranchers. However, the last 30 years have seen the evolution of a quieter but no less formidable expression of Indian power.

The process of organising for change started in Amazonia in the early 1960s with the creation of the Federation of Shuar Centres, by which the Shuar people united to defend their lands on the Ecuadorean frontier. Within twenty years land title had been gained for the majority of Shuar communities; they established their own radio station broadcasting in their own language and developed bilingual and bicultural education programmes. Primary health care programmes administered by the Indians were developed with State assistance.

The Shuar experience has been repeated with numerous variations all over Amazonia. Clusters of communities along the same river valley have come together to form local cultural associations. Regionally they have grouped their new community-based organizations into national confederations. The majority of Amazonian Indian communities are now linked to these kinds of institutions, some of which have become so well organized and respected that western governments are directly financing their work from their overseas development budgets. In some places, enlightened missionaries have also helped organise Indian political resistance.

National governments have also come to respect the strength and legitimacy of these Indian organisations. Most compare very favourably, in terms of their accountability and their representativeness, with the often corrupt local government structures which they parallel. Mass mobilisations of Indians, under the leadership of these organisations, has also obliged governments to heed their demands (see Box 3).

In Amazonia, these national confederations have also united as an Amazon-wide organisation, the Coordinating Body for the Indigenous Organisations of the Amazon Basin (COICA), in order to be heard directly by the international community. Indians have taken their concerns to inter-governmental agencies such as the United Nations, the World Bank and the International Tropical Timber Organisation to press for a recognition of their rights.

In Central America, the Indians are no less organised into local, national, regional and international organisations. Recently, both they and the Amazonian groups have linked together with indigenous organisations from all around the tropics into an International Alliance of the Indigenous-Tribal Peoples of the Tropical Forests, which has entered into dialogue with the UNCED process, the European Commission, the Global Environment Facility and many national Governments.

The increasing power of indigenous organisations is reflected in advances made in international law. A new Convention (No. 169) of the International Labour Organisation, which clearly recognises Indian rights to their territories, comes into force this year. A Declaration of the Rights of the Indigenous Peoples of the Americas is expected from the Organisation of American States in 1993, and a Universal Declaration of the Rights of Indigenous Peoples is already going through its third draft at the United Nations (Davis, 1988; UN, 1991).

New Models

The Indians' struggle to reassert their traditions and control their lives and environment has important implications for the future of the forests in the Neotropics. It implies — in areas subject to their control — an end to major road-building, min-

ing, hydropower and colonisation schemes and the application of another model of development more sensitive to human needs and the limitations of the forests (Chirif *et al.*, 1991).

As the Coordinating Body for the Indian Organisations of the Amazon Basin has put it: '*Development can only occur when the people it affects participate in the design of proposed policies, and the model which is implemented thereby corresponds to the local people's aspirations. Development can be guaranteed only when the foundations are laid for the sustained well-being of the region, only continued poverty can be guaranteed when the policies lead to the pillage and destruction of local resources by those coming from outside. The indigenous people of the Amazon have always lived there: the Amazon is our home. We know its secrets well, both what it can offer us and what its limits are. For us, there can be no life if our forests are destroyed. We want to continue living in our homelands.*'

Clear evidence is emerging that, under Indian management, forests have a better chance of being sustained (Smith, 1987; but see Redford and Maclean Stearman, 1993). For example, studies in the highlands of Guatemala have shown that communal forests under Indian control are better 'policed' and are less overexploited than either individually owned forests, which tend to be "cashed-in" for short term personal gains, or municipal forests, which are either corruptly opened to outside interests or treated by locals and outsiders alike as 'open access' areas.

Even where Indians themselves undertake logging, they provide examples of far superior management than is the norm in other parts of Latin America, where forest management is almost unknown. The Amuesha Indians of the Yanesha Cooperative in Palcazu in Peru have developed an innovative shelterbelt logging system that makes maximum use of the forests — the larger, high quality timbers being processed for sale on the international market, while smaller poles are chemically treated and sold locally as fencing posts. Similar projects have started up in Quintana Roo in Mexico and in the coastal forests of Ecuador (Anderson 1990; WWF 1991).

Timber is far from the only product that Indian communities are marketing from their forests. Tannins, dyes, oils, honey, wild fruits, nuts, basketry, artwork, canoes, treecrops and agricultural produce are among the varied goods that Indian communities are bringing to the local and wider markets. Much more needs to be learned about these community management schemes before

MARCHING FOR TERRITORIAL RECOGNITION

In 1988, the International Tropical Timber Organisation gave US$1.26 million to the Government of Bolivia to promote the sustainable management of the Chimanes forests of the Beni, part of Bolivia's Amazon territory. The project formulated by the Bolivian Government and the Washington-based NGO Conservation International was designed to complement the management of the Chimanes Biosphere Reserve, which encloses the El Beni Biological Station, secured under a debt-for-nature swap financed by Conservation International.

The project, however, was flawed. It made no provisions to secure the territorial rights of the Indians, nor did it provide a real political mechanism for controlling the rampant logging of mahogany that was already underway in the region.

Indian protests culminated in 1989 with a month-long, 750 kilometre trek to the national capital, La Paz, by thousands of

Indians. The pressure forced the Government to declare the whole area of the Chimanes forest as Indian territory and secured about half the forest as 'indigenous areas' for exclusive Indian use. The loggers were supposed to halt the extraction of timber from these 'indigenous areas' and restrict their cutting to the rest of the territory, which would be finally restored to the Indians after some 70 years.

However, continued illegal timber extraction from the 'indigenous areas' and accelerating logging in the rest of territory obliged the Indians to send delegates to Yokohama to raise their concerns with the International Tropical Timber Organisation. The ITTO suspended funding for the project until new management plans for the now reduced logging areas were designed and the Indians were brought into the decision-making process. The Indians have yet to declare victory, but their position has begun to improve.

they can be declared 'sustainable', but the evidence is already clear that they are far preferable to the destructive short-term exploitation of outsiders (Counsell and Rice, 1992; Gray, 1991).

Governments and development agencies are beginning to get the message. Already some 200,000 sq. km of Colombia's Amazonian forests have been redefined as Indian *resguardos*, as the Government has explicitly recognised the Indians to be the forests' best guardians (Bunyard, 1989). In Peru, Indian land demarcation projects are restoring Indian territories through a patchwork quilt of community titling programmes, condoned by Government and assisted by national and international NGOs and bilateral aid agencies. In Ecuador, pressured by a country-wide Indian mobilisation, the Government has recognised large swathes of Indian territory, while retaining rights to petroleum exploitation. In Brazil, land demarcation processes have again speeded up. Some 90,000 sq. km of forests have been recognised as Yanomami Indian lands, while Kayapo areas have been considerably expanded and those of the Tikuna and Xavante increased slightly (Hosken, 1990). In all, well over 500,000 sq. km of Amazonian forests are now recognised as Indian lands.

A parallel programme in Brazil is also securing areas of forests as 'extractive reserves' for rubber tappers. Under this process forests remain under State ownership, but are leased to registered rubber tapper cooperatives. The real innovation in these reserves lies in the wholly new management regimes that the tappers have instituted; they no longer produce rubber to pay-off debts to the rubber barons who used to run the trade, but market it themselves through self-run cooperatives. Even so, the tappers are finding it hard going as real prices for latex are abysmally low. Politically, the tappers have united with the Indians to push for development policies that protect their interests and they are seeking wider alliances with other non-Indian groups who also live in the forests — river-dwellers, nut-collectors, fisherfolk and palm-workers (LAB, 1990).

Conservation initiatives are also paying increasing attention to Indian rights. The Venezuelan Government recently decreed the whole of the Upper Orinoco, an area inhabited by Yanomami and Yekuana Indians, a Biosphere Reserve — at over 80,000 sq. km the world's largest tropical forest conservation zone. The legislation explicitly recognises Indian use rights throughout the reserve and promises them a direct role in the management of the area.

Most recently the Inter-American Development Bank, supported by the World Bank and working with the Spanish Government and Governments from Latin America, has established a special facility — the Fondo Indigena, already capitalised with US$40 million — to develop projects in Indian areas, including land demarcation schemes. An advisory body for the new Fund will be drawn half from Government and half from indigenous representatives.

Kayapo family on medicinal trail, Gorotire, Brazil.
(WWF/Mauri Rautkari)

Recognition of indigenous rights is now readily admitted as being socially just, environmentally prudent and necessary for the sound development of Indian territories. The challenge for the future is to ensure that external support for these areas goes to the communities in the forests, that it remains under local control and that local initiatives are built on (Beauclerk and Narby, 1988). In the past the Indians have suffered from externally imposed problems; great sensitivity is now required to prevent externally imposed solutions doing just as much harm.

References

Anderson, A.B. (1990). *Alternatives to Deforestation: steps toward sustainable use of the Amazon rain forest.* Columbia University Press, New York.

Annis, S. (1987). *God and Production in a Guatemalan Town.* University of Texas Press, Austin.

Beauclerk, J. and Narby, J. with Townsend, J. (1988). *Indigenous Peoples: a field guide to development.* Oxfam, Oxford.

Bodley, J.B. (1982). *Victims of Progress.* Mayfield, Palo Alto.

Branford, S. and Glock, O. (1985). *The Last Frontier: Fighting over land in the Amazon.* Zed Books, London.

Brooks, E., Fuerst, R., Hemming, J. and Huxley, F. (1973). *Tribes of the Amazon Basin 1972.* Report for the Aborigines Protection Society. Charles Knight and Co., London.

Bunyard, P. (1989). *The Colombian Amazon: policies for the protection of its indigenous peoples and their environment.* Ecological Press, Bodmin.

Burger, J. (1987). *Report from the Frontier: the State of the World's Indigenous Peoples.* Zed Books, London.

Chirif, A., Garcia, P. and Smith, R.C. (1991). *El Indigena y Su Territorio son uno solo: estrategias para la defensa de los pueblos y territorios indigenas en la cuenca Amazonica.* COICA and Oxfam (America), Lima.

CEDI (1985). *Povos Indigenas no Brasil.* Centro de Documentacao e Informacao, Sao Paulo, 23 volumes (in progress).

CEDI/CONAGE, (1988) *Empresas de Mineracao e Terras Indigenas na Amazonia.* Centro de Documentacao e Informacao, Sao Paulo.

CEDI/PETI, (1990). *Terras Indigenas no Brasil.* Centro de Documentacao e Informacao, Sao Paulo.

Clad, J. (1984). Conservation and Indigenous Peoples. *Cultural Survival Quarterly* 8(4): 68–73.

Clay, J. (1988). *Indigenous Peoples and Tropical Forests: models of Land Use and Management from Latin America.* Cultural Survival, Cambridge, Mass.

Cohen, J.M. (1969). *The Four Voyages of Christopher Columbus.* Penguin, Harmondsworth.

Colchester, M. (1981). Ecological Modelling and Indigenous Systems of Resource Use: some examples from the Amazon of South Venezuela. *Antropologica* 55: 51–72.

Colchester, M. (1982a). *The Economy, Ecology and Ethnobiology of the Sanema Indians of South Venezuela.* Doctoral Dissertation, University of Oxford.

Colchester, M. (1982b). Amerindian Development: the search for a viable means of surplus production in Amazonia. *Survival International Review* 41/42: 5–16.

Colchester, M. (ed.) (1984). *The Health and Survival of the Venezuelan Yanoama.* International Work Group on Indigenous Affairs, Copenhagen, 1984.

Colchester, M. and Lohmann, L. (eds.) (1992). *The Struggle for Land and the Fate of the Forests.* World Rainforest Movement, Penang, with Zed Books.

Coppens, W. (1983–1989). *Los Aborigenes de Venezuela.* 3 vols. Fundacion La Salle, Caracas.

Counsell, S. and Rice, T. (eds.) (1992). *The Rainforest Harvest: Sustainable Strategies for Saving the Tropical Forests?* Friends of the Earth, London.

Davis, S.H. (1977). *Victims of the Miracle.* Cambridge University Press, Cambridge.

Davis, S.H. (1988). *Land rights and indigenous peoples: the role of the Inter-American Commission on Human Rights.* Cultural Survival, Cambridge.

Denevan, W.M. (ed.) (1976). *The Native Population of the Americas in 1492.* University of Wisconsin Press, Madison.

Fried, J.L., Gettleman, M.E., Levenson, D.T. and Peckenham, N. (1983). *Guatemala in Rebellion: Unfinished History.* Grove Press, New York.

Gray, A. (1987). *The Amerindians of South America.* Minority Rights Group, London.

Gray, A. (1991). *Between the spice of life and the melting pot: biodiversity conservation and its impact on indigenous peoples.* International Work Group on Indigenous Affairs, Copenhagen.

Hecht, S. and Cockburn, A. (1989). *The Fate of the Forest.* Verso, London.

Hemming, J. (1978). *Red Gold: the conquest of the Brazilian Indians.* Macmillan, London.

Hemming, J. (1987). *Amazon Frontier. The defeat of the Brazilian Indians.* Macmillan, London.

Hicks, J.F., Daly, H.E., Davis, S.H. and de Freitas M.L. (1990). *Ecuador's Amazon Region.* World Bank, Washington.

Hosken, L. (1990). *A Tribute to the Forest People of Brazil.* Gaia Foundation, London.

Johnson, C., Knowles, R. and Colchester, M. (1989). *Rainforests: Land Use Options in Amazonia.* Oxford University Press, Oxford.

LAB (1990). *Fight for the Forest: Chico Mendes in his own Words.* Latin America Bureau, London.

Leonel, M. (1992). *Roads, Indians and the Environment in the Amazon: from Central Brazil to the Pacific.* International Work Group on Indigenous Affairs, Copenhagen, Document 72.

Lizot, J. (1986). *Tales of the Yanomami.* Cambridge University Press, Cambridge.

Monbiot, G. (1991). *Amazon Watershed.* Michael Joseph, London.

Moody, R. (1988). *The Indigenous Voice: Vision and Realities.* Volume 1. Zed Books, London.

Moran, E. (ed.) (1983). *The Dilemma of Amazonian Development.* Westview Press, Boulder.

Nelson, R. (ed.) (1977). *Popol Vuh: the great mythological book of the ancient Maya.* Houghton Mifflin Co., Boston.

Nietschmann, B. (1973). *Between Land and Water.* Seminar Press, New York.

Plant, R. (1978). *Guatemala: Unnatural Disaster.* Latin America Bureau, London.

Posey, D. (1983). Indigenous ecological knowledge and development of the Amazon. In: *The Dilemma of Amazonian Development.* Moran, E. (ed.). Westview Press, Boulder. Pp. 225–257.

Redford, K.H. and Maclean Stearman, A. (1993). Forest-dwelling native amazonians and the conservation of biodiversity: interests in common or in collision? *Conservation Biology* 7 (2): 248–255.

Reichel-Dolmatoff, G. (1976). Cosmology as ecological analysis: a view from the rain forest. *Man* 11(3): 307–318.

Roosevelt, A.C. (1980). *Parmana: Prehistoric Manioc and Maize Cultivation along the Amazon and Orinoco.* Academic Press, New York.

Smith, R.C. (1987). Indigenous autonomy for grassroots development. *Cultural Survival Quarterly* XI(1): 8–12.

Stephen, D. and Wearne, P. (1984). *Central America's Indians.* Minority Rights Group, London.

Survival International France (1990). Bresil: Indiens et Developpement en Amazonie. *Ethnies* 11–12, Survival International France, Paris.

Taussig, M. (1987). *Shamanism, Colonialism and the Wild Man: a study in terror and healing.* University of Chicago Press, Chicago.

Treece, D. (1987). *Bound in Misery and Iron: the impact of the Grande Carajas Programme on the Indians of Brazil.* Survival International, London.

UN (1991). *Draft Declaration of the Universal Rights of Indigenous Peoples.* United Nations, E/CN.4/Sub.2/1991/40.

Utting, P. (1991). *The Social Origins and Impact of Deforestation in Central America.* Discussion Paper, United Nations Research Institute on Social Development, Geneva.

WWF (1991). *Views from the Forest: Natural Forest Management Initiatives in Latin America.* World Wildlife Fund (USA), Washington DC.

Wilbert, J. (1972). *Survivors of El Dorado.* Praeger Press, New York.

Authors: Marcus Colchester, World Rainforest Movement, Oxford, U.K and Jeremy Narby, Moudon, Switzerland, with contributions from John Hemming, Royal Geographical Society and Steven Hugh-Jones, Cambridge University.

7 Agricultural Colonization Policies and Deforestation in Amazonia

INTRODUCTION

The Malthusian forces of natural resource destruction by local people, market-oriented agricultural expansion and the need to generate foreign exchange were not the major factors behind the occupation and deforestation of Amazonia. The real problem stemmed from growing numbers of landless peasants and small farmers arriving from areas outside Amazonia and the geopolitical goals and speculative interests of the ruling elites.

The areas from where agricultural colonists arrived were not excessively populated, but land ownership was concentrated in a few influential hands. It was this unequal land distribution that caused problems. Inducing landless workers and peasants to move into the "empty" Amazonian region offered a means of avoiding these problems. Additionally, the fear — shared by most Amazonian countries — that vast uninhabited areas would tempt foreign occupation, stimulated colonization programmes. The fact that Amazonia was already inhabited by Amerindians was either ignored altogether or else concerns about these peoples were subordinated to national developmental and territorial aspirations.

The occupation of Amazonia and the economic integration of the region have emphasised the settlement of land by peasants and landless workers. Large agricultural schemes undertaken by individual entrepreneurs or corporations have also been encouraged. This chapter considers the evolution, since World War II, of the colonization policies of the main countries sharing the Amazonian ecosystem. Particular reference is made to Brazil, as a large portion of Amazonia falls within its boundaries. Moreover, since 1970, this country has pursued an array of colonisation policies which have contributed significantly to large-scale deforestation.

The Limits of Amazonia and its Deforestation

Radically different limits of Amazonia were proposed until the 1950s (Daly and Prance, 1989) and even now estimates of its size vary between five and six million square kilometres (Sioli, 1984; Pires, 1972), but there is no doubt that most of it lies in Brazil. Smaller areas occur in Bolivia, Colombia, Ecuador, Peru, Venezuela and the Guianas. The approximate limits of the natural boundaries of the area are shown in Figure 7.1. It must

be noted that, in Brazil, this does not correspond with the broader economic/political boundaries set by the government as "Amazonia Legal" in 1953 (Oliveira, 1983).

Neither the area nor the rate of deforestation in Amazonia are well known. Probably best studied is the forest in Brazil and here it is estimated by Skole and Tucker (1993) that 230,000 sq. km of closed canopy forest (6 per cent) had been cleared as of 1988, while INPE (1992) estimated about 280,000 sq. km had been cleared in the Legal Amazon at that time — this, though, included the cerrado vegetation. The estimate increases to 377,600 sq. km if the degraded secondary forests in Pará and Maranhão are included, where "the original forest was removed in great part many years ago" (INPE, 1992). The figure given by Fearnside in Table 25.5 for deforestation in the Brazilian Legal Amazon is very similar to INPE's larger figure.

In absolute terms, Brazil has certainly lost the greatest area of Amazonian rain forest, but the losses in Venezuela and Ecuador, in proportion to the area of Amazonian forest they contain, have been higher (Schubart, 1991).

Agricultural Colonization in Amazonia

Until the middle of this century, most of Amazonia was sparsely populated. The exploratory incursions, begun centuries ago, had reduced the Amerindian population considerably, decreasing it by perhaps as much as 90 per cent. However the extractive booms (mainly of rubber) of the 19th and early 20th centuries did attract tens of thousands of migrants to some areas, such as western Amazonia. There were attempts to introduce large scale exploitation of tropical products, such as the Ford rubber plantations set up in Brazil, but most of these failed and were abandoned. As a result, until the mid-1940s, much of this immense region was inhabited only by native peoples and the colonizers who had settled some of its more accessible areas. Little development or deforestation had taken place.

The 1950s marked the beginning of a complete reversal of this situation, with considerable influxes of migrants and attempts to develop Amazonia as rapidly as possible. Public policies were fundamental in bringing about these changes.

Figure 7.1 The limits of Amazonian vegetation

Source: Daly and Prince (1989)

Brazil

Most early deforestation in Brazil resulted from agricultural expansion outside Amazonia, particularly in the south and southeast. For instance, before the coffee boom started in the mid-18th century, São Paulo was 82 per cent forested, but by 1973 only 8.3 per cent of the forest remained. Similarly, at the end of the 1940s, almost 90 per cent of the northern region of Paraná state was covered in forests. This area is now one of Brazil's most important agricultural regions and only two per cent of it remains under forest (Mueller, 1991).

Until the late 1960s, agriculture expanded 'spontaneously'. The main government action to stimulate the process before that time was improvement of the transportation system. However, recent expansion in the Brazilian Amazonia has been greatly influenced by social policies. These policies reflect an approach to development in recent decades that has tended to favour city dwellers and has led to a highly unequal distribution of benefits (Mueller, 1992). Since 1968, the ruling elites and those with powerful economic interests have received numerous advantages. Modernisation of agricultural methods, without redistribution of land, has meant that a growing number of people have been expelled from the main farming areas in the centre-south of the country. Many of these migrants moved to the large urban industrial centres, but a considerable number went to the agricultural frontier which had, by then, reached the Amazonian rain forest. Other people, from the poverty-stricken north-east of Brazil, joined the migrants from the rural areas of the centre-south and together they were responsible for a major onslaught on the Amazonian forests.

Both Brazil's corporate sector and government agencies have embarked upon major Amazonian ventures. Mining, hydroelectric and industrial investments have all contributed to forest clearance but large agricultural enterprises and cattle ranches have been the leading causes of deforestation.

The policies which have directly affected frontier expansion in Brazilian Amazonia since the mid-1960s have gone through several distinct phases.

The Early Phase, up to 1965. Policies which sought to integrate Amazonia into the Brazilian economy were attempted prior to the 1960s, but they had little effect (Mahar, 1978). However, in the late 1950s, the first major road to link Amazonia to the centre-south of the country — the Belém-Brasília highway — was built. It connected the more dynamic areas of Brazil with the southeast margin of the rain forest which later became an important agricultural frontier area.

Formation of the Amazonian Strategy (1965–1969). T h e military regime, which came into power in 1964, drew up a specific Amazonian strategy. Contrary to current belief, it was geopolitical considerations, rather than the prospect of exploiting the region's abundant resources, that motivated this strategy. It was argued that by establishing a demographic and economic stronghold in Brazilian Amazonia, and by promoting settlement of the country's extensive international borders to the north and west of it, foreign powers would be discouraged from staking claims there. A frequently voiced motto in the 1970s was, "integrate it or lose it". The main objective of the military regime was, therefore, to induce rapid occupation of some of Amazonia's huge "empty spaces", regardless of the economic or environmental sustainability of the process.

Occupation was based on the hope that it would be possible to integrate the region into the mainstream of the country's economy. However, the projects undertaken in the region did not undergo any form of economic viability analysis. Even for large investments, cost-benefit analysis was generally not carried out (Torres, 1990). The first major natural resource survey did not begin until after the projects had started.

Operation Amazônia was launched in 1965 to implement the new strategy. Its main component was a regional development programme based chiefly on the provision of tax rebates and other financial incentives aimed at stimulating private investment in Amazonia. Most of the investment projects took the form of huge livestock ranches. Between 1966 and 1969, a total of 166 livestock enterprises were approved; these made up over one fifth of all schemes approved as of 1988 (Yokomizo, 1989).

The construction of the Cuiabá-Porto Velho highway began in 1968. This brought floods of land-hungry settlers, mostly rural migrants from the centre-south, into the state of Rondônia.

Intensification of the Amazonian Strategy (1970–1975). In 1970, the military government created the National Integration Programme (PIN) which aimed to boost occupation of Amazonia by funding road building and settlement projects. Through this programme, resources were made available to construct some 15,000 kilometres of road and, on either side of these roads, a 20 km strip of land was reserved for agricultural settlement projects (Mahar, 1989). At the same time, virtually all state-owned land was transferred to the federal government, which thereby acquired control over very large areas. In addition, PIN increased fiscal incentives for private investment in Amazonia.

The road construction programme was extremely ambitious. It was intended that one highway (the Transamazon) would cross the region from east to west, another (Cuiabá-Santarém) would cross it from the north to south and a third would be built along most of the northern boundary of Brazilian Amazonia. In addition, other trunk roads were to be built or improved to provide the more developed central-southern regions with access to strategic portions of Amazonia.

Only part of the projected road network was actually built. The Manaus-Porto Velho and Cuiabá-Santarém trunk roads and the Cuiabá-Porto Velho highway were completed, while the Transamazon highway was not finished and the border road never materialised (Figure 7.2). Nonetheless, the roads were responsible for the opening up of large densely forested areas for agricultural colonization.

Colonization projects, intended as "model" settlements, were set up in two areas of the country. The then federal state of Rondônia in the north-west of Brazil was one of these. Settlements here were intended to attract farmers from the south who were experienced in modern agricultural methods. The other was along the eastern part of the Transamazon highway. Here the aim was to settle people from the poverty stricken northeast and thereby alleviate population and social pressures in that area.

The fiscal incentives were stepped up by PIN so that, between 1966 and 1972, substantial areas of land were incorporated into agricultural projects, many involving cattle rearing. This was partly because of the high prices for beef in the world market in the early 1970s which led to hopes that Amazonia would become a world exporter of this commodity.

The intention of PIN was that the settlers would produce subsistence goods and provide manpower for various secondary developments, while private initiatives, aided by the fiscal incentives, were to furnish a growing quantity of agricultural products for both the domestic and export markets. This strategy aimed to incorporate Amazonia into the national economy and reduce the danger of foreign domination of the region.

Loss of Impetus and Change in Strategies (1975–1979).
Events did not materialize as expected, however. The oil crises of the 1970s reduced Brazil's economic growth and made it more difficult to obtain resources for the road construction programme. The high oil prices also accentuated the problems of having settlements in such remote areas. The road construction programme for Amazonia was therefore cut back considerably.

This period also witnessed a major change in the strategy for occupying Amazonia. The public colonization schemes had proved unsuccessful for a number of reasons. There were serious administrative problems, inappropriate agricultural techniques were applied by the migrants, and the settlers generally experienced difficulty in adapting to their new environment. As a result public colonisation schemes were phased out. Instead, in order to make the best use of limited governmental resources, efforts after 1974 focussed on areas with high potential, rather than on the region in general.

Even though the public colonization schemes had failed, a much larger flow of spontaneous immigration into parts of eastern Amazonia and Rondônia began. The migrants were small farmers and workers displaced from the centre-south of Brazil. This compelled the government to support the orientation and control of spontaneous colonisation (Martine, 1990; Mueller, 1980). Despite government efforts, the pressure of this migra-

Figure 7.2 Amazonia: Main Federal Highways and Development Projects

Source: Mahar (1989)

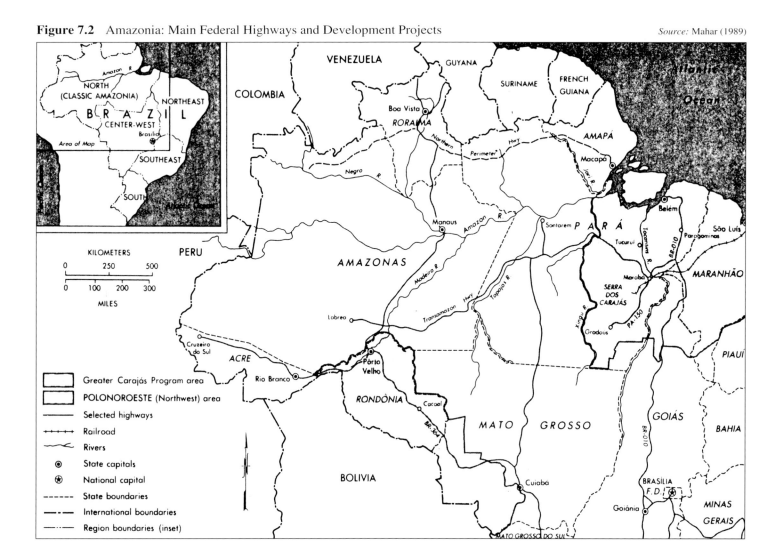

tion was such that the demand for plots in colonization areas far exceeded supply. As a result, wherever there was road access, large numbers of migrants settled on public and private land. The authorities were unable to control the process and this invasion of public land was eventually condoned and legitimised by the government. In contrast, settlement on private or disputed land frequently led to violence (Mueller, 1983; Sawyer, 1990).

It was hoped that government-sponsored, private schemes could replace the public colonisation projects. The government started providing private ventures and cooperatives with access to public lands and subsidized credit. These schemes were intended mainly for settlers from the south of Brazil who had some capital and farming experience. Most of the projects were implemented in the north of the state of Mato Grosso, in the rain forest-savanna transition zone.

Private colonization gained impetus, particularly in the period from 1976 to 1981. Of the 104 private colonization projects started between 1970 and 1986, almost 67 per cent were established between 1976 and 1981. The total area covered was 29,000 sq. km, of which 68 per cent was settled in 1976–1981. Most of the farms developed were between one and five sq. km. The settlers were mainly interested in cultivating commercial crops and in the 1980s the private colonization areas become an important producer of soybeans (Mueller, 1990).

The large-scale fiscal incentive projects also fell far short of original expectations and their number was reduced considerably. Thus from 1973 to 1979, only 56 projects were approved, compared to 312 projects in the previous seven year period (Yokomizo, 1989). In addition, new regulations came into force which prohibited projects in the core of the Amazonian forest and provided for stricter controls over development in the area.

Nevertheless, some individuals still believed that large investment projects could suceed in Amazonia and that these were the key to developing the area. It was during this time that Daniel Ludwig's huge Jarí complex in eastern Amazonia began to take shape. Over 1000 sq. km of the 15,000 sq. km owned by Ludwig were cleared and planted with *Gmelina arborea* and *Pinus caribea*. These were to be used as raw material for a large pulp plant that had been imported from Japan. The scheme included rice cultivation on 40 sq. km of flood-plain and minerals exploitation (Fearnside and Rankin, 1979, 1985). Ludwig used his own money for these activities, but was encouraged by the government.

Major Programmes and the Expansion of Fiscal Incentives (1980–1988). The principal development projects in Amazonia between 1980 and 1988 were the Northwest Brazil Integrated Development Programme (POLONOROESTE) in western Amazonia and the Grande Carajás Programme in eastern Amazonia (Figure 7.2).

The POLONOROESTE programme, financed by the World Bank, was an attempt to impose some order on the chaotic occupation of Rondônia and part of western Mato Grosso. A principal objective of the programme was to reduce forest clearance on land with little long-term agricultural potential and, instead, to promote sustainable farming systems based on tree crops (Mahar, 1989). The programme sought to assist the 30,000 or so families already settled in the region as well as the 15,000 families waiting to be settled there (Mahar 1989). It aimed to reduce the environmental degradation which was taking place and to protect Indian populations (World Bank, 1981). However, most of these goals were not achieved; some people believe that the government's main objective in seeking loans for

POLONOROESTE was to obtain funds for paving the Cuiabá-Porto Velho highway (Martine, 1988).

The Grande Carajás Programme began in 1980 as a massive multisectoral project based on the extraction, transformation and exportation of the enormous mineral wealth (principally iron ore) of the Carajás. The numbers of migrants attracted to the region inevitably caused quite extensive deforestation, particularly outside the concession area. One of the project's most controversial components is the production of pig-iron using charcoal made from timber from the natural forest. The proposed pig-iron plants would require 1.2 million tons of charcoal per year and the wood required for this would result in the clearing of between 5,400 and 12,000 sq. km of forest (Mahar, 1989). Many billions were invested in this programme, but it is not now expected to yield a net profit.

As well as developing these two programmes, the government also increased its fiscal incentives scheme dramatically after 1980. Between 1980 and 1986, 353 agricultural projects were approved. Political pressure from the groups benefiting from the incentives, rather than the inherent worth of any of the projects, forced the government to continue the scheme. The beneficiaries profited both directly from the incentives and subsidies and indirectly from the increased value of their land. Land prices were driven up by the scheme and by high inflation which increased the demand for real estate (Binswanger, 1991). The size of the projects approved after 1980 tended to be smaller than the earlier ones, and most of them were on the periphery of the rain forest rather than within it. However, the federal agency responsible for the scheme became extremely lax in its management of the enterprise and incentive monies were frequently misused (Yokomizo, 1989).

The fiscal incentive scheme for agricultural projects was reduced in 1987 and temporarily suspended by government decree in 1989. However, fiscal incentives for regional development have been maintained by the 1988 Constitution, and there is a danger that inappropriate agricultural projects will be resumed in Amazonia. At present, projects can still be undertaken in the already degraded or savanna area of Legal Amazonia whereas those in the core of Amazonia can be resumed only upon completion of a detailed zoning study, which is currently underway.

This period also saw the failure of the Jarí project. In 1982, having experienced increasing problems with his enterprise, Ludwig transferred control to a government-backed Brazilian group (Mueller, 1983).

Summary
Brazil's vast array of measures to encourage colonization have had very negative impacts on Amazonia. In general, they have failed to achieve sustainable agricultural and livestock production or economic development. They have also resulted in vast demographic shifts, social dislocation, distress for Amazonian Indian peoples, forest clearance and pervasive environmental disruption.

Colonization in Other Latin American Countries
The Amazonian region of most of the other countries discussed in this chapter are covered with lowland rain forest or, on the eastern slopes of the Andes, with montane forest. The montane forest, commonly known as *selva alta* (upland forest), occurs from 600 to 3500 m. It covers a smaller proportion of Amazonia than does lowland forest, but has been the prime target for colonization in the Andean countries. Indeed, in contrast to Brazil, the Andean lowlands of Bolivia, Colombia, Ecuador, Peru and Venezuela remain largely untouched (Coomes, 1991).

Bolivia

Bolivia is considered an Andean country, although two-thirds of its territory is Amazonian. Some of its upland forests were colonised as long ago as the 16th Century, with attendant extermination, expulsion or absorption of Indian populations by the invading Europeans. Nevertheless, these upland areas were not intensively exploited until the early 1950s.

In 1952 the Movimiento Nacional Revolutionario (MNR) seized power and embarked upon a programme of agrarian reform, nationalization of mines and abolition of feudalism. However, as Green (1980) notes, the impact of the agrarian reform legislation on the Amazonian region was not as great as it might have been since there was little demand for land there.

The MNR also pursued an Amazonia colonization policy, the main objectives of which were expansion of agricultural production, alleviation of demographic pressures in the highlands and integration of the Bolivian Amazonia into the country's economy. The construction of a highway, completed in 1954, which linked La Paz and Cochabamba with the forest city of Santa Cruz, was an important element of this policy. Between 1954 and 1956, four colonies were founded in this region and were followed by more modest attempts at colonization of other high forest areas made accessible by road construction.

Bolivia had frequent changes in its political regime and, consequently, in its administrative policies, but the public colonisation schemes to resettle landless peasants from the highlands in Amazonia were maintained. Many landless people migrated to the Oriente of their own accord. The objectives set by MNR for the Oriente were gradually achieved and parts of the forest, particularly the area around Santa Cruz, experienced considerable economic development. The role of government colonization schemes in this was minor, though as Stearman (1984) points out, the schemes used up considerable monetary and human resources and were a significant feature of Bolivia's development plans for many years. Other factors such as the discovery and exploitation of oil, the establishment of large farms and ranches, industrialization and, more recently, the cocaine trade were far more significant for the development of the region. In addition, international financial support encouraged a flow of domestic and foreign settlers to the Amazonian highlands.

Only those colonization programmes involving foreign settlers and international finance had any real success. Public colonization programmes performed poorly (Rivière d'Arc, 1980; Stearman, 1984). They were undermined by inadequate transportation and marketing, unstable and inefficient administration, and corruption. In the 1960s the Instituto Nacional de Colonizacion (National Colonization Institute) was created to administer the official programmes, but still they did not improve markedly. However, colonists who abandoned agriculture were an important element in the expansion of other activities in the Santa Cruz area.

By the mid-1980s, colonization in Bolivia had become largely spontaneous or semi-directed, with the National Colonization Institute providing secondary or tertiary roads, technical assistance, water supplies and some schools (Stearman, 1984).

In Bolivia, unlike other Andean countries, the demographic and economic results of settlement within Amazonia were considerable. The number of inhabitants is estimated to have reached 3.7 million in 1990, which is around 51 per cent of the country's total population. This is a considerable increase from 1960 when only 38 per cent of the population lived in the area (Butts and Bogue, 1989). The Santa Cruz region has became an important agricultural centre, generating growing surpluses for both domestic and export markets. This Amazonia region has become Bolivia's major area of economic development.

Peru

In Peru, as in Bolivia, the Spanish conquistadores explored Amazonia, but failed to colonise it. However, in the 1940s, population increases in the country's coastal and highland areas and unequal land distribution led to urban saturation, food deficits and political unrest and these stimulated rural exodus. Political elites opposed land redistribution, and as new roads made the Peruvian Amazonia accessible, landless peasants from the Sierras moved in.

It was not until the 1960s that a concerted colonization policy was established. Peasants had been settled previously in Amazonia but had not been sponsored by the government. In 1954, for instance, le Tourneau, an American millionaire, obtained 4000 sq. km of Peruvian Amazonia for a colonization project. In spite of large expenditure, this failed and was abandoned. The government granted land to companies constructing roads in the upland forest, and to their employees, for sale to colonists from the Andes (Chirif, 1980).

It was during the first mandate of President Belaunde Terry that a strategy for settlement and development in Amazonia was introduced; access roads were to be constructed and colonization projects promoted. A highway, the Carretera Marginal de la Selva, was to be built along the eastern flank of the Andes with other new roads leading from it. Belaunde Terry hoped that by linking the Venezuelan-Colombian border with southeast Bolivia, through the Ecuadorian and Peruvian forests, the Carretera Marginal would facilitate the development and economic integration of the Amazonian region of all the Andean countries. In the event, only the Peruvian sector of the road was constructed. A large colonisation project, financed by a US$41 million loan from the Interamerican Development Bank (IDB), was started in 1966 in the Huallaga Valley. Two other smaller projects were also attempted (Schuurman, 1980). However, all three ran into difficulties and were phased out.

In the 1960s and early 1970s, both government-sponsored and, more importantly, spontaneous colonization resulted in the settlement of eleven important river basins on the eastern slopes of the Andes (Aramburú, 1984). Spontaneous colonization by landless peasants and entrepreneurs, the latter interested in cattle ranching and commercial agriculture, brought people from the highlands and coastal areas. Large numbers of Indians were

Charcoal making from mahogany, used to smelt iron ore from Carajás. Amazonia, Brazil. (WWF/Mark Edwards)

pushed off their land during this process. Some moved to remote lowland areas and others were assimilated by the new communities and exploited as labourers.

A military coup in 1968 changed the Amazonian strategy. Colonization was downplayed, an Indian rights policy was established and there was a short-lived attempt to deal directly with the agrarian problems in the coastal and highland areas. However, changes within the military leadership and the re-election of Belaunde Terry in 1980 meant that the Amazonian development strategy was resurrected. Assistance programmes for the region's settlers were established and colonization schemes were revived with American aid. Between 1981 and 1985, USAID allocated US$167 million for this purpose, but with disappointing results (Aramburú and Garland, 1986). There were also incentives for settlers to move north to consolidate the disputed border with Ecuador (Stocks, 1984).

In the 1970s, the Peruvian Oriente experienced an oil boom. Exploration companies moved into parts of the region, creating temporary employment, but also generating substantial social dislocation. When the boom ended, unemployment became a serious problem for some areas.

More recently, there has been a sharp increase in the illegal cultivation of coca, creating a problem of almost unmanageable proportions. The United States pushed for eradication of this crop, but the wisdom of their pouring abundant foreign aid into areas already settled, but of low agricultural potential, is now being questioned (Aramburú, 1984). The results of the aid for colonisation were poor and both state and foreign aid has now been phased out. Further problems in many of these areas have been created by the presence of the Sendero Luminoso (Shining Path) guerilla group.

In 1978 a decree annulled the law recognizing the rights of Amazonian indigenous communities. It also introduced a concessions system for the exploitation of national forest reserves, which had previously been controlled by the state (Chirif, 1980). The decree established safeguards to protect forests, but legislation of the Belaunde Terry government has since eliminated most of them and made it much easier for national and foreign companies to gain access to reserve lands. According to Stocks (1984), as much as 90 per cent of national forests in some areas have been given in concessions to the private sector. In addition, the Amazonian strategy of the 1980s provided generous incentives for entrepreneurs willing to invest in the region's remoter areas.

Spontaneous colonization and entrepreneurial activity were responsible for a considerable increase in the number of occupants of Peruvian Amazonia; they grew from little more than 400,000 in 1940 to over 1.8 million in 1981. This is an increase from 6.7 per cent to 10.6 per cent of the country's total population living in Amazonia. The upland forests have absorbed most of this population increase but there has also been an inflow of migrants into other parts of the Peruvian Amazonia. However, transportation and other difficulties have meant that the rate of growth in these areas has been lower than that occurring in upland forest areas (Aramburú, 1984), while migration into the coastal areas, especially into large cities, has been most significant.

Ecuador

Official support for the settlement of Ecuadorian Amazonia is a fairly recent phenomenon. As a result of the 1941 war between Ecuador and Peru over petroleum, Ecuador lost part of its Amazonian territory. It, therefore, came to view colonization of the remainder and its integration into the national economy as matters of considerable urgency. Military posts and colonization projects were established, regardless of economic considerations. The aim was simply to gain control of the country's borders (Bromley, 1980; Uquillas, 1984).

Spontaneous population movements in Ecuador began to gain pace in the late 1940s. The migrants were from the more densely populated areas in the Andean highlands and from the coast; they moved because of overcrowding and land pressures in those areas. They were attracted to Amazonia by the prospect of jobs and the availability of land.

The oil boom which began in parts of Amazonia in the late 1940s was an added factor. Roads to oil areas facilitated migration, which was spurred on by the employment opportunities in both the oil and timber industries. Land was available and agricultural products were required by the people working in the area. Entrepreneurs saw opportunities for cattle-ranching and the production of crops such as coffee.

The government favoured spontaneous colonization and also created several official colonization projects. By 1981 there were seven of these official schemes in Ecuadorian Amazonia. They were located in the provinces of Napo (the main oil area), Morona-Santiago and Zamora-Chinchipe (near the Peruvian border). Gradually, settlements were consolidated throughout the high forest and in the intermontane valleys. The majority were dedicated to farming and ranching (Uquillas, 1984). Initially, the official colonization projects were intended to attract people to "empty" areas, but later they became attempts to control the rapid spontaneous occupation.

Costs associated with the settlement of the Ecuadorian Amazonia included the usual social dislocation of frontier areas, environmental problems and the displacement of Indian communities, who were forced to find land elsewhere. However, only a relatively small area of Amazonia was affected by colonization. One of the main reasons for this was the region's poor transportation system. There were plans to construct more highways, and even railroads, but these were never realized. In 1976 there were only four relatively short penetration roads, either associated with oil exploration or constructed for strategic reasons (Bromley, 1980). The result was a comparatively minor increase in the region's population, from 1.6 per cent of the country's total in 1960, to 3.0 per cent in 1980 and still only 4.2 per cent in 1990. Of the 460,000 people inhabiting the region in 1990, 76.1 per cent lived in the forested provinces of Napo and Morona-Santiago (Butts and Bogue, 1989).

Colombia

The Colombian Amazonia was explored several centuries ago, but was only recently settled by non-Indians. Here, as in other countries of the region, population pressure in the uplands stimulated its settlement. However, two events led the government to intervene decisively in the process. The first was during the 1930s and 1940s, when Colombia and Peru were laying claim to the same territory and tensions ran high. As a result, the government built a road into strategic areas near the Colombian-Peruvian border and introduced incentives to encourage settlers to move into parts of the provinces of Putumayo and Caquetá (Carrizosa, 1983). The second event was the insurrection and conflict (the Violência) which erupted in 1948. When a truce was finally reached in 1953, it was decided that peasants who had lost their land, and other victims of the Violência, should be settled on public lands in Amazonia.

The settlement process was stepped up in the 1960s. After the meeting of the Organization of American States (OAS) in Punta del Este in 1960, foreign aid was sought and the Instituto Colombiano de la Reforma Agraria (INCORA) created to manage colonization of Amazonia (Dominguez, 1984). The OAS meeting had recommended strong commitment to agrarian reform in Latin America, but Colombia, together with most other countries in the region, decided that politically it was easier to settle landless peasants in the "empty" spaces of Amazonia.

The results of the public and private colonisation schemes that took place in the 1950s and 1960s, in the forests of the provinces of Putumayo and Caquetá and, later in the province of Guaviare, were generally poor. Reasons for this included bad planning, inefficient administration, malaria outbreaks and lack of support for the settlers. Many people moved back to the highlands or set-off in search of less hostile areas elsewhere in Amazonia (Ortiz, 1984). The scheme in Caquetá seems to have been an exception. There the colonization project attained such a high growth rate that it prompted INCORA to concentrate most of its resources in this region and use it as a model of agrarian reform (Dominguez, 1984).

The discovery of petroleum in the late 1960s led to the improvement of the transportation system, generated jobs and markets for agricultural products and encouraged spontaneous migration into Putumayo. Caquetá also attracted wealthier settlers and farmers drawn by the province's improved conditions and the availability of land which was not only cheap, but had been cleared by previous settlers (Ortiz, 1984). In this way, large landholdings were created in the high forest zone in the two regions. Urban centres and heterogeneous agricultural sectors, producing both subsistence and market oriented goods, also developed in both provinces.

As in other Latin American countries, the first- and second-generation settlers took over land previously used by Indian peoples. The latter moved to other areas of Amazonia, or became acculturated, joining the poorest migrants as a source of cheap labour.

Difficulties of access and the inhospitable nature of Colombian Amazonia have restricted colonization to a limited geographical area and its impact has accordingly been fairly small. Similarly, the region's contribution to the national economy remains meagre and its population increase insignificant. It is estimated that by 1990, the number of people in Colombian Amazonia was a mere 533,000, or 1.7 per cent of the country's total population. The provinces of Caquetá and Putumayo hold 76.1 per cent of the people living in Amazonia, while Guaviare contains another 10 per cent of the area's inhabitants. Although the other three provinces in the region are very extensive, they have only small populations.

Venezuela

Venezuela's Amazonian region is mostly within the Territorio Federal do Amazonas situated in the southern tip of the country. The state of Bolivar, to the south of the Orinoco, includes a relatively small portion of Amazonia (Butts and Bogue, 1989; Esteves, 1986), but this area is not included in the following discussion.

The Federal Territory of Amazonia covers 178,000 sq. km, or 20 per cent of Venezuela, but its estimated population in 1990 was only 83,000 (Butts and Bogue, 1989). Nevertheless, this is a large increase from 1960 when there were a mere 11,000, or thereabouts, people in the area (Butts and Bogue, 1989). One of the Territory's most striking characteristics is its isolation from the more developed parts of the country. No major roads have been constructed and the extensive river network still constitutes the main transportation system (Esteves, 1986).

Around 30 per cent of the tropical forest originally covering Venezuela was in the Territory, with most of the remainder in Bolivar. Although a considerable area of forest has been cleared, only a very small proportion of this has been from the Territory. This is because colonization in the region has been negligible. However, this does mean that its rain forest is not under pressure. To some extent, Venezuela is at the stage the other Andean countries were at forty years ago. Although prosperity was created by petroleum until the late 1970s, its influence, in terms of increased economic activities and a rise in population, was restricted almost exclusively to the area north of 6° latitude (Benacchio, 1982). When the revenue from oil declined in the 1980s, Venezuela was compelled to search for new avenues of development, and occupation of Amazonia was one possibility. In addition, settlement of this area was advocated as a means of protecting the immense "empty" areas to the south of the country from the expansionist ambitions of Venezuela's neighbours.

Expansion into Amazonia has had a major impact on the Indian communities in the region. Expropriation of the Indians' land began in the early colonial period, but it was not until the late 1950s that this occurred in Amazonia. Initially, the process was slow, but according to Arvelo-Jiménez (1984, 1986) it speeded up dramatically and many Indian communities lost land they had occupied for generations. The reasons for this change, which can be traced back to the late 1960s, were the real or supposed geopolitical strategies of Venezuela's neighbours. These aroused nationalistic feelings and made the country's military forces uneasy. This led to the inception of the "Conquista del Sur" (Conquest of the South), a strategy for the development and integration of Amazonia into the country's economy, which received strong backing from the corporate sector. As well as proposing settlement and development of the region, it envisioned the "civilization" of the Indians. It was claimed that, in their primitive state, the Indians held no allegiance to Venezuela and were potential pawns of foreign interests. They should, therefore, be acculturated and incorporated into the national society. Arguments such as these provided an excuse for land grabbing, but by corporations rather than landless peasants.

The Venezuelan Amazonian debate features two opposed groups: the developers, armed with arguments such as those outlined above, and the Indian Rights movement, which argues against measures which destroy the identity of the Indians and/or expropriate their land. Until the early 1970s the former prevailed, but since then the influence of the Indian Rights movement has increased markedly. Legislation which favours the interests of the Indians has been passed and extensive areas of forest have been allocated for conservation and traditional use. However, these actions have been strongly criticized by the developers on the grounds that they risk endangering national security.

The economic crisis of the 1980s lent further support to arguments for developing Amazonia and gave added impetus to groups keen to see an Amazonian geopolitical strategy implemented. These groups were at one with vociferous politicians and segments of the media who pointed to the supposed inherent danger in the nomadic behaviour of the Amazonian Indians and the neglected state of Venezuela's southern international borders. It was claimed that, with the aid of more modern agricultural techniques, the Indians would be able to subsist in much smaller areas of land and live in permanent settlements. This 'reorganization' would then make extensive areas available for development and enable the corporate sector to exploit any minerals or other resources in the "freed" land (Arvelo-Jiménez, 1986).

Venezuela's Amazonian frontier is still not opened and settled, but the belief that it should be is gaining increasing acceptance in Venezuela. Nationalistic feelings are stronger than ever, particularly as the discovery of alluvial gold has brought a flood of Brazilian gold-diggers into the Venezuelan Amazonia. Events such as this highlight the danger that the regulations protecting both the environment and the interests of Indian communities will be abandoned. Instead, roads will be opened and the landless and poor induced to move into Amazonia as has happened in the other Latin American countries. A major factor preventing this to date is the Territory's dense river network, which makes road construction there an arduous and very expensive task (Esteves, 1986).

Conclusions

There are common elements in the colonization experiences of all the countries reviewed above. In most, the land holding class of the old, settled areas has successfully resisted attempts to carry out land reform by persuading governments to direct the peasants and landless workers to the "empty" Amazonian region. Typically, geopolitical considerations have played a central role in defining strategies for Amazonia. In addition, the discovery of petroleum in Amazonia, with its knock-on effects on transportation systems, job and market creation and increased settlement, has been a important factor. The corporate sector has also had a significant influence on policies concerned with development of Amazonia.

The effects of the strategies and the colonization policies of the different countries also exhibit common features. Relative to the total area of Amazonia in each country, the land areas affected by settlers and agricultural ventures are not large. Similarly, except in Bolivia, the population increase due to the colonization of Amazonia has not been great. Much the same can be said of the contribution the schemes have made to the economies of the countries concerned. The difficulty of access to the rain forest, which renders economic exploitation problematic, has in itself moderated the impact of human activities. Nevertheless considerable resources have been poured into colonization schemes in all countries except Venezuela, with generally very poor results. Moreover, there has been senseless destruction of tropical forests and native populations have suffered violence and expropriation of their land.

The conclusion, for both Brazil and the Andean countries, is that the colonization schemes have caused enormous economic, social and environmental problems and have yielded only modest benefits.

References

Aramburú, C.E. (1984). Expansion of the agrarian and demographic frontier in the Peruvian selva. In: *Frontier Expansion in Amazonia.* Schmink, M. and Wood, C.H. (eds), pp. 153–230. University of Florida Press, Gainesville, Florida, U.S.A.

Aramburú, C.E. and Garland, E.B. (1986). Poblamiento y uso de los recursos en la Amazonía Alta: el caso del Alto Huallaga. In: *Desarollo Amazónico: Una Perspectiva Lationamericana.* Aramburú, C.E. and Mora, C. (eds), pp. 115–177. CIPA-INANDEP, Lima, Peru.

Arvelo-Jiménez, N. (1984). The politics of cultural survival in Venezuela: beyond indigenismo. In: *Frontier Expansion in Amazonia.* Schmink, M. and Wood, C.H. (eds), pp. 105–126. University of Florida Press, Gainesville, Florida.

Arvello-Jiménez, N. (1986). Se dice que son contradictorios . . . los indígenas y la seguridad nacional. In: *Desarollo Amazónico: una Perspectiv Lationamericana.* Aramburú, C.E. and Mora, C. (eds), pp. 391–423. CIPA-INANDEP, Lima, Peru.

Benacchio, S. (1982). Agricutural development in Venezuela's Amazon region. *In: Amazonia — Agriculture and Land Use Research.* Hecht, S. (ed.), pp. 115–134. Centro Internacional de Agricultura Tropical, Cali, Colombia.

Binswanger, H.P. (1991). Brazilian policies that encourage deforestation in the Amazon. *World Development* 19 (7): 821–29.

Bromley, R. (1980). The role of tropical colonization in the twentieth century economic development of Ecuador. In: *Land, People and Planning in Contemporary Amazonia.* Barbira-Scazzochio, F. (ed.), pp. 174–184. Cambridge University Press, Cambridge, U.K.

Butts, Y. and Bogue, D.J. (1989). *International Amazonia — Its Human Side.* Social Development Center, Chicago, U.S.A.

Carrizosa, J. (1983). La ampliacion de la frontera agricola en el Caqueta (Amazonia Colombiana). In: *Expansion de la Frontera Agropecuária y Medio Ambiente en America Latina.* ECLA/UNEP (eds), pp. 237–310. UN/CIFCA, Madrid, Spain.

Chirif, A. (1980). Internal colonialism in a colonised country: the Peruvian Amazon in a historical perspective. In: *Land, People and Planning in Contemporary Amazonia.* Barbira-Scazzocchio, F. (ed.), pp. 185–192. Cambridge University Press, Cambridge, U.K.

Coomes, O.T. (1991). *Rain Forest Extraction, Agroforestry, and Biodiversity Loss: an Environmental History from the Northeastern Peruvian Amazon.* Proceedings of the XVI International Congress of the Latin American Studies Association, April 6, 1991, Washington, D.C., 28 pp.

Daly, D.C. and Prance, G.T. (1989). Brazilian Amazon. In: *Floristic Inventory of Tropical Countries: the status of plant systematics, collections, and vegetation, plus recommendations for the future.* Campbell, D.G. and Hammond, H.D. (eds). Pp. 401–426. The New York Botanical Garden, New York.

Domínguez, C.A. (1984). National expansion and development policies in the Colombian Amazon. In: *Frontier Expansion in Amazonia.* Schmink, M. and Wood, C.H. (eds), pp. 405–18. University of Florida Press, Gainesville, Florida, U.S.A.

Esteves, J. (1986). Manejo ambiental de los recursos: plan de la Amazonía Venezoelana. In: *Desarollo Amazonico: Una Perspectiva Latinoamericana.* Aramburú, C.E. and Mora, C. (eds), pp. 21–57. CIPA-INANDEP, Lima, Peru.

Fearnside, P.M. and Rankin, J. (1979). Avaliação da Jarí Florestal e Agropecuária Ltda. como modelo para o desenvolvimento da Amazônia. *Acta Amazonica* 9 (3): 609–616.

Fearnside, P.M. and Rankin, J. (1985). Jarí revisted: changes and the outlook for sustainability in Amazonia's largest silvicultural estate. *Interciencia* 10(3): 121–129, 160.

Fearnside, P.M., Tardin, A.T. and and Meira, L.G.M. (1990). Deforestation rate in Brazilian Amazonia. National Secretariat of Science and Technology, Brasília, Brazil.

Green, M. (1980). The development of the Bolivian Oriente since 1950 and the 'Junkers' transition to capitalism in Bolivian agriculture. In: *Land, People and Planning in Contemporary Amazonia.* Barbira-Scazzocchio, F. (ed.). Pp. 171–173. Cambridge University Press, Cambridge, U.K.

INPE (1992). Deforestation in Brazilian Amazon. Instituto Nacional de Pesquisas Espaciaias, São Jose dos Campos, Brazil.

Mahar, D. (1978). Políticas de desenvolvimento para a Amazônia: passado e presente. In: *Dimensões do Desenvolvimento Brasileiro.* Baer, W., Geiger, P.P. and Haddad, P.R. (eds.). Editora Campus Ltda, Rio de Janeiro, Brazil.

Mahar, D.J. (1989). *Government Policies and Deforestation in Brazil's Amazon Region.* The World Bank, Washington, D.C.

Martine, G. (1988). Frontier expansion, agricultural modernization and population trends in Brazil. In: *Population, Food and Rural Development.* Lee, R.D., Arthur, W.B., Kelly, A.C., Srinivasan, G. and Rogers, T.N. (eds). Pp. 187–203. Clarendon Press, Oxford, U.K.

Martine, G. (1990). Rondônia and the fate of small producers. In: *The Future of Amazonia — Destruction or Sustainable Development.* Goodman, D. and Hall, A. (eds), pp. 23–48. Macmillan, London, U.K.

Mueller, C. (1980). Frontier based agricultural expansion: the case of Rondônia. In: *Land, People and Planning in Contemporary Amazonia.* Barbira-Scazzocchio, F. (ed.), pp. 141–153. Cambridge University Press, Cambridge, U.K.

Mueller, C. (1983). El estado y la expansion de la frontera agricola en la Amazonia. In: *Expansion de la Frontera Agropecuaria y Medio Ambiente en America Latina.* ECLA/UNEP (eds), pp. 37–78. UN/CIFCA, Madrid, Spain.

Mueller, C. (1990). Políticas governamentais e expansão recente da agropecuária no Centro Oete. *Planejamento e Políticas Públicas, Brasília,* 3: 45–73.

Mueller, C. (1991). *Dinâmica, Condicionantes e Impactos Sócio-ambientais da Evolução da Fronteira Agrícola no Brasil.* Working Document No. 7. Institute for the Study of Society, Population and Nature, Brasília. 29 pp.

Mueller, C. (1992). *Agriculture, Urban Bias and the Environment.* Paper presented at the conference on Natural Resources and Environment Management in an Interdependent World. January 22–24, 1992. Costa Rica.

Oliveira, A.E. de (1983). Ocupação humana. In: *Amazônia: desenvolvimento, integração, e ecologia.* Salati, E., Schubart, H.O.R., Junk, W, and Oliveira, A.E. de (eds). Editora Brasiliense/CNPq, São Paulo.

Ortiz, S. (1984). Colonization in the Colombian Amazon. In: *Frontier Expansion in Amazonia.* Schmink, M. and Wood, C.H. (eds), pp. 204–230. University of Florida Press, Gainesville, Florida, U.S.A.

Pires, J.M. (1972). Tipos de vegetação de Amazônia. *Publicacoes Avulsas Museu Paraense Emilio Goeldi* 20: 179–202.

Rivière d'Arc, H. (1980). Public and private agricultural policies in Santa Cruz (Bolivia). In: *Land, People and Planning in Contemporary Amazon.* Barbira-Scazzocchio, F. (ed.), pp. 154–161. Cambridge University Press, Cambridge, U.K.

Sawyer, D. (1990). The future of deforestation in Amazonia: a socioeconomic and political analysis. In: *Alternatives to Deforestation — Steps Towards Sustainable use of the Amazon Rain Forest.* Andernson (ed.), pp. 265–274. Columbia University Press, New York, U.S.A.

Schubart, H.O.R. (1991). *A Amazônia e os Temas Ecológicos Globais — Mitos e Realidade.* Working Document no. 6. Institute for the Study of Society, Population and Nature (ISPN), Brasília. 24 pp.

Schuurman, F. (1980). Colonization policy and peasant economy in the Amazon Basin. In: *Land, People and Planning in Contemporary Amazonia.* Barbira-Scazzocchio, F. (ed.), pp. 106–113. Cambridge University Press, Cambridge, U.K.

Sioli, H. (1984). The Amazon and its main affluents: hydrography, morphology of the river courses, and river types. In: *The Amazon. Limnology and Landscape Ecology of a Mighty Tropical River.* Sioli, H. (ed.). Dr W. Junk, Dordrecht.

Skole, D. and Tucker, C. (1993). Tropical deforestation and habitat fragmentation in the Amazon: satellite data from 1978 to 1988. *Science* 260: 1905–1910.

Stearman, A.M. (1984). Colonization in Santa Cruz, Bolivia: a comparative study of the Yapacaní and San Julian Projects. In: *Frontier Expansion in Amazonia.* Schmink, M. and Wood, C.H. (eds), pp. 231–260. University of Florida Press, Gainesville, Florida, U.S.A.

Stocks, A. (1984). Indian policy in Eastern Peru. In: *Frontier Expansion in Amazonia.* Schmink, M. and Wood, C.H. (eds), pp. 33–61. University of Florida Press, Gainesville, Florida, U.S.A.

Torres, H.G. (1990). A experiência de planejamento e desenvolvimento regional da Amazônia. In: *O Aproveitamento Integrado das Principais Bacias Hidrográficas da Amazônia como Estratégia Espacial de Desenvolvimento Regional.* SUDAM/OAS, Belém. (Mimeograph).

Uquillas, J. (1984). Colonization and Spontaneous Settlement in the Ecuadorian Amazon. In: *Frontier Expansion in Amazonia.* Schmink, M. and Wood, C.H. (eds), pp. 261–284. University of Florida Press, Gainesville, Florida, U.S.A.

World Bank, (1981). *Brazil, Integrated Development of the Northwest Frontier.* The World Bank, Washington, D.C., U.S.A.

Yokomizo, C. (1989). *Incentivos Financeiros e Fiscais na Pecuarização da Amazônia.* Texto para Discussão No. 22. IPEA/IPLAN, Brasília. 30 pp.

Author: Charles C. Mueller, University of Illinois, with contributions from David Cleary, Cambridge University; Michael Eden, Royal Holloway and Bedford College and Nigel Sizer, World Resources Institute.

8 Protected Areas

INTRODUCTION

As forest loss in the Americas accelerates and its economic and social consequences are increasingly felt, protected areas (or as often referred to in this atlas, conservation areas) have assumed greater importance as a means to conserve viable, representative portions of intact forest and other ecosystems. The process has taken different forms in different countries and to generalise across the Neotropics is difficult given the great diversity of countries and the variety of forces which have influenced protected area creation and management. Yet within this context of diversity, which makes it imperative to consider each country individually, there are also important common factors — similar socioeconomic conditions, for example — which have forged the protected area systems we see today.

Although there has been a large increase in the number and extent of protected areas over the last decade (see Figure 8.1), the success of those in the Americas has been rather mixed. The great majority of parks and reserves are subject to encroachment, poaching and similar threats. Conflicts between local communities and national or global interests have been solved in only a very few cases, and with increasing population these conflicts will intensify. More effective means are required for linking protected areas with national development, territorial planning and, at the most fundamental level, the needs of humans. It is in this field that Neotropical protected area managers are learning most and within which there will be exciting developments in the future. This chapter presents a history of protected areas in tropical America, examines the current situation and analyses the issues confronting protected area managers.

History of Protected Areas in the Americas

Protection of natural areas as we conceive it today is a recent phenomenon in the Americas. Of course, there are notable exceptions: the Aztecs maintained botanical gardens, those constructed and cared for by the sovereigns Netzahualcóyotl and Moctezuma being amongst the most well known (Alcérreca et al., 1988). The Maya on the other hand developed a very efficient and complex shifting agricultural system based on silviculture. They made extensive use of terraces and designed irrigation systems to supply raised fields. They also managed and protected "natural" forest blocks in order to speed reforestation of their fallow plots, a system which can still be seen today in the rich and diverse forest gardens of the present day Maya (Gómez-Pompa, 1991).

It is important to understand the history of Neotropical forests and the processes responsible for their present day composition and distribution in order to set conservation criteria (McNeely, 1993). Before the arrival of the Europeans in 1492,

there are thought to have been about 30 million people living in the tropical forests of the Americas (see Chapter 6 — but note that there is debate about these figures). Many were hunter-gatherers, but agriculture was also widespread. The large populations living in the forests had profound effects upon the ecological processes, species composition and structure of the forest itself. Amazonia's eight million inhabitants, like the Kayapo in Brazil of today, were collecting and cultivating food plants such as tubers and beans as well as managing the densities and distributions of useful tree species (Posey, 1982). In Central America, 75 per cent of the Yucatan forest had been modified by A.D. 800. However, with the collapse of the Maya civilisation, the forests in the central lowlands had largely recovered when the Spaniards arrived 700 years later. Nevertheless, when the first European settlers arrived, far from encountering a "pristine" environment, they found a landscape which had been profoundly altered by man (McNeely, 1993).

The European colonists, bringing diseases and forced labour with them, caused a severe reduction in the indigenous population: 75 per cent of the native people of the Americas south of present-day USA are thought to have been eliminated between 1492 and 1650 (Denevan, 1992). This demographic collapse was not compensated for until the recent immigration of settlers, and it left large areas of agricultural land to revert to forest once more.

The conquest also modified traditional resource management systems or replaced them with non-sustainable, export-oriented ones (Alcérreca et al., 1988; Pérez-Gil and Jaramillo, 1992). In response to environmental degradation, the first protected areas were established: Tobago's Main Ridge Reserve and St. Vincent's King's Hill Reserve were declared in 1765 and 1791 respectively, both to protect watersheds (Putney, 1992). A century passed before the first true protected area, Mexico's Desierto de los Leones Forest Reserve, was established in Middle America, and not until the start of the 19th Century did the first ones appear in South America (Torres, 1992; Ugalde and Godoy, 1992).

In 1872, Yellowstone in the United States was declared the world's first national park. The first Neotropical national parks were a product of the efforts of particular individuals, such as Francisco ('Perito') Moreno in Argentina and Henri Pittier in Venezuela (Amend and Amend, 1992a). Parque Nacional del Sur (now called Nahuel Huapi) in Argentina, set up in 1903, was the first national park to be declared in South America. It was followed by Uruguay's F.D. Roosevelt in 1916, Chile's Vicente Pérez Rosales in 1926, Kaietur in Guyana in 1929 and Pico Cristal National Park in Cuba in 1930 (Oltremari, 1992; Putney, 1992; Torres, 1992). Barro Colorado Biological

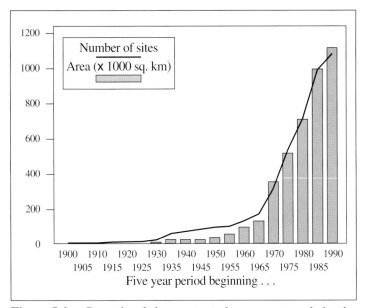

Figure 8.1 Growth of the protected areas network in the Americas

Source: WCMC, unpublished data

Reserve in Panama, the Islas Galápagos National Park in Ecuador and Henri Pittier National Park in Venezuela were all established during the 1920s and 1930s.

To begin with, protected areas were declared by the enactment of legislation specific to each site. Brazil's Royal Charter of 1797 was the first general legislation to protect forests. The first Forest Laws providing for the creation of protected areas appeared in 1905 (Amend and Amend, 1992b; Ugalde and Godoy, 1992; IUCN, 1992). Management was usually assigned to either forest or agriculture departments. However, in some countries in the absence of more appropriate agencies, this fell, for example, on the Central Bank in Nicaragua and on the Institute of Tourism in El Salvador. Protection of natural areas was often associated with laws on agrarian reform, as both were linked to a rational territorial planning process. Indeed, the most successful reformers were often the best conservers. For example, in Mexico President Lázaro Cárdenas, famous for his land reform programmes, established 58 per cent of the current protected areas system and made major improvements in natural resource management during his term of office from 1934 to 1940 (Alcérreca *et al.*, 1988).

Protected areas continued to be created throughout the first half of this century, mainly as a means of safeguarding watersheds, outstanding natural landscapes and areas for tourism. In Central America, many were declared to preserve the region's impressive Precolumbian heritage. These included Tikal National Park in Guatemala, which protects the remains of the largest Mayan city in Mesoamerica, Ruinas de Copán Cultural Monument in Honduras, and numerous areas on the Yucatán Peninsula in Mexico. However, there was no clear concept of how a national park should be managed; each country followed a different philosophy according to its historical, social and geographical background. Efforts to unify philosophy and practice began through international agreements in the 1930s. The 1940 Convention on Nature Protection and Wildlife Preservation in the Western Hemisphere (Western Hemisphere Convention) did much to encourage and direct protected area legislation throughout the Americas. By the 1960s, all of the South and Central American nations had declared protected areas of some sort (Torres, 1992; Ugalde and Godoy, 1992).

In the 1970s, environmental concern on a world scale stimulated the appearance of new criteria for the creation and management of protected areas. This world concern was reflected in the elaboration and ratification of treaties such as the World Heritage and Ramsar Conventions and the establishment of UNESCO's Man and the Biosphere Programme (see Table 8.1 and Figure 8.2). These initiatives marked the emergence of conservation and protected areas as international issues and not just national concerns.

In the 1980s, concern revolved around the ability to conserve natural areas as a resource to sustain human societies in the future. Conserving the diversity of genes, organisms and ecosystems was seen as a legitimate aim in order to maintain nature's ability to change and adapt whilst also keeping open people's options for developing new crops and drugs.

Throughout the region, major legislative strengthening took place in the 1980s. In Central America, protected area laws were enacted in Belize and Guatemala and there was a considerable strengthening of Costa Rica's protected areas system. Panama declared 14 out of its 20 existing protected areas, accounting for 95 per cent of the area of the national system. Honduras declared its three most important protected areas and Guatemala and Nicaragua each declared their countries' two biggest biosphere reserves (Ugalde and Godoy, 1992). At this time in South America, many countries made an important step by producing plans for consolidation of their protected areas into systems, rather than treating them as independent units (Torres, 1992). Similar changes also took place in the Caribbean, where the establishment of protected areas was more prolific during the 1980s than ever before (Putney, 1992).

The 1980s also saw the establishment of Conservation Data Centres (CDCs) by governments, universities and non-governmental organisations (NGOs) in several countries in the Americas. These CDCs, assisted by the US NGO The Nature Conservancy (TNC), collect, store and analyze information for use in siting and managing protected areas (Norris, 1988).

In addition, the 1980s saw the beginning of a movement to integrate local communities into protected areas, from which they had become divorced by the traditional concept of national parks as inviolable sanctuaries. Local communities were a key issue at the Third World Parks Conference in Bali in 1982 (McNeely and Miller, 1984). Biosphere reserves and indigenous reserves were a product of the realisation that protected areas would simply not function without the support and participation of the local people.

Unfortunately, the 1980s also saw the deepening of the severe economic and social crises which still afflict many nations in the Neotropics today. In the face of falling commodity prices on world markets, burgeoning national debt, hyperinflation and commitments to austerity programmes, many governments had little possibility of strengthening their environment departments and protected area agencies. This seriously hampered attempts to expand and consolidate protected area systems in the Americas. Legislation could not be enforced and parks could not be managed effectively (Putney, 1992; Torres, 1992; Ugalde and Godoy, 1992).

The Coverage of Protected Areas in the Americas

Reviews of regional protected area coverage have been carried out by Oltremari (1992), Putney (1992), Torres (1992) and Ugalde and Godoy (1992). Older reviews, which give a historical perspective, include Hartshorn and Green (1985) on Central America, and Wetterberg (1974) and Wetterberg et al. (1985) for South America. In addition, there are country-by-country analyses for South America (Amend and Amend, 1992b) and

Central America (Morales and Cifuentes, 1989). Excellent national studies have also been carried out in many countries, for example, Alcérreca *et al.* (1988) for Mexico, APN (1991) for Argentina, CDC-UNALM (1991) for Peru and SEA/DVS (1990) for the Dominican Republic.

At present, **terrestrial** protected areas under IUCN management categories I–IV (those receiving a higher degree of protection — see Box 1) in the countries being considered in this Atlas, cover 4.8 per cent of South America, 4.3 per cent of Central America (but 9.5 per cent if Mexico is excluded) and 7.1 per cent of the Caribbean (WCMC, unpublished data — see Table 8.2). Over 900 category I–IV protected areas have been

established in the countries covered in this Atlas. They are not, however, evenly distributed amongst the countries. Again considering categories I–IV, the Dominican Republic has 23.6 per cent of its land area protected, Panama has 17.5 per cent, Venezuela has 16.2 per cent; while El Salvador, Jamaica, Haiti, French Guiana and Guyana all have one per cent or less of their land area protected within categories I–IV (WCMC, unpublished data — see Table 8.2).

These figures by themselves give little clue as to the "value" of protected areas in different countries. To get an idea of this one must also consider how areas have been selected for protection and how they are managed.

Table 8.1 State parties to international and regional conventions or programmes concerned with the conservation of natural areas

Country	World Heritage Convention[1]	International Biosphere Reserves[2]	Ramsar Convention[3]	Western Hemisphere Convention[4]	Cartagena Convention[5]	SPAW Protocol[6]	Amazon Cooperation Treaty[7]
SOUTH AMERICA							
Bolivia	4 Oct 76	3	27 Oct 90 (1)	Y			Y
Brazil	1 Sep 77 (1)	2	24 Sep 93 (5)	Y			Y
Colombia	24 May 83	3		Y	Y	Y	Y
Ecuador	16 June 75 (2)	2	7 Jan 91 (2)	Y			Y
French Guiana (France)	27 Jun 75		1 Dec 86 (2)		Y	Y	
Guyana	20 Jun 77			Y			Y
Paraguay	28 Apr 88			Y			
Peru	24 Feb 82 (4)	3	30 Mar 92 (3)	Y			Y
Surinam			22 Nov 85 (1)	Y			Y
Venezuela	3 Oct 90	1	23 Nov 88 (1)	Y	Y	Y	Y
CENTRAL AMERICA							
Belize	6 Nov 90						
Costa Rica	23 Aug 77 (1)	2	27 Apr 92 (3)	Y			
El Salvador	8 Oct 91			Y			
Guatemala	16 Jan 79 (1)	2	26 Oct 90 (1)	Y			
Honduras	8 Jun 79 (1)	1	23 Oct 93 (1)				
Mexico	23 Feb 84 (2)	10	4 Nov 86 (1)	Y	Y	Y	
Nicaragua	17 Dec 79			Y			
Panama	3 Mar 78 (2)	1	26 Nov 90 (3)	Y			
CARIBBEAN							
Antigua and Barbuda	1 Nov 83				Y	Y	
Cuba	24 Mar 81	4		Y	Y	Y	
Dominica							
Dominican Republic	12 Feb 85			Y			
Grenada					Y		
Guadeloupe (France)	27 Jun 75	1	1 Dec 86 (1)		Y	Y	
Haiti	18 Jan 80			Y			
Jamaica	14 Jun 83				Y	Y	
Martinique (France)	27 Jun 75		1 Dec 86		Y	Y	
Puerto Rico (USA)	7 Dec 73	2	18 Dec 86	Y	Y	Y	
St. Kitts and Nevis	10 Jul 86				Y	Y	
St. Lucia	14 Oct 91				Y	Y	
St. Vincent and the Grenadines					Y	Y	
Trinidad and Tobago			21 Apr 92 (1)	Y	Y	Y	

Source: WCMC, unpublished

1 — World Heritage Convention: date of becoming a party, with number of sites (December 1993 baseline) inscribed in brackets

2 — Number of International (MAB) Biosphere Reserves (June 1994 baseline)

3 — Ramsar Convention: date Convention came into force, with number of sites recognised in brackets (June 1994 baseline)

4 — Western Hemisphere Convention: Y = signed

5 — Convention for the Protection and Development of the Wider Caribbean Region (Cartagena Convention): Y = signed

6 — SPAW Protocol: protocol concerning Specially Protected Areas and Wildlife: Y = signed

7 — Amazon Cooperation Treaty: Y = signed

Table 8.2 Protected areas classified under IUCN categories I–IV (marine reserves are not included)

Country	No. of protected areas	Protected area coverage (sq. km)	Land area (sq. km)	Percentage of land area covered
CARIBBEAN				
Antigua and Barbuda	8	41*	440	9.3
Cuba	37	3,139	110,860	2.8
Dominica	4	75	750	10.0
Dominican Rep	16	11,435	48,380	23.6
Grenada	0	0	340	0
Guadeloupe	2	210	1,690	12.4
Haiti	2	75	27,560	0.3
Jamaica	0	0	10,830	0
Martinique	4	12	1,060	1.1
Puerto Rico	22	181	8,860	2.0
St Kitts and Nevis	2	26	272	9.6
St Lucia	5	16	610	2.6
St Vincent and the Grenadines	27	44	390	11.3
Trinidad/Tobago	12	177	5,130	3.5
Total	141	15,431	217,172	7.1
CENTRAL AMERICA				
Belize	15	2,477	22,800	10.9
Costa Rica	34	6,341	51,060	12.4
El Salvador	2	52	20,720	0.3
Guatemala	21	8,334	108,430	7.7
Honduras	77	8,636*	111,890	7.7
Mexico	85	56,994	1,908,690	3.0
Nicaragua	65	9,050	118,750	7.6
Panama	18	13,272	75,990	17.5
Total	317	105,156	2,418,330	4.3
SOUTH AMERICA				
Bolivia	28	92,200	1,084,390	8.5
Brazil	274	249,131	8,456,510	2.9
Colombia	43	90,157	1,038,700	8.7
Ecuador	11	31,254	276,840	11.3
French Guiana	0	0	88,150	0
Guyana	1	586	208,419+	0.3
Paraguay	15	13,954	397,300	3.5
Peru	18	41,196	1,280,000	3.2
Surinam	14	7,361	143,662+	5.1
Venezuela	69	143,131	882,050	16.2
Total	473	668,970	13,856,021	4.8
Grand total	931	789,557	16,491,523	4.8

* For a large number of sites, size of protected area is not known

\+ Land area has been derived from Mundocart, which is based on the Operational Navigation Charts (1:1 million), rather than from FAO

Effectiveness of Legislation and Management

Ideally protected areas should be managed under a comprehensive protected areas law. Such laws now exist in Bolivia and Guatemala. More often protected areas are covered under more general environmental legislation such as land reform laws (El Salvador), forest laws (Costa Rica, Panama), territorial planning laws (Venezuela), environment laws (Brazil, Colombia, Cuba, Mexico), or under a range of different acts (Nicaragua). Some countries (Costa Rica, Panama, Venezuela) are in the process of passing protected areas laws (IUCN, 1992; Marchetti *et al.*, 1992).

Lack of coherent legislation has been cited, both by state management agencies and by NGOs, as a major cause of protected area deficiencies in almost all Neotropical countries. In many cases, legislation is internally inconsistent and protected area legislation conflicts with that governing other types of resource use, most commonly mineral/hydrocarbon extraction (IUCN, 1992). In Ecuador for example, the 1981 Law of Forestry and the Conservation of Wildlife prohibits all commercial activities in protected areas whilst the 1988 Hydrocarbon Law allows for oil exploitation (Cabarle *et al.*, 1989; MAG, n.d.). Similar situations are to be found in Chile (Gutiérrez, 1992), Peru (Ferreyros, 1988), Bolivia (Marconi, 1989) and the Dominican Republic (SEA/DVS, 1990).

As discussed previously, international conventions have helped a great deal in standardising legislation throughout the region, but their effectiveness depends on whether their spirit is embodied in national legislation. For example, Mexico has signed the Washington and World Heritage Conventions, although its tenets have not been fully incorporated into national legislation (Ramos, 1988).

The results of recent analyses of quality of management are sobering (Putney, 1992; Torres, 1992; Ugalde and Godoy, 1992). In Central America, the majority of protected areas, including Darién National Park in Panama and Zapatera and Cerro Saslaya National Parks in Nicaragua, are not adequately managed. Many parks are not delimited in the field. For the majority (60 per cent), the management agency has not acquired land-rights. Many have no resident staff. In all, 30 per cent of Central American protected areas are "paper parks", in other words a decree is the only token of their creation (Ugalde and Godoy, 1992). In South America the situation is little better. Whilst 30 per cent of protected areas do have management plans, only five per cent implement them. Some 70 per cent receive no government support and less than 1 per cent have sufficient personnel. As a result, 86 per cent are affected by incompatible activities, ranging from agriculture to oil exploitation (Amend and Amend, 1992a; Torres, 1992). In 1991, a study of 148 of South America's national parks, revealed that the main problems were extraction of natural resources from the park, lack of qualified personnel and infrastructure, and unresolved land-rights (Amend and Amend, 1992a). A similar situation is found in the Caribbean: two-thirds of protected areas are not achieving the objectives for which they were established. Some 24 per cent are protected in name only and another 43 per cent are only partially managed (Putney, 1992).

In Mexico, dispersion of responsibilities for protected areas and repeated changes in the structure of agencies managing the areas have meant that the national management agency SEDUE has been unable to apply adequate management regimes to its protected areas (Ramos, 1988). Changes in management structures continue, but do not necessarily lead to improved protection in the field (Pérez-Gil and Jaramillo, 1992).

Few countries have totally satisfactory protected area systems. In Central America, practically all countries have preliminary drafts of plans for a protected area system. Costa Rica is the most advanced country in this respect and has even analyzed its protected areas at a regional level. However, El Salvador is the only country to have developed a true system plan (Ugalde and Godoy, 1992). Argentina, Ecuador and Peru have produced system strategies (APN, 1991; CDC-UNALM, 1991; Cifuentes *et al.*, 1989), whilst Paraguay and Venezuela are defining systems (DPNVS/CDC-Paraguay, 1990; MARNR, 1989). System plans have been produced for eight out of the 25 Caribbean

Figure 8.2 Distribution of protected areas designated under international conventions and programmes
Source: WCMC, unpublished data

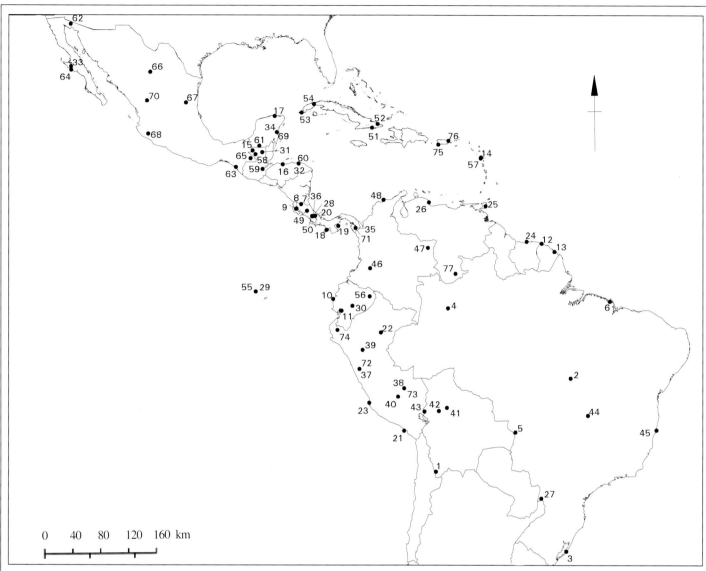

0   40   80   120   160 km

Ramsar Sites

Bolivia
1   Laguna Colorada

Brazil
2   Ilha do Bananal
3   Lagoa do Peixe
4   Mamirauá
5   Parque Nacional do Pantanal
6   Reentrancias Maranhenses

Costa Rica
7   Caño Negro
8   Palo Verde
9   Tamarindo

Ecuador
10   Machalilla
11   Manglares Churute

French Guiana
12   Basse-Mana
13   Les Marais De Kaw

Guadeloupe
14   Grand Cul-de-Sac Marin de la Guadeloupe

Guatemala
15   Laguna del Tigre

Honduras
16   Barras de Cuero y Salado

Mexico
17   Ría Lagartos

Panama
18   Golfo de Montijo
19   Punta Patiño
20   San San — Pond Sak

Peru
21   Lagunas de Mejía
22   Pacaya Samiria
23   Paracas

Surinam
24   Coppenamemonding

Trinidad and Tobago
25   Nariva Swamp

Venezuela
26   Cuare

World Heritage Sites

Brazil
27   Iguaçu National Park

Costa Rica
28   Talamanca Range-La Amistad Reserves

Ecuador
29   Galapagos Islands
30   Sangay National Park

Guatemala
31   Tikal National Park

Honduras
32   Río Platano WHS

Mexico
33   'El Vizcaino Whale Lagoon'
34   Sian Ka'an Biosphere Reserve

Panama
35   Darién National Park
36   La Amistad International Park

Peru
37   Huascaran National Park
38   Manu National Park
39   Rio Abiseo National Park
40   Sanctuario Historico de Macchu Picchu

Biosphere Reserves

Bolivia
41   Estación Biológica Beni
42   Parque Nacional Pilón-Lajas
43   Reserva Nacional de Fauna "Ulla Ulla"

Brazil
44   Cerrado
45   Reserva da Biósfera da Mata Atlântica (stretching along the Atlantic coast of Brazil)

Colombia
46   Cinturón Andino Cluster Biosphere
47   El Tuparro Nature Reserve
48   Sierra Nevada de Santa Marta

Costa Rica
49   Cordillera Volcánica Central
50   Reserva de la Biósfera de la Amistad

Cuba
51   Baconao
52   Cuchillas del Toa
53   Península de Guanahacabibes
54   Sierra del Rosario

Ecuador
55   Archipiélago de Colón (Galápagos)
56   Reserva de la Biósfera de Yasuni

Guadeloupe
57   Guadeloupe Archipelago

Guatemala
58   Maya
59   Sierra de las Minas

Honduras
60   Río Plátano Biosphere Reserve

Mexico
61   Calakmul
62   El Pinacate y Gran Desierto de Altar
63   El Trifinio
64   El Vizcaíno
65   Monte Azules
66   Reserva de Mapimí
67   Reserva de la Biósfera "El Cielo"
68   Reserva de la Biósfera Sierra de Manantlán
69   Reserva de la Biósfera de Sian Ka'an
70   Reserva de la Michilía

Panama
71   Parque Nacional Fronterizo Darién

Peru
72   Reserva de Huascarán
73   Reserva del Manu
74   Reserva del Noroeste

Puerto Rico
75   Guanica Commonwealth Forest Reserve
76   Luquillo Experimental Forest (Caribbean)

Venezuela
77   Alto Orinoco — Casiquiare

CATEGORIES AND MANAGEMENT OBJECTIVES OF PROTECTED AREAS

I   Scientific Reserve/Strict Nature Reserve: to protect nature and maintain natural processes in an undisturbed state in order to have ecologically representative examples of the natural environment available for scientific study, environmental monitoring, education and for the maintenance of genetic resources in a dynamic and evolutionary state.

II   National Park: to protect natural and scenic areas of national or international significance for scientific, educational and recreational use.

III   Natural Monument/Natural Landmark: to protect and preserve nationally significant natural features because of their special interest or unique characteristics.

IV   Managed Nature Reserve/Wildlife Sanctuary: to assure the natural conditions necessary to protect nationally significant species, groups of species, biotic communities, or physical features of the environment where these require specific human manipulation for their perpetuation.

Abridged from IUCN (1984)

Note: In 1994 IUCN adopted a revised protected area management classification system. For practical reasons the protected areas data given here is classified according to the former system. For further details of the revised categories see IUCN (1994).

countries, including the Dominican Republic (SEA/DVS, 1990) and the British Virgin Islands (Putney, 1992).

Lack of a clearly defined environmental policy is often responsible for a poor system of protected areas. In countries with no such policy, protected area legislation is frequently a response to conflicting priorities and emergency situations. In other countries, where laws exist, regulations for their implementation may be absent. Alternatively, the laws may rarely be applied, penalties may be inadequate, or communication between government departments may be limited (Ramos, 1988). The result of all these problems is inadequate protection of the environment.

Protected area managers in the Americas are quick to point out that the problems discussed above will not be solved until the environment is given a higher position on national agendas, and that this in turn depends on changes in economic policies, nationally and internationally (Putney, 1992; Torres, 1992; Ugalde and Godoy, 1992).

The 1980s saw the appearance of many more NGOs in all Neotropical countries and, in response to weaknesses in the public sector, many of them now manage protected areas. There are at present around 50 NGOs in Ecuador, 80 in Peru and 500 in Brazil (IUCN, 1992). Those administering protected areas include Fundación para la Conservación de la Naturaleza which manages eight of Peru's protected areas, the Venezuelan foundation FUDENA which manages the Cuare Faunal Refuge and Ramsar site, Ecuador's Fundación Natura which is responsible for two areas and participates in many others, Defensores de la Naturaleza which manages Guatemala's Sierra de las Minas

MONTEVERDE CLOUD FOREST, COSTA RICA

Monteverde is a private reserve of 105 sq. km established in 1972 located between 800 m and 1860 m above sea level in the Tilaran mountains of north-west Costa Rica. The reserve is owned and managed by the Tropical Science Centre, a non-profitmaking Costa Rican organisation. In 1987, nearly 13,000 people visited the reserve. They stayed in small hotels in forest and agricultural land below the reserve boundary. The number of hotels is growing as visitors increase, and associated services such as souvenir shops and restaurants are being developed.

Agricultural encroachment on the lower Pacific slopes below the reserve was destroying forest and leading to erosion in the areas where the tourist facilities were located. These lower lying forests are seasonally important habitats for the reserve's fauna. In 1986, local biologists and farmers formed the Monteverde Conservation League with the aim of protecting the lower Pacific slopes as a buffer zone for the reserve. They raised money locally from visitors and from international conservation organisations, some of the latter in the form of debt swaps.

The League has purchased farmland in the buffer zone and is restoring natural forest cover on it, as well as trying to improve the conservation practices of local farmers. The League is also running educational programmes for local children. A guided trail has been established in a farmland/forest mosaic in order that visitors can observe the impact of past agriculture on the forest as well as the process of forest restoration. A recent initiative is the "children's rainforest" campaign. Children in Sweden, Canada, United Kingdom, Japan and Germany are raising money for the purchase of additional land for the reserve. Some of these chil-

Monteverde cloud forest, Costa Rica (WWF/Michèle Dépraz)

dren visit Monteverde to have a look at what they have purchased. It is hoped that this initiative might grow into a loose network of private forest reserves located throughout the tropics, each adopted by a children's group.

The Monteverde Conservation League provides a forum for debate of issues affecting the reserve and its surroundings. There is considerable discussion of the economic impact of tourism. Income to the reserve exceeded US$30,000 in 1987, and a cooperative craft shop selling local handicrafts has annual sales in excess of US$50,000. Many residents would like tourism to remain small-scale and are concerned that its benefits should not be excessively concentrated in the hands of a minority of people. Land prices are escalating and this is restricting traditional activities in the area. *Source:* Jim Crisp

Biosphere Reserve, Liga de Monteverde managing the Monteverde Cloud Forest Reserve in Costa Rica (see Box 2) and Eco-Activo 20-30 (FESA) which runs El Imposible National Park in El Salvador (IUCN, 1992). Mexico had 200 conservation NGOs by 1986 and the Montes Azules Biosphere Reserve was established as a result of their action (Ramos, 1988). In addition, organisations such as Monarca A.C. and Pronatura A.C. in Mexico have been responsible for the inclusion of environmental considerations in the government's planning process and political agendas.

Additions to Protected Area Systems

Siting of protected areas has often been influenced more by socioeconomic conditions than by biological considerations (Leader-Williams *et al.*, 1990). In other words, protected areas have almost always been established in areas not in demand for other land uses.

In the Caribbean, Puerto Rico had only 0.4 per cent of its original forest left untouched by 1903 (Brash, 1987), but the forest has now expanded somewhat, while Cuba had lost all but 15 per cent by 1959. In contrast, most of Middle America was still covered in forest in 1950, but as human population has doubled over the last 30 years, only 60 per cent of this region remained forested in 1980. In both the Caribbean and Central America, protected areas were declared to preserve what remained. South America has a much bigger land area and lower population: consequently pressure has not been nearly so severe and even now there is still great scope for decisions over where to site new protected areas to ensure representative systems. The South American coastal areas, which were settled first by Europeans, are less well represented in protected areas

than the largely uncolonised Amazonian region. Large Amazonian protected areas have been established, for example, in Bolivia (Carrasco Ichilo and Isiboro Sécure National Parks), Brazil (Amazonia, Jau, Pico da Neblina and Xingu National Parks), Colombia (El Tuparro and Amacayacu National Parks), Peru (Manú Biosphere Reserve) and Venezuela (Alto Orinoco-Casiquiare Biosphere Reserve).

Ideally, conservation priorities should be determined by identifying and classifying the various elements of biological diversity within the country/region (Burley, 1988); then examining the existing system of protected areas; and finally, using various classifications, identifying which elements (major ecosystems, habitat types, species) are unrepresented or poorly represented. Many countries have begun this process, often with assistance from international agencies such as TNC, WWF, IUCN or WCMC. Peru is a good example of where this has occurred (CDC-UNALM, 1986, 1991, 1992).

Before meaningful recommendations can be made, however, detailed analysis must be undertaken at national and local levels (Putney, 1992; Ugalde and Godoy, 1992). Coverage of protected areas is often assessed using a habitat classification system such as Holdridge's Life Zone system (Holdridge, 1967), or by systems developed by and tailored to national requirements. Monitoring of protected areas is being carried out in many Neotropical countries through the Conservation Data Centres, a good example of which is CDC-UNALM in Peru. Although Peruvian biologists had long known that Andean cloud forests and coastal habitats were important areas for conservation, the analysis carried out by CDC-UNALM revealed these priorities in a much more systematic, quantified way and identified specific areas for protection and management (CDC-UNALM, 1986).

PEOPLE AND PARKS

According to recent studies of South American national parks (Amend and Amend, 1992a), some 50 per cent contain subsistence agriculturalists, while a mere 14.1 per cent are totally uninhabited. Colombia has most closely linked protected areas with safeguarding indigenous cultures. One quarter of its national territory has been protected in indigenous reserves: in 16 cases, indigenous "resguardos" overlap with national parks. Argentina and Chile are taking similar steps (Amend and Amend, 1992a).

Land-tenure in protected areas seems to present a particular problem. Theoretically, in most South American countries the possibility of expropriating land for the creation of protected areas exists. However, money and political will for expropriation are usually lacking. In addition, most people recognise that expropriation is socially unacceptable and that the results are usually negative in the long term (Amend and Amend, 1992a; Pérez Hernández, 1992). In Argentina, the law grants the land-owner total dominion over his land, even to the extent that he may degrade or destroy it, even within a national park. He may also deny access to park authorities, thereby making management impossible. In Chile, this problem has been avoided by including private areas in proposals for national parks only if there is a guarantee of a quick acquisition of the land after the area has been declared. Even so, around 50 per cent of South American national parks have been created, at least partially, on existing private lands. This situation is

unlikely to change very much in the near future, and Amend and Amend (1992b), Janzen (1989) and Pérez Hernández (1992) recommend revising the concept of strict protection within national parks as set out in the Western Hemisphere Convention.

Since the legal situation is often unclear, few park managers have been able to manage communities within parks, and even fewer management agencies are prepared to make funds available for resolving conflicts with local communities (Amend and Amend, 1992a).

Enforcement by itself will not preserve protected areas in the face of relentless human pressures. Many fieldworkers have, therefore, tried to set up projects linking biodiversity conservation in protected areas to local social and economic development. Projects of this type have been termed Integrated Conservation-Development Projects (ICDPs), and they range from community forest management in the Fundación Neotrópica's Boscosa project in the Osa Peninsula in Costa Rica to improvement of farming systems in the Central Selva Resource management Project in Peru's Palcazu Valley. An excellent, but sobering, evaluation of ICDPs has been carried out by Wells *et al.* (1992). This study concludes that the impact of ICDPs is limited because they do not address the powerful forces generated far from the national parks themselves, forces which can only be diminished through macro-economic policy changes. Nevertheless, even the limited success of these projects is encouraging.

The Central American protected area system has largely been directed towards conserving mountain ecosystems including high peaks and volcanoes where cloud forests are the dominant forest type. Nevertheless, the forests of Los Morrales de Chalatenango in El Salvador, the Maya Mountains of Belize and the Volcán de Ometepe in Nicaragua would be important potential additions to the system. In contrast, in the central highland and Pacific coastal lowlands, the protected areas are amongst the region's smallest and most threatened because of long settlement and high population pressure there. Deforestation in Mesoamerica has been most acute in the dry forests of the Pacific slope. All but two per cent of original 550,000 sq. km of Mesoamerican dry forest (an area the size of France) has been cleared for farms or pasture and only 0.08 per cent is protected. These forests support almost as many species as neighbouring rain forests (Janzen, 1986). Protection needs to be strengthened and additional areas declared in this region. Overall, Nicaragua and Guatemala have the greatest potential for declaring new areas, particularly in the mountains and on the Atlantic lowlands (Ugalde and Godoy, 1992).

In South America, four clear priorities are: the Atlantic forests and semi-deciduous forests of Brazil, the Colombian Chocó, the Pacific dry forests of Ecuador and Peru and the Eastern Andean forests in Bolivia, Colombia, Ecuador and Peru. All of these areas are home to a highly endemic flora and fauna (da Fonseca, 1985; ICBP, 1992; Torres, 1992). The Caribbean, in contrast to the other two regions, already has a reasonably representative protected area system (Putney, 1992).

The Coverage of Neotropical Forests by Protected Areas

In an attempt to estimate the area of protected forest, the boundaries of protected areas within IUCN's categories I–IV have been overlain onto the forest data for each country mapped in this Atlas. Ideally, the area of forest within each protected area for all countries should be measured, but this has not been done here for a number of reasons. Firstly, for most countries in the Caribbean, no forest maps were found; in this region, only Cuba, Jamaica and Trinidad (excluding Tobago) have been mapped. Secondly, in some cases location data were not available, so a number of protected areas have not been mapped at all. Thirdly, boundary information was not available for all protected areas; some are identified only with a centre point derived from latitude and longitude data.

Instead, in Table 8.3, each total area in column 6 is the sum of the sizes of the protected areas that are shown as containing forest on the respective country maps, rather than an area of actual protected forest. In other words, if a protected area encloses any forest, the total extent of the reserve has been included in the column 6 figure. In this way, some countries will be shown as holding more protected forest than they actually do (for instance, where only a small proportion of a protected area includes forest), while others will be shown as holding less (if, for instance, a particular protected area has not been mapped due to lack of information).

Table 8.3 shows that about 8.4 per cent of the remaining forest in Central America (including Mexico) is protected; if Mexico is excluded, then the percentage is much higher at 19.3 per cent. In South America 9.1 per cent of remaining forest is protected. It is interesting to note that two of the countries with the highest percentages of remaining forest cover have the lowest percentages of forest protection — Guyana (87.8 per cent remaining forest and only 0.3 percent protected) and French Guiana (92.4 percent remaining with no protection). Panama and

TRANSFRONTIER PROTECTED AREAS

There are ten transfrontier parks in the Americas (Figure 8.3). Reasons for their establishment range from the need to control the spread of cattle disease in the Los Katíos-Darién park between Colombia and Panama, to acting as symbols for peace in the SI-A-PAZ (Sistema de Areas Protegidas para la Paz) system between Nicaragua and Costa Rica. Transfrontier areas are valuable from the biological standpoint because they protect much larger areas of contiguous ecosystems than would be possible within one country alone. Their large size provides for greater genetic and species diversity and allows populations of rare species to be maintained well above minimum viable population levels. Management of transfrontier parks is often based on informal collaboration as in the El Tamá park where researchers from both Colombia and Venezuela work freely throughout the park without the need for border controls. Collaboration is at its strongest in La Amistad where both Costa Rican and Panamanian parks services have developed complimentary management plans for the entire park (Marchetti *et al.*, 1992)

1　Gran Petén — Belize/Guatemala/Mexico
2　Chiquibul/Montañas Mayas — Belize/Gratemala
3　Trifinio — El Salvador/Guatemala/Honduras
4　SI-A-PAZ — Costa Rica/Nicaragua
5　La Amistad — Costa Rica/Panama
6　Los Katíos/Darién — Colombia/Panama
7　El Tamá — Columbia/Venezuela
8　Do Pico da Neblina/La Neblina — Brazil/Venezuela
9　Manuripi Heath/Pampas del Heath — Bolivia/Peru
10　Sajama/Lauca — Bolivia/Chile
11　Iguazú/do Iguaçu — Argentina/Brazil
12　Lanin/Villarica — Argentina/Chile
13　Nahuel Huapi/Puyehue y Vincente Pérez Rosales — Argentina/Chile
14　Los Glaciares/B. O'Higgins y Torres del Paine — Argentina/Chile

Figure 8.3　Map of transfrontier protected areas in the Americas
Source: Marchetti *et al.* (1992)

Table 8.3 Protected area coverage of tropical forest as shown on the Maps in this Atlas

Country	Land area (sq. km)	Remaining area of tropical forest as defined in this Atlas (sq. km)	Remaining area of tropical forest as a percentage of land area	Total area of protected areas within IUCN categories I–IV (sq. km)	Total area of protected areas with forest (sq. km)[11]	Percentage of remaining forest protected (sq. km)
CARIBBEAN[1]						
Cuba	110,860	25,035	22.6	3,139	2,922	11.9
Jamaica	10,830	3,181	29.4	0	0	0
Trinidad and Tobago	5,130	1,683[3]	32.8[3]	177[9]	159[3]	9.4
CENTRAL AMERICA						
Belize	22,800	18,393	80.7	2,477	2,452	13.3
Costa Rica	51,060	15,049	29.5	6,341	5,770	38.3
El Salvador	20,720	1,555	7.5	52	52	3.3
Guatemala	108,430	48,244	44.5	8,334	8,318	17.2
Honduras	111,890	52,735[4]	47.1	8,636[10]	6,425	12.2
Mexico	1,908,690	515,000[5]	27.0	56,994	18,240	3.5
Nicaragua	118,750	57,450	48.4	9,050	7,628	13.3
Panama	75,990	33,053[6]	43.5	13,272	13,200	39.9
Total	2,418,330	741,479	30.7	105,156	62,085	8.4
SOUTH AMERICA						
Bolivia	1,084,390	451,426	41.6	92,200	83,655	18.5
Brazil	8,456,510	3,415,308	40.4	249,131	179,835	5.3
Colombia	1,038,700	510,935	49.2	90,157	88,469	17.3
Ecuador	276,840	142,370	51.4	31,254	23,485	16.5
French Guiana	88,150	81,490	92.4	0	0	0
Guyana	208,419[2]	183,025	87.8	586	586	0.3
Paraguay	397,300	47,488[7]	12.0	13,954	1,151	2.4
Peru	1,280,000	674,340[8]	52.7	41,196	40,298	6.0
Surinam	143,662[2]	133,284	92.8	7,361	7,090	5.3
Venezuela	882,050	542,682	61.5	143,131	135,928	25.0
Total	13,856,021	6,182,348	44.6	668,970	560,497	9.1

[1] Forest maps were obtained for only three of the Caribbean islands. It is not, therefore, possible to give a total protected forest area for the Caribbean, nor, consequently, for the whole of the Neotropical region.

[2] The borders between the Guianas are disputed and in this instance figures from Map 29.1 for Guyana and Map 23.1 for Surinam have been used, rather than FAO's figures of 196,850 sq. km and 156,000 sq. km respectively.

[3] For Trinidad only

[4] Not including mangroves

[5] Masera et al. (1992) – see Chapter 21

[6] INRENARE (1990) – see Chapter 23

[7] In eastern Paraguay only

[8] FAO (1993) – see Chapter 31

[9] Including Tobago

[10] For a large number of sites, the size of protected area is not known

[11] This area is derived from overlaying protected area boundary information onto the forest maps shown in this Atlas. As explained in this chapter, there will be a degree of error due to the way in which this figure has been calculated.

Costa Rica have the highest percentages of forest protected, (39.9 per cent and 38.8 per cent respectively), about twice as much as any country other than Venezuela, which is the next highest with 25 per cent protected. In Central America, it is only El Salvador and Mexico which have less than 10 per cent of their remaining forest protected, while in South America only Bolivia, Colombia, Ecuador and Venezuela have over 10 per cent.

New Sources of Finance for Protected Areas

In response to growing economic crises and the consequent short-fall of state support, many countries have had to rely on international NGOs and aid agencies for funding. The Nature Conservancy programme for establishing national Conservation Data Centres has already been mentioned. In addition, TNC runs a "Parks in Peril" Programme, an emergency effort to safeguard imperiled natural areas. TNC plans to bring on-site man-

agement to 200 critical protected areas in the Americas between 1990 and 2000 (TNC, 1990). The Wildlife Conservation Society (WCS, previously WCI) has long been funding small scale projects in protected areas throughout the Neotropics. Paseo Pantera, a consortium formed by WCS and the Caribbean Conservation Corporation, aims to preserve biological diversity and enhance wildlands management in Central America. Its programme for protected areas includes linking forest fragments into wildlife corridors, protecting watersheds, setting up buffer-zones and promoting ecotourism and environmental education (Anon., n.d.).

Some NGOs have raised revenues by debt-purchasing arrangements as a means of funding protected areas at little cost to the state. In 1987, through the world's first debt-swap, Conservation International purchased US$650,000 of Bolivian debt for US$100,000. The debt was then surrendered in exchange for a commitment from the Bolivian government of 15,000 sq. km of land and US$250,000 maintenance funds to expand existing protected areas in north west Bolivia to form the Río Beni Biosphere Reserve. However, some Neotropical countries have been reluctant to agree to debt-swaps because they may be seen to imply a surrender of national sovereignty to foreign organisations.

Less problematic debt-swaps were carried out between 1987–1989 by the Fundación Natura of Ecuador, aided by TNC and WWF. The foundation bought US$10 million of Ecuador's national debt and converted the proceeds into conservation bonds which are used by the foundation and the government in the management of protected areas. The interest from these bonds, for 1987 alone, was equivalent to the funding provided by the state. By 1991, six protected areas had benefited from the scheme (Oviedo, 1991; Torres, 1992). Even these relatively large amounts of money are small in comparison with the US$135 million which has accrued to Costa Rica through debt-for-nature-swaps (Ugalde and Godoy, 1992).

Tourism has become an important way of earning foreign revenue for Neotropical countries. It is currently the Caribbean's only growth industry (Putney, 1992). There has been particular growth in the sector of the business which includes adventure tourism, nature tourism and ecotourism. The possibilities of linking revenue from these types of tourism with financing protected areas has been studied in depth (Boo, 1990),

but clear examples of how tourism has been successfully harnessed to this end are infrequent. Some obvious beneficiaries have been the protected areas of Costa Rica and to some extent the Caribbean, partly because of their close proximity to the USA and also because of the well-developed tourism infrastructure in these countries.

Protected areas owned and administered by private individuals or organisations began to appear very recently in the Neotropics. They collectively comprise an insignificant proportion of national territories, nevertheless, they are well funded in comparison with state areas and some are of high conservation value. It seems that their importance will increase as concern about the environment grows. Well-known examples of private protected areas are Monteverde and La Selva in Costa Rica, the ranches in the Venezuelan llanos where tourism is used to finance the management of natural and man-made habitats for wildlife, and the growing network of reserves managed by the Fundación Moisés Bertoni in Paraguay.

Priorities for Action

Regional priorities for action were summarised in the IV World Parks Congress held in Caracas in February 1992 (Putney, 1992; Torres, 1992; Ugalde and Godoy, 1992). Four common themes emerge, they are:

1) Improving management: Systems to monitor protected areas and evaluate their management are needed so that prob-

EXTRACTIVE RESERVES IN BRAZIL

The exploitation of rubber from the tree *Hevea brasiliensis* began in earnest in the middle of the last century, spreading from the mouth of the Amazon up-river and westward into the headwaters of tributaries in Bolivia, Colombia and Peru. Collection and processing of the tree's latex was carried out by migrant labourers, or "seringueiros", from Northeast Brazil who lived in a state of debt-bondage. They traded rubber for the food and tools necessary for survival (Alegretti, 1988).

In the early part of this century, the Brazilian rubber industry was all but destroyed by a combination of competition from synthetic rubbers, rubber from newly-established Malaysian plantations and the attacks of a fungus (*Microcyclus ullei*) which thwarted attempts to establish

Rubber tapper scoring the bark of a wild rubber tree in Alto Jurua extractive reserve, Acre, Brazil.
(WWF/Edward Parker)

plantations in Amazonia (May, 1992). Indeed, were it not for government subsidies and protection, the industry would no longer exist. Today, some rubber tappers still pay rent to a patron — or "seringalista" — for usufruct rights. Others, however, have broken free of this system and achieved a measure of independence. They have also diversified into collection of other latexes, Brazil nuts and palm hearts. Until recently, however, they did not possess land rights and many seringalistas sold their land to speculators who converted large areas to poor quality cattle pasture (May, 1992).

In the late 1970s, the rubber tappers of Acre State and other parts of western Amazonia began a nonviolent campaign known as "empate" (stalemate) in order to impede land clearance in areas with economically important trees. In 1985, representatives of a number of rural workers unions and producer associations met in Brasília to found the National Council of Rubber Tappers and demand the creation of extractive reserves ("reservas extrativistas") that would legitimise producers' property rights over the forest resources on which they depend. Such reserves would be common property, managed by forest-dwelling communities in recognition of their traditional patterns of occupation. This alternative form of resource ownership has been increasingly recognised by state and national governments as a useful mechanism for resolving conflicts over access to and use of extractive resources (see UICN, 1993).

As a result of the 1985 meeting, 24 extractive reserves have now been declared in Brazil covering over 40,000 sq. km. Today there are some 68,000 families involved in rubber tapping in Amazonia, each usually managing 3–5 sq. km of forest with at least 120 rubber trees along the collecting trails (Bunyard, 1992).

lems can be identified and corrective action be taken. Training of protected area managers and field personnel is urgent. Both these needs are being addressed by, for example, the cooperation programmes of FAO/UNEP, the Amazon Cooperation Treaty and CATIE in Central America.

2) Enhancing revenue generation: Innovative means of revenue generation are needed — these must include more international participation. Emphasis should be placed on long-range finance mechanisms, such as the establishment of trust funds. In the Caribbean, much of this additional revenue can be generated from tourism, whereas Central and South America will depend more on financial transfers from rich countries as payment for the conservation of "global environmental values".

3) Achieving more effective cooperation: Improving communications between protected area managers in the Neotropics is a priority. Once this is achieved, regional support will be required in order to promote technical cooperation and set up pilot projects. In addition, increased cooperation with international agencies is required, particularly in the fields of technology transfer and information exchange.

4) Integrating local communities: Protected area managers must identify mechanisms to allow local people to participate in protected area design and management. Meanwhile parks should be geared to provide socioeconomic benefits to surrounding communities or else mechanisms must be found to compensate people for costs that they incur when protected areas are established on their land.

Conclusions

The Neotropics are fortunate enough to have fairly extensive (although not always representative) systems of protected areas already established. Legislation is good on the whole and new areas are being designated at a rapid rate. Unfortunately, mainly as a result of difficult economic conditions, many of these areas are not adequately managed. Nevertheless, the conservation community in the Neotropics, both governmental and non-governmental, is extremely resourceful and there have been exciting developments in the search for support for protected areas. It is to be hoped that innovations such as extractive reserves (see Box 3) and CDCs will have relevance beyond the borders of the Neotropics in conserving the world's natural heritage.

References

Alcérreca, C., Consejo, J.J., Flores, O., Gutiérrez, D., Hentschell, E., Herzig, M., Pérez-Gil, R., Reyes, J.M., and Sánchez-Cordero, V. (1988). *Fauna silvestre y áreas naturales protegidas.* Universo Veintiuno. 193 pp.

Alegretti, M.H. (1988). *Reservas Extrativistas: Implementaçao de uma alternativa ao desmatamento na Amazonia.* Paper presented in the symposium "Alternativas Ao Desmatamento", Belém PA, January 1988.

Amend, S. and Amend, T. (1992a). ¿Habitantes en los parques nacionales ¿una contradicción insoluble? In: *¿Espacios sin Habitantes? Parques nacionales de América del Sur.* Amend, S. and Amend, T. (Eds). IUCN/Editorial Nueva Sociedad, Caracas, Venezuela. Pp. 457–472.

Amend, S. and Amend, T. (1992b). (Eds) *¿Espacios sin Habitantes? Parques nacionales de América del Sur.* IUCN/Editorial Nueva Sociedad, Caracas, Venezuela. 497 pp.

Anon. (n.d.). *Paseo Pantera: Preserving biological diversity in Central America.* WCI/CCC. 4 pp.

APN (1991). *El sistema nacional de áreas protegidas de la República Argentina: diagnóstico de su desarrollo institucional y patrimonio natural.* Administración de Parques Nacionales, Buenos Aires, Argentina. 127 pp.

Boo, E. (1990). *Ecotourism: The Potentials and Pitfalls.* WWF, Washington DC. 72 pp (Vol I) and 155 pp (Vol II).

Brash, A.R. (1987). The history of avian extinction and forest conversion on Puerto Rico. *Biological Conservation* 39(2): 97–111.

Bunyard, P. (1992). *Sustainable Economies in the Tropical Forest.* (Unpublished). 21pp.

Burley, F.B. (1988). Monitoring biological diversity for setting priorities for conservation. In: *Biodiversity.* Wilson, E.O. (ed.). National Academic Press, Washington. Pp. 227–230.

Cabarle, B.J., Crespi, M., Calaway, H.D., Luzuriaga, C.C., Rose, D. and Shores, J.N. (1989). *An Assessment of Biological Diversity and Tropical Forests for Ecuador.* Prepared for US-AID/Ecuador as an Annex to the Country Development Strategy Statement 1989–1990. 110 pp.

CDC-UNALM (1986). *Ecosistemas críticos del Perú.* Informe al World Resources Institute (WRI). Centro de Datos para la Conservación-Universidad Nacional La Molina, Lima, Perú.

CDC-UNALM (1991). *Plan director del Sistema Nacional de Unidades de Conservación (SINUC): una aproximación desde la diversidad biológica.* Centro de Datos para la Conservación-Universidad Nacional La Molina, Lima, Perú.

CDC-UNALM (1992). *Estado de Conservación de la Diversidad Natural de la Región Noroeste del Perú.* Centro de Datos para la Conservación-Universidad Nacional La Molina, Lima, Perú.

Cifuentes, M., Ponce, A., Albán, F., Mena, P., Mosquera, G., Rodríguez, J., Silva, D., Suárez, L., Tobar, A. and Torres, J. (1989). *Estrategia para el Sistema Nacional de Areas Protegidas del Ecuador, II Fase.* DINAF-MAG/Fundación Natura, Quito, Ecuador. 196 pp.

da Fonseca, G.A.B. (1985). The vanishing Brazilian Atlantic Forest. *Biological Conservation* 34: 17–34.

Denevan, W.M. (1992). *The Native Population of the Americas in 1492.* Second edition. University of Wisconsin Press, Madison.

DPNVS/CDC-Paraguay (1990). *Areas Prioritarias para la Conservación en la Región Oriental del Paraguay.* Dirección de Parques Nacionales-Centro de Datos para la Conservación, Asunción, Paraguay. 99 pp.

Ferreyros, A. (1988). *Situación actual de los parques nacionales y otras unidades de conservación en el Perú.* Asociación de Ecología y Conservación (ECCO), Lima. 21 pp.

Gómez-Pompa, A. (1991). Learning from traditional ecological knowledge: insights from Mayan silviculture. In: *Rain Forest Regeneration and Management.* Gómez-Pompa, A., Whitmore, T.C. and Hadley, M. (eds). UNESCO/Parthenon, Paris. Pp. 335–341

Gutiérrez, D. (1992). Legislación chilena sobre parques nacionales: uso de los recursos naturales. In: *¿Espacios sin Habitantes? Parques Nacionales de América del Sur.* Amend, S. and Amend, T. (eds). IUCN and Editorial Nueva Sociedad, Caracas. Pp. 159–172.

Hartshorn, G.S. and Green, G.C. (1985). *Wildlands*

Conservation in Northern Central America. CATIE/Tropical Science Centre, Costa Rica.

Holdridge, L.R. (1967). *Life Zone Ecology.* Tropical Science Center, San José. 206 pp.

ICBP (1992). *Putting Biodiversity on the Map: priority areas for global conservation.* International Council for Bird Preservation, Cambridge, UK. 90 pp.

IUCN (1984). *Categories and criteria for protected areas.* In: National Parks, Conservation and Development. The role of protected areas in sustaining society. McNeely, J.A. and Miller, K.R. (Eds). Smithsonian Institution Press, Washington. Pp. 47–53.

IUCN (1992). *Protected Areas of the World: a review of national systems.* Volume 4: Nearctic and Neotropical. Compiled by WCMC for IUCN, Gland, Switzerland and Cambridge, UK.

IUCN (1994). *Guidelines for Protected Area Management Categories.* CNPPA with the assistance of WCMC. IUCN, Gland, Switzerland and Cambridge, UK. 261 pp.

Janzen, D.H. (1986). *Guanacaste National Park: tropical ecological and cultural restoration.* San José, Costa Rica EUNED-FPN-PEA. 104 pp.

Janzen, D.H. (1989). The evolutionary biology of national parks. *Conservation Biology* 3 (2): 109–110.

Leader-Williams, N., Harrison, J. and Green, M.J.P. (1990). Designing protected areas to conserve natural resources. *Science Progress* 74: 189–204.

MAG (n.d.). *Diagnóstico — Plan de acción forestal 1991–1995.* Subsecretaría Forestal y de Recursos Naturales, Ministerio de Agricultura y Ganadería, Quito, Ecuador. 126 pp.

Marchetti, B., Oltremari, J. and Peters, H. (1992). *Manejo de Areas Silvestres Protegidas Fronterizas en América Latina.* FAO/PNUMA, Santiago, Chile. 120 pp.

Marconi, M. (1989). *Base Legal del Sistema de Areas Protegidas de Bolivia, Evaluación General.* Centro de Datos para la Conservación, CDC-Bolivia, La Paz. 40 pp.

MARNR (1989). *Marco Conceptual del Plan del Sistema Nacional de Areas Naturales Protegidas.* Serie Informes Técnicos DGSPOA/IT/295. Unpublished draft.

May, P. (1992). Common property resources in the neotropics: theory, management progress, and an action agenda. In: *Conservation of Neotropical Forests. Working from Traditional Resource Use.* Redford, K.H. and Padoch, C. (eds). Columbia University Press, New York. Pp. 359–378.

McNeely, J.A. (1993). *Lessons from the Past: Forests and Biodiversity.* Paper presented to Global Forest Conference, Bandung, Indonesia, 17–20 February 1993. 19pp.

McNeely, J.A. and Miller, K.I. (1984). *National Parks, Conservation and Development: The Role of Protected Areas in Sustaining Society.* Smithsonian, Washington DC. 825 pp.

Morales, R. and Cifuentes, M. (1989) (eds). *Sistema regional de áreas silvestres protegidas en América Central: plan de acción 1989–2000.* CATIE, Turrialba, Costa Rica. 122 pp.

Norris, R. (1988). Data for diversity: Conservation Data Centres underlie protection efforts in the tropics. *TNC News* 38(1): 4–10.

Oltremari, J.V. (1992). Situación actual de las áreas protegidas de América Latina y el Caribe. *Flora, Fauna y Areas Silvestres* Año 6 No. 14. FAO/PNUMA, Santiago, Chile. Pp. 17–24

Oviedo, G. (1991). *Lineamientos y acciones de conservación con fondos de canje de deuda externa.* Fundación Natura: Programa de Conservación, Quito, Ecuador. 15 pp.

Pérez-Gil, R. and Jaramillo, F. (1992). *Natural Protected Areas in Mexico.* A Report for IUCN-BID by P.G.7 Consultores, S.C. 21 pp.

Pérez Hernández, R. (1992). La ocupación de los parques nacionales: una alternativa de solución. In: *¿Espacios sin Habitantes? Parques nacionales de América del Sur.* Amend, S. and Amend, T. (eds). IUCN/Editorial Nueva Sociedad, Caracas, Venezuela. Pp. 423–428.

Posey, D.A. (1982). The Keepers of the Forest. *Garden* 6: 18–24.

Putney, A. (1992). *Regional Review: Caribbean.* Paper presented at IV World Congress on National Parks and Protected Areas, Caracas, Venezuela. 10–21 February, 1992. 28 pp.

Ramos, M.A. (1988). The conservation of biodiversity in Latin America: a perspective. In: *Biodiversity.* Wilson, E.O. (ed.). National Academic Press, Washington. Pp. 428–436.

Sayer, J. (1991). *Rainforest Buffer Zones: Guidelines for Protected Area Management.* IUCN, Gland, Switzerland and Cambridge, U.K. 104 pp.

SEA/DVS (1990). *La Diversidad Biológica en la República Dominicana.* Report prepared for the Departamento de Vida Silvestre by the Servicio Alemán de Cooperación Social-Técnica (DED) and the World Wildlife Fund. Secretaría de Estado de Agricultura, SURENA/DVS, Santo Domingo, República Dominicana. 266 pp.

TNC (1990). *Parks in Peril: a conservation partnership for the Americas.* The Nature Conservancy, USA. 24 pp.

Torres, H. (1992). *Regional Review: América del Sur.* Paper presented at IV World Congress on National Parks and Protected Areas, Caracas, Venezuela. 10–21 February, 1992. 29 pp.

Ugalde, A. and Godoy, J.C. (1992). *Regional Review: Centroamérica.* Paper presented at IV World Congress on National Parks and Protected Areas, Caracas, Venezuela. 10–21 February, 1992. 26 pp.

UICN (1993). *El Extractivismo en América Latino. Recomendaciones del Taller UICN-CEE, Amacayacu, Colombia, Octubre, 1992.* Ruiz Pérez, M., Sayer, J. and Cohen Jehoram, S. (Eds). IUCN, Gland, Switzerland and Cambridge, UK.

Wells, M. Brandon, K., and Hannah, L. (1992). *Parks and People: linking protected area management with local communities.* The World Bank/WWF/USAID. Washington DC, USA. 99 pp.

WCMC (1993). *Protected area summary statistics: Neotropical and Caribbean.* Unpublished report. World Conservation Monitoring Centre, Cambridge, UK.

Wetterberg, G.B. (1974). *The History and Status of South American National Parks and an Evaluation of Selected Management Options.* Unpublished Ph.D. thesis, University of Washington, 1974. 253 pp.

Wetterberg, G.B., Jorge Pádua, M.T., Tresinari, A. and Ponce, C.F. (1985). *Decade of Progress for South American National Parks.* US National Park Service, Washington DC. 125 pp.

Author: Chris Sharpe, Protected Areas Data Unit, WCMC, Cambridge with contributions from Jerry Harrison, WCMC, Cambridge, Jeff McNeely and Jim Thorsell, IUCN, Gland, Switzerland, Hernan Torres, Corporación, Nacional Forestal, Chile and Jim Crisp, President, Monteverde Conservation League.

9 A Future for Neotropical Forests

INTRODUCTION

The two years that have elapsed since the United Nations Conference on Environment and Development (UNCED) in Rio de Janeiro, Brazil have seen a deepening of the rift between rich and poor countries on forest issues. For instance, the renegotiation of the International Tropical Timber Agreement (ITTA) has been difficult because of fears that the standards being applied to the forests of the richer, Northern countries were different from those being applied in the tropical countries. In addition, the domination of the Tropical Forestry Action Plan (TFAP) by the developed Northern countries has been challenged by nationals of the Southern countries. As a result, the latter have established a Forestry Forum for Developing Countries, feeling that this will be more sympathetic to their problems. Similarly, an initiative to set-up an International Commission on Forestry and Sustainable Development is foundering on the perception that it has no political legitimacy without support from the Southern countries. There is also a rift between the technologically driven Bretton Woods Institutions and the more participatory, politically sensitive UN institutions, which has been highlighted by the negotiations for a Global Environment Facility (GEF).

The *non-legally binding authoritative Statement of Principles for a global consensus on the management, conservation and sustainable development of all types of forests* that was adopted by the UNCED Conference disappointed many by failing to engage the parties in real commitments to immediate direct action to halt deforestation. Nevertheless, the fact that the Statement was hedged in cautious qualifications was a recognition of the depth and complexity of the factors that lead to the mismanagement of forest lands. The UN Commission on Sustainable Development, the follow-up to the Rio Conference, will not discuss forests until 1995.

The key issues at the Rio Summit were the same as those confronting everybody trying to conserve Neotropical forests. Can the forests be used in ways which will enhance the material and social development of the countries of the region? Will protecting the so-called global values of the forests, as demanded by rich Northern countries, require a slowing of the economic growth that most of the population of Latin America would certainly aspire to? If it is indeed a question of Latin American people foregoing the use of their sovereign resources in order to protect the biodiversity and climatic functions which the industrial world values, can equitable ways be found for the North to pay the South a "rent" for the services that the forests provide? Article 9a of the Statement (see Box) suggests some of the topics that should be taken into consideration by the international community.

The conclusions of Rio are consistent with those of the *World Conservation Strategy* (IUCN/UNEP/WWF, 1980), its successor *Caring for the Earth* (IUCN/UNEP/WWF, 1991), *Our Common Future (Bruntland Report)* (WCED, 1987) and others. The goods and services provided by forests with high biological diversity and high biomass are, over extensive areas of the humid tropics, valuable resources for sustained economic development. There are global benefits to be derived from conserving a high proportion of the biological and environmental values of these forests which can be maintained only if the tropical countries which possess the forests incur significant "opportunity costs". In these circumstances it is only right that the global beneficiaries of forest conservation compensate the people of poor countries for these opportunity costs. The Rio Summit endorsed an expanded GEF to be administered by the World Bank as a first attempt to pay for global conservation benefits. Statements by leaders of several industrialised nations at Rio affirmed a "willingness to pay" for environmental benefits from poor Southern nations.

The forests in the Americas are by far the most extensive remaining in the humid tropics (see Chapter 1). They are richer in plant and animal species than rain forests in Africa and Asia and those in South America, at least, are subject to much less pressure from population growth and resource demand than those elsewhere in the tropics. Popular claims that virgin forests will disappear within a human lifetime seem exaggerated. Nevertheless, in many areas the forests are being used abusively, cleared to meet the short-term needs of poor farmers or the greed of speculators and industrialists. An understanding of the ecological, social and economic forces underlying this process is essential if investments in conservation are to be effective and the negative impacts of "development" are to be minimised.

The Prehistory of Forests in The Americas

As with the world's other tropical forests, those of the Americas have been affected by periods of marked climatic change during the Pleistocene. The most recent dry period associated with glacial advances in high latitudes came to an end less than 10,000 years ago. This concluded a period of several hundred thousand years during which the rain forests had been repeatedly reduced to relatively isolated refuges in localities where edaphic or relief features allowed these forests to sustain them-

---

ARTICLE 9 (A) OF THE STATEMENT AGREES THAT:

"The efforts of developing countries to strengthen the management, conservation and sustainable development of their forest resources should be supported by the international community, taking into account the importance of redressing external indebtedness, particularly where aggravated by the net transfer of resources to developed countries, as well as the problem of achieving at least the replacement value of forests through improved market access for forest products, especially processed products. In this respect, special attention should also be given to the countries undergoing the process of transition to market economies."

---

selves during periods of low rainfall (Haffer, 1969; Prance, 1982; and see Chapter 2). The last of these dry periods occurred after human beings colonised South America via the Bering land bridge and the Central American isthmus (see Chapter 6). This means that the expansion of the forest over the past 10,000 years occurred in an environment where humans were a significant ecological force. Fire may not have had the impact in the Americas that it has had in Africa and Asia, but it had significantly modified the vegetation found by Europeans at the end of the 15th century. Wood ash has been found in soil profiles in many areas of Amazon forest where fire no longer occurs. This is one indication of the very extensive impact of shifting cultivators and hunter-gatherers on the vegetation. The extensive savannas on the Guyana Shield in Venezuela and Colombia and in parts of Brazil are thought to have existed throughout the Holocene and to have been maintained by modest levels of human activity in areas where soils and rainfall conditions made the forests particularly susceptible to fire. In the absence of humans, these areas would almost certainly have reverted to forest under the relatively humid climate that has prevailed for the past 10,000 years (Dourojeanni, 1990).

With the exception of these savanna areas, most of the potential forest land in the Americas was covered by natural or only slightly modified forests when the first Europeans arrived 500 years ago. There were, though, some exceptions. For example, in Central America, Spanish explorers found evidence of extensive forest modification by the Mayas although Mayan civilisation had, by then, been in decline for a couple of centuries (Dourojeanni, 1990). Similarly, when the conquistadors first "visited" the Andean kingdoms in their quest for Eldorado in the 16th century, they discovered extensive deforestation around the indigenous cities of the inter-Andean valleys, where modern-day Quito and Bogotá are now found; and Francisco de Orellana, on his epic voyage down the Amazon in 1542, was impressed by the densely settled agricultural areas on some of the *várzea* floodplains. It is, indeed, highly likely that the Amerindian population at that time was considerably higher than the eight million people who occupied Amazonia in 1960 or even the 16 million people who occupy the basin today. It is, therefore, a myth, that the Neotropical forests have evolved in pristine isolation. An indication of how the Amerindian populations altered both lowland and submontane forests can be gained from the extensive and sophisticated irrigation systems present along the lower course of the Magdelena river in Colombia and the widespread deforestation of parts of Bolivia and Peru, both these environmental modifications took place long before the arrival of

Europeans. However, there is evidence that the agricultural methods used by the native peoples of Amazonia 500 years ago were less harmful to the environment than those practised by present-day populations. It seems then, that the present diversity of the forests exists in spite of, or possibly because of, this past disturbance (see McNeely, 1994).

European Influence and Forest Depletion

European colonists occupied those parts of South America where the environment most resembled their continent of origin. This meant that they settled, almost exclusively, in those areas that had dry climates or were at high elevations or both. Significant settlement occurred mainly in the "Southern Cone" of present day Chile and Argentina and in the cool temperate highlands of the Andes; it was in the Andean valleys that most deforestation took place during the first four centuries of European occupation.

Trading settlements were established on the coast, and cities such as Cartagena, Guayaquil and Caracas developed as gateways to the high elevation interior. The cities on the Brazilian coast were transit centres for tropical crops such as rubber and significant forest clearance occurred in their hinterland. The process of deforestation of the Mata Atlantica, the dry Brazilian north-east and parts of the Caribbean also began early as land was cleared for sugar cane and to feed the African slaves who were brought in to tend the plantations.

In contrast, the early colonists did not occupy the lowland rain forests, nor did they make significant demand on their resources. Although rubber, harvested from wild trees of *Hevea brasiliensis*, was exported from the Amazon basin for several hundred years, this never led to significant deforestation, not even when the development of the process of vulcanisation led to the sudden expansion of world demand for this commodity in the late 19th century. The rubber boom was a major event in the history of Amazonian forests, but the prosperity of the area was based on extractive economies that were dependent on natural forests, hence the lack of deforestation. The saga of the feudal and often cruel bondage systems under which the *seringueros* worked, the growth and prosperity of the cities of Manaus and Iquitos, and the collapse of the rubber-based economy following the establishment of far more productive rubber plantations in Malaysia, is now familiar. It was these events that made the rubber boom important as a social phenomenon, laying the foundations for relations between different ethnic and social groups which have conditioned many development issues during the 20th century.

Europeans first arrived in the Neotropics 500 years ago, yet most of the deforestation in the moist lowlands of the region has occurred in the last 30 years. The information that is now emerging on the impact of indigenous Indian populations on the forests and the decline of these impacts during the colonial period make it possible to speculate that the forests in the lowlands of South America may have been more extensive in 1952 than in 1492.

This is not true of the Caribbean and parts of Central America where different processes were at work. Much of the Caribbean was colonised early and the region became a major source of tropical agricultural commodities. Markets in North America and Europe were relatively accessible and the slave trade had enormous demographic and cultural impacts. Many Caribbean islands were deforested early. For example, the forest cover of Puerto Rico was reduced to only 10 per cent of the island's land area at the end of the 19th century and most of this was very disturbed, with coffee bushes planted beneath it. However, the forest area has increased significantly since (see

Chapter 15). Similarly in Cuba, most deforestation took place between 1900 and 1959, with the land being cleared for sugar cane plantations and for intensive cattle ranching, so that by the 1950s as little as 14 per cent of the forest cover remained (see Chapter 10).

In the countries of Central America, with the exception of El Salvador, deforestation has been highest in the past four decades. In the region as a whole, forests have tended to be looked upon as an obstacle to development (Utting, 1993). With the boom in demand for several agricultural products, such as coffee, that occurred from the 1950s onwards, forests have been converted to pastures and crop land to reap short-term benefits with little regard for the long-term sustainability of the production systems (Utting, 1993).

Although there was little deforestation for agriculture in the humid Neotropics compared with that in the Old World tropics, the commodities that allowed demographic expansion and forest clearing in Africa and Asia almost all originated in the forests of South America. Maize, cassava, cacao, yams, rubber and a wide variety of fruits, which had major ecological impacts in West Africa and Southeast Asia, all came from the Americas. A further irony is that the tropical crops that have been associated with significant deforestation in the Americas, coffee, sugar and bananas, all originated in the Old World.

Development and the Environment in the Late 20th Century

The dramatic developments that have occurred in the forests of the tropical Americas in the past 30–40 years are the main subject of this Atlas. Few major biomes of the world have suffered such dramatic change in so short a time. Extrapolation from limited observation has led people to predict widespread doom and destruction. Others have pointed out the vastness of the forests and invoked the sovereign right of nations to develop their resources to improve the welfare of their populations.

The country chapters in this Atlas provide information on forest extent and this is summarised here in Table 9.1. For each country, the total forest area measured from the relevant Map within this Atlas is given, along with the figure of forest area for that country from FAO (1993). These two figures are very different in some cases and, for each, the percentage of land area still covered with tropical forest has been calculated. Maps from which statistics for total forest cover could be measured were not obtained for all countries, this was the case for most of the Caribbean countries and for Panama, Mexico and Peru. As a result no figure for total forest cover in the Caribbean has been obtained from the Maps in this Atlas. For Central and South America, to obtain the total figures, the areas from FAO (1993) have been used for Panama, Mexico and Peru (Table 9.1).

In the other two Atlases in this series, it was possible to obtain figures for original forest cover in each country, but this has not been done for The Americas because no potential vegetation map was found that covered all three regions. It can, however, be assumed that the Caribbean islands considered here were once more or less completely covered in forest whereas now only two (Dominica and Guadeloupe) have more than half left, while Haiti has lost almost all its forest. Similarly, in Central America, most of each country, except Mexico, will have been forest covered (Leonard, 1987); although the driest areas (east-central Nicaragua and the Oriente Region of Guatemala) will probably have contained some natural non-forest areas. Now only Belize has most of its land covered in forest, forest in El Salvador covers less than 10 per cent of its land, Costa Rica is reduced to only 30 per cent cover, while the other countries on the isthmus all

have between 40 and 50 per cent of their land covered in forest. In South America, the Guianas are all still more or less totally covered in forest, while the rest of the countries, other than Paraguay, have at least 40 per cent of their land covered. It is, however, more difficult to know the original extent of forest in these countries. In the case of Brazil, the remaining extent as estimated by FAO compared to the area measured from Maps here, is very different. The reason for this is unclear, but is almost certainly due to the inclusion of open formations in the figure given by FAO (1993). The difference between the area measured here and that given by FAO for closed broadleaved forests (3,871,210 sq. km) is not so great, especially as the figure measured here is for 1992 as opposed to 1990.

As with the figures for forest area remaining within a country, estimates of rates of deforestation also vary. Fearnside (see Box and Chapter 25) has introduced some rigour into the debate on deforestation in the Brazilian Amazon by attempting to analyse and interpret the causes of major discrepancies between some of the earlier estimates.

Along with the extent and speed of deforestation being difficult to assess, the underlying causes are also subject to varied interpretation. People's perception of the problem of forest misuse is very much influenced by their culture. The perception of forests by urban North Americans and Europeans is different from that of the urban rich of São Paulo, the *favelas* dwellers of Rio, the cattle ranchers of Rondonia or the Indians of the upper Orinoco. South Americans of all ethnic and social groups have at various times felt attacked by outside conservationists and developers whose judgements reflect an alien culture. This has been manifest in a belief that industrialised nations were promoting an "internationalisation" of Amazonia. The contradictory perceptions concerning Amazonia are discussed in *Amazonia Without Myths* (Latin America, Caribbean, Commission on Development and Environment for Amazonia, nd). Somewhat more analytical accounts are given in Eden (1990) and Mahar (1989).

A major focus of debate has been the extent to which government policies have acted in a perverse way to promote unsustainable and destructive use of forest lands. It is still unclear whether such policies drove the process of frontier expansion or whether they simply acted to subsidise the entrepreneurial aspirations of governing elites. Rich people throughout the tropical Americas have colonised and cleared land as a speculative venture and as a potential hedge against high inflation. Poor people have colonised forests to escape the feudal conditions found in more accessible agricultural areas, to escape civil strife and political conflict and to escape the grinding poverty of over-populated coastal and upland areas. There is increasing evidence that government fiscal measures aimed at encouraging colonisation of forests have had less real impact than had previously been thought (see Chapter 7). The single most significant intervention by governments and outside agencies has been the provision of infrastructure. Road construction throughout the forests of tropical America has inevitably been followed by land colonisation and forest clearance. The extent and pattern of deforestation is profoundly influenced by the planning and financing of transportation networks. Ministries of Transport are more important than Ministries of Environment in determining the fate of forests.

Forest colonists of all classes have practised very extensive agricultural systems and small numbers of people have had a major, and largely deleterious, impact on forests over large areas. Most agricultural colonisation has been followed by abandonment of the land as soil nutrient levels declined under low input farming systems. The only exceptions are in the more prosperous

Table 9.1 Remaining extent of tropical forest as judged from the country maps in this Atlas and by FAO (1993).

Country	Land area (sq. km)	Remaining extent of forest for 1990 according to FAO (1993) in sq. km[2]	Remaining area of tropical forest as mapped in this Atlas (sq. km)	Date of the forest cover data shown in this Atlas[7]	Remaining area of tropical forest as a percentage of land area	
					From FAO (1993)	From map data
CARIBBEAN						
Antigua and Barbuda	440	100	nd	–	22.7	nd
Cuba	110,860	17,150	25,035	date unknown	15.5	22.6
Dominica	750	440	nd	–	58.7	nd
Dominican Republic	48,380	10,770	nd	–	22.3	
Grenada	340	60	nd	–	17.7	nd
Guadeloupe	1690	930	nd	–	55.0	nd
Haiti	27,560	230	nd	–	0.8	nd
Jamaica	10,830	2,390	3,181	1989	22.0	29.4
Martinique	1,060	430	nd	–	40.6	nd
Puerto Rico	8,860	3,210	nd	–	36.2	nd
St Kitts and Nevis	272	130	nd	–	47.8	nd
St Lucia	610	50	nd	–	8.2	nd
St Vincent & Grenadines	390	110	nd	–	28.2	nd
Trinidad and Tobago	5,130	1,550	1,683[3]	1980	30.2	32.8
Total	217,172	37,550	nd	–	17.3	nd
CENTRAL AMERICA						
Belize	22,800	19,960	18,393	1992	87.5	80.7
Costa Rica	51,060	14,280	15,049	1988	28.0	29.5
El Salvador	20,720	1,230	1,555	1981	5.9	7.5
Guatemala	108,430	42,250	48,244	1992	39.0	44.5
Honduras	111,890	46,050	52,735[4]	1990	41.2	47.1
Mexico	1,908,690	448,120	448,120[5]	FAO 1990	23.5	23.5
Nicaragua	118,750	60,130	57,450	1990	50.6	48.4
Panama	75,990	31,170	31,170	FAO 1990	41.0	41.0
Total	2,418,330	663,190	672,716		27.4	27.8
SOUTH AMERICA						
Bolivia	1,084,390	419,670	451,426	1992	38.7	41.6
Brazil	8,456,510	5,322,440	3,415,308	1993	62.9	40.4
Colombia	1,038,700	540,460	510,935	1985	52.0	49.2
Ecuador	276,840	119,190	142,370	1987	43.0	51.4
French Guiana	88,150	79,970	81,490	1979	90.7	92.4
Guyana	208,419[1]	184,160	183,025	1992	93.6[2]	87.8
Paraguay	397,300	60,640	47,488[6]	1985	15.3	12.0
Peru	1,280,000	674,340	674,340[5]	FAO 1990	52.7	52.7
Surinam	143,662[1]	147,680	133,284	1978	94.6[1]	92.8
Venezuela	882,050	454,570	542,682	1982	51.5	61.5
Total	13,856,021	8,003,120	6,182,348		57.8	44.6

[1] The borders between the Guianas are disputed and in this instance we have used figures from Map 23.1 and Map 29.1 rather than FAO's figures of 156,000 sq. km and 196,850 sq. km respectively. Per cent cover using FAO's figure for forest area is calculated by using the land area given by FAO.

[2] FAO's figures given here includes the areas of forest within the tropical rain forest zone, the moist deciduous forest zone and the hill and montane zone. Forests in the dry deciduous forest zone, very dry forest zone and desert zone have not been included as it is inferred that they are open formations, and these are not covered in this Atlas.

[3] Trinidad only

[4] Not including mangrove

[5] As it has not been possible to obtain forest statistics from the Map in this Atlas, the forest area given by FAO (1993) has been used here.

[6] In Eastern Paraguay only

[7] Where known, this is the actual date of the forest data, rather than the publication date of the source map.

CLIMATE CHANGES

Deforestation in Brazilian Amazonia releases gases to the atmosphere that contribute to global warming. While the releases from current deforestation are significant, the unique feature of Brazil is the vast area of its forests that still remain uncut. This makes the potential for future greenhouse gas emissions from Amazonia far greater than for other tropical areas.

Greenhouse gas emissions from Amazonian deforestation are the subject of considerable controversy. Sources of differences among the estimates have included wide discrepancies in the rates of deforestation used in the calculations — a source of variation that has decreased greatly as errors have been clarified in some of the deforestation estimates. Another source of the differences comes from differing estimates for forest biomass, and part from inappropriate use of existing biomass estimates (as by using above-ground live biomass for total biomass; see review in Fearnside *et al.*, 1993). Some estimates, including Brazil's official estimates at the time of UNCED in Rio de Janeiro in June 1992, have indicated very low levels of emissions because only gases released from burning at the time of clearing were considered, while the larger "inherited" releases from decay and combustion of the biomass that was left unburned in the areas deforested in previous years were omitted. Emissions values also differ depending whether carbon dioxide alone is considered, or if trace gases such as methane, carbon monoxide and nitrous oxide are included.

Significant differences can also stem from the way the global warming impact of the various trace gases is calculated, including the treatment of indirect effects and choices of the time horizon and representation of time preference (such as discounting). Different indices of emissions also contribute to the variety of estimates. For example, "net committed emissions" expresses the effect of clearing in a given year, including delayed emissions and uptakes, over an infinite or very long time horizon as the deforested area approaches an equilibrium replacement landscape, while the "annual balance of net emissions" expresses the gas fluxes in a single year over the entire regional landscape (not only the area cleared in a given year).

The net committed emissions from deforestation in 1990 are estimated to be 234 million t of carbon in terms of carbon dioxide only, and 260–266 million t of CO_2-equivalent carbon for low and high trace gas scenarios if trace gases are included using the Intergovernmental Panel on Climate Change (IPCC) 1992 global warming potentials for direct effects with a 100-year time horizon and no discounting. The annual balance was 321–324 million t of carbon for CO_2 only or 339–371 million t with trace gases. The annual balance for 1990 was higher than the net committed emissions because of delayed emissions from the period of rapid deforestation in the 1980s. The annual flux represents approximately 4 per cent of the global total CO_2 flux from fossil fuel combustion and tropical deforestation (Fearnside,n.d.-a, n.d.-b).

Halting global warming cannot be achieved without significantly reducing global fossil fuel use. The emissions from deforestation in Brazil are nevertheless substantial: at the 1990 level, halting deforestation in Brazilian Amazonia would contribute more to combatting global warming than doubling the fuel efficiency of all of the automobiles in the world (see Fearnside, 1992)

While global warming has its greatest impacts outside Brazil, one of the consequences of widespread Amazonian deforestation that has the greatest likely impact on Brazil itself is potential alteration of the water cycle. These changes threaten the remaining Amazonian forests that are not directly cleared. In patches of forest isolated by cattle pasture, the trees on the edges of forest patches die at a much greater rate than do those in continuous forest (Rankin-de-Merona *et al.*, 1990). Dry conditions in the air or soil near the reserve edges is a likely explanation for the mortality (Kapos, 1989).

Precipitation in Amazonia is characterized by tremendous variability from one year to the next, even in the absence of massive deforestation. Were the forest's contribution to dry season rainfall to decrease, the result would probably be a very severe drought once in, say, 20 or 50 years that would kill many trees of susceptible species. The result would be replacement of the tropical moist forest with more drought-tolerant forms of scrubby, open vegetation resembling the *cerrado*. Such a change could set in motion a positive feedback process leading to less dense forests that transpire less, increasing the severity of droughts, thereby causing even more tree mortality and forest thinning (Fearnside, 1985). Simulations incorporating this feedback indicate large parts of the region becoming unsuitable for closed forest (Shukla *et al.*, 1990). The reductions in rainfall potentially affect not only Amazonia but also Brazil's major agricultural regions in the central-south part of the country (Salati and Vose, 1984). In addition, drier climatic conditions are likely to result in fires entering the forest surrounding agriculture and pasture areas, a phenomenon that already occurs on a more modest scale under present climatic conditions (Uhl and Buschbacher, 1985).

The example of tropical forest burned in Indonesia during the El Niño/Southern Oscillation drought of 1982–1983 (Malingreau *et al.*, 1985) serves as a warning of the potential for much more widespread impact from this source in Amazonia in the future. *Source:* Philip Fearnside

---

regions of Central America (Costa Rica), the forested hinterlands of São Paulo and Rio de Janeiro, and the forested slopes of the Andes, where access to markets for cash crops has enabled farmers to develop tree crops and agroforestry systems which are stable and productive even on poor forest soils. It is claimed that 80 per cent of the forested land cleared for agriculture, especially for cattle raising, in lowland moist forests is abandoned within 10 years, but there are also plenty of examples of productive and stable agriculture on forest lands. The success of colonisation has been conditioned by the selection of sites, the skills and resources of the colonists and the availability of markets (de Onis, 1992).

Realisation of the severe ecological constraints to development in moist forest areas is now widespread. Schemes to promote large scale deforestation for extensive agriculture are being viewed with caution in most countries. There is, however, a growing appreciation that forest lands do have considerable development potential if they are used appropriately. The promotion of uses which are consistent with the maintenance of biological and environmental values has been a major focus of IUCN's work in the humid tropics. The principles are set out in Poore and Sayer (1991) and are reflected in a resolution adopted by the IUCN General Assembly in Perth, Australia in 1990. The resolution was adopted without opposition by IUCN's 450 non-governmental organisation members and by representatives of governments or government agencies from a further 114 countries. Its essential message is that ecologically sound development of some forest areas is needed to alleviate poverty and thus diminish the pressure for unsustainable use of more extensive areas. It recognises the solutions to deforestation as lying in creating industrial employment and generating wealth for society at large. Markets must exist for cash crops which will allow small farmers to invest in the higher input farming systems needed to achieve sustainability on marginal soils. The resolution is significant because a broad section of the conservation community of both Northern and Southern countries recognised that forests will not be saved by measures to diminish access to their resources (timber boycotts, etc), but rather by measures to promote more appropriate use of those resources. The resolution suggests that attempts by conservation lobbyists to constrain development of mineral or timber resources in forest areas may be counterproductive.

Resources derived from restricted sources (minerals) or from forest systems (tree crops or timber) are generating wealth and employment for people who would otherwise practice extensive agriculture and destroy far more forest. The test of good development in the humid tropics is the amount of wealth and employment it can create per unit area of land; thus the extent to which it can advance social and economic well-being without incurring extensive deforestation. These issues are reviewed in considerable detail in the thought-provoking book *The Green Cathedral* (de Onis, 1992).

These ideas are reflected in the UNCED Statement of Principles on Forests and in Agenda 21. They are also consistent with the revised goals and objectives of the TFAP and the targets and guidelines established under the International Tropical Timber Agreement. The translation of these concepts into practical development options for any specific locality is much more difficult. The questions of the carrying capacity of land under different uses are examined for Amazonia by Fearnside (1986, 1990). The principles of economic zoning are recognised by several countries in the American tropics. For instance, a major study of land capability carried out in Brazil formed the basis of the maps in Chapter 25 (Brazil, Projeto RADAMBRASIL, 1973–83). Policies promoted by the Amazon Pact and the Brazil Pilot Project and supported by the major industrial powers are consistent with this developmental approach to conservation. The issues addressed in this Atlas and the information provided for each country attempt to demonstrate the potential synergies between conservation and development at a continental level.

The Future

There is no inherent demand for forest land or forest resources that need condemn the forests of Amazonia to disappear. The population density of the region is only a fraction of that found in tropical Asia. Investments in improved use of land outside the forests will yield far more than will attempts to extend the agricultural frontier. This is not true for the Pacific seaboard of continental South America, nor for parts of Central America and the Caribbean where population density is much higher. Indeed in countries such as El Salvador and Haiti it is already largely too late to save the forests and a major proportion of these countries' biodiversity is already extinct (Goodland, 1992).

For the Caribbean as a whole, the situation is precarious for the natural resources, and consequently also for the well-being of the people (Lugo *et al.* 1981). The islands are mostly small

and densely populated and there is intense competition for the flat land in particular. The great diversity of forest types complicates the problems of forest management since it is difficult to develop management techniques which can be applied successfully over wide areas (Lugo *et al.*, 1981). In addition, not only are there man-made disruptions to the forests, the natural disturbances, such as hurricanes, can also cause considerable damage to the forest.

In some cases, knowledge exists of the sites and management regimes needed to conserve the region's biodiversity (see Chapters 3, 4 and 8). In South America at least, there is room to conserve biodiversity and to allocate adequate forest lands for sustainable development. There are nutrient rich soils in the region which could support productive, sustainable and intensive agriculture if technologies and inputs were available. This could most readily be achieved by more efficient use of the large area of land that has already been deforested.

Sustainable extraction of forest products, both timber and non-timber, is consistent with the retention of much of the biological and environmental value of the forests. It is likely that this extractivism will gradually disappear as other lifestyle options become available to its practitioners; but extractivism may be useful in building a bridge for certain sectors of rural society into the 21st century (UICN, 1993; Redford and Padoch, 1992). The past practise of spending conservation money on repressing the activities of hunters and gatherers in pursuit of protection of pristine ecosystems is no longer viable. Nevertheless, it is also evident that it may not be possible to expect the large vertebrates, at least, to survive in a forest where hunting is unrestrained (see Chapter 5).

We must be cautious, however, in assuming that the future will be a linear extrapolation of the past. Fossil fuel reserves are being depleted, and the climate changes caused by carbon released during their combustion are becoming intolerable (see Box). The world is inevitably going to turn more towards renewable sources of hydrocarbons. Ethanol is already substituting for fossil oil in Brazil and demand for this product can be expected to increase in the future. Tropical tree plantations can produce hydrocarbons, and also fibres, to substitute for those of the slow growing natural forests and plantations of northern temperate zones (Sawyer, 1993; Davidson, 1987). The major reforestation schemes on the llanos of Venezuela and in the Vale de Rio Doce in Brazil may be a foretaste of the future. Some see such industrial forest development as a threat to natural systems; others argue that it will channel development into a few circumscribed areas and diminish pressure on the bulk of the forest estate.

We exist at a time when thoughtful people are more and more concerned at the ever accelerating consumerism and search for economic growth in the industrialised North. In the medium term, the single most important requirement for halting the abuse of forest lands in the tropical Americas is that the economies of the countries of the region must grow. This must not be growth at any cost. It must be sustained, consistent growth of all sectors of the economy and it must be associated with greater democracy, improved social facilities (particularly health and education) and greater predictability of markets. Virtually everybody agrees that these forests need to be conserved. The need is to create an economic and social environment in which this will be possible. As this Atlas is being finalised, in mid-1994, there is, at last, the beginning of agreement between tropical and temperate countries that a global convention on forests might, after all, be in everyone's interest.

References

Brazil, Projeto RADAMBRASIL (1973–83). *Levantamento de Recursos Naturais Vols 1–23*. Ministério das Minas e Energia, Departamneto Nacional de Perdação Mineral, Rio de Janeiro, Brasil.

Davidson, J. (1987). *Bioenergy Tree Plantations in the Tropics: Ecological Implications and Impacts*. Commission on Ecology Paper No 12. IUCN, Gland, Switzerland.

Dourojeanni, M.J. (1990). *Amazonia que hacer?*. Centro de Estudios Teologicos de la Amazonia, Iquitos, Peru. 444 pp.

de Onis, J. (1992). *The Green Cathedral: sustainable development of Amazonia*. Oxford University Press, Oxford, U.K.

Eden, M.J. (1990). *Ecology and Land Management in Amazonia*. Belhaven Press, London. 269 pp.

Fearnside, P.M. (1985). Environmental change and deforestation in the Brazilian Amazon. In: *Change in the Amazon Basin: Man's Impacts on Forests and Rivers*. Pp. 71–88. Hemming, J. (ed). Manchester University Press, Manchester, U.K. 222 pp.

Fearnside, P.M. (1986). *Human Carrying Capacity of the Brazilian Rainforest*. Columbia University Press, New York, E.U.A. 293.

Fearnside, P.M. (1990). Predominant land uses in the Brazilian Amazon. In: *Alternatives to Deforestation: Towards Sustainable Use of the Amazon Rain Forest*. Pp. 235–251. Anderson, A.B. (ed.). Columbia University Press, New York. 281 pp.

Fearnside, P.M. (1992). *Greenhouse Gas Emissions from Deforestation in the Brazilian Amazon*. Carbon Emissions and Sequestration in Forests: Case Studies from Developing Countries. Volume 2. LBL-32758, UC-402. Climate Change Division, Environmental Protection Agency, Washington, DC and Energy and Environment Division, Lawrence Berkeley Laboratory (LBL), University of California (UC), Berkeley, California. 73 pp.

Fearnside, P.M. (n.d.-a). *Greenhouse gases from deforestation in Brazilian Amazonia: Net committed emissions*. Unpublished manuscript.

Fearnside, P.M. (n.d.-b). *Amazonia and global warming: Annual balance of greenhouse gas emissions from land use change in Brazil Amazon region*. Unpublished manuscript.

Fearnside, P.M., Leal, N. and Fernandes, F.M. (1993). Rainforest burning and the global carbon budget: Biomass, combustion efficiency and charcoal formation in the Brazilian Amazon. *Journal of Geophysical Research* 98: 16,733–16,743.

Goodland, R.J.A. (1992). Neotropical moist forests: priorities for the next two decades. In: *Conservation of Neotropical Forests: working from traditional resource use*. Redford, K.H. and Padoch, C. (eds). Columbia University Press, New York. Pp. 475.

Haffer, J. (1969). Speciation in Amazonian forest birds. *Science* 165: 131–137.

IUCN/UNEP/WWF (1980). *World Conservation Strategy: living resource conservation for sustainable development*. IUCN, Gland, Switzerland.

IUCN/UNEP/WWF (1991) *Caring for the Earth: a strategy for sustainable living*. IUCN, Gland, Switzerland.

Kapos, V. (1989). Effects of isolation on the water status of forest patches in the Brazilian Amazon. *Journal of Tropical Ecology* 5: 173–185.

Latin America, Caribbean, Commission on Development and Environment for Amazonia (nd). *Amazonia Without Myths*. Inter-American Development Bank, Washington, D.C. 99 pp.

Leonard, H.J. (1987). *Natural Resources and Economic Development in Central America: A Regional Environmental Profile*. International Institute for Environment and Development. Transaction books, Oxford, U.K.

Lugo, A.E., Schmidt, R. and Brown, S. (1981). Tropical forests in the Caribbean. *Ambio* 10(6): 318–324.

Mahar, D.J. (1989). *Government Policies and Deforestation in Brazil's Amazon Region*. The World Bank, Washington, D.C.

Malingreau, J.P., Stephens, G. and Fellows, L. (1985). Remote sensing of forest fires: Kalimantan and North Borneo in 1982–83. *Ambio* 17(1): 314–321.

McNeeley, J.A. (1994). Lessons from the past: forests and biodiversity. *Biodiversity and Conservation* 3: 3–20.

Prance, G.T. (1982). Forest refuges: evidence from woody angiosperms. In: *Biological Diversification in the Tropics*. Prance, G.T. (ed.). Columbia University Press, New York: pp. 137–157.

Poore, D. and Sayer, J. (1991). *The Management of Tropical Moist Forest Lands: Ecological Guidelines*. Second edition. IUCN, Gland, Switzerland and Cambridge, UK. 78 pp.

Rankin-de-Merona, J.M., Hutchings, R.W. and Lovejoy, T.E. (1990). Tree mortality and recruitment over a five-year period in undisturbed upland rainforest of the Central Amazon. In: *Four Neotropical Rainforests*. Pp. 573–584. Gentry, A.H. (ed.) Yale University Press, New Haven, Connecticut, U.S.A.

Redford, K.H. and Padoch, C. (1992). *Conservation of Neotropical Forests*. Colombia University Press.

Salati, E. and Vose, P.B. (1984). Amazon Basin: a system in equilibrium. *Science* 115: 129–138.

Sawyer, J. (1993). *Plantations in the Tropics: Environmental Concerns*. IUCN, Gland, Switzerland and Cambridge, U.K. 83 pp.

Shukla, J., Nobre, C. and Sellers, P. (1990). Amazon deforestation and climate change. *Science* 247: 1322–1325.

UICN (1993). *El Extractivismo en América Latino. Recomendaciones del Taller UICN-CEE, Amacayacu, Colombia, Octubre, 1992*. Ruiz Pérez, M., Sayer, J. and Cohen Jehoram, S. (Eds). IUCN, Gland, Switzerland and Cambridge, UK.

Uhl, C. and Buschbacher, R. (1985). A disturbing synergism between cattle-ranch burning practices and selective tree harvesting in the eastern Amazon. *Biotropica* 17(4): 265–268.

Utting, P. (1993). *Trees, people and power*. Earthscan Publications Ltd, London.

WCED (1987). *Our Common Future (Bruntland Report)*. Oxford University Press, Oxford, UK.

Author: Jeff Sayer, Centre for International Forestry Research, Bogor, Indonesia, with contributions from Marc Dourojeanni, Inter American Development Bank; Philip Fearnside, INPA, Manuas, Brazil and W. Veening, European Working Group in Amazonia, Amsterdam, Netherlands

PART II

10 Cuba

Country area 110,860 sq. km
Land area 110,860 sq. km
Population (mid-1994) 11.1 million
Population growth rate 0.8 per cent
Population projected to 2025 12.9 million
Gross national product per capita (1992) US$2458
Forest cover, date unknown (see Map) 25,035 sq. km
Forest cover for 1990 (FAO, 1993) 17,150 sq. km
Annual deforestation rate 1981–1990 1.0 per cent
Industrial roundwood production 611,000 cu. m
Industrial roundwood exports —
Fuelwood and charcoal production 2,529,000 cu. m
Processed wood production 279,000 cu. m
Processed wood exports 21,000 cu. m

The island of Cuba is the largest of the Caribbean islands, accounting for over half the land area of the Antilles and, as such, has the greatest area of forest remaining on it. Nevertheless, only around 15 to 20 per cent of the island is forested. Most forest destruction has occurred in the last hundred years, with cattle pasture and sugar cane plantations replacing the forests. There is little tradition of conservation in Cuba, but recent efforts, including a law for the protection of the environment and the rational use of natural resources, have established the basis for success in preserving the remaining flora and fauna.

INTRODUCTION

The Republic of Cuba comprises the main island of Cuba, 1300 km long and 190 km wide with an area of 104,945 sq. km, the Isla de la Juventud (formerly the Isla de Pinos) covering 2200 sq. km, and some 1600 further small cays and islands.

Topographically, the island of Cuba consists of three main regions: the plains, foothills and the highland area. The plains make up two thirds of the island. There are four principal mountain systems, which are, from west to east, the Guaniguanico system, the Guamuhaya system, the Sierra Maestra system (which contains Pico Real the highest point in the country at 1974 m), and the extensive Sagua-Baracoa massif.

The mean annual temperature is about 24.5°C, with a mean minimum of 10°C and mean maximum of 35°C. January is the coldest month and July the hottest. The main rainy season is from May to October. Mean annual precipitation in most areas is in the range 1100–1600 mm, but some places receive as little as 300 mm and some as much as 3000 mm rainfall in a year (Capote *et al.*, 1989).

The island is thought to have been inhabited since 6000 BP although it was reportedly only sparsely populated when the Spaniards first settled in the 16th century. Estimates for the pre-Colombian population vary from 200,000 to 1,000,000. Within 50 years of Spanish settlement, the indigenous inhabitants had been almost entirely exterminated by epidemics. Until the 19th century Spanish settlements were largely concentrated along the north-west coast in and around Havana, the country's capital. The country has remained largely urban and at present 73 per cent of the population live in towns with Havana having a population of over 2 million. Overall population density is quite low at 100 people per sq. km, but around half the people live in less than 10 per cent of the island.

Arable land occupies 44,000 sq. km of the island and 24,000 sq. km is permanent pasture (MINAG, 1991). Principal exports are sugar, minerals, tobacco, citrus fruit and fish.

The Forests

The variable topography, geology and climate of Cuba together with the effects of humans, particularly in the past century, have resulted in the existence of a wide and complex range of vegetation types. The impact of humans has in many cases made it very difficult to identify and classify the original vegetation cover (Smith, 1954). For this reason, the extent of original forest cover remains a matter of conjecture, with estimates varying from 60 per cent (Smith, 1954) to 90 per cent of the country (Anon., 1992). Existing forests on the island are divided principally into rain, cloud, semi-deciduous, swamp, gallery, mangrove and pine (Capote *et al.*, 1989). Original forest cover is believed to have been largely evergreen and semi-deciduous, the latter particularly frequent in central and western regions (Borhidi and Muñíz, 1980).

The typical rain forest formations occur below 400 m in close association with river valleys in the northeast extremity of Cuba. Three tree strata are present with heights ranging between 15 and 35 m. *Carapa guianensis* is dominant in the first stratum, other important tree species are *Calophyllum utile*, *Buchenavia capitata*, *Manilkara albescens*, *Micropolis polita* and *Terminalia nipensis*. In the second storey are *Ochroma pyramidale*, *Guarea guidonia*, *Oxandra laurifolia*, *Diospyros caribaea* and the palms *Prestoea montana* and *Calyptronoma orientalis* (Capote *et al.*, 1989). Tree ferns, lianes and epiphytes are abundant.

Lowland seasonal rain forests formerly occupied the most extensive areas in the island. Although this forest type is still widespread on Cuba, it is rarely found in undisturbed stands and much has been replaced by agricultural land. Two canopy layers are found, at 20–25 m and at 8–15 m, typically with emergents of the deciduous species *Ceiba pentandra*. Common trees of the upper canopy are *Roystonea regia*, *Guazuma ulmifolia*, *Bucida buceras*, *Chlorophora tinctoria*, *Cordia collococca*, *Ficus* spp. and *Samanea saman*. In the lower storey *Oxandra lanceolata*,

Ateramnus lucidus, Andira inermis and *Crescentia cujete* are characteristic (Borhidi, 1991).

Between 400 and 900 m elevation in the Cristal and Moa Mts and in the valleys of the Nipe Mts are serpentine rain forests with an open upper canopy at 15–22 m composed of such species as *Calophyllum utile, Podocarpus ekmanii, Dipholis jubilla, Ocotea leucoxylon* and *Byrsonima coriacea*, often mixed with *Pinus cubensis*. The lower stratum is only 5 to 12 m high and has species such as *Bactris cubensis, Tetrazygia cristalensis, Tapura cubensis, Byrsonima biflora* and *Ilex berteroi* within it (Borhidi, 1991).

Sub-montane rain forests occur in the Moa Mts and in the Toa, Jaguani and Duaba Basins. The upper canopy layer, at 30–35 m, is closed and is composed of *Carapa guianensis*, and only rarely mixed with other species. The second storey, with a canopy at 20–25 m high, is composed of *Calophyllum utile, Sloanea curatellifolia, Dipholis jubilla, Guarea guidonia, Cupania americana, Buchenavia capitata, Ficus wrightii* and *Roystonea regia*. Palms such as *Bactris cubensis* and *Prestoea montana* are commonly found along creeks. The third canopy layer is 6–15 m high and *Oxandra lanceolata, Cordia sulcata* and *Miconia elata* are some of the characteristic species.

The submontane seasonal forests occur between 200 and 800 m in altitude. They are similar to the lowland seasonal forests in structure but tree composition differs from those forests and between the mountains (Borhidi, 1991).

Montane forest is the climax vegetation over 800 m altitude in Sierra Maestra, Escambray Mts and Sierra del Purial and in some areas of Moa, Sierra del Crista and Baracoa. It is 20–25 m high with a closed upper canopy. Species found in this storey include *Magnolia cubensis, Ocotea cuneata, O. leucoxylon, O. floribunda, Myrsine coriacea* and *Cyrilla racemiflora*. Characteristic species of the second tree layer include *Clusia*

tetrastigma, Alchornea latifolia, Garrya fadyenii, Miconia punctata and tree ferns such as *Cyathea arborea* and *C. cubensis* (Borhidi, 1991). Epiphytes are abundant in both storeys.

Cloud forests in Cuba are confined to the high altitude regions of Sierra Maestra and to the high mountains of the Pico Turquino and Pico Bayamesa group between 1600 and 1900 m. The canopy layer is dense and closed but only 6–12 m high. Some of the characteristic species of this layer are *Myrsine microphylla, Nectandra reticularis, Sapium maestrense, Persea anomala, Symplocos leonis, Cyrilla racemiflora, Weinmannia pinnata, Torralbasia cuneifolia, Alsophila aspera* and *Lophosoria quadripinnata* (Borhidi, 1991). There is also a dense, almost impenetrable shrub layer. Orchids and bryophytes are common.

Coniferous forests are restricted to the eastern and western ends of the island where they are the dominant vegetation type. In the Sierra Maestra, *Pinus occidentalis* is found between 900 and 1500 m. In western Cuba, *Pinus caribaea* predominates, *P. tropicalis* is also present and often associated with *Colpothrinax wrightii* (Capote *et al.*, 1989).

Mangroves

Mangroves, of which Cuba is estimated to have around 5300 sq. km (IFF, 1989; Padron *et al.*, 1993), the tenth largest area in the world, constitute roughly one quarter of the country's existing forest domain (Anon., 1992). The mangroves shown on Map 10.1 cover an area of 7665 sq. km, a somewhat larger figure than that reported by IFF (1989) and other authors. They form zones 2–3 km wide along Cuba's shallow muddy beaches. The largest extent is in the Peninsula de Zapata. In the intertidal zone, *Rhizophora mangle* forms a belt between low tide and mid tide levels, whereas *Avicennia nitida* is dominant between mid and high tide levels. *Laguncularia racemosa* may be inter-

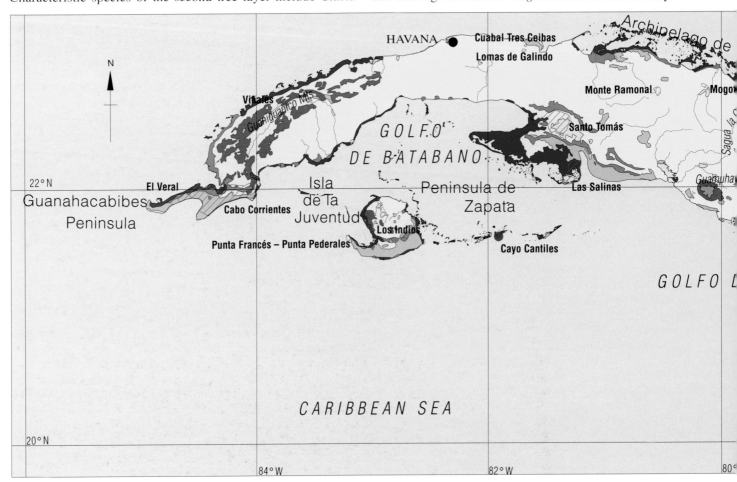

mingled with *Avicennia* in some stands. In the uppermost sections of the intertidal region the extremely salt-resistant species *Conocarpus erectus* forms pure stands or may be mixed with *Avicennia* and *Laguncularia*.

Mangroves have traditionally played a very important role in the forest economy of the country and have recently become a focus of reafforestation efforts. Between 1988 and 1990 nearly 180 million mangrove seedlings were planted, mostly of red mangrove *Rhizophora mangle* (Anon., 1992).

Forest Resources and Management

Cuba's forest estate was estimated by the country's Ministry of Agriculture (MINAG, 1991) and the total area of natural forest was reported to be 17,103 sq. km (see Table 10.1). In Cuba's country report to the 1992 United Nations Conference on Environment and Development (UNCED), the area of natural forests was given as 16,882 sq. km (Anon., 1992 and see Table 10.4). FAO (1993) gives the similar figure of 17,150 sq. km of forest, distributed between the rain (1140 sq. km), moist deciduous (12,470 sq. km), dry deciduous (20 sq. km) and hill and montane zones (3520 sq. km). The area of closed broadleaved forest is also given as 17,150 sq. km (FAO, 1993), therefore in this instance the dry deciduous forest has been included in the statistics at the head of the chapter.

The forests shown on Map 10.1 cover 25,035 sq. km, distributed within the forest types as indicated in Table 10.2. This is a somewhat higher figure than that given in Tables 10.1 and 10.4 or by FAO (1993). It is unclear when or how the data were collected for the source map, which was published in 1989 in the *Nuevo Atlas Nacional de Cuba* (see Map legend). It is, therefore, quite probable that the forest cover shown on Map 10.1 is an overestimate of the present day situation. Another reason for the differences may, as usual, be the definitions of "forest"

Table 10.1 Cuba's forest estate in 1991

Forest	*Area in sq. km*
Total forest resource*	28,198
Total forested	20,185
Natural forest	17,103
Plantation	3,082
Deforested area	3,090
Non-forest	4,923

* Forest resource covers all areas slated for forest development purposes, including some deforested and some non-forested areas.
Source: MINAG (1991)

used. For instance, FAO (1993) indicates that all the forest in Cuba is closed broadleaved forest (the figure in Table 5c of *Forest resources assessment 1990* for closed broadleaved forest is the same as that for Cuba's total forest in this and other tables in the same publication), whereas the source map shows conifer forests which, when measured on Map 10.1, cover 2719 sq. km. It is also not clear whether mangroves are included as forest in MINAG (1991).

Policies for forest resource use are formulated by the National Institute for Forest Development (INDAF) and the forested land is overseen by the Forest Administration within the Ministry of Agriculture (MINAG). There are separate departments for silviculture, protection of forests and fauna and industrial forestry, while forest inventories are carried out by a different unit.

Forest inventories were carried out in the 1960s in two phases, the first, running from 1961 to 1963, covered pine forest while the second, from 1966 to 1970, covered broadleaved

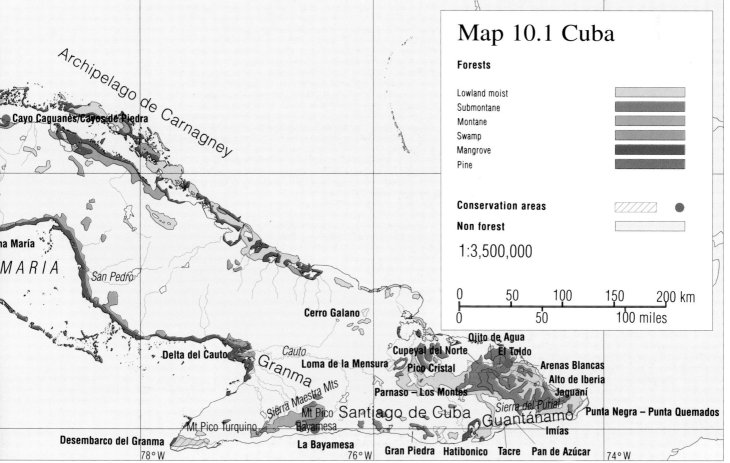

Map 10.1 Cuba

Forests

Lowland moist	
Submontane	
Montane	
Swamp	
Mangrove	
Pine	

Conservation areas

Non forest

1:3,500,000

0   50   100   150   200 km
0   50   100 miles

Table 10.2 Estimates of forest extent in Cuba

Forest type	Area (sq. km)	% land area
Lowland moist	7,833	7.1
Sub-Montane	2,513	2.3
Montane	716	0.6
Pine	2,719	2.5
Inland Swamp	3,589	3.2
Mangrove	7,665	6.9
Total	25,035	22.6

Based on analysis of Map 10.1. See Map Legend on p. 101 for details of source

forests. In 1973 the results of this were used to draw up a national forest census. This led to the development of a forest management strategy under whose aegis have been drawn up plans for the exploitation and development of the forest resource. These plans were complete at local and provincial level by 1985 (CIF, 1985). Elaboration of a national forest plan (the Plan de Accion Forestal Para Cuba) was begun in 1989. The ultimate aim is to see 23–25 per cent of the country forested (MINAG, 1991), compared with the current level of about 18 per cent (15 per cent natural forest and 3 per cent plantations).

Reafforestation has proceeded actively since 1959. Both plantation forestry and enrichment planting are used. Between 1959 and 1983 just over 2000 sq. km of plantation were established, with a total of nearly 1.4×10^9 trees planted (CIF, 1985). Roughly the same number of trees is reported to have been planted between 1985 and 1990 (MINAG, 1991). In 1987 a new scheme, known as Plan Manati was launched. This has involved massive popular participation and is particularly concerned with the planting of fruit and coffee trees in marginal agricultural land (IFF, 1989). Of the total planted up to 1983, around 37 per cent were conifers, mainly *Pinus caribaea*, 12 per cent *Eucalyptus*, 15 per cent *Casuarina* and 36 per cent broadleaved trees. Some 64 species of broadleaf have been planted, of which the most abundant are mahogany (*Swietenia macrophylla, S. mahagoni* and *Khaya nyasica*), cedar *Cedrela odorata*, blue mahoe *Hibiscus elatus* and *Calophyllum brasilense* var *antillanum*. Most of the broadleaf species are used for enrichment planting rather than for plantation forestry (CIF, 1985).

Because of previous overexploitation and lack of forest management, the standing crop of timber is relatively low, averaging 47.6 cu. m per ha. Mature hardwood trees are now very rare. Around 70 per cent of total wood volume is in stands less than 30 years old; for coniferous species this proportion increases to 84 per cent (CIF, 1985).

As of 1985 there were 105 sawmills. Just under half of timber harvested in 1983 was hardwood. Thinnings, mostly from plantations, but since 1979 also from natural forests, are a major source of construction wood in rural areas as well as firewood and charcoal. *Casuarina* is used mainly for sugar refineries and for charcoal production (CIF, 1985).

Deforestation

FAO (1988) estimated that Cuba had one of the lowest net annual deforestation rates (0.2 per cent) in Latin America between 1981 and 1985. However, the latest figures from FAO (1993) indicate that between the years of 1981 and 1990, Cuba lost forest at a rate of 1 per cent per annum, an annual loss of 173 sq. km. As can be seen from Table 10.3, forest cover actu-

ally increased between 1959 and 1987, although this is mostly through an increase in the extent of plantations. Between 1900 and 1959 the country suffered very serious deforestation and forest degradation, with forest cover decreasing from about 54 per cent in 1900 to 14 per cent in 1959. Western Cuba was the most degraded region. Much of the destruction was due to clearing land for intensive cattle raising and sugar cane plantations. The forests themselves were also seriously over-exploited, with more than 130 species regularly used by the commercial timber trade and areas often clear-felled for firewood and charcoal. Forest fires have also had an important impact, particularly in the pine forests where they inhibit natural regeneration. Overall this has resulted in there being very few mature forest stands remaining on the island (Anon., 1992; CIF, 1985; Smith, 1954).

Biodiversity

Cuba has the highest species diversity and the highest degree of endemism in the West Indies. Just over 50 per cent of the flora and 32 per cent of the vertebrate fauna are endemic. The island has an estimated 6200 species of flowering plants, 450 vertebrates and 7500 insects and arachnids (Santana, 1991).

Among the best represented plant families are Poaceae, Asteraceae, Rubiaceae, Euphorbiaceae, Orchidaceae and Leguminosae (Capote *et al.*, 1989; Vales *et al.*, 1992). There are no endemic families but over 70 endemic genera. Most of the endemic taxa are found in the montane regions; in the east, the flora of the Sagua-Baracoa montane system is 80 per cent endemic. The second highest number of endemics is found on the Cordillera of Guaniguanico in the west.

Almost all the amphibians on Cuba (36 of 41) are endemic (WCMC, 1992), but little is known of their status. Excluding marine turtles, there are 100 reptile species on the island, with 79 endemics (WCMC, 1992; Garrido and Jaume, 1984). Four of these reptile species have been assigned IUCN threatened species categories: the Cuban tree boa *Epicrates angulifer* (Indeterminate) and the Cuban crocodile *Crocodylus rhombifer* (Endangered), both endemic, the comparatively widespread American crocodile *Crocodylus acutus* (Vulnerable) and the Cuban ground iguana *Cyclura nubila* (Vulnerable), which also occurs on the Cayman Islands (Groombridge, 1993).

There are 159 breeding bird species recorded in the country, 22 are endemic (WCMC, 1992). Collar *et al.* (1992) list 13 threatened birds in Cuba, of which nine are endemic. Of the endemics, the forest living species are Gundlach's hawk *Accipiter gundlachi*, the blue-headed quail dove *Starnoenas cyanocephala* and the giant kingbird *Tyrannus cubensis*. The ivory-billed woodpecker *Campephilus principalis*, which formerly also occurred in the south-eastern USA, is the most endangered bird on the island and may even now be extinct.

The surviving native mammalian fauna is a relict of that which is believed to have existed before human settlement. It is

Table 10.3 Forest cover in Cuba between 1812 and 1987

Year	Forested area (sq. km)*	Per cent forested
1812	99,000	89
1900	60,000	54
1959	15,000	14
1987	20,000	18

* includes plantations

Source: Adapted from MINAG (1991)

difficult to be precise about the number of extant species as the taxonomy of the most important non-volant group, the hutias (family Capromyidae, order Rodentia), is uncertain. Estimates for the number of recent species, all in the genus *Capromys*, vary from four (Morgan and Woods, 1986) to ten (Woods, 1989). Of the latter all except two are listed as threatened by IUCN and several, which have only been recorded on a few cays and islets, may already be extinct (Groombridge, 1993). The only other native terrestrial mammal is the Cuban solenodon *Solenodon cubanus*, a large, primitive, endemic insectivore confined to montane rainforests in the east and classified as Endangered by IUCN.

There are around 25 bat species on Cuba, of which 3 are endemic (*Mormopterus minutus*, *Phyllops falcatus* and *Lasiurus insularis*); the Cuban flower bat *Phyllonycteris poeyi*, also recorded on Hispaniola, is listed by IUCN as possibly threatened (Groombridge, 1993).

There are 23 recorded freshwater fish species in Cuba, all except two (*Ophisternon aenigmaticum* and *Gambusia puncticulata*) are endemic. Some of these are apparently highly localized (Lee *et al.*, 1983). The number of invertebrates is unknown, four butterflies (*Papilio caiguanabus*, *Anetia briarea*, *A. cubana* and *A. pantheratus*) and one dragonfly (*Hypolestes trinitatis*) are listed as threatened by IUCN (Groombridge, 1993).

Conservation Areas

The protection status of the forests as of 1990 is outlined in Table 10.4.

This classification follows a decree promulgated in 1988 which divided all forests into two types: production forests and protection forests, with several different categories of the latter (enumerated in the table above).

The first national park (Pico Crystal) was established in 1930 and five more protected areas were established between then and 1958 with a further nine gazetted in 1959.

The National Network of Protected Areas in Cuba was established in 1981 and there are now around 100 conservation areas that cover approximately 20 per cent of the land, but only a few of these are strictly protected. Categories within the national network of conservation areas are national park, natural reserve, national monument, faunal refuge and "other categories". There are, however, no clear definitions of the management of each type of area (IUCN, 1992) and the network does not function as a structured national system (Ottenwalder *in litt.*, 1993). Those areas in IUCN's categories I–IV are listed in Table 10.5.

Table 10.4 The status of forest in Cuba in 1990

Status	Area (sq. km)		
	total	natural	plantn
PRODUCTION FOREST	6,549	4,500	2,049
PROTECTION FOREST	13,661	12,382	1,279
National parks	1,003	794	209
Recreational areas	252	134	118
Areas for fauna conservation	5,372	5,213	159
National reserves	515	501	14
Protection of water and soils	2,842	2,217	625
Shoreline protection	3,677	3,523	154
Total	20,210	16,882	3328

Source: Anon. (1992)

Table 10.5 Conservation areas of Cuba

Existing protected areas in IUCN's categories I–IV are listed below. Marine national parks are not listed or mapped. For information on Biosphere Reserves see Chapter 8.

National Parks	*Area (sq. km)*
Desembarco del Granma*	258
Gran Piedra*	34
La Bayamesa*	165
Pico Cristal*	150
Punta Francés – Punta Pederales*	174
Turquino*	175
Viñales*	134

Ecological Reserves	
Los Indios*	33
Mogotes de Jumagua	4
Punta Negra – Punta Quemados*	40

Natural Reserves	
Cabo Corrientes*	16
Cupeyal del Norte*	103
El Veral*	75
Imías	26
Jaguaní*	49
Loma de la Mensura*	24
Tacre	12

Managed Flora Reserves	
Arenas Blancas+	15
Cayo Caguanes/Cayos de Piedra*	15
Cerro Galano	28
Cuabal Tres Ceibas*	4
El Toldo*	56
Lomas de Galindo	6
Monte Ramonal	26
Pan de Azúcar*	3
Parnaso – Los Montes*	95

Faunal Refuges	
Alto de Iberia*	57
Cayo Cantiles*	38
Cayos de Ana María*	69
Delta del Cauto*	600
Hatibonico*	52
Las Salinas*	318
Ojito de Agua*	37
Río Máximo+	100
Santo Tomás*	148
Total	3,139

* Area with forest within its boundaries as shown on Map 10.1

+ not mapped

Source: WCMC (unpublished data)

Forests are protected within the Viñales National Park. A view of the Viñales Valley. (WWF/Vithal Rajan)

Legislation for protected areas management is laid down in Law 33 of 1981 for the Protection of the Environment and Rational Use of Natural Resources and Decree No. 67 of 1983. Under these regulations, natural reserves are managed by the Cuban Academy of Sciences, national parks, faunal refuges and hunting or game areas by the Directorate for the Protection of Fauna and Flora of the Ministry of Agriculture, national monuments by the Ministry of Culture and 'natural and touristic areas' by the National Institute of Tourism.

Cuban conservation policies are directed by the National Commission for Environmental Protection and Rational Use of Natural Resources (COMARNA).

Initiatives for Conservation

The major initiative at present is a large-scale conservation and sustainable development project which is being implemented in eastern Cuba. This is the Gran Parque Nacional Sierra Maestro,

which is a multiple use area in the provinces of Granma, Santiago de Cuba and Guantánamo covering 5280 sq. km; 64 per cent is government land and the rest private. The area has its own management authority and legislation and is administered and managed by a Ruling Commission which is assisted by a Technical Advisory Council formed by a number of Government Ministries and agencies. Within the area there are three national parks (Desembarco del Granma, Turquino and La Gran Piedra), nine faunal refuges, nine natural reserves, four natural tourist areas and 28 tourist sites. An environmental education programme has been implemented in primary schools in the area. Ecologically sound projects on beekeeping, forestry, aquaculture and the production of cacao, coffee and fruit trees have been started and incentives to persuade peasants to form production cooperatives and move off the hillsides to less fragile areas are being provided (Santana, 1991).

References

Anon. (1992). *Cuba.* Country report to UNCED, Rio de Janiero, Brazil.

Borhidi, A. (1991). *Phytogeography and Vegetation Ecology of Cuba.* Akadémiai Kiadó, Budapest.

Borhidi, A. and Muñíz, O. (1980). Die vegetationskarte von Kuba. *Acta Botanica Hungarica* 26: 25–53.

Capote, R.P., Berazaín, R. and Leiva, A. (1989). Cuba. In: *Floristic Inventory of Tropical Countries: The Status of Plant Systematics, Collections, and Vegetation, plus Recommendations for the Future.* Campbell, D.G. and

Hammond, D. (Eds). The New York Botanical Garden, New York. Pp. 315–335.

CIF (1985). *Breve Caracterización de la Actividad Forestal en Cuba.* Centro de Investigación Forestal, Ministerio de la Agricultura, La Habana, Cuba.

Collar, N.J., Gonzaga, L.P., Krabbe, N., Madroño Nieto, A., Naranjo, L.G., Parker III, T.A. and Wege, D.C. (1992). *Threatened Birds of the Americas. The ICBP/IUCN Red Data Book.* ICBP, Cambridge, U.K.

IFF (1989). *Breve Caracterización de la Actividad Forestal en*

Cuba. Instituto de Investigaciones Forestales, Centro de Información y Documentación Agropecuario, La Habana, Cuba.

FAO (1988). *An Interim Report on the State of the Forest Resources in the Developing Countries*. FAO, Rome, Italy.

FAO (1993). *Forest resource assessment 1990: tropical countries*. FAO Forestry Paper 112. FAO, Rome, Italy.

Garrido, O.H. and Jaume, M.L. (1984). Catalogo descriptivo de los anfibios y reptiles de Cuba. *Donana Acta Vertebrata* 11 (2): 1–128.

Groombridge, B. (Ed) (1993). *1994 IUCN Red List of Threatened Animals*. IUCN, Gland, Switzerland and Cambridge, U.K. 286 pp.

IUCN (1992). *Protected Areas of the World: A review of national systems. Volume 4: Nearctic and Neotropical.* IUCN, Gland, Switzerland and Cambridge, U.K.

Lee, D.S., Platania, S.P., Burgess, G.H. (1983). *Atlas of North American Freshwater Fishes*. 1983 Supplement. North Carolina Biological Survey Constribution No. 1983–6.

MINAG (1991). *Plan de Accion Forestal para Cuba: documento base*. Ministerio de la Agricultura, Ciudad de la Habana, Cuba.

Morgan, G.S. and Woods, C.A. (1986). Extinction and the zoogeography of West Indian land mammals. *Biological Journal — Linnean Society* 28: 167–203.

Padrón, C.M., Llorente, S. and Menendez, L. (1993). Mangroves of Cuba. In: *Conservation and Sustainable Utilization of Mangrove Forests in Latin America and Africa Regions. Part 1: Latin America*. ITTO/ISME Project PD114/90(F). Pp. 147–154.

Santana, E. (1991). Nature conservation and sustainable development in Cuba. *Conservation Biology* 5(1): 13–16.

Smith, E.E. (1954). *The Forests of Cuba*. Maria Moors Cabot Foundation Publication No. 2.

Vales, M.A., Montes, L. and Alayo, R. (1992). Estado del conocimiento de la biodiversidad en Cuba. In: *La Biodiversidad Biológica de Iberamérica*. Halffter, G. (Ed.). Acta Zoológica Mexicana (n.s.). Programa Iberoamericano de Ciencia y Tecnologia para el Desarrollo.

WCMC (1992). *Global Biodiversity: Status of the Earth's Living Resources*. Chapman and Hall, London xx + 594pp.

Woods, C.A. (1989). Endemic rodents of the West Indies: the end of a splendid isolation. In: *Rodents: A World Survey of Species of Conservation Concern*. Lidicker Jr., W.Z. (Ed.). Occasional Papers of the IUCN Species Survival Commission, No. 4.

Authors: Martin Jenkins and Caroline Harcourt, Cambridge with contributions from Jose Ottenwalder, Florida State Museum and Julio Figueroa-Colon, International Institute of Tropical Forestry, Puerto Rico.

Map 10.1   Cuba

Forest data for Cuba have been digitised from the *Nuevo Atlas Nacional de Cuba: X Flora y Vegetacion: 1 Vegetacion Actual* 1:1 million Academia de Ciencias de Cuba (1989). The vegetation map was prepared by Capote Lopez, R.P., Ricardo Napoles, N.E., Gonzalez Areu, A.V., Garcia Rivera, E.E., Vilamajo Alberdi, D. and Urbino Rodriguez, J.

There are 32 vegetation types depicted on the source map. Out of these, 17 classes (listed below), classified under *Vegetación Natural* (natural vegetation), have been digitised to illustrate the forests on Map 10.1.

1. ***Bosques Tropicales Latifolios (Perennifolios and Subperennifolios):*** *Pluvial — de baja altitud (menor de 400 m), Siempreverde — mesófilo de baja altitud (menor de 400 m), microfilo costero subcostero (monte seco)* and *Semideciduo — mesófilo típico* — have been classified as lowland moist forest; *Pluvial — submontano (400–800 m)*, and *Siempreverde — mesófilo submontano (400–800 m)* — classified as submontane forest; *Pluvial — montano (800–1600 m), Nublado — típico (1600–1900 m)* and *Nublado — bajo, sobre serpentinita (800–1300 m)* — classified as montane forest; *Siempreverde — de ciénaga típico & bajo* and *Semideciduo — mesófilo con humedad fluctuante* — inland swamp forest; and mangroves were digitised directly from the *Siempreverde — de mangles* vegetation category.

2. ***Bosques Tropicales Aciculifolios (Perennifolios):*** *Pinar —- con Pinus caribaea, con caribaea y P. tropicalis, con P. cubensis* and *con P. maestrensis* were amalagamated and are shown as pine forest.

Protected areas boundaries were derived from a printed map (nd, no title) at a scale of 1: 1 million, provided by Antonio Perera Puga (pers comm, 1991) of the *Comisión Rectora del Gran Parque Nacional Sierra Maestra*, Havana, Cuba with accompanying annotations for the mapped conservation areas.

11 Hispaniola

DOMINICAN REPUBLIC		HAITI	
Country area	49,730 sq. km	**Country area**	27,750 sq. km
Land area	48,380 sq. km	**Land area**	27,560 sq. km
Population (mid-1994)	7.8 million	**Population (mid-1994)**	7.0 million
Population growth rate	2.2 per cent	**Population growth rate**	2.3 per cent
Population projected to 2025	11.4 million	**Population projected to 2025**	13.1 million
Gross national product per capita (1992)	US$1040	**Gross national product per capita (1992)**	US$380
Forest cover for 1990 (FAO, 1993)	10,770 sq. km	**Forest cover for 1990 (FAO, 1993)**	230 sq. km
Annual deforestation rate (1981–1990)	2.8 per cent	**Annual deforestation rate (1981–1990)**	4.8 per cent
Industrial roundwood production	6000 cu. m	**Industrial roundwood production**	239,000 cu. m
Industrial roundwood exports	—	**Industrial roundwood exports**	—
Fuelwood and charcoal production	976,000 cu. m	**Fuelwood and charcoal production**	5,812,000 cu.m
Processed wood production	—	**Processed wood production**	14,000 cu. m
Processed wood exports	—	**Processed wood exports**	—

The forested habitats of the Dominican Republic and Haiti, which comprise the island of Hispaniola, are undergoing accelerating degradation. The prospects for conservation are particularly poor in Haiti, but even in the Dominican Republic the forested lands face virtually unrestricted development for tourism and agriculture.

INTRODUCTION

The island of Hispaniola includes Haiti and the Dominican Republic. The topography of the Dominican Republic is dominated by four principal mountain ranges which run northwest to southeast and parallel to each other. The northern most one is the Cordillera Septentrional; the Cordillera Central extends into Haiti and it is in this range that the highest point in the Antilles, Pico Duarte at 3087 m, is found. The ranges in the southern part of the country are the Sierra de Neiba and Sierra de Bahoruco, both reaching more than 2000 m. There is also one minor range, the Cordillera Oriental, in the northeast with an altitude of about 600 m. Much of the island is over 1000 m. The three valleys between the principal ranges are major agricultural regions. A low area, Llanura Costera, in the east of the country is also agricultural land where rice and sugar cane are grown and cattle are pastured.

The deep valley between the mountain ranges of Sierra de Neiba and Sierra de Bahoruco was once a marine channel dividing the area into a large northern and a small southern island. A relic of this is left as Lago Enriquillo, a large saltwater lake 40 m below sea level.

Haiti is also dominated by mountain chains. The Massif de la Hotte in the southwest, the Massif de la Selle in the southeast (this range continues eastwards as the Sierra de Bahoruco), the Chaine des Matheux and Montagnes du Trou-d'Eau in the centre, the Montagnes Noires in the north-centre and the Massif du Nord in the north. The highest point is Pic la Selle (2674 m) in the Massif de Selle. The major valleys are in the northeast and centre of the country. The northwestern peninsula, Presqu'île du Nord-Ouest, is a low ridge with arid areas associated with it (Zanoni, 1989).

Hispaniola's climate is influenced mainly by humid northeast trade winds and as a result, annual precipitation is very variable. In the Dominican Republic, only 350 mm fall in the Neiba Valley while 2750 mm fall at Laguna Limon. In Haiti, rainfall varies from less than 300 mm in the northwest to over 2800 mm, the greatest precipitation falls on the highest mountain summits in the southwest (Ehrlich *et al.*, 1985). There are two rainy and two dry seasons. October and November are usually the wettest months, January and February the driest. Mean annual temperature is around 26°C. A major hurricane occurs every ten to 20 years, causing tremendous damage both environmentally and economically.

Columbus landed on Hispaniola in 1492 and was followed by Spanish colonists who more or less wiped out the Amerindian population (Cook and Borah, 1971; Deagan, 1985; Keagan, 1992). In the late 17th century, French colonists began to establish themselves in the western half of the island, then in 1697, the Treaty of Ryswick divided the island between France and Spain. Both countries became independent in the early 19th century, though Haiti in particular has been plagued by uprisings and coups right up to the present.

Sixty per cent of the Dominican Republic's population are urban dwellers in comparison to 31 per cent in Haiti. The population of the Dominican Republic is multiracial with 68 per cent mulattos, 20 per cent Europeans, 11 per cent Afroamericans and one per cent Asian (SEA/DVS, 1990). Overall population density in the Dominican Republic is 161 people per sq. km; the country's most densely populated regions are the southern coast around the capital city of Santo Domingo and the Cibao Valley in the north. In Haiti, most of the population is of African origin. Overall density, at 254 inhabitants per sq. km, is higher than in the Dominican Republic. Around half a million Haitians are earning a meagre wage working in the Dominican Republic, mainly in the agricultural sector.

The socioeconomic trends in the Dominican Republic have been changing over the last twenty years. The society has shifted from being rural and agriculture-dependent to become urban and services orientated. Sugar was the backbone of the economy and the main export in the 1970s, but with the drop in demand many areas were converted to grow fruit and vegetables. The tourist industry is now an important source of income for the country. In Haiti, the most important crop is coffee, followed by sugar.

The Forests

The vegetation of Hispaniola is usually described in terms of Holdridge's Life Zone System (Holdridge, 1947). Hartshorn *et al.* (1981) and Ehrlich *et al.* (1985) use this classification in their descriptions of the forests of the Dominican Republic and Haiti respectively. However, Hager and Zanoni (1993) have recently published a description of the natural vegetation of the Dominican Republic based on data from botanical field work. They distinguish between dry, semi-deciduous, broadleaved evergreen, pine, gallery and mangrove forests, as well as describing several non-forest formations. Their forest descriptions are used in this chapter.

The dry forests in the Dominican Republic are generally found between elevations of 40 m and 500 m, in areas with rainfall of between 500 and 1000 mm. They are mostly very disturbed. This forest type is now found in the country's southwestern lowlands around Azua, in the Neiba valley and on the Barahona Peninsula and in the northwest in the Ciabo Valley between Monte Cristi and Santiago. It is only on the Barahona Peninsula that large areas of relatively undisturbed dry forest remain.

The dry forests have a canopy at around 10 m with little in the way of a shrub or herb layer. Among the characteristic trees and shrubs are *Guaiacum sanctum*, *G. officinale*, *Phyllostylon rhamnoides*, *Ziziphus rignoni*, *Maytenus buxifolia*, *Capparis* spp. and *Acacia skleroxyla*. On very dry, rocky or sandy ground, arborescent species of Cactaceae such as *Opuntia moniliformis*, *Lemaireocereus hystrix* and *Pilosocereus polygonus* are very frequent. Cactus species are also common in disturbed dry forests where the dominant tree species are the spiny *Prosopis juliflora* and *Acacia macracantha*.

The semi-deciduous forests are transitional between the dry forests and the broadleaved evergreen forests. They are found in the coastal plains and in mountainous regions at elevations between 400 and 900 m. They occur in areas with a distinct arid period and an annual precipitation of 1000 to 1800 mm. In the coastal plains, two different formations can be distinguished —those on rocky ground and those in swampy areas. The characteristic rocky ground formation can be found in Del Este National Park and in the eastern coastal zone between Macao and Cape San Rafael. This forest type has a canopy only 3–10 m high and contains trees such as *Krugiodendron ferreum*, *Coccoloba diversifolia*, *Bursera simaruba*, *Sideroxylon* spp. and *Ateramnus lucidus*. The herb layer is poorly developed and nearly always dominated by *Zamia pumila*. The semi-deciduous forest on swampy ground is characterised by two canopy layers. Generally the upper canopy reaches 20 m and is dominated by *Bucida buceras*. The lower canopy is around 5 m in height and commonly contains *Annona glabra* and *Calophyllum calaba*. Representative formations of this forest are found near the southern part of Bávaro Lagoon and by Hoyo Claro Lagoon. The mountainous semi-deciduous forests are found on the southern slopes of the Sierra de Neiba, the northern slopes of the Cordillera Central and in large areas of the Sierra de Bahoruco. In the Sierra de Neiba,

these forests are dominated by *Swietenia mahagoni* and *Coccoloba diversifolia*.

Two types of broadleaved evergreen forests are distinguished in the Dominican Republic — the rain forests and the cloud forests. The former are mostly found below 500 m; patches occur between Puerto Plata and Miches on the slopes of the Cordillera Septentrional and Cordillera Oriental, on Samaná Peninsula and in the basin of Río Yuma. However, in the Cordillera Central, they may be found as high as 1500 m. Annual precipitation exceeds 2000 mm in the areas where rain forests occur. The upper canopy of this forest type is usually about 25 m high, but in those forests dominated by *Sloanea ilicifolia* (such as in Armando Bermúdez National Park) it can reach 40 m.

The evergreen rain forest formations are quite variable. For instance, in Los Haitises National Park the rain forest occurs on a limestone karst and two associations occur: the *mogote* association of *Coccothrinax* spp., *Leptogonum molle* and *Sapium daphnoides* amongst others; and the valley association including *Oxandra laurifolia*, *Tetragastris balsamifera* and *Dendropanax arboreus*. In other areas, the rain forests are dominated by *Mora abbottii*. This species occurs on the northeastern slopes of the Cordillera Septentrional between Moca and Nagua, in places on the eastern Cordillera Central and particularly in the forests of Loma Quita Espuela and Loma Guaconejo. In Loma La Herradura in the Cordillera Oriental another formation is found; it includes *Buchenavia* spp., *Didymopanax morototoni* and *Omosia krugii*.

Cloud forests are found in the high mountains, between 600 m and 2300 m. They are characterised by an abundance of epiphytes. In areas between 600 and 1250 m in elevation, on steep northern slopes and in mountain valleys, the palm cloud forest, or *manaclar*, is common. This forest type is dominated by *Prestoea montana* and tree ferns *Cyathea* spp. In areas of the eastern Sierra Bahoruco and in parts of the Cordillera Central above 1200 m the cloud forests are dominated by *Didymopanax tremulus*, often in association with species of *Magnolia*. In the western part of the Sierra de Neiba and in the Valle Nuevo Scientific Reserve at altitudes between 1800 and 2200 m the cloud forest is dominated by *Podocarpus aristulatus*.

Elfin woodlands are known only from the top of Loma Nalga de Maco between 1800 and 1900 m. They have a canopy at only 5 m and are characterised by an association of *Coccoloba pauciflora* and *Podocarpus hispaniolensis*.

Pine forests of the native *Pinus occidentalis* are the natural vegetation in high altitude zones of the Cordillera Central, Sierra de Bahoruco and, to a lesser degree, in the Sierra de Neiba.

In Haiti, the subtropical moist forest life zone is the most extensive zone. The natural vegetation of this zone is a well developed heterogenous forest of broadleaved trees, but clearing for agriculture has reduced the forest to mere remnants. *Catalpa longisiliqua* and mahogany *Swietenia* sp. are characteristic tree species, while the royal palm *Roystonea regia* is very common on limestone soils (Ehrlich *et al.*, 1985).

In Haiti, the dry forest zone is the second largest life zone. It is characterised by *Phyllostylon brasiliense*, *Prosopis juliflora* and *Guaiacum officinalis* (Ehrlich *et al.*, 1985).

The subtropical lower montane rain forest includes most of the remaining pine (*Pinus occidentalis*) forest in Haiti.

The natural vegetation of the other zones has not been described by Erhlich *et al.* (1985), little if any of the forest remains.

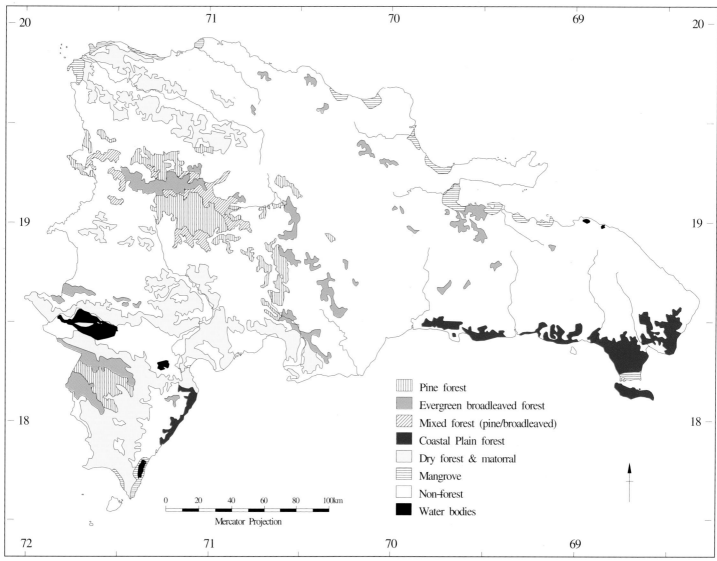

Figure 11.1   The forest ecosystems in the Dominican Republic, based on 1984 aerial photographs.
Source: after Schubert (1993)

Mangroves

The largest areas of mangrove are found in the northeast of the Dominican Republic at Manzanillo, Montecristi and Samaná Bay. Analysis of aerial photographs taken between 1983 and 1984 indicated that approximately 325 sq. km of mangroves remained in the Dominican Republic (SEA/DVS, 1990). Common species include *Conocarpus erectus*, *Rhizophora mangle*, *Laguncularia racemosa* and *Avicennia germinans*.

Mangrove forests in the Dominican Republic are particularly threatened by development for the tourist trade. Extensive areas are being devastated in Punta Cana, one of the largest resorts in the eastern portion of the country, between Puerto Plata and Samaná in the north and northeast and between La Romana and Boca de Yuma in the southeast. The development of Montecristi and the Barahona Peninsula is expected to cause further devastation on the northwest and southwest coasts.

Ehrlich *et al.* (1985) reported that there were a total of 224 sq. km of mangrove in Haiti, with major areas in the Bay of Caracol and L'Estère. In later papers (Thorbjarnarson, 1988; Paryski *et al.*; 1989), it was estimated that there were about 180 sq. km of mangroves. Mangroves are used for charcoal and polewood, but this does not yet have a significant impact. It is forbidden by law to cut these forests, but this is not enforced. Nevertheless, the mangrove forests are one of the least threatened ecosystems in Haiti (Paryski *et al.*, 1989).

Forest Resources and Management

When Columbus arrived in Hispaniola, the island was almost entirely forested. Today, about 90 per cent of the forests in the Dominican Republic have vanished due to human activities (SEA/DVS, 1990). At the beginning of this century, 40,000 sq. km or 85 per cent of the country was forested, this was reduced to 34,000 sq km by 1940, to 11,000 sq. km in 1973 and to only 5000 sq. km or 10 per cent of the Dominican Republic by 1986 (SEA/DVS, 1990). FAO (1993) gives the considerably higher estimate of 10,770 sq. km remaining in 1990, of which 8540 sq. km was closed broadleaved forest.

DIRENA, using aerial photographs from 1983–84, detailed the land use in the Dominican Republic as shown in Table 11.1 (Republica Dominica, 1992). According to this report, there were approximately 3000 sq. km each of both pine and broadleaved forests remaining in the country at that time. No recent, accurate map of the forests in the country has been found for this Atlas, therefore a sketch map based on 1984 aerial photographs (Schubert, 1993) has been reproduced here as Figure 11.1.

The first documented attempt to regulate clearing of forests in the Dominican Republic was in 1884, when all clearing near river beds and springs was banned and farmers were ordered to keep five per cent of their property in forest (Reynoso *et al.*, 1988). Since then, a total of 63 laws, two executive orders, three resolutions and several decrees have been legislated for the protection of forests (J. Ottenwalder, in litt. 1993).

While about 26 government agencies are involved in the management of natural resources in the Dominican Republic, in an administrative and/or advisory capacity, two institutions — the General Directorate of Forests (DGF) and the National Forestry Technical Commission (CONATEF) — are directly invested with management authority for the administration and management of the forests. A third institution, the Directorate of National Parks (DPN), is involved when the forests occur in conservation areas.

DGF was created in 1962 both to enforce legislation prohibiting tree cutting and to preserve national security in forest areas. The DGF is also responsible for Government reafforestation projects and controls the production and distribution of charcoal. It, however, lacks an adequate budget and trained personnel.

The National Technical Forestry Commission (CONATEF) was established in 1982 to develop a national plan for the organisation of the forestry sector. In 1985, the role of CONATEF was expanded to include forest preservation, development and policy and it thereby became the primary institution for the administration of forest resources, while DGF became the agency for implementing forest policy.

In 1967, in an attempt to enforce forestry regulations, all sawmills were closed and the cutting of trees was declared illegal throughout the country. In 1986, Operación Selva Negra was launched by the government of the Dominican Republic to enforce these regulations (Ottenwalder, 1989). It was intended to stop illegal, indiscriminate deforestation and to give CONATEF time to develop a programme for the sustainable utilisation of dry forests. It lasted for several months and, although cosmetic in nature and achievements, it was highly

Figure 11.2   Land in Haiti covered with forest having at least 60% tree coverage.

Source: Ehrlich *et al.* (1985)

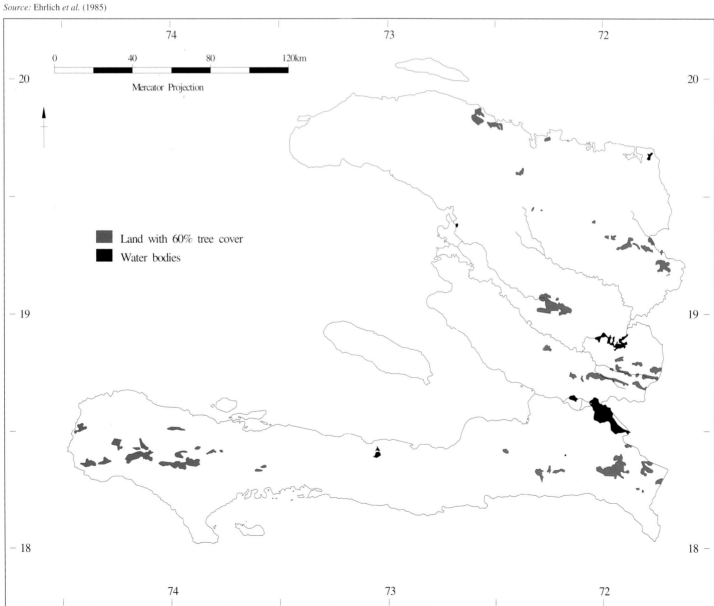

Table 11.1   Land use in the Dominican Republic

Land Use	Area (sq. km)	% of land
Urban zone	361	0.8
Sugar cane	4,074	8.4
Other agriculture	12,883	26.6
Pastures	13,736	28.4
Pine forests	2,950	6.1
Broadleaved forests	2,893	6.0
Dry forests	8,055	16.7
Matorral/Brushland	2,094	4.3
Wetlands	210	0.4
Others	1,124	2.3
Total	48,380	100

Source: Republica Dominica (1992)

successful as an extension and public relations exercise (J. Ottenwalder, in litt, 1993).

Interest and efforts to develop a national programme for forest management rose during the late 1960s. Inventories of forest resources were conducted between 1967 and 1974 by OEA and FAO, while integrated conservation-development projects, targeting important watersheds and rural areas and often including reafforestation plans, began in 1970.

From its inception to 1985, DGF has reforested about 79 sq. km, mostly with the exotic *Pinus caribea* rather than the indigenous *P. occidentalis*. Few follow-up evaluations of the plantations occur, but it is estimated that about 65 per cent of them survive (Peña, 1988). The reafforestation programme has been hampered by a scarcity of trained professionals, a lack of financial and technical support and inadequate institutional support.

FAO (1994) reported that production of fuelwood and charcoal in the Dominican Republic was less than one million cubic metres in 1992. However, the government (Republica Dominica, 1992) has calculated that yearly consumption is 3.9 million cu. m and that it will increase at an annual rate of 1.4 per cent. Forests with a potential for fuelwood production are estimated to cover between 2000 and 3000 sq. km, but average yields are so low (about 2 cu. m/ha/year) that, even if the forests were managed, they could not satisfy the projected demand. In the year 2000, the annual demand for firewood is expected to be 4,760,000 cu. m (Republica Dominica, 1992). Around 75 per cent of the energy for domestic use comes from the forests; they supply, overall, about 29 per cent of the country's total energy demands.

As from January 1987, a five year ban was passed on the capture, killing or exploitation of all native wild vertebrates in the Dominican Republic (Ottenwalder, 1989). This was extended in February 1992 for another ten years. Excluded from the decree are species considered to be agriculture pests and exotic predators. Enforcement of these regulations is poor.

In Haiti, Holdridge (1947) calculated that forests, in the absence of humans, could potentially occupy 55 per cent of the land area. However, very little of this remains. Even as early as 1954, it was reported that only eight or nine per cent of the land surface was forested (Burns, 1954). In 1978, it was estimated that 6.7 per cent of the land was covered with forest having at least 60 per cent tree coverage (Figure 11.2); 659 sq. km (36 per cent) had a canopy cover of 80–100 per cent; while 1188 sq. km had a canopy cover between 60 and 80 per cent (Ehrlich *et al.*,

1985). The single largest stretch of forest remaining in the mid-1980s was the 264 sq. km stand of pine forest in the southeast of the country. Paryski *et al.*, (1989) reported that forest cover in the country was less than 1.5 per cent, while FAO (1993) estimates that only 230 sq. km of forest (0.8 per cent of the country's land area) remained in 1990.

In Haiti it is the Division of Natural Resources (DNR) within the Ministry of Agriculture (MARNDR — Ministere de L'Agriculture, des Ressources Naturelles et du Developpement Rural) which is responsible for the protection of forests, watersheds, coastal resources and other natural resources. Most of its efforts so far have been restricted to regulating hunting and fishing and to very limited reforestation projects (Paryski et al., 1989). Low budgets, a lack of trained personnel, no clear policies and changing government priorities have prevented any serious conservation efforts.

Deforestation

The earliest Amerindian settlers on Hispaniola were primarily hunter gatherers who had little impact on the forest. Even though the Tainos, who arrived later, were practising intensive agriculture by the time they were discovered, they were concentrated along the coast and their population density was low so that they too had a minimal effect on the forests (Lugo *et al.*, 1981).

The forests have diminished only since European colonisation. Between 1630 and 1880s, as in many of the Caribbean islands, the lowland forests were gradually converted to plantations of sugar cane and African slaves were brought in to work on the land. After this period, following the abolition of slavery and the economic collapse of monocultures, some destruction of montane forests took place as many of the freed slaves moved to the mountains (Lugo *et al.*, 1981). The scarcity of lowlands and valleys in Haiti meant that the upland forests there were exploited early on. In both countries, the temporary rise in the price of sugar cane at the end of the First World War meant that some plantations were extended considerably (J. Ottenwalder, in litt. 1993).

In the Dominican Republic, devastation of pine and broadleaved forests is mostly caused by clearing for agriculture and pasture and by the demand for forest products. Deterioration of the dry forests is due mainly to collecting of wood for charcoal and fuel, for both domestic and industrial purposes (Ottenwalder, 1989). If the government's estimates (Republica Dominica, 1992) of annual consumption of firewood are correct, the outlook for the dry forests in particular is extremely bleak. FAO (1993) estimates deforestation in the Dominican Republic to be 351 sq. km each year, an annual rate of 2.8 per cent.

Table 11.2 Status of locally threatened species within the Dominican Republic

	Endangered	Vulnerable	Rare	Unknown
Fish	–	–	–	2
Amphibians	–	–	–	–
Reptiles	8	13	6	–
Birds	4	24	6	21
Mammals	3	–	1	1
Total	15	37	13	24

Source: SEA/DVS, 1990

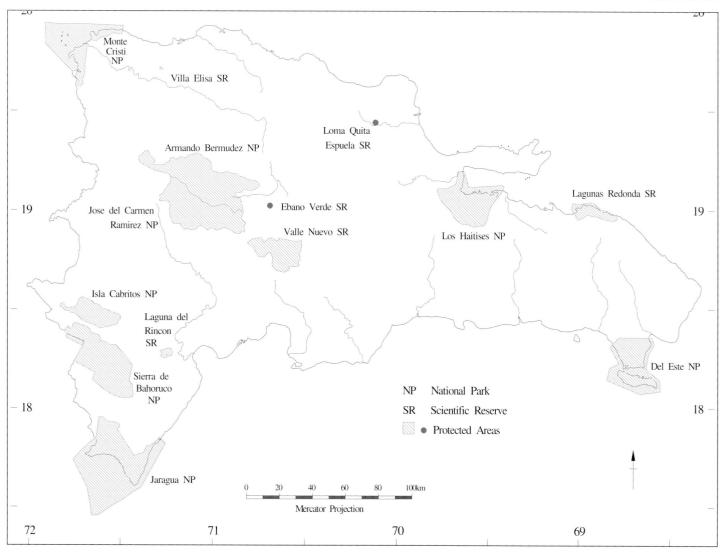

Figure 11.3   Protected areas in the Dominican Republic in IUCN's categories I–IV

Russell (1988) attempted to measure the rate of deforestation in the western half of the Dominican Republic by comparing satellite photographs taken in 1972, 1979 and 1986. He calculated that 2115 sq. km of hardwood and pine forests disappeared between 1972 and 1986, giving an annual deforestation of 141 sq. km per year. During the same period, annual deforestation of the subtropical dry and thorn forests was calculated to be 106 sq. km. Most of the forested land was cleared for agriculture and pasture.

The same problems occur in Haiti where, after many generations of land abuse, there is now a tradition of land stewardship in the country by which most peasants expect to exploit the land. Indeed, peasant life is almost totally dependent on cutting trees for construction, fuelwood and charcoal and for clearing new agricultural land to replace that rendered unproductive by overuse and erosion (Paryski *et al.*, 1989).

In addition, large quantities of timber were cut and exported from Haiti as early as the 19th century, for instance in 1845, 18,600 cu. m of mahogany alone were exported (Paryski *et al.*, 1989). It is estimated that by 2008 only one of Haiti's river basins will have any forest cover remaining. Paul Paryski (in litt., 1993) working for UNDP in Haiti, estimates annual deforestation rate in the country to be 3.8 per cent. However FAO (1993) give the higher figure of 4.8 per cent; this, though, is only 15 sq. km each year.

Biodiversity

The flora of the island of Hispaniola is the second most diverse for the Caribbean islands. Of the estimated 5000 flowering plants and conifers, 30–33 per cent are considered endemic (Zanoni, 1989). The areas with highest rainfall are the most diverse with the highest number of endemics.

There is little monitoring of the status of the plants on Hispaniola, but a considerable number are threatened. For instance, on the Dominican Republic the endemic *Cryptorhiza haitiensis* and the palm cacheo *Pseudophoenix ekmanii* are being eliminated by commercial use.

Hispaniola has the highest faunal diversity and levels of endemism of the West Indies, with the Dominican Republic having the highest diversity and endemism in vertebrate groups of all the Caribbean islands. As on the other islands, most (18 of 20) of the native mammals remaining on Hispaniola are bats. Haiti used to have at least 28 species of native terrestrial mammals, but now only two survive (Woods, 1983; Paryski *et al.*, 1989). These are the endangered Haitian solenodon *Solenodon paradoxus* and the rare Hispaniolan huita *Plagiodontia aedium*. A species recovery plan has been completed for *S. paradoxus* and a major reserve on the north side of Pic Macaya has been proposed to protect it; this species is considered to be the highest priority for con-

Montane rain forests in the Ebano Verde Area, Central Dominican Republic.   (WWF/Mauri Rautkari)

servation in Haiti (Ottenwalder, 1992a; Woods *et al.*, 1992; Woods and Ottenwalder, 1992). The other species on the island listed as threatened by IUCN (Groombridge, 1983) is the Cuban flower bat *Phyllonycteris poeyi*. There are 12 introduced species of mammal (Woods and Ottenwalder, 1992) of which the mongoose *Herpestes auropunctatus* and rat *Rattus norvegicus* have a considerable adverse impact on the native fauna.

A total of 136 resident and 118 migratory birds have been recorded in the Dominican Republic, 22 of these are endemic to the island (SEA/DVS, 1990). The same eight bird species (five endemics) are listed as threatened in Haiti as in the Dominican Republic; four are at risk mainly as a result of deforestation. (Collar *et al.*, 1992). The Hispaniolan hawk *Buteo ridgwayi* and white-winged warbler *Xenoligea montana* have all but vanished from Haiti as most of their forest habitat has been cut down; the latter is, however, found in some protected areas. La Selle thrush *Turdus swalesi* and the chat tanager *Calyptophilus frugivorus* are in protected areas in both countries, but neither species is considered safe (Woods and Ottenwalder, 1992). The fifth endemic species, the rufous-breasted cuckoo *Hyetornis rufigularis* is found in many habitat types and over a wide range of altitudes. It is hunted, as medicinal food, and its scarcity may be due to the impact of pesticides and fertilizers as well as to the general degradation of the island's natural vegetation (Collar *et al.*, 1992). The ground warbler *Microligea montana* and the Hispaniolan parrot *Amazona ventralis* are also considered to be threatened in Haiti (P. Paryski, in litt.), although they are not listed by Collar *et al.* (1992) as globally threatened. Species recovery plans have been completed for the black-capped petrel *Pterodroma hasitata*, the white-winged warbler and the Hispaniolan crossbill *Loxia megaplaga* (Ottenwalder, 1992b, 1992c, 1992d; Woods *et al.*, 1992; Woods and Ottenwalder, 1992).

Sixty species of amphibian have been recorded on the island, all belong to the order Anura, while 43 belong to the genus *Eleutherodactylus* (Schubert, 1993). *Hyla vasta* is threatened in both countries, while *E. semipalmatus* is threatened in Haiti (Groombridge, 1993). The cane toad *Bufo marinus* and the frog *Rana catesbeiana* have been introduced.

There are 141 reptiles on the island, 117 of which are endemic and two lizards are introduced (Schubert, 1993). There is still a significant number of the threatened American crocodile *Crocodylus acutus* on the island. However, numbers in Lake Enriquillo, which was considered to be one of the largest concentrations of the species, have declined from an estimated 500 in 1980 to only 100 in 1992 (J. Ottenwalder, in

litt. 1993). A recovery plan is being implemented by a consortium of government institutions and NGOs. Six other reptiles (excluding the marine turtles) are threatened in the Dominican Republic, three of these are also listed for Haiti (Groombridge, 1993).

There are 70 species of fresh or brackish water fish recorded on the island of which 22 are endemic. Numbers of invertebrates are not known. Eight species are listed as threatened in the Dominican Republic, with six of these given for Haiti also (Groombridge, 1993). The two listed as vulnerable are *Phylolestes ethelae* and *Battus zetides*, the latter is in both countries.

There are 89 species or subspecies of vertebrates in the Dominican Republic that are considered to be locally threatened, their status is shown in Table 11.2 (SEA/DVS, 1990). Of these, 13 reptiles and one bird, the spotted rail *Pardirallus maculatus*, are not found in a protected area.

Conservation Areas

The first of the Dominican Republic's conservation areas were set up in the 1950s when two stretches of montane forest in the Cordillera Central were gazetted as national parks. There is now a network of 24 conservation areas, although not all of these are in IUCN's categories I–IV (Table 11.3, Figure 11.3), and they protect representative areas of the country's ecosystems. Nevertheless, these protected areas do not exist as a structured national system at present. A systematic, comprehensive evaluation of them and their legislation is required to achieve national conservation objectives. The government has failed to allocate the financial and administrative resources necessary to implement the laws adequately and truly protect the conservation areas (Reynoso *et al.*, 1988). Park guards are generally underpaid and inadequately trained. Monte Cristi National Park is considered to be the most threatened of the conservation areas.

Fifteen new conservation areas have been proposed (SEA/DVS, 1990). These areas were selected for their potential contribution to national biodiversity conservation and include habitat types that are not under protection in the existing network. There are also proposals to expand some of the present protected areas, and to manage others as Biosphere Reserves.

The National Park Directorate (DNP) in the Dominican Republic was created in 1974. It is responsible for developing, managing, regulating and protecting the country's conservation areas. The institution has been affected by budget limitations, political influences and its role overlapping with that of DGF.

In various protected areas, a co-management strategy has been developed with local or national NGOs cooperating with DNP to protect natural resources, develop and implement management plans for the conservation areas or work in surrounding buffer zones. For instance, Fundación Quito Espuela works in Loma Quita Espuela Scientific Reserve, Progressio in Ebano Verde Scientific Reserve and Grupo Jaragua in Jaragua National Park.

Management plans have been written for three of the national parks (Jaragua, Los Haitises and Del Este) and there are draft plans for two others: José del Carmen Ramírez and Armando Bermudez. The management plan for Jaragua has, since 1991, been successfully implemented; the plan for Del Este was scheduled for implementation beginning in 1993/1994. All the conservation areas have suffered some form of exploitation (Reynoso *et al.*, 1988) and, in addition, government agencies

Table 11.3 Conservation areas of the Dominican Republic

Existing conservation areas in IUCN's categories I–IV are listed. The large wildlife sanctuary (for whales) is not listed.

National Parks	Area (sq. km)
Del Este	420
Isla Cabritos	24
Jaragua	1,374
José Armando Bermùdez	766
José del Carmen Ramírez	738
Los Haitises	1,600
Monte Cristi+	1,310
Sierra de Bahoruco	800

Scientific Reserves	
Ebano Verde	23
Laguna del Rincón	48
Lagunas Redonda y Limón	101
Loma Quita Espuela	73
Valle Nuevo	409
Villa Elisa/Dr Orlando Franco	0.2

Historic National Parks	
La Isabela°	0.3
La Vega Vieja°	nd

Total	11,435

+   includes Cayos Siete Hermanos Bird Sanctuary
°   not shown on Figure 11.3
Source: WCMC (unpublished data)

other than DNP often carry out programmes which foster the invasion of parks and reserves.

As well as the areas controlled by DNP, there are three *Zonas Vedadas*, two managed by the General Directorate of Forests and the third, the Rio Nizao watershed, managed jointly by DNP and DGF. The sizes and IUCN category of these are unknown.

In Haiti, a decree of 1968 declared eight sites as national parks or nature sites (IUCN, 1992), but these were mostly small areas of historic interest. They were all less than 50 hectares except for the 22 sq. km La Citadelle. In 1979, the Institut de Sauvegarde du Patrimoine National (ISPAN) was created to protect and conserve Haiti's natural and cultural heritage and in 1983 two new parks (La Viste and Pic Macaya) were gazetted by presidential decree, with financial help from USAID. However, the decree creating the new parks failed to assign final responsibility for them to a single government agency and there has been some conflict between ISPAN and MARNDR as a result. Neither organisation have the staff or budget to adequately protect the parks. Both areas suffer from invasion by peasants, who clear the forests to plant crops. The eight areas designated earlier are still protected, but they are not listed in Table 11.4 as they are not in IUCN's categories I–IV.

Management plans have been written for Haiti's three largest protected areas — La Citadelle (22 sq. km, category V), La Visite and Pic Macaya (Woods *et al.*, 1992 — shown on Figure 11.2). The World Bank's Forestry and Environmental project proposes to consolidate the management of all the parks in Haiti under the administrative control of the Service for the Protection of the Environment (SPE) of MARNDR.

A national marine park at Les Arcadins, about 30 km from Port-au-Prince, has been proposed as a conservation and eco-tourism site by WWF.

Conservation Initiatives

In 1991, a Forestry Code for the management and administration of the Dominican Republic's forest resources and a Strategy for the Conservation of Biological Diversity in the Dominican Republic were prepared; the former by CONATEF/SURENA and the latter by the NGO Grupo Jaragua. A Forestry Action Plan is currently under review. In addition, a Coastal Zone Management Plan for the entire coast of the country was prepared and released by the Oficina Nacional de Planificación (ONAPLAN) in 1993.

Participation of Dominican NGOs in environmental issues has increased considerably, particularly since the mid-1980s. Today about 50 of these organisations are directly or indirectly involved in the sector. About 20 are committed to the protection, conservation and promotion of natural resources and biological diversity, with programmes involving protected areas, endangered species, environmental education, community development, sustainable development and control of pollutants amongst other things.

Over the past 25 years there has been aid to the forestry sector from a variety of international organisations. This includes assistance with resource assessment, forest management, education, technical training, watershed management and institutional strengthening from organisations such as OAS, FAO, UNDP and IICA.

There are also other international governmental and non-governmental organisations involved in the promotion and support of biodiversity conservation and sustainable development in the Dominican Republic. The groups involved at present include USAID, TNC, WWF, World Bank, IUCN, OEA, the Center for Marine Conservation, GTZ and the Spanish Cooperation Agency.

USAID has financed a massive reafforestation and agroforestry project in Haiti through the Pan American Development Foundation. A number of private environmental lobby groups have been established in the last few years and they have helped the public become aware of Haiti's enormous environmental problems. The Haitian government also prepared an environmental plan which was presented to UNCED in 1992.

An environmental unit has been established recently by UNDP in Haiti. Its activities include: facilitating and coordinating the programmes, strategies and projects of the donor community, the NGOs and the private sector in Haiti, mainly through an inter-agency committee; monitoring and documenting the status of the environment in Haiti using databases, a GIS, satellite imagery and useful environmental indicators; fulfilling UNDP directives concerning the environment, especially those resulting from UNCED and Agenda 21; and facilitating the preparation and execution of environmental projects.

Table 11.4 Conservation areas of Haiti

Existing conservation areas in IUCN's categories I–IV are listed.

Natural National Parks	
La Visite	20
Pic Macaya	55

Total	75

Source: WCMC (unpublished data)

Unfortunately the September 1991 coup d'etat and the consequent political crisis have resulted in the suspension of most of the local government and internationally funded programmes that were established to address conservation and environmental problems. For instance, in 1992, USAID terminated funding to the University of Florida Biosphere Reserve Project, which was set up to establish a functional biosphere reserve around Pic Macaya (2347 m) to protect its exceptional biodiversity, its last relictual cloud forests and the watercatchment zone for Haiti's southern peninsula. However, after a major lobbying effort, USAID agreed to continue conservation activities in the Pic Macaya area by funding a local NGO, and the Haitian government has assigned soldiers to protect the reserve, a measure which has halted much of the destruction of the remaining forests there.

The situation in Haiti remains very difficult due to the continuing and unresolved political crisis and an OAS trade embargo which has further impoverished the peasant farmers, forcing them to destroy their environment and Haiti's forests merely to survive.

References

Burns (1954). *Report to the Government of Haiti on Forest Policy and its Implementation.* Report 346, United Nations, Fao, Rome.

Collar, N.J., Gonzaga, L.P., Krabbe, N., Madroño Nieto, A., Naranjo, L.G., Parker III, T.A. and Wege, D.C. (1992). *Threatened Birds of the Americas. The ICBP/IUCN Red Data Book.* ICBP, Cambridge, U.K.

Cook, S.F. and Borah, W. (1971). The aboriginal population of Hispaniola. In: *Essays in Population History. Volume I: Mexico and the Caribbean.* Cook, S.F. and Borah, W. (eds). University of California Press, Berkeley. Pp. 376–410.

Deagan, K. (1985). Spanish-Indian interactions in sixteenth century Florida and the Caribbean. In: *Cultures in Contact.* Fitzhugh, W. (ed.). Smithsonian Institute Press, Washington, D.C. Pp. 281–318.

Ehrlich, M., Conway, F., Adrien, N., Le Beau, F., Lewis, L. Lauwerysen, H., Lowenthal, I., Mayda, Y., Paryski, P., Smucker, G., Talbot, J. and Wilcox, E. (1985). *Haiti: Country Environmental Profile, a field study.* USAID.

FAO (1993) *Forest resources assessment 1990: Tropical countries.* FAO Forestry Paper 112. FAO, Rome, Italy.

FAO (1994). *FAO Yearbook: Forest Products 1981–1992.* FAO Forestry series No. 27, FAO Statistics Series No. 116. FAO, Rome, Italy.

Groombridge, B. (Ed). (1993). *1994 IUCN Red List of Threatened Animals.* IUCN, Gland, Switzerland and Cambridge, U.K.

Hartshorn, G., Antonini, G., DuBois, R., Harcharik, D., Heckadon, S., Newton, H., Quesada, C., Shores, J. and Staples, G. (1981). *The Dominican Republic: Country Environmental Profile, a field study.* USAID

Hager, J. and Zanoni, Th.A. (1993). La vegetación natural de la Republica Dominica: Una nueva clasificación. *Moscosoa* 7: 39–81.

Holdridge, L.R. (1947). *The Pine Forest and Adjacent Mountain Vegetation of Haiti Considered from the Standpoint of a New Climatic Classification of Plant Formations.* Unpublished PhD dissertation. University of Michigan, Anne Arbor, Michigan.

IUCN (1992). *Protected Areas of the World: A review of national systems. Volume 4: Nearctic and Neotropical.* IUCN, Gland, Switzerland and Cambridge, U.K.

Keagan, W.F. (1992). *The People Who Discovered Columbus: The Prehistory of the Bahamas.* University Press of Florida, Gainseville, Florida.

Lugo, A.E., Schmidt, R. and Brown, S. (1981). Tropical forests in the Caribbean. *Ambio* 10(6): 318–324.

Ottenwalder, J.A. (1989). A summary of conservation trends in the Dominican Republic. In: *Biogeography of the West Indies: past present and future.* Woods, C.A. (ed.). Sandhill Crane Press, Inc., Gainseville, Florida, U.S.A. Pp. 845–850.

Ottenwalder, J.A. (1992a). *Recovery Plan for the Hispaniola Solenodon in the Massif de la Hotte, Haiti.* Unpublished technical report prepared for the Macaya National Park Project/University of Florida and MacArthur Foundation. 37pp.

Ottenwalder, J.A. (1992b). *Recovery Plan for the Black-capped petrel* (Pterodroma hasitata) *in Southern Haiti.* Unpublished technical report prepared for the Macaya National Park Project/University of Florida and MacArthur Foundation. 18pp.

Ottenwalder, J.A. (1992c). *Recovery Plan for the White-winged warbler* (Xenoligea montana) *in Southern Haiti.* Unpublished technical report prepared for the Macaya National Park Project/University of Florida and MacArthur Foundation. 13pp.

Ottenwalder, J.A. (1992d). *Recovery Plan for the Hispaniolan crossbill* (Loxia megaplaga) *in Southern Haiti.* Unpublished technical report prepared for the Macaya National Park Project/University of Florida and MacArthur Foundation. 13pp.

Paryski, P., Woods, C.A. and Sergile, F. (1989). Conservation strategies and the preservation of biological diversity in Haiti. In: *Biogeography of the West Indies: past present and future.* Woods, C.A. (ed.). Sandhill Crane Press, Inc., Gainseville, Florida, U.S.A. Pp. 855–878.

Peña, J.M, (1988). *Informe Tecnico del Día de Campo Forestal, December 11, 1988.* Fundación Miguel L. de Peña Garcia Inc. Santo Domingo.

Republica Dominica (1992). *Republica Dominica: Informe Nacional 1991.* Conferencia Mundial de las Naciones Unidas sobre medio ambiente y desarrollo, Brasil. Santo Domingo, Editora Taller.

Reynoso, F.A., Dotzauer, H., Herrera, H.C., Garcia, J.R., Rodriguez, A.A., Geraldes, F.X. and McCluskey, D. (1988). *The Dominican Republic: Biological Diversity Assessment.* USAID.

Russell, A.F. (1988). *Uso del Suelo y Degradación Ambiental en la Zona Occidental de la Republica Dominicana Durante el Periodo 1972–1986: Una Evaluación Cuantitativa de las Variaciones de la Cobertura Vegetal con la Ayuda de Imágenes de Saélites Landsat.* Unpublished thesis, Universidad Católica Madre y Maestra, Santiago, Dominican Republic.

Schubert, A. (1993). Conservation of biological diversity in the Dominican Republic. *Oryx* 27(2): 115–121.

SEA/DVS (1990). *La Diversidad Biológica en la República Dominicana.* Reporte preparado por el Departamento de Vida Silvestre para el Servicio Alemán de Cooperación Social-Técnica y WWF-US. Secretaría de Estado de Agricultura, SURENA/DVS, Santo Domingo. 266 pp.

Thorbjarnarson, J.B. (1988). The status and ecology of the

American crocodile in Haiti. *Bulletin Florida State Museum Biological Science* 33(1): 1–86.

Woods, C.A. (1983). Biological survey of Haiti: status of the endangered birds and mammals. *National Geographic Society Research Reports* 15: 759–768.

Woods, C.A. and Ottenwalder, J.A. (1992). *The Natural History of Southern Haiti*. Special Publication, Florida Museum of Natural History. Pp. 211.

Woods, C.A., Sergile, F.E. and Ottenwalder, J.A. (1992). *Stewardship Plan for the National Parks and Natural Areas of Haiti*. Special Publication, Florida Museum of Natural History. Pp. 334.

Zanoni, T. (1989). Hispaniola. In: *Floristic Inventory of Tropical Forests: the Status of Plant Systematics, Collections, and Vegetation, plus Recommendations for the Future*. Campbell, D.G. and Hammond, H.D. (eds). The New York Botanical Garden, New York, U.S.A. Pp. 336–340.

Authors: Caroline Harcourt and Jose Ottenwalder, of Florida Museum of Natural History; with The Forest section and other information contributed by Andreas Schubert and Dieter Hoener of Servicio Alemán, further contributions from Paul Paryski, UNDP, Haiti and Charles Woods, Florida Museum of Natural History.

12 Jamaica

Country area	10,990 sq. km
Land area	10,830 sq. km
Population (mid-1994)	2.5 million
Population growth rate	1.8 per cent
Population projected to 2025	3.5 million
Gross national product per capita (1992)	US$1340
Forest cover for 1989 (see Map)	3181 sq. km
Forest cover for 1990 (FAO, 1993)	2390 sq. km
Annual deforestation rate (1981–1990)	7.2 per cent
Industrial roundwood production	156,000 cu. m
Industrial roundwood exports	—
Fuelwood and charcoal production	13,000 cu. m
Processed wood production	28,000 cu. m
Processed wood exports	—

Centuries of deforestation caused by clearing land for farming and settlement has reduced the area of natural, undisturbed forest on Jamaica to a tiny proportion of the original. It is only the forest in the most remote, inaccessible and steepest part of the island that has survived undisturbed.

In spite of concern about Jamaica's forests being first expressed over a century ago, lack of funds has meant that little has ever been done to preserve them. The major destructive element has been widespread agriculture mismanagement.

INTRODUCTION

Jamaica is the third largest island in the Caribbean, it is 236 km long and between 35 and 82 km wide. The island has a central backbone of peaks and plateaux running the length of the island, which reaches 2256 m at Blue Mountain Peak in the east. The high mountains are flanked by limestone plateaux and hills, occupying the central and western two thirds of the island. This highland interior is surrounded by a flatter coastal strip that is narrow in the north, while the southern coastal plains are broad and include flat alluvial areas, swamps and dry hills.

Over half the island is above 300 m, approximately 80 per cent is hilly or mountainous and more than 50 per cent has slopes exceeding 20 degrees. The impact of years of shifting agriculture and removal of forest cover on steep slopes with high rainfall and erodible soils has created a situation of severe environmental degradation in many watersheds. Most of the rivers in the country are short and fast flowing.

Temperatures in the coastal lowlands are fairly uniform with an average of 27°C, ranging from 23°C in the coldest months of January and February to 28°C in July and August, the warmest months. On Blue Mountain Peak, the mean annual average temperature is only 13°C. Precipitation is very varied both within and between years and on the different parts of the island. Mean annual rainfall over the whole island is about 1960 mm, with the capital city of Kingston receiving less than 1300 mm and the Blue Mountains and north-east coast having over 3300 mm (CEP, 1987). May and October are the wettest months, March and June the driest. Hurricanes occur fairly frequently and can cause considerable damage.

Jamaica's population is 48 per cent rural and the incomes of these people are generally low. Most are small farmers living in the hilly interior. Approximately half a million people live in the capital city of Kingston. Population density overall is high, around 231 individuals per sq. km. The original inhabitants were Arawaks; Spanish colonists arrived in 1494 and by 1655 the Indians had all but disappeared, decimated by disease. When the British took control of the island they brought African slaves to labour on the plantations and now most of the population are of African origin. The island became independent in 1962.

Tourism is the country's largest foreign exchange earner. Main export crops are sugarcane, bananas, citrus and cocoa. Blue Mountain coffee is also exported. Jamaica is the world's third largest producer of alumina and bauxite and these are major sources of income.

The Forests

Jamaica's forests are as species rich as any on the other Caribbean islands, but not as diverse or as tall as those on the continent (Kelly et al., 1988). The first comprehensive account of the island's plant communities was that of Asprey and Robbins (1953); their system largely followed that of Beard (1944, 1955). An updated, expanded classification scheme has been proposed by Grossman et al., (1992) and expanded on by Iremonger et al. (in press). However, their vegetation categorisation is too detailed to be described here. Similarly, the detailed descriptions of forest types in the Blue Mountains provided by Grubb and Tanner (1976) and Tanner (1986) are too lengthy for inclusion. Instead, most of the following is from the simplified version in FAO/UNEP (1981).

Wet limestone forests occur mainly between 300 and 750 m with the largest areas remaining in the Cockpit Country and John Crow Mountains; other areas are located in Mt Diablo and on Dolphin Head. Their canopy is more or less closed with a height of 15–18 m, though in deep valleys emergents of *Terminalia latifolia* and *Cedrela odorata* rise to 25–30 m in height. Other common large trees include santa maria *Calophyllum brasiliense*, *Pithecellobium alexandri*, breadnut *Brosium alicastrum*, sweetwoods *Nectandra* spp. and bulletwoods *Dipholis* spp.. The trees are generally evergreen. A dense understorey of small trees is present but undergrowth is generally lacking (FAO/UNEP, 1981).

Much of the original lower montane rain forest on the Blue Mountain range has been cleared and there are now only relict patches in inaccessible places. This forest type has a canopy of 20–22 m high, though emergents such as *Psidium montanum*, *Ficus suffocans* and *Symphonia globulifera* can reach 40 m. There is a lower tree layer at 9–15 m and the shrub layer is sparse. Lianes are uncommon and epiphytes are confined to the higher branches of trees (FAO/UNEP, 1981).

The upper slopes of the Blue Mountains still have some montane mist forests on them and elfin woodland is found on the exposed summits and northern ridges of the range. Montane mist forest has few emergents and the canopy is only 12–14 m high. Dominant trees are *Podocarpus urbani*, *Cyrilla racemiflora* and *Alchornea latifolia*. Tree ferns are frequent. A sub-canopy is found at 10 m and the shrub layer is scattered. The low canopied, gnarled trees of which elfin woodland is composed are covered in many mosses, lichens, ferns and epiphytes. *Clusia clarendonensis* and *Clethra occidentalis* are common (FAO/UNEP, 1981). Also present on the Blue Mountains, between 750 and 1200 m, is montane sclerophyll forest. This is a low shrubby community, mostly very disturbed by humans.

There are a number of small areas of swamp forest in the country with the canopy dominated by *Symphonia globulifera* and *Roystonea princeps*. Climbers are a prominent feature in some of the swamps.

Other woody formations found in Jamaica include the dry limestone forest (see Kapos, 1986) which is a sparse cover of low forest and tall scrub growing on bare limestone rock. Red birch *Bursera simaruba* is common as an emergent tree. In the few remaining undisturbed areas, mahogany *Swietenia mahagoni*, *Spondias mombin* and *Plumiera* sp. are found as deciduous emergents. Most of the vegetation is made up of a diverse array of small xerophytic trees and shrubs.

Mangroves

Mangroves are more common on the south coast, but most of the coastal forests have been destroyed and the wetlands drained (FAO, 1990). FAO/UNEP (1981) gives a figure of 70 sq. km for mangroves around the island. Iremonger *et al.* (in press) report only 22 sq. km of mangrove forest, but a further 73 sq. km of mangrove scrub. Bacon (1993) reports the higher figure of 106 sq. km; this, though, includes areas on offshore islands — he recorded 101 sites with mangrove. Map 12.1, a simplified version of the digital data supplied by Iremonger (see Map Legend), shows 19 sq. km of mangrove remaining in the country.

Red mangrove *Rhizophora mangle* is dominant and frequently can be found in monospecific stands with a canopy of up to 25 m. Other common species are white mangrove *Laguncularia racemosa*, black mangrove *Avicennia germinans* and buttonwood *Conocarpus erectus*.

Forest Resources and Management

Jamaica was almost entirely covered in forest before human settlement in the first century AD and when Columbus discovered the island in 1494 the island was still substantially forested. Indeed the name Jamaica is derived from the Arawak word *Xamayca* meaning the land of wood and water. Now only the most inaccessible of the forests are in a pristine condition. Estimates of the proportion of land under well-stocked natural forest were 32 per cent in the early 1920s (Zon and Sparhawk, 1923), 18 per cent in the early 1950s (Asprey and Robbins, 1953) and only six per cent in 1980 (FAO, 1988).

In the 1990 National Forestry Action Plan, forests with a commercial potential were estimated to cover 2670 sq. km. Of these, only 770 sq. km were natural forest, while 210 sq. km

Remnants of terraces constructed during the 1950s and 60s with the forested Main Ridge of the Blue Mountains in the background. (Mark Aldrich)

were plantations and 1690 (or 63 per cent) were ruinate forests, ones that had been cut over and the secondary growth had not attained the status of a developed forest (FAO, 1990). Most of the relatively undisturbed natural forests and the plantations are publicly owned, while 80 per cent of the ruinate forests are under private ownership. FAO (1993), using 1985 baseline data, estimates Jamaica's forest cover (and its closed broadleaved forest cover) at 2390 sq. km. This includes forest in the tropical rain, moist deciduous and hill and montane zone.

The Nature Conservancy (TNC), in conjunction with the Conservation Data Centre-Jamaica, have recently carried out a Rapid Ecological Assessment of the island. The main purpose of this was to provide a classification of Jamaican vegetation communities and a map of their current extent (Iremonger *et al.*, in press). It is these data that have been used as a source for Map 12.1. Measurements from this map of the different forest types are shown in Table 12.1 and give a total of 3182 sq. km of forest on the island — a somewhat higher figure than the 2842 sq. km reported by Iremonger *et al.* (in press). As cloud is obscuring parts of the Blue and John Crow Mountains, there is actually slightly more lower and upper montane forest than is reported by Iremonger *et al.* (in press), or indicated in Table 12.1 and shown on Map 12.1.

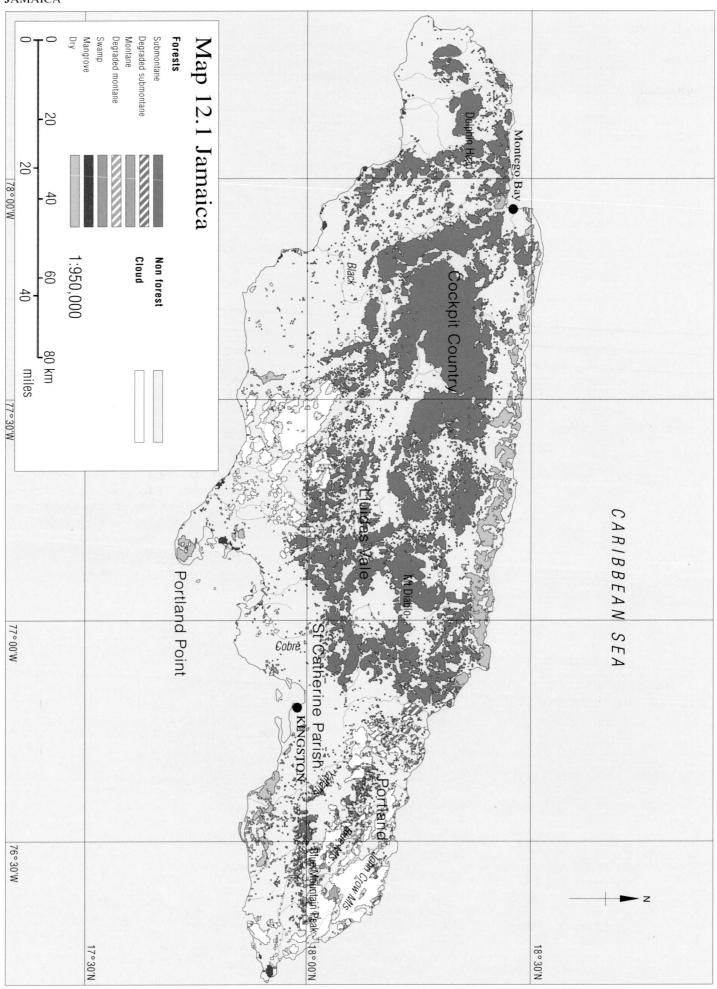

Map 12.1 Jamaica

Forests

Submontane
Degraded submontane
Montane
Degraded montane
Swamp
Mangrove
Dry

Non forest
Cloud

1:950,000

0 20 20 40 40 60 40 80 km
0 20 40 miles

CARIBBEAN SEA

Montego Bay
Dolphin Head
Black
Cockpit Country
Lluidas Vale
Mt Diablo
Cobré
St Catherine Parish
KINGSTON
Portland Point
Portland
Blue Mountain Peak
John Crow Mts
Blue

78°00'W
77°30'W
77°00'W
76°30'W

18°30'N
18°00'N
17°30'N

N

Table 12.1 Estimates of forest extent in Jamaica

Forest type	Area (sq. km)	% land area
Submontane*	2,657	24.5
Degraded submontane	80	0.7
Montane	28	0.3
Degraded montane	2	<0.1
Dry	363	3.4
Swamp	33	0.3
Mangrove	19	0.2
Total	3,182	29.4

* This includes over 2,000 sq. km of evergreen seasonal forest, much of which may be disturbed.
Based on analysis of Map 12.1. See Map Legend on p. 119 for details of sources.

Muchoney *et al.* (in press) have looked in more detail at the Blue and John Crow Mountains National Park, including a 1 km buffer zone, and give figures for lower and upper montane forest as well as the modified formations of each of these. It has been suggested (S. Iremonger, *in litt.*) that the figures from Muchoney *et al.* (in press) for the montane and lower montane formations, combined with the evergreen seasonal, dry semi-evergreen, swamp and mangrove forest from Iremonger *et al.* will give the most accurate figure for Jamaica's forest cover (Table 12.2). However, it must be noted that all these estimates include modified and secondary forest — there is a much smaller area of pristine forest left on the island.

The majority of the forest plantations have been established in the east of the island. *Pinus caribaea* is most commonly used; these plantations are frequent in the Blue Mountains and in the centre of Jamaica (Iremonger *et al.*, in press), but a few areas of hardwood have also been planted. The most successful of these is blue mahoe *Hibiscus elatus*, although West Indian mahogany *Swietenia mahagoni*, cedar *Cedrela odorata* and santa maria *Calophyllum antillanum* are also planted. However, most of these broadleaved plantations now lie idle and are reverting to secondary forest, or have been underplanted with coffee, as in the Blue Mountains (Iremonger *et al.*, in press). The pine plantations, covering 100 sq. km in 1985, are managed by a Government agency, the Forest Industry Development Corporation (FIDCO). However, a combination of hurricanes

Table 12.2 Estimates of forest cover on Jamaica

Forest type	Area (sq. km)
Lower montane	182
Modified lower montane	104
Upper montane	186
Modified upper montane	41
Evergreen seasonal	2,112
Dry semi-evergreen	323
Swamp	46
Mangrove	22
Total	3,016

Sources: Muchoney *et al.* (in press); Iremonger *et al.* (in press).

and fires have made these plantations unprofitable. Indeed, over a decade, the area of pines ravaged by arson exceeded plantings by 40 per cent (Eyre, 1991).

Jamaica's National Forestry Action Plan (FAO, 1990) reported that an estimated 725,441 cu. m of wood was cut for fuel and charcoal (a very much larger quantity than that reported in FAO, 1994 and indicated at the head of this chapter). This is 84 per cent of the total wood harvest and is consequently a major contributor to the loss of forest resources. Charcoal burning is a US$3.3 million industry, providing employment for 10,000 people (Eyre, 1991). Hardwood made up 10 per cent of the industrial roundwood produced in 1988, it is used mostly by the local furniture and building industries. Softwood, five per cent of the harvest, is also used for building. Poles and posts are cut from both soft and hard woods (FAO, 1990). There are around 150 sawmills in the country, cutting rough timber of poor quality with low levels of efficiency and high wastage (FAO, 1990). Timber felling is not subject to licence and many of the mills are not registered. Only 20 per cent of the country's timber needs are met locally and imports are increasing (Headley and Thompson, 1986).

Although forest reserves were developed on Crown Lands over 100 years ago, funds were not provided to effect the proposals and the laws supporting the reserves were repealed. An Afforestation Law was passed in 1927, the Blue Mountain Forest Reserve was gazetted and a Forest Officer appointed, but, again, lack of funds prevented the implementation of the law. The Forest Act of 1937 repealed and replaced the Afforestation Law and since then there has been no revision or amendment to the Act (FAO, 1990). The forest reserves lack management plans and the authority for protection and development of these areas has, in the past, not been clear. Major problems stem from the lack of a formally constituted national system of protected areas, no legal requirement for environmental impact assessments and the ineffective implementation of environmental laws.

In response to the environmental situation, the sector of the Jamaican government concerned with the environment recently underwent some rearrangement. This was the result of the Protected Areas Resource Conservation Project (PARC) a joint effort of the Planning Institute of Jamaica (representing the country's government) and USAID. This project was initiated in 1989 and was designed to promote tourism and sustainable development, as well as protect biological diversity on the island. The Forestry and Soil Conservation Department (FSCD) of the Ministry of Agriculture which was responsible for development, research and protection of forest resources, is now also responsible for the Blue Mountain/John Crow Mountain National Park. The Natural Resource Conservation Authority (NRCA) superseded the Natural Resources Conservation Department (NRCD), and became the primary agency for national environmental management. NRCA is part of the newly created Ministry of Tourism and the Environment. Its brief includes enforcement of the Act protecting the country's wildlife.

Deforestation
Concern about the adverse impact of excessive deforestation was expressed in Jamaica as long ago as 1885 when E.D.M. Hooper of the Indian Forest Service reported to the government on the situation (Swaby, 1945).

Jamaica has been a considerable exporter of fine timbers, but this does not seem to have been a major cause of deforestation.

Basic soil conservation measures using bamboo and wooden poles. (Mark Aldrich)

Those exported included West Indian mahogany, ebony *Brya ebenus*, and lignum vitae *Guaiacum officinale*, as well as dye-woods such as fustic *Chlorophora tinctoria*, logwood *Haematoxylum campechianum* and braziletto *Peltophorum brasiliense*. At higher elevations in the Blue Mountains, the cultivation of *Cinchona* spp. for quinine was another element in forest destruction, but also never a major one.

In a report published in 1990, FAO estimated that Jamaica's forests were disappearing at a rate of 3.0 per cent per annum. However, in the recent FAO (1993) publication, *Forest resources assessment 1990*, the rate of deforestation in Jamaica between the years of 1981 and 1990 is estimated at 7.2 per cent per year, considerably higher than in any of the other countries covered in this Atlas. This rate represents an annual loss of 268 sq. km.

Clearing for settlement and agricultural land has always been the main cause of deforestation on the island. The forests are presently being diminished for subsistence crop cultivation and pasture, for charcoal production and for the establishment of plantations of exotic pine and coffee. In areas surveyed by Eyre (1987), commercial lumber production constituted only a small portion of the deforestation that had occurred between the years of 1980 and 1986, the main cause was cultivation by the rural people (Table 12.3).

Hurricanes have also caused some damage to the island's forest; the last one to do so was Hurricane Gilbert in September 1988. The severity of the damage caused led to UNDP implementing their "Forestry Rehabilitation Programme" on the island. After this hurricane, there were 500 new landslides mapped along 100 km of road (Eyre, 1991).

Between 1980 and 1988, 20 sq. km of coffee were planted in the Blue Mountains with approximately 9 sq. km of this replacing natural forests and plantations in the Yallahs watershed alone. The land-clearing operations and road construction are frequently poorly done and create intense surface erosion and landslides. For instance, over 400 million tonnes of soil were lost by erosion between the years of 1981 and 1990 — a rate of 13,071 tonnes per sq. km per year and, islandwide, over 200 major landslides have been reported, almost all of them due to deforestation (Eyre, 1991).

Indeed, one of the most serious aspects of deforestation is the clearing of steep, unstable slopes for cultivation. This has occurred particularly in the tract of forest northwest of Lluidas

Table 12.3 Causes of deforestation between the years of 1980 and 1986 in 55.7 sq. km of surveyed forest.

Cause of deforestation	Percentage of deforested land 1986
Peasant agriculture	52.2
Pasture	11.0
Coffee	9.3
Residential etc.	8.8
Horticulture	6.5
Logging and fuelwood	4.5
Bananas	2.9
Marijuana	2.7
Other commercial agriculture	2.2
Conifer plantations	0.2

NB   In some places the principal cause of deforestation could not be identified.

Source: Eyre (1987)

Vale in St Catherine parish and places in Mount Rosanna Range (Eyre, 1987). Even if adequate funding were forthcoming for forest conservation/regeneration, the severity of soil erosion and consequent degradation is such that traditional plantation practises may not be suitable. Almost all the soil conservation projects on the island have ended in failure (Eyre, 1991).

Biodiversity

The Jamaican landmass moved eastwards with the Proto-Antillean island arc but, unlike Cuba and Hispaniola, Jamaica was completely submerged from the late Middle Eocene to the early Middle Miocene and emerged only 10–15 million years ago. The island has never been connected to the North American mainland and it did not rejoin any of the other islands, consequently endemism on Jamaica is high. Indeed, the country ranks among the first ten islands of the world for degree of endemism; about 27 or 28 per cent of the approximately 3000 species of flowering plant are endemic (Adams, 1972; Proctor, 1982; Kelly, 1988). Of these endemics, 256 are listed as threatened, of which 52 are apparently extinct (Kelly, 1991). The Pteridophyte flora is also rich with 579 species and 82 endemics (Adams, 1990; Davis *et al.*, 1986). Numerous (47) local endemics are found in the isolated limestone massif of the John Crow Mountains (Kelly, 1988). Proctor (1986) reports the occurrence of 101 endemic vascular plants in Cockpit Country and a further five that are found there and nowhere else in Jamaica.

The country has 24 native mammal species of which all but one are bats; three or four of the bat species are endemic including *Artibeus flavescens*, *Phyllonycteris aphylla* and *Eptesicus lynni* (Johnson, 1988; CEP, 1987). The endemic hutia *Geocapromys brownii* is threatened by over hunting and habitat destruction.

Over 250 species of birds have been recorded in Jamaica (CEP, 1987; Downer and Sutton, 1990), though only 106 extant native species breed there (Wiley, 1990). There are at least 25 (AOU, 1983; Johnson, 1988) and maybe 27 (Lack, 1976; CEP, 1987; Haynes *et al.*, 1989) single-island endemics. Five species are listed as threatened by Collar *et al.* (1992) of which two endemics, the Jamaican petrel *Pterodroma caribbaea* and Jamaican pauraque *Siphonorhis americanus*, may be extinct. The other threatened species are the West Indian whistling-duck *Dendrocygna arborea*, the plain pigeon *Columba inornata* and the endemic ring-tailed pigeon *Columba caribaea*. The pigeons are threatened by hunting and habitat loss.

There are 27 single-island endemic reptiles and another four shared with a few other islands (Schwartz and Thomas, 1975; Schwartz *et al.*, 1978). The Jamaican boa *Epicrates subflavus* is listed as vulnerable by IUCN, while the black racer *Alsophis ater* is endangered (Groombridge, 1993). The endemic Jamaican iguana *Cyclura collei*, assumed to be extinct or exceedingly rare, was rediscovered in the Hellshire Hills in 1990 (Oryx, 1991). Other reptiles listed as threatened by IUCN are *Celestus duquesneyi*, *C. fowleri* and *C. microblepharis*. The endangered American crocodile *Crocodylus acutus* also occurs on Jamaica and there are five species of marine turtles in the area, only three nest on the island. Schwartz and Thomas (1975) record 20 amphibians endemic to Jamaica. Schwartz and Henderson (1991) give distributions, descriptions and the natural history of the Caribbean's amphibians and reptiles.

Little is known about numbers or status of the fish and invertebrates on the island. Two endemic swallowtail butterflies, the Homerus *Papilio homerus* and the Jamaican kite *Eurytides mar-*

cellinus, are listed as threatened in Collins and Morris (1985) and another six threatened invertebrates are listed by IUCN (Groombridge, 1993). Information on some other invertebrates is given in Farr (1984).

Conservation Areas

There is no legislation in Jamaica to authorise the establishment of national parks and other protected areas. There is, however, some legislation covering specific aspects of environmental management. This includes laws covering marine protected areas under the Beach Control Act, caves and monuments under the Jamaican Natural Heritage Trust Act, game sanctuaries and watershed areas under the Wildlife Protection Act, forest protection and tree preservation orders under the Forestry Act and the Town and Country Planning Act, and fish sanctuaries under the Fishing Industry Act.

There have been about 40 protected areas, mostly forest reserves, proposed or "gazetted" (without boundaries) in Jamaica since the 1930s, but these are not managed or protected. They may be invaded by squatters, leased for coffee growing or be plantation areas. Some of these are described in CEP (1987).

Although there is a national park on the island — Blue Mountain/John Crow Mountain — this has an IUCN category of VIII and is, therefore, not shown on Map 12.1. It was created recently as a result of the first stage of the PARC project. It is 780 sq. km and contains Jamaica's largest expanse of continuous, undisturbed forest. FSCD is responsible for the management of this park. There is also one marine park, Montego Bay (15 sq. km — not mapped), developed as a pilot management activity and controlled by NRCA.

The Jamaica Conservation and Development Trust (JCDT), a NGO formed in 1987, is dedicated to the promotion and financial support of national parks in the country, to setting up a National Park Trust Fund and to assisting in the development of a national park system plan.

Initiatives for Conservation

The National Environmental Societies Trust (NEST), which is an umbrella organisation for environmental NGOs and community based organisations, was established in 1989 and currently comprises 22 supporting members. These include JCDT, the Gosse Bird Club and the Natural History Society of Jamaica. In 1991, NEST became the National Committee of UNEP.

A Jamaican Environmental Strategy was developed in 1991 with the support of USAID. The Strategy provided an analytical background for the design of the DEMO Project. This project was devised to confer a framework for USAID collaboration with a wide range of interested parties in the government and private sector. It was concerned with addressing institutional deficiencies and the need to focus attention on the management of the natural resource base as the precondition for future economic growth. The ultimate goal of the project is to promote stable, sustainable economic development. Its purpose is to strengthen the capabilities of public and private environmental organisations to manage Jamaica's natural resources.

As part of the DEMO project, NRCA, which is responsible for the centralisation of all environmental activities for the Government of Jamaica, is receiving assistance in environmental policy reform, strategic planning, organisational development, financial management and enforcement of environmental regulations.

Other DEMO project components include institutional support to NEST and other Jamaican NGOs; development of field activities in selected "areas of environmental concern", starting in Negril and Montego Bay; and expansion of the national parks and protected areas, this is PARC II — the second phase of the Protected Areas Resource Conservation (PARC), planned to build on the successes of phase one. The first task of PARC II will be to manage the two existing national parks while the second major objective is to develop proposals to establish and manage additional parks in other pristine areas. Among the leading candidates for early inclusion are the Black River wetlands areas.

In addition to USAID, several international bodies are actively participating in the development and organisation of Jamaica's environmental sector. Among the most important are the Canadian International Development Agency (CIDA), the Organisation of American States (OAS), UNEP, TNC and WWF.

A Conservation Data Centre has recently been established by the University of the West Indies, the Planning Institute of Jamaica, JCDT and TNC. This will allow the systematic collection, storage and dissemination of data on the island's flora and fauna.

A National Forestry Action Plan, under the auspices of the Tropical Forestry Action Plan, was initiated in 1989 at the request of the Jamaican government. The resulting report contains 30 project proposals (FAO, 1990).

References

Adams, C.D. (1972). *Flowering Plants of Jamaica.* University of West Indies, Mona. Pp. 848.

Adams, C.D. (1990). Phytogeography of Jamaica. In: *Biogeographical Aspects of Insularity.* Accademia Nazionale de Lincei, Rome. Pp. 681–693.

AOU (1983). *Check-list of North American Birds* 6th edition. American Ornithologists' Union.

Asprey, G.F. and Robbins, R.G. (1953). The vegetation of Jamaica. *Ecological Monographs* 23: 359–412.

Bacon, P.R. (1993). Mangroves in the Lesser Antilles, Jamaica, Trinidad and Tobago. In: *Conservation and Sustainable Utilization of Mangrove Forests in Latin America and Africa Regions. Part 1: Latin America.* ITTO/ISME Project PD114/90(F). Pp. 155–209.

Beard, J.S. (1944). Climax vegetation in tropical America. *Ecology* 25: 127–158.

Beard, J.S. (1955). The classification of tropical American vegetation types. *Ecology* 36: 89–100.

CEP (1987). *Country Environmental Profile: Jamaica.* Prepared on behalf of IIED by the Natural Resources Conservation Division, Ministry of Agriculture and Ralph M. Field Associates, Inc., Kingston Jamaica.

Collar, N.J., Gonzaga, L.P., Krabbe, N., Madroño Nieto, A., Naranjo, L.G., Parker III, T.A. and Wege, D.C. (1992). *Threatened Birds of the Americas. The ICBP/IUCN Red Data Book.* ICBP, Cambridge, U.K.

Collins, N.M. and Morris, M.G. (1985). *Threatened Swallowtail Butterflies of the World: The IUCN Red Data Book.* IUCN, Gland, Switzerland and Camnridge, U.K.

Davis, S.D., Droop, S.J.M., Gregerson, P., Henson, L., Leon, C.J., Villa-Lobos, J.L, Synge, H. and Zantovska, J. (1986). *Plants in Danger. What do we know?* IUCN, Gland, Switzerland and Cambridge, U.K.

Downer, A. and Sutton, R. (1990). *Birds of Jamaica: a photographic field guide.* Cambridge University Press, Cambridge, U.K.

Eyre, L.A. (1987). Jamaica: test case for tropical deforestation? *Ambio* 16(6): 338–343.

Eyre, L.A. (1991). Jamaica's crisis in forestry and watershed management. *Jamaica Naturalist* 1(1): 27–34.

FAO/UNEP (1981). *Proyecto de Evaluacion de los Recursos Forestales Tropicales. Los Recursos Forestales de la Amaerica Tropical.* FAO, Rome, Italy.

FAO (1988). *An Interim Report on the State of the Forest Resources in the Developing Countries.* FAO, Rome, Italy.

FAO (1990). *National Forestry Action Plan: Jamaica. Main report with project profiles and budgets.* Government of Jamaica, UNDP, FAO, Kingston, Jamaica. Technical report – FOD:JAM/88/016.

FAO (1993). *Forest resources assessment 1990: Tropical countries.* FAO Forestry paper 112. FAO, Rome Italy.

FAO (1994). *FAO Yearbook: Forest Products 1981–1992.* FAO Forestry series No. 27, FAO Statistics Series No. 116. FAO, Rome, Italy.

Farr, T. (1984). Land animals of Jamaica. Origins and endemism. *Jamaican Journal* 17(1): 38–48.

Groombridge, B. (Ed.) (1993). *1994 IUCN Red List of Threatened Animals.* IUCN, Gland, Switzerland and Cambridge, U.K. 286 pp.

Grossman, D.H., Iremonger, S. and Muchoney, D.M. (1992) Jamaica: *A Rapid Ecological Assessment. Phase 1. An Island-Wide Characterization and Mapping of Natural Communities and Modified Vegetation Types.* The Nature Conservancy, Virginia, U.S.A. Pp. 41.

Grubb, P.J. and Tanner, E.V.J. (1976). The montane forests and soils of Jamaica: a reassessment. *Journal of the Arnold Arboretum* 57: 313–368.

Haynes, A.M., Sutton, R.L. and Harvey, K.D. (1989). Conservation trends, and the threats to endemic birds in Jamaica. In: *Biogeography of the West Indies: past present and future.* Woods, C.A. (ed). Sandhill Crane Press Inc., Gainseville, Florida.

Headley, M.V. and Thompson, D.A. (1986). Forest management in Jamaica. In: *Forests of Jamaica.* Thompson, D., Bretting, P. and Humphries, M. (eds). The Jamaican Society of Scientists and Technologists, Kingston, Jamaica. Pp. 91–96.

Iremonger, S., Muchoney, D., Wright, R. (in press). *Jamaican Vegetation Types: a new classification and map.*

Johnson, T.H. (1988). *Biodiversity and Conservation in the Caribbean: profiles of selected islands.* ICBP Monograph No. 1, ICBP, Cambridge, U.K.

Kapos, V. (1986). Dry limestone forests of Jamaica. In: *Forests of Jamaica.* Thompson, D., Bretting, P. and Humphries, M. (eds). The Jamaican Society of Scientists and Technologists, Kingston, Jamaica. Pp. 49–58.

Kelly, D.L. (1988). The threatened flowering plants of Jamaica. *Biological Conservation* 46: 201–216.

Kelly, D.L. (1991). The threatened flowering plants of Jamaica: a reappraisal. *Jamaica Naturalist* 1(1): 19–26.

Kelly, D.L., Tanner, E.V.J., Kapos, V., Dickinson, T.A., Goodfriend, G.A. and Fairburn, P. (1988). Jamaican limestone forests: floristics, structure and environment of three examples along a rainfall gradient. *Journal of Tropical Ecology* 4: 121–156.

Lack, D. (1976). *Island Biology.* Blackwell, Oxford.

Muchoney, D.M., Iremonger, S. and Wright, R. (in press). *A Rapid Ecological Assessment of the Blue and John Crow Mountains National Park Jamaica.* The Nature Conservancy, Virginia, U.S.A.

Oryx (1991). Jamaican iguana rediscovered. *Oryx* 25: 133.

Proctor, G.R. (1982). More additions to the flora of Jamaica. *J. Arnold. Arbor.* 63(3): 199–315.

Proctor, G.R. (1986). Cockpit Country and its vegetation. In: *Forests of Jamaica.* Thompson, D., Bretting, P. and Humphries, M. (eds). The Jamaican Society of Scientists and Technologists, Kingston, Jamaica. Pp. 43–47.

Schwartz, A. and Henderson, R.W. (1991). *Amphibians and Reptiles of the West Indies: Descriptions, Distributions and Natural History.* University of Florida Press, Gainesville.

Schwartz, A. and Thomas, R. (1975). *A Checklist of West Indian Amphibians and Reptiles.* Carnegie Museum of Natural History, Pittsburgh.

Schwartz, A., Thomas, R. and Ober, L.D. (1978). *First Supplement to a Checklist of West Indian Amphibians and Reptiles.* Carnegie Museum of Natural History, Pittsburgh.

Swaby, C. (1945). *Forestry in Jamaica.* Forestry Bulletin No. 1. Forestry Department, Jamaica.

Tanner, E.V.J. (1986). Forests of the Blue Mountains and the Port Royal Mountains of Jamaica. In: *Forests of Jamaica.* Thompson, D., Bretting, P. and Humphries, M. (eds). The Jamaican Society of Scientists and Technologists, Kingston, Jamaica. Pp. 15–30, 127–132.

Wiley, J.W. (1990). A profile of Jamaica and its birds. *El Pitirre* 3(1): 2–6.

Zon, R. and Sparhawk, W.N. (1923). *Forest Resources of the World.* Volume 1. McGraw-Hill, New York.

Author: Caroline Harcourt, Cambridge and Jose Ottenwalder, Florida Museum of Natural History with contributions from E.V.J. Tanner, The Botany School, Cambridge, Dan Chalmers, Taverham, Norfolk and Mark Aldrich, Cambridge.

Map 12.1 Jamaica

Digital data of Jamaica's vegetation were kindly made available by Doug Muchoney and Susan Iremonger of TNC, who, with Robb Wright and in collaboration with the Conservation Data Centre — Jamaica, have compiled vegetation cover information for the whole of the country. A written report titled, *Jamaican Vegetation Types: a new classification and map* (in press), details the findings of their data collection and research. The vegetation classes were mapped using Landsat TM satellite imagery (1988–89), supplemented by digital and hard copy maps of the island's soils, geology and elevation. As a result of this work, as well as extensive fieldwork and analysis of the literature, they have produced a comprehensive classification of the island's vegetation.

The classification scheme is hierarchical and is grouped into four major formations: closed forests, woodlands, scrub and herbaceous communities. Only the higher categories in the classification are mapped in this source dataset, although a few copies of the islandwide vegetation have been produced in greater detail and at a scale of 1:250,000.

Map 12.1 illustrates the natural closed forest communities and includes only 11 of the higher categories within the TNC classification, including occurrence of cloud. The patch of lowland rain forest, a tiny area on the north-west coast near Portland, is obscured by cloud and therefore is not shown.

The following forest types have been harmonised into the broad forest classes used in this Atlas:

Submontane rain forest:	*Lower montane rain forest over limestone; Lower montane forest over shale; Evergreen seasonal forest*
Degraded submontane rain forest:	*Modified lower montane rain forest*
Montane rain forest:	*Upper montane rain forest over shale; Upper montane rain forest over limestone*
Degraded montane rain forest:	*Modified upper montane rain forest*
Dry forest:	*Dry semi-evergreen forest*
Inland swamp forest:	*Swamp forest*
Mangrove:	*Mangrove forest*

The wet limestone forest of the Cockpit country (*Evergreen seasonal forest — mesic forest over limestone*) also includes modified formations. The forests in the Cockpit range generally occur between 300–1000 m, therefore these forests have been grouped under a submontane heading. The dry forest also includes modified or degraded formations.

Mapped conservation areas were derived from spatial data held on file at WCMC.

13 Lesser Antilles

ANTIGUA AND BARBUDA
Country area   440 sq. km
Land area   440 sq. km
Population (mid-1994)   0.1 million
Population growth rate   1.2 per cent
Population projected to 2025   0.1 million
Gross national product per capita (1992)   US$4870
Forest cover in 1990 (FAO, 1993a)   100 sq. km
Annual deforestation rate (1981–1990)   0
Industrial roundwood production   —
Industrial roundwood exports   —
Fuelwood and charcoal production   —
Processed wood production   —
Processed wood exports   —

DOMINICA
Country area   750 sq. km
Land area   750 sq. km
Population (mid-1994)   0.1 million
Population growth rate   1.3 per cent
Population projected to 2025   0.1 million
Gross national product per capita (1992)   US$2520
Forest cover in 1990 (FAO, 1993a)   440 sq. km
Annual deforestation rate (1981–1990)   0.7 per cent
Industrial roundwood production   —
Industrial roundwood exports   —
Fuelwood and charcoal production   —
Processed wood production   —
Processed wood exports   —

GRENADA
Country area   340 sq. km
Land area   340 sq. km
Population (mid-1994)   0.1 million
Population growth rate   2.5 per cent
Population projected to 2025   0.2 million
Gross national product per capita (1992)   US$2310
Forest cover in 1990 (FAO, 1993a)   60 sq. km
Annual deforestation rate (1981–1990)   +4.3 per cent
Industrial roundwood production   —
Industrial roundwood exports   —
Fuelwood and charcoal production   —
Processed wood production   —
Processed wood exports   —

GUADELOUPE
Country area   1710 sq. km
Land area   1690 sq. km
Population (mid-1994)   0.4 million
Population growth rate   1.2 per cent
Population projected to 2025   0.5 million
Gross national product per capita (1992)   US$4539
Forest cover in 1990 (FAO, 1993a)   930 sq. km
Annual deforestation rate (1981–1990)   0.3 per cent
Industrial roundwood production   7000 cu. m
Industrial roundwood exports   —
Fuelwood and charcoal production   15,000 cu. m
Processed wood production   1000 cu. m
Processed wood exports   —

MARTINIQUE
Country area   1100 sq. km
Land area   1060 sq. km
Population (mid-1994)   0.4 million
Population growth rate   1.1 per cent
Population projected to 2025   0.4 million
Gross national product per capita (1992)   US$4223
Forest cover in 1990 (FAO, 1993a)   430 sq. km
Annual deforestation rate (1981–1990)   0.5 per cent
Industrial roundwood production   3000 cu. m
Industrial roundwood exports   —
Fuelwood and charcoal production   10,000 cu. m
Processed wood production   1000 cu. m
Processed wood exports   —

ST KITTS AND NEVIS
Country area   272 sq. km
Land area   272 sq. km
Population (mid-1994)   0.04 million
Population growth rate   1.3 per cent
Population projected to 2025   0.1 million
Gross national product per capita (1992)   US$3990
Forest cover in 1990 (FAO, 1993a)   130 sq. km
Annual deforestation rate (1981–1990)   0
Industrial roundwood production   —
Industrial roundwood exports   —
Fuelwood and charcoal production   —
Processed wood production   —
Processed wood exports   —

ST LUCIA
Country area   620 sq. km
Land area   610 sq. km
Population (mid-1994)   0.1 million
Population growth rate   2.0 per cent
Population projected to 2025   0.2 million
Gross national product per capita (1992)   US$2900
Forest cover in 1990 (FAO, 1993a)   50 sq. km
Annual deforestation rate (1981–1990)   5.2 per cent
Industrial roundwood production   —
Industrial roundwood exports   —
Fuelwood and charcoal production   —
Processed wood production   —
Processed wood exports   —

ST VINCENT AND GRENADINES
Country area   390 sq. km
Land area   390 sq. km
Population (mid-1994)   0.1 million
Population growth rate   1.7 per cent
Population projected to 2025   0.1 million
Gross national product per capita (1992)   US$1990
Forest cover in 1990 (FAO, 1993a)   110 sq. km
Annual deforestation rate (1981–1990)   2.1 per cent
Industrial roundwood production   —
Industrial roundwood exports   —
Fuelwood and charcoal production   —
Processed wood production   —
Processed wood exports   —

The islands of the Lesser Antilles considered here cover in total a very small area compared with most of the other countries or regions dealt with in this volume. They comprise several different countries or colonies which, although politically separate, share several important characteristics.

Floristically and physiognomically the forests of the archipelago form a single unit, albeit one with a large number of different plant associations within it. This unit is characterised by moderate species richness and a high degree of endemism, with nearly 25 per cent of the tree species of the Lesser Antilles being endemic to the region. Most of these are found on more than one island, although there are also significant numbers of single-island endemics. This high level of regional endemism is also reflected in the fauna and other components of the flora.

The islands also share many similar problems in the conservation and management of their forest resources. In common with other island ecosystems, they have shown themselves to be vulnerable to disturbance from humans. The region has been inhabited for at least 6000 years and during this time a significant part of the original fauna has been exterminated, almost certainly as a result of mankind's activities. It is not clear whether plant species have suffered similar extinction rates. However, it is evident that there has been large scale disturbance and destruction of natural habitats, including the forest ecosystems which are believed to have originally covered most of the islands. Habitat destruction has been most marked since the region was settled by European colonists in the early 16th century. Most clearance has been for agricultural production. Remnant forest areas are generally in montane, inaccessible areas.

INTRODUCTION

The Lesser Antilles comprises a chain of islands running in an arc from the easternmost point of the Greater Antilles to the north-eastern part of South America. The islands of the principal arc are volcanic and mountainous; the outlying islands are composed mainly of limestone and are of low relief (Table 13.1). Volcanoes on three of the islands (Martinique, Guadeloupe and St Vincent) have erupted this century.

Putney (1982) records the largest remaining contiguous areas of relatively unaltered ecosystems on the islands of the Lesser Antilles. Table 13.2 gives his figures for mangroves, moist, rain and cloud forest. He adds the caution that the boundaries between the vegetation types have not been drawn using consistent criteria for all the islands so that the area of each should be considered a relative indication of approximate magnitude, not as an exact figure.

The eight Lesser Antillean countries that Putney (1982) and FAO (1993a) list as containing forest will be briefly described here. They are: Antigua and Barbuda, Dominica, Grenada, Guadeloupe, Martinique, St Kitts and Nevis, St Lucia and St Vincent and the Grenadines.

Tourism, agriculture and fisheries are the major economic activities on these islands and they are all dependent on the integrity of the natural resource base.

The Forests

Floristically and physiognomically the forests of the entire Lesser Antillean archipelago form a single unit, albeit one with a large number of different plant associations within it. There are minor geographical variations in floristic composition owing to the differences in range of some of the component species and the occurrence of localized endemics on some islands or combinations of islands (see Figure 13.1).

The natural vegetation of the Lesser Antilles has been comprehensively described by Beard (1949). This remains the standard work on the subject in English and most subsequent

Table 13.1 Islands of the Lesser Antilles (from north to south)

Main volcanic arc	Area in sq. km	Limestone islands	Area in sq. km
Saba	13	Sombrero	2
St Eustatius	23	Anguilla	91
St Kitts	174	St Martin	98
Nevis	98	St Bartholomew	21
Redonda	2	Barbuda	91
Montserrat	86	Antigua	280
Guadeloupe	1,603	La Désirade	26
Les Saints	2	Marie Galante	155
Dominica	787	Barbados	430
Martinique	984		
St Lucia	604		
St Vincent	337		
The Grenadines	130		
Grenada	311		

Source: Howard (1989)

Table 13.2 Largest remaining contiguous areas of relatively unaltered ecosystems in the Lesser Antilles

Forest type/place	Island	Area (sq. km)
MANGROVES		
Eastern Central Grand Cul de Sac Marin	Guadeloupe	28
Fort de France Bay	Martinique	22
Codrington Lagoon	Barbuda	9
Northeastern Coast	Antigua	6
MOIST FOREST		
Southern	Dominica	51
Central	Guadeloupe	13
Central	Martinique	13
Northwest of Mt Pelee	Martinique	10
Central Western	St Lucia	10
Mt Misery	St Kitts	7
Southwestern	St Vincent	6
Central eastern	St Vincent	6
Nevis Peak	Nevis	4
RAIN FOREST		
Central	Guadeloupe	123
Central	Dominica	92
Piton du Corbet/Mt Pelee	Martinique	90
Central	St Lucia	85
Central	St Vincent	39
Central	Grenada	18
CLOUD FOREST		
Morne Trois Pitons	Dominica	46
Central	St Vincent	32
Mt Misery	St Kitts	14
Morne Diablotin	Dominica	13
Soufriere	Guadeloupe	10
Central	Grenada	10
Mt Pelee	Martinique	8
Western central	Martinique	7

Source: Putney (1982)

descriptions of the Lesser Antillean forests are derived from it. The following is a brief summary.

Lowland rain forest

Lowland rain forest (referred to by Beard purely as rain forest) is found at elevations of between about 60 and 1000 m, usually on sites sheltered from the prevailing wind.

Climax rain forest has an uppermost stratum forming a more or less closed canopy at 28–35 m, a discontinuous middle layer of trees at 12–25 m and a lower tree layer at 5–12 m. There are shrub, sub-shrub and ground layers although in general the forest is relatively open underneath the canopy. There are 300–370 trees of 10 cm dbh per hectare.

Dacryodes excelsa is the principal dominant, accounting for up to 40 per cent of the standing crop on some islands. Other dominant species include *Sloanea dentata*, *S. truncata*, *S. berteriana*, *Pouteria semecarpifolia*, *P. multiflora*, *Chimarrhis*

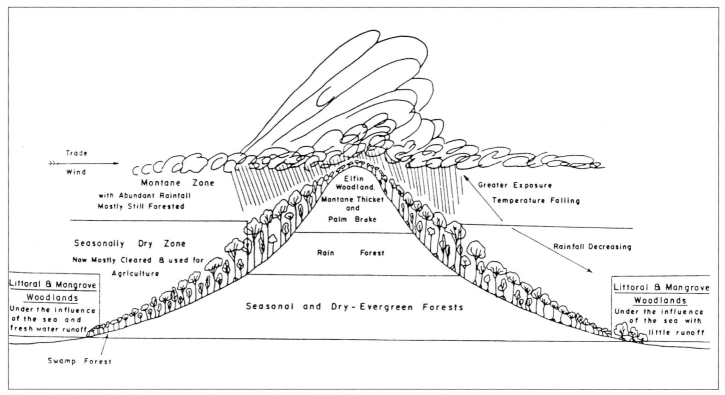

Figure 13.1 An idealised transect through a Caribbean island in the Lesser Antilles. *Source:* Lugo *et al.* (1981)

cymosa, *Dussia martinicensis*, *Talauma dodecapetala*, *Ormosia monosperma*, *Meliosma herbertii*, *Hyeronima caribaea*, *Phoebe elongata* and *Beilschmiedia pendula*.

A variety of second growth communities following destruction of the forest can be recognized, of which the most readily distinguished are: tree-fern brake, dominated by groves of *Cyathea arborea* and *Hemitelia grandifolia*; *Miconia* thicket, dominated by *Miconia guianensis*; and pioneer forest, dominated in the initial stages by species such as *Cecropia peltata*, *Ochroma lagopus*, *Hibiscus tulipiflorus*, *Freziera hirsuta* and *Acmistus arborescens* and at later stages by members of the Lauraceae, notably *Nectandra antillana* and *Ocotea leucoxylon*.

MONTANE FORMATIONS

There are marked changes in forest physiognomy and floristic composition between the lowland forests and those at higher altitudes. However, the distribution of the different montane formations appears to be determined by exposure to wind rather than by changes in temperature or rainfall with altitude.

a. Lower montane rain forest

Lower montane rain forest is found on mountain slopes and ridges from 60 m to 500 m elevation, generally more or less exposed to the wind. It is dominated by a variable though closed and often very dense stratum of trees 20–30 m in height, below which is an understorey of trees up to 12 m in height. Shrub, sub-shrub and ground layers also occur, merging into each other and into the lower tree storey.

The major dominants are *Licania ternatensis* and *Oxythece pallida*, with *Amanoa caribaea* locally important (e.g. in the wetter parts of Dominica where it is the commonest species in this formation). Other dominants are *Dacryodes excelsa*, *Tapura antillana*, *Ternstoemia oligostemon*, *Micropholis chryosphylloides*, *Manilkara bidentata*, *Guatteria caribaea*, *Sloanea caribaea*, *Sterculia caribaea*,

Diospyros ebenaster and *Symphonia globulifera*. Palms of the genus *Euterpe* are among the commonest understorey trees.

Second growth on cleared areas is essentially similar to that of the rain forest described above although tree-fern brake and *Miconia* thicket are commoner than pioneer forest.

b. Montane thicket

Typical montane thicket is found on ridge tops and steep slopes facing to windward, between elevations of around 300 m and 600 m. It generally has a dense canopy of around 12–20 m height composed largely of slender trees (under 1 m girth) with small crowns at a density of from 500 to nearly 900 stems over 0.3 m girth per hectare. There is virtually no woody understorey. There is a heavy growth of moss on the trees and ground, and there are large numbers of epiphytes. A slightly atypical form is found on Dominica on swampy flats of 450–600 m elevation. It is distinguished by an open canopy, markedly thin stems and small crowns and the presence of aerial roots on over half the trees.

Montane thicket has a much less consistent species composition across the different islands of the Lesser Antilles than do lower montane rain forest and (lowland) rain forest. Typical component species are *Micropholis chrysophylloides*, *Richeria grandis*, *Podocarpus coriaceus*, *Byrsonima martinicensis*, *Licania oligantha*, *Tovomita plumieri*, *Myrica* spp., *Ilex* spp, *Cyrilla racemiflora*, *Pisonia fragrans*, *Hedyosmum arborescens*, *Rondeletia* spp., *Rapanea guianensis*, *Licania ternatensis* and *Cassipourea elliptica*.

c. Palm brake

Palm brake appears to be a natural community sub-climax to montane thicket and is found on ridge tops and steep slopes facing windward between 300 and 600 m. The forest is not stratified, nor is there a true canopy but rather agglomerations of trees occurring in patches of different heights, from

6 m to 20 m, averaging around 12 m. Two-thirds of the trees are palms of the genus *Euterpe*, with the mountain cabbage *Euterpe globosa* being dominant and characteristic on most islands. Other trees present are both elfin woodland and rain forest species, including *Sloanea truncata*, *Richeria grandis*, *Marila racemosa*, *Hedyosmum arborescens*, *Freziera undulata*. *F. hirsuta*, *Ilex sideroxyloides*, *Dacryodes excelsa*, *Byrsonima martinicensis*, *Micropholis chrysophylloides*, *Miconia guianensis*, *Nectandra* and *Ocotea* spp.

There is no shrub layer, but the herbaceous ground layer is usually very luxuriant.

d. Elfin woodland

Elfin woodland is the highest of the montane formations and occurs on the summits and upper slopes of the principal peaks and ridges, above 450 m and usually above 600 m, in areas which are continuously wet and severely exposed to wind.

There is a single woody stratum of low, gnarled, almost impenetrable epiphyte-covered trees 3–6 m in height. Dominance is not consistent from island to island, although *Didymopanax attenuatum* and several *Charianthus* species are the most regularly found common trees. On some islands (notably Gaudeloupe and Dominica) *Clusia venosa* is the principal dominant, forming half the standing crop.

SEASONAL FORMATIONS

Beard noted that because of the pressure of cultivation there were no longer any undamaged examples of forests in dry or seasonal areas in the Lesser Antilles. Nevertheless several different forest types could be conjectured to have existed on the basis of more or less damaged remnants.

a. Seasonal evergreen forest

Two areas of what appeared to have been evergreen seasonal forest were recorded, in northern Martinique and at Morne Delice in Grenada, both areas being below 300 m with an annual rainfall of 2000 mm or more. The principal dominants in the former were Andira inermis and *Lonchocarpus latifolius*, in the latter *Manilkara bidentata*, *Buchenavia capitata* and *Tabebuia pallida*. These areas appeared to be unique in the Lesser Antilles.

b. Semi-evergreen seasonal forest

Forests of this type, all now disturbed, appear to have been considerably more widespread than seasonal evergreen forests, being found for example in Barbados (Turner's Hall Wood), St Vincent (King's Hill forest), St Lucia (Gros Piton), Cannouan and Carriacou (the Grenadines), south-west Dominica, Antigua (Walling's Reservoir) and southern Martinique. These areas are generally below 200 m elevation with 130–200 cm annual rainfall and a moderately severe dry season.

Dominants, which vary in importance in different sites, include *Hymenaea courbaril*, *Inga laurina*, *Pisonia fragrans*, *Citharexylum spinosum*, *Bursera simaruba*, *Simarouba amara*, *Brosimum alicastrum*, *Pouteria multiflora* and *Fagara martinicensis*.

c. Deciduous seasonal forest

Some low-lying areas in the Leeward Islands, St Vincent, the Grenadines and Grenada, characterised by an annual rainfall of 1000–1500 mm and a severe dry season, have degraded examples of what appears to have been deciduous seasonal woodland, with a closed upper canopy at 9–12 m and a layer of shrubs below. *Bursera* and *Pisonia* are the only common trees, usually making up 90 per cent of the stand between them.

d. Dry evergreen forests

Such dry evergreen forests as exist have almost all been very severely degraded. Larger trees in the surviving remnants include *Pimenta racemosa*, *Coccoloba pubescens*, *Tabebuia pallida*, *Manilkara bidentata*, *Eugenia* spp. and *Pisonia fragrans*.

e. Littoral Woodland

Littoral woodland is found widely on the windward shores of the islands. On the seaward edge it generally consists of a littoral hedge whose height varies from a few centimetres to several metres, in which typical species are *Coccoloba uvifera*, *Chrysobalanus icaco*, *Conocarpus erectus*, *Erithalis fruticosa*, *Jacquinia barbasco* and *Plumeria alba*. Behind this, and therefore partially sheltered from the wind, there may develop woodland with dominant trees 18–25 m tall not forming a closed canopy, underneath which is a lower tree stratum and a shrub layer. Typical components of this woodland are *Tabebuia pallida*, *Rheedia lateriflora*, *Calophyllum antillanum*, *Pisonia fragrans*, *Manilkara bidentata*, *Diospyros ebenaster*, *Coccolobis diversifolia*, *C. pubescens* and *Pisonia fragrans*. *Terminalia catappa* is introduced and naturalized.

f. Swamp Forest

Stands of *Pterocarpus officinalis* reaching 20 m in height are found in freshwater swamp areas.

g. Mangrove

Mangroves, generally of low growth, are widely found. Species are *Rhizophora mangle*, *Avicennia germinans*, *Laguncularia racemosa* and *Conocarpus erectus*.

INTRODUCTION – ANTIGUA AND BARBUDA

Antigua and Barbuda comprise three islands: Antigua (280 sq. km), Barbuda (160 sq. km) 40 km northwards and the tiny, uninhabited Redonda. In Antigua, dry flat limestone plains in the north and east give rise to gently rolling hills in the centre of the island and to a higher volcanic area in the west. Boggy Peak at 1319 feet (402 m) is the highest point on Antigua (CCA/IRF, 1991a). Barbuda's topography is lower and more uniform. Most of this limestone island is only a few feet above sea level.

The islands have high year round temperatures, 29°C in summer and 24°C in winter. A dry season extends from January to March or April, with the wettest time occurring from August to November. Annual precipitation in Antigua is 107–114 cm. Barbuda, in contrast, is one of the driest islands in the Caribbean with only 76–99 cm rain per year.

Most people live on Antigua, where the capital, St John's, has 36,000 inhabitants. Codrington is the only settlement on Barbuda; 1500 people or thereabouts live on this island. Agriculture used to be the mainstay of the country's economy, with sugar and cotton being important crops, but tourism is now the primary economic activity.

Forest Resources and Management

Clearing of the forests in Antigua and Barbuda began with the colonisation of the islands in the early 17th century. In the space of a few decades, much of the natural vegetation had been cleared for the cultivation of tobacco, indigo, cotton and then sugar cane

(CCA/IRF, 1991a). On Antigua, only 22 sq. km (5500 acres) are reported to have been spared from cane production (Cater, 1944). Many reports refer to woodlands, as opposed to forests, on Antigua and Barbuda (e.g. OAS, 1990), while others state that all the forest on the islands is secondary (FAO, 1993b).

Only small areas of humid forest exist on Antigua; the remaining patches are found in the southwest of the island. It does not occur on Barbuda (Morello, 1983). In the volcanic region of Antigua and on the highlands of Barbuda are some areas of deciduous forest, most of it greatly degraded by collection of firewood. Barbuda has some scleromorphic forests of red cedar *Tabebuia pallida*, as well as fairly extensive mangrove edge forests, which are leguminous forests dominated by *Haematoxylum* and *Pithecellobium*. Neither of these formations are common on Antigua. Both islands have some areas of mangrove. The most common species are red *Rhizophora mangle*, white *Laguncularia* spp., and black *Avicennia* spp.

The Caribbean Conservation Association (CCA) report that the forests on Antigua and Barbuda — including the mangroves — occupy 15 per cent of the islands' land area (CCA/IRF, 1991a). FAO's (1993a) estimate is that 100 sq. km remain, all in the moist deciduous forest zone.

Although there have been attempts at reforestation on the islands, none has been very successful (CCA/IRF, 1991a).

Deforestation

FAO (1993a) reports that there is now no deforestation in Antigua and Barbuda. However, CCA indicate that slash and burn cultivation, uncontrolled fires and excessive grazing by livestock destroy much of the secondary forest in an early stage of its development, leading to soil erosion and general degradation of the environment. Cutting down trees for fuel and fenceposts is another source of forest disturbance.

Large scale hotel and related recreational developments along Antigua's coastline have destroyed considerable areas of mangrove swamps. In addition, some sizeable areas of mangrove are used as rubbish dumps, notably Crooks and Fitches Creek on Antigua.

Biodiversity

Nearly three centuries of degradation and land clearing for intensive agriculture have contributed to loss of species diversity on the islands. In addition the introduction of such species as fallow deer *Dama dama*, the indian mongoose *Herpestes auropunctatus* and rats (*Rattus rattus* and *R. norvegicus*) have altered the native biodiversity through competition, habitat modification and depredation.

There are no comprehensive floral lists for the islands and the number of indigenous species remaining is unknown.

There are three amphibians on Antigua and one on Barbuda. Both islands have the small tree frog *Eleuthrodactylus johnstonei*; while *E. martinicensis* is also present on Antigua. The only other amphibian is the introduced toad *Bufo marinus*.

Seventeen reptiles have been recorded from Antigua and 12 from Barbuda, these include four marine turtles (Faaborg and Arendt, 1985). Some of these reptiles are no longer found on the islands. Threatened species include the endemic snake *Alsophis antiguae* and the iguana *Iguana delicatissima*. The latter has been decimated by human exploitation and the introduced mongoose and may even be extinct (CCA/IRF, 1991a).

There have been 106 bird species reported from Antigua and 74 from Barbuda (Faaborg and Arendt, 1985). Several land birds have become extinct on the islands. These include an owl, *Speotyto cunicularia armaura*, a parrot *Amazona* sp. and trem-

Coastal woodland of Antigua. (Mark Spalding)

bler *Cinclocerthia ruficaudata* (CCA/IRF, 1991a). The only species listed as endangered by Collar *et al.* (1992) is the West Indian whistling-duck *Dendrocygna arborea*.

The only indigenous mammals remaining on Antigua and Barbuda are bats, of which there are seven species.

Conservation Areas

Although there is an institutional framework for a protected areas system in the form of the National Parks Act of 1984, no formal system exists. At present, only one protected area — Nelson's Dockyard National Park on Antigua, is managed. Those areas in IUCN's categories I–IV are listed in Table 13.3.

Two authorities are involved with the management of protected areas. These are the National Parks Authority and the Fisheries Division of the Ministry of Agriculture, Fisheries and Lands.

Initiatives for Conservation

NGOs on the islands are particularly knowledgeable and committed and have been very active despite their lack of resources (FAO, 1993b).

The first draft of the country's National Forestry Action Plan was completed in November 1991 and it is expected to be finalised in 1994. The main emphasis of the Plan is on land use, conservation and institution building, but none of the proposed projects has yet been implemented (FAO, 1993b).

INTRODUCTION – DOMINICA

Dominica is one of the larger islands in the Lesser Antilles. It is volcanic and largely mountainous. The highest peak, Morne Diablotin, in the north central part of the island, rises to 1447 m above sea level. The only relatively flat areas are river valleys on the north-east coast and on the small central plateau.

Rainfall is heaviest from July to January. Annual precipitation ranges from 1250 mm on the northwest coast to 10,000 mm in the high mountains. Melville Hall on the northeast coast experiences mean monthly minimum temperatures of 18–20°C and mean monthly maxima of 28–31°C.

Dominica was initially settled by Arawak Indians and then by Caribs. The island is now the major homeland of the last survivors of the Caribs. Control of the island passed from the French to the British in 1783; it became independent in 1978.

Population density at 133 people per sq. km is fairly low compared to most of the other large islands in the Lesser Antilles. Some 90 per cent of the population live along the coast, most on the leeward side. The main urban areas are the capital city of Roseau in the south-west and Portsmouth in the north-west. About 40 per cent of the people are rural inhabitants, mostly subsistence farmers (CCA/IRF, 1991b).

The economic mainstay of the island is still agriculture, with crops providing 30 per cent of the gross domestic product in 1988. Bananas and root crops each make up about 30 per cent of agricultural production. Bananas are the main export followed by coconut products, primarily soap. Tourism is a growing source of income.

Forest Resources and Management

Forests originally covered almost the entire island; as late as 1945 around 80 per cent of Dominica was forested, much of it secondary although with large expanses of primary forest (Beard, 1949). The country still has some of the largest expanses of forest in the Lesser Antilles, with around 520 sq. km of natur-

Table 13.3 Conservation areas in Antigua and Barbuda

Existing conservation areas in IUCN's categories I–IV are listed. Marine national parks are not listed or mapped.

National Park	*Area sq. km*
Betty's Hope	nd
Half Moon Bay	nd
Nelson's Dockyard	41
Other Area	
Mamoura Reef	nd
Park Reserve	
Darkwood	nd
Devil's Bridge	nd
Green Island Reefs	nd
Northeast Archipelago	nd
Total	41*

* Note that for a majority of these areas sizes are not known.
Source: WCMC (unpublished data)

al forest, woodland and bush (CCA/IRF, 1991b), just over half of which is relatively undisturbed rain forest and lower montane rain forest (*sensu* Beard) or montane forest (Table 13.4). However, the figures in Table 13.4 are from an OAS map which must be treated with caution as the aerial photographs on which it is based are far from perfect (EARTHSTAT, 1986). FAO (1993a) estimates that there are 440 sq. km of forest on the island, all in the tropical rain forest zone.

The littoral woodland is confined to a narrow strip along the windward coast, while the scrub woodland, now all considerably disturbed and degraded, is found on the leeward coast. No primary stands of semi-evergreen forest remain.

Swamp forests border the river estuaries from Portsmouth to Marigot. There are only four small areas of mangrove in Dominica, near Cabrits, in the Canefield Pool, at Calibashie and at Hampstead. White mangrove *Laguncularia racemosa* and black mangrove *Avicennia germinans* are both present.

A 1986–1987 FAO inventory of the merchantable timber of the island reported 4.9 million cu. m of timber on 160 sq. km of land of which, at most, 3.7 million cu. m was considered marketable (De Milde, 1987; CCA/IRF, 1991b). About 3 million cu. m of the timber was on government lands. Timber richness was found to be 200 cu. m per hectare on 125 sq. km and as high as 600 cu. m per hectare on the remaining 35 sq. km. Three species, *Dacryodes excelsa*, *Amanoa caribaea* and *Tapura latifolia* made up 50 per cent of the trees enumerated and these with a further seven species comprised over 90 per cent of the total volume (Prins, 1987).

Timber exploitation is carried out by two relatively mechanized companies, Dominica Timbers Limited (DTL) and Northeastern Timber Cooperative Ltd (NET), as well as around 100 pitsawyers. Annual output from the two companies is about 4 million board-feet (ca 9500 cu. m), while that from the pitsawyers is between one and two million board-feet (ca 2400–4800 cu. m) (CCA/IRF, 1991b). Combined, this provides about 75 per cent of the timber used locally for furniture and house construction.

On all state lands there is a minimum girth limit, between one and two metres, before a tree may be harvested. NET was recently allowed to cut a 8 ha area of the Northern Forest

Table 13.4 Areas of the different forest types remaining on Dominica

Forest Type	Area (sq. km)	Per cent of land
Mature inc. lower montane	244.9	31
Montane	36.4	4.6
Montane thicket	8	1.0
Elfin woodland	1.7	0.3
Littoral woodland	1.4	0.2
Scrub woodland	62.4	7.9
Secondary rain forest	90.9	11.5
Semi-evergreen forest	71.7	9.1
Swamp	0.3	0.1
Total	517.7	65.6

NB   The land area used to calculate the figures in column 3 appears to be 790 sq. km.
Source: EARTHSTAT (1986)

Reserve and here it was stipulated that reforestation had to be undertaken. This has occurred in about half the area cut, using exotics, mostly mahogany.

The Forestry and Wildlife Division within the Ministry of Agriculture and the Environment is responsible for the protection and management of forests, wildlife and watersheds as well as for the national parks and for environmental education.

Deforestation

A 1987 study concluded that at that time some 237 sq. km or 46 per cent of the island had been deforested. Much of the clearing has occurred since 1945 (Figure 13.2). FAO (1993a) estimates that 3 sq. km of forest are cleared annually, a rate of 0.7 per cent. The main motivation is land clearance for agriculture, particularly for banana plantations. Forested state land is still being sold into private ownership, often to small farmers, without consultation with the Forest Department; these areas, including steep slopes and watersheds, are being deforested, usually for cultivation of bananas and other crops. Many of the trees cut are allowed to rot where they fall rather than being used more productively. Cutting wood for charcoal is also still extensively practised.

Biodiversity

Dominica has at least 1000 species of native flowering plants (CCA/IRF, 1991b) of which twelve are endemic (WCMC, 1992).

There are two native amphibian species, *Eleutherodactylus martinicensis* and *Leptodactylus fallax* (Corke, 1992). Twelve of the 14 reptiles on the island are native, of which two (*Anolis*

Table 13.5 Conservation areas in Dominica

Existing conservation areas in IUCN's categories I–IV are listed

National Park	Area (sq. km)
Morne Trois Pitons	69
Cabrits	5
Wildlife Reserve	
Dyer Estate	1
Natural Monument	
Indian River	nd
Total	75

Source: WCMC (unpublished data)

oculatus and *Ameiva fuscata*) are endemic (Corke, 1992), however neither of these lives in moist forests. *Iguana delicatissima*, the Lesser Antiguan iguana, which is listed as vulnerable by IUCN (Groombridge, 1993) occurs on the island.

There have been 166 species of birds recorded on Dominica, of which 59 species breed there (Johnson, 1988). Species diversity is highest in the lowland and montane rain forest (Evans, 1986). There are two single-island endemics, the red-necked amazon *Amazona arausiaca* and the imperial amazon *A. imperialis*; both are threatened, are dependent on rain forest and are now concentrated on Morne Diablotin (Collar *et al.*, 1992). Nine other species are restricted to the Lesser Antilles (Johnson, 1988).

The only native mammals are bats. With 12 species Dominica has the highest bat diversity in the Lesser Antilles. One species *Myotis dominicensis* is endemic to the island and three are restricted to the Antilles: *Monophyllus plethodon*, *Ardops nichollsi* and *Brachyphylla cavernarum*. There are six introduced mammals, including the agouti *Dasyprocta antillensis* which was probably brought in by the Arawak indians.

Conservation Areas

Legally established conservation areas cover 171 sq. km or about 23 per cent of Dominica, but only four of these areas are in IUCN's categories I–IV (Table 13.5). The largest is the Northern Forest Reserve (category VIII) at 88 sq km — all others, except Morne Trois Piton, are 5 sq. km or less. A ten year management plan has been drafted for Morne Trois Pitons National Park by Scheele (1989). Morne Diablotin has been proposed as a site for a new national park of about 25 sq. km.

The degree of protection of Dominica's forests is not clear. There is, for instance, a proposal to put a principal highway through the east side of the Northern Forest Reserve. There is also a hydropower scheme being developed in Morne Trois Pitons National Park which includes transformation of one of the main attractions of the area — Freshwater Lake — into a reservoir. In addition, squatters are tolerated in this park, because of the country's need for agricultural land (CCA/IRF, 1991b).

Initiatives for Conservation

An environmental monitoring programme, the Dominica Multiple Land Use Project, has been in progress for ten years. This study has two main objectives: an assessment of the impact of different forms of land use on the flora and fauna of the island and a study of how best to improve the economy by developing particular forms of agriculture, forestry, industry and tourism without conflicting with conservation interests (Evans, 1986).

Non-governmental organisations include the Dominica Conservation Association. This society is working on a development plan for the country. It has received funding from the Caribbean Conservation Association and the MacArthur Foundation. The Caribbean Natural Resources Institute has sponsored a cottage forest industries programme, organising sawyers and serving as a timber marketing outlet.

INTRODUCTION – GRENADA

The State of Grenada includes the large island of Grenada and the much smaller islands of Carriacou and Petit Martinique in the Grenadines, as well as a number of tiny islands off the main ones. Only the island of Grenada is discussed here as the others have no rain forest on them.

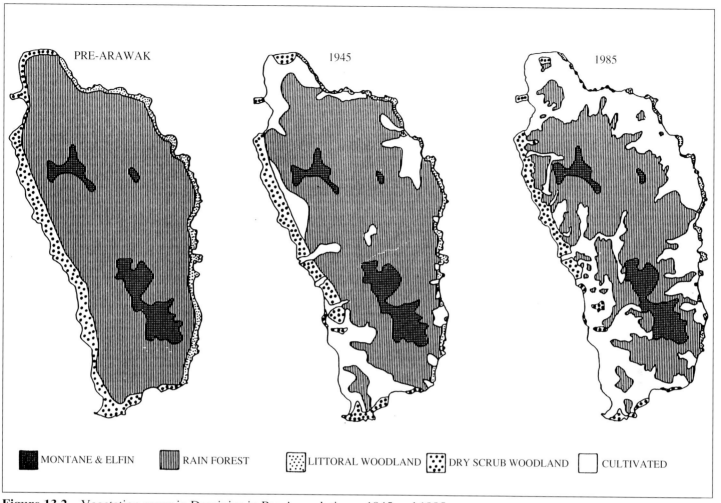

MONTANE & ELFIN   RAIN FOREST   LITTORAL WOODLAND   DRY SCRUB WOODLAND   CULTIVATED

Figure 13.2   Vegetation cover in Dominica in Pre-Arawak times, 1945 and 1985.   *Source:* Evans (1986)

Grenada is dominated by mountain peaks, steep ridges and deep, narrow valleys. The island's principal peak, Mount St Catherine (833 m), is located in the northern half of the ridge that runs north-south through the centre of the island. The slopes are comparatively gentle in the east where there are some fairly extensive coastal plains. The western side is more rugged. There are low hills in the north-east and south-west.

June to December is the wetter season, with some risk of hurricanes. On the coast rainfall is about 1500 mm, in the mountains it may reach 5000 mm. Average annual temperature at sea level is about 30°C (CCA/IRF, 1991c).

The Carib Indians living on the island at the time of French occupation in 1650 were more or less completely exterminated by 1654. The island was taken over by the British in 1762, won back by the French in 1779, returned to Britain in 1783 and then became an independent nation within the Commonwealth in 1974. The population is mostly of African origin, descendants of the slaves brought in to tend the sugar cane. There are six major settlements located in the coastal area of the island, the largest is the capital, St George's. Average population density is 294 people per sq. km.

In the early eighteenth and nineteenth centuries, sugar cane was the main crop on the island. Agriculture is still the single most important sector of Grenada's economy. Nowadays, the principal export crops are cocoa, bananas, nutmeg and mace.

Forest Resources and Management
Figure 13.3 shows the distribution of the vegetation on Grenada

as indicated by Beard in 1949. The most recent map of actual vegetation cover was compiled from interpretation of aerial photographs taken in 1982 (Eschweiler, 1982). At that time there were 17 sq. km of "montane rain forest" (this includes Beard's (1949) categories of montane thicket, elfin woodland and palm brake) and 23 sq. km of "closed evergreen rain forest" (including Beard's primary and secondary rain forest and lower montane forest). There was also 18 sq. km of "moist deciduous and semi-deciduous forest", 28 sq. km of ruinate cropland and grazing land reverting to secondary growth and 2 sq. km of mangrove. Eschweiler estimated that as little as a quarter (10 sq. km) of the 40 sq. km of rain forest on Grenada was relatively undisturbed. The remaining forests are all in steep inaccessible areas. The montane thicket is found on the summit of the main watersheds from Mount Qua Qua south towards Mount Sinai and on lesser ridges in the area, while the evergreen and semi-evergreen forest is found in a small patch on Morne Delice. Mangroves occurred mainly at Levera Pond in the northeast and also at the head of deep inlets along the south coast. FAO (1993a) reports the same area (60 sq. km) of forest remaining on the island, though all of it is considered to be in the moist deciduous zone.

About 48 sq. km of nominally "forested" land belongs to the Government (CCA/IRF, 1991c); 32.6 sq km of this is Crown land and 15.4 sq. km is Grand Etang Forest Reserve.

There has been little forestry on the island except in the Grand Etang Forest Reserve. Much of the timber in this reserve was severely damaged by Hurricane Janet in 1955. A few small government plantations of, principally, blue mahoe *Hibiscus*

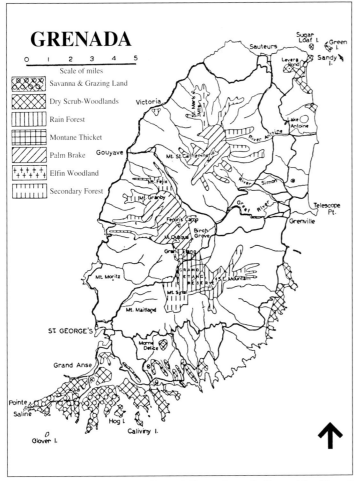

GRENADA

Scale of miles 0 1 2 3 4 5

Savanna & Grazing Land
Dry Scrub-Woodlands
Rain Forest
Montane Thicket
Palm Brake
Elfin Woodland
Secondary Forest

Figure 13.3 The vegetation of Grenada as indicated by Beard in 1949. *Source:* CCA/IRF (1991c) based on Beard (1949)

elatus exist, covering a total of 165 ha (CCA/IRF, 1991c). Two nurseries are operated by the Forestry department for the production of timber and Christmas tree seedlings.

Most roundwood is imported, primarily for the construction industry. There are four local sawmills but at least up to 1986 none had secondary processing equipment, there was no drying kiln on the island and only one saw capable of processing logs from old-growth forests of mature plantations (CCA/IRF, 1991c).

Deforestation

The early European colonists cleared most of the low altitude forest to plant sugar, along with some indigo and cotton. Later many of the higher areas were also cleared for cash crops or shifting agriculture.

The forests have also been degraded for many centuries by extensive collecting of wood for fuel. Large quantities were needed to fuel the sugar factory boiling houses and rum distilleries. Charcoal is traditionally the primary cooking fuel in Grenada and the demand for this and firewood still contributes to the overall exploitation of the forest. There is, however, no reliable information on the use of these fuels or the extent of their contribution to deforestation.

According to FAO (1993a), Grenada is one of the two countries in the Americas where the area of forest is increasing rather than decreasing — the other is Puerto Rico. It is reported that the island is gaining 2 sq. km of forest each year, an annual increase of 4.3 per cent.

Biodiversity

Beard (1949) recorded 120 tree species, of which 15 were Lesser Antillean endemics. One rain forest tree, *Maytenus grenadensis*, is endemic to the island.

Grenada has three native amphibian species, *Eleutherodactylus johnstonei*, *E. urichi* and *Leptodactylus wagneri*, the last two of which are found in the Grand Etang forests (Corke, 1992). In addition, the cane toad *Bufo marinus* has been introduced, originally to control pests in sugar-cane fields.

There were 15 terrestrial reptile species on the island, but two snakes (*Liophis melanotus* and *Pseudoboa neuwiedi*) are believed extirpated (Corke, 1992). There is one endemic, a worm snake *Typhlops dominicana*. Three other species, the lizards *Anolis aeneus* and *A. richardi* and the snake *Mastigodryas bruesi* are regional endemics (Corke, 1992) and there are two introduced species (a tortoise and a gecko).

About 150 species of birds have been recorded in Grenada (Groome, 1970) but only 35 of these are resident species of land bird (Blockstein, 1988). The only species listed as threatened by Collar *et al.* (1992) is the endemic Grenada dove *Leptotila wellsi*, of which only 100 or so remain. It is threatened principally by habitat destruction. It is not, however, an inhabitant of the rain forest, but is found in lowland dry-scrub woodland.

The only native mammals in Grenada are its eleven species of bat; none is endemic and little information exists on their status. Introduced mammals on the island include the greater and lesser Chapman's murine opossums — *Marmosa robinsoni chapmani* and *M. fuscata carri* respectively — and the nine-banded armadillo *Dasypus novemcinctus* (CCA/IRF, 1991c). Several other species have been introduced more recently, including the mona monkey *Cercopithecus mona* and the mongoose *Herpestes auropunctatus*, both of which are considered serious pests.

Conservation Areas

There are, at present, no officially designated national parks in Grenada. A plan for a nationwide system of national parks and protected areas has been prepared (GOG/OAS, 1988), but has not yet been officially accepted by the government. There is one 15.5 sq. km forest reserve in the country, Grand Etang, which was established in 1906 and enlarged in 1963 (CCA/IRF, 1991c). However, logging can occur in the reserve and although hunting and trapping are prohibited there is little protection of the area.

Initiatives for Conservation

There is a National Trust and Historical Society in Grenada which is concerned with the island's flora and fauna as well as its historical and cultural heritage.

INTRODUCTION – GUADELOUPE

The two large islands of Basse-Terre and Grande-Terre, separated by the Rivière Salée, make up most of Guadeloupe. A few smaller islands (Marie Galante, la Désirade and Saintes archipelago) are also associated. The islands of Saint Barthélémy and Saint Martin, situated about 200 km north, are part of the same administrative unit.

Grande-Terre, a flat limestone island, has no forest and virtually no natural vegetation remaining on it. Basse-Terre is volcanic and mountainous, rising to 1467 m at La Soufrière volcano, the highest peak in the Lesser Antilles. Most land below 400 m on this island has been developed but there is still untouched rain forest and lower montane forest at higher altitudes (Davis *et al.*, 1986).

The climate on Guadeloupe is warm and humid. In the town of Basse-Terre, mean monthly maximum temperatures vary from 24.4°C in February to 27.7°C in August. Average annual rainfall is 1814 mm and the wettest months are from June to September.

A French colony was established on Guadeloupe in 1635 and the country has remained a French possession. It is an overseas department and an administrative region of France. About half the population live in urban areas, with concentrations at the main port of Pointe-à-Pitre and its suburb of Les Abymes, as well as in the capital town of Basse-Terre.

Bananas, sugar and rum are the main agricultural exports. However, tourism, not agriculture, is the main economic activity of Guadeloupe.

Forest Resources and Management

FAO (1993a) estimates that there is as much as 930 sq. km of forest in Guadeloupe, all in the tropical rain forest zone. The Office National des Forêts, in contrast, reports only 650 sq. km of forest on the island (ONF, 1990). Of these, 388 sq. km, comprising 280 sq. km of "forêt départementalo-domaniale", 15 sq. km of littoral "forêt domaniale", 13 sq. km of departmental forest and 80 sq. km of mangrove, are controlled by ONF. The remaining 262 sq. km of forest is either in private hands or is public forest not managed by the ONF. The mangrove area is the largest in the Lesser Antilles (Putney, 1982). The main area is around Grand Cul de Sac Marin. There are also swamp forests in the north of Basse-Terre. Figure 13.4 maps the vegetation on Guadeloupe as shown on a Centre d'Etude de Géographie Tropicale map published in 1980.

Under a management plan which ran from 30 May 1979 to 31 December 1990, 150 sq. km of the forêt départementalo-domaniale at higher altitudes was designated a protected zone where no silviculture was to be undertaken. A further 80 sq. km was designated a production area for mahogany and 50 sq. km was designated a production area for local timbers.

A proposed management plan to follow on from this designated 10 sq. km to be planted with mahogany, 10–15 sq. km to be reafforested with a mixture of mahogany and local tree species, 5 sq. km to be reafforested with local tree species following the effects of Hurricane Hugo and 5 sq. km to be allowed to regenerate naturally.

Deforestation

Forests on Guadeloupe were seriously affected by Hurricane Hugo in September 1989. There is little information on the causes of deforestation on the island but FAO (1993a) estimates that 3 sq. km are lost each year, an annual rate of 0.3 per cent.

Biodiversity

Ten bat species are found on Guadeloupe, two of them (*Eptesicus guadeloupensis* and *Sturnira thomasi*) restricted to the island (Honacki *et al.*, 1982). The racoon *Procyon minor* may be an endemic species on Guadeloupe, but it may be conspecific with the North American *P. lotor* (Honacki *et al.*, 1982); it is almost certainly a human introduction.

There is one endemic bird, the Guadeloupe woodpecker *Melanerpes herminieri*. It is most commonly found in areas of moist forest on Basse-Terre (Short, 1974).

The numbers of reptiles and amphibians on the island is unknown. Two reptiles, excluding the marine turtles, are listed as threatened. These are *Iguana delicatissima* and the snake *Alsophis rijersmai* (Groombridge, 1993).

Table 13.6 Conservation areas in Guadeloupe

Existing conservation areas in IUCN's categories I–IV are listed. For information on Biosphere Reserves and Ramsar Sites, see Chapter 8.

National Park	*Area (sq. km)*
Guadeloupe	173
Nature Reserve	
Grand Cul de Sac Marin	37
Total	210

Conservation Areas

There is one national park and one nature reserve (Table 13.6). Management of reserves is the responsibility of the Parc National de Guadeloupe under the control of the Ministry of the Environment. The national park, which is mostly forested, is co-managed by ONF. Several new sites are proposed.

INTRODUCTION – MARTINIQUE

Martinique is the second largest island in the Lesser Antilles. It is mountainous, particularly in the northern half. The highest peak, Mt Pelee (1397 m), is an active volcano in the far north. Other major massifs are Morne Jacob and Carbet.

There is a well defined dry season from November to March. Average annual rainfall on high ground in the north is ca 7500 mm. The south is much drier, with ca 500 mm annual rainfall. The island is within the hurricane belt.

Martinique was already inhabited by Caribs when discovered by Columbus in 1493. A French colony was first established in 1635. Since then, apart from intermittent periods under English control, it has been governed by France of which it became an Overseas Department in 1946.

Population density is high (around 400 people per sq. km); over 30 per cent are concentrated in three adjacent urban areas in the western-central part of the island — Fort-de-France (the capital), Schoelcher and Lamentin. As many as 81 per cent of the population are urban dwellers. Of the economically active population, numbering ca 130,000 in 1989, only 10 per cent are involved in agriculture.

Principal exports are agricultural products (bananas, rum and sugar) and petroleum products, synthesised from imported crude petroleum. In 1988, 83 sq. km of land were under banana cultivation, and 34.6 sq. km under sugar-cane.

Forest Resources and Management

Forest of some description reportedly covers approximately 44 per cent of the island (D. Chalmers, in litt). There are said to be some areas of virtually pristine rainforest in the remote mountain district of Plateau de la Concorde at about 600 m (D. Chalmers, in litt.). Elsewhere, forests at lower elevations are secondary with some montane thicket, palm brake and elfin woodland at higher elevations (Davis *et al.*, 1986). Some of the forests in the south are privately owned. FAO (1993a) reports that there is 430 sq. km of forest on Martinique.

The second largest mangrove area in the Lesser Antilles, covering 22 sq. km, is found in Fort-de-France Bay. There are also reportedly almost pristine well-developed mangrove areas in the south-east.

Martinique's forest policy emphasises three roles for the forest: production, conservation and recreation. Commercial

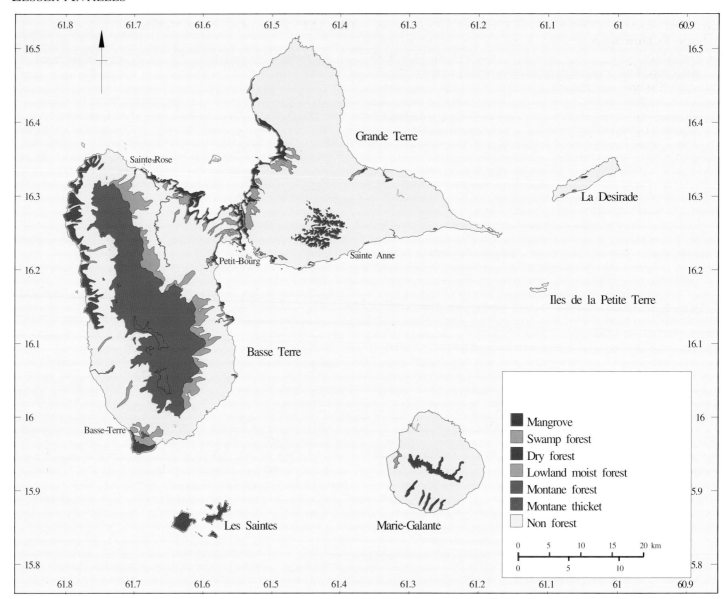

Figure 13.4   The vegetation on Guadeloupe as shown on a Centre d'Etude de Géographie Tropicale map published in 1980.

Source: Centre d'Etude de Géographie Tropicale (1980)

exploitation is limited in scale and restricted to around 12 species. Production was quoted in 1983 as around 6000 cu. m, compared with imports of 40,000 cu. m. Plantations of mahogany Swietenia have been established since 1960. There is active charcoal production, mainly in the private forests in the south.

In 1960 the rôle of the Office Nationale des Forêts (ONF — the National Forest Office), which had until then been purely protection of national and public forests, was expanded to cover the accommodation of leisure activities within forest areas. In 1981 their rôle was further extended to include the management of all littoral forest, including mangrove and any forest associated with the 120 beaches fringing the island. To meet the increasing demand for leisure activities there are now 350 km of forest roads and trails of which 170 km are maintained by the forest service.

Deforestation
One of the major problems on the island is the pressure exerted on the fragile littoral forest by the large number of campers using sites near the beaches. The annual rate of deforestation is estimated to be 0.5 per cent, or 2 sq. km per year (FAO, 1993a).

Biodiversity
Martinique has 24 recorded endemic plant species. Several tree species are considered in need of monitoring, including the endemics *Didymopanax urbanianum* (syn. *Schefflera urbaniana*) (Araliaceae), found at ca 800 m, *Sloanea dussii* (Elaeocarpaceae) and *Drypetes dussii* (Fiard, 1992; D. Chalmers, *in litt*). The endemic dwarf shrub *Tibouchina chamaecistus* which occurs at high altitude is classified as Vulnerable because of picking of flowers and uprooting. *Avicennia schauerana* and *Pterocarpus officinalis* are also of note (D. Chalmers, *in litt*).

Five single-island endemic reptiles have been recorded; two of these (*Ameiva major* and *Leiocephalus herminieri*) are believed extinct, while a third, *Liophis cursor*, was last seen in the 1960s. The other two endemic species are *Anolis roquet* and *Bothrops lanceolatus*. The threatened *Iguana delicatissima* is found on the island. One regionally endemic amphibian, *Eleutherodactylus martinicensis*, occurs.

The one recorded native terrestrial mammal, the endemic Martinique rice rat *Megalomys desmarestii*, is extinct. Nine chiropterans have been recorded. Introduced mammals include the agouti *Dasyprocta aguti* and mongoose *Herpestes auropunctatus*.

Some 53 breeding birds have been recorded of which one, the Martinique oriole *Icterus bonana*, is endemic; it is classified as endangered by Collar *et al.* (1992), its decline being chiefly attributable to brood-parasitism by the shiny cowbird *Molothrus bonariensis*. The oriole inhabits all the island's forest types except cloud-forest. Eight other species confined to the Lesser Antilles occur, including the endangered white-breasted thrasher *Ramphocinclus brachyurus*, which is found in dry forest on Martinique and St Lucia only.

Conservation Areas

Since 1976, 70 per cent of Martinique has been classified as a Regional Nature Park which has an IUCN category of V; within the park, areas are zoned to safeguard different land uses, although it is unclear how effective or comprehensive protection is. There is a 4 sq. km nature reserve on the Caravelle Peninsula on the east coast, also established in 1976; it is not known how much of this is forested. Other conservation areas within IUCN category I–IV are listed in Table 13.7. Both the nature park and nature reserve are administered by a board composed of representatives of the municipalities, the region and the department. The administration is separate from the ONF.

Conservation Initiatives

An arboretum with over 60 indigenous tree species has been established at La Donis, close to a popular forest recreation area. Two botanical trails have been created, one in mesophytic forest in the north and the other in xerophytic forests at Grand Macabou.

INTRODUCTION – ST KITTS AND NEVIS

The main part of St Kitts has a rugged backbone dominated by the Northwest Range and including the Central and Southeast Ranges. There are three linked volcanoes in the Northwest Range, the highest, Mt Liamuiga, reaching 1156 m. The steeper part of the mountainous interior of St Kitts is surrounded by an upland forest belt which grades into a gradually sloping coastal plain. This plain is covered primarily by sugar cane with expanding patches of diversified agricultural crops and some pasture land.

Nevis is approximately circular and is dominated by the 985 m high Nevis Peak which forms the central part of a north-south spine completed by Windy Hill in the north and Saddle Hill in the south.

The climate of both islands is tropical and heavily influenced by steady northeast trade winds. Mean annual temperature is about 27°C. Annual precipitation is 1625 mm on St Kitts and 1170 mm on Nevis.

The Carib Indians remained on St Kitts until the early 17th century. A small number of British established a settlement there in 1624 and were followed soon after by the French. Within a few years all the resident Caribs had been killed or enslaved. Nevis was settled by a group of Englishmen in 1628. France ceded St Kitts to the British in the early 18th century. The federation of St Kitts and Nevis became an independent nation in 1983. Most of its population are descendants of the slaves brought in to work in the sugar cane fields. The chief town on St Kitts is the capital, Basseterre; on Nevis the major town is Charlestown. About half of the population are urban dwellers.

On St Kitts the main economic activity was sugar production,

Table 13.7 Conservation areas in Martinique

Existing conservation areas in IUCN's categories I–IV are listed.

Bird Reserve	Area (sq. km)
Ilets de Ste Anne	<0.1
Littoral Conservation Area	
Caravelle	2.5
Précheur/Gd Rivière	5
Nature Reserve	
Caravelle	4
Total	11.5

Source: WCMC (unpublished data)

now tourism is gradually replacing agriculture as the major economic sector. Agriculture (fruit and vegetables), fisheries and tourism are important on Nevis.

Forest Resources and Management

The present vegetation of St Kitts and Nevis is greatly disturbed by human activities. In most lowland areas all traces of natural vegetation have been removed. Although the mountain peaks are covered in forest, it is unlikely that this is virgin. Storms undoubtedly have an impact on the forest and maintain much of it in a pre-climax condition (CCA/IRF, 1991d). Vegetation cover as recorded by Beard in 1949 is shown on Figure 13.5.

There is an estimated 65 sq. km of woodland/forest on St Kitts, of which 23 sq. km is cloud and rainforest, 21 sq. km moist forest and the remaining 21 sq. km dry forest (Mills, 1988). Forest on Nevis covers an estimated 19 sq. km. The upland forested areas on both St Kitts and Nevis appear to be increasing in extent as abandoned agricultural land reverts to secondary forest. FAO (1993a) estimate a total cover of 130 sq. km, all in the moist deciduous zone.

Traditionally, the management of forested areas on St Kitts was undertaken by the sugar estate owners. Although initially conserving the forests, they began to cut them down to increase the area of sugar cane. As a result, in 1904 a Forest Ordinance established a Forestry Board to control the cutting. This was never very effective and in 1987 a National Conservation and Environmental Protection Act was passed. This covers numerous aspects of conservation including the establishment and administration of protected areas, protection of forests, soil and water conservation, reforestation, control of charcoal production and control of logging. At present forestry falls under the Director of Agriculture.

The Forest Ordinance of 1904 declared all forested lands on both St Kitts and Nevis above 1000 feet (330 m) in elevation as crown lands and even now nearly all forested areas, except the dry forest on the Southeast Peninsula of St Kitts, are owned by the government.

The only substantial stand of tall forest on Nevis is on the northwestern side of the mountain above Jessups (Davis *et al.*, 1986). Palm brake is found on Nevis's mountain slopes above 550 m on the eastern and southern slopes and above 700 m on the northern and western slopes (CCA/IRF, 1991d). Elfin woodland is on the summits of the mountains. Good stands of white mangrove *Laguncularia racemosa* still exist on Nevis at

Newcastle Bay, Pinneys Estate and the mouth of the Bath Stream (Rodrigues, 1990).

There is no forest management or protection programme on Nevis and the island has no active forestry unit despite proposals for forest management having been prepared by the Caribbean Development Board as long ago as 1983.

Deforestation

Most of Nevis below 600 m has been cultivated since the late 1600s and as early as 1687 it was reported by Sloane (1707) that "the clearing of land extended almost to the top of the central mountain". The area under cultivation (for sugar and subsequently mainly for cotton) has declined dramatically on Nevis during this century, resulting in large areas of fallow land. Figures for the rate of deforestation in St Kitts and Nevis in the recent FAO publication (FAO, 1993a) are not consistent. In Table 4c of this report, deforestation is given as nil, but the annual rate of deforestation is 0.2 per cent. In Table 8c, area deforested is zero, but it is reported that 100 per cent of the deforestation occurs in the moist deciduous zone.

Charcoal was reported in the 1940s to be the principal forest product, much of it produced in Nevis resulting in the destruction of large areas of forest on the leeward side of the island. A 1980 household census revealed that just under 30% of households used wood and/or charcoal for cooking. Residential encroachment is a threat to the higher elevation forest in Nevis

(CCA/IRF, 1991d). Uncontrolled grazing reportedly hampers any forest regeneration (D. Chalmers, *in litt.*).

One of the major mangrove locations on St Kitts, Great Heeds Pond, which is also an important habitat for wildlife, particularly migratory birds, is under stress from solid waste dumping and other industrial activities.

Biodiversity

Beard (1949) reported 121 tree species on St Kitts and Nevis. The islands have two endemic plant species (WCMC, 1992).

St Kitts and Nevis has five lizards, four geckos and two snakes (CCA/IRF, 1991d). IUCN (Groombridge, 1993) lists two of these as threatened — these are *Iguana delicatissima* and *Alsophis rufiventris*. There are two native amphibians, *Eleutherodactylus johnstonei* and *Leptodactylus fallax*, although the latter may be extinct on the islands, and the cane toad has been introduced.

There are at least 35 resident breeding bird species on St Kitts; Morris and Lemon (1982) recorded 77 bird species during a survey in 1982. A minimum of 70 species of birds has been sighted on Nevis (Hilder, 1989). The only globally threatened bird listed as occurring on the islands by Collar *et al.* (1992) is the West Indian whistling duck *Dendrocygna arborea*. It appears likely that this marsh-dwelling duck no longer occurs there.

The only native mammals on St Kitts and Nevis are bats. At

Figure 13.5   The vegetation of St Kitts and Nevis as recorded by Beard in 1949.

Source: Beard (1949)

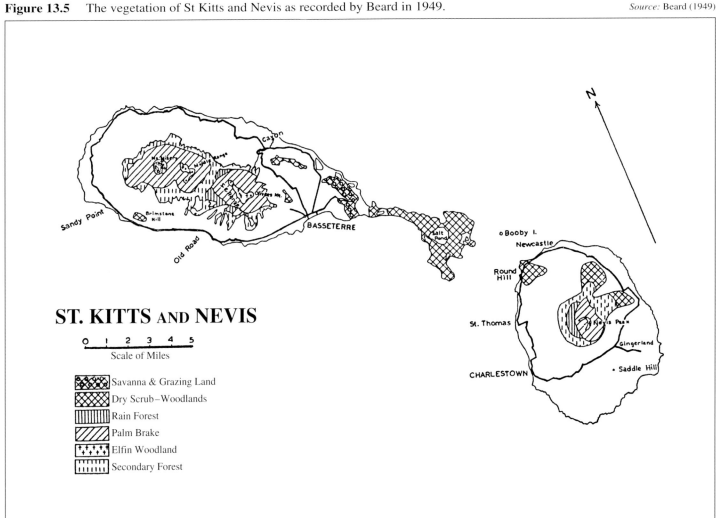

ST. KITTS AND NEVIS

0 1 2 3 4 5
Scale of Miles

Savanna & Grazing Land
Dry Scrub–Woodlands
Rain Forest
Palm Brake
Elfin Woodland
Secondary Forest

least seven species occur on St Kitts including the regional endemics *Ardops nichollsi*, *Brachyphyllum cavernarum* and *Monophyllus plethodon*. Two species have been identified on Nevis, *Artibeus jamaicensis* and *Molossus molossus*. Introduced species on St Kitts and Nevis are the vervet monkey *Cercopithecus aethiops* and the mongoose *Herpestes auropunctatus* as well as rats and mice. There is a small feral herd of white-tailed deer *Odocoileus virginianus* on St Kitts.

Conservation Areas

The only protected areas on St Kitts are the small Brimstone Hill Fortress National Park, which is a historical monument, and the Southeast Peninsula (Table 13.8). Neither plays any part in conserving moist forest. There are no protected areas on Nevis. The recent National Conservation and Environmental Protection Act provides for the establishment of other conservation areas. A total of fourteen or so sites on both islands have been proposed for protection.

Conservation Initiatives

A recent OAS Natural Resource Management Planning Project for St Kitts was concerned with the identification, propagation and outplanting of suitable forest species in multi-purpose plantations (CCA/IRF, 1991d).

The 1987 National Conservation and Environmental Protection Act allows for greater involvement by NG0s in the management of some protected areas. It is hoped that this will allow for improved public awareness and education.

INTRODUCTION – ST LUCIA

The island of St Lucia is volcanic with an irregular, steep terrain and very little flat land. About 90 per cent of the island has a slope greater than 1:10. The south-central mountain cluster rises to 950 m at Mt Gimie.

Mean annual temperature is 27°C with little seasonal variation. January to May are the drier months, hurricanes may occur from late June to early October and there are often severe tropical storms in November. Rainfall is uneven over the island, ranging from about 1500 mm annually in the extreme north and south to around 3700 mm at Quiless and Edmond in the mountainous south-central area.

Most of the population lives on or near the coast and is concentrated in the north-west. Urban centres are located on river mouths on the generally flatter coastal plain. Over 90 per cent of landholdings are 4 ha or less in size and these produce about 60 per cent of the country's agricultural produce. Agricultural output accounted for 17 per cent of GDP in 1986, with bananas being the dominant cash crop (CCA/IRF, 1991e). Tourism is becoming increasingly important in the island.

St Lucia was first occupied by Amerindians, the Ciboneys, about 2500 years ago. The Arawaks became established about

Table 13.8 Conservation areas in St Kitts and Nevis

Existing conservation areas in IUCN's categories I–IV are listed.

National Park	Area (sq. km)
Brimstone Hill Fortress	0.2
Southeast Peninsula and Recreation Area	26
Total	26.2

200 AD, but by the 13th century were displaced by the Carib indians. It was 1663 before the Caribs were expelled and the island then changed hands 14 times before finally being ceded to Britain in 1814.

Forest Resources and Management

The forests are now mostly confined to the more inaccessible mountainous areas in the interior of St Lucia. Figure 13.6 illustrates the vegetation cover on St Lucia as mapped by the Organisation of the American States (OAS) in 1984. In March 1988, CIDA estimated that approximately 77 sq. km (13 per cent) of the island was occupied by primary forest. Rain forest covered around 68 sq. km, while the rest was montane thicket, elfin woodland or other small climax forest associations. Around 60 per cent of the forest is on slopes of between 20° and 30°, with another 9 per cent on slopes over 30° (Piitz, 1983). Montane thicket is found principally at La Sociere, Piton Flore, Morne Locombe, Piton St Esprit and Grand Magazin. The only remaining area of elfin woodland, or cloud forest, of any size is on Mt Gimie (CCA/IRF, 1991e). FAO (1993a) reports only 50 sq. km of forest remaining.

There are very small patches of mangrove scattered mainly round the east and northwest coasts, few of which are still intact (CCA/IRF, 1991e). Approximately 2 sq. km are thought to exist of which those at Savannes Bay and Praslin are least degraded (CCA/IRF, 1991e). The largest area is at Man Kote but here, in particular, overharvesting of the mangroves for charcoal is a problem.

Lowland and lower montane forests account for nearly all the commercial timber land. Half of the merchantable timber volume is collected from six species within these forests: gommier *Dacryodes excelsa*, chataignier *Sloanea* sp., balata chien *Oxytheca pallida*, bois de masse *Licania ternatensis*, bois pain marron *Talauma dodecapetala* and mahaut cochon *Sterculia caribaea*. Forest reserves cover 75 sq. km of land. Exploited forests cover 16 sq. km of Protection Production Forest, of which 14 sq. km are in forest reserves, and 6.7 sq. km of Exploitation Forest on private land. It is estimated that the sustainable timber production from natural forests on the island is only 1200 cu m per year (FAO, 1991).

Plantations on the island are mostly small and cover only 3 sq. km or thereabouts. The most commonly used species are mahogany *Swietenia macrophylla*, blue mahoe *Hibiscus elatus* and Caribbean pine *Pinus caribaea*.

Deforestation

There is little information available on the rate of deforestation in St Lucia. FAO (1993a) estimates an annual loss of 3 sq. km between 1981 and 1990, which gives the very high rate of 5.2 per cent per year. In 1980, Hurricane Allen damaged an estimated 40 per cent of trees in 80 per cent of the island's forests. Increasing population pressure and a rising demand for agricultural land are the main causes of forest clearing, and these have been exacerbated by the development of roads into formerly inaccessible forests (CCA/IRF, 1991e). These roads have enabled quite large tracts of forest to be illicitly removed for banana cultivation.

Firewood and charcoal are important fuels on the island; they are used by over 80 per cent of households, and the demand for these contributes to the exploitation of the forests.

Biodiversity

The number of plant species on St Lucia is unknown, but Beard

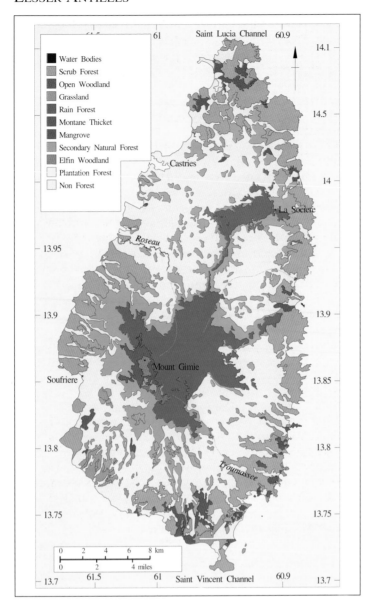

Figure 13.6 The vegetation on St Lucia as mapped by the Organisation of the American States (OAS) in 1984.

threatened, the latter may even be extinct, probably exterminated by the introduced mongoose. The other endangered bird on the island is the white-breasted thrasher *Ramphocinclus brachyurus*, which is found in semi-arid woodland on St Lucia and also on Martinique.

There are 17 species of reptile on the island, excluding marine turtles, five of these are endemic and three are introduced (Corke, 1992). The endemics are three lizards (*Anolis luciae, Cnemidophorus vanzoi* and *Sphaerodactylus microlepis*), and two snakes (*Bothrops caribbaeus* and *Liophis ornatus*). *C. vanzoi* and *L. ornatus* are found only on the Maria Islands; they are listed as vulnerable and endangered respectively by IUCN (Groombridge, 1993).

There are two native amphibians, *Eleutherodactylus johnstonei* and *Ololygon rubra*, neither of which is endemic. The former is reportedly abundant, the latter apparently not. The introduced *Bufo marinus* is also common (Corke, 1992).

Conservation Areas

Excluding the Forest Reserves, the amount of protected land in St Lucia is very small (Table 13.9). There is no national parks legislation. A good, broad conservation policy was articulated in 1977 but has yet to be implemented. Many of the tiny islands in the area have been proposed for protection.

Conservation Initiatives

There are a number of NGOs on the island and these have heightened public awareness about environmental issues. For instance, St Lucia Natural Trust has done much to encourage the conservation and development of national parks, while the Caribbean Natural Resources Institute has been working on community conservation and sustainable use of mangroves and other forests for several years.

INTRODUCTION – ST VINCENT AND THE GRENADINES

The Grenadines, made up of 31 islands and cays, contain no moist forest and will not be considered further in this account. The 345 sq. km island of St Vincent is dominated by a large volcanic cone, La Soufriere, which rises to almost 1220 m; it last erupted in 1979. This is separated from the Morne Garu Mountains and the rest of the central massif by a deep trough. The leeward side of the island is characterised by deep-cut val-

(1949) reported 151 trees on the island. Following Howard (1974–89) there are eleven plant species endemic to St Lucia. Regional endemism is about 12 per cent in the coastal dry zone but increases to 40–50 per cent in the flora of the primary rain forest and montane forest (CCA/IRF, 1991e).

There are nine bat species recorded on the island (Varona, 1974). These include three regional endemics, *Monophyllus plethodon, Ardops nichollsi* and *Brachyphylla cavernarum* (Johnson, 1988). There are also several introduced mammals including the opossum *Didelphis marsupialis insularis*, agouti *Dasyprocta aguti*, mongoose *Herpestes auropunctatus* and some rat and mice species.

There are 51 resident bird species on St Lucia (WCMC, 1992) of which four are endemic. These are the St Lucia parrot *Amazona versicolor*, Semper's warbler *Leucopeza semperi*, St Lucia black finch *Melanospiza richardsoni* and St Lucia oriole *Icterus laudabilis*. Of these, the parrot and warbler are

Table 13.9 Conservation areas in St Lucia

Existing conservation areas in IUCN categories I–IV are listed. Marine reserves are not included.

National Park	*Area (sq. km)*
Pigeon Island	0.2
Nature Reserve	
Maria Island	0.1
Fregate Island	0.1
Reserve	
Marigot	0.1
Sanctuary	
Parrot Sanctuary	15
Total	15.5

leys and high vertical coastal cliffs, while on the windward side the valleys tend to be wider and flatter, opening onto a fairly flat coastal plain.

The climate on the island is similar to that of St Lucia. Highest elevations receive most rainfall, up to 7000 mm in some places, while the valleys and coastal plains receive only 2000 mm or thereabouts. Hurricanes cause extensive damage.

St Vincent's early history of occupation is similar to that of St Lucia. Arawak indians were conquered by Caribs who, in turn, were forcibly ousted by the British in 1797, even though St Vincent was one of the islands the French and British had in 1748 agreed to designate as "neutral territory" for the sole benefit of the Caribs. The islands became an independent state within the British Commonwealth in 1979. Most (65 per cent) of the population are descendants of African slave labour and only two per cent are Amerindians (Birdsey *et al.*, 1986). The population in 1989 was estimated at 104,000, making the island one of the two most densely populated in the Lesser Antilles, the other being Grenada. The population is largely concentrated along the less steep coastal areas, particularly around Kingstown, the capital, but also in Mesopotamia Valley and on the leeward coast in Layou and Barrouallie (CCA/IRF, 1991f).

St Vincent's economy has traditionally been dependent on export crops. Bananas support approximately 85 per cent of St Vincent's population and account for the majority of exports (CCA/IRF, 1991f).

Forest Resources and Management

The distribution of the vegetation on St Vincent as indicated by Beard in 1949 is shown on Figure 13.7. Birdsey *et al.* (1986) estimated that, in 1984, around 130 sq. km of St Vincent was forested. However, only 16 sq. km of this was undisturbed primary forest (Table 13.10). FAO (1993a) reports that by 1990, the forest had been reduced to 110 sq. km.

A small area of mangrove occurs around a pond at Milkin Bay on the south coast, and a few other smaller areas are present on the island. It is, however, probable that mangroves were never very extensive on St Vincent. Somewhat larger areas are found on the Grenadines, the biggest at 21 ha on Union Island.

The primary forest remains only on the largely inaccessible interior mountain ridges and at the heads of deep steep valleys of the leeward coast. Due to the steep, rugged terrain and lack of access, it is unlikely that these forests will be harvested in the near future. The term secondary forest was applied to a broad spectrum of forests disturbed either by natural occurrences such as hurricanes and volcanic eruptions or by humans (Birdsey *et al.*, 1986).

Dacroydes excelsa, Ormosia monosperma, Actinostemen caribeus and *Talauma dodecapetala* together comprise 59 per cent of all sawtimber (Birdsey *et al.*, 1986). There is only a small primary forest industry on the island which supplies about 15 per cent of the lumber demand via a few pit sawyers. The secondary forest industry, though well developed, makes most of its products from imported wood.

There is very little plantation on the island, around 5 sq. km. Most of this (70 per cent) is blue mahoe *Hibiscus elatus*, with Caribbean pine *Pinus caribaea* and mahogany *Swietenia macrophylla* and *S. mahagoni* making up much of the remainder. With little possibility of harvesting timber from the remaining natural forests, the best hope for increasing timber production is through increasing the area of plantations (CCA/IRF, 1991F). Annual planting has ranged from only 2 to 4 ha per year (Prins, 1986).

There is no formal written forest policy and no forest management plans have been prepared for the island.

Deforestation

Most of the land below 300 m has been cultivated for many years as have many of the deep valleys at higher elevations. However, in recent years, much upslope expansion of agriculture has occurred, mostly to plant bananas. Many very steep slopes have been cleared and planted by shifting agriculturalists as land is in very short supply and the population is increasing. Collection of wood for fuel may be a serious problem but no data exist on the extent of this. Deforestation is estimated to be 3 sq. km per year, a rate of 2.1 per cent (FAO, 1993a).

Natural hazards such as volcanic eruptions, hurricanes and severe tropical storms have also caused deforestation on the island. For instance, almost 28 sq. km, or eight per cent of the island was deforested by the 1979 eruption of Soufriere (Birdsey *et al.*, 1986).

Biodiversity

There are four amphibian species on St Vincent: the introduced cane toad *Bufo marinus*, two tree frogs *Eleutherodactylus johnstonei* and *E. urichi*) and a foam-nesting frog *Leptodactylus fallax* (Corke, 1992). None is endemic to the island but *E. johnstonei* is found only in the West Indies.

Twelve reptiles are found on the island of which eleven are native and three endemic to St Vincent (Corke, 1992). The endemics are the tree lizards *Anolis griseus* and *A. trinitatis* and a snake *Chironius vincenti*. The snake is considered to be rare (Groombridge, 1993).

St Vincent and the Grenadines are reported to hold 95 species of breeding land birds (Faaborg and Arendt, 1985), with four seabird species breeding on St Vincent and 12 on the Grenadines (Halewyn and Norton, 1984). Only one species, the St Vincent parrot *Amazona guildingii*, is listed as threatened by Collar *et al.* (1992). The whistling warbler *Catharopeza bishopi* is the only other bird endemic to the island.

Most of the native mammals on St Vincent and the Grenadines are bats, eight species occur of which three are regional endemics. There are also seven introduced mammal species, including the opossum *Didelphis marsupialis*, the mongoose *Herpestes auropunctatus* and the agouti *Dasyprocta aguti*. The only native, non-flying mammal was the now extinct endemic rice rat *Oryzomys victus*.

Conservation Areas

The St Vincent Botanical Garden, established in 1765, is the oldest such site in the Western hemisphere. In 1791, it was also

Table 13.10 Area of forest and woodland in St Vincent in 1984

Forest type	Area (sq.km)	Area (per cent)
Young secondary forest	35.7	10.5
Secondary forest	37.06	10.9
Primary forest	16.32	4.8
Plantation forest	0.34	0.1
Palm forest	17.34	5.1
Elfin woodland	9.52	2.8
Dry scrub forest	13.26	3.9
Total	129.54	38.1

Source: Birdsey *et al.* (1986)

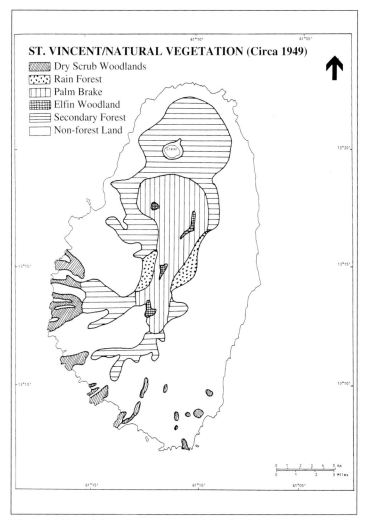

ST. VINCENT/NATURAL VEGETATION (Circa 1949)

- Dry Scrub Woodlands
- Rain Forest
- Palm Brake
- Elfin Woodland
- Secondary Forest
- Non-forest Land

Figure 13.7   The vegetation on St Vincent as recorded by Beard in 1949.   *Source:* CCA/IRF (1991f) based on Beard (1949)

the first Eastern Caribbean island to establish a forest reserve. Indeed, the Order setting King's Hill aside is thought to be the first piece of legislation providing for protected areas in the Americas (IUCN, 1992). In 1912, all land above 1000 feet in elevation was designated as crown property, reserved by law to protect forests in the upper watershed. However much encroachment, legal and illegal, has occurred and little protection of the area takes place.

A national parks system is being considered but is not fully approved. There are six forest reserves, three designated as category IV, and 23 wildlife reserves, all in category IV and all gazetted in 1987, but for none of these is the size known so they have not been listed here. Almost all of the wildlife reserves are islands within the Grenadines. An area of 44 sq. km in the centre of St Vincent was declared a reserve in 1987, particularly for the protection of St Vincent's parrot.

Conservation Initiatives

At the end of the 1980s the Government took significant steps to focus public attention on environmental concerns. A new Ministry of Health and the Environment was created in 1989. The Prime Minister designated the 1990s as the Decade of the Environment in St Vincent and established an Environment Protection Task Force to assist the government in developing an environmental agenda and programme.

A five year forestry assistance programme (1989–1994) funded by CIDA is currently addressing many of St Vincent's problems. A National Forest Management Plan is being prepared as part of this programme. The boundaries of the forest reserves will be surveyed and marked and the number of people working in the Forestry Division will be increased. Forest management policies and a draft Forest Resources Conservation Act have been prepared. The new act, replacing a 1945 law, will greatly expand the power of the Forestry Division. An environmental education programme is also part of the CIDA project.

References

Beard, J.S. (1949). The natural vegetation of the Windward and Leeward Islands. *Oxford Forestry Memoirs* No. 21. Clarendon Press, Oxford, U.K.

Birdsey, R., Weaver, P. and Nicholls, C. (1986). *The Forest Resources of St Vincent, West Indies.* Research Paper SO-229. U.S. Department of Agriculture, Forestry Service, Southern Forest Experimental Station, New Orleans, LA.

Blockstein, D.E. (1988). Two endangered birds of Grenada, West Indies: Grenada dove and Grenada hook-bill kite. *Caribbean Journal of Science* 24: 127–136.

Cater, J. (1944). *Forestry in the Leeward Islands.* Development and Welfare in the West Indies Bulletins, No. 7. Advocate Co., Ltd., Bridgetown, Barbados.

CCA/IRF (1991a). *Antigua and Barbuda Environmental Profile.* Caribbean Conservation Association, St Michael, Barbados/Island Resources Foundation, St Thomas, U.S. Virgin Islands.

CCA/IRF (1991b). *Dominica Environmental Profile.* Caribbean Conservation Association, St Michael, Barbados/Island Resources Foundation, St Thomas, U.S. Virgin Islands.

CCA/IRF (1991c). *Grenada Environmental Profile.* Caribbean Conservation Association, St Michael, Barbados/Island Resources Foundation, St Thomas, U.S. Virgin Islands.

CCA/IRF (1991d). *St Kitts and Nevis Environmental Profile.* Caribbean Conservation Association, St Michael,

Barbados/Island Resources Foundation, St Thomas, U.S. Virgin Islands.

CCA/IRF (1991e). *St Lucia Environmental Profile.* Caribbean Conservation Association, St Michael, Barbados/Island Resources Foundation, St Thomas, U.S. Virgin Islands.

CCA/IRF (1991f). *St Vincent and the Grenadines Environmental Profile.* Caribbean Conservation Association, St Michael, Barbados/Island Resources Foundation, St Thomas, U.S. Virgin Islands.

Centre d'Etudes de Géographie Tropical (1980). *La Guadeloupe — Planche 9 — Végétation.* Scale 1:150,000. Atlas des Départements d'Outre-Mer.

Collar, N.J., Gonzaga, L.P., Krabbe, N., Madroño Nieto, A., Naranjo, L.G., Parker III, T.A. and Wege, D.C. (1992). *Threatened Birds of the Americas. The ICBP/IUCN Red Data Book.* ICBP, Cambridge, U.K.

Corke, D. (1992). The status and conservation needs of the terrestrial herpetofauna of the Windward Islands (West Indies). *Biological Conservation* 62: 47–58.

Davis, S.D., Droop, S.J.M., Gregerson, P., Henson, L., Leon, C.J., Villa-Lobos, J.L, Synge, H. and Zantovska, J. (1986). *Plants in Danger. What do we know?* IUCN, Gland, Switzerland and Cambridge, U.K.

De Milde, R. (1987). *Inventory of the Exploitable Forests of Dominica.* FAO, Rome, Italy.

EARTHSTAT (1986). Preparation of natural vegetation map for Dominica, West Indies from 1:26,000 scale, black and white aerial photography, final report. Prepared by Earth Satellite Corporation for OAS, Washington, DC.

Eschweiler, J. (1982). *Explanatory Note to the Land Use Maps of Grenada, Carriacou and Petite Martinique (1982 Scale 1:25,000).* Land Use Division, Ministry of Agriculture, St Georges, Grenada.

Evans, P.G.H. (1986). Dominica multiple land use project. *Ambio* 15(2): 82–89.

Faaborg, J. and Arendt, W. (1985). St Lucia. In: *Wildlife Assessments in the Caribbean*, pp. 127–157. Institute of Tropical Forestry, USDA. Forest Services, Rio Piedras, Puerto Rico.

FAO (1991). *Tropical Forestry Action Plan: St Lucia.* FAO, Rome Italy.

FAO (1993a). *Forest resource assessment 1990: tropical countries.* FAO Forestry Paper 112. FAO, Rome, Italy.

FAO (1993b). *TFAP Update* 30. FAO, Rome, Italy.

Fiard, J.-P. (1992). *Arbres rares et menacés de la Martinique.* Collection régionale connaissance du patrimoine No 1.

GOG/OAS (1988). *Plan and Policy for a System of National Parks and Protected Areas.* Government of Grenada and Organisation of American States, Department of Regional Development, OAS, Washington, DC.

Groombridge, B. (Ed) (1993). *1994 IUCN Red List of Threatened Animals.* IUCN, Gland, Switzerland and Cambridge, U.K. 286 pp.

Groome, J. (1970). *A Natural History of the Island of Grenada.* Caribbean Printers Ltd., Arima, Trinidad.

Halewyn, R. van and Norton, R. (1984). The status and conservation of seabirds in the Caribbean. In: *Status and Conservation of the World's Seabirds.* Croxall, J., Evans, P. and Schreiber, R. (eds). ICBP Technical Publication No. 2, ICBP, Cambridge, U.K. Pp. 169–222.

Hilder (1989). *The Birds of Nevis.* Nevis Historical and Conservation Society, Charlestown, Nevis.

Honacki, J.H., Kinman, K.E. and Koeppl, J.W. (1982). *Mammal Species of the World.* Allen Press Inc. and The Association of Systematics Collections, Lawrence, Kansas, U.K.

Howard R.A. (ed.) (1974–1989). *Flora of the Lesser Antilles, Leeward and Windward Islands.* 6 vols. Arnold Arboretum, Jamaica Plain, Massachusetts, U.S.A.

Howard, R.A. (1989). The Lesser Antilles. In: *Floristic Inventory of Tropical Forests: the Status of Plant Systematics, Collections, and Vegetation, plus Recommendations for the Future.* Campbell, D.G. and Hammond, H.D. (eds). The New York Botanical Garden, New York, U.S.A. Pp. 347–349.

IUCN (1992). *Protected Areas of the World: A review of national systems. Volume 4: Nearctic and Neotropical.* IUCN, Gland, Switzerland and Cambridge, U.K.

Johnson, T.W. (1988). *Biodiversity and Conservation in the Caribbean: Profiles of Selected Islands.* ICBP Monograph No. 1. ICBP, Cambridge, U.K.

Lugo, A.E., Schmidt, R. and Brown, S. (1981). Tropical forests in the Caribbean. *Ambio* 10 (6): 319–324.

Mills, F. (1988). Wildlife Management in St Kitts. Proceedings of the fourth workshop of Caribbean foresters, Dominica, April 4–6, 1988. Institute of Tropical Forestry, Rio Pedras, Puerto Rico.

Morello, J. (1983). *Ecological Diagnosis of Antigua and Barbuda.* Organisation of American States, Department of Regional development, Washington, D.C.

Morris, M. and Lemon, R. (1982). *The Effects of Development on the Avi-fauna of St Kitts, West Indies.* McGill University, Montreal, Quebec.

OAS (1984). *Saint Lucia — Land Use and Vegetation.* Scale 1:50,000. Prepared by the Department of Regional Development of the Organisation of American states, with the collaboration of the Ministry of Agriculture, Lands, Fisheries, Co-operatives and Labour of the Government of St Lucia.

OAS (1990). *Natural Resources Assessment, Application and Projects for the Agricultural Sector of Antigua and Barbuda.* Department of Regional Development, Organisation of American States, Washington, DC.

ONF (1990). *Note sur la Politique Forestière de L'Office National des Forêts en Guadeloupe.* Unpublished report, L'Office National des Forêts

Piitz, P. (1983). *Forest Inventory Report.* Prepared for CIDA for the St Lucia-CIDA Forest Management Assistance Project, Ottawa, Canada.

Prins, P. (1986). *St Vincent and the Grenadines Forestry Sector Analysis: revision and update.* Canadian International Development Agency.

Prins, P. (1987). *Forestry Policy and Administration 1987–1997. Natural Resources and Rural Development Project, Commonwealth of Dominica.* Department of Regional Development, OAS, Washington, DC.

Putney, A.D. (1982). *Survey of Conservation Priorities in the Lesser Antilles: Final Report.* Eastern Caribbean Natural Area Management Program, St Croix, US Virgin Islands.

Rodrigues, D. (1990). *Dominant Flora and Vegetation Zones of Nevis.* Vanier College Press, St Laurent, Quebec, Canada.

Scheele, R. (1989). *Morne Trois Pitons National Park Management Plan 1990–2000.* Draft report prepared for the Division of Forestry and Wildlife, Dominica. OAS, Washington, DC.

Short, L.L. (1974). Habits of three endemic West Indian woodpeckers (Aves: Picidae). American Museum Novitates 2549.

Sloane, H. (1707). *A Voyage to the Islands of Madera, Barbados, Neives, St Christopher and Jamaica.* Volume 1. London, England.

Varona, L.S. (1974). *Catálogo de los Mamíferos Vivientes y Extinguidos de las Antillas.* Academia de Ciencias de Cuba.

WCMC (1992). *Global Biodiversity: Status of the Earth's Living Resources.* Chapman & Hall, London, U.K.

Authors: Martin Jenkins and Caroline Harcourt, Cambridge with contributions from Steve Bass, IIED, London; Dan Chalmers, Taverham, Norfolk and Frank Wadsworth, Southern Forest Experiment Station, Puerto Rico.

14 Puerto Rico

Country area   8900 sq. km
Land area   8860 sq. km
Population (mid-1994)   3.6 million
Population growth rate   1.0 per cent
Population projected to 2025   4.7 million
Gross national product per capita (1992)   US$6610
Forest (FAO, 1993)   3210 sq. km
Annual deforestation rate (1981–1990)   +1.4 per cent
Industrial roundwood production   —
Industrial roundwood exports   —
Fuelwood and charcoal production   —
Processed wood production   —
Processed wood exports   —

By the beginning of this century, Puerto Rico had already lost over 80 per cent of its forest cover. By the middle of the century, there was as little as 34 sq. km of virgin forest remaining. However, in the past 40 years, following the collapse of the sugar cane industry and the abandonment of much of the agricultural land, there has been a dramatic increase in the forest cover.

INTRODUCTION

The island of Puerto Rico is the easternmost and smallest of the Greater Antilles. It can be divided into three main physiographic units: a south-central volcanic mountainous region varying from 600–1338 m in elevation forming the Central Cordillera; a belt of rugged karst topography in the north-central and north-western parts of the island; and a discontinuous fringe of coastal plains.

Daily and annual temperature changes are minor although there are variations over the island. The lowest mean annual temperature is 18°C at Pico del Este and Cerro Maravilla and the highest is 27°C at Guayama on the south coast (Birdsey and Weaver, 1982). Average annual precipitation is 1800 mm, with coastal areas receiving 750 mm, while the summit of Luquillo receives over 4000 mm. A relatively dry season occurs from mid-December to the end of March (Birdsey and Weaver, 1982). Hurricanes occur quite commonly.

Puerto Rico was originally colonised by Igneris Amerindians around 100 AD. Late in the 15th century, the aggressive Tainos tribe colonised the east of the island, but they were displaced by the arrival of Europeans in 1508. Puerto Rico's population density, at 406 inhabitants per sq. km, is one of the highest in the world. The greatest population centres are located in the coastal plains, with over half the island's inhabitants concentrated in the metropolitan area surrounding the capital city of San Juan (Vivaldi, 1989). About 74 per cent of the people are urban dwellers. The island is a self-governing commonwealth in free association with the USA, and many Puerto Ricans live in the USA.

The major agricultural product is sugar cane, but there has been a change in emphasis from an agrarian economy to one based on light industry and business. Tourism is the third most important industry, after manufacturing and agriculture.

The Forests

Little and Wadsworth (1964) give a description of the different types of forest that used to occur on Puerto Rico and show eight climax forest types on their map — reproduced here as Figure 14.1. Not shown on this figure are the small patches of littoral woodland or mangrove.

Holdridge's Life Zone system has been used in this chapter to classify the forests of Puerto Rico (Ewel and Whitmore, 1973; Figure 14.2).

The Subtropical Dry Forest is characterized by deciduous vegetation, often with small and succulent leaves and spines or thorns. Canopy height is rarely above 15 m. Common trees include *Bursera simaruba*, *Prosopis juliflora*, *Cephalocereus royenii* and *Pictetia aculeata*. This zone covers 18 per cent of the island.

The Subtropical Moist Forest zone is the most widespread, occupying over 58 per cent of the island, but little forest remains in the area. The trees in this forest type are up to 30 m in height, many are deciduous and epiphytes are common. *Guassi attenuata*, an endemic palm species, is a conspicuous component of the limestone hill forests. The serpentine-derived soils in the south-west of the island support a unique vegetation which contains a number of endemics. The trees tend to be slender and only 12 m or so high. Species common in the moist forest zone include *Roystonea borinquena*, *Tabebuia heterophylla*, *Erythrina poeppigiana*, *Inga vera* and *I. laurina*. Species of *Nectandra* and *Ocotea* are prominent in many of the older secondary forests. Inland from the mangroves in this zone are remnants of swamp forests dominated by *Pterocarpus officinalis*.

The Subtropical Wet Forest zone covers about 23 per cent of the island. The forests contain more than 150 species of trees and have a closed canopy at around 20 m. Dominant trees are *Dacryodes excelsa*, *Sloanea berteriana* and *Manilkara bidentata*. Epiphytic ferns, bromeliads and orchids are abundant.

The Subtropical Rain Forest zone is found in only a small area on the Luquillo Mountains. Species composition is similar to that in the wet forest, but there is a high frequency of the palm *Prestoea montana* and more epiphytes.

The Subtropical Lower Montane Wet Forest life zone occurs in both the central and eastern parts of the island up to the summits of most mountains above 1000 m and occasionally extend-

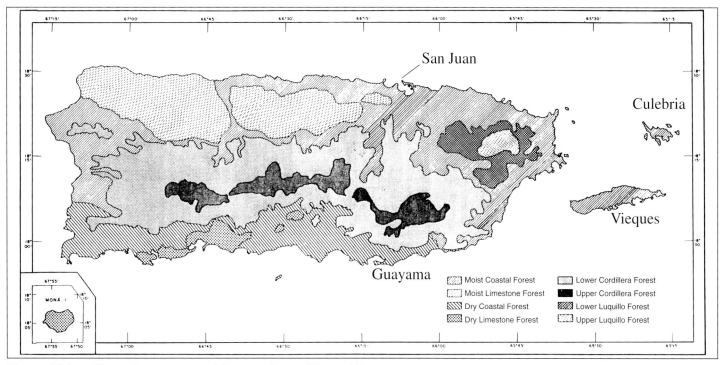

Figure 14.1 Climax forest types and forest regions of Puerto Rico

Source: Little and Wadsworth (1964)

ing down to almost 700 m. The forest is less rich than the sub-tropical wet forest with only 53 tree species recorded. *Cyrilla racemiflora* is probably the most abundant tree, though *Ocotea spathulata*, *Micropholis chrysophylloides* and *M. garciniaefolia* are also common, at least in eastern Puerto Rico (Wadsworth, 1951). Elfin woodland and palm brake associations are found in this forest zone.

The Subtropical Lower Montane Rain Forest is present only on the Luquillo Mountains. Species are similar to those in the Lower Montane Wet Forest, but epiphytes, palms and tree ferns are more common in the Rain Forest.

Mangroves

It is estimated that mangroves may have once covered about 240 sq. km in Puerto Rico (Wadsworth, 1968). Exploitation of the trees for fuel and wood during the Spanish period, a series of destructive hurricanes and reclamation of land for agriculture meant that the mangroves were reduced to around 64 sq. km by the 1930s (Carrera, 1975; Martinez *et al.*, 1979). Although this had increased slightly by 1959, urban development and industrialisation caused further destruction in the 1960s (Wadsworth, 1959). In 1979, Martinez *et al.* (1979) estimated that less than 60 sq. km remained.

Forest Resources and Management

When European colonists arrived on Puerto Rico in 1508, the island was almost completely forested (Wadsworth, 1950; Birdsey and Weaver, 1987). From 1815, when the island was opened to international trade, clearing took place at a geometric rate (Table 14.1) so that Dansereau (1966) reported *"The plant cover of the Island of Puerto Rico is now entirely controlled by man. There is no such thing as virgin vegetation, whether forest, savana, scrub, or grassland"*. However, other writers report that a few tiny areas of virgin forest, covering 0.4 per cent of the island or 34 sq. km, did survive to the middle of the 20th century (Table 14.2). Some 22 sq. km of this was in the Luquillo Mountains, while other areas were left in Carite, Toro

Negro, Guilarte, Maricao and on a few mountain tops that were in private ownership (Wadsworth, 1950; Birdsey and Weaver, 1982).

Puerto Rico's forest area has increased dramatically in the last 40 years as shown in Table 14.1. Although the different definitions of "forest" used by the various authors make the estimates not entirely comparable or reliable, they do give an indication of the trends over time. The increase in forest is a result of the new growth on the marginally productive pastures and croplands which have been deserted as a result of the migration of the rural population. Nevertheless, Table 14.1 gives an optimistic estimate of the present forest extent. A comparison with Table 14.2 from Brash (1987) gives an indication of how little **virgin** forest is left on the island.

Using a 1985 survey as a baseline, FAO (1993) estimates forest cover in Puerto Rico to be 3210 sq. km, with 490 sq. km in

Table 14.1 Historical Estimates of Forest Area for Puerto Rico.

Year of estimate	Forest Area (sq. km)	References
c. 1500	8,500	1 and 2
1828	5,870	2
1899	1,820	2
1912	1,690	1
1916	1,780	1
1931	810	3
1948	570	4
1960	820	5
1972	2,840	6

NB Different definitions of "forest" were used for these estimates, which makes comparisons somewhat unreliable.

References: 1. Murphy, 1916; 2. Wadsworth, 1950; 3. Gill, 1931; 4. Koenig, 1953; 5. Englerth, 1960; 6. Department of Natural Resources, 1972.

Source: Birdsey and Weaver (1982)

Table 14.2   Per cent of the island covered in different woody vegetation between the years of 1770–1978.

Cover	Year						
	1770	1830	1899	1912	1949	1972	1978
Virgin	94.0	60.2	0.9	0.9	0.4	0.4	0.4
Coffee shade	0.01	0.4	8.9	7.8	7.8	8.5	4.7
Brush and scrub	–	–	–	18.8	17.3	–	–
Secondary growth	0	0.0	0.0	0.0	11.4	33.0	32.3
Total*	94.0	60.6	9.8	27.5	36.9	41.9	37.4

* Total area of the island used here is 8,628 sq. km, this excludes offshore islands

Source: Brash (1987)

Table 14.3   Areas of different forest types in Puerto Rico in 1980

Forest Zone	All forest land*	Timberland+	Noncommercial forest land
Dry forest	405		405
Moist forest	1,224	604	620
Wet forest	1,037	701	336
Rain forest	13		13
LM Wet forest	96		96
LM Rain forest	12		12
Total	2,787	1,305	1,482

LM — Lower Montane
* Forest land — Land at least 10 per cent stocked by forest trees of any size, or formerly having had such forest tree cover and not currently developed for nonforest use.
+ Timberland — Forest land that is producing or is capable of producing crops of industrial wood and is not withdrawn from timber utilisation. Coffee shade is included in this category.

Source: Birdsey and Weaver (1982)

the tropical rain forest zone, 1510 sq. km in the moist deciduous zone and 1210 sq. km in the hill and montane forest zone. FAO's "forest" figures include any area with trees having over 10 per cent canopy cover. Birdsey and Weaver (1982) give a breakdown of the different forest types in the country in 1980 (Table 14.3), which is somewhat different from that given by FAO.

Forest plantations have had a significant role in reforestation. The major species planted is *Pinus caribaea,* with mahogany *Swietenia macrophylla* and *Swietenia mahagoni,* eucalyptus *Eucalyptus robusta,* teak *Tectona grandis* and others also being planted. Most reforestation is, however, occurring naturally.

Although consumption of wood and wood products on the island continues to rise, almost all of these are imported. The harvesting of wood from the forests is almost negligible at present, but it is suggested that with proper management the regenerating forests could provide Puerto Ricans with some wood in the future (Wadsworth and Birdsey, 1985).

Deforestation

Extensive clearing of the forests began when Puerto Rico was opened to international trade, with the clearing peaking at a rate of 0.86 per cent per year between 1830 and 1899 (Hill, 1899; Murphy, 1916; Gill, 1931; Wadsworth, 1950). Much of the forest was cleared for sugar cane and coffee plantations or other agricultural use.

Puerto Rico's forests also suffer damage from hurricanes; Hurricane Hugo in 1989 caused damage ranging from defoliation to breaking and even overturning of trees (Basnet *et al.,* 1992). However, according to FAO (1993), Puerto Rico is one of only three countries in Latin America and the Caribbean to be gaining forest at the present time. FAO (1993) estimates annual regeneration of forest between the years of 1981 and 1990 to be 42 sq. km, an annual increase of 1.4 per cent.

Figure 14.2   Holdridge's Life Zones of Puerto Rico   *Source:* Ewel and Whitmore (1973)

- ☐ Water bodies
- ⊠ Subtropical dry forest
- ▦ Subtropical moist forest
- ◩ Subtropical wet forest
- ▨ Subtropical rain forest
- ⊞ Lower montane wet forest
- ▤ Lower montane rain forest

Biodiversity

There are slightly over 3000 vascular plants on Puerto Rico and its adjacent islands, these include introduced species (Davis *et al.*, 1986). There are estimated to be 234 endemics; the highest numbers are found on the white sands of Tortuguero and on the Luquillo Mountains (Vivaldi, 1989). There are 547 tree species known to be native to Puerto Rico and another 203 species naturalized there (Little and Wadsworth, 1964; Little *et al.*, 1974).

The only native mammals on the island are fifteen species of bat (Starrett, 1962). None is endemic to Puerto Rico and none is listed as threatened by IUCN (Groombridge, 1993).

There are 46 reptiles (20 endemic) and 22 amphibians (14 endemic) in Puerto Rico (WCMC, 1992; Rivero, 1978). Of the five reptiles listed as threatened by IUCN (Groombridge, 1993), four are found on the small islands, rather than on the main island of Puerto Rico, and three of these are endemic. The Mona blind snake *Typhlops monensis* and the rhinoceros iguana *Cyclura cornuta* occur on Mona, the former is endemic; the Monito gecko *Sphaerodactylus micropithecus* occurs only on Monito and giant anole *Anolis roosevelti* occurs only on Culebra island and may even be extinct. The Puerto Rican boa *Epicrates inornatus* is endemic to the main island. There are also three amphibians listed as threatened, the golden coqui frog *Eleutherodactylus jasperi* and *E. karlschmidtii*, both endemic, and the Puerto Rican crested toad *Peltophryne lemur*, which occurs also on the British Virgin islands.

Around 275 bird species have been recorded on the island (Raffaele, 1989) of which 94 are resident breeding birds — there are 12 endemic species. Six bird species on Puerto Rico are listed as threatened by Collar *et al.* (1992), of which three are endemic to the island. Numbers of the endangered *Amazona vittata* dropped to 13 in 1975, due mainly to destruction of its habitat but also as a result of hunting, the pet-trade and a variety of other factors; further losses occurred as a result of Hurricane Hugo in 1989. In 1992, after an intensive conservation programme, wild populations were estimated at 40 and there were 58 in captivity. The other threatened endemics are the Puerto Rican nightjar *Caprimulgus noctitherus*, a species of the dry limestone forests, and the yellow-shouldered blackbird *Agelaius xanthomus*. The main cause of the decline of the once widespread blackbird appears to be parasitism of its nest by the shiny cowbird *Molothrus bonariensis*, which is a recent invader of the island (Wiley *et al.*, 1991).

The numbers of fish and invertebrates are unknown. Two of the latter are listed as threatened, the Mona cave shrimp *Typhlatya monae* and the Tuna cave roach *Aspiduchus cavernicola*, both are endemic (Groombridge, 1993).

Conservation Areas

Four US federal agencies and three Puerto Rican agencies are involved in protected area administration. Private conservation organisations also play a part.

Three categories of protected area have been created under US federal legislation in Puerto Rico: national forest, national wildlife refuge and national estuarine research reserve. The Department of Natural Resources (DRN) is the local governmental organisation responsible for nature conservation. The Commonwealth Forest Service administers the 14 commonwealth forests (covering around 240 sq. km; in IUCN's category VIII), while the wildlife refuges and natural reserves are managed by the Division of Sanctuaries and Natural Reserves — both are part of DRN.

The Spanish proclaimed forest reserves on Puerto Rico as early as 1876, before it was ceded to the US. However, the first of the existing reserves to be established (in 1907) was the Caribbean National Forest. This is now called the Luquillo Experimental Station and, at 113 sq. km, is the largest reserve on the island, but is classified as category VIII by IUCN and is consequently not included in Table 14.4. It is, however, shown on Figure 14.3, along with the Commonwealth Forests and those protected areas in IUCN's categories I–IV for which data are available.

Initiatives for Conservation

Several NGOs work in conservation including the Puerto Rico Conservation Foundation and the Conservation Trust of Puerto Rico. The former group, along with The Nature Conservancy and Conservation International provide support to run the conservation data centre of the Natural Heritage Programme of Puerto Rico. This Programme, established in 1988, encourages coordination between governmental institutes and NGOs in order to improve selection and management of protected areas.

Table 14.4 Conservation areas in Puerto Rico

Existing conservation areas in IUCN's categories I–IV.

Natural Areas

Ballena	1
Cabezas de San Juan	1
Canon de San Cristobal	3
Hacienda Buena Vista	0.3
Hacienda La Esperanza	9
Laguna Guaniquilla	2
Lands adjacent to the Bioluminescent Bay	1
Punta Yegua	0.3

Natural Reserves

Cayos de la Cordillera	1
Estuarina Nacional Bahia Jobos	11
Isla Caja de Muertos	2
Isla de Mona	56
La Parguera	50
Laguna Tortuguero	10
Puerto Mosquito (Vieques)	4

Wildlife Refuge

Boqueron	2
Embalse de Guajataca	3
Embalse de Luchetti	6
Humacao	10

National Wildlife Refuge

Cabo Rojo	2
Culebra	6
Desecheo	1
Total	180.6

Source: WCMC (unpublished)

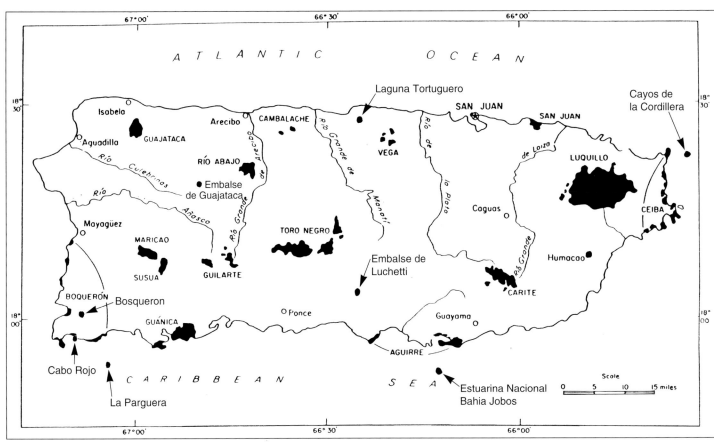

Figure 14.3 Protected areas of Puerto Rico, including Commonwealth Forests and Luquillo Experimental Station

Source: Little and Wadsworth (1964) and WCMC (unpublished)

References

Basnet, K., Likens, G.E., Scatena, F.N. and Lugo, A.E. (1992). Hurricane Hugo: damage to a tropical rain forest in Puerto Rico. *Journal of Tropical Ecology* 8: 47–55.

Birdsey, R.A. and Weaver, P.L. (1982). *The Forest Resources of Puerto Rico.* U.S. Department Agricultural Forest Service Resource Bulletin SO-85. Pp. 59. Southern Forest Experiment Station, Louisiana, New Orleans.

Birdsey, R.A. and Weaver, P.L. (1987). *Forest Area Trends in Puerto Rico.* Research Note SO-331. U.S. Department of Agriculture, Forest Service, Southern Forest Experiment Station.

Brash, A.R. (1987). The history of avian extinction and forest conversion on Puerto Rico. *Biological Conservation* 39(2): 97–111.

Carrera, C.J. (1975). *Efectos historicos de la interaccion entre los factores socioeconomicos y los manglares: el caso de Puerto Rico.* Memorias del Segundo Simposio latinoamericano sobre Oceanografia Biologica. Universidad de Oriente, Cumuna, Venezuela.

Collar, N.J., Gonzaga, L.P., Krabbe, N., Madroño Nieto, A., Naranjo, L.G., Parker III, T.A. and Wege, D.C. (1992). *Threatened Birds of the Americas. The ICBP/IUCN Red Data Book.* ICBP, Cambridge, U.K.

Dansereau, P. (1966). Description and integration of the plant-communities. In: *Studies on the Vegetation of Puerto Rico.* Institute of Caribbean Science. Special Publication No. 1.

Davis, S.D., Droop, S.J.M., Gregerson, P., Henson, L., Leon, C.J., Villa-Lobos, J.L, Synge, H. and Zantovska, J. (1986). *Plants in Danger. What do we know?* IUCN, Gland, Switzerland and Cambridge, U.K.

Department of Natural Resources (1972). *Natural, Cultural and Environmental Resources Inventory. Land Use in Puerto Rico.* Unpublished document cited in Birdsey and Weaver (1982).

Englerth, G.H. (1960). *Forest Utilization in Puerto Rico.* Unpublished document cited in Birdsey and Weaver (1982).

Ewel, J.J. and Whitmore, J.L. (1973). *The Ecological Life Zones of Puerto Rico and the U.S. Virgin Islands.* Research Paper ITF-18. Department of Agriculture, Forest Service, Southern Forest Experiment Station, Rio Piedras, Puerto Rico.

FAO (1993). *Forest resources assessment 1990: Tropical countries.* FAO Forestry Paper 112. FAO, Rome, Italy.

Gill, T. (1931). *Tropical Forests of the Caribbean.* The Read-Taylor Co., Baltimore, U.S.A. 318 pp.

Groombridge, B. (Ed) (1993). *1994 IUCN Red List of Threatened Animals.* IUCN, Gland, Switzerland and Cambridge, U.K. 286 pp.

Hill, R.T. (1899). Notes on the forest conditions of Porto Rico. *USDA Bulletin* No. 25, Washington.

Koenig, N.A. (1953). *A Comprehensive Agricultural Program for Puerto Rico.* Department of Agriculture and Commonwealth of Puerto Rico, Washington, DC, USA. 290 pp.

Little, E.L. and Wadsworth, F.H. (1964). *Common Trees of Puerto Rico and the Virgin Islands.* Agriculture Handbook No. 249. U.S.D.A. Forest Service, Washington, D.C. 548 pp.

Little, E.L., Woodbury, R.O. and Wadsworth, F.H. (1974). *Trees of Puerto Rico and the Virgin Islands. Second Volume.* USDA Handbook No. 449. USDA Forestry Service, Washington, D.C. Pp. 1024.

Martinez, R., Cintron, G. and Encarnacion, L.A. (1979). *Mangroves in Puerto Rico: a structural inventory.* Area of Scientific Research, Department of Natural Resources, San Juan, Puerto Rico.

Murphy, L.S. (1916). Forests of Puerto Rico, past, present, and future. *USDA Bulletin* No. 354, Washington.

Raffaele, H.A. (1989). *A Guide to the Birds of Puerto Rico and the Virgin Islands.* Princeton University Press, Princeton, USA.

Rivero, J.A. (1978) *Los Anfibios y Reptiles de Puerto Rico.* Editorial Universitaria, Universidad de Puerto Rico, Mayaguez, Puerto Rico. 148 pp.

Starrett, A. (1962). The bats of Puerto Rico and the Virgin Islands, with a check list and keys for identification. *Caribbean Journal of Science* 2(1): 1–7.

Vivaldi, J.L. (1989). Puerto Rico. In: *Floristic Inventory of Tropical Countries: The Status of Plant Systematics, Collections, and Vegetation plus Recommendations for the Future.* Campbell, D.G. and Hammond, H.D. (eds). The New York Botanical Garden, New York, USA. Pp. 341–346.

Wadsworth, F.H. (1950). Notes on the climax forests of Puerto Rico and their destruction and conservation prior to 1900. *Caribbean Forester* 11 (1): 38–47.

Wadsworth, F.H. (1951). Forest management in the Luquillo Mountains, 1:The setting. *Caribbean Forester* 11: 38–47.

Wadsworth, F.H. (1959). Growth and regeneration of white mangrove in Puerto Rico. *Caribbean Forester* 20 (3 and 4): 59–71.

Wadsworth, F.H. (1968). Clean water for the nation's estuaries. In: *Proceedings of the Puerto Rico Public Meeting, National and Estuarine Pollution Study.* Federal Water Pollution Control Administration, Atlanta. Pp. 78–91.

Wadsworth, F.H. and Birdsey, R.A. (1985). A new look at the forests of Puerto Rico. *Turrialba* 35(1): 11–17.

WCMC (1992). *Global Biodiversity: Status of the Earth's Living Resources.* Chapman and Hall, London. 594 pp.

Wiley, J.W., Post, W. and Cruz, A. (1991). Conservation of the yellow-shouldered blackbird *Agelaius xanthomus*, an endangered West Indian species. *Biological Conservation* 55: 119–138.

Author: C. Harcourt, with contributions from F.N Scatena and P.L. Weaver, International Institute of Tropical Forestry, Rio Piedras, Puerto Rico.

15 Trinidad and Tobago

Country area	5130 sq. km
Land area	5130 sq. km
Population (mid-1994)	1.3 million
Population growth rate	1.2 per cent
Population projected to 2025	1.8 million
Gross national product per capita (1992)	US$3940
Forest cover in 1980 (see Map)*	1683 sq. km
Forest cover in 1990 (FAO, 1993)	1550 sq. km
Annual deforestation rate 1980–1990	2.4 per cent
Industrial roundwood production	65,000 cu. m
Industrial roundwood exports	3000 cu. m
Fuelwood and charcoal production	22,000 cu. m
Processed wood production	58,000 cu. m
Processed wood exports	—

* For Trinidad only

Compared to many of the Caribbean islands, Trinidad and Tobago still have a considerable percentage of their forest cover remaining. Trinidad is the only country of tropical America with a substantial history of professional management of natural forests; the first management plan was prepared almost 100 years ago. Although there are severe economic and social pressures facing the country, the Forestry Division is optimistic that proposals in the National Forest Resources Plan and the planned comprehensive system of conservation areas will protect the forests.

INTRODUCTION

Trinidad is the most southerly of the West Indian islands; it is separated from the South American mainland by only 11 km. This island is about 80 km long, 59 km wide and covers an area of 4828 sq. km. Tobago is 42 km long, 12 km wide and has an area of about 300 sq. km.

Trinidad has three mountain ranges which decrease in altitude from the north. Cerro del Aripo in the Northern Range is the highest point, rising to 914 m. The Central Range reaches 310 m at Mount Tamana, while Trinity Hills in the Southern Range rises to 308 m. Undulating land, plains and swamps separate the ranges and overall the island is relatively flat. Tobago is a more rugged island; it has a central Main Ridge running the length of the island, reaching 576 m at Centre Point. There is only a small area of coastal plain; this is in the south-west of the island.

The dry season is from January to May, with the wet season from June to December, but this is broken by a short dry period of about three weeks between September and October. Rainfall in Trinidad averages 2880 mm in the north and north-east and 1200 mm in the west and south-west. Average annual temperatures are about 29°C during the day and 21°C at night. The islands lie on the border of the hurricane zone; Tobago is occasionally affected by hurricanes while they are very rare in Trinidad.

Columbus sighted Trinidad in 1498 and the island was colonised by the Spaniards in the 16th century, but was conquered by a British force and annexed to the British Crown in 1797 (Beard, 1945). Although Tobago was sighted at the same time, it never became a Spanish colony. It was fought over by the Dutch, English and French for more than 100 years until it was recaptured by the English and ceded to Britain in 1763. It continued to change hands until 1803 when the British won it permanently. It was declared a ward of the combined colony of Trinidad and Tobago in 1889.

People of African descent make up 41 per cent of the population, Indians make up another 41 per cent, a further 16 per cent are of mixed race, while Chinese, Europeans and others make up the remainder. Most of Trinidad's population reside in the west coastal area (James *et al.*, 1984), 64 per cent of them in urban areas. Greatest population pressure occurs along a corridor from west of the capital, Port of Spain, skirting the foothills of the Northern Range, to Sangre Grande in the east.

Oil is one of the country's leading industries; it represented 66 per cent of exports in 1990 (NRED, 1992). The importance of agriculture to the economy is declining; it contributed only four per cent to GDP in 1990. The major commodities are sugar cane, cocoa, coffee and citrus (NRED, 1992).

The Forests

Beard (1945) classified the vegetation types of Trinidad as shown in Table 15.1.

Most of the forests are seasonal — varying from evergreen to deciduous depending on moisture. The following descriptions are from Beard (1945) and FAO/UNEP (1981).

Evergreen seasonal forest is the most widespread in Trinidad. It is found up to 250 or 300 m in altitude. This forest is three storeyed with emergents up to 40 m, a closed canopy at between 12 and 30 m and a lower almost continuous canopy of shrubs and small trees at 3 to 9 m in height. Lianes are fairly well developed and epiphytes are common above 6 m. The two characteristic trees of the upper layer are *Carapa guianensis* and *Eschweilera subglandulosa*. Other important species of the upper canopy are *Licania biglandulosa, Pachira insignis, Sterculia caribaea, Mora excelsa* and two palm trees *Maximiliana caribaea* and *Sabal manritiiformis*. There are around 100 tree species per hectare. In some places, *Mora excelsa* forms almost homogenous stands which are intensively managed.

Semi-evergreen moist forest is found in drier areas. The upper layer at around 24 m is discontinuous; there are a few taller trees up to 30 m. A closed canopy occurs at 6–12 m. Lianes are very common, but epiphytes are not luxuriant.

Table 15.1 Vegetation types in Trinidad

Seasonal Formations	**Intermediate Formations**
Evergreen Seasonal Forest	Seasonal Montane Forest
Semi-evergreen Seasonal Forest	
Deciduous Seasonal Forest	**Swamp Formations**
	Swamp Forest
Dry Evergreen Formations	Palm Swamp
Woodland	Herbaceous Swamp
Littoral Woodlands	Mangrove
Montane Formations	**Marsh Formations**
Lower Montane Rain Forest	Marsh Forest
Montane Rain Forest	Palm Marsh
Elfin Woodland	Savanna

Important species are *Peltogyne porphyrocardia, Trichilia smithii, Brosimum alicastrum, Bravaisia intergerrima, Mouriri marshali, Guarea guara* and *Ficus tobagensis.*

Even by 1945, there was virtually no undisturbed deciduous seasonal forest remaining in Trinidad. The few surviving patches are in the Northern Range. There is a highly discontinuous emergent layer at 13–20 m and a lower storey at 3–10 m. Characteristic species include *Bursera simaruba, Lonchocarpus latifolius* and *Machaerium robinifolium.*

The dry evergreen formations have a limited distribution, mostly along the east coast. The trees are generally small, often bent and have thick leaves.

Lower montane forest has an upper continuous canopy at about 30 m with no emergents. Understorey trees are at any height between 3 and 16 m with no marked layering. Neither lianes nor epiphytes are common. *Licania ternatensis, L. biglandulosa, Sterculia caribaea* and *Byrsonima spicata* are dominant in the canopy layer. *Calliandra guildingii* and *Cassipourea latifolia* occur commonly in the lower storey. This forest type is confined to the Northern Range and occurs between altitudes of about 300–800 m.

The montane or cloud forest occupies only a very small area above 800 m on the Aripo Massif. The more or less closed canopy reaches only 20 m and the trees are smaller in diameter and less diverse than those lower down the mountains. Small palms and tree ferns are common, climbers and epiphytes occur. The dominant tree species in the canopy include *Richeria grandis, Eschweilera trinitensis* and *Licania biglandulosa.* The last of these is of localized abundance and is primarily characteristic of the transitional zone to lower montane forest. The seasonal montane forest is confined to limestone outcrops in the Northern Range — *Inga macrophylla* and *Guarea guara* are common.

There is a small area of elfin woodland on the Cerro del Aripo. The canopy is formed of a dense layer of tree ferns and small palms at about 3 m. There is also a discontinuous tree layer emerging to reach about 7 m; *Clusia intertexta* is the major species in this layer — few other species are present. The tree ferns *Cyathea tenera* and *C. caribaea* and the palms *Euterpe broadwayana* and *Prestoea pubigera* are present.

Swamp forest, found in areas on the east coast, consists of almost homogenous stands of *Pterocarpus officinalis* forming a canopy at about 20 m. Palm swamps are also found on the island. Main species are *Roystonea oleracea* and *Mauritia* spp. No canopy is present, rather the palms (25–30 m tall) are scattered above an understorey that varies between scrubby bush and 20 m tall forest. Marsh forests, containing mostly palm

species, are of only local occurrence and are found mainly in Trinidad's northern plain.

In Tobago, rain forest is found in sheltered valleys on interior mountains. The principal species in the upper storey of this formation are *Carapa guianensis, Andira inermis, Hyeronima caribaea* and *Eschweilera decoloram. Tresanthera pauciflora* and *Styrax glaber* are dominant species in the lower storey. Some lower montane forest occurs. The major species in its upper storey are *Brysonima spicata, Licania biglandulosa, Ternstroemia oligostemon* and *Eschweilera decolorans,* while the lower level is occupied mainly by *Euterpe broadwayana, Styrax glaber* and by species of the Myrtaceae family. Drier elfin woodland also occurs on the island.

Mangroves
Faizool (1990) lists 17 locations of mangroves, varying in extent from 9 ha in Godineau Swamp to 37.3 sq. km in Caroni Swamp. He estimates the total area as 74.1 sq. km, including 1.7 sq. km in Tobago. Bacon (1991, 1993), however, lists 36 locations in Trinidad, 11 in Tobago and 2 on offshore islands with a total area of 71.5 sq. km (Lacerda *et al.*, 1993). Somewhat lower figures are given by Taylor (1989) and by Saenger *et al.* (1983); they estimate 53 and 40 sq. km respectively. On Map 15.1, mangroves cover 51 sq. km, but this was in 1980 or earlier (see Map Legend).

The main species present are *Rhizophora mangle, Avicennia nitida* and *Laguncularia racemosa. R. harrisonii, A. schaueriana* and *Conocarpus erectus* also occur. Those mangroves in the Nariva Swamp in the east of Trinidad are relatively undisturbed, whereas those in the west, in Caroni Swamp, have been more disturbed by man. Housing, roads and industrial development have considerably reduced the area of mangroves in Caroni Swamp. There is, however, now a much greater awareness of the benefits provided by mangroves and a consequent reduction in the wood cut from them for firewood and charcoal. Caroni Swamp, with its magnificent colony of scarlet ibis *Eudocimus ruber* is a major attraction for locals and tourists.

Forest Resources and Management
According to some estimates, approximately 3075 sq. km or 60 per cent of the total land area of Trinidad and Tobago can be classified as forest land, 80 per cent of this is state land (Bacchus and McVorran, 1990; Table 15.2). According to NRED (1992) this 60 per cent includes "natural and secondary forests and swamps". Other authors suggest a somewhat lower forest cover. For instance Faizool (1990) estimates a total of 2300 sq. km of proclaimed and unproclaimed forest reserves and other forested state lands, while the estimate in FAO (1993) is of only 1550 sq. km of forest remaining, all of which is considered to be closed broadleaved forest in the tropical rain forest

Table 15.2 Distribution of land in Trinidad and Tobago under forest cover

Classification	Area (sq. km)
Forest reserves	1,444
Other state lands	1,113
Private lands	518
Total	**3,075**

Source: Bacchus and McVorran (1990)

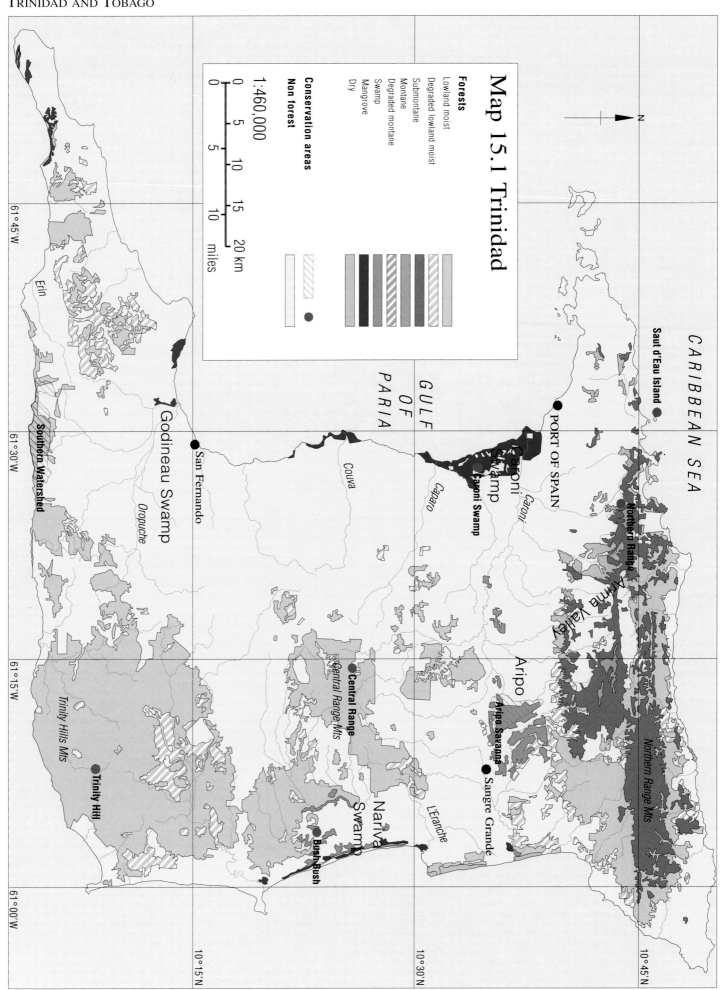

Map 15.1 Trinidad

Forests

Lowland moist
Degraded lowland moist
Submontane
Montane
Degraded montane
Swamp
Mangrove
Dry

Conservation areas
Non forest

1:460,000

0   5   10   15   20 km
0   5   10   miles

N

CARIBBEAN SEA

GULF
OF
PARIA

Saut d'Eau Island

PORT OF SPAIN

Caroni
Swamp
Caroni Swamp
Caroni

Northern Range

Maracas Valley

Aripo

Aripo Savanna

Northern Range Mts

Sangre Grande

L'Eranche

Couva

Caparo

Caroni

San Fernando

Godineau Swamp

Oropuche

Central Range
Central Range Mts

Nariva
Swamp

Bush Bush

Southern Watershed

Erin

Trinity Hills Mts

Trinity Hill

61°45'W
61°30'W
61°15'W
61°00'W

10°45'N
10°30'N
10°15'N

Extensive mangroves are found in Caroni Swamp, Western Trinidad. (Mark Spalding)

zone. Map 15.1 shows the forests in Trinidad covering 1683 sq. km (Table 15.3), but the source map is 14 years old and there is no indication of when the data for this map were collected (see Map Legend). No map or information on the extent of the forests on Tobago has been found for this project.

An analysis of aerial photographs covering most of the State-owned forest land during the 1978–1980 forest inventory gave the areas of the forest types as shown in Table 15.4. This indicates that state-owned natural forests covered around 35 per cent of the islands at that time. The area of private forests is disputed (Chalmers and Faizool, 1992). For many years, up to 1971, the annual reports of the Forestry Division gave a figure of 105 sq. km for these forests. However, in the 1972 report a figure of 544 sq. km was quoted, of which only 72 sq. km was high forest and timber plantations while the rest was secondary growth — the source for this information was a 1963 agricultural census.

The forest resources can be divided into protection and production forests. Approximately 29 per cent of the state controlled forests in Trinidad are devoted to environmental conservation, while almost all of Tobago's forests are designated as protection forests.

About 750 sq. km of Trinidad's natural forest have been classified as productive — i.e. intended for long term production of

timber — of which 160 sq. km are intensively managed. However, Synnott (1988, 1989) considers all 750 sq. km to be sustainably managed in that they are protected to a degree by resident forest guards, there are defined management objectives and working plans for the forests and the logging activities are subject to at least some planning, supervision and control. This professional management began in the 1920s and working plans were written from 1935 onwards (Synnott, 1988). Continuous forest inventory using permanent sample plots started in 1983 in the natural forests. This is the only system of its kind established as a tool of tropical forest management rather than as a research study (Synnott, 1988).

Logging operations on public land in the natural forests are controlled through the granting of conservators licences. Ideally, this license system takes into account both silvicultural and industrial considerations. Exploitation is controlled on a basis of minimum girth limits and much of the forest has been subject to area control using designated blocks of predetermined size to ensure a sustained yield in the future. The timber is sold on an individual tree basis and is sold only to registered licensees. The annual reports of the Forest Department list the top 30 tree species by volume cut and then give the volume cut from all other species; the latter varies between 70 and 87 species. In 1955, the volume harvested was 151,600 cu. m, but this has declined steadily so that in 1960, 100,680 cu. m were cut and in 1971 only 64,674 cu. m. One factor has been the decline in the use of firewood and charcoal. FAO (1994) estimated that in 1992 around 65,000 cu. m of industrial roundwood were harvested from the islands.

Over the period 1955–65, when timber production was probably at its peak, local forests provided an average of 72 per cent of the annual timber requirements; by the 1980s this had fallen to an average of 11 per cent. In 1983, imports of sawlogs reached as high as 492,100 cu. m, with an annual average of 242,640 cu. m over the period of 1983–1988.

At present the Forest Act is very limited in relation to protection and management of timber; it is more concerned with the sale of the resources (Bacchus and McVorran, 1990). Although existing methods of harvest are wasteful, it is intended that the timber resources be carefully developed to avoid environmental degradation. One of the main risks of over-exploitation of the natural forests arises from the fact that there are over 100 marketable species. This emphasises the need for thorough silvicultural and management control on the ground to ensure that

Table 15.3 Estimates of forest extent in Trinidad

Forest type	Area (sq. km)	% of land area°
Lowland moist	1,101	22.8
Degraded lowland moist	193	4.0
Submontane	244	5.1
Montane	7	<0.1
Degraded montane	1	<0.1
Dry	37	0.8
Swamp	49	1.0
Mangrove	51	1.1
Total	1,683	34.9

° Area of Trinidad only — 4828 sq. km.

Based on analysis of Map 15.1. See Map Legend on p. 150 for details of sources.

Table 15.4 Areas of the different forest types found in the state-owned forest lands of Trinidad and Tobago

Forest Type	Area (sq. km)
Edaphic swamp forest	164
Montane forest	225
Evergreen seasonal	1,152
Semi-evergreen seasonal	141
Dry evergreen seasonal	5
Deciduous seasonal	37
Plantations, inc non-timber	214
Secondary Forest	60
Total	1,998

Source: Synnott (1988)

exploitation does not irrevocably change the composition of the forest. Greatest concern relates to the exploitation of mora *Mora excelsa*. It has topped the sales list for many years, even though the annual volume cut has dropped — from 21,875 cu. m between 1971–79 to 11,860 cu m between 1983–88 — its contribution in those years remained around 27 per cent of the total volume sold. Another over-exploited species is matchwood *Didymopanax morototoni*. This can no longer supply the demand from the local match factory — its wood has had to be replaced entirely by aspen splints from Scandinavia.

For many years an undesirable feature of the local forestry scene has been the excessive number of sawmills that are licensed, from a peak of 91 in 1958 to an average of 65 in the 1980s. Most of them operate on a part-time basis and are not very efficient in terms of converting roundwood into sawn timber. There have been no recent studies, but the loss on conversion is thought to average 35–40 per cent. With modern equipment and good management, six to eight sawmills could cope with the logs harvested locally, particularly since the State-owned enterprise TANTEAK Ltd has a virtual monopoly on the raw material harvested from the government's pine and teak plantations.

The plantations are found almost wholly within forest reserves. In 1990, Chalmers and Faizool (1992) estimated that the total area of plantations was 152.5 sq. km, comprising 90.1 sq. km of teak *Tectona grandis*, 42.1 sq. km of pine *Pinus caribaea* and 20.3 sq. km of mixed hardwoods. It was estimated that around 16,000 cu. m of timber were harvested annually from these plantations between 1986 and 1989, approximately 60 per cent of this was teak (Bacchus and McVorran, 1990). Although the establishment of plantations used to involve the clearing of degraded natural forest, they are now developed only on non-forest land.

Tree cutting on private land is generally not controlled and there is little management of these areas. Some species require permits from the Forestry Division before they can be transported along public roads, and it is only for these species that outputs can be estimated (Bacchus and McVorran, 1990).

The severe economic and social pressures facing a large proportion of the population has made it increasingly difficult to maintain traditional levels of management and protection of the forests. Indeed, the management plans for most forest reserves are now in need of revision. Nevertheless, the Forestry Division is optimistic that proposals contained in the National Forest Resources Plan (Anon, 1989) will soon be formally adopted. Supporting legislation and funding in conjunction with the TFAP project is also expected in the near future.

Deforestation

The most obvious and some of the most severe deforestation has taken place throughout the Northern Range, mainly as a result of encroachment by squatters, shifting cultivation and the inevitable burning of forest; the overall impact is exacerbated by similar activities on many abandoned cacao estates. The same occurs in parts of the Central Range Reserve, in the large Victoria Mayaro Reserve and in the reserves in the drier south-western area of Trinidad. Here the almost annual bush fires spread into the teak plantations and the constant burning has resulted in some of the worst soil erosion in the country.

A considerable volume of wood used to be sold for firewood and charcoal. In the 1940s, around 60,000 cu. m were used annually for this purpose, with the annual average volume being 38,500 cu. m between 1949 and 1960, of which about 85 per cent was used for charcoal (Forestry Dept/Division Annual Reports 1955–88). However, at this time the operation was well controlled and officially monitored so it was generally not destructive of the natural forest, but it became so in the 1960s and 1970s when much of the cutting was illegal. Fortunately with the increasing use of kerosene and gas the demand for wood has declined. Since 1976 the Forestry Division annual reports have not provided detailed information on the subject.

There is some illegal clearfelling of natural forests, but this is usually on State Lands outside the forest reserves. FAO (1993) estimates annual deforestation in Trinidad and Tobago between the years of 1980 and 1990 to be as much as 2.4 per cent or 37 sq. km each year.

Biodiversity

Trinidad has one of the highest levels of biodiversity per unit area of the Americas. Bacon (1978) gives a general overview of the ecology of the country. There are 2281 flowering species recorded on the islands of which 215 are endemic (Adams and Baksh, 1981). Their main affinities are with South America rather than the Antilles (Beard, 1945).

These islands are the richest in the Caribbean as far as number of mammal species goes — over 100 occur there, almost half of which are bats.

Around 420 species of bird have been recorded on the islands: these include 160 North and South American migrants (ffrench, 1986; NRED, 1992). Only 180 or so of these birds are seen on Tobago, but 18 of the species recorded on this island have not been sighted on Trinidad (Tomlinson, 1981). Collar *et al.* (1992) list only two threatened species for Trinidad and Tobago. One of these, the Trinidad piping-guan *Pipile pipile* is endemic and is considered endangered. It is found in primary forest and now occurs only in two small, well separated populations on Trinidad. Hunting and habitat destruction are the causes of its decline. The white-tailed sabrewing *Campylopterus ensipennis* is found in montane forest on Tobago, but also occurs in north-east Venezuela. On Tobago, it is threatened by forest destruction.

There are 70 species of reptiles, including 38 snakes, and 26 amphibians on the islands (NRED, 1992; see also Underwood, 1962 and Boos and Quesnel, 1969). As would be expected, more of these species occur on Trinidad than on Tobago, but there are three species of amphibians and two of reptiles that occur in Tobago and not in Trinidad. There are two endemic species in each of these groups (WCMC, 1992). No terrestrial species are listed as threatened by IUCN (Groombridge, 1993). There are 76 species of freshwater fish on the islands.

Most of the invertebrate fauna remains to be identified, but

Table 15.5   Conservation areas in Trinidad and Tobago

Existing conservation areas in IUCN's categories I–IV. For information on Ramsar Sites see Chapter 8.

Game Sanctuaries

Bush Bush*	16
Central Range*	22
Little Tobago[1]	1
Northern Range*	9
Saut d'Eau Island	0.1
Soldado Rock+	>0.1
Southern Watershed*	19
St Giles Island[1]	0.3
Trinity Hill*	82

Prohibited Areas

Aripo Savanna*	18
Caroni Swamp*	2

Nature Reserve

Bucco Reef[1]	7

Total	176.5

* Area with forest within its boundaries as shown on Map 15.1
+ Not mapped
[1] See Figure 15.1 for location of these areas in Tobago

there are at least 600 butterfly species present (NRED, 1992). One beetle *Aglymbus bromeliarum* is listed as threatened by IUCN (Groombridge, 1993).

Conservation Areas

The country's first protected area, a game sanctuary, was created on Tobago in 1928 (Bacchus and McVorran, 1990). There are now 13 game sanctuaries in which the fauna receive total protection all year round. Most of these sanctuaries are within forest reserves and a small amount of logging may be allowed in them (Bacchus and McVorran, 1990). The nine in IUCN's categories I–IV are listed in Table 15.5. The remaining four — with no category allocated — are Caroni Swamp (2 sq. km), Kronstadt Island (5 ha), Morne l'Enfer (3 sq. km) and Valencia (28 sq. km).

It was not until 1980 that a policy for the establishment and management of a national park network was initiated. Although the government agreed in principle with the proposals in this policy, no legislation has yet been enacted nor have the 61 proposed protected areas been set up (James *et al.*, 1984; Bacchus and McVorran, 1990).

An important aspect of the proposed National Parks policy is the active encouragement of community involvement in all aspects of the development and management of the parks.

There are also 35 forest reserves on the islands, but hunting occurs in these and many are intended for long-term timber production (James *et al.*, 1984; Synnott, 1988). There are also some small, private but very actively run nature reserves. In the absence of government clarity as to its conservation policy, several NGOs are very concerned with conservation and management of reserves.

The new Ministry of the Environment and National Service, which was established in 1989, is responsible for the protected areas. However, management of most areas, except Caroni Swamp, is inadequate (IUCN, 1992).

Conservation Initiatives

There are a number of active, long-running conservation groups on the islands. The Trinidad and Tobago Field Naturalists Club (TTFNC) was founded in 1891 and is still going strong. In the early 1950s, the New York Zoological Society established a tropical research station in the Arima Valley which attracted many established and young scientists to the island. The station has been taken over recently by the Asa Wright Nature Centre, which is operated by a local Trust and has itself organised regular seminar programmes over the last 25 years. The Pointe-a-Pierre Wildfowl Trust has been functioning for nearly 30 years, encouraging the conservation of wildlife on the refinery reservoirs of a local petroleum company. More recently, the Caribbean Forest Conservation Association (CFCA) was established in Trinidad. Along with other organisations, it prepared a substantial submission for consideration by the TFAP Country Mission Team and it is very active in lobbying the government and the public. The University of the West Indies (UWI) is also a powerful voice in conservation issues.

The Northern Range Reforestation Project, started in 1971 as an UNDP Technical Assistance Project, now with government funding, continues to achieve its principal objectives — the conservation and regeneration of the natural forest in the Northern Range. To date, 14.8 sq. km have been regenerated with an acceptable level of survival and growth. Of equal importance are the many initiatives that have been developed to persuade the shifting cultivators/squatters to adopt more acceptable, less damaging forms of land-use.

Some years ago, the Forestry Division made a long-term decision that any teak plantations located within a protected area would, at rotation age, be replaced with local hardwood species to provide a much more beneficial environment for wildlife.

A revision of the legislation addressing the conservation of natural resources is underway (NRED, 1992).

Perhaps the most important conservation initiative in the country is the proposal for the establishment of a Caribbean International Institute for Forestry and the Environment (CIIFE) at the Trinidad and Tobago Campus of UWI. It is planned that this institute will provide training at undergraduate and postgraduate levels in forestry/natural resources management, provide leadership and extension services throughout the region in silviculture, forest management, wildlife conservation and watershed management and organise and sustain the research initiatives that are vital in solving the region's environmental problems.

Figure 15.1   Tobago's protected areas

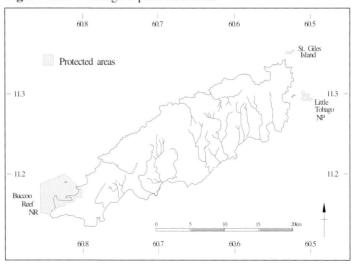

References

Adams, C.D. and Baksh, Y.S. (1981). What is an endangered plant? *Living World* 1981–2: 9–14.

Anon (1989). *The National Forest Resources Plan*. Forestry Division, Ministry of the Environment and National Service, Trinidad.

Bacchus, C.F. and McVorran, G.M. (1990). *The Role of Forestry in Biological Diversity Conservation in Trinidad and Tobago*. Unpublished manuscript.

Bacon, P.R. (1978). *Flora and Fauna of the Caribbean. An Introduction to the Ecology of the Caribbean*. Key Caribbean Publications, Trinidad and Tobago.

Bacon, P.R. (1991). *The Status of Mangrove Conservation in the CARICOM Islands of the Eastern Caribbean*. Report to the EEC as part of the TFAP for the Caribbean Region.

Bacon, P.R. (1993). Mangroves in the Lesser Antilles, Jamaica, Trinidad and Tobago. In: *Conservation and Sustainable Utilization of Mangrove Forests in Latin America and Africa Regions. Part 1: Latin America*. ITTO/ISME Project PD114/90(F). Pp. 155–209.

Beard, J.S. (1945). The natural vegetation of Trinidad. *Oxford Forestry Memoirs* 20: 1–152.

Boos, H. and Quesnel, V. (1969). *Reptiles of Trinidad and Tobago*. Ministry of Education and Culture, Trinidad and Tobago. Pp. 39.

Chalmers, W.S. and Faizool, S. (1992). *Trinidad and Tobago National Forestry Action Programme. Report of Country Mission Team*. FAO/CARICOM TFAP. GCP/RLA/098, U.K.

Collar, N.J., Gonzaga, L.P., Krabbe, N., Madroño Nieto, A., Naranjo, L.G., Parker III, T.A. and Wege, D.C. (1992). *Threatened Birds of the Americas. The ICBP/IUCN Red Data Book*. ICBP, Cambridge, U.K.

Faizool, S. (1990). *Some Forestry and Related Statistics*. Forestry Resource Inventory and Management Unit, Forestry Division, Trinidad and Tobago.

FAO/UNEP (1981). *Proyecto de Evaluacion de los Recursos Forestales Tropicales. Los Recursos Forestales de la America Tropical*. FAO, Rome, Itlay.

FAO (1993) *Forest resources assessment 1990: Tropical countries*. FAO Forestry Paper 112. FAO, Rome, Italy.

FAO (1994). *FAO Yearbook: Forest Products 1981–1992*. FAO Forestry Series No. 27, FAO Statistics Series No. 116. FAO, Rome, Italy.

ffrench, R. (1986). *Birds of Trinidad and Tobago*. Macmillian Caribbean. 87 pp.

Groombridge, B. (Ed) (1993). *1994 IUCN Red List of Threatened Animals*. IUCN, Gland, Switzerland and Cambridge, U.K. 286 pp.

James, C., Nathai-Gyan, N. and Hislop, G. (1984). *Neotropical Wetlands Project. National Report on Trinidad and Tobago*. Prepared for IWRB/ICBP. Forestry Division, Ministry of Agriculture Lands and Food Production.

IUCN (1992). *Protected Areas of the World: A review of national systems. Volume 4: Nearctic and Neotropical*. IUCN, Gland, Switzerland and Cambridge, U.K.

Lacerda, L.A., Conde, J.E., Bacon, P.R., Alarcón, C., D'Croz, L., Kjerfve, B., Polanía and Vannucci, M. (1993). Mangrove ecosystems of Latin America and the Caribbean: a Summary. In: *Conservation and Sustainable Utilization of Mangrove Forests in Latin America and Africa Regions. Part 1: Latin America*. ITTO/ISME Project PD114/90(F). Pp. 1–42.

NRED (1992). *National Report on Environment and Development*. Report presented to the United Nations Conference on Environment and Development, Rio de Janero, Brazil.

Saenger, P., Hegerl, E.J. and Davie, J.D.S. (1983). (eds). *Global Status of Mangrove Ecosystems*. Commission on Ecology Papers No. 3. IUCN, Gland, Switzerland.

Synnott, T. (1988). *Natural Forest Management for Sustainable Timber Production: South America and the Caribbean*. IIED, London.

Synnott, T. (1989). South America and the Caribbean. In: *No Timber Without Trees*. Poore D. (ed). Earthscan, London.

Taylor, J.G. (1989) (ed.) *Manglares. La importancia económica de los manglares en la política, planeamiento y manejo de los recursos naturales costeros*. FUDENA, Caracas.

Tomlinson, D. (1981). Treasures of sea and swamp: a naturalist in Trinidad — II. *Country Life* October 8: 1227–1228.

Underwood, G. (1962). Reptiles of the Eastern Caribbean. *Caribbean Affairs, New Series* 1: 1–192.

WCMC (1992). *Global Biodiversity: Status of the Earth's Living Resources*. Chapman and Hall, London xx + 594pp.

Author: Caroline Harcourt with contributions from Steve Bass, IIED and Dan Chalmers, Taverham, Norfolk.

Map 15.1   Trinidad

Forest data for Trinidad (no data were found for Tobago) have been digitised from the map *Inventory of the Indigenous Forest of Trinidad — Forest Resource Inventory and Management Section*, which was published in 1980. This was prepared for the Government of Trinidad and Tobago by Institutional Consultants (International) Ltd. in cooperation with the Forestry Division Ministry of Agriculture, Lands and Fisheries and the Canadian International Development Agency (CIDA). It is unclear how old the actual data are, but as the source map itself is 14 years old, the estimates of forest extent should be treated with caution.

A variety of forest types are illustrated and have been amalgamated to form estimates of forest extent on Map 15.1. Harmonisation of the forest types is as follows:

Mangrove	*Edaphic Swamp Forest* — mangrove
Swamp forest	*Edaphic Swamp Forest* — palm swamp; swamp forest; marsh forest
Montane forest	*Montane Forest* — bois bande-mountain-guatecare (rain); mountain mangrove (elfin)
Degraded montane forest	*Montane Forest* — secondary mountain forest
Submontane forest	*Montane Forest* — serrette-bois gris (lower) *Seasonal Montane Forest* — pois doux-redwood
Lowland moist forest	*Evergreen Seasonal Forest* — crappo-debasse; crappo-fineleaf-carat; crappo-fineleaf-cocorite; crappo-blackheart-cocorite; mora *Semi Evergreen Seasonal Forest* — purpleheart-incense-poui; purpleheart-bois lissette; acurel-moussara-jiggerwood; acurel-gommier; moussara-figuier
Degraded lowland moist forest	*Evergreen Seasonal Forest* — secondary evergreen seasonal forest; secondary mora forest *Semi Evergreen Seasonal Forest* —secondary semi evergreen seasonal forest
Dry forest	*Dry Evergreen* and *Deciduous Seasonal* formations (excluding the secondary formation)

Non-forest comprises teak, pine and other plantation crops, agriculture, clear cut sites, fire burn sites and non-forested areas.

Conservation area boundaries were taken from a 1:150,000 scale map compiled by the Forestry Division, Ministry of Agriculture Lands and Fisheries, Government of Trinidad and Tobago: *Trinidad — National Parks and Other Protected Areas*, which was published in 1980.

16 Belize

Country area   22,960 sq. km
Land area   22,800 sq.km
Population (mid-1994)   0.2 million
Population growth rate   3.3 per cent
Population projected to 2025   0.4 million
Gross national product per capita (1992)   US$2210
Forest cover for 1992 (see Map)   18,393 sq. km
Forest cover for 1990 (FAO, 1993)   19,960 sq. km
Annual deforestation rate (1981–1990)   0.2 per cent
Industrial roundwood production   62,000 cu. m
Industrial roundwood exports   1000 cu. m
Fuelwood and charcoal   126,000 cu. m
Processed wood production   14,000 cu. m
Processed wood exports   10,000 cu. m

Although physically part of Central America, Belize more closely resembles a Caribbean island in both culture and economy. For three hundred years, forestry was the mainstay of its economy. However, the highly selective extraction of only a few valuable species has not radically altered the vegetation and extensive natural forests still remain. Agriculture is gradually becoming more important, but the very low human population means that there is much less forest destruction in Belize than in any other country in the region. Increasing economic pressure and a huge influx of immigrants threaten this state of affairs. There has, however, been a dramatic increase in environmental awareness within the country and a number of initiatives by both the government and non-governmental organisations aim to direct Belize's development along a more sustainable pathway.

INTRODUCTION

Belize is the second smallest of the Central American countries but, because it is mostly still covered with relatively undisturbed vegetation, it retains much of the wildlife that has vanished from other areas. Formerly British Honduras, the country became self-governing in 1964 and fully independent of Britain in 1981.

The northern half and the eastern fringe of the southern half of the country consists of level, low lying plains. The Maya Mountains, mostly between 300 m and 1000 m in altitude, occupy the south-centre of Belize. These mountains rise steeply to a maximum of 1200 m at Doyles Delight in the south-east and slope down to the Vaca Plateau in the west. North and west of the Maya Mountains is a hilly or rolling karst landscape. There are approximately 1100 offshore islands and coral cays, many of these lying in a chain along the country's spectacular barrier reef, the second longest in the world.

Mean monthly temperatures range from a minimum of 16°C to a maximum of 33°C, the cool season is from November to January. The north of Belize receives about 1500 mm of rain per year, while in the south precipitation is over 4000 mm in a year. In the north and centre of the country there is a pronounced dry season from January to April or May with less than 100 mm of rain per month. In the south, the dry season is from February to April. Hurricanes are frequent and can be devastating.

Belize's population has grown by an estimated 30,000 in the last ten years as a result of an influx of refugees from other Central American countries. Nevertheless, the country has an exceptionally low overall population density of less than nine individuals per sq. km. About half the people live in urban areas, most on the low-lying coastal region. Around 75 per cent of the country is virtually uninhabited. The population is diverse; although predominantly Creole or mestizo, there are also descendants of the Maya and Caribs, as well as people with

Chinese, East Indian, European and North American ancestry in the country (Hartshorn *et al.*, 1984). English is the official language, but Spanish is widely and increasingly spoken.

Forestry used to be the mainstay of the country's economy; although still important, it is in decline. Agriculture and fisheries are other leading productive sectors of the economy. Sugar and citrus fruit are the main agricultural exports. The tourist industry is increasing and is presently second to agriculture as a foreign exchange earner.

The Forests

The subtropical moist forests (Holdridge *et al.*, 1950) of northern and western Belize are similar to those covering Guatemala's northern Petén and Mexico's Yucatán Peninsula (Pennington and Sarukhán, 1968). Characteristic species include *Swietenia macrophylla, Manilkara zapota, Brosimum alicastrum, Pouteria izabalensis, Pimenta dioica, Manilkara chicle, Drypetes brownii, Pseudolmedia spuria, Dialium guianense, Calophyllum brasiliense, Orbignya cohune* and *Terminalia amazonia* (Hartshorn *et al.*, 1984).

There are two major areas of *Pinus caribaea* in Belize: one is north of the Western Highway and the other is on the lower, western part of Mountain Pine Ridge. These are included in the subtropical moist forest zone (Hartshorn *et al.*, 1984).

At an elevation of 650–700 m, the subtropical moist forests change floristically to lower montane forests. *Quercus* spp., *Pinus oocarpa* and *Podocarpus guatemalensis* are representative species. This forest type is found in the Mountain Pine Ridge, on higher parts of the Vaca Plateau and along the upper western slopes of the Maya Mountains. In wetter areas such as on the high points of Mountain Pine Ridge and the upper windward ranges of Maya Mountains, *Pinus patula* predominates. Other characteristic species are the mountain cabbage palm

Euterpe macrospadix and the tree ferns *Alsophila myosuroides* and *Hemitelia multiflora* (Hartshorn *et al.*, 1984).

The subtropical wet forest zone occurs below about 600 m on the windward side of the Maya Mountains. Upper Stann Creek, the Cockscomb Basin and much of Toledo district also fall into this zone. Tree species found in the zone include *Virola koschnyi*, *Symphonia globulifera*, *Schizolobium parahybum*, *Vochysia hondurensis*, *Simarouba amara*, *Calophyllum brasiliense* and *Dalbergia stevensonii*.

In southern Toledo district, the wettest area of Belize, the transitional zone from subtropical to tropical wet forest is found. Cotton trees *Ceiba pentandra* can reach a height of 50 m in this area. Extensive swamp forest is dominated by *Pterocarpus officinalis* while *Manicaria saccifera* dominates the freshwater palm swamp.

Mangroves

Mangroves fringe most of Belize's coastline. Many cays are also covered in mangroves or have been colonised on the lagoon side, principally by the red mangrove *Rhizophora mangle*. ODA (1989) estimated the area of mangroves to be 748 sq. km. In 1992, S.A. Zisman of the Forest Planning and Management Project estimated a very similar area; he reported, in an unpublished paper (Zisman, 1992), that mangroves, including those on the cays, covered 772 sq. km. The cays are not included in the figure of 523 sq. km estimated by the Belize Forest Department (1993) and shown in Table 16.1. The mangroves shown on Map 16.1, cays included, cover 670 sq. km (Table 16.2).

Forest Resources and Management

The true extent of forest cover in Belize is uncertain. Although the annual reports of the Forestry Department give a figure for "forest land", this figure includes all but urban land and that zoned as "agribusiness" land. In 1981, the Department regarded 21,322 sq. km or 93.5 per cent of the country's land area as "forest land", but that was obviously an overestimate of actual forest cover (Hartshorn *et al.*, 1984). FAO (1993) estimates 19,960 sq. km, or 87.5 per cent of the country, to be forested, but this includes areas with as little as 10 per cent canopy cover and the survey used as a baseline was from 1979. The figure given by FAO (1993) for closed broadleaved forest in Belize is 18,680 sq. km. However, FAO/UNEP (1981) points out that: *it*

Table 16.1 Estimates of vegetation cover in Belize

Vegetation Class	Area (sq. km)	Per cent canopy cover	Per cent of land covered
Broadleaf cover	13,725	>75	63
Open broadleaf cover	469	25–75	2
Mixed broadleaf and pine	378	>75	2
Pine woodland	360	>75	2
Pine woodland savanna	637	50–75	3
Pine tree savanna	1,227	5–50	6
Marsh/swamp forest	553	>75	2
Mangrove forest	523	>5	2
Non-forest cover	1,536	<5	7
Agricultural/urban land	2,323	–	11
Total	21,731*		100

* NB   This is a different figure for total land area than that noted at the head of this chapter.

Source: Belize Forest Department (1993).

Table 16.2 Estimates of forest extent in Belize

Forest type	Area (sq. km)	% land area
Lowland[1]	14,325	62.8
Pine[2]	1,348	5.9
Swamp[3]	521	2.3
Mangrove[4]	670	2.9
Total	16,864	74.0

[1]   Includes broadleaf and open broadleaf category from Table 16.1 but some of this, as noted above, is low scrubby vegetation rather than true forest.

[2]   This is the pine woodland, pine woodland savanna and mixed broadleaf and pine from Table 16.1 — the pine tree savanna has been mapped as non-forest on the advice of D. Gray from the Belize Forest Department.

[3]   This is the marsh/swamp forest from Table 16.1.

[4]   This is the mangrove from Table 16.1 but also includes mangroves on the cays.

Based on analysis of Map 16.1. See Map Legend on p. 159 for details of sources.

is estimated that there are no virgin forests left in the country, all having been creamed mainly for mahogany, cedar and pine.

The distribution of the forest types given in Table 16.1 and shown in a generalised way on Map 16.1 was derived from the Land System maps of the Land Resources Assessments of King *et al.* (1986, 1989, 1992). The land use data come from aerial photographs and satellite images produced between 1985 and 1988. Belize Forest Department (1993) note that the map they have produced should be seen only as a first approximation at estimating the present forest resources of Belize.

The broadleaf cover shown on Map 16.1 is a mixture of a wide range of forest types, ranging from low scrubby woodlands to tall, species-rich forests. Its area, in Table 16.1, was arrived at by subtracting the area of the other classes from the land area of Belize. The pine tree savanna, which occurs over large areas of the coastal plain, consists of scattered pine trees and clumps of pine distributed amongst extensive grassland. On the advice of D. Gray, it has been shown as non-forest on Map 16.1.

Excluding the pine-tree savanna, non-forest and agricultural/urban land, Table 16.1 suggests a forest cover of 16,645 sq. km, i.e. 73 per cent of the country, though this includes some low scrubby vegetation which would not normally be included as forest in this atlas.

Measurements taken from Map 16.1 are shown in Table 16.2. The Map was compiled from a digital data set provided by the Belize Forest Department so the areas of the different forest types measured from it are very similar to those in Table 16.1. The total forest area shown on Map 16.1 is 16,864 sq. km, a 74 per cent forest cover. It must be reiterated that Belize's Forest Department regard their figures as indicative only, but, whatever the true forest area, it is clear that Belize has a considerably higher percentage of its land under forest than does any other Central American country.

The largest single block of intact broadleaved forest extends over the remote, steep, terrain of the Maya Mountains. Of the 11 per cent of the country covered with some natural pine vegetation (Table 16.1), only two per cent (the pine woodland) is closed forest (Belize Forest Department, 1993). The pine tree savannas consist of scattered pine trees and clumps of pine distributed amongst extensive grassland. This formation occurs over large areas of the coastal plain.

Neil Bird, of the Belize Forest Planning and Management

Project, reports that there are 16 forest reserves in the country covering an area of 4487 sq. km or about 20 per cent of the country's land area. These reserves contain about 73 per cent and 25 per cent of the country's pine woodland and broadleaf category forests respectively (Belize Forest Department, 1993). Management of the reserves is based upon the principle of multiple use, allowing sustainable use of forest products but ensuring values such as watershed protection and wildlife conservation. The Belize Forest Department (1993) has calculated the area of land in Belize with a potential for timber extraction to be 11,501 sq. km; most of this is outside the Forest Reserves (Table 16.3). Those areas unavailable for timber production are either protection forest or are considered inaccessible (ODA, 1989). There are also some privately-held forests and there is little information available on these.

As can be seen from Table 16.3, 72 per cent of the exploitable pine woodland are within forest reserves, whereas only 11 per cent of the exploitable broadleaf forests are within these reserves. About one fifth of this area is regarded by the Forest Department to be protection forest and a greater area is considered "inaccessible" and therefore unusable for timber production (ODA, 1989). Most of the exploitable pine woodland is within Mountain Pine Ridge Forest Reserve. If managed sustainably, this would be sufficient to guarantee the long-term domestic supply of softwood.

Belize's geopolitical identity is directly related to its forest resources. The country was declared the Crown Colony of British Honduras in 1862. Its settlers were principally interested in exploiting logwood *Haematoxylon campechianum* for dye. Exploitation of the species continued at a reduced level until early this century, although it was gradually superseded as Belize's principal export by mahogany *Swietenia macrophylla*.

Output of forest products was initially predominantly in the form of logs for export; this declined rapidly from 1950 and had almost ceased by 1970. Production of mahogany and pine sawnwood expanded until the mid-1950s. Most trees were cut in repeated cycles of selective logging, with only the larger individuals of a few commercially sought-after species being taken.

The majority of logging is now carried out by private concessionaires. Most forest permits and licences are issued for one year at a time with an option for renewal if performance is satisfactory. However, some licences can be issued for as long as 10 years. There are 1940 sq. km of private forest land and an estimated 2500 sq. km of Crown land under licence (ODA, 1989).

Although there are 46 sawmills in the country, some 75 per cent of the country's lumber production comes from only five or six mills (ODA, 1989). In 1986–87, three species, mahogany, pine and cedar *Cedrela odorata* accounted for 58 per cent of sawnwood production. Production of cedar and mahogany has declined considerably this century. In 1928–29, 2.5 million cu. feet were harvested each year, but between 1983 and 1987 only 350,000 cu. feet were cut annually. It is, however, estimated that even the much lower levels of pine and hardwood now being cut cannot be sustained with the present management and harvesting systems.

Plantation forestry began over 45 years ago, but only a very small area of plantations exists today. *Pinus caribaea* is planted most commonly, but teak *Tectona grandis*, *Gmelina arborea* and *Swietenia macrophylla* are also used.

A number of non-timber forest products are harvested in the wild on a commercial basis. Up to the middle of this century or thereabouts, the production of chicle from sapodilla trees

Table 16.3   The amount of land in Belize with potential for timber extraction

Vegetation Class	Extent				
	Areas inside FRs		Areas outside FRs		Total Area
	sq. km	per cent	sq. km	per cent	sq. km
Broadleaf	990	11	7,864	89	8,854
Open broadleaf	10	2	460	98	470
Mixed Bl & pine	31	22	107	78	138
Pine woodland	254	72	98	28	352
Pine woodland savanna	105	18	485	82	590
Pine tree savanna	269	25	828	75	1,097
Marsh/swamp	0		0		0
Mangrove	0		0		0
Non-forest	0		0		0
Total	1,659		9,842		11,501

Manilkara zapota was one of the country's main forest industries, but competition from synthetic gums has meant that there is now only a small vestigial trade in this product. Recent Japanese interest in chicle may, however, revive the trade. Seeds from *Pinus caribaea* are collected and exported by the Forest Department. Allspice from *Pimenta officinalis* is exported to Europe and used locally.

Responsibility for most aspects of forestry and conservation rests with the Forest Department in the Ministry of Natural Resources. Belize now has comprehensive laws regulating activities that have an impact on the environment. New legislation that has been passed includes laws to protect wildlife, establish national parks and reserves, regulate the use of land, control pesticides and ensure that the extraction of minerals and petroleum is done in an environmentally sensitive manner. However, there are still weaknesses in the application of the laws.

Deforestation

There was comparatively widespread deforestation in Belize when the Maya civilization was at its peak over 1000 years ago and extensive areas of the country were farmed. The decline of the Maya led to the abandonment of much of the farmed land, allowing the vegetation to regenerate so that the forest is now widely found as a climax formation (ODA, 1989).

In spite of the long history of logging, it is only in areas of traditional slash and burn agriculture (southern Toledo and western Cayo districts) and in the northern sugar cane region that the country has suffered significant deforestation (Hartshorn *et al*, 1984). Nevertheless, the large influx of refugees, mainly from Guatemala, in the 1980s, and the consequent rise in the number of small farmers, has been a major cause of the recent increase in deforestation. FAO (1993) estimates average deforestation between the years of 1981 and 1990 to be only 50 sq. km per year, a rate of 0.2 per cent.

The boom in the citrus industry has meant that in the four years between 1986 and 1990, the land under cultivation for citrus fruit more than doubled from around 75 sq. km to 162 sq. km. Most of this is in Stan Creek district (BNF, 1992). However, an IUCN study showed that this clearing for citrus caused comparatively little deforestation and that the benefits from increased employment and general prosperity probably outweigh the environmental costs of the industry.

153

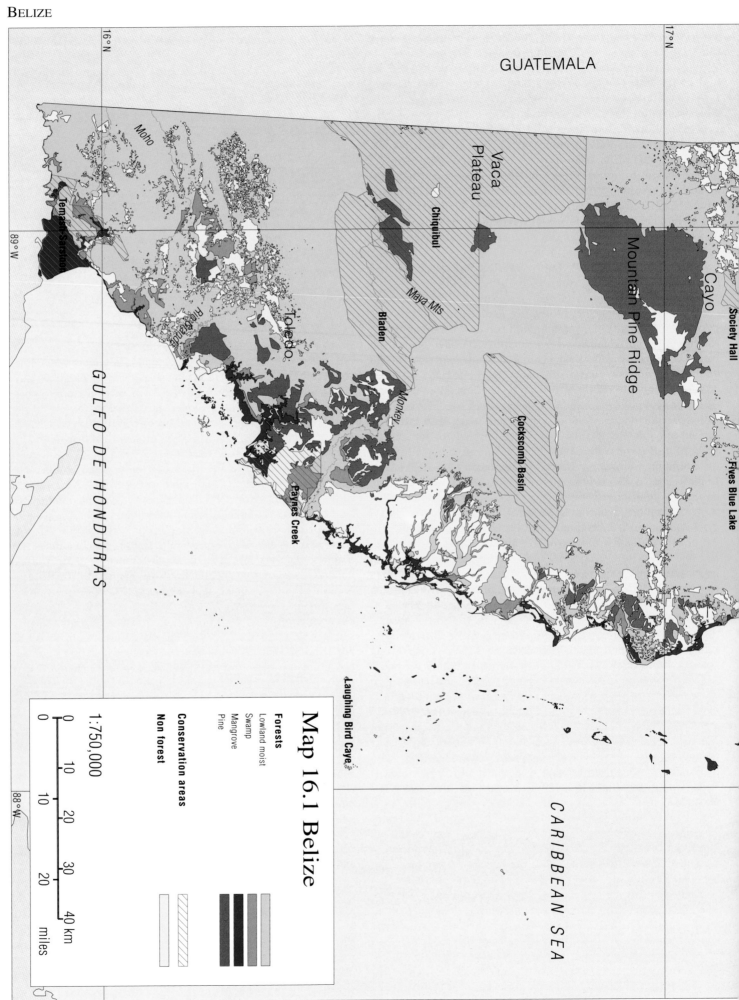

GUATEMALA

Vaca Plateau

Chiquibul

Maya Mts

Bladen

Monkey

Cockscomb Basin

Mountain Pine Ridge

Cayo

Society Hall

Fives Blue Lake

Moho

Temash-Sarstoon

Rio Grande

Toledo

Paynes Creek

Laughing Bird Caye

GULFO DE HONDURAS

CARIBBEAN SEA

Map 16.1 Belize

Forests
Lowland moist
Swamp
Mangrove
Pine

Conservation areas

Non forest

1:750,000

| 0 | 10 | 20 | 30 | 40 km |
| 0 | 10 | 20 | 30 | miles |

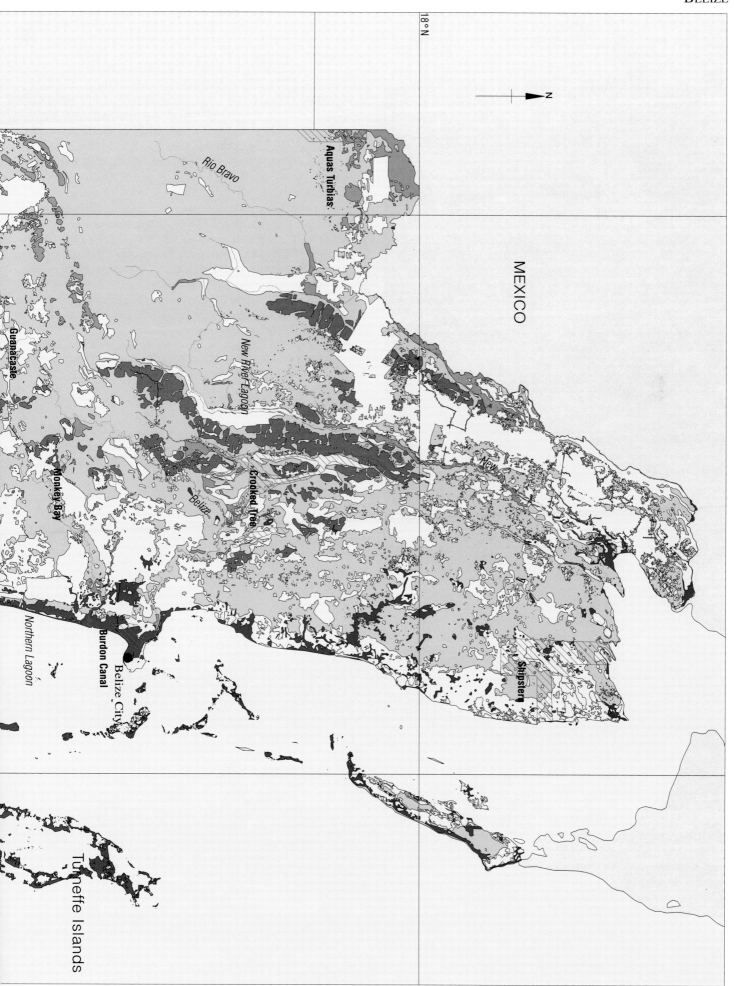

Columbia River forest, Belize.   (WWF/Tony Rath)

In recent years, several thousand hectares of land have been transferred out of reserved forests including some from Columbia River Forest Reserve for shifting agriculture (ODA, 1989).

Biodiversity

Although a small country, Belize has a high diversity of plant and animal life. Since much of its habitat is relatively undisturbed at present, the populations of many species are more stable here than in other countries. The flora is estimated to include about 4000 species of flowering plants, with 700 tree species, but there are few endemics (Hartshorn *et al.*, 1984). There are 135 species of mammals, 513 bird species, 107 reptiles and 32 amphibians (N. Bird, pers. comm.). The country's spectacular barrier reef is the second longest in the world and has been nominated for listing under the World Heritage Convention.

Two crocodile species are threatened in Belize, *Crocodylus acutus* and *C. moreletii*, though only the former is listed as globally threatened by IUCN (Groombridge, 1993). *C. acutus* is widely distributed along the coastline and the latter, which is rarer, is found in inland lagoons and rivers, including in the upper streams of the Maya Mountains (Hartshorn *et al., 1984).* The threatened Central American river turtle *Dermatemys mawii* is comparatively common in Belize. It is, however, hunted for food everywhere it occurs.

There are two bird species listed as threatened in Belize by Collar *et al.* (1992): the yellow-headed Amazon *Amazona oratrix* and the keel-billed motmot *Electron carinatum*. The Amazon lives in a variety of habitats including humid forest, but the motmot is confined to moist forest. Habitat destruction is one of the causes of the decline in both species.

Forest mammals listed as threatened by IUCN (Groombridge, 1993) that occur in Belize are the howler monkey *Alouatta pigra*, the spider monkey *Ateles geoffroyi*, the tapir *Tapirus bairdii*, the margay *Leopardus wieldii* and the olingo *Bassariscus sumichrasti*.

Conservation Areas

Provision for the gazettement and management of conservation areas lies within the National Parks System Act of 1981, which is administered by the Ministry of Natural Resources. Wildlife sanctuaries are no-hunting zones that are set aside to preserve important habitats or migration stop-over sites. National parks and monuments are for the enjoyment of the people of Belize and are open to the public. Nature reserves are set aside for scientific research.

The government does not have the resources to manage or protect its system of national parks adequately. However, it con-

Table 16.4   Conservation Areas in Belize

Existing conservation areas in IUCN's categories I–IV are listed below. Marine reserves have been excluded. Private reserves and forest reserves (category VIII) are shown on Figure 16.1.

National Park	Area (sq.km)
Aquas Turbias*	35
Blue Hole*	3
Chiquibul*~	1029
Guanacaste	0.2
Fives Blue Lake*	4
Laughing Bird Caye*	0.1
National Monument	
Half Moon Caye+	4
Wildlife Sanctuary	
Crooked Tree*	174
Cockscomb Basin*	402
Monkey Bay*	7
Paynes Creek*	123
Temash-Sarstoon*	170
Nature Reserve	
Bladen*	402
Burdon Canal	21
Society Hall*	27
Private Reserve	
Shipstern*	76
Total	2477.3

*   areas with forest (including mangroves) within their boundaries according to Map 16.1
~   Includes Caracol Archaeological Reserve of 18 sq. km
+   Not mapped — data not available to this project.

Source: D. Gray for sizes and designations (in litt., 1993) WCMC for IUCN's categories (unpublished data)

tracts the Belize Audubon Society (BAS), a private NGO, to provide management plans and train park wardens. BAS has access to domestic and international funding sources that the government does not, so this relationship works quite well.

As well as the protected areas with IUCN's categories I–IV listed in Table 16.4, there are also three other privately held reserves in the country (Figure 16.1). The Community Baboon Sanctuary was established in 1985 to protect one of the few healthy black howler monkey *Alouatta villosa* populations in Central America. Landowners from eight villages included in the area contribute to the maintenance of the sanctuary which now covers 53 sq. km. Rio Bravo Conservation and Management Area (926 sq. km), is being managed to integrate forestry and conservation by the Programme for Belize (see Box). There is also a 4 sq. km reserve at Monkey Bay (separate from the wildlife sanctuary). Shipstern is the only private reserve in Belize listed in IUCN's categories I–IV; it is a category IV reserve. It is being run along the same lines as Rio Bravo and is also being used as a production area for butterflies for export.

The 16 forest reserves, most in the south of Belize (see Figure 16.1), are managed for multiple use. Sustainable extraction of forest products and tourist recreation are permitted where these are consistent with protection of wildlife and environmental values. These reserves cover a total area of 4487 sq. km (N. Bird, in litt).

Figure 16.1 Private reserves and forest reserves of Belize
Source: unpublished data held at WCMC

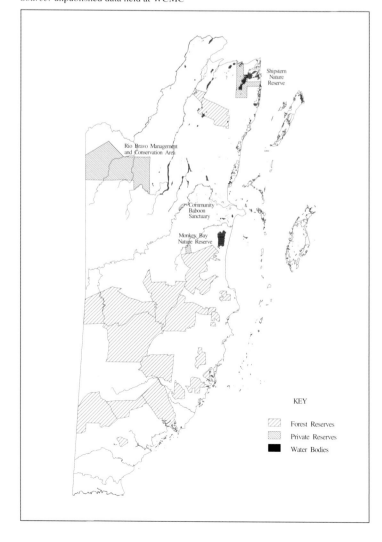

A boat-billed heron Cochlearius cochlearius *on nest with young in Cockscomb Basin Wildlife Sanctuary.* (WWF/Tony Rath)

Conservation Initiatives

A comprehensive land-use study, funded by the Overseas Development Administration of the UK, is nearly complete. This will provide Belize's government with information which will enable it to zone agricultural and infrastructural development so as to minimise environmental risks.

International and local NGOs working in conservation have a high profile in Belize. The Belize Audubon Society is involved with environmental education, conservation of wildlife and, as mentioned above, in the financing, development and management of protected areas. The overall goal of the Programme for Belize is to assist in the conservation and economic development of the natural resources of the country. The Nature Conservancy assisted with the purchase of Rio Bravo.

The Nature Conservancy of the US and the NGO CARE International include Belize in their regional "Proyecto Ambiental para Centro America". This is a project to promote conservation and sustainable use of resources in Central America. The main emphasis in Belize is on the district of Toledo in the south of the country.

Programme for Belize and the Rio Bravo Conservation and Management Area

In the late 1980s, some 2830 sq. km of land in north-western Belize came on the open market after the break-up of a much larger holding. The land, mostly covered with sub-tropical moist forest, but also with significant tracts of wetland and pine-oak savanna, had been selectively logged (mainly for *Cedrela* and *Swietenia*) for well over a century. Nonetheless it was still in excellent condition, containing healthy populations of a wide range of species that were becoming rare in Central America. In addition, although no indigenous people had lived in the area since the mid-19th century, ancient Mayan settlements were common.

As it was feared that the area would be totally cleared for agriculture, Programme for Belize (PFB) was set up with the express purpose of acquiring as much of the land as possible for conservation purposes. PFB is a Belizean controlled, non-profit making company which is dedicated to promoting wise use of the nation's natural resources. Around 445 sq. km of land were purchased with funding from foundations, bilateral aid agencies, commercial sponsors and — through a sponsorship scheme for purchase and endowment of individual plots — from private donors including schools. A further 370 sq. km were subsequently donated by Coca-Cola Inc. after the company abandoned its original plan for a large-scale citrus plantation on the land. Additional land purchases means that, as of September 1993, PFB controlled a total of slightly over 926 sq. km (Programme for Belize, 1993).

This area constitutes the Rio Bravo Conservation and Management Area (RBCMA), where Programme for Belize demonstrates the practical application of its principles. The ultimate objective is to achieve financial self-sufficiency for conservation management of Rio Bravo through revenues generated by wise use of its natural resources. In doing so, PFB will also show that retention of forest is a viable economic use of the land. Meanwhile, although several (20–30) thousand hectares, mostly owned by Mennonites, has since been turned over to intensive agriculture, much of the original holding remains under forest cover and the PFB maintains its policy of purchasing such land as it can when it comes onto the market. The RBCMA already has a shared boundary with the Guatemalan Rio Azul National Park and it is hoped that it may ultimately form the Belizean portion of a tri-national conservation area in the northern Petén/southern Yucatan area.

As of 1993, Programme for Belize has completed preliminary management, land-use and action plans. It is now emphasising development of land management activity, based on a provisional zoning system, whilst refining its planning approach for the post-1995 period. It has a fully-functioning research station, and long-term programmes for pure and applied ecological research, archaeological work, environmental monitoring and survey work are in place. There is also beginning to be effective control over the illegal resource theft, looting of Mayan sites and hunting that have long taken place in this border zone. An education and outreach programme is operating and subsidised visits by local groups are rapidly increasing. PFB also runs a professional training scheme, giving a year of practical work experience to Belizeans contemplating a career in natural resource management.

At present, educational tourism is the sole revenue-earning activity established on the RBCMA, but this already provides some 20 per cent of annual financial requirements. Other means of raising money are planned. The provisional zoning system allows for harvesting of non-timber forest products over the wide area buffering RBCMA's central core and trials for chicle-tapping and production of honey, essential oils, resins, logwood dyes and other products are currently being devised. Zoning on the lands donated by Coca-Cola allow for harvest of the timber, therefore the potential for sustainable forestry is being investigated; this is subject to the production of an appropriate forestry plan and the results of an independent environmental impact assessment. PFB's remit also allows for experimental agricultural and agro-forestry activities, but these have not been developed as yet.

The combination of conservation and economic development and the determination to achieve self-sufficiency, the last within a specific and limited time-frame and within the constraints set by wise-use, are important features of Programme for Belize and its work on the Rio Bravo Area. Perhaps the most important feature, however, is the demonstration that a local NGO, by making judicious use of the full range of support mechanisms available to it, can develop its own approach to sustainable natural resource management on an ambitious scale.

Source: John Burton, Programme for Belize

References

Belize Forest Department (1993). *The Forests of Belize: a first approximation at estimating the country's forest resources.* 10 pp. Unpublished.

BNF (1992). *Belize National Report.* Presented to the UN Conference on Environment and Development, Rio de Janerio, Brazil.

Collar, N.J., Gonzaga, L.P., Krabbe, N., Madroño Nieto, A., Naranjo, L.G., Parker III, T.A. and Wege, D.C. (1992). *Threatened Birds of the Americas. The ICBP/IUCN Red Data Book.* ICBP, Cambridge, U.K. 1150 pp.

FAO/UNEP (1981). *Proyecto de Evaluacion de los Recursos Forestales Tropicales: Los Recursos Forestales de la America Tropical.* FAO, Rome, Italy.

FAO (1993). *Forest resources assessment 1990: Tropical countries.* FAO Forestry paper 112. FAO, Rome, Italy.

Groombridge, B. (Ed.) (1993). *1994 IUCN Red List of Threatened Animals.* IUCN, Gland, Switzerland and Cambridge, U.K. 286 pp.

Hartshorn, G., Nicolait, L., Hartshorn, L., Bevier, G., Brightman, R., Cal, J., Cawich, A., Davidson, W., DuBois, R., Dyer, C., Gibson, J., Hawley, W., Leonard, J., Nicolait, R., Weyer, D., White, H. and Wright, C. (1984). *Belize Country Environmental Profile: A Country Study.* USAID Contract No. 505-0000-C-00-3001-00. 150 pp.

Holdridge, L.R., Lamb, F.B. and Mason, B. (1950). *Los Bosques de Guatemala.* IICA/Inst. Fom. Prod, Guatemala. 249 pp.

King , R.B., Baillie, I.C., Bissett, P.G., Grimble, R.J., Johnson, M.S. and Silva, G.L. (1986). *Land Resource Survey of Toledo District, Belize.* Tolworth Land Resources Development Centre, ODA. Pp. 65.

King , R.B., Baillie, I.C., Dunsmore, J.R., Grimble, R.J., Johnson, M.S. and Wright, A.C.S. (1989). *Land Resource Assessment of Stann Creek District, Belize.* Natural Resources Institute, Bulletin 19. ODA, Chatam. Pp. 262.

King , R.B., Baillie, I.C., Abell, T.M.B., Dunsmore, J.R., Gray, D.A., Pratt, J.H., Versey, H.R., Wright, A.C.S. and Zisman, S.A. (1992). *Land Resource Assessment of Northern Belize.* Natural Resources Institute, Bulletin 43. Volumes I and II. ODA, Chatam. Pp. 174 and 513.

ODA (1989). *Belize Tropical Forestry Action Plan.* Overseas Development Administration, London.

Pennington, T.D. and Sarukhán, J. (1968). *Arboles Tropicales de Mexico.* INAF/FAO, Mexico. 413 pp.

Programme for Belize (1993). Going forward in Belize — the new river wildlife corridor. *Programme for Belize Newsletter* 9: 1.

Zisman, S.A. (1992). *Mangroves in Belize: their characteristics, use and conservation.* Unpublished report for the Forest Planning and Management Project.

Author: Caroline Harcourt, WCMC, Cambridge with contributions from Neil Bird and David Gray of the Belize Forest Planning and Management Project, John Palmer of CIFOR and John Burton, Programme for Belize.

Map 16.1   Belize

Forest cover data for Belize was made available to WCMC by the Land Information Centre (LIC) of the Ministry of Natural Resources, Belmopan. David Gray, of LIC, kindly provided a digital dataset of forests at a scale of 1:500,000, harmonised into simplified broad forest categories to facilitate use in this Atlas. The distribution of each forest type in the LIC dataset was derived from land system maps of the Land Resource Assessments compiled by Bruce King *et al.* (1986, 1989 and 1992) of the Natural Resources Institute (NRI), UK. It must be noted, however, that because the forest cover has been estimated from the NRI Land Systems survey (i.e. the extent of each forest type was estimated by extracting land known to be under cultivation from 1985–1989), this map should be seen only as a first approximation at measuring the forest resources of Belize.

Mangrove cover for the outlying cays has been added from a supplementary file provided by the Land Information Centre, and is based on Zisman, S. (1992) *Mangroves in Belize: their characteristics, use and conservation,* an unpublished report for the Forest Planning and Management Project.

The NRI land system units, mapped to show agricultural potential of Belize, were assigned to the following forest classification: broadleaf cover (>75% tree canopy cover); open broadleaf cover (25%–75%); mixed broadleaf and pine (>75%); pine woodland (>75%); pine woodland savanna (50%–75%); pine tree savanna (5%–50%); marsh/swamp forest (>75%); mangrove (>5%) and non-forest cover (<5%). Canopy cover was determined by interpreting a sample of 1:40,000 scale aerial photographs, however determination was indicative only. It is important to note that the broadleaf category is very generalised. This class is a mixture of a wide range of forest types ranging from low scrubby woodlands to tall species-rich forests. The match between land system units and forest types varied, with good correlations for pine forests, marsh/swamp forest and non-forest. However, because the broadleaf classification is so general, the only way the extent of this class could be derived was by subtracting the area of all the other classes from the total area of Belize. This inevitably will have introduced inaccuracies.

The following forest classes have been amalgamated into the broad forest types shown on Map 16.1. Lowland rain forest — *Broadleaf forest* and *Open broadleaf forest*; pine forest — *Pine woodland, Pine woodland savanna* and *Mixed broadleaf/pine forest*; inland swamp forest — *Marsh/swamp*; mangrove — *Mangrove*; and non-forest — *Pine tree savanna* and *Non-forest*.

A map compiled at a 1:350,000 scale by the Belize Centre for Environmental Studies, Belize City, *Belize — Protected Lands of Belize* (1992), was used to portray the protected areas.

17 Costa Rica

Country area 51,100 sq. km
Land area 51,060 sq. km
Population (mid-1994) 3.2 million
Population growth rate 2.3 per cent
Population projected to 2025 5.4 million
Gross national product per capita (1992) US$2000
Forest cover for 1988 (see Map) 15,049 sq. km
Forest cover for 1990 (FAO, 1993) 14,280 sq. km
Annual deforestation rate (1981–1990) 2.9 per cent
Industrial roundwood production 1,170,000 cu. m
Industrial roundwood exports —
Fuelwood and charcoal production 3,136,000 cu. m
Processed wood production 462,000 cu. m
Processed wood exports 28,000 cu. m

Within a period of only 50 years, Costa Rica has reduced its forest cover from 80 per cent of the total territory to less than 30 per cent. Since 1950, the area deforested each year has exceeded 500 sq. km. The main cause of the deforestation is the conversion of forest to pasture for raising beef cattle. Most of the remaining forests are in the country's extensive protected areas system; all other forests are likely to be cleared before the end of this century.

The critical situation of the forests has become a subject of considerable public concern. As a result, in 1984 a law was passed to make it illegal to cut down forest on land that is unsuitable for agriculture. In addition, the national parks system is currently being reorganized and a National Institute for Biodiversity has been established. This institute aims to encourage the conservation, management and appropriate use of biodiversity in the country. However, despite these changes, Costa Rica's forests are still shrinking every year.

INTRODUCTION

Costa Rica is the third smallest Central American country, extending only 460 km or so at its greatest length, with as little as 118 km between coasts. The flat, open, 210 km stretch of Caribbean coast contrasts sharply with the irregular and hilly Pacific coast, which is some 1016 km long. Geographically the country can be divided into three distinct regions: the Pacific coast, a central mountainous backbone and the Caribbean lowlands.

The Pacific coast consists mainly of steep cliffs with occasional narrow beaches. The two major coastal peninsulas, Nicoya to the north and Osa to the south, are mostly rugged hills with small fringing plains; they are sparsely populated. The highest points on these peninsulas are Cerro Azul at 1018 m on Nicoya peninsula and Cerro Tigre at 782 m on Osa peninsula. The mountain chain in the interior is divided into four ranges which include several volcanoes, some of which are still active. Indeed, volcanic activity is a frequent cause of deaths, displacement and economic disruption in the country. The highest peak, in the Cordillera de Talamanca, is Chirripo Grande at 3810 m. The capital city of San José is situated in the agriculturally productive upland basin of Valle Central in the highland area. The Caribbean lowlands, below 500 m elevation, make up about one fifth of the country. The land is mostly flat with scattered hills. This area has always been inaccessible and sparsely populated. However, the Tortuguero waterway now provides access to the northern coastal area and a road has been built to the border with Panama. Puerto Limón remains the only port on the Caribbean coast and it is the site of the largest eastern settlement.

Although entirely within the tropics, Costa Rica possesses great climatic diversity with extreme regional differences.

Average annual rainfall is 3300 mm, but it varies considerably throughout the country. The length of the rainy season also varies, from all year round in the Caribbean lowlands to six months (May to October) in regions of Guanacaste Province on the Pacific coast. Mean annual maximum and minimum temperatures in San José (at 1172 m) are 26°C and 15°C respectively. Temperatures in the Caribbean lowlands tend to be lower than those on the Pacific coast. For instance, Siquirres at around 100 m elevation on the east coast has a mean annual temperature of 24.7°C, while Esparta at the higher elevation of 208 m on the Pacific coast has a mean annual temperature of 26.5°C.

The Costa Rican people are strikingly homogenous and generally tolerant of the few minorities within the nation. Most Costa Ricans claim European, particularly Spanish, ancestry. Of this group a small portion are "mestizo", that is of mixed Spanish and Indian blood. There are also some Afro-americans on the Caribbean coast, descendants of immigrants or slaves. The indigenous Amerindians now make up less than 0.5 per cent of the population.

Costa Rica's population growth rate has slowed from over 3.6 per cent in the early 1960s to 2.3 per cent in 1994. The population has nevertheless increased significantly, rising from 862,000 in 1950 to over 3 million at present. A considerable number of these people, more than 10 per cent, are refugees from political conflict in Guatemala, Nicaragua and El Salvador. Overall population density is around 63 inhabitants per sq. km, but the majority of the people live in the highland Valle Central. Around 45 per cent of Costa Ricans are urban dwellers.

The amount of land devoted to agriculture has risen considerably in the past four decades with a consequent decrease in for-

Table 17.1   Land use in Costa Rica in 1984

Land Use	Area (sq. km)	Percent of country
Pasture	22,290	43.9
Forest	16,385	32.3
Permanent crops	3,150	6.2
Annual crops	2,102	4.1
Other natural veg.	5,949	11.7
Urban areas	266	0.5
Lakes and reservoirs	163	0.3
Others	452	0.9
Total	50,757*	100

* NB   This is a slightly lower total land area than given at the head of the chapter
Source: MIRENEM/PAFCR (1990)

est cover. Table 17.1 shows land use in Costa Rica in 1984. Major agricultural exports from the country are coffee and bananas followed by beef and sugar. Beef production occupies a disproportionately large share of agricultural land (Leonard, 1987). Costa Rican society is regarded as the most equitable in the region, nevertheless access to land and resources is very unequal with 36 per cent of the land in large farms of over 5 sq. km and these are held by only one per cent of the landowners (Leonard, 1987).

The Forests

Different systems have been used in Costa Rica for the ecological classification of vegetation (e.g Tosi, 1969; Gómez, 1986). The most widely used is the system of "Life Zones" described by Holdridge et al. (1971), which is based on land form and climate. The system divides the forest types dealt with in this Atlas into tropical lowland, tropical premontane, lower montane and tropical montane. Each category is further sub-divided into moist, wet and rain forest types. In addition, mangroves and tropical dry forests exist in closed formations.

Tropical moist forest is the most widespread, but also the most discontinuous, Life Zone in Costa Rica (Holdridge et al., 1971). It is found in large areas of the north, east and southeast. The forest is composed of tall (40 to 50 meters), semideciduous or evergreen trees, with wide crowns and slender unbranched boles (mostly less than 100 cm dbh). There are also understorey trees 15–18 m high and a moderately dense undergrowth of 1–3 m high shrubs. Typical tree species include *Anacardium excelsum*, *Brosimum* spp., *Luehea seemannii*, *Cordia alliodora*, *Castilloa* spp., *Virola* spp., *Guarea* spp., *Calophyllum brasiliense*, *Terminalia amazonia*, *Dialium guianense*, *Tabebuia pentaphylla*, *Ochroma lagopus*, *Minquartia guianensis*, *Coumarouna panamensis*, *Vitex* spp. and *Eschweilera calyculata*. Palms, especially *Scheelea rostrata*, are usually abundant.

Holdridge's tropical wet forest is most extensive in the high rainfall areas of the Sarapiquí and Tortuguero plains in the northeast and in the Golfo Dulce lowlands in the southwest. The forest is multistoried and evergreen, the canopy is 45 to 55 meters high, while understorey trees are 10–25 m tall and the shrub layer is only 1.5–2.5 m. Overall, the trees are taller and denser than those in the moist forests and they include numerous stilt-rooted palms. It is the most species rich of the Life Zones with as many as 100 tree species in a single hectare.

The vegetation in Holdridge's tropical premontane moist forest zone in the centre of the country has mostly been destroyed and replaced with coffee bushes. It is a two-layered semidecidu-ous forest with a canopy at about 25 m and an understorey of evergreen trees 10–20 m tall. Typical species included *Persea caerulea*, *Phoebe mexicana*, *Erblichia odorata* and *Albizzia adinocephala*.

The tropical premontane wet forest occurs on the lower slopes of the El General Valley, in the Turrialba area and in a broad arc on the lower slopes of the Valle Central, extending in a narrow band along the Pacific flank of the Tilarán and Guanacaste Cordilleras. The forest is semi-evergreen with a canopy 30–40 m high, understorey trees are 10–20 m high and there is a dense undergrowth 2–3 m tall. Various species of the family Lauraceae characterise the forests, while *Talauma gloriensis* and *Lafoensia* spp. and *Mauria* spp. are also common.

The evergreen tropical premontane rain forest occurs mainly along the Atlantic slopes of the Talamanca, Central and Tilarán Cordilleras. Canopy trees are mostly 30–40 m high and the sub-canopy is dense, with trees 15–25 m tall. Palms are common in well-drained situations. Epiphytes, woody vines and herbaceous climbers are very abundant.

Lower montane moist forest occurs in only small areas of the country: north and southwest of Cartago and around the town of Zacero. It is an open evergreen forest. Canopy trees are mostly *Quercus*, 30–35 m high. The lower montane wet forest occurs chiefly on the Cordillera de Talamanca. It is primarily an evergreen oak forest with *Quercus oocarpa* at lower elevations, *Q. copeyensis* in the upper elevations and *Q. tomentocaulis*. *Cornus disciflora*, *Cedrela tonduzii*, *Alnus jorullensis* and *Magnolia poasana* also occur. Tropical lower montane rain forest occurs extensively on the windward flanks of the Central Cordillera, both flanks of the Talamanca Cordillera, the top of the Tilarán Cordillera and around the volcanic summits in the Guanacaste Cordillera. It too is an evergreen forest with *Quercus* species occurring commonly and these may reach 50 m although the general canopy height is only 25–30 m tall.

Tropical montane wet forest is restricted to the summit and upper southwest slopes of Irazú volcano but most of the vegetation here was destroyed by the volcanic eruptions of 1963–65. It would have been an evergreen forest with the canopy dominated by *Quercus* species. Tropical montane rain forest is found in the high Talamancas and occurs as small outliers around the summits of Turrialba, Irazú, Barba and Poás volcanoes. Rains, heavy mists and low cloud cover occur daily in these areas and there is no dry season. Trees are 25–30 m tall with small, often open crowns. Epiphytes are abundant and there is a dense shrub layer. Only 12 or 13 tree species occur including *Buddleia alpina*, *Escallonia poasana*, *Oreopanax xalapense*, *Weinmannia pinnata*, *Quercus costaricensis* and *Podocarpus standleyi*.

Dry tropical forest once covered extensive areas in the northern Pacific coastal plain. Most has now been cleared for agriculture but some remnant areas in the Guanacaste National Park have become the focus for a major international conservation programme (Janzen, 1986). The forest is semi-deciduous with a canopy at 20–30 m, an understorey of trees 10–20 m high and a 2–5 m tall, dense shrublayer. Common trees include *Bombacopsis quinatum*, *Casearia arguta*, *Chomelia spinosa*, *Eugenia salamensis*, *Piper amalago* and *Zanthoxylum setulosum* (Hartshorn, 1983).

Mangroves

Costa Rica's mangroves are found mostly along the Pacific coast of Costa Rica, where they occupy 35 per cent of the shoreline (WRI, 1991). In the Gulf of Nicoya, they cover 152 sq. km

NICARAGUA

Guanacaste Cordillera

Guanacaste

Caño Negro

Volcan Rinco del Viejo

Liberia

Piedras

Arenal Lagoon

Arenal

Lomas Barbudal

Tilarán Cordillera

Las Baulas de Guanacaste

Palo Verde

Poas V

Tamarindo

Penas Blancas

Isla Pájaros

Valle Ce

Ostional

Mt Cerro Azul

Esparta

Nicoya peninsula

Islas Guayabo y Negritos

Grande de Tárcales

Curú

Carara

Islas Guayabo

Negritos

Cabo Blanco

Map 17.1 Costa Rica

Forests

Lowland moist

Submontane

Montane

Mangrove

Dry

Conservation areas

Non forest

1:1,400,000

| 0 | 20 | 40 | 60 | 80 km |

| 0 | 20 | 40 | miles |

PACIFIC OCEAN

86° W

85° W

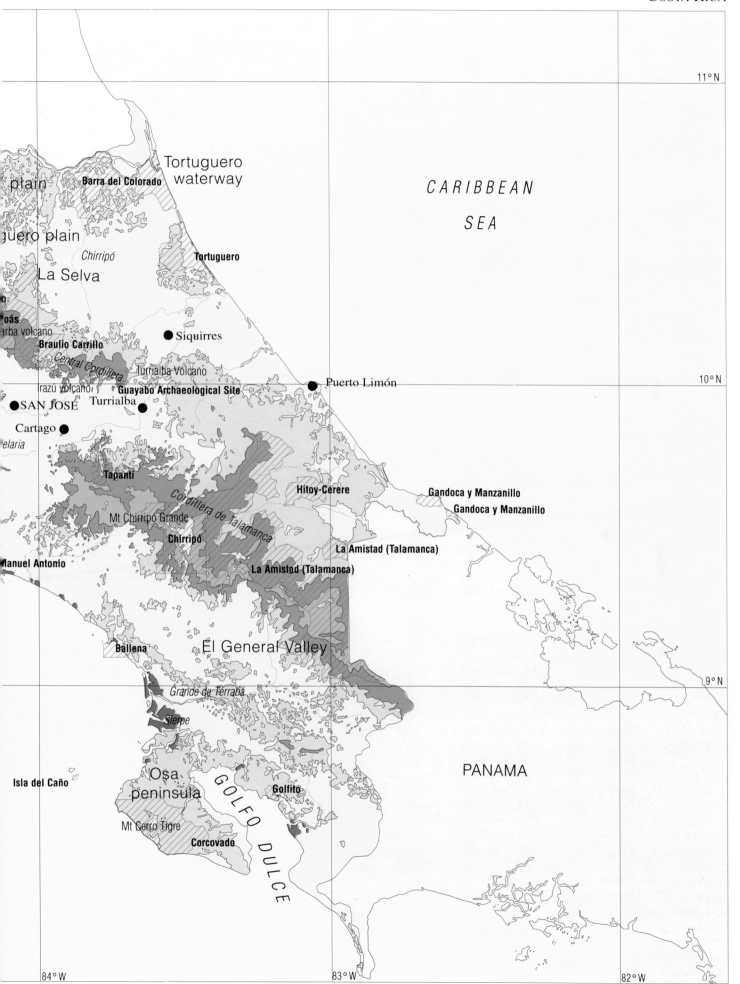

plain

Tortuguero
waterway

Barra del Colorado

CARIBBEAN

SEA

guero plain

Chirripó

Tortuguero

La Selva

oás

rba volcano

Braulio Carrillo

● Siquirres

Central Cordillera

Turrialba Volcano

razú volcano

Guayabo Archaeological Site

● SAN JOSÉ   Turrialba ●

Puerto Limón

Cartago ●

elaria

Tapantí

Hitoy-Cerere

Gandoca y Manzanillo

Gandoca y Manzanillo

Cordillera de Talamanca

Mt Chirripó Grande

Chirripó

La Amistad (Talamanca)

anuel Antonio

La Amistad (Talamanca)

El General Valley

Ballena

Grande de Térraba

Sierpe

PANAMA

Isla del Caño

Osa
peninsula

Golfito

GOLFO

Mt Cerro Tigre

DULCE

Corcovado

11° N

10° N

9° N

84° W   83° W   82° W

Table 17.2 Estimates of forest extent in Costa Rica

Forest type	Area (sq. km)	% land area
Lowland moist	10,306	20.2
Submontane	3,176	6.2
Montane	1,037	2.0
Dry	120	0.2
Mangrove	530	1.0
Total	15,169	29.7

Based on analysis of Map 17.1. See Map Legend on p. 170 for details of sources.

(WRI, 1991) and are also found in the estuaries of the Río Grande de Térraba and the Río Sierpe and to the east of Quepos (Leonard, 1987). In 1981, FAO/UNEP reported that mangroves on the Caribbean coast occurred on Río Chirripó and in a small area north of Puerto Limón.

FAO/UNEP (1981) estimated that 390 sq. km of mangroves were present in the country in 1981, while a decade later WRI (1991) reported an area of 400 sq. km. The area given by Jimenez (1992) is 413.3 sq. km. The 530 sq. km of mangroves (Table 17.2) indicated on Map 17.1 were digitised from hand drawn additions to the source map (see Map Legend) and consequently may not be an accurate representation.

Leonard (1987) reported that even as early as 1979, at least 40 per cent of the country's original mangrove area had been cleared. The clearance is for the construction of shrimp ponds, salt pans and coastal development. In addition, mangroves have been degraded by the over-collecting of their bark for the tanning industry. The harvesting of the bark of red mangroves *Rhizophora* has now been made illegal.

Forest Resources and Management

Costa Rica's original vegetation was virtually all forest; the exceptions were the fresh-water marshes and the sub-alpine páramo on the highest mountains (Holdridge, 1967). Before the Spanish arrived, the forest was broken by only a few dispersed Indian settlements and even as late as 1900, forest dominated over 90 per cent of the land (WRI, 1991). However, since 1922, deforestation has increased exponentially (WRI, 1991).

According to Garita (1989), forest covered only 14,760 sq. km in 1989, which is less than 29 per cent of the country. Of this, 9726 sq. km were in protected areas and 2350 sq. km received some protection in buffer zones. That left only 2684 sq. km, merely 5.3 per cent of the national territory, available for production forests. This area, at present covered by natural commercial forests, will be depleted before the end of the century. It is estimated that Costa Rica will then need to import wood, with an annual cost of approximately US$375 millions (WRI, 1991). FAO (1993) estimated that 14,280 sq. km of forest remained in the country in 1990, this was distributed between the tropical rain forest and hill and montane zones. Table 17.2 gives the area of each forest types as shown on Map 17.1. The differences between the estimates of FAO (1990 forest cover), Garita (1989 forest cover) and Table 17.2 (1988 forest cover), can probably be accounted for by the very high annual deforestation rate of 500 sq. km (but see the section on deforestation below).

The Directorate General of Forests (Dirección General Forestal-DGF) is responsible for forest management. Since 1986, DGF has fallen under the Ministry of Natural Resources,

Energy and Mines (MIRENEM — Ministerio de Recursos Naturales, Energía y Minas). According to the Forestry Law (Law No. 7174 of 1990) all harvesting operations should be regulated through a forest permit. These are issued by DGF, which also regulates timber through transportation permits and requires the timber owner to pay a forestry tax as well as municipal taxes. The dimensions of the trees that can be harvested from natural forests are legally restricted; they have to be more than 60 cm dbh in the Atlantic and northern regions of the country and over 80 cm dbh in the southern region (Lutz *et al.*, 1993). Permits for the main categories of exploitation require a forest inventory and a management plan prepared by a professional. However the management plans tend to have limited technical foundation; instead they are essentially "plans for cutting" (Lutz *et al.*, 1993). Cutting of more than the authorized volume appears to be quite common and this illegal logging is hard to detect (Lutz *et al.*, 1993).

A survey by Lutz *et al.* (1993) found that less than 20 per cent of the species from primary tropical forests were used by the internal timber market and that prices were low for species that are unknown or have little structural resistance. The most exploited species were found to be caobilla *Carapa guianesis*, laurel *Cordia alliodora* and lechosa *Brosimun* spp. in the Atlantic zone; caobilla and cedro *Cedrela odorata* in the northern region; and caobilla and cristobal *Platymiscium polystachyum* in the southern region of Costa Rica (Lutz *et al.*, 1993).

In recent years, forest laws have been amended to encourage greater private sector activity in forestry. There are now more than 175 public, private and non-governmental organisations engaged in different aspects of forestry or forest conservation. Many are still quite weak but some reforestation companies, both large scale and farmer-owned, have been relatively efficient. These have contributed to increased reforestation rates in recent years (Table 17.3).

Matamoros (1988) reports that 6 million cu. m of wood is cut annually; of this, 33 per cent is used for fuel, less than 25 per cent is used in the timber industry and more than 42 per cent is wasted. These figures are somewhat higher than those reported by FAO (1994) and indicated at the head of this chapter. According to Flores (1985), the average volume of wood cut in the commercial forests is 50.8 cu. m per ha. About 310 sq. km are logged each year. This should yield 1,574,800 cu. m of timber but only about 850,000 cu. m reaches sawmills and as little as 382,000 cu. m of processed wood is produced

Table 17.3 Reafforestation in Costa Rica from 1964 to 1989

Year	Annual (sq. km)	Cumulative (sq. km)
1964–1979	0.44 (mean)	7.0
1980	8.1	15.1
1981	11	26
1982	13.6	39.6
1983	9.8	49.4
1984	12.9	62.2
1985	25	87.2
1986	41.7	129
1987	53	182
1988	48.3	230.4
1989	50	280.4

Source: WRI (1991)

(MIRENEM/DGF, 1988). At present, it is far more profitable for landowners to clear their land and produce agricultural crops for export than it is for them to try and manage forests for a sustained yield of timber.

The direct economic value of forest exploitation is very low, only 3.6 per cent of the value of agricultural (MIRENEM, 1989). The forest sector is considered to contribute only one per cent to GNP. This is due to the fact that the only element taken into account is the value of timber supplied to industry. Other factors, such as the creation of jobs and the production of firewood and other direct and indirect forest products, are being ignored (Flores, 1985). In addition, forests are immensely important for the protection of catchments, both of agricultural areas and of hydro-electric schemes, and are valuable for tourism.

A recent study indicates that the depreciation of the value of the forest resource is very high, exceeding 100 million dollars in 1989 (WRI, 1991). If this loss of forest capital were to be taken into account when calculating Gross National Product then, instead of an annual growth of three per cent in GNP (World Bank, 1991), a decline of almost two per cent per year could be demonstrated in recent years.

A Tropical Forest Action Plan was completed in 1991, but the implementation of the plan has been limited by the failure of international development assistance agencies to provide financial support for it.

Deforestation

Within a period of only 50 years, the forest cover of Costa Rica has declined from 80 per cent of the total territory to under 30 per cent. More than 99 per cent of tropical dry forest, 77 per cent of the tropical moist forest and 54 per cent of the tropical wet forest have been cleared.

Several studies indicate that deforestation has increased dramatically since 1922, but that it has been most severe in the four decades from 1950 (see Figure 17.1). During this period, average annual deforestation has exceeded 500 sq. km. The root of the problem is a combination of official policies aimed at expanding the economy, liberal laws of land possession and a high rate of population growth (WRI, 1991). FAO (1993) estimates annual deforestation between the years of 1981 and 1990 to have been 496 sq. km, a rate of 2.9 per cent, which is considerably higher than that in any other Central or South American country except Paraguay. However in their recent report, Lutz *et al.* (1993) estimate that clear cutting in Costa Rica is now only 50 to 100 sq. km per year, as opposed to their estimate of 300 sq km being cleared each year in the past. They also report that since their survey was completed in 1992, a government analysis of LANDSAT data for the period 1986 to 1992 found average annual deforestation to be 170 sq km. They consider that the decrease can be explained by the fact that conversion historically occurred on land most suitable for agricultural use, and that the remaining forest lands are of increasingly marginal use for agriculture. In addition to this conversion, Lutz *et al.* estimate that the authorized change from primary to secondary forest, from secondary to logged-over secondary forest or from tree stands to solely pastureland may reach 310 to 360 sq. km per year. Including estimates of overcutting at authorized sites and cutting at unauthorized sites, Lutz *et al.* consider that selective logging could reach between 510 and 590 sq. km per year.

Most forest depletion has been caused by an increase in the area cleared for pasture. In other words, deforestation has been mainly the consequence of the expansion of livestock produc-

tion. This process started in the 1950s and was based on policies designed to encourage the export of beef. The generous credit programmes supporting beef production were funded almost exclusively by external sources. From 1950 to 1984, land used for livestock production increased by 10,264 sq. km (MIRENEM/PAFCR, 1990); pasture now occupies more than 54 per cent of the land. In spite of this, meat exports have never exceeded 8.6 per cent of Costa Rica's total exports.

This increase in livestock production, which required large areas of land and a small labour force, was not of benefit to the poor campesinos; instead it turned them into land speculators (WRI, 1991). They settled in uncultivated public lands, cleared some of the forest then sold the 'improved' lands to buyers who had economic power and access to bank credit. These buyers turned the areas into livestock farms. This process occurred so fast that it was not possible to extract and make good use of the trees that were cut down on the land. As a consequence, more than 90 per cent of the wood was wasted. This led to the "culture" of squandering that still prevails among Costa Rican campesinos and loggers. However, Lutz *et al.* (1993) consider that smallholders squatting on public or private land play only a minor role in current land clearing or logging.

Lutz *et al.* (1993) regard economic motives of the owners of forested land to be the current driving force behind most of the conversion and selective logging; the main objective being to realize the gains from timber harvesting or from subsequent agricultural production or both. Forest clearing to establish a stronger claim to the land no longer appears to be a motive, as it was in the past (Lutz *et al.*, 1993).

The rate of deforestation has been accelerated by the increase in road building in the country. For instance, the completion of the Interamerican Highway meant that clearing of the forest rose five fold along the Pacific slope. Similarly, deforestation on the Atlantic slope increased after the construction of the San José to Limón road. As a result of the clearance, erosion, flooding, falling river levels and weed infestation are causing difficulties in many areas. These problems are widespread along the entire central and south Pacific slope.

Until 1984, the forest was generally considered an obstacle to agriculture and cattle raising and deforested land was regarded as more valuable than forested. However, at that time a law was passed prohibiting the clearance of forest from land that was unsuitable for agriculture. Recently, there has been an increase in public concern about the destruction of the forests, with many more people in favour of the conservation of nature.

Biodiversity

The rich flora and fauna present today in Costa Rican forests are the result of the dispersion of biota from the two large continental masses of North and South America. These two blocks were separated until the end of the Pleistocene, when the Central American isthmus containing Costa Rica was formed.

This geographical situation, the variety of landscapes (mountain ranges with peaks over 3800 m, intermountain valleys of different altitudes and coastal plains and prairies of various characteristics and sizes), its condition as a barrier separating two oceans and the consequent five different climatic regions has resulted in Costa Rica containing more species per unit area than most other countries in the world (MIRENEM, 1992; Quesada, 1990). Containing some 10,000 plant species, 850 bird species, 228 species of mammals (about half of these are bats), 215 reptile species, 160 species of amphibians, 130 species of fresh water fishes and around 360,000 species of insects, it is

Figure 17.1 Deforestation in Costa Rica between the years of 1940–1987

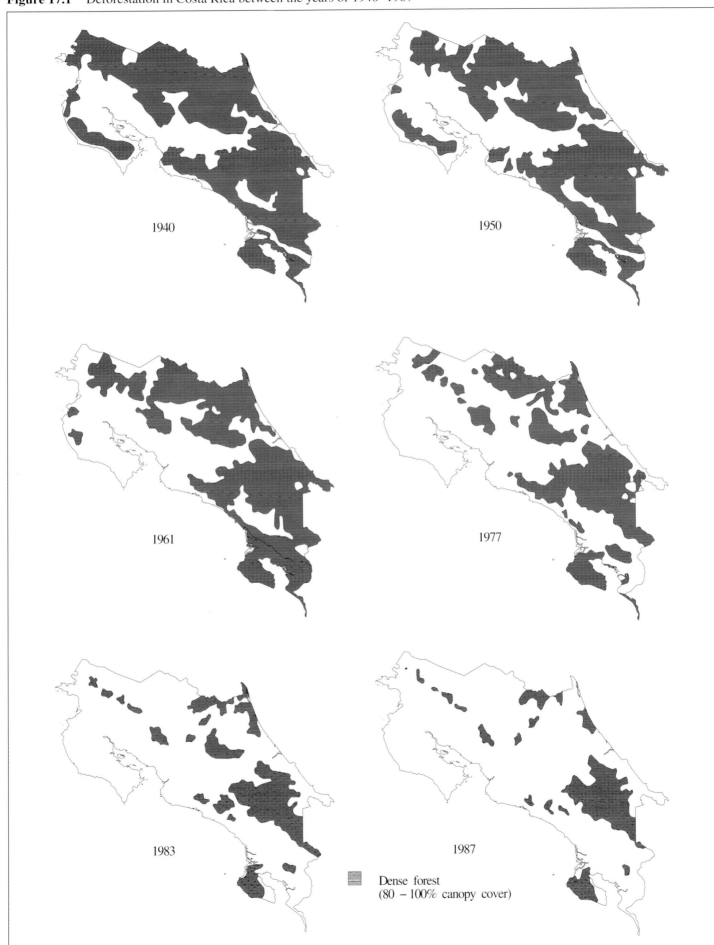

Dense forest
(80 – 100% canopy cover)

Source: Fundación Neotrópica (1988)

Logging in the Golfo Dulce Forest Reserve, Osa Peninsula.
(WWF/Olga Sheean)

home to between four and five per cent of the world's terrestrial animal and plant species (Quesada, 1990).

Many of Costa Rica's species, both plants and animals, have still not been described and, with the current rate of habitat destruction, it is likely that they will disappear before they are known (MIRENEM/SPN, 1992). The tropical moist and wet forests have the highest biodiversity in the country and these ecosystems are vanishing rapidly.

For its size, Costa Rica may have the most diverse plant life in the world (Davis *et al.*, 1986). For instance, La Selva Private Reserve, an area of only 14 sq. km, contains as many as 1740 vascular plants (Hammel, 1990). Gentry (1978) estimated that a total of 8,000 species occur in the country, while L.D. Gómez (1984, cited in Davis *et al.*, 1986) considers that 10,000 occur. Of these, 1393 are believed endemic (Davis *et al.*, 1986).

Forty-five commercial timber species are threatened, nine of these are endemic (CEAP.ECO., 1991; MIRENEM, 1992). Among the threatened species are the mahoganies *Swietenia humilis* and *S. macrophylla*, cocobolo *Dalbergia retusa*, balsamo *Myroxylon balsamum*, Belize yellowwood *Podocarpus guatemalensis, Cordia gerascanthus, Parkia pendula* and *Mora oleifera* (MIRENEM, 1992).

The *1994 IUCN Red List of Threatened Animals* (Groombridge, 1993) contains 37 species (12 mammals, seven birds, seven reptiles, one amphibian and ten invertebrates) that are found in Costa Rica. Few, however, are restricted to the country. The threatened non-endemics include the Central American squirrel monkey *Saimiri oerstedii*, the giant anteater *Myrmecophaga tridactyla*, the Central American tapir *Tapirus bairdii* and the American crocodile *Crocodylus acutus*; these are all relatively widespread. In contrast, the threatened mountain squirrel *Syntheosciurus brochus* and eight-spotted skipper *Dalla octomaculata* are found otherwise only in Panama. Excluding birds, the golden toad *Bufo periglenes* is the only endangered vertebrate endemic to the country. Many of the invertebrates listed are endemic, including most of the Odonata such as *Palaemnema gigantula, P. melanota, Diaphlebia pallidistylus* and *Epigomphus camelus*.

Collar *et al.* (1992) list only four threatened bird species in Costa Rica. One of these, the mangrove hummingbird *Amazilia boucardi* is endemic. The other three species are the keel-billed motmot *Electron carinatum*, the bare-necked umbrella bird *Cephalopterus glabricollis* and the yellow-billed cotinga *Carpodectes antoniae*. Destruction of their forest habitat —

including mangroves — is the cause of the decline of all of these species. Hunting and the cagebird trade are also a threat in Costa Rica (Stiles, 1985). The species most affected by hunting is the great curassow *Crax rubra*, while the scarlet macaw *Ara macao*, yellow-headed amazon *Amazona ochrocephala*, dark-backed goldfinch *Carduelis psaltria*, yellow-bellied siskin *C. xanthogastra* and yellow-tailed oriole *Icterus mesomelas* are all commonly kept in cages by the local people and are threatened as a result (Stiles, 1985).

Luis Elizondo of the National Institute of Biodiversity (INBio) has produced an unpublished list of the amphibians, reptiles, birds and mammals that are threatened in Costa Rica (rather than being globally threatened as listed by IUCN). He considers 76 bird and 18 mammal species to be threatened and 11 birds and three mammals to be in danger of extinction in the country (Elizondo, 1991). As well as the golden toad, he lists the toad *Atelopus senex* as heading for extinction, possibly due to the introduction of exotic fish such as the trout *Salmo gairdneri*. The reptiles he lists as threatened are the marine turtles.

A recent study (MIRENEM/SPN, 1991) identifies the areas of highest endemism in the country. They are the Talamanca region, the highlands of the central volcanic mountain range, the Golfo Dulce area and the Isla del Coco (these regions are all under the protection of the national parks system). This same study assessed the contribution of biodiversity to the country's development and the cost of conserving it. It demonstrated that the most effective mechanism to conserve biodiversity in the long term is the *National System of Conservation Areas*, which is the new pattern of management of protected areas in Costa Rica.

Conservation Areas

Costa Rica is internationally known for its efforts in the field of conservation. Although the first national park was created in 1945 (Hartshorn *et al.*, 1982), it was in the 1970s that the process effectively began. Now over 70 areas (excluding the anthropological reserves) have been established (see Table 17.4) and more than 20 per cent of the country's territory has been legally declared as belonging to some kind of conservation area. Only the national parks, biological reserves, wildlife refuges and national monuments are listed in Table 17.5 and shown on Map 17.1 as these are the only ones in IUCN's categories I–IV. Three of the national parks (Barra Honda — 23 sq.

Table 17.4 The establishment of protected areas in Costa Rica

Categories	Before 1971	71–75	76–80	81–85	86–90	1991	Total
National Park	2	8	2	2	1	3	18
Biological Reserve*	2	3	3	0	1	0	9
National Monument	0	1	0	0	0	0	1
Wildlife Refuge	0	0	0	9	0	0	9
Forest Reserve	2	4	3	0	0	0	9
Protection Zone	1	0	8	9	4	6	28
National Forest	0	0	0	0	0	1	1
Total	7	16	16	20	6	10	75

* including the private reserves

Source: MIRENEM/SPN (1992)

167

km, Cahuita — 11 sq. km and Volcan Irazu — 23 sq. km) have also been excluded as these are in category V. There are two private biological reserves, La Selva (14 sq. km) and Monteverde (105 sq. km — see Box in Chapter 8), which are not mapped or listed.

The administration of the protected areas falls under a variety of different organisations. The National Parks Service (Servicio de Parques Nacionales — SPN) manages national parks, biological

Table 17.5 Conservation areas in Costa Rica

Existing conservation areas in IUCN's categories I–IV are listed below. For information on World Heritage sites, Ramsar sites and Biosphere reserves see Chapter 8.

National Parks

Arenal	20
Ballena*	42
Braulio Carrillo*	441
Chirripó*	502
Corcovado*	546
Guanacaste*	325
Isla del Coco Marine+	24
Juan Castro Blanco*	143
La Amistad (Talamanca)*	1,939
Manuel Antonio*	7
Palo Verde*	132
Santa Rosa+	372
Tapantí*	61
Tortuguero*	189
Volcán Poás*	56
Volcan Rincón de la Vieja*	141

Biological Reserves

Cabo Blanco*	12
Carara*	47
Hitoy-Cerere*	92
Isla Pájaros	<0.1
Isla del Caño	2
Islas Guayabo y Negritos	1
Lomas Barbudal	23

Wildlife Refuges

Barra del Colorado*	980
Baulas	1
Caño Negro*	100
Curú*	0.8
Gandoca y Manzanillo	94
Golfito*	14
Isla Bolaños+	1
Ostional	2
Penas Blancas	24
Tamarindo	5

National Monument

Guayabo Archaeological Site	2

Total	6,341

* area with moist forest within its boundaries as shown on Map 17.1
+ not mapped

reserves and national monuments. The Forest Service (DGF) manages the forest reserves and protection zones, which cover about 4600 sq. km, but are all in IUCN's category VIII as exploitation of natural resources is permitted with permission from DGF. The Wildlife Department (Departamento de Vida Silvestre — DVS) is responsible for the wildlife refuges. The National Commission for Indian Affairs (Comisión Nacional de Asuntos Indígenas — CONAI) supervises the 30 or so indigenous reserves, which cover around 5800 sq. km. In addition, the private sector is becoming involved in the management of conservation areas. For instance, Monteverde Biological Reserve is administered by the Centro Científico Tropical (CCT), while La Selva Biological Reserve is run by the Organisation for Tropical Studies (OTS).

Many of Costa Rica's conservation areas were established without scientific studies of their natural or cultural features or an analysis of their socioeconomic situation. Instead, such factors as political or personal interest strongly influenced the identification of the areas to be protected (Hartshorn *et al.*, 1982). There are still problems within the protected areas system. In many cases, the boundaries of the areas are not marked on the ground and frequently private property occurs within the supposedly protected area. For example, the SPN owns only one hectare of Cahuita National Park (Hartshorn *et al.*, 1982). Most areas do not have management plans and exploitation of timber, fuelwood and wildlife is common, particularly in forest reserves. Almost all of Costa Rica's remaining forest is now found in its protected areas system.

A new strategy for the management of protected areas called the *National System of Conservation Areas* has been recently designed. Its purpose is to achieve management of the protected areas in a regional context and to integrate the neighbouring communities in an effective manner. The system has given rise to new features such as the development of resource management programmes involving non-profit, private conservation organizations (MIRENEM/SPN, 1992).

The development of protected areas has promoted the "ecotourism industry", which is today the country's second largest foreign income generating activity.

Conservation Initiatives

The Conservation Strategy for Sustainable Development in Costa Rica (MIRENEM, 1989) aims at defining long and medium term policies which would lead to the integration of conservation and sustainable development. The strategy promotes a

Forest protected in Corcovado National Park.

(WWF/H. Jungius)

new, integrated approach to conservation and development, but it has not yet been given any official recognition by the government.

The Forestry Action Plan for Costa Rica (MIRENEM/PAFCR, 1990) was based on a diagnosis of the forest situation in the country. It demonstrated that the present pattern of farming was causing a "significant deterioration" of natural resources. It has been officially acknowledged and has served as a base for the National Development Plan of the current government. External technical and financial cooperation in the forest sector is linked to the plan's implementation.

An important recent initiative was the creation of the National Institute for Biodiversity. This institute is a private, non-profit-making organization, the purpose of which is to carry out a national inventory of biodiversity and improve the information on biodiversity and its uses for the benefit of the country.

The development of new mechanisms to support conservation activities (such as the "foreign debt-for-nature swap") has provided conservation programmes with large amounts of money and, therefore, with greater long term stability. NGOs have played an important role in this field. Two of the most outstanding NGOs are the National Parks Foundation and the Foundation for the Development of the Central Volcanic Mountain Range, which jointly administer some US$50 million.

The government has provided a series of incentives to strengthen management of the private forest sector. These incentives help national, regional and campesino organizations to plant and manage forests.

References

CEAP.ECO (1991). *Informe Nacional de Costa Rica (Borrador de Discusión)*. Fundación Neotrópica y Comisión del Nuevo Orden Ecológico Internacional, Ministerio de Relaciones Exteriores y Culto. San Jose, Costa Rica.

Collar, N.J., Gonzaga, L.P., Krabbe, N., Madroño Nieto, A., Naranjo, L.G., Parker III, T.A. and Wege, D.C. (1992). *Threatened Birds of the Americas. The ICBP/IUCN Red Data Book*. ICBP, Cambridge, U.K.

Davis, S.D., Droop, S.J.M., Droop, Gregerson, P., Henson, L., Leon, C.J., Villa-Lobos, J.L., Synge, H. and Zantovska, J. (1986). *Plants in Danger: What do we know?* IUCN, Gland, Switzerland and Cambridge, U.K.

Elizondo, L.H. (1991). *Especies de Anfibios, Reptiles, Aves y Mamíferos Amenazadas o en Peligro de Extinción en Costa Rica: Breve Reseña*. Base de Datos de Biodiversidad, Instituto Nacional de Biodiversidad. Heredia, Costa Rica. 63 pp (unpublished).

FAO (1993) *Forest resources assessment 1990: Tropical countries*. FAO Forestry Paper 112. FAO, Rome, Italy.

FAO (1994). *FAO Yearbook: Forest Products 1981–1992*. FAO Forestry Series No. 27, FAO Statistics Series No. 116. FAO, Rome, Italy.

FAO/UNEP (1981). *Tropical Forest Resources Assessment Project. Los Recursos Forestales de la America Tropical*. FAO, Rome, Italy.

Flores, J. (1985). *Diagnóstico del Sector Forestal Industrial*. San Jose, Costa Rica. Editorial UNED.

Fundación Neotrópica (1988). *Desarrollo Socioeconómica y el Ambiente Natural: Sitación Actual y Perspectives*. Ramirez, A. and Maldonado (Eds). San José, Costa Rica.

Garita, D. (1989). *Mapa de cobertura boscosa de Costa Rica (scale 1:200,000)* MIRENEM/DGF, San Jose, Costa Rica.

Gentry, A. (1978). Floristic knowledge and needs in Pacific Tropical America. *Brittonia* 30 134–153.

Gomez, L.D. (1986). Vegetación de Costa Rica. In: *Vegetación y Clima de Costa Rica*. Gomez, L.D. and Herrera, W. (eds). EUNED, San Jose, Costa Rica.

Groombridge, B. (Ed.) (1993). *1994 IUCN Red List of Threatened Animals*. IUCN Gland, Switzerland and Cambridge, U.K. 286 pp.

Hammel, B. (1990). The distribution of diversity among families, genera, and habitat type in the La Selva flora. In: *Four Neotropical Rainforests*. Gentry, A. H. (ed). Pp. 75–84. Yale University Press, New Haven.

Hartshorn, G.S. (1983). Plants. In: *Costa Rican Natural History*. D. Janzen (ed.). The University of Chicago Press, Chicago. Pp. 118–350.

Hartshorn, L. *et al.* (1982). Costa Rica: Country Environmental Profile. Tropical Science Centre. San José, Costa Rica.

Holdridge, L.R. (1967). Life Zone Ecology. Tropical Science Centre. San José, Costa Rica

Holdridge, L.R., Grenke, W.H., Hatheway, W.H., Liang, T. and Tosi, J.A. (1971). *Forest Environment in Tropical Life Zones: A Pilot Study*. Pergamon Press, Oxford. 747 pp.

Janzen, D. H. (1986). *Guanacaste National Park: Tropical Ecological and Cultural Restoration*. Editorial Universidad a Distancia. San José, Costa Rica.

Jiménez, J.A. (1992). Mangrove forests of the Pacific coast of Central America. In: *Coastal Plant Communities of Latin America*. Seeliger, U. (ed). Academic Press, San Diego. Pp. 259–267.

Leonard, H.J. (1987). *Natural Resources and Economic Development in Central America: A Regional Environmental Profile*. Transaction Books, Oxford, U.K.

Lutz, E., Vedova W., M., Martínez, H., San Román, L., Vazquez L., R., Alvarado, A., Merino, L., Celis, R., and Huising, J. (1993). *Interdisciplinary Fact-Finding on Current Deforestation in Costa Rica*. Environment Working Paper No. 61. The World Bank Sector Policy and Research Staff.

Matamoros, A. (1988). *Documento de trabajo: Sector Forestal y Areas Silvestres. Estrategia Nacional para el Desarrollo Sostenible de Costa Rica*. San José, Costa Rica.

MIRENEM (1989). *Memorias 1er Congreso: Estrategia de Conservación para el Desarrollo Sostenible de Costa Rica, octubre de 1988*. Comp. y d. por Quesada, C. y Solis, V. San Jose, Costa Rica.

MIRENEM (1992). *Estudio Nacional de Biodiversidad. Costos, beneficios y Necesidades de la Conservación de la Diversidad Biológica*. Primer Borrador. San José, Costa Rica.

MIRENEM/DGF (1988). *Censo de la Industria Forestal*. San José, Costa Rica.

MIRENEM/PAFCR (1990). *Plan de Acción Forestal para Costa Rica. Documento Base, Area 1: Foresteria en el Uso de la Tierra; Area 2: Desarrollo Industrial Basado en Bosques; Area 3: Lena y Energia; Area 4: Conservación de Ecosistemas*. San José, Costa Rica.

MIRENEM/SPN (1991). *Estudio de diagnóstico de las Areas Protegidas de Costa Rica*. San José, Costa Rica.

MIRENEM/SPN (1992). *Sistema Nacional de Areas Conservación. Un nuevo enfoque*. San José, Costa Rica.

Quesada, C. (1990). *Estrategia de Conservación para el Desarrollo Sostenible de Costa Rica*. ECODES. MIRENEM, San José, Costa Rica.

Stiles, F. (1985). Conservation of forest birds in Costa Rica: problems and perspectives. In: *Conservation of Tropical Forest Birds*. Diamond, A.W. and Lovejoy, T.E. (eds). Pp. 141–168. ICBP Technical Publication No. 4, ICBP, Cambridge.

Tosi, J.A. (1969). *Mapa Ecológica de Costa Rica*. Tropical Science Centre, San José, Costa Rica.

World Bank (1991). *The World Bank Atlas, 1991*. World Bank, Washington, D.C. Pp. 1–25.

WRI (1991). *Accounts Overdue: Natural Resource Depreciation in Costa Rica*. Tropical Science Center, San José, Costa Rica/World Resources Institute, Washington, D.C. 110 pp.

Author: Alonso Matamoros Delgado, San José, Costa Rica; with contributions from Luis H. Elizonda Castillo, INBio, Costa Rica.

Map 17.1   Costa Rica

Costa Rica forest data have been derived from two main sources. Forest cover has been digitised from a dyeline map (in nine sheets covering different regions), entitled *Mapa de Cobertura Boscosa de Costa Rica (+60% densidad)*. The source map was compiled by the Ministerio de Recursos Naturales, Energia y Minas, Direccion General Forestal (1988), at a scale of 1:200,000. Forests, at >60% canopy cover, are shown and are classified as *Area de Bosque Natural*. These natural forest areas have been digitised to compile the forest cover data shown on Map 17.1.

An ecological map, *Mapa Ecologico — Republica de Costa Rica*, using Holdridge Life Zones, has been selectively digitised and overlaid onto the forest cover information, to delimit the submontane and montane forest types of Costa Rica. The source map, published in 1969 and produced by Joseph A. Tosi Jr., Centro Cientifico Tropical, San José, depicts 19 Life Zones. Of these, five zones have been digitised, from the *Piso Montano Bajo* and *Piso Montano* forest formations, to locate submontane and montane moist forest. The source classes have been digitised and harmonised in the following way: submontane rain forest comprises *Lower montane moist forest*, *Lower montane wet forest* and *Lower montane rain forest*; montane rain forest includes *Montane wet forest* and *Montane rain forest*. The limits of dry forest (*tropical dry forest*) have also been derived from this map. The location and extent of remaining mangroves were supplied by the author.

Spatial data for the protected areas of Costa Rica have been extracted from a 1:500,000 scale dyeline map *Mapa de Areas Silvestres* (1989), prepared by the *Ministerio de Recursos Naturales, Energia y Mínas and Dirección General Forestal*, Costa Rica. Additions and updates have been made to protected area boundaries from information hand drawn onto large 1:200,000 scale maps (Instituto Geografico Nacional, 1969), and kindly made available to WCMC by the Servico de Parques Nacionales, Costa Rica.

18 El Salvador

Country area	21,040 sq. km
Land area	20,720 sq. km
Population (mid-1994)	5.2 million
Population growth rate	2.7 per cent
Population projected to 2025	9.1 million
Gross national product per capita (1992)	US$1170
Forest cover for 1981 (see Map)	1555 sq. km
Forest cover for 1990 (FAO, 1993a)	1230 sq. km
Annual deforestation rate (1981–1990)	2.2 per cent
Industrial roundwood production	146,000 cu. m
Industrial roundwood exports	—
Fuelwood and charcoal production	4,526,000 cu. m
Processed wood production	70,000 cu. m
Processed wood exports	—

The high population density in El Salvador has resulted in most of the country being deforested, with little of the land still in its natural state. A considerable area was deforested even before the beginning of this century. Most of the country's remaining forest is in the montane area on the border with Honduras. The persistent civil strife has disrupted conservation efforts. Nonetheless, some areas of natural forest are under protection.

INTRODUCTION

El Salvador is the smallest of the Central American countries and the only one without a Caribbean coast. Most of the country consists of rugged volcanic highlands of moderate elevation. The highest point, 2730 m, is Cerro El Pital on the northwestern border with Honduras. A narrow coastal plain, interrupted by mountains and deep ravines, runs parallel to the Pacific ocean.

May to October is the rainy season and precipitation is high throughout the country during these months; there is little rain for the rest of the year. San Salvador, the capital, receives 1600 mm in the rainy season and 150 mm in the dry. Temperatures rarely fall below 18°C except in the highest mountains. In San Salvador, the average is 23°C with a variation of only 3°C between the warmest and coldest months.

Population density in El Salvador, at 251 people per sq. km, is considerably higher than that in any other Central American country. About 93 per cent of the population are mestizo, five per cent are Indian and two per cent are of European origin. Most of the Indians are descended from the Pipil tribes who came from Mexico and inhabited almost two thirds of El Salvador before the Spanish arrived. Another important group are the Lenca, descendants of the early Mayas. Few of the Indians retain their native way of life. About 45 per cent of the population are urban inhabitants, with around one quarter of these living in San Salvador.

The country is primarily agricultural but it is, nevertheless, more highly industrialised than the other Central America nations. Major exports include pharmaceuticals, cardboard and manufactured goods as well as agricultural products such as coffee, sugar and cotton.

The Forests

Most of El Salvador's natural vegetation was destroyed before it could be studied by botanists. Daugherty (1974) lists the forest formations that occur in the country: mangroves, evergreen, gallery and deciduous forests occur in the lowlands and in the highlands are found cloud forests and mixed pine-oak forests. The hypothetical distribution of these formations is shown in Figure 18.1.

The lowland formations extended from sea level to about 800–1000 m. The evergreen forests occurred primarily in a narrow band along the coast and on the moister floodplains of the main rivers. Characteristic tree species of this forest type include *Bombax ellipticum, Brosimum terrabanum, Castilla gummifera, Ceiba pentandra, Chlorophora tinctoria, Enterolobium saman, Myroxylon balsamum, Sideroxylon tempisque, Ficus* spp. and *Terminalia obovata* (Daugherty, 1974).

The most common species found in El Salvador's gallery forests are *Ceiba pentandra, Enterolobium cyclocarpum, Ficus* spp. and *Terminalia obovata*. Only small patches of this forest type remain.

Deciduous forests originally covered around 90 per cent of El Salvador. Characteristic species of this formation include *Bursera simaruba, Cedrela* spp., *Cordia alliodora, Gliricidia sepium, Myroxylon balsamum, Piptadenia constricta, Poeppigia procera, Swietenia* spp. and *Tabebuia alliodora* (Daugherty, 1974).

The pine-oak formation extends from between 800–1000 m up to 1800–2000 m in elevation. It was formerly widespread on the slopes of the volcanic chain in the Centre-South and on the mountains on the border with Honduras but has now mostly been cleared. It is dominated by species of *Quercus* and *Pinus oocarpa*. Other species include *Cedrella mexicana, Clethra vulcanicola, Permymenium* spp. and *Nectandra sinuata*. In areas where the soil is richer, *Liquidambar styraciflua* also occurs. Epiphytes are common in this forest type (Daugherty, 1974).

Cloud forests are generally found above 1800 m. The trees are 20–30 metres tall and are dominated by the families Fagaceae and Lauraceae. Epiphytes, including bromeliads and orchids, mosses, lichen and ferns are abundant. These forests are best developed in the northwest, on Montecristo and El Pital, but can also be found on the volcanoes of Santa Ana, San Salvador and San Vicente.

Mangroves

In the country's Environmental Profile, mangrove forests are estimated to cover 453 sq. km (Perfil Ambiental, 1985), but Jimenez (1992) reports an area of only 352.4 sq. km. On Map 18.1, the

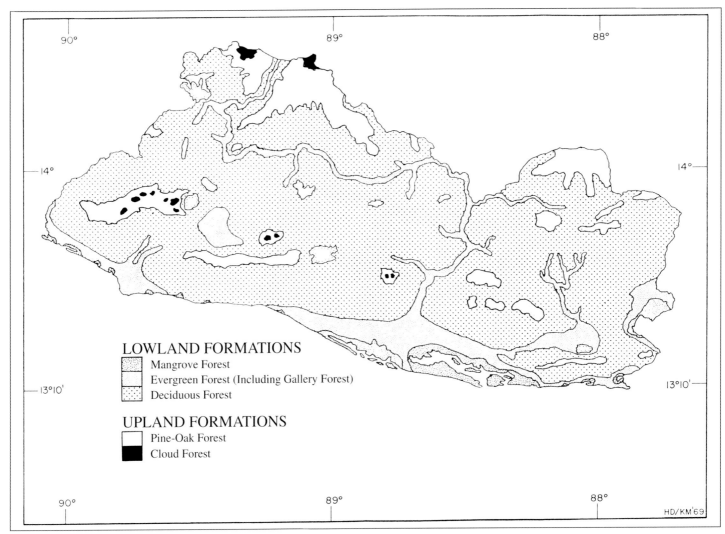

Figure 18.1 Hypothetical climax vegetation of El Salvador

Source: Daugherty (1969) from field observations, 1968–1969; Laver (1955)

mangroves cover 446 sq. km. They are concentrated in four areas: Bahía de Jiquilisco, Barra de Santiago, Estero de Jaltepeque and Bahía de La Unión. The main species are *Rhizophora mangle, Avicennia germinans* and *Laguncularia racemosa*. Although they are, by law, inalienable government domain, the mangroves suffer exploitation for poles, posts, firewood and tannins. In addition, they are threatened by the encroachment of agriculture, the construction of shrimp and salt ponds, drainage for mosquito control and the influx of agricultural pesticides (USAID, 1988).

Forest Resources and Management

El Salvador is thought to have been almost completely forested at the time of European settlement in the 16th century. In a 1985 study, using data from 1978 and 1979, it was estimated that only 2682 sq km or 13 per cent of the country's land area was covered with "forest" (Perfil Ambiental, 1985). However, in this report "forest" included plantations and shrubland (Table 18.1) and very little undisturbed natural forest (as defined in this Atlas) remained. Excluding shrubland and plantations from Table 18.1, the area of natural closed forest remaining in 1978/79 was only 1846 sq. km or 9 per cent of El Salvador's land area.

FAO (1993a) indicates that 1230 sq. km of forest remained in El Salvador in 1990, 64 per cent of this is in the hill and montane zone of the country. FAO (1993a) gives no figure for closed broadleaved forest in the country. The distribution of the forests shown on Map 18.1 have been taken from a map that

was published more than a decade ago — in 1981. The area of the forests given in Table 18.2 (1555 sq. km) is, therefore, almost certainly an overestimate of the present day situation.

The broadleaved forests are scattered in relatively small patches throughout the country and include riparian forests along the streams. The most important, for biological diversity and as watershed protection, are the cloud forests of Montecristo, Volcan Santa Ana and El Pital (USAID, 1988). Cloud forests are estimated to cover approximately 39 sq. km.

As of 1982, El Salvador imported 90 per cent of its wood. Extensive reforestation over the last several years may help remedy this situation but any gains are offset by the high rate of

Table 18.1 Areas of Forest Vegetation in El Salvador

Type of Forest	Area (sq. km)	% of total forest	% of land area
Coniferous	485	18	2.3
Broadleaved	908	34	4.4
Mangroves	453	17	2.2
Shrubland	778	29	3.8
Plantations	58	2	0.3
Total	2,682	100	13

Source: Adapted from Perfil Ambiental (1985).

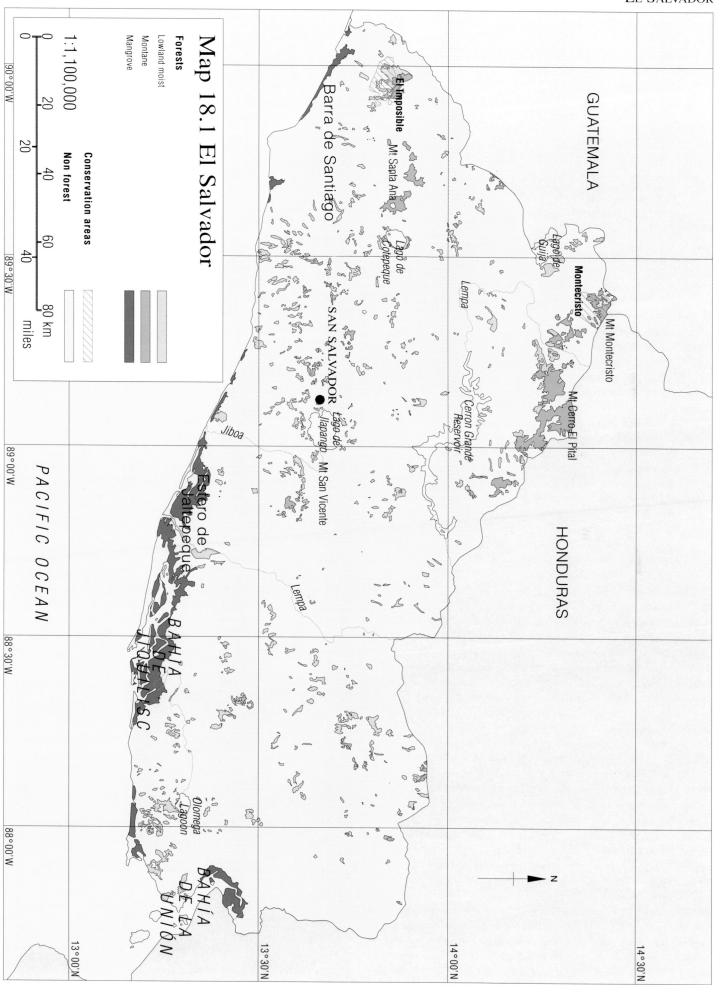

Map 18.1 El Salvador

1:1,100,000

Forests
Lowland moist
Montane
Mangrove

Conservation areas
Non forest

Table 18.2   Estimates of forest extent in El Salvador

Forest type	Area (sq. km)	% of land area
Lowland*	746	3.6
Montane+	363	1.8
Mangrove	446	2.2
Total	1,555	7.5

*   includes deciduous, evergreen and gallery forests (see Figure 18.1)
+   includes cloud forest and pine-oak forest (see Figure 18.1)

Based on analysis of Map 18.1. See Map Legend on p. 175 for details of sources.

deforestation (USAID, 1988). Given the small size of the public forest lands and the dense population of rural areas, the major potential for forestry in El Salvador lies in plantations of commercially valuable species such as teak, and the use of fast-growing, multi-purpose trees in social and agroforestry programmes (USAID, 1988). At present, sustained yield management of natural forest is almost non-existent.

The minimum legal diameter for harvesting pine trees is 45 cm but although permits have to be obtained from the forest service before any tree is cut, enforcement is lax. Neither the finances nor the organisation exist to manage the pine forests and this is exacerbated by the fact that they are mostly located in the north of the country where there is much unrest.

Responsibility for implementation of the forest law and for encouraging sustained use of forest and other natural resources is vested in the Centre of Natural Resources (CENREN — Centro de Rescursos Naturales), the National Forest Service is one of CENREN's subdivisions.

Fuelwood is the most important forest product, more than 80 per cent of the harvested wood is used as fuel (USAID, 1988). It provides about 64 per cent of El Salvador's energy requirements.

Deforestation

Deforestation has been faster and more complete in El Salvador than in any other Central American country (USAID, 1988). Most of the land originally covered by broadleaved forests was cleared for agriculture or cattle pastures long ago. After 1840, the oak-pine forests were progressively cleared for coffee plantations (Daugherty, 1972). In addition, El Salvador took the lead in road and bridge building as early as the beginning of this century, and these developments facilitated the ease with which migrants colonised forest areas and partially explain why El Salvador lost most of its forest several decades earlier than other countries in the region (Utting, 1993). FAO (1993a) estimates that between the years of 1981 and 1990, 31 sq. km of forest were cleared each year, a rate of 2.2 per cent, which is higher than in any other Central American country except Costa Rica.

The density of population and the consequent demand for land, logging and uncontrolled fires have been other, more recent, causes of deforestation. As a result, three quarters of the national territory is now exposed to severe erosion conditions and decreasing land productivity (Núñez et al., 1990).

Biodiversity

It is generally thought that El Salvador is the least diverse of the Central American countries. There are estimated to be 2500 flowering plants (Hampshire, 1989) with 700 tree species and 365 orchids. The vertebrate fauna consists of 30 amphibians, 80 rep-

tiles, 450 birds, 110 mammals and 400 fresh water fish (Perfil Ambiental, 1985). Numbers of invertebrates are unknown, but 400 butterfly species have been recorded (Perfil Ambiental, 1985).

Many of the larger mammals that are found in other Central American countries are no longer present in El Salvador. These include the black howler monkey *Alouatta villosa*, jaguar *Panthera onca*, puma *Felis concolor* and tapir *Tapirus bairdii*. Many other species may well disappear in the near future as their habitat is destroyed. The ocelot *Leopardus pardalis*, the peccaries *Tayassu tajacu* and *T. pecari*, agouti *Dasyprocta punctata*, red brocket deer *Mazama americana* and white-tailed deer *Odocileus virginia* are all species threatened in El Salvador, though none is considered to be globally threatened by IUCN (Groombridge, 1993). Mammals listed by IUCN are the spider monkey *Ateles geoffroyi*, the margay *Leopardus wiedii*, the olingo *Bassariscus sumichrasti* and the bat *Leptonycteris curasoae*.

There are no endemic birds in El Salvador and Collar *et al.* (1992) list no globally threatened bird species in the country. There are, though, some locally threatened species. One of these, in the highland forests, is the highland guan *Penelopina nigra*. The considerable loss of forest in all Central American countries is of particular concern as many of the birds that breed in North America overwinter in Central America.

There are four endemic reptiles in the country, but no endemic amphibians are listed (WCMC, 1992). The only globally threatened reptiles, other than the marine turtles, listed by IUCN (Groombridge, 1993) in El Salvador are the American crocodile *Crocodylus acutus* and the endemic lizard *Abronia montecristoi*. One invertebrate, a dragonfly *Amphipteryx agrioides*, is listed by IUCN (Groombridge, 1993).

Conservation Areas

El Salvador has only two protected areas (Table 18.3). Over 30 other small areas — almost all less than 20 sq. km — are proposed. There are currently no official national policies regarding the use or protection of the environment and natural resources. The Forestry Law of 1973 allows for the formation of different categories of protected areas but no detailed definitions of the categories are given, nor are the regulations governing the use of the areas outlined (Núñez *et al.*, 1990). In 1981, the National Parks and Wildlife Section, a department within the Forest Service, became the National Parks and Wildlife Service and is, as such, the first institute in El Salvador specifically responsible for national park management (IUCN, 1992).

Montecristo cloud forest, El Salvador.   (WWF/Peter Thomas)

Table 18.3 Conservation Areas in El Salvador

Existing conservation areas for El Salvador in IUCN categories I–IV are listed below

National Parks	Area (sq. km)
El Imposible*	32
Montecristo*	20
Total	52

* areas with forest within their boundaries according to Map 18.1
Source: WCMC (unpublished data)

Initiatives for Conservation

There have been relatively few conservation organisations active in El Salvador and very little international financial and technical assistance has been received by the country.

By the end of 1993, El Salvador's government had reactivated the Tropical Forestry Action Plan exercise with a view to completing the planning phase by early 1994. The TFAP Coordinating Unit of FAO is assisting the government in the preparation of a project document for capacity building, in order to strengthen the recently created National Forestry Institute. The exercise has helped to revise Forest Act and integrate forestry into the National Reconstruction Plan and the National Environment Agenda (FAO, 1993b).

References

Collar, N.J., Gonzaga, L.P., Krabbe, N., Madroño Nieto, A., Naranjo, L.G., Parker III, T.A. and Wege, D.C. (1992). *Threatened Birds of the Americas. The ICBP/IUCN Red Data Book*. ICBP, Cambridge, U.K.

Daugherty, H.E. (1969). *Man-Induced Ecologic Change in El Salvador*. Unpublished PhD thesis, University of California, Los Angeles. 248 pp.

Daugherty, H.E. (1972). The impact of man on the zoogeography of El Salvador. *Biological Conservation* 4(4): 273–278

Daugherty, H.E. (1974). *Conservación Ambiental en El Salvador con un Plan Maestro para Parques Nacionales y Reservas Equivalentes*. Desarrola Forestal y Ordenacion de Cuencas Hidrgraficas. Informe Tecnico No. 1. FO:DP/ELS/73/004. UNDP, FAO.

FAO (1993a). *Forest resource assessment 1990: tropical countries*. FAO Forestry Paper 112. FAO, Rome, Italy.

FAO (1993b). El Salvador. *TFAPulse No. 22:3*.

Groombridge, B. (Ed.) (1993). *1994 IUCN Red List of Threatened Animals*. IUCN, Gland, Switzerland and Cambridge, U.K. 286 pp.

Hampshire, R.J. (1989). El Salvador. In: *Floristic Inventory of Tropical Countries: the status of plant systematics, collections, and vegetation plus recommendations for the Future*. Campbell, D.G. and Hammond, D. (eds). New York Botanical Garden, New York. Pp. 295–298.

IUCN (1992). *Protected Areas of the World: A review of national systems. Volume 4: Nearctic and Neotropical*. IUCN, Gland, Switzerland and Cambridge, U.K.

Jiménez, J.A. (1992). Mangrove forests of the Pacific coast of Central America. In: *Coastal Plant Communities of Latin America*. Seeliger, U. (ed) Academic Press, San Diego. Pp 259–267.

Núñez, R.D., Serrano, F., Martínez, A.C. and Guerra, H. (1990). *El Salvador Natural Resource Policy Inventory*. USAID/ROCAP Project. Technical report No. 113, prepared for USAID. Pp. 78–98.

Perfil Ambiental (1985). *El Salvador Perfil Ambiental, Estudio de Campa*. USAID.

USAID (1988). *El Salvador Action Plan FY 1989–1990*. Agency for International Development Washington, D.C., U.S.A.

Utting, P. (1993). *Trees, People and Power: social dimensions of deforestation and forest protection in Central America*. Earthscan Publications, Ltd, London. Pp. 206.

WCMC (1992). *Global Biodiversity: Status of the Earth's Living Resources*. Chapman and Hall, London xx + 594 pp.

Author: Caroline Harcourt, WCMC, Cambridge, U.K.

Map 18.1 El Salvador

The spatial data for El Salvador's forests were digitised from *Mapa de Vegetacion Arborea de el Salvador*, a map prepared at a scale of 1:200,000 by the Ministerio de Agricultura y Ganaderia, Direccion General de Recursos Naturales Renovables, Programa Determinacion del Uso Potential del Suelo. This map was published in 1981; more recent information has not been traced. The source map is a land use map, illustrating the remaining natural forests as well as cash crops. Only the *Bosque* category, which has been mapped as lowland or montane forest (demarcated by a 3000' contour taken from the Digital Chart of the World) and the *Bosque hidrohalofito (Manglares)* category, mapped as mangrove, have been illustrated on Map 18.1. The lowland forest comprises deciduous, evergreen and gallery forest; the montane forest includes pine-oak and cloud forests; it has not been possible to categorise the forests in greater detail than this. The *Bosque irregular (Matorral y Manchones Dispersos de Arboles)* has not been mapped as forest in this Atlas.

The boundaries of El Salvador's protected area were derived from a photocopy of an A3 map, *Ubicación de Areas para el Establecimento de Parques Nacionales y Reservas Equivalentes en El Salvador*, which was compiled in 1987 by the *Departmento de Planes y Proyectos del Servicio Forestal* and the *Centro de Recursos Naturales, Servicio de Parques Nacionales y Vida Silvestre*.

19 Guatemala

Country area 108,890 sq. km
Land area 108,430 sq. km
Population (mid–1994) 10.3 million
Population growth rate 3.1 per cent
Population projected to 2025 21.7 million
Gross national product per capita (1992) US$980
Forest cover in 1992 (see Map) 48,244 sq. km
Forest cover in 1990 (FAO, 1993) 42,250 sq. km
Annual deforestation rate (1981–1990) 1.7 per cent
Industrial roundwood production 114,000 cu. m
Industrial roundwood export 1000 cu. m
Fuelwood and charcoal production 11,142,000 cu. m
Processed wood production 26,000 cu. m*
Processed wood exports 23,000 cu. m*
* Figures for 1991 (FAO, 1994)

Guatemala holds a special position as a bridge between two continents and two oceans; it is endowed with a great biological diversity and has many endemic species.

The highlands of Guatemala are home to a colourful blend of Amerindian cultures and a rich Spanish American heritage. Handicrafts, architecture, landscapes and the people themselves retain a special national identity which has been lost in many of the more cosmopolitan centres of the region.

The largest area of undisturbed tropical and subtropical forest in the country occurs in the north, in the department of El Petén. Inland, on the high plateau, there are vast conifer forests and remnants of rainforests. Mangrove forests occur on the Pacific coast. At present about 30 per cent of the country is reported to be covered with mature forest. Some estimates suggest that as much as 45 per cent of the country is forested. However, all the remaining forests, whatever their area, are under pressure due to the demand for agricultural land and fuelwood.

Forestry institutions are weak and, although considerable international aid is now flowing to forest conservation, achievements on the ground have been modest. A National Conservation Strategy has been adopted officially, but little progress has been made in putting it into practice.

INTRODUCTION

Guatemala can be divided into four basic physical regions (Nations *et al.*, 1988). In the south, lies the Pacific coastal plain, with an average altitude of 850 m above sea level. Although the area used to be covered in dense forest, it is now mostly pasture and swamp land. Inland of this region is the Pacific mountain chain consisting of a strip of 33 volcanoes running parallel to the west coast. They rise to a height of 4211 m at the peak of Volcán Tajumulco, the highest point in Central America. Two sub-regions are recognised within this area: the *boca costa* or foot of the mountains, and the cloud forests at higher elevations. A central highland region (the Altiplano) occupies almost half of the country, extending from the Pacific chain in the south to the Sierra de los Cuchumatanes, Sierra de Chama and Sierra de las Minas to the north. This region has complex topography consisting of hills and volcanoes, mesas and valleys. The middle valley of Rio Motagua includes the driest spot in Central America (Nations *et al.*, 1988). The Petén-Caribbean lowlands occupy the northern third of Guatemala and extend along its short Caribbean coast. The region is mostly flat with karst relief (CONAMA, 1991; Nations *et al.*, 1988). It is here, in the eastern Caribbean area, that the most humid tropical rain forest is found.

Geologically speaking, Guatemala, along with the rest of the Central American isthmus, is young. Twenty million years ago there was only a chain of volcanic islands in the area. The straits between them began to close gradually due to the movement of tectonic plates, but it was only five million years ago that the isthmus was finally formed. Guatemala lies over several tectonic plates of slow but continuous movement and is unstable as a result. The Pacific mountain chain is located in the converging zone of two of the most important plates: the Cocos and the Caribbean. Consequently, earthquakes are frequent and often very intense. Guatemala City has been severely damaged by them on 19 occasions, most recently in 1976, when 25,000 people died.

Hydrographically the country is divided into two main systems: the Pacific System (23,990 sq. km), with short rivers and steep slopes, and the Atlantic System, with longer rivers and milder slopes. The latter is subdivided into two sub-systems, one draining into the Gulf of Mexico (50,803 sq. km) and the other into the Caribbean (34,096 sq. km). There are 18 main river catchments in the Pacific system and 17 in the Atlantic system (CONAMA, 1991; PAFG, 1991).

Only 26.4 per cent of the country's land is considered to have agricultural potential. A further 21.4 per cent is suitable for pastures, perennial crops or tree plantations, 37.1 per cent for production forest and 14.1 per cent for protection forest and wildlife. More than 300 water bodies cover the remaining one per cent of the country.

The average annual temperature varies from 28°C on the coast to 10°C in the mountains, with maximum and minimum extremes of 42°C and -7°C respectively. There is a dry season from November to April and a rainy season from May to October, with maximum precipitation in June and September.

Average annual rainfall is 1708 mm, but this is not distributed evenly throughout the country. The east receives around 300 mm precipitation annually with 45 to 60 rainy days, while in the north there are up to 200 days of rain per year with total precipitation of about 6000 mm.

Overall, population density is 95 inhabitants per sq. km, which makes Guatemala the second most densely populated country in Central and South America. The highest density, 872 inhabitants per sq. km, is in the central region in the department of Guatemala and the lowest, only 6 people per sq. km, is found in the department of El Petén (CONAMA, 1991). The indigenous population makes up 37 per cent of the inhabitants. There are 19 Mayan ethnic groups who use 61 different dialects. Around 82 per cent of these Mayans live in rural areas (Instituto Nacional de Estadística, cited in PAFG, 1991). Only 38 per cent of the total population live in urban areas.

Agricultural products are the country's major exports. These include coffee, sugar, bananas, cardamon and cotton. Cultural tourism is an important and growing industry in Guatemala.

The Forests

There are four main forest types in Guatemala: conifer, broadleaved, mixed and mangroves.

The conifer forests are located over a wide altitudinal gradient, between 100 and 4000 m above sea level. They contain such species as pine *Pinus* spp., fir *Abies guatemalensis*, cypress *Cupressus lusitanica* and ahuehuete *Taxodium mucronatum*. The classification of the pines varies, ranging from seven species and two varieties according to Mittak (1977) to ten species in the taxonomy used by Schwerdtfeger (1953) and Veblen (1978).

The broadleaved forests are characteristic of low areas such as Petén, Izabal, the north of Huehuetenango, Quiché and Alta Verapaz. The most important commercial species include cedar *Cedrela odorata*, mahogany *Swietenia macrophylla*, chichique *Aspidosperma megalocarpum*, palo blanco *Tabebuia donnell-smithii* and Santa María *Calophyllum brasiliense*. An inventory recently carried out in the department of El Petén revealed the existence of some 300 tree species, of which 50 are timber species (AHT/APESA, 1991).

The mixed forests are located in a transition area between the conifer and broadleaved forest. Pines, oaks *Quercus* spp., liquidambar *Liquidambar styraciflua* and some species from the Betulaceae family (*Ostrya* sp. and *Alnus* spp.) are the dominant species in this forest type but other genera, including *Ocotea*, *Nectandra* and *Persea*, are also important.

Mangroves

The mangrove forests are located mainly on the Pacific coast, where they cover an area of 174 sq. km or 0.2 per cent of the country's land area. On Map 19.1, the mangroves cover an area of 161 sq. km.

The mangrove swamps are composed of species of the genera *Rhizophora*, *Avicennia*, *Conocarpus* and *Laguncularia*. In spite of being the essential breeding and feeding grounds for countless species of marketable crustaceans, molluscs and fish, the mangroves are still being used to produce charcoal, firewood, dyes, medicines and construction materials. The wood is valued for building as it is resistant to water. Mangrove areas have been converted into shrimp and salt ponds and drained for agriculture (Morales, 1979).

Mangroves are protected in the Monterrico Biotope on the Pacific coast (not shown on Map 19.1 as it is in IUCN's category VIII) and the Chocón Biotope on the Caribbean coast. Both of these sites are managed by the Centro de Estudios Conservacionistas (CECON) of the San Carlos University. Other reserves, at Manchón and Punta de Manabique, have been proposed.

Forest Resources and Management

The figures for area of forest remaining in Guatemala are very varied. In the 1991 *Plan de Acción Forestal para Guatemala*, it was reported that forests covered 40 per cent of the country, 81.5 per cent of this being broadleaved forest and the remainder conifer forest (PAFG, 1991). Figures from the authors of this chapter indicate that, in 1992, mature forest formations covered 31,843 sq. km, or only 30 per cent, of the country. Of this, the conifer forests covered 2190 sq. km, broadleaved forests covered 28,209 sq. km, mixed forests covered 1270 sq. km and the remainder (174 sq. km) was mangrove forest. The recent report by FAO (1993), indicates that forest cover in Guatemala was 42,250 sq. km in 1990, but this figure includes areas with as little as 10 per cent canopy cover. FAO's (1993) estimate for the area of closed broadleaved forest in the country at the end of 1990 is 39,460 sq. km.

The source map (see Map Legend) for Map 19.1 includes a legend showing the areas of different vegetation types within the country. This has been translated and is reproduced here as Table 19.1. It is noted on the source map that the categories are subject to revision and should not be taken as definitive. The source map is undated, but is based on one published in 1992 and was sent to WCMC in mid-1993.

The total forest area shown on Map 19.1 is, at 48,244 sq. km (Table 19.2), slightly higher than the total of the first eight categories given in Table 19.1. It is, however, not clear how much of this is forest as defined in this Atlas. The open forests (which measure 9462 sq. km on Map 19.1) may be degraded or may be naturally open formations, and the *humedal* certainly includes wet grassland as well as swamp forests. As explained in the Map Legend, the figure given in Table 19.2 for montane forests includes all broadleaved and mixed forests above 1000 m, but

Table 19.1 Areas of different vegetation formations in Guatemala

Forest type°	Area (sq. km)	Per cent of country*
Conifers	2,699	2.48
Open conifers	1,982	1.82
Marsh, wetground (*humedal*)	5,734	5.27
Broadleaf	28,370	26.05
Open broadleaf	6,170	5.67
Mixed	874	0.80
Open mixed	1,065	0.98
Mangroves	167	0.15
Not determined (clouds/shadows)	5,102	4.68
Marsh, swamp (*pantano*)	1,914	1.76
Other+	54,812	50.43
Total	108,889	100.00

° *Tipo de Bosque* — obviously not all of these are actually forests

* Note this is country, not land, area.

+ includes urban areas, agricultural land, pastures, waterbodies and scrubland (*matorrales*)

Source: PAFG (nd)

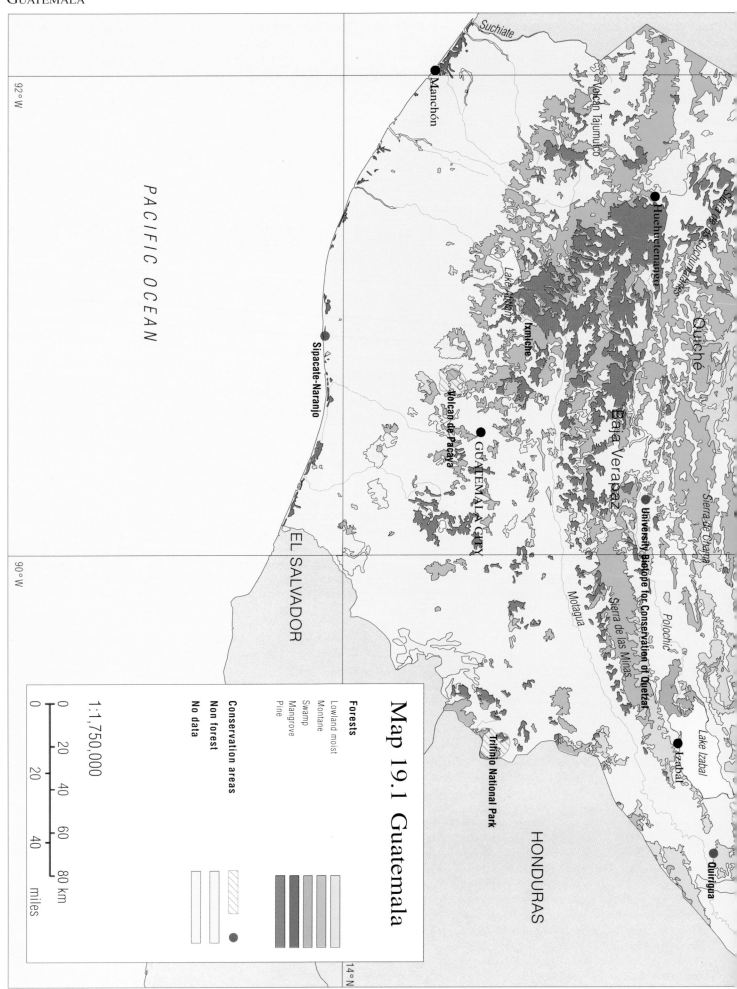

Map 19.1 Guatemala

Forests

Lowland moist
Montane
Swamp
Mangrove
Pine

Non forest

No data

Conservation areas

1:1,750,000

| 0 | 20 | 40 | 60 | 80 km |
| 0 | 20 | 40 | 40 | miles |

PACIFIC OCEAN

EL SALVADOR

HONDURAS

92°W

90°W

14°N

Manchón

Suchiate

Volcán Tajumulco

Huehuetenango

Sierra de los Cuchumatanes

Quiché

Lake Atitlán

Ixniché

Volcán de Pacaya

GUATEMALA CITY

Baja Verapaz

University Biotope for Conservation of Quetzal

Sierra de Chama

Sipacate-Naranjo

Motagua

Sierra de las Minas

Polochic

Lake Izabal

Izabal

Trifinio National Park

Quiriguá

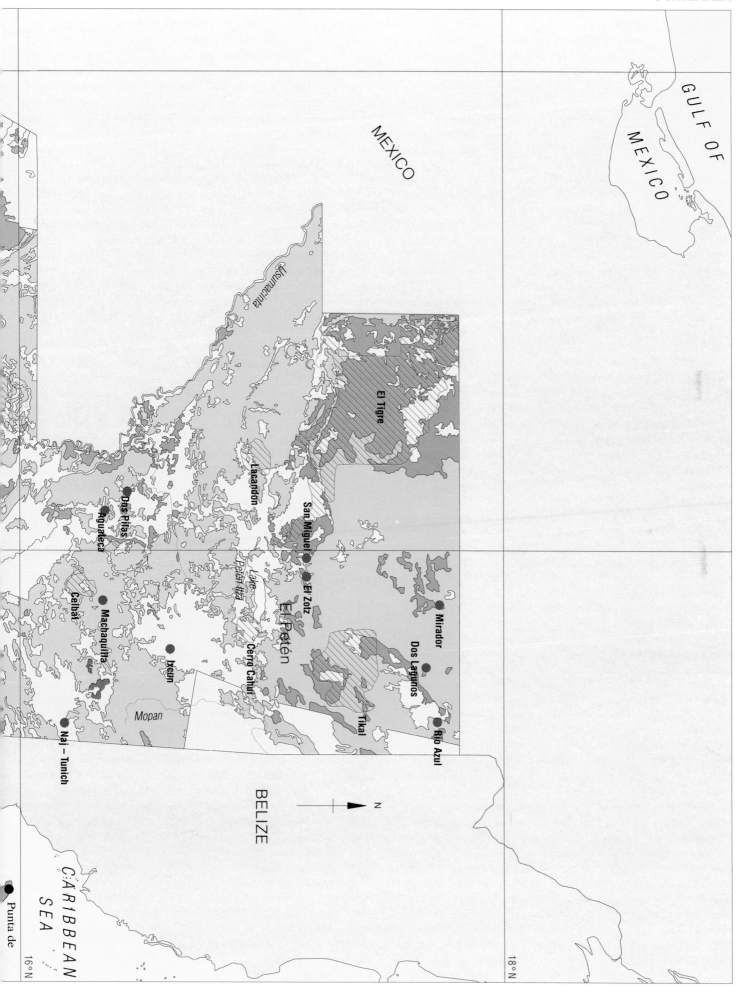

GULF OF

MEXICO

MEXICO

Usumacinta

El Tigre

Lacandón

Dos Pilas

Aguateca

San Miguel

El Zotz

Ceibal

Machaquilá

Lake Petén Itzá

El Petén

Mirador

Dos Lagunos

Ixcun

Cerro Cahuí

Mopan

Tikal

Río Azul

Naj – Tunich

N

BELIZE

CARIBBEAN

SEA

Punta de

16°N

18°N

Table 19.2 Estimates of forest extent in Guatemala

Forest type	Area (sq. km)	% land area
Lowland moist	27,913	25.7
Montane	10,208	9.4
Swamp	5,708	5.3
Pine (conifer)	4,254	3.9
Mangrove	161	0.1
Total	48,244	44.5

Based on analysis of Map 19.1. See Map Legend on p. 184 for details of source.

not any conifer forest. Similarly, these two categories have been incorporated into the lowland moist forest type if they occur below 1000 m.

Forest management, the use of timber and non-timber products and the conservation of fauna and flora, are the responsibility of DIGEBOS, the Dirección General de Bosques y Vida Silvestre (Forests and Wildlife General Office). This was established in June 1988 to replace INAFOR, the Instituto Nacional Forestal (The National Institute for Forestry). DIGEBOS is under the Ministerio de Agricultura, Ganadería y Alimentación (MAGA) (Ministry of Agriculture, Livestock and Food).

The conifer forests are an important source of fuel. During 1990, these forests yielded six million cu. m of firewood. This wood was used for home heating (especially in the cold regions of the Altiplano), cooking, bread-making, the production of lime and the manufacture of earthenware tiles, pots and blocks. The communities that live in the country's colder areas are especially dependent on the conifer forests. They use the wood for house construction (balks); the pine needles are used for the manufacture of adobe (bricks of unburned clay), as fastening material, as ornaments in family reunions and religious parties, as bedding for animals and as packing material for fragile agricultural products; while the copal resin is mixed with the bark of the pine tree to make an aromatic material that is burned in religious rites.

Closed broadleaved forests are found mainly in the sparsely populated northern lowlands. These forests have been subject to industrial logging, with mahogany and cedar being extracted selectively. Even though the number of trees taken is low, only two or three per hectare, a considerable amount of damage is done to the residual stand. In consequence, regeneration is poor. In El Petén, extensive, long-term concessions were granted by Empressa Nacional de Fomento y Desarrollo Económico de El Petén (FYDEP). Between 1985 and 1989, 51,000 cedar and mahogany trees were extracted by 13 large sawmills and these produced 41 million cu. m of wood.

The forests also yield non-timber products, such as leaves, stems, fruits, seeds and latex. These include the xate palm tree (*Chamaedorea elegans* and *C. oblongata*), allspice (*Pimenta dioica*), tropical pine seed (*Pinus caribaea*), latex from the chicozapote or chicle tree (*Manilkara zapota*), wicker (*Philodendron* sp.), corozo stems, flax and guano palm trees. Harvest of xate palm leaves, for use in the European and North American floral industry, provides jobs for more than 6000 people, while the export of this species earns US$3.7 millions. In 1988, the production of chicle (used in chewing gum) totalled about 136,054 kg, which represented earnings of US$333,000. Exports of allspice are worth US$16 million retail in the United

States and Europe, but only US$1–2 million accrues to Guatemalans (Nations *et al.*, 1988).

In 1975, the government began providing tax incentives for reforestation. Between 1981 and 1983, a total of 55 sq. km were reforested. Between 1984 and 1988, the average area reforested reached 20 sq. km per year. Recently a large scale reforestation programme was launched in the northeast of the country. It is estimated that 80 sq. km of plantations are now established each year.

One of the most important reforestation programmes is the DIGEBOS/CARE/Peace Corps agroforestry programme, which operates in 69 sites in 15 forest subregions. This programme promotes the establishment of forest and fruit nurseries, agroforestry, plantations, construction and maintenance of equipment for soil conservation, pasture improvement and community forest management. In the period 1990–1991, DIGEBOS contributed US$45,000 cash, plus the salaries of regional coordinators and promoters. CARE, the Cooperativa Americana de Remesas al Exterior (The American Cooperative for Foreign Remittances), donated US$250,000, and the Peace Corps provided some 40 volunteers.

Another community forest project, supported by the US Agency for International Development, began in 1985. It aims to carry out reforestation, extension and training for the establishment of community forest plantations and nurseries in the western Altiplano.

The German Association for Technical Cooperation (GTZ) supports a community forest project in the department of Baja Verapaz in the northern part of the country. The project involves forestry and agroforestry training, improvement of resin tapping and distillation methods, establishment of demonstration smallholdings and silvicultural techniques.

Deforestation

As with the figures for forest cover, the estimates for deforestation in Guatemala vary quite considerably. However, it is evident that the last few decades have seen extensive clearance of the forests, and if present trends continue, Guatemala's forest cover will disappear within 25 to 40 years.

According to FAO figures reported by Leonard (1987), 77 per cent of Guatemala's surface area was covered by forests in 1960 and only 42 per cent remained in 1980. Studies carried out by IPGH, the Instituto Panamericano de Geografía e Historia (Panamerican Institute of Geography and History), gave a figure of 40,700 sq. km of forest present between 1985 and 1987 and indicated that this was a decrease of 16.4 per cent with respect to the preceding decade.

FAO/UNEP (1981) estimated forest loss at 712 sq. km per year, although Lanly (1981) implies this may be an overestimate as he notes that *this study did not take into account those deforested areas that were abandoned and reverted to secondary forest*. Méndez Domínguez (1988) reported deforestation at between 1080 and 1620 sq. km, or 1 to 1.5 per cent annually. The most recent FAO (1993) estimate is that 813 sq. km are lost each year, a rate of 1.7 per cent.

According to Rose (1988), 63 per cent of forest destruction in Guatemala is due to over-harvesting of firewood, 29 per cent to agricultural colonization, 6.5 per cent to forest fires and pests and 1.1 per cent to industrial use of wood. However, Escobar (1990) indicated that 90 per cent of the destruction is due to colonization, eight per cent to fires and two per cent to the use of forest products. He reported that 23 per cent of the deforestation occurs in the conifer forest (126 sq. km per year) and 77 per cent in the broadleaved forest (430 sq. km per year) and that most of the destruction (380 sq. km per year) occurs in El Petén and the Verapaces.

Molinos (1991) reported that of the 19 million cubic meters of wood cut in 1990, 12 million cu. m (63 per cent) were used as firewood for both domestic and industrial use, six million (32 per cent) rotted or burned in the field and one million (5 per cent) was used as industrial logs. Fifty per cent of the wood used as firewood came from the conifer forests, 25 per cent from mixed forests and the remaining 25 per cent from the broadleaved forests. It is calculated that this wood "saves" the country US$300 million in oil-generated energy (Molinos, 1991). The figure given in FAO (1994) for industrial round-wood used in 1990 is the same as that at the head of the chapter and is somewhat lower than that reported by Molinos (1991).

The main cause of depletion of the conifer forest in the Altiplano is firewood collection (Méndez Domínguez, 1988). This is not the case in the wet forests of El Petén. There, the destruction of the forest is due to the expansion of the agricultural frontier. The trees are cut and burned to clear the land for the use of settlers and livestock breeders (Nations et al., 1988). Land is cleared by both small-scale farmers, who practice shifting agriculture, and large-scale farmers, who sell their products to local and foreign markets.

The most important forest pest is the pine weevil *Dendroctonus* sp., which lives as a parasite of *Pinus rudis* in the Guatemalan Altiplano (Pisano, 1991).

Biodiversity

Guatemala's location on the "Indo-American Biological Bridge", the meeting point of the nearctic and neotropical flora and fauna, results in high biological diversity. There is also a high degree of endemism in the country. Guatemala contains 14 of the Life Zones described by Holdridge (Figure 19.1 and Table 19.3) and is home to one of the well-known Vavilov Centres (the postulated centres of the origin of domestic crops).

The flora is diverse with an estimated total of 8000 vascular plants, with over 1000 endemic species (Davis et al., 1986). This includes 17 conifers, 450 broadleaved trees, 527 orchids — with 57 endemics, 110 ferns and 519 mosses (55 endemics). A number of plants in Guatemala are listed on Appendix I of CITES. These include the fir tree *Abies guatemalensis*,

Figure 19.1 Holdridge's Life Zones of Guatemala

Honduras mahogany *Swietenia humilis*, palo colorado *Engelhardtia pterocarpa*, copey oak *Quercus copeyensis*, Skinner's orchid *Cattleya skinneri*, *Balmea stormiae*, the country's national flower "monja blanca" or white nun *Lycaste skinneri* var. *alba* and the "madera santa" or saint wood *Guaiacum sanctum* (Nations et al., 1988).

According to D'Arcy (1977), as much as 70 per cent of the high mountain vascular flora is endemic. The Altiplano is one of the few regions in the tropics where conifers are well represented in the flora. There are two *Juniperus* species (*J. comitana* and *J. standleyi*) in Guatemala and 26 *Quercus* species. Some of the latter, such as the *Q. acatenangensis*, are among the world's tallest oak trees, competing with the well-known copey oak.

There have been 1464 species of vertebrates recorded — this excludes the marine species. There are 250 species of mammals, 664 species of birds, 231 reptile species, 99 amphibian species and 220 species of fresh water fish (Nations et al., 1988).

The larger mammals of the forests of El Petén include the jaguar *Panthera onca*, puma *Felis concolor*, tapir *Tapirus bairdii*, spider and howler monkeys *Ateles geoffroyi* and *Alouatta palliata*, kincajous *Potus flavus* and peccaries *Tayassu pecari* and *Tayassu tajacu*. Many of these species were previously found on the southern coast of Guatemala but their forest habitat has now been destroyed in that region. Forty species of mammals are considered to be endangered within the country though only eight globally threatened mammals are listed by IUCN as occurring in Guatemala (Groombridge, 1993). These are the spider and howler monkeys, the margay *Leopardus wiedii*, olingo *Bassasicyon sumichrasti*, tapir *Tapirus bairdii*,

Table 19.3 The extent of Holdridge's Life Zones in Guatemala

Life Zones	Extent (sq. km)	per cent
Subtropical spiny bush	928	0.85
Tropical dry forest	216	0.20
Subtropical dry forest	3,964	3.64
Subtropical warm moist forest	12,320	11.31
Subtropical hot moist forest	27,000	24.80
Subtropical hot wet forest	40,780	37.45
Subtropical cold wet forest	2,584	2.37
Subtropical rain forest	1,144	1.05
Tropical wet forest	2,636	2.42
Subtropical lower montane moist forest	9,769	8.97
Subtropical lower montane wet forest	5,512	5.06
Subtropical lower montane rain forest	908	0.83
Subtropical moist montane forest	88	0.08
Subtropical wet montane forest	1,040	0.96

two bats *Leptonycteris curasoae* and *L. nivalis* and the manatee *Trichechus manatus*.

There is more information about birds than about any other animal group in Guatemala. Of the 664 species reported, 480 are resident and 184 are migratory. Although no detailed studies have been conducted on the conservation status of Guatemala's birds, many species are considered endangered due, in particular, to hunting and habitat destruction. One, a non-forest species, the Atitlán giant grebe *Podilymbus gigas*, may even be extinct. Collar *et al.* (1992) list four species (*Oreophasis derbianus, Electron carinatum, Tangara cabanisi* and *Dendroica chrysoparia*) as threatened in the country, none is endemic. Some birds, including the quetzal *Pharomachrus mocinno*, the horned turkey *Oreophasis derbianus* and the ocellated turkey *Agriocharis ocellata,* are protected by the country's game laws.

At least 480 bird species live in the forests of the El Petén, including the scarlet macaw *Ara macao*, the harpy eagle *Harpia harpyja* and the ocellated turkey. Migratory species such as the stork *Jabiru mycteria* and the orange-breasted falcon *Falco deiroleucus* nest in the forests.

The most endangered of the amphibians are the frogs from the family Hylidae and the salamanders from the family Plethodontidae which live in the moist lowland forests and the cloud forests. None, though, is listed as threatened by IUCN (Groombridge, 1993). The montane forests contain several endemic species of amphibians, such as the salamander *Agalychnis moreletii* and the frogs *Eleutherodactylus bocourti, E. daryi* and *E. xucanebi.*

There are three groups of reptiles that are economically important: the sea turtles, the crocodiles and caimans and the iguanas. Of these, the sea turtles such as *Lepidochelys olivacea, Dermochelys coriacea, Eretmochelys imbricata* and *Chelonia mydas agassizi* and the crocodile *Crocodylus moreletti* of El Petén, are seriously endangered due to indiscriminate hunting. The iguanas *Iguana iguana* and *Ctenosaura similis* are in great demand for food in both urban and rural areas and this is leading to a decline in their numbers. IUCN (Groombridge, 1993) lists nine threatened reptiles: five marine turtles, the river turtle *Dermatemys mawii*, the American crocodile *Crocodylus acutus*, the beaded lizard *Heloderma horridum* and the endemic snake *Adelphicos daryi.*

Five threatened dragonflies occur in Guatemala (Groombridge, 1993), but the total number of invertebrates is unknown.

Conservation Areas

Guatemala's first protected areas were created in 1955 when 10 areas were designated as national parks under the direction of INAFOR. Their designation was based on the beauty of the scenery rather than on the presence of particular habitats or species. As a result, many are not listed in IUCN's categories I–IV. During the 60s another two areas were added and a further eight in the 70s. In the next decade, national interest and pressure from international conservationists meant that many other areas were protected (Table 19.4 shows all existing areas in categories I–IV) and a further 13 have been proposed. The rate of creation of protected areas is, nevertheless, still well below the general rate of 4.5 per year in Central America. In addition, land ownership conflicts have not been resolved for many of the areas and few of them are delimited on the ground. A large number has no permanent management staff on site (Godoy and Ugalde, 1992).

The legal framework for protected areas is Decree 4-89, issued by the Congress of the Republic on February 14th, 1989. This was modified by Decree 18-89 and promulgated by Governmental Agreement No. 759-90, in force since August 27th, 1990. Decree 4-89 and its modifications appoint the State as the Administrator and Guarantor of the use and conservation of the natural and cultural resources enclosed in the protected areas. They state that any use of these areas requires an authorization from the Consejo Nacional de Areas Protegidas (CONAP), (National Board for Protected Areas). Protected areas may be managed by organisations other than CONAP only through a legal agreement with CONAP and under its supervision. Other institutions concerned with protected areas include the Guatemalan Tourism Institute (INGUAT), the Institute of Anthropology and History (IDAEH), CECON and the National Council for Urban and Rural Development, as well as some NGOs.

In Guatemala, there are still very few people properly trained in the management of protected areas. There is also not enough money to run the protected areas. Although some is provided by the state, this barely covers the payment of salaries. International development agencies, foundations, and conserva-

Table 19.4 Conservation Areas of Guatemala

Existing conservation areas in IUCN's categories I–IV. For information on World Heritage Sites, Biosphere Reserves and Ramsar Sites see Chapter 8.

National Parks	Area(sq. km)
El Tigre*	3,500
Lacandon*	2,000
Laguna Lachúa*	100
Mirador/Dos Lagunos/Rio Azul*	1,470
Sipacate-Naranjo*	20
Tikal*	574
Trifinio National Park*	40
Volcan de Pacaya*	20
Biotopes	
Cerro Cahui*	8
Chocon-Machacas*	63
Mario Dary Rivera Quetza+	112
San Miguel – El Zotz*	420
University Biotope for Conservation of Quetzal*	12
Cultural Monuments	
Aguateca*	17
Ceibal*	21
Dos Pilas*	32
Ixcun	4
Ixmiche*	0.5
Machaquilla*	20
Naj – Tunich	0.5
Quirigua*	0.3
Total	8,334.3

*   Area with forest within its boundaries as shown on Map 19.1
+   not mapped

Source: WCMC (unpublished data)

tion organizations donate some funds. Debt-for-nature swaps have not had much impact.

Threats to the protected areas include disputes over land titles, poaching, expansion of the agricultural frontier and firewood extraction. Another problem is that most of the conservation areas are less than 100 sq. km with only four over 1000 sq. km. The larger ones are generally those created in the last ten years or so and the four largest were established as recently as 1990 (UICN/CNPPA, 1992).

Initiatives for Conservation

Since the creation of the National Commission for the Environment (CONAMA) in 1986, and the proclamation of the Law for the Protection of the Environment (Decree 68-86), the conservation sector has become much more dynamic. The Law for Protected Areas was passed in 1989.

In 1991, governmental agencies from the U.S.A, Germany and Sweden gave their support to conservation projects in the country. Other institutions, such as WWF, The Nature Conservancy (TNC), Conservation International (CI) and IUCN have projects in Guatemala. UNESCO, FAO, Instituto Interamericano de Cooperación para la Agricultura (IICA) and Centro Agronómico Tropical de Investigación y Enseñanza (CATIE) also work in Guatemala.

In 1987, the Guatemalan Government asked IUCN's Central American office for its support in the creation of a Strategy for Sustainable Development in El Petén. The region of Nakum-Yaaxjá-Naranjo, which includes large expanses of natural forest, archaeological sites and sites of recent and rapidly increasing colonization, was identified as one of the priority areas for a protection programme.

IUCN's project aims at establishing a model of sustainable development in the region, based on the conservation of the natural resources base, the community self-administration, and the use of appropriate technologies (UICN/ORCA, 1988).

Lately, IUCN and the WWF have been working on strengthening local initiatives for the development of the National Park of Laguna Lachúa.

Another important protection initiative is the agreement signed between the Guatemalan Government and USAID to develop the Mayan Biosphere Reserve; this was formerly known as the Mayarema Project. The project will help achieve better management of the natural renewable resources and protection of the biological diversity and tropical forests in the reserve. The cost of the project totals US$22,410,000, of which 46.5 per cent will be provided by USAID, 33.5 per cent by the Guatemalan Government and the remaining 20 per cent is expected from international NGOs (Agency for International Development, 1990).

A German funded Emergency Programme for areas south of El Petén aims to extend protection to those places where the forests are in immediate danger of destruction because of agri-

Rain forest among the ruins of Tikal, El Petén. (Mark Spalding)

cultural immigration. The southern Petén still has large areas of relatively undisturbed forest, and the combination of this with the wetlands, archaeological sites and beautiful landscapes means that the area has a significant tourism potential. The whole emergency programme would cost D.M. 27.23 millions if it is carried out within five years, and D.M. 45.03 millions if carried out within ten years. It will be financed by the KfW (Kreditonstalt für Wiederaufbau — German Bank for Reconstruction), through the system of direct debt purchase.

With the support of TNC and WWF, "Defensores de la Naturaleza" (Nature Defenders) is developing the Sierra de las Minas Biosphere Reserve, which has a significant forest component. The first permit to carry out debt-for-nature swap in the country was granted to these two foundations.

References

Agency for International Development (1990). *Convenio de Donación para el Proyecto de la Biósfera Maya.* Guatemala.
AHT/APESA (1991). *Plan de Desarrollo Integrado de El Petén. Programa de Emergencia de Protección de la Selva Tropical en El Petén.* Convenio Gobiernos Alemania/Guatemala. Santa Elena, Petén. Guatemala. 176 pp.
Collar, N.J., Gonzaga, L.P., Krabbe, N., Madroño Nieto, A., Naranjo, L.G., Parker III, T.A. and Wege, D.C. (1992).

Threatened Birds of the Americas. The ICBP/IUCN Red Data Book. ICBP, Cambridge, U.K.
CONAMA (1991). *Agenda Ambiental de la República de Guatemala (Versión Preliminar).* Guatemala. 94 pp.
D'Arcy, W.G. (1977). Endangered landscapes in Panama and Central America: the threat to plant species. In *Extinction is Forever.* Prance, G.T. and Elias, T.S. (eds). New York Botanical Garden, Bronx, New York. Pp. 89–104.

Davis, S.D., Droop, S.J.M., Gregerson, P., Henson, L., Leon, C.J., Villa-Lobos, J.L., Synge, H. and Zantovska, J. (1986). *Plants in Danger: What do we know?* IUCN, Gland, Switzerland and Cambridge, U.K. Pp. 461.

Escobar, M. (1990). *Modelo de Dumulación Forestal Basico de la República de Guatemala.* INFORDE/CAEM/DIGEBOS, Guatemala. 26 pp.

FAO (1993) *Forest resources assemment 1990: Tropical countries.* FAO Forestry Paper 112. FAO, Rome, Italy.

FAO (1994). *FAO Yearbook: Forest Products 1981–1992.* FAO Forestry Series No. 27, FAO Statistics Series No. 116. FAO, Rome, Italy.

FAO/UNEP (1981). *Proyecto de Evaluacion de los Recursos Forestales Tropicales. Los Recursos Forestales de La America Tropical.* FAO, Rome, Italy.

Godoy, J.C. and Ugalde, A. (1992). *Informe Centroamericano sobre el Estatus de las Areas Protegidas.* IV World Congress of National Parks, San José, Guatemala. 66 pp.

Groombridge, B. (Ed) (1993). *1994 IUCN Red List of Threatened Animals.* IUCN, Gland, Switzerland and Cambridge, U.K. 286 pp.

Lanly, J-P. (1981). *Evaluación de Recursos Forestales Mundiales.* FAO, Rome, Italy.

Leonard, H.J. (1987). *Natural Resources and Economic Development in Central America: a regional environmental profile.* IIED. Pp. 279.

Méndez Domínquez, A. (1988). *Population Growth, Land Scarcity and Environmental Deterioration in Rural Guatemala.* Final Report. The Futures Groups, RAPID II Project and the University del Valle of Guatemala. Publication No 5337.210 UNIVA201.

Mittak, W.L. (1977). *Fortalecimiento del Sector Forestal Estudios para la Reforma Nacional.* FO:DP/GUA/72/006 Documento de trajabo No. 25 — Guatemala.

Molinos, S. (1991). *Las Iniciativas y la Conservación de Recursos Natuales en Guatemala.* IInd Forestry Congress, Guatemala.

Morales, J.V. (1979). *Importancia Nacional del uso y Manejo Racional para la Conservación del Mangle* (Rhizophora mangle) *en el litoral del Pacifico.* Unpublished thesis. University of San Carlos of Guatemala, Agronomy Faculty, Guatemala.

Nations, J.D., Houseal, B., Ponciano, I., Billy, S., Godoy, J.C., Castro, F., Miller, G., Rose, D., Rosa. M.R., Azurdia, C. (1988). *Biodiversidad en Gutemala. Evaluación de la Diversidad Biológica y los Bosques Tropicales.* World Resources Institute, Washington, D.C. U.S.A.I.D. Project number LAC-5517-A-00-5077-00. 185 pp.

PAFG (1991). *Plan de Acción Forestal para Guatemala. Documento base y Perfiles de Proyectos.* Guatemala 227 pp. and annexes.

PAFG (nd) *Cubierta Forestal de la Republica de Guatemala.* Scale 1:500,000. Plan de Accion Forestal de Guatemala.

Pisano, I. Valenzuela de (1991). *La Dinámica Social de la Deforestación en Totonicapán, Guatemala.* Instituto de Investigaciones sobre el Desarrollo Social de las Naciones Unidas (UNRISD), Guatemala. 95 pp. and annexes.

Rose, D. (1988). *Economic Assessment of Biodiversity and Tropical Forest.* Background paper prepared for the Biodiversity and Tropical Forest Assessment Project. Center for International Development (IIED) and Guatemala: U.S.A.I.D., Washington, D.C.

Schwerdtfeger, F. (1953). Los pinos de Guatemala. *Informe FAO/ETAP* 202: 57, ff 139.

UICN/CNPPA (1992). *Areas Protegidas de Centroamérica, Informe de la Reunión de Trabajo de Jefes de Parques Nacionales de Centroamérica.* Guatemala. 29 pp. and annexes.

UICN/ORCA (1988). *Proyecto Yaaxjá-Nakum-Naranjo (PYNN), Manejo Integrado de Patrimonio Natural y Cultural y Desarrollo Sostenible en Petén, Guatemala.* UICN/ORCA.

Veblen, T.T. (1978). Guatemalan conifers. *Unysylva* 29(118): 25–30.

Authors: Juan Carlos Godoy and C.R. Quiroa, IUCN, Guatemala

Map 19.1   Guatemala

Forest cover data were digitised from a dyeline map prepared as part of Guatemala's Forestry Action Plan (*Plan de Accion Forestal de Guatemala*)(PAFG). The map, *Cubierta Forestal de la Republica de Guatemala — Plan de Accion Forestal de Guatemala* (nd), at a scale of 1:500,000, is based on an earlier map *Mapa Preliminar de la Cubierta Forestal de Guatemala* at a scale of 1:250,000 (1992).

The source vegetation categories have been harmonised in the following manner: lowland moist and montane forest (distinguished by overlaying a 3000' contour from the Digital Chart of the World) include *Latifoliadas, Mixto, Latifoliadas Abierto* and *Mixto Abierto*; pine forest comprises *Coniferas, Coniferas Abierto*; inland swamp forest consists of *Humedal*, and mangrove — *Manglar*. Non-forest comprises *Urbano, Agricultura, Pastos, Matorrales* and *Pantano*; No data comprises *Non determinados (nubes, sombras).*

Several important points should be noted. 1. Open ('*abierto*') broadleaved, mixed and pine forest formations have been included with the naturally occurring forest categories. It is possible that some may represent degraded forest. 2. Mixed forests which are a transition formation containing broadleaved and coniferous species, have been mapped within the broadleaved forest classes. The mixed forests are more commonly found in the Altiplano and rarely in El Petén. 3. '*Humedal*' has been mapped as swamp forest but this is likely to give an over-estimate of forest cover as the formation includes other wetland vegetation such as marsh/swampy grassland. 4. On the source map, the vegetation type in 4.68 per cent of the country could not be determined.

Boundary information for the protected areas of Guatemala originate from a regional map compiled by CATIE (Centro Agronómico Tropical de Investigación y Enseñanza) and IUCN, entitled *Areas Silvestres Protegidas de Centro America* (1987), Costa Rica.

20 Honduras

Country area	112,090 sq. km
Land area	111,890 sq. km
Population (mid-1994)	5.3 million
Population growth rate	3.1 per cent
Population projected to 2025	9.7 million
Gross national product per capita (1992)	US$580
Forest cover in 1990 (see Map)	52,735 sq. km*
Forest cover in 1990 (FAO, 1993a)	46,050 sq. km
Annual deforestation rate (1981–1990)	2.1 per cent
Industrial roundwood production	558,000 cu. m
Industrial roundwood export	9000 cu. m
Fuelwood and charcoal production	5,671,000 cu. m
Processed wood production	333,000 cu. m
Processed wood export	40,000 cu. m

* does not include mangroves

Honduras is the second largest of the Central American countries. It is a very poor country, with the third lowest GNP per capita in Latin America and the Caribbean.

The extensive conifer forests provide about 90 per cent of forest products. However, most of the deforestation occurs in the country's broadleaved forests. It is here, and in the mangrove areas, that the majority of Honduras' conservation areas are found, but many of these are threatened by deforestation. The major underlying causes of this high deforestation rate are population growth, poverty, skewed land tenure patterns and development policies that have promoted extensive agricultural practices.

There is an urgent need to strengthen forest management and conservation organizations in Honduras. Development and land tenure patterns need to be changed and conservation awareness must be enhanced, amongst both decision makers and society in general.

INTRODUCTION

Honduras is a mountainous country that lies in the centre of the Central American isthmus. More than three quarters of the territory has slopes greater than 25 per cent. The isthmic character of Honduras, its abrupt topography and its variable soils have resulted in a wide range of ecosystems. Eight of Holdridge's life zones occur in the country. Its major physical regions are the Caribbean coastal plain in the north, the Pacific lowlands in the south and the mountains and intermontane valleys of the interior.

The interior highlands make up more than 80 per cent of the country. Mountains above 600 m occupy 79 per cent of this highland region, while hills between 150 and 600 m make up a further 15 per cent; valleys close to sea level constitute the remainder. The highlands are mostly covered by open pine forests and the soils are generally shallow, rocky, acid and eroded. These soils cannot support intensive agriculture. Cattle ranching is the major economic activity in this area and fire is used to keep the extensive pastures open.

The northeastern region, where it is influenced by the Caribbean, has an annual rainfall that ranges from 1750 to 2000 mm. Holdridge's humid and very humid tropical life zones are found here. Tropical hardwood forests cover 75 per cent of the area. The intermountain western watersheds, valleys and mountains that are not exposed to the Caribbean's humid influence, are predominantly covered with pine and oak/pine stands. On slopes or plateaux above 1800 m, cloud forests are present. In the central area, however, valleys to the north and east are almost desert-like, in stark contrast to the green cloud forests above them.

The Gulf of Fonseca, on the Pacific coast, is surrounded by relatively low, but steep, mountains of volcanic origin that stand out from the coastal plains and also form islands in the gulf. The extensive coastal plain has been formed by sediments from its five main rivers (the Goascorán, Nacaome, Choluteca, Sampile and Negro); these drain around 13 per cent of the total area of Honduras. The coast is characterized by narrow areas of mangroves and by tropical dry forests further inland.

Sixty per cent of Honduras' population inhabit rural regions, where more than two-thirds are living in extreme poverty (GOH/SECPLAN, 1991). Population growth rate is high at 3.1 per cent per annum; some of this is caused by immigrants from war-torn Nicaragua and El Salvador. Overall population density has increased from 30.6 people per sq. km in 1980 to 47 people per sq. km in 1994. Density is very varied however as over two thirds of the inhabitants live in the southern and western highlands, while another quarter lives in the eastern area of the Sula Valley (Leonard, 1987).

The Honduran economy is based on the export of primary products, mainly from the agricultural, fisheries and forestry sectors. More than half the labour force is employed in the agricultural sector. In 1990, the forestry sector contributed some 2 per cent to GDP with exports of forest products making up almost 4 per cent of total exports and totalling US$33.7 million (FAO 1993b). Coffee, bananas and beef are the most important agricultural exports.

The Forests

Tropical rain forest, corresponding to Holdridge's humid tropical forest, is located on the Caribbean lowlands. The region of La Mosquitia, in the east of the country, contains the largest portion of this forest. The rain forest is generally limited to

Table 20.1 Coastal resource alterations

Resource Type	Area (hectares)	
	1987	1989
Mangroves	46,710	45,988
Estuaries	14,240	3,363
Shrimp farms	8,291	20,021
Salt exploitation	1,292	1,292
Artisan fishing	624	493
Managed plantations	111	111
Sand	58	58
Total	71,326	71,326

Source: Molina (1992)

regions with more than 2000 mm of annual rainfall with hardly any dry season and to areas lower than 750 m. These forests are primarily composed of evergreen hardwood species with a dense canopy around 60 m high; the understoreys are open. Common species include *Vochysia hondurensis, Virola koschnyi, Terminalia amazonia, Cordia alliodora, Swietenia macrophylla, Ceiba pentandra* and *Cedrela mexicana* (FAO/UNEP, 1981).

Elsewhere in the lowlands of La Mosquitia, forests of *Pinus caribaea* occur. These are fire climax formations, restricted to highly leached, sandy soils.

A dry deciduous tropical forest replaces the rain forest where rainfall is distinctly seasonal. Dry forests still occur in the Pacific lowlands, but only in small degraded fragments, mostly scattered along rivers and creeks, in stands too small to show on Map 20.1. The bulk of the remaining dry forest species occurs as individual trees left standing in pastures and agricultural land and along fencelines.

Cloud forests occur between 1400 m and 2800 m. They are replaced by drier oak/pine/liquidamber forests at lower elevations. Between 2200 m and 2800 m, very wet cloud forests are found with many mosses and *Hepatica*. On a few mountains, stunted elfin forest is found on windswept ridges or exposed peaks. Conifer species found in the cloud forest include *Abies guatemalensis, Cupressus lusitanica, Pinus ayacahuite, P. maximinoi, P. patula tecunumanii, P. pseudostrobus* and *Podocarpus oleifolius*. Hardwood trees include *Alfaroa hondurensis, Alnus arguta, Brunellia mexicana, Cornus disciflora, Drimys granadensis, Hedyosmum mexicanum, Ilex leibmanii, Magnolia hondurensis, Matudaea trinervia, Olmediella betscheleriana, Pithecellobium vulcanorum, Weinmannia pinnata, W. tuerckheimii* and species from the genera *Dendropanax, Nectandra, Oreopanax, Persea, Phoebe, Quercus* and *Symplocos*.

Pine and oak-pine associations, corresponding to Holdridge's humid subtropical life zone, occur between 600 m and 1800 m over most of central and western Honduras. The predominant species is *Pinus oocarpa*, often associated with oak *Quercus* spp. at lower elevations and with *Pinus pseudostrobus* and *Liquidambar styraciflua* at higher elevations.

Mangroves

There are areas of mangrove in the Gulf of Fonseca. These support important local and commercial estuarine fishing industries. Mangroves are also present in the large river outlets and in the extensive coastal lagoons of the north coast around Laguna Quemada, Laguna de Caratasca near Puerto Lempira and east of

Table 20.2 Forest resources in Honduras

Forest type	Area (sq. km)	% of total cover
Dense pine	28,353	55.0
Dense hardwoods	23,434	45.0
Total	51,787	100

Source: COHDEFOR/OAS (1992)

La Ceiba. Common species include *Avicennia bicolor, Rhizophora mangle, Laguncularia racemosa* and *Bravaisia integerrima*.

It was estimated that in 1989 mangroves covered 460 sq. km (Molina, 1992). However, a 1981 report by Saenger *et al.*, gave the much higher figure of 1450 sq. km of mangroves in the country and in a very recent report, Jimenez (1992) estimated that there were 1213.4 sq. km of mangrove in Honduras. On Map 20.1, the mangroves cover 2310 sq. km, but as their distribution has been digitised from a dyeline map (see Map Legend) with a coastline very different from that used here, errors have almost certainly been introduced. This estimate has not, therefore, been included in Table 20.3 or in the forest statistics at the head of the chapter.

Considerable changes in coastal habitat have occurred in recent years (Table 20.1). In particular, many of the mangroves are being destroyed by the construction of shrimp farms.

Forest Resources and Management

A recent report by the Honduran Forest Development Corporation COHDEFOR/OAS (1992) estimates that 51,787 sq. km of forest are found in Honduras, 55 per cent of this is dense pine forest and 45 per cent is dense hardwoods (Table 20.2). Together, they cover 46 per cent of the country's land area.

FAO (1993a) estimates that in 1990 there was only 46,050 sq. km of forest in Honduras, of which 24,060 sq. km was closed broadleaved forest.

The forest cover shown on Map 20.1 was taken from a map produced by COHDEFOR in 1992 (see Map Legend) and gives a total forest cover of 52,735 sq. km. This excludes the area of mangroves (see above).

In 1974, Honduran legislation created a Forest Development Corporation (COHDEFOR), which is an autonomous state forest corporation with the power and authority to regulate and manage all forests in Honduras, regardless of land tenure. Until 1982, COHDEFOR also had the mandate to transform and export all primary timber products. In 1992, all forestry activities were privatized. COHDEFOR's activities were limited to a regulatory and advisory role in forest management on private and municipal lands, whilst retaining a full mandate and authority over forests on national lands.

In Honduras, the forest estate is divided into protection

Table 20.3 Estimate of forest extent in Honduras

Forest type	Area (sq. km)	% of land area
Lowland moist	11,614	10.4
Montane	12,785	11.4
Pine	28,336	25.3
Total	52,735	47.1

Based on analysis of Map 20.1, but excluding the mangrove area. See Map Legend on p. 192 for details of sources.

Table 20.4 Area deforested in Honduras between 1965 and 1990

	Area (sq. km)		
Forest type	1965	1990	Deforested
Pine	36,094	28,353	7,741
Hardwood	37,592	23,434	14,158
Total	73,686	51,787	21,899

Source: COHDEFOR/OAS (1992)

forests and production forests. The former category is intended to protect hydrological functions, recreational opportunities and other environmental services; the forests are not used for commercial purposes. The latter category, on the other hand, is intended primarily for commercial production of timber. There are legal stipulations that the forest management plans prepared and implemented by COHDEFOR take into account the value and management of non-timber resources. However, in practice, logging activities are planned and implemented without consideration being given to the value of wildlife or any other non-timber resource and there is no attempt to protect rare or endangered species.

Honduran pine timber, particularly *Pinus caribaea* and *P. oocarpa* is an important source of foreign exchange. Ninety per cent of all timber production and forest management activities occur in pine forest areas, namely in the central, western and eastern regions of the country. The remaining 10 per cent of timber production comes from selective cutting of generally unmanaged hardwood forests.

There has been a decline in production of industrial roundwood, from 958,400 cu. m in 1987, to 752,200 cu. m in 1990, a 21.5 per cent drop in four years. FAO (1993c, 1994) shows a similar decline in output — from 990,000 cu. m in 1987 to 558,000 cu. m in 1992, but also shows that there was a decline from 1980 to 1983 (1,112,000 cu. m to 571,000 cu. m) and then an increase until 1987. Most of this roundwood is consumed by the sawmilling industry and this too has declined, from 109 sawmills in operation in 1986 to 85 in 1990. In 1990, as well as the sawmills, there were two plywood and veneer plants and two resin and gum plants in Honduras.

Exports of forest products have also decreased in value and importance, dropping from a 6 per cent contribution to total exports in 1987 to 3.6 per cent in 1990. This means that forest product exports have dropped in importance from fourth to fifth place (BCH, 1992). In 1989, forestry contributed 2.8 per cent of the gross domestic product (GDP) and 10.6 per cent of the agricultural GDP. This contribution decreased in the 1986–90 period. Similar declines occurred in non-timber forest industries such as those using gum and resin.

Forest-based industries are increasing in importance. There are 152 furniture manufacturers, concentrated primarily in Tegucigalpa and San Pedro Sula. As a result, higher value added timber products have increased their share in total forest product exports, from 33 per cent in 1987 to 40 per cent in 1990.

The social importance of forestry is reflected in the fact that almost five per cent of the economically active population work in this subsector. These jobs are essential for the rural population where unemployment is extremely high. Non-timber values for local communities vary according to the nature of the forest resource. For instance, for the indigenous communities in the north and northeast, wildlife and medicinal plants from the surrounding rain forest are of very high value, both for local use and for commercial exploitation.

Honduras has pioneered a system of community operated Integral Management Areas (AMIs). These allow communities to retain the benefits from log sales and from primary and secondary processed products. They operate in both rain forests and pine areas. They could be a useful model for replications in other countries, although some land tenure and management issues still have to be fully worked out.

In spite of the present decline, the prospects for the forestry sector are good. Honduras has large volumes of uniform, high quality timber, an abundant supply of cheap labour and is geographically located so as to benefit from future regional economic integration.

Deforestation

The area deforested in Honduras between the years of 1965 and 1990 has been estimated at 21,899 sq. km (Table 20.4), an average of 876 sq. km per annum. Previous estimates have indicated that deforestation rates have been around 800 sq. km per year, with 81 per cent (645 sq. km) occurring in the broadleaved and the remaining 19 per cent (150 sq. km) in the pine forests (Daugherty, 1989). FAO (1993a) estimates that 1116 sq. km of forest was cleared each year between 1981 and 1990, an annual rate of 2.1 per cent.

The major areas affected by deforestation have been the hardwood forests (65 per cent). Deforestation has primarily affected the Papaloteca, Kruta and Segovia watersheds, the outlets of Motagua and Choluteca Rivers and the drainages between the Caratasca Lagoon and the Kruta River. The Caribbean watersheds have been particularly affected. Some have completely lost their vegetation cover; such is the case of the high part of the Patuca River watershed and the lower part of the Ulúa River watershed.

The major land use changes that have taken place over the last thirty years have been the expansion of agriculture and, especially, the increase in pasture for cattle ranches (Table 20.5). Considerable areas of forest have been cleared for these purposes.

Development policies, promoting and subsidising industrial cattle raising and other extensive agricultural activities, have tended to displace populations and expand production on the basis of increased area and not on improved productivity. These policies, along with population growth and excessive concentration of land in a few large holdings have been primary causes of deforestation.

Recent studies reveal that more than 20 per cent of the country's territory is over-utilised (in terms of its land-use capacity) and 12 per cent under-utilised (COHDEFOR/OAS, 1992). Coincidentally, the over-utilised proportion is almost equal to the area that has been deforested in the 1960–1990 period. Crop pro-

Table 20.5 Land use changes in Honduras (1960–1990)

	Area (sq. km)		
Land Use	1960	1990	% change
Forests	73,686	51,787	-29.7
Pastures	20,265	34,000	+67.8
Crops	14,500	17,770	+22.6
Undifferentiated*	3,637	8,531	–
Total	112,088	12,088	–

* Undifferentiated in satellite imagery, or unaccounted for, and includes water bodies.
Sources: Leonard (1987) and COHDEFOR/OAS (1992)

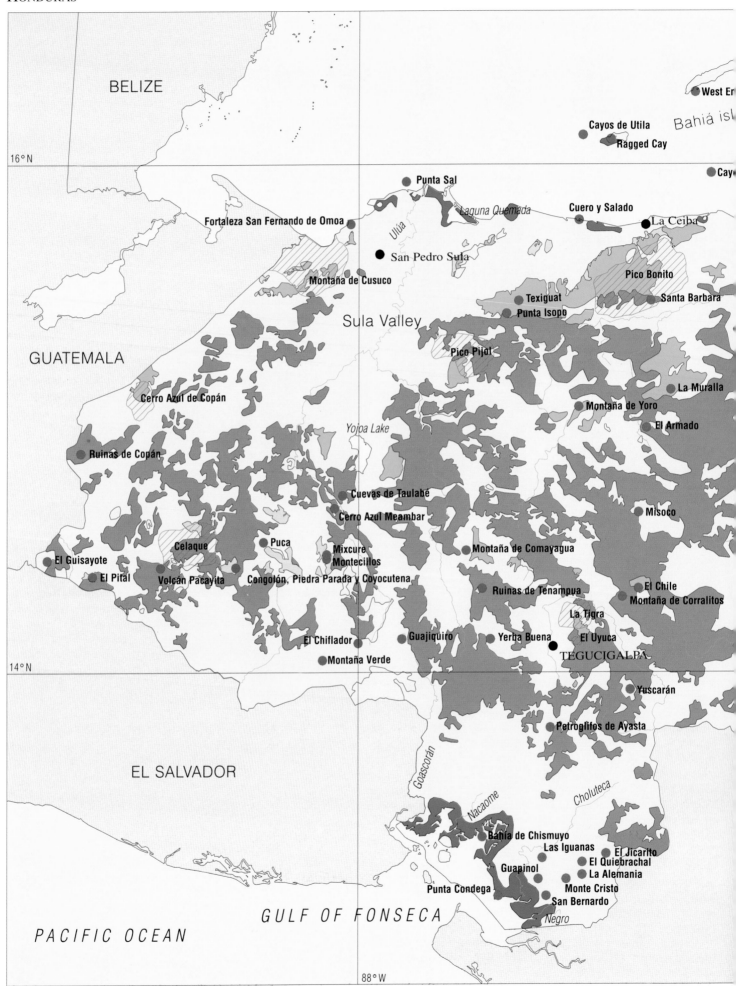

BELIZE

16°N

West En

Cayos de Utila

Bahiá isl

Ragged Cay

Cay

Punta Sal

Laguna Quemada

Cuero y Salado

Fortaleza San Fernando de Omoa

La Ceiba

Ulúa

San Pedro Sula

Pico Bonito

Montaña de Cusuco

Texiguat

Santa Barbara

Punta Isopo

Sula Valley

GUATEMALA

Pico Pijol

La Muralla

Cerro Azul de Copán

Montaña de Yoro

Yojoa Lake

El Armado

Ruinas de Copán

Cuevas de Taulabé

Misoco

Cerro Azul Meambar

Celaque

Puca

Montaña de Comayagua

El Guisayote

Mixcure

Montecillos

El Pital

El Chile

Volcán Pacayita

Congolón, Piedra Parada y Coyocutena

Ruinas de Tenampua

Montaña de Corralitos

La Tigra

El Chiflador

Guajiquiro

Yerba Buena

El Uyuca

Montaña Verde

TEGUCIGALPA

14°N

Yuscarán

Petroglifos de Ayasta

EL SALVADOR

Goascorán

Nacaome

Choluteca

Bahía de Chismuyo

Las Iguanas

El Jicarito

El Quiebrachal

Guapinol

La Alemania

Punta Condega

Monte Cristo

San Bernardo

GULF OF FONSECA

Negro

PACIFIC OCEAN

88°W

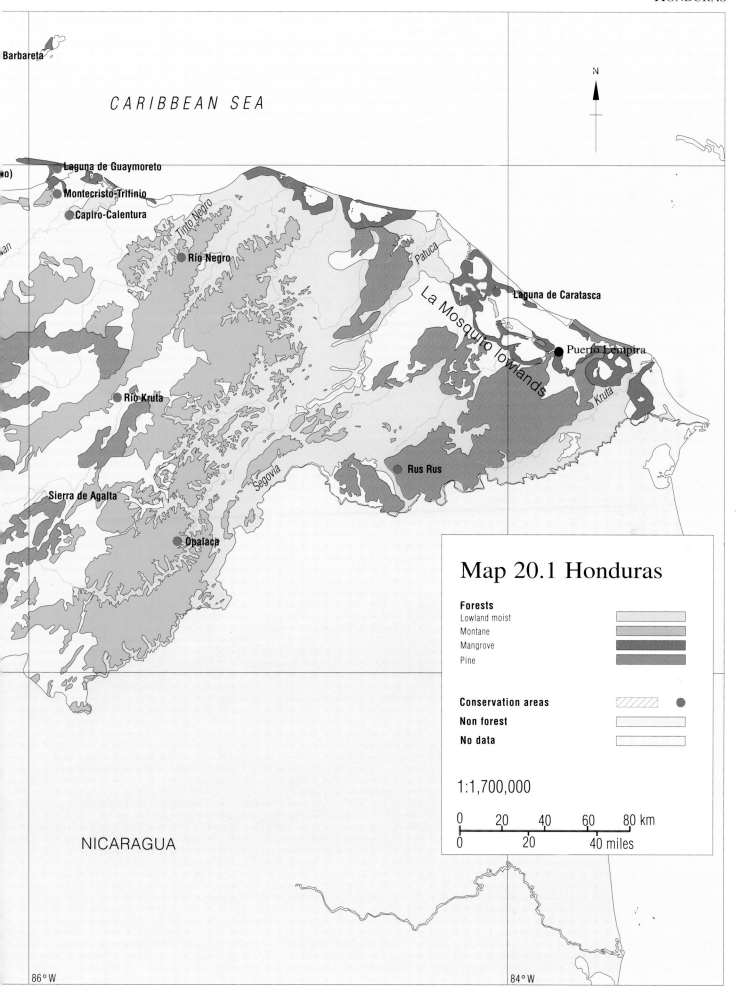

CARIBBEAN SEA

Barbareta

o)

Laguna de Guaymoreto

Montecristo-Trifinio

Capiro-Calentura

Tinto Negro

Río Negro

Patuca

La Mosquito lowlands

Laguna de Caratasca

Puerto Lempira

Kruta

Río Kruta

Rus Rus

Sierra de Agalta

Segovia

Opalaca

NICARAGUA

86° W

84° W

Map 20.1 Honduras

Forests
Lowland moist
Montane
Mangrove
Pine

Conservation areas

Non forest

No data

1:1,700,000

0   20   40   60   80 km

0   20   40 miles

ductivity is very low on this land, some studies showing it to be less than one-third the productivity of those same crops in some developed countries (Leonard, 1987). Cattle raising is especially inefficient in its use of land. It also deprives small farmers of land and displaces poor rural people, forcing them to migrate to forested hillsides, where they practice shifting agriculture.

In Honduras, a large proportion of forested lands has traditionally belonged to the state, even forest on private lands was considered a public resource until 1992. However, little effective control has been exerted over the expansion of the agricultural frontier and over logging areas. This has, in effect, resulted in forests being an open access resource, free to be exploited on a first-come, first-serve basis. The lack of control has increased the rate of forest resource depletion.

Honduras has begun a period of policy reform that has returned forest property to landowners and has reduced to a minimum the participation of the State in the national economy and the market place. However, tenure and wealth distribution issues still remain, and these continue to have an adverse effect on the conservation of Honduran natural forests.

Biodiversity

The flora and fauna of North and South America intermix in Honduras. The forests are inhabited by some fauna that is characteristic of North America (such as the white-tailed deer *Odocoileus virginianus*) and others characteristic of South America (such as the tapir *Tapirus bairdii*, sloth *Bradypus variegatus*, monkeys *Alouatta palliata* and *Cebus capucinus* and ocelot *Leopardus pardalis*). Indeed, due to some large climatic variations in relatively small extensions of abrupt terrain and in the mountains, tropical and temperate species of plants and animals can be found sharing the same habitat. For instance, white-tail deer and

monkeys can be found in the high mountains of the Department of Yoro, in north central Honduras (Hartshorn and Green, 1985).

Honduras has at least 700 species of breeding birds, 173 mammals and 208 reptiles and amphibians (Hartshorn and Green, 1985; WCMC, 1992). Another 225 or so migratory bird species use the Central American isthmus as a seasonal area, while at least 53 species of birds that breed in the United States and Canada spend the rest of the year in the forests and open areas of Central America (Millington, 1984). The green turtle *Chelonia mydas*, the hawksbill turtle *Eretmochelys imbricata* and the loggerhead turtle *Caretta caretta* are found along the Caribbean coast. The green turtle, in particular, is overexploited off the north coast of Honduras, as its large size make it a favoured food source (Campanella *et al.*, 1982). Very few wildlife species in Honduras are sufficiently abundant to allow for commercial or intensive exploitation and many are scarce or even close to extinction (Barborak *et al.*, 1983). Nevertheless, sport hunting is becoming important in some regions of Honduras, such as Choluteca on the Pacific, where American sport hunters pay about US$1 million per year to hunt white-winged doves *Zenaida asiatica*, jaguars *Panthera onca*, pumas *Puma concolor* and ocelots.

Globally threatened species occurring in Honduras include the spider monkey *Ateles geoffroyi*, the tapir *Tapirus bairdii*, the margay *Leopardus wiedii*, the endemic Honduran emerald *Amazilia luciae*, the keel-billed motmot *Electron carinatum*, the golden-cheeked warbler *Dendroica chrysoparia*, the American crocodile *Crocodylus acutus* and two dragonflies *Amphipteryx agrioides* and *Heteragrion eboratum* (Groombridge, 1993).

The least exploited biological resource in Honduras is its abundant plant species. There is great promise in the future for this immensely rich resource, particularly for the manufacture of pes-

Forests along the banks of the Río Plátano, Río Plátano Biosphere Reserve, Honduras.   (WWF/Craig MacFarland)

ticides and for medicinal purposes. Thus far, the only significant research that has been funded in Honduras has been for the use of the calaguala fern, *Polypodium leucotomas*, in cancer research.

Honduras is also a rich source of many internationally important timber and multipurpose tree species such as *Gliricidia sepium*, many *Leucaena* and *Albizia* species, *Pinus patula tecunumanii*, *Swietenia macrophylla*, *Cedrela odorata*, *Calliandra calothyrsus* and *Pinus caribaea*. Particularly in the dry forest areas, these species are being severely reduced in number, which represents a loss of genetic material of great potential value.

Conservation Areas

Since 1991, COHDEFOR has been responsible for formulating and implementing national policies and laws regarding the protection, conservation and management of wildlife and wildlands. COHDEFOR has a Protected Areas Section (Sección de Areas Protegidas) within its Department of Natural Areas and Faunas (Departamento de Areas Silvestres y Fauna). However, the exact distribution of responsibilities for protected areas is unclear as is the distinction between the different categories used. Protected areas are state owned, but there is provision for private individu-

Table 20.6   Conservation areas of Honduras

Existing conservation areas in IUCN's categories I–IV. For information on World Heritage Sites, Biosphere Reserves and Ramsar Sites see Chapter 8. Marine reserves are not listed or mapped here.

National Parks	Area (sq. km)
Capiro-Calentura*	55
Cayos Cochinos (Marino)	nd
Celaque*	270
Cerro Azul de Copán*	155
Cerro Azul Meambar*	200
Isla de Exposición+	2
La Muralla*	249
La Tigra*	238
Montaña de Comayagua	180
Montaña de Cusuco*	184
Montaña de Yoro*	300
Montecristo-Trifinio*	54
Pico Bonito*	1125
Pico Pijol	114
Port Royal	nd
Punta Sal	782
Santa Barbara*	130
Sierra de Agalta*	655

Biological Reserves	
Cayo Saint Joshs+	nd
El Arenal+	nd
El Cedro+	nd
El Chiflador	5
El Chile*	120
El Guisayote	70
El Pacayal+	nd
El Pital*	38
El Uyuca*	11
Guajiquiro	70
Jardin Botanico de Lancetilla+	17
Las Trancas+	nd
Misoco	40
Mogola+	nd
Montecillos*	125
Opalaca*	145
Río Kruta	500
Río Negro*	600
Rus Rus*	nd
Sabanetas+	nd
San Pablo+	nd
San Pedro+	nd
Volcán Pacayita*	97
Yerba Buena	36
Yuscarán	24

Wildlife Refuge	
Bahía de Chismuyo	nd
Barbareta	nd
Cayos de Utila	nd
Cuero y Salado	132
El Armado*	35
El Jicarito	nd
El Quiebrachal	nd
Erapuca+	65
Guameru+	nd
Guapinol	nd
La Alemania	nd
La Chaparrosa+	2
Laguna de Caratasca*	1200
Laguna de Guaymoreto*	50
Las Iguanas	14
Mixcure*	80
Montaña de Corralitos*	55
Montaña Verde	83
Monte Cristo	nd
Puca	49
Punta Condega*	39
Punta Isopo*	112
Ragged Cay*	nd
San Bernardo	26
Teonostal+	nd
Texiguat*	100
West End	nd

Cultural Monument	
Fortaleza San Fernando de Omoa	nd
Parque Arqueológico El Puente+	nd
Petroglifos de Ayasta	nd
Ruinas de Copán*	3
Ruinas de Tenampua*	nd

Natural Monument	
Congolón, Piedra Parada y Coyocutena*	nd
Cuevas de Taulabé*	0.2

Total	8636.2°

° but note that the size of many of the conservation areas is unknown
* Area with forest within its boundaries as shown on Map 20.1
+ not mapped

Source: WCMC (unpublished data)

als or a foundation to manage conservation areas. For instance, Uyuca Biological Reserve is managed by the Escuela Agricola Panamericana with the authority of COHDEFOR.

Although a few protected areas were gazetted earlier, most (37) of the conservation areas in Honduras were designated in 1987 to protect cloud forests. A further 24 areas (including three marine reserves) were proclaimed by presidential decree in 1992. There are also around 30 officially proposed sites, with many others suggested for protection. Table 20.6 lists protected areas in IUCN's categories I–IV.

Most of the conservation areas do not have a management plan, and illegal hunting and timber cutting commonly occurs within them. In spite of the problems, the Honduran Government is making an effort to delimit the protected areas and to begin flora and fauna inventories, particularly in the case of La Muralla National Park and the World Heritage Site of Río Plátano.

Initiatives for Conservation

There are encouraging signs of support for conservation in Honduras. US aid is funding studies in La Muralla National Park. There are plans to establish the Honduran portion of a biological corridor that would extend from Río Plátano through the Bosawas (Honduran-Nicaraguan border) as far as Tortuguero in Costa Rica. The NGO movement is also beginning to show some promise particularly in conservation for development efforts, for example in La Mosquitia (Mosquitia Pawisa, MOPAWI), and in Cuero y Salado Refuge (FUCSA) near La Ceiba, on the north coast.

Honduras established the beginnings of an environmental action plan, in preparation for UNCED 1992, but has yet to initiate the process for the formulation of a National Conservation Strategy.

Honduras was one of the first countries to prepare a Tropical Forest Action Plan. The Honduran TFAP identified numerous projects, of which 15 are presently being implemented with a total external donation of US$70.6 million (FAO, 1993b). However, the Honduran TFAP failed to tackle the fundamental policy issues influencing forests and has now lost much of its credibility. A new and very recent diagnostic study carried out for a regional forestry project may serve as a basis for the reformulation of a new and participatory TFAP.

References

BCH (1992). *Indicadores Economicos de Corto Plazo 1988–1990*. Banco Central de Honduras, Departamento de Estudios Economicos, Tegucigalpa, Honduras.

Barborak, J., Morales, R., MacFarland, C. and Swift, B. (1983). *Status and Trends in International Trade and Local Utilization of Wildlife in Central America*. CATIE, Turrialba, Costa Rica.

Campanella, P., Dickinson, J., DuBois, R., Dulin, P., Glick, D., Merkel, A., Pool, D., Rios, R., Skillman, D. and Talbot, J. (1982). *Honduras II, Country Environmental Profile, A Field Study*. Agency for International Development, McLean, Virginia.

COHDEFOR/OAS (1992). *Programa Nacional de Manejo de Cuencas*. Corporacion Hondureña de Desarrollo Forestal, Tegucigalpa, Honduras.

Daugherty, H.E. (ed) (1989). *Perfil Ambiental de Honduras 1989*. DESFIL, Washington D.C., U.S.A.

FAO/UNEP (1981). *Proyecto de Evaluacion de los Recursos Forestales Tropicales: Los Recursos Forestales de la America Tropical*. FAO, Rome, Italy.

FAO (1993a). *Forest resource assessment 1990: tropical countries*. FAO Forestry Paper 112. FAO, Rome, Italy.

FAO (1993b). *TFAP (Tropical Forests Action Programme) Update 30*. TFAP Coordinating Unit, Forestry Department. FAO, Rome, Italy.

FAO (1993c). *FAO Yearbook: Forest Products 1980–1991*. FAO Forestry Series No. 26, FAO Statistics Series No. 110. FAO, Rome, Italy.

FAO (1994). *FAO Yearbook: Forest Products 1981–1992*. FAO Forestry Series No. 27, FAO Statistics Series No. 116. FAO, Rome, Italy.

GOH/SECPLAN (1991). *Urgencias y Esperanzas. Datos Prioritarios para los Retos de los Noventa*. Government of Honduras Proyecto SECPLAN/OIT/FUAP-HON/87-009, Tegucigalpa, Honduras.

Hartshorn, G.S. and Green, G. (1985). *Wildlands Conservation in Northern Central America*. Draft Paper: The Nature Conservancy International Program, Washington, D.C.

Jiménez, J.A. (1992). Mangrove forests of the Pacific coast of Central America. In: *Coastal Plant Communities of Latin America*. Seeliger, U. (ed). Academic Press, San Diego. Pp. 259–267.

Leonard, H.J. (1987). *Natural Resources and Economic Development in Central America. A Regional Environmental Profile*. International Institute for Environment and Development. Transaction Books, Oxford, U.K.

Millington R.S. (1984). *The Effect of Land-Use Changes in Central America on the Population of some Migratory Bird Species*. Unpublished draft manuscript. The Nature Conservancy, Washington, D.C.

Molina, M. (1992). *Diagnóstico Integral del Sector Forestal de Honduras*. Unpublished manuscript. IUCN/Intercooperation, San José, Costa Rica.

Saenger, P., Hegeri, E.J. and Davie, J.D.S. (eds) (1981). *First Report on the Global Status of Mangrove Ecosystems*. IUCN/Commission of Ecology.

WCMC (1992). *Global Biodiversity: Status of the Earth's Living Resources*. Chapman and Hall, London xx + 594pp.

Author: Jose Flores Rodas, IUCN Regional Office, Costa Rica with contributions from Graham Chaplin and Ernesto Ponce, CONSEFORH, Siguatepeque, Honduras.

Map 20.1   Honduras

The forests shown on Map 20.1 were digitised from a map *Cobertura Forestal y Deforestacion (1965–1990)* compiled by COHDEFOR (1992) at a scale of 1:500,000. The source map illustrates existing forest cover and areas deforested since 1965. Only the existing forests have been digitised for this Atlas which include *Cobertura bosque latifoliado* digitised to show lowland moist and montane forest and *Cobertura bosque pinar* to depict pine forest. The montane forest has been delimited by a 1000 m contour.

Mangroves are not mapped on the above mentioned source map. Those shown on Map 20.1 are derived from an unpublished map (nd) *Mapa de Recursos Costeros* compiled by COHDEFOR at a scale of 1:1 million. Area measurements of mangrove cover from this map have not been included in the forest statistics in Table 20.3 (see text).

Boundary information for the protection areas of Honduras originate from a regional map compiled by the Centro Agronómico Tropical de Investigación y Enseñanza (CATIE) in Costa Rica and IUCN, entitled *Areas Silvestres Protegidas de Centro America* (1987). Point data are derived from the WCMC protected areas database.

21 Mexico

Country area 1,958,200 sq. km
Land area 1,908,690 sq. km
Population (mid-1994) 91.8 million
Population growth rate 2.2 per cent
Population projected to 2025 137.5 million
Gross national product per capita (1992) US$3470
Forest cover in 1990 (FAO, 1993)* 448,120 sq. km
Annual deforestation rate 1981–1990 1.3 per cent
Industrial roundwood production 7,516,000 cu. m
Industrial roundwood exports 6000 cu. m
Fuelwood and charcoal production 15,450,000 cu. m
Processed wood production 3,341,000 cu. m
Processed wood exports 638,000 cu. m
* excluding forests in the dry deciduous, very dry and desert zones

Mexico, the third largest country in Latin America after Brazil and Argentina, houses the northernmost tropical forests in the Americas. As a result of its latitudinal range and topography, the country contains a remarkable climatic complexity and biotic richness that make it one of the most ecologically diverse countries in the world.

The country's economy, the second largest in Latin America after Brazil, is clearly very much influenced by its trade relations with its northern neighbour, the USA. Agriculture contributes more to domestic product than in most of the other countries in the region, and foreign investment is a major economic factor. This has led to skewed development patterns, with some parts of the country dominated by modern intensive agriculture, while elsewhere extensive subsistence agriculture persists.

Mexico's tropical forests are rapidly being fragmented as a result of policy incentives that for the last two decades have promoted population resettlement, cattle ranching and other forms of forest conversion in the lowlands. However, conservation is now prominent on the political agenda, to the extent that the president has made strong commitments to preserve the country's biodiversity. Indeed, Mexico may have reached the development threshold when society at large will begin to demand forest conservation.

INTRODUCTION

Two of the major biological regions of the world, the nearctic and the neotropical, meet in Mexico. The distribution of the different vegetation types, is, however, strongly influenced by the country's complex topography. Mexico is framed by three major mountain ranges: the two Sierras running north-south, one (Sierra Madre Oriental) parallel to the coast of the Gulf of Mexico and the other (Sierra Madre Occidental-Sierra Madre del Sur) parallel to the Pacific coast; and the central range (Eje Neovolcanico) running east-west. This range has three of the five highest peaks in North America, including Mexico's highest peak, Citlaltepetl, at 5699 m. The projection of the Sierras south of the Tropic of Cancer results in the occurrence of temperate forests at latitudes where tropical vegetation thrives in the lowlands. Most of the vegetation south of the Tropic is a mosaic of temperate and tropical plant associations with a wide range of physiognomic variation, apart from that in the flat and low Yucatan Peninsula in the east and on the southern Gulf coast plains and piedmont where the vegetation is eminently tropical.

A federal republic, Mexico is divided into 32 states displaying a rich mosaic of cultures, landscapes and natural resources. However, only the eight southern states of Yucatan, Campeche, Quintana Roo, Tabasco, Chiapas, Oaxaca, Veracruz and Guerrero have significant areas of tropical vegetation. This region accounts for 21 per cent of Mexico's population and the formal economy of the area is strongly dependent on oil, cattle ranching, logging and tourism. These eight states also contain the richest ethnic ancestry of Mexico. Fifty eight per cent of the country's indigenous population live in them (Toledo *et al.*, 1989), and 24 of the 38 indigenous languages spoken in Mexico are spoken there (INEGI, 1984). As it is often the case with indigenous communities in Mesoamerica, many of these groups inhabit the more remote forested areas of the region, both temperate and tropical, and their cultural practices are closely linked to the resources contained in those forests.

The Forests

The two main systems of vegetation classification used in Mexico, Miranda and Hernández (1963) and Rzedowski (1978), tend to differentiate forest types by their physiognomy and phenology rather than by using the Holdridge Life Zone system (Holdridge *et al.*, 1971), which classifies the forests by the climate and elevation of the areas where they are found. In the following description of Mexico's forests, forest types in the Miranda/Hernández (1963) and Rzedowski (1978) classifications are grouped into: Tropical rain forests, Tropical seasonal forests, Tropical montane forests and Conifer and oak forests (Table 21.1).

"Tropical" refers to vegetation growing in a warm, humid and frost-free climate — Koeppen's A climate — (Koeppen, 1948). Within this climatic zone, "seasonal" refers to vegetation subjected to a dry season of three months or more, and "montane" to vegetation growing in frost-free areas between 1000 and 1500 m.

Table 21.1   Classification of different forest types in Mexico

This chapter	Miranda/Hernández (1963)	Rzedowski (1978)
Tropical rain forests	Selva alta perennifolia, Selva alta subperennifolia, Selva mediana subperennifolia	Bosque tropical perennifolia
Tropical seasonal forests	Selva alta/mediana subcaducifolia, Selva baja caducifolia, Selva baja subperennifolia, Selva baja espinosa perennifolia, Selva baja espinosa caducifolia	Bosque tropical subcaducifolia, Bosque tropical caducifolio, Bosque espinoso
Tropical montane forests	Selva mediana/baja perennifolia, Bosque caducifolio	Bosque mesofilo de montaña
Coniferous and oak forests	Pinares, Encinares, Bosque de oyameles	Bosque de coniferas y de Quercus

Tropical Rain Forests

Tropical rain forests are differentiated by canopy height and degree of deciduousness. Truly tall, evergreen forests (*selva alta perennifolia*) are confined to approximately 10,000 sq. km (Anaya *et al.*, 1992), mostly in the premontane Lacandon forest and the lowland and premontane forests of the Chimalapas-El Ocote region. These areas represent 10 per cent of the original distribution of the *selvas altas* in Mexico (Rzedowski, 1978). *Selvas altas* grow on volcanic soils in areas with the wettest and warmest climates. Dominant trees in these forests are higher than 30 m, have buttressed trunks and, not uncommonly, diameters of two to three metres.

Shorter rain forests with a noticeable degree of canopy deciduousness (*selva alta/mediana subperennifolia*) have a greater geographic range than the taller rain forests. They occur from northern Veracruz to Yucatan. However, most of the areas along the Gulf coast originally covered by these forests have been converted to grasslands or are highly degraded, and today significant tracts of forest occur only in southern Yucatan. These *selvas medianas* commonly grow in areas characterized by karstic terrain and a seasonal rainfall of 1200 to 1500 mm per year. Dominant trees are 30 to 35 m high and up to 50 per cent of them may be deciduous for two to three months a year. In Campeche and Quintana Roo, it is common to find relatively large areas with deficient drainage, known as *bajos*, covered by a semi-evergreen forest (*selva mediana/baja subperennifolia*) often dominated by *Haematoxylum campechianum* (Pennington and Sarukhán, 1968).

A considerable degree of canopy dominance by a single species is common in Mexican rain forests, especially in the northernmost and driest associations, such as in ramonales (*Brosimum alicastrum*), caobales (*Swietenia macrophylla*), tintales (*Haematoxylum campechianum*) and guapacales (*Dialium guianense*). Tree species frequently found in other rain forests in the country include *Brosimum alicastrum*, *Terminalia amazonia*, *Dialium guianense*, *Guatteria anomala*, *Pseudolmedia oxyphyllaria*, *Swietenia macrophylla* and *Manilkara zapota*.

Tropical Seasonal Forests

Seasonal forests — shown on Map 21.1 as dry forests — fall along a continuum between relatively tall forests subjected to a short, but well defined, dry season during which 50 per cent of the species lose their leaves, and short forests (less than 10 m) subjected to dry seasons of six months or more during which all trees lose their leaves. The two main types of seasonal forests recognized in Mexico are: *selvas subcaducifolias* (semi-deciduous forests) and *selvas caducifolias* (deciduous forests). The driest formations are scrub forests dominated by short and spiny trees and cacti (*selvas espinosas*).

The phenology and species composition of this seasonal vegetation varies considerably even within relatively short distances as a result of changes in soil depth, slope, aspect, and land-use history. Since most of the seasonal forests in Mexico thrive on hilly terrain and have been subjected to various degrees of human intervention, large tracts of forest with a homogenous physiognomy are uncommon. The landscape of the seasonal tropics often displays a patchy distribution of short to medium forest, thorn scrub, savanna and secondary associations. Seasonal forests are commonly dominated by a few species. A well-defined understorey of shade tolerant trees occurs only in the tallest and most moist of these associations. Common tree species in seasonal forests include *Bursera simaruba*, *Vitex gaumeri*, *Tabebuia* spp., and numerous Leguminosae, especially in the driest associations.

Tropical Montane Forests

Tropical montane forests represent the altitudinal limit of tropical vegetation. The original distribution of these forests follows an altitudinal belt between 1000 and 1500 m on the western slopes of the Sierra Madre Oriental, and include areas at a similar elevation in parts of the Sierra Madre del Sur and northern and central Chiapas. Associated with altitudinal gradients, the montane forest is often found in the most humid and warm areas of transition between oak-pine forests and lowland rain forests. In the drier and cooler areas, this ecotone is typified by mesophyllous forests with a greater dominance of oaks.

Montane humid forests are dense stands frequently dominated by *Liquidambar styraciflua* with canopy heights between 20 m and 35 m and tree diameters between 30 cm and 50 cm. Canopy deciduousness is apparent in the cooler, but not necessarily drier, months of the year and is rarely complete. The understorey is lush, and epiphytes (bromeliads and orchids), vines and arborescent ferns are well represented. The confluence of the nearctic and the neotropical regions in Mexico is strongly evidenced in the floristic affinities of these forests. Characteristically, canopy species belong to temperate genera, while those in the understorey are typically tropical (Pennington and Sarukhán, 1968). Common tree species, in addition to *L. styraciflua*, include various species of *Quercus*, *Juglans*, *Carpinus*, *Cornus*, *Eugenia*, *Dalbergia* and *Podocarpus*. A more tropical canopy flora has been described (Miranda, 1952) in warmer and moister montane forests in restricted areas of Veracruz, Oaxaca and Chiapas (*selva mediana/baja perennifolia*). These forests are physiognomically more similar to cloud and elfin forests of other tropical areas, with a dense vegetation covered by mosses, lichens and ferns.

Conifer and Oak forests

These forests are found over a wide range of ecological conditions and associated with this is the remarkable species richness of the genera *Pinus* and *Quercus* (see section on Biodiversity).

Table 21.2 Areas of mangroves in Mexico

Region	Area (sq.km)
1: NW	698
2: NE	76
3: Centre	1,066
4: SE	3,474
Total	5,315

Source: SARH (1992a).

Pines tend to dominate the cooler and higher parts of the forests, while oaks are more common in the drier and lower areas. Pine and oak forests also occur at lower elevations in areas subjected to a clearly tropical climate. Tropical pine forests include stands of *P. oocarpa*, found in the area of Los Tuxtlas in Veracruz, Arriaga in Chiapas and in parts of the isthmus of Tehuantepec, and *P. caribaea*, found in restricted patches in Quintana Roo (Rzedowski, 1978). Stands of *Q. oleoides* used to be relatively common along the Gulf coast, but they were mostly cleared by cattle ranchers in the 1960s (Gómez Pompa, 1966). These are mapped as pine forest on Map 21.1.

Mangroves
Mexico's mangroves are being lost very rapidly. In the mid-1970s the estimated area of mangroves was 15,000 sq. km, but by 1990 this cover had been reduced to slightly over 5000 sq. km (Almada, 1992; SARH, 1992a — see Table 21.2). They form fringes along the coast that may range from a few metres to a few kilometres in width (Lot and Novello, 1990).

The most important mangrove formations in the Pacific are Marismas Nacionales in Nayarit and the Panzacola system in Chiapas. In the Gulf, major mangrove areas occur on the northern coast of Yucatan, Laguna de Terminos in Campeche, Pantanos de Centla in Tabasco and Laguna Madre in Tamaulipas. The northernmost limit of mangroves in Mexico is the eastern shores of the Sea of Cortez.

The floristic composition of the mangroves is relatively constant along both the Atlantic and Pacific oceans. Most are dominated by *Rhizophora mangle,* which often forms monospecific stands. Following a predictable zonation, other common species are *Avicennia germinans, Laguncularia racemosa* and *Conocarpus erecta.*

Mangroves are lost mainly as a result of clearing for agriculture, aquaculture, the development of urban areas and tourist facilities. They are also being increasingly used for firewood in the coastal areas (Yañez-Arancibia and Lara, 1993).

Forest Resources and Management
The exact area of Mexico's tropical forests remains unknown. One of the major problems is that different sources use different definitions for the term forest. The most reliable sources (Masera *et al.*, 1992; SARH, 1992a, 1992b) indicate that about a quarter of Mexico's territory is presently covered with closed-canopy forests, although the actual figures given in these publications vary. Approximately half of the area is conifer and oak forest, 19 per cent is rain forest and 31 per cent is seasonal (dry) tropical forest (Masera *et al.*, 1992; Table 21.3).

FAO (1993) estimates that there is a total of 448, 120 sq. km of forest within the rain, moist deciduous and hill and montane zones as of 1990. A further 37,730 sq. km is found in the dry deciduous, very dry and desert zones — none of which is con-

sidered to be forest in this Atlas. Closed broadleaved forest covers only 81,770 sq. km (FAO, 1993).

Map 21.1 has been produced from a digital dataset compiled by the Southern Forest Experiment Station of the US Forest Service. However, this dataset gives only an approximation of the distribution of the different forest types and therefore, measurements of the formations could not be taken from the Map. As a result, no statistic of forest cover as shown on this Map is given in this chapter.

The digital dataset was produced by classifying AVHRR data for 1990 and 1991 using information from 1:1,000,000 vegetation maps, Landsat TM prints and aerial photographs and other ancillary information such as the personal experience of foresters and botanists from the Secretariat of Agriculture and Water Resources (SARH — Secretaría de Agricultura y Recursos Hidráulicos) and the National Institute of Statistics, Geography and Information — INEGI (Evans *et al.*, 1992; Eggen-McIntosh *et al.*, 1992). Eggen-McIntosh *et al.* (1992) estimate that total forest area in the country, as measured from the AVHRR classification, is 663,115 sq. km, but this includes considerable areas of fragmented forest. Including the areas covered by cloud on the AVHRR imagery, which are, in general, forested areas, increases the estimate to 671,622 sq. km. This is quite similar to the estimate by SARH (1992a). SARH (1992a) reports that there are 496,477 sq. km of forest with a canopy cover of 20 per cent or more and 180,831 sq. km of disturbed (fragmented) forest giving a total of 677,308 sq. km. In addition, SARH (1992a) estimates that there are 35,480 sq. km of severely disturbed forest land in the country.

Rain forests in Mexico were originally found along the piedmont and coastal plains of the Gulf of Mexico from the Huasteca region in northern Veracruz to Tabasco, northern Oaxaca and Chiapas and into the Yucatan Peninsula (Rzedowski, 1978; Toledo, 1988).

The three most significant vestiges of rain forest are the Chimalapas-El Ocote forest between Oaxaca and Chiapas, the Lacandon forest in northeastern Chiapas and the Yucatan forests in Campeche and Quintana Roo. The Yucatan forests are an extension into Mexico of a larger expanse of lowland tropical forest in the Petén region in Guatemala. Along Mexico's Pacific coast, rain forests remain only in isolated tracts in southern

Table 21.3 Area of forest in Mexico and percentage of each type remaining.

Forest type[1]	Original cover[2]	Present cover[3]	% of land area	% of original area
Tropical Rain	212,000	97,000	5.1	46
Tropical Seasonal	397,000	161,000	8.4	41
Tropical Montane	16,000	–	–	–
Conifer and oak	377,000	257,000	13.5	68
Total	972,000	515,000	27.0	53

1. Forest type according to grouping of vegetation types described above.
2. Original cover (in sq. km) calculated from cover of potential vegetation types indicated in SARH (1971) — other sources report different figures.
3. Present forest cover in sq. km (Masera *et al.*, 1992)

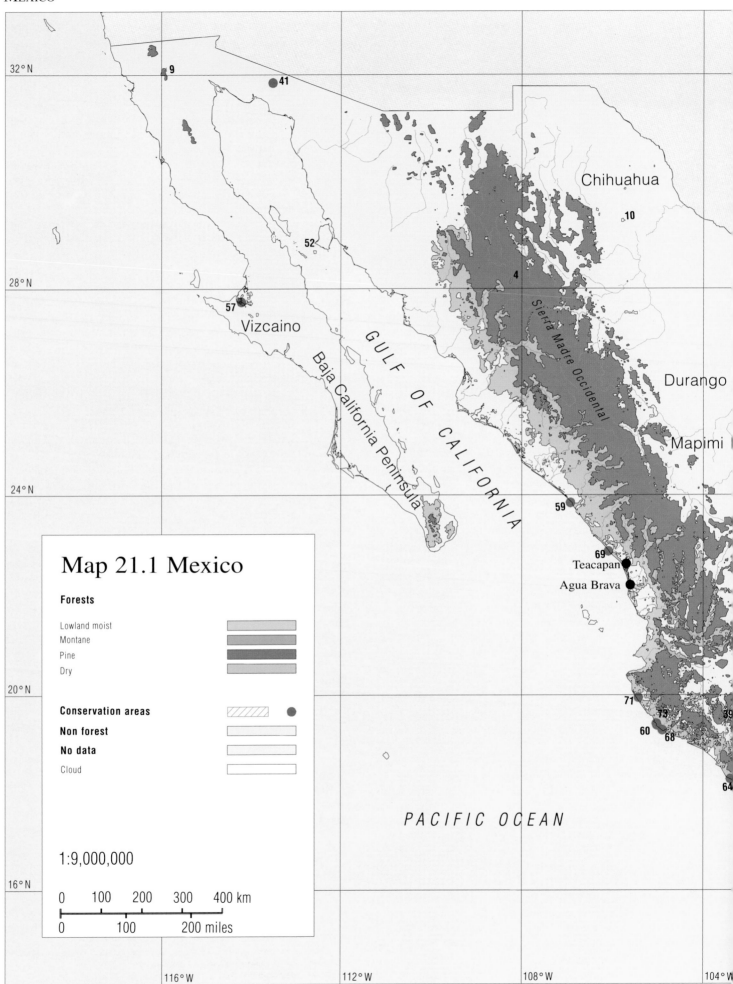

Map 21.1 Mexico

Forests

Lowland moist
Montane
Pine
Dry

Conservation areas

Non forest

No data

Cloud

1:9,000,000

| 0 | 100 | 200 | 300 | 400 km |

| 0 | 100 | 200 miles |

Chiapas and Oaxaca. Elsewhere, rain forest areas have been substantially converted, altered or degraded to a mosaic of secondary vegetation.

Seasonal forests represent the most extensive of the tropical plant associations of Mexico. On the Gulf coast, seasonal forests occur in parts of central and northern Veracruz and in the northern part of the Yucatan Peninsula. Their greatest distribution is along the Pacific coast in Chiapas, Oaxaca and Guerrero, continuing north between the coast and the Sierra Madre Occidental, well above the Tropic of Cancer. Inland, the largest tract of seasonal forest is found along the Balsas basin, between the Eje Neovolcanico and the Sierra Madre del Sur.

It is difficult to assess the extent to which the Mexican montane rain forest has been degraded or lost. Significant areas have been converted to coffee plantations. Since these plantations commonly include shade trees, some of which belong to the original forest canopy, aerial imagery often fails to differentiate the plantations from natural forest. It is estimated that the few remnants of this forest, scattered throughout Chiapas, Oaxaca and Veracruz, comprise an area perhaps no larger than 10 per cent of its original extent (Rzedowski, 1978).

The most widely distributed and extensive forests in Mexico are the oak and pine forests of medium and high elevations, covering an estimated total of 250,000–257,000 sq. km (SARH, 1991; Masera *et al.*, 1992). Although the greatest extent of these forests is in the Sierra Madre Occidental in the northern states of Chihuahua and Durango, oak and pine forests are amply represented in the south and are one of the dominant vegetation types in Oaxaca, Guerrero and Chiapas. They cover most areas above 1800 m in Eje Neovolcanico and Sierra Madre del Sur and on the mountains of Chiapas and Oaxaca. They are also found in Sierra Madre Oriental, in a mosaic with tropical montane forests and other tropical vegetation.

While 15 per cent of the Mexico's forest lands are private and five per cent are public, the vast majority is communal land (*ejidos*) or subject to use-rights by indigenous communities. The amount of forest land in each *ejido* varies widely across the country, and so do the uses that *ejidatarios* (communal land holders) make of their forests. Some may be converted to agricultural land, while activities in others include extraction of timber, non-timber forest products and firewood, and cattle grazing.

The Mexican Constitution establishes that all forests, regardless of their tenure, belong to the nation. Timber harvesting, either by concessionaires or by *ejido* cooperatives, is regulated by the federal government through the Undersecretariat for Forestry within SARH. With some exceptions, state governments are not substantially involved in forestry policy or regulation within their jurisdictions.

As established by the forestry law of 1986, logging permits are granted by SARH on the basis of annual harvest volumes, and need to be applied for every logging season. Up until the late 1970s, forestry in Mexico was carried out following an officially sanctioned method prescribed for all forests, the Metodo Mexicano de Ordenamiento de Montes (MMOM). This was a polycyclic system based on the selective extraction of a small number of trees of a minimum diameter. The MMOM was designed to preserve the forest "capital" while extracting the "interest" (Rodríguez, 1958). In tropical forests, the use of minimum diameters has probably been critical in the persistence of stands of valuable species, but selective timber harvesting in stands of shade intolerant pine species has often resulted in mixed oak-pine stands with a lower commercial value (Jardel, 1985).

For most of this century, commercial logging was carried out through concessions granted by the federal government. The valuable tropical species, mahogany and cedar, were harvested in extensive areas of Quintana Roo and Campeche first by American contractors and then by Mexican private and parastatal companies (Snook-Cosandey, 1986). With the forestry law

---

PLAN PILOTO FORESTAL

Plan Piloto Forestal (PPF) illustrates the potential of community forestry to control tropical deforestation in Mexico. The PPF started in 1983 as an officially-sponsored initiative to transfer forest utilization in the state of Quintana Roo from concessionaires to *ejidatarios* (communal land holders). The main objectives of PPF were the promotion of social and economic development in the region and the curbing of the accelerated deforestation brought by the colonization programs promoted in the 1960s.

Under the PPF, *ejidos* are organized in forestry cooperatives that provide technical assistance and strengthen the producers' capacity to negotiate better prices for their timber. Today 25 *ejidos* organized in two cooperatives control 2670 of the state's 4200 sq. km of forests. This forest area is the sum of the permanent forest areas (PFA) demarcated by consensus in each *ejido*. The PFA is spared from conversion to agriculture and is dedicated to an integrated forest management that includes not only logging, but also the extraction of non-timber products (chicle gum, spices and honey) which contribute significantly to the *ejido* economy.

Forest management is planned at the *ejido* level and is supervised by PPF foresters licensed by SARH. Logging is selective, based on minimum diameters, and is planned around the extraction of the most valuable species: mahogany and cedar. Harvesting schedules follow a 25-year cutting cycle in rotations of 75 years. While this silvicultural scheme seems to insure sustained yields of mahogany within the current rotation, its sustainability beyond 2060 depends on whether current practices insure the seed regeneration of mahogany and other commercial species. Dependence on mahogany, however, is seen in PPF as an initial stage that will be reduced as markets for lesser-known timber species and specialty products expand and become more reliable.

In less than ten years, forest *ejidatarios* in Quintana Roo have gone from leasing their resources to concessionaires, to harvesting and selling roundwood and now to processing boards and exploring new markets. In the process, income in the *ejidos* has increased substantially, rural communities have reclaimed control of their lands and deforestation in Quintana Roo has been noticeably reduced. While long-term sustainable forest management in Quintana Roo still faces substantial challenges, PPF has provided a foundation to meet them in the context of equitable rural development and forest conservation.

Sources: Galleti and Arguelles (1987); Richards (1992); and Snook (1992).

of 1986, concessions have been phased out and, in their place, *ejidatarios* and indigenous communities, through cooperative arrangements, have become more active and independent in wood production and processing. However, the decades of concession forestry, when the largest pine trees were removed and there was intense extraction of mahogany and cedar, has meant that the forestry cooperatives have commonly been left with degraded and impoverished stands whose silvicultural needs are often beyond the *ejidatarios* technical and financial resources.

There are some instances where community tenacity, political will and adequate technical assistance are promoting sustainable *ejido* forestry. The Association of Forestry Communities and Ejidos of Oaxaca (UCEFO), which manages 700 sq. km of pine forest, has started introducing shelterwood, seed-tree and other silvicultural methods designed to increase forest productivity and to help recover degraded stands that were exploited for decades by a paper company. In Quintana Roo, several associations of forest *ejidos* — collectively known as Plan Piloto Forestal — are developing silvicultural and marketing strategies to increase utilization of the lesser known timber species, thus reducing their dependence on the already creamed stands of mahogany and cedar (see Box 1). In tropical forests, the extrac-

A casque-headed lizard Laemanctus longipes, *found throughout Mexico, Honduras and probably Nicaragua.*

(WWF/Tony Rath)

tion of non-timber forest products, such as chicle *Manilkara zapota*, allspice *Pimenta dioica*, barbasco *Dioscorea* spp. and xate *Chamaedorea* spp., often provide a critical incentive to *ejidatarios* to maintain their lands under forest cover.

According to SARH (1992b), wood production in Mexico was 32.3 million cu. m in 1989, of which 23.5 million cu. m was firewood, and 8.8 million cu. m pulpwood and lumber. These figures, however, are questionable given the occurrence of illegal logging and the difficulty of quantifying unregulated firewood collection. The figures, particularly for fuelwood and charcoal, estimated by FAO (1994) and given at the head of the chapter, are considerably lower. Up to 80 per cent of the industrial wood is supplied by pine forests, mostly in the Sierra Madre Occidental and to a lesser extent in the Sierra Madre del Sur. Tropical timber accounts for less than five per cent of Mexico's annual timber production (i.e. less than 250,000 cu. m); most comes from Quintana Roo and Campeche (Toledo *et al.*, 1989). The principal tropical timber products are sawnwood and plywood from mahogany and a few other species, and railway sleepers and floorboards from lesser-known hardwoods.

The forestry sector in Mexico has been slow to recover from the economic crisis of the 1980s. Timber production rates have decreased by 25–35 per cent since 1980, reflecting a decreasing demand for construction wood (SARH, 1992b). On the other hand, pulpwood imports increased by 80 per cent between 1988 and 1990, and softwood prices in Mexico are now up to 35 per cent higher than those in the international market (Lara, 1991). Without a major revamping of the current production scheme, the forestry sector is likely to be weakened by the eventual incorporation of Mexico into the North America free trade zone. Canada and the United States, the world's largest timber producers, have a combined production of over 500 million cu. m per year and a highly developed processing industry with which Mexican producers and industry can hardly compete (Merino, 1992). Some people predict that Mexico's forest sector may eventually become restricted to the production of pulpwood on large-scale plantations established in tropical moist areas that have already been deforested (Sedjo, 1992).

Responding to this situation, and following a determined policy of deregulation and privatization, the government passed a new forestry law in 1992. This law is intended to strengthen the forestry sector by providing incentives for private investment in forest plantations and industries. The new law also emphasizes the environmental value of forests, particularly those in the lowland moist tropics, and establishes strict limits on the conversion of forest lands. In spite of this legislation, the challenge to the forestry sector under NAFTA, privatization and deregulation remains significant. Forestry policies have traditionally been superseded by agrarian reform, agricultural credit policies and development schemes which have promoted forest conversion to agriculture and cattle ranching.

Deforestation

Degradation and rapid loss of forest cover, particularly in the lowland tropics, is a critical issue in Mexico. Estimates of annual forest loss country wide vary from 6150 sq. km (FAO, 1988) to 15,000 sq. km (Toledo, 1988). A more recent estimate, based on state-level information adjusted with data from recent satellite images, indicate an annual loss of forest cover of 8040 sq. km, a rate of 1.6 per cent per year (Masera *et al.*, 1992). According to this study, tropical forests are the most affected, with an estimated annual loss of 2370 sq. km (2.4 per cent) in rain forests and 3220 sq. km (2.0 per cent) in seasonal forests. These estimates do not, however, take into account forest recovery that is expected to take place after forest fires or abandonment of agricultural lands. FAO (1993) estimates annual deforestation between 1981 and 1990 in the tropical rain, moist deciduous, hill and montane zones to be 5977 sq. km, a rate of 1.2 per cent. Around 62 per cent of this occurs in the hill and montane forests. Across all formations, FAO (1993) estimates an annual loss of 6781 sq. km.

Truly tall, evergreen forests have disappeared dramatically in the last two decades. In the mid-1960s up to 40 per cent of the original area of these forests remained (Pennington and Sarukhán, 1968), but by the late 1980s only 10 per cent had survived (Rzedowski, 1992).

Studies show that up to 60 per cent of the loss of tropical forests in Mexico can be attributed to the expansion of cattle ranching (Masera *et al.*, 1992; Toledo, 1990). Cattle ranching is a multimillion dollar industry that has benefited from specific incentives provided by the federal and state governments; these include credits, tax breaks, technical assistance, infrastructure and land tenure arrangements (Toledo, 1990). In some cases, cattle pastures are established directly after forest clearing, whereas in others, a short agricultural period precedes them.

Massive deforestation in Mexico's tropical area has also resulted from the grand colonization and development schemes promoted by the federal government in the second part of this century. Colonization projects in federal lands have been in response either to the demand for arable land or for specific political purposes, such as the protection of the national territory along the Guatemalan border. The projects have usually included an initial stage where logging operations by private concessionaires facilitate penetration and removal of the forest cover (Gómez Pompa *et al.*, 1993).

Rain forests along the lowlands and piedmont on the Gulf coast have been the most affected, notably in the state of Tabasco. From 1940 to 1985, the state's area dedicated to cattle ranching increased from 3500 sq. km to 16,500 sq. km, destroying in the process nearly 7500 sq. km of lowland rain forest (Morales, 1990). In addition, in 1972, the federal government instituted a major social development plan for the area of Balancan-Tenosique (adjacent to the Guatemalan border). This failed in its social objectives, but resulted in a further expansion of cattle ranching (Tudela, 1989). It is estimated that primary rain forest in Tabasco now occupies about two per cent of its original area.

This process is not atypical of the rest of the Gulf plains, from northern Veracruz to the isthmus of Tehuantepec, where the original rain forest cover has been reduced to less than 10 per cent (Dirzo, 1992). Other areas of particularly intensive deforestation in the humid tropics are the Lacandon forest in northeastern Chiapas, Los Tuxtlas area in southern Veracruz, and parts of the southern half of the Yucatan Peninsula. Slash-and-burn agriculture is another important factor in deforestation in the humid tropics, particularly when it is practised by landless *colonos* in previously logged areas (Gómez Pompa, 1990).

Not all of this deforestation is permanent; considerable areas of secondary forest are found throughout the tropics in Mexico. Management and protection of these tracts is essential. Enrichment planting and multiple-use extractive schemes are particularly promising (del Amo, 1991).

In the seasonal tropics, cattle ranching is the leading cause of

forest loss, followed by firewood extraction, agriculture and fires. However, structural and functional degradation is less evident in these dry forests and the extent of their alteration more difficult to quantify than in moist forest.

Biodiversity

Although Mexico covers only one percent of the earth's land area, it contains about one tenth of all terrestrial vertebrates and plants known to science. The meeting of the nearctic and neotropical biotic regions, the abundance of topographic islands and the wide climatic variation across its territory are significant factors in Mexico's biodiversity.

In the Americas, the country is the richest in reptiles (717 species) and mammals (449 species), third richest in flowering plants (c. 25,000 species) and fourth in amphibians (284 species) (Fa and Morales, 1993; McNeely *et al.*, 1990; Table 21.4). Mexico's biota is also conspicuous for its high endemism, particularly among reptiles and amphibians and the floras of dry and temperate montane habitats (Flores-Villela and Gerez, 1989; Rzedowski, 1991a, chapters in Ramamoorthy *et al.*, 1993; Table 21.4).

Mexico's natural habitats range from deserts and alpine grasslands to tropical rain forests and coral reefs. The various biomes contribute differently to the overall biodiversity of the country. While arid areas tend to be high in endemic genera (Rzedowski, 1991b), forests contribute significantly to species numbers and, in many cases, to endemism as well. Out of the estimated 25,000 vascular plant species and 1352 vertebrate species that can be sorted by habitat, 81 per cent and 75 per cent respectively are found in lowland rain, seasonal, montane or pine/oak forests (Flores-Villela and Gerez, 1989).

The floras of the lowland and montane rain forests are conspicuously rich, harbouring up to one third of the country's vascular plants (Rzedowski, 1991b). In the case of the lowland rain forest, floristic richness increases markedly with decreasing latitude. While moist forests in the Huasteca region of northern Veracruz tend to be dominated by one or two canopy species, dominance in the southern rain forests is shared by many more. The number of species of vascular plants in Los Tuxtlas region in southern Veracruz is estimated at 1300, in an area of less than 100 sq. km (Dirzo, 1992). The flora of the Yucatan moist forest is significantly poorer in vascular plants than forests subjected to similar climatic conditions in the Gulf plains (Pennington and Sarukhán, 1968), probably due to the edaphic constraints of the Peninsula.

Floristic diversity is most conspicuous in tropical montane forests. They probably cover less than one per cent of Mexico's area, but contain almost 10 per cent of the country's species of vascular plants (Rzedowski, 1991b). Well-preserved tracts of montane forests in the Sierra Madre Oriental can have up to eight times more species of vascular plants than other forested areas in the region (González-Medrano, 1972).

Mexico's tropical seasonal forests are reportedly richer than

Table 21.4 Total number of vertebrate and vascular plant species and number of endemic and threatened species in Mexico

	Birds	Mammals	Reptiles	Amphibians	Plants
Total no.	961	449	717	284	25,000
Endemics	78	142	368	173	3,624
Threatened	123	32	35	4	477

Sources: Flores-Villela and Gerez (1989), Fa and Morales (1993)

Table 21.5 Diversity and endemism in different forest types in Mexico

Forest type	Flora[1]	Fauna[2]	Restricted species[3]
Rain	5,000	197	62
Seasonal*	6,000	229	34
Montane	3,000	nd	nd
Coniferous	nd	119	13
Oak	nd	468	134
Conifer & Oak	7,000	nd	nd

1. Approximate number of species of vascular plants found in each forest type (Rzedowski, 1991b; Rzedowski, 1993).
2. Numbers of vertebrate species in Mexico that can be assigned to a particular forest type (Flores-Villela and Gerez, 1989).
3. Species "restricted" to the ecological system (Flores-Villela and Gerez, 1989).
* Includes thorn forests
nd Data not reported separately for this forest type.

similar forests elsewhere. According to Dirzo (1992), the floristic richness of seasonal forests in Mexico is about 30 per cent higher than would be expected from the observed floristic patterns among similar vegetation types. The biological significance of Mexican seasonal forests is further increased by their high degree of endemism. The Balsas basin, one of the largest areas originally covered by seasonal forests, is considered a Pleistocene refugium. It has a larger number of species from the common neotropical genus *Bursera* than does any other area; most of them are endemic to the basin.

The contribution of the oak-pine forest to Mexico's biodiversity is also significant. It is estimated that nearly one third of all vascular plant species found in forest habitats are housed in oak-pine forests. The diversity of these forests is typified by *Quercus* and *Pinus*. Out of Mexico's reported 55 species of pines and estimated 130 species of oaks, 85 per cent and 70 per cent respectively are endemic (Mittermeier and Goettsch, 1992). The overall importance of the oak forest is emphasized by the fact that of the vertebrate species endemic to Mesoamerica which can be categorised according to habitat, 468 live in oak forests, compared with 229 in tropical seasonal forests and 197 in rain forests (Flores-Villela and Gerez, 1989; see Table 21.5).

Of the 961 bird species recorded in the country, 22 are listed as threatened by Collar *et al.* (1992); most of these are forest species. There are 14 threatened endemic species. They include the bearded wood-pigeon *Dendrortyx barbatus*, the Oaxaca and white-tailed hummingbirds *Eupherusa cyanophrys* and *E. poliocerca* and the white-throated jay *Cyanolyca mirabilis*, all of which are inhabitants of cloud forest and threatened by the destruction of this habitat.

Bats and rodents together account for 79 per cent of the total number of mammal species in Mexico (Fa and Morales, 1993). There are 30 threatened mammal species listed by IUCN in Mexico (Groombridge, 1993), but few of these are forest species. They include two primates — the black howler monkey *Alouatta pigra* and Geoffroy's spider monkey *Ateles geoffroyi*; the margay *Leopardus wiedii* and Baird's tapir *Tapirus bairdii*.

There are 20 reptile species listed as threatened by IUCN (Groombridge, 1993) comprising six marine turtles, six freshwater turtles (five endemics), three tortoises (one endemic), three lizards, one snake and one crocodile. Three amphibians are listed as threatened by IUCN; these are the Sonoran green toad *Bufo*

retiformis and the two endemic salamanders *Ambystoma lermaense* and *A. mexicanum*. The number of fish in the country is unknown, but around 100 are listed as threatened. There are also 42 globally threatened invertebrates in the country, mostly mesogastropods (12), isopods (11) and dragonflies (9).

Conservation Areas

The legal protection of wildlands in Mexico started in the late 19th century with the demarcation of watersheds and other areas of environmental and economic value around Mexico City. During the first part of this century, dozens of protected areas were established along the Eje Neovocanico, mostly as recreational areas, with some as forest reserves.

In the 1970s, the accelerated development of the lowland tropics, the inadequacy of the traditional park approach, and the involvement of the academic community drastically changed Mexico's approach to the protection of natural areas. Based on the conservation strategy promoted by UNESCO's Man and Biosphere program, the first biosphere reserves in Mexico were established in 1977 in Mapimi in Durango and in 1978 in the Lacandon forest (Montes Azules). Since then, large size, ecological representation and multiple-use objectives have been recognized as important factors in the selection and design of new protected areas.

In 1983, the federal government instituted the National System of Natural Protected Areas (SINAP) to secure habitat representation, management capacity and funding for protected areas. SINAP controls the national parks, special biosphere reserves and biosphere reserves, which together represent approximately three per cent of Mexico's land area (Perez Gil and Jaramillo, 1992). All those conservation areas within IUCN's categories I–IV are listed in Table 21.6. Many sites are not given in this list, including the forest reserves and protection forests which cover approximately 85,000 sq. km.

Until the 1960s, the vegetation type most favoured for parks was the pine-oak forest; the conservation of tropical forests and arid habitats occurred only by default as the result of their remoteness from the main centres of development (Alcérraca *et al.*, 1988; Gutierrez Palacio, 1989). However, many reserves have been established since then and these have significantly enhanced habitat representation in protected areas, particularly in the desert scrub (Mapimi), coastal ecosystems (Sian Ka'an, Pantanos de Centla) and moist tropical forests (Montes Azules, Calakmul, Selva El Ocote). Rain forests are now the best represented terrestrial habitat in SINAP. Approximately thirteen per cent of the estimated current cover of these forests is protected (Table 21.7). Most of this is accounted for by three reserves: Calakmul (7232 sq. km), in Campeche State and Montes Azules and Selva El Ocote in Chiapas State. In contrast, less than one per cent of seasonal tropical forests in Mexico is legally protected (Table 21.7). Under representation of these forests is a remarkable shortcoming of SINAP since seasonal forests account for a third of the country's forest cover, and almost a third of its floristic richness.

Being listed as a protected area does not, however, guarantee the conservation of an area. Most of Mexico's parks and protected areas are subjected to neglect and abuse (Perez Gil and Jaramillo, 1992). Montes Azules, Calakmul and Selva El Ocote are under considerable pressure from cattle ranching, slash-and-burn agriculture and illegal logging; there are no reliable data on the actual cover of undisturbed vegetation within these areas. Efforts to protect them effectively are critical, since together with the Chimalapas region in Oaxaca, they contain a consider-

Table 21.6   Conservation areas in Mexico

Existing conservation areas in IUCN's categories I–IV are list-ed. Marine reserves are not listed or mapped. For information on World Heritage Sites, international designated Biosphere Reserves and Ramsar Sites see Chapter 8.

Map Ref	National Park	Area (sq. km)
1	Balneario de los Novillos	<0.5
2	Benito Juárez*	27
3	Bosencheve*	150
4	Cascada de Bassaseachic*	58
5	Cañón de Río Blanco*	557
6	Cañón del Sumidero*	218
7	Cerro de Garnica*	10
8	Cerro de la Estrella	11
9	Constitución de 1857*	50
10	Cumbres de Majalca*	48
11	Cumbres de Monterrey*	2,465
12	Cumbres del Ajusco	9
13	Desierto del Carmen*	5
14	El Chico*	27
15	El Cimatario	24
16	El Gogorrón	250
17	El Potosí	20
18	El Sabinal	<0.1
19	El Sacromonte	<0.5
20	El Tepeyac	3
21	El Tepozteco*	240
22	El Veladero	32
23	Insurgente José María Morelos y Pavón*	18
24	Insurgente Miguel Hidalgo y Costilla*	18
	Isla Isabela+	2
25	IztaccihuatlPopocatepetl*	257
26	La Malinche*	457
27	Lago de Camecuaro	<0.1
28	Lagunas de Chacahua*	142
29	Lagunas de Montebello*	60
30	Lagunas de Zempoala*	47
31	Los Mármoles*	232
32	Los Remedios	4
33	Molino de Flores Netzahualcoyotl	1
34	Nevado de Toluca*	510
35	Pico de Orizaba*	198
36	Pico de Tancitaro*	293
37	Rayón	<0.5
38	Sacromonte	<0.5
39	Volcán Nevado de Colima*	222
40	Zoquiapán y Anexas*	194

	Private Reserve	
	El Morro de la Mancha (INIREB) Biological Station+	<0.5

	Refuge	
	La Mojonera+	92
	La Primavera+	305
	Sierra de Alvarez+	169
41	Sierra del Pinacate	287
	Valle de los Cirios+	35,000

	Natural and Typical Biotope	
42	La Encrucijada	300

Map Ref	Natural Monument	
43	Bonampak*	44
	Cerro de la Silla+	60
	Grutas de Coconá+	4
	Yaxchilán+	26

	Protection Area for Wild Flora and Fauna	
44	ChanKin*	122
45	Corredor Biológico Chichinautzin	373

	Park	
46	Omiltemi*	36

	Biosphere Reserve	
47	El Triunfo*	1,192
48	Montes Azules (Selva Lacandon)*	3,312
49	Sian Ka'an*	5,281
	Special Biosphere Reserve	
50	Cascadas de Agua Azul*	26
51	Isla Contoy	2
	Isla Guadalupe+	250
52	Isla Rasa	<0.1
	Islas del Golfo de California+	1,500
53	Mariposa Monarca*	161
54	Ría Celestún*	591
55	Ría Lagartos*	478
56	Selva El Ocote*	481

	Reserve Zone for Migratory Fauna	
57	Laguna Ojo de Liebre y San Ignacio	nd

	Reserve Zone for Sea Turtle Protection	
58	Playa adyacente a Rio Lagartos	2
59	Playa Ceuta	2
60	Playa Cuitzmala*	<0.5
61	Playa de Escobilla*	1
62	Playa de Isla Contoy	0.5
63	Playa de la Bahía de Chacahua*	1
64	Playa de Maruata y Colola*	1
65	Playa de Puerto Arista	2
66	Playa de Rancho Nuevo	1
67	Playa de Tierra Colorada*	1
68	Playa El Tecuan*	<0.5
69	Playa El Verde Camacho*	2
70	Playa Mexiquillo*	1
71	Playa Mismaloya*	3
72	Playa Piedra de Tlacoyunque*	1
73	Playa Teopa*	<0.5

	State Park	
	Agua Blanca+	20

	Total	56,993.8

*   Area with moist forest within its boundaries as shown on Map 21.1
+   not mapped

Source: WCMC (unpublished data)

MAJOR PROTECTED AREAS WITH TROPICAL FORESTS

Selva El Ocote Special Biosphere Reserve in Chiapas (481 sq. km). The abrupt topography of Selva El Ocote results in a diversity of habitats including dry forests, rain forests, pine-oak forests and montane elfin forests. Fauna in the area includes river crocodile, spider and howler monkeys, jaguars, tapir and harpy eagles.

Montes Azules (Selva Lacandon) Biosphere Reserve in Chiapas (3312 sq. km). A part of the Lacandon forest, Montes Azules includes premontane and montane tropical forest as well as oak-pine forests. The area has high species diversity and numerous endemic species, including an endemic plant family. The fauna of Montes Azules includes several primates, tapir and harpy eagle.

El Triunfo Biosphere Reserve in Chiapas (1192 sq. km). Situated in the slopes of the Sierra Madre, El Triunfo covers a wide range of vegetation types, from lowland dry forest to oak-pine forests, and is best known for its magnificent cloud forests. El Triunfo is rich in endemic and endangered species such as the Horned Guan, the Quetzal and several snakes and amphibians. Jaguars, tapirs and howler and spider monkeys are common.

Calakmul Biosphere Reserve in Campeche (7231 sq. km). This area is not shown on Map 21.1 or listed in Table 21.6 as it is in IUCN's category V. Calakmul is mostly covered with dry and moist lowland tropical forests It is part of a significant forest tract that extends south of the border to the Petén in Guatemala and Belize. Because of its size and strategic location, Calakmul provides a critical habitat for migratory birds (18 species of wood warblers) and endangered birds

(ocellated turkey and great curassow), and serves as a sanctuary for several species of felines, monkeys, tapir and two species of deer.

Sian Ka'an Biosphere Reserve in Quintana Roo (5281 sq. km). Situated on the Caribbean coast, Sian Ka'an contains numerous habitats: coral reefs, coastal dune vegetation, mangroves, lowland dry tropical forests and rain forests. Sian Ka'an provides costal habitats that are critical for migratory birds and the endangered manatee.

El Cielo Biosphere Reserve in Tamaulipas (1300 sq. km). This area is not shown on Map 21.1 or listed in Table 21.6 as it has not been assigned a category by IUCN. El Cielo is one of the best preserved and richest cloud forests in Mexico. Canopy trees are mostly temperate while orchids, bromeliads and other epiphytes are tropical. At lower elevations, the vegetation is drier and includes nine species of endangered cacti.

Sierra de Manantlán Biosphere Reserve in Jalisco (1395 sq. km). This area is not shown on Map 21.1 or listed in Table 21.6 as it is in IUCN's category V. The reserve, established in 1987, harbours a remarkable variety of habitats, including large tracts of tropical seasonal forest and some of western Mexico's northernmost montane tropical forest. It contains an endemic population of the perennial corn *Zea diploperennis*, one of the most important genetic and agricultural discoveries of this century.

Sources: The Nature Conservancy (1990); WWF (1990); SEDUE (1988).

---

able portion of the rain forest left in Mexico (see Box 2). Calakmul is a projection into Mexico of Guatemala's Mayan Biosphere Reserve, which contains the largest contiguous tract of protected rain forest in the Petén.

Other important protected areas containing tropical forests are the Sian Ka'an Biosphere Reserve, the El Triunfo Biosphere Reserve and the Manantlan Biosphere Reserve (see Box 2). Mangrove forest is amply represented, mostly in Ría Celstun, Ría Lagartos and Pantanos de Centla (3027 sq. km in Tabasco) Special Biosphere Reserves and in Sian Ka'an Biosphere Reserve.

Conservation Initiatives

Programa de Accion Forestal Tropical (PROAFT) is the current version of the Mexican TFAP, the main objective of which is

Table 21.7 Area and percent of Mexico's forest formations in conservation areas

Forest type	No. of CA[1]	Area in CA[2]	% in CA[3]
Rain	7	12,170	12.5
Seasonal	9	870	0.5
Montane	nd	210	nd
Oak & Conifer	35	5,870	2.3

[1] Number of conservation areas (Flores-Villela and Gerez, 1989)

[2] Area (sq. km) of each forest type contained in conservation areas (Alcérreca *et al.*, 1988; Perez Gil and Jaramillo, 1992).

[3] Percentage of present estimated forest cover in conservation areas.

the reduction of deforestation. The mission of PROAFT is to provide SARH with a blueprint for a conservation/development strategy for tropical forests. PROAFT is in the process of developing such a strategy using an approach that includes both field projects and policy analysis. Field projects, called Alianzas Tripartitas (AT), are structured as a collaboration between local communities, SARH and NGOs (which include academic and research institutions). The projects are on forest management, wildlife use, reforestation, etc., and are designed as experimental approaches to resolving specific sets of conservation needs. In contrast, policy analysis will focus on a larger scale and will explore the impacts of the current institutional and legislative framework determining resource use in tropical areas. The combination of the lessons learned from the AT and the major findings of the policy analyses should provide PROAFT with the elements needed to make sound recommendations on concrete actions that the federal government can take in its fight against deforestation and resource degradation (PROAFT, 1991).

A new concept for the management of the Chimalapas area in eastern Oaxaca is being developed which could provide important lessons for the conservation of other areas in Mexico. The Chimalapas area contains one of the largest expanses of tropical moist forest in the country. It is considered a conservation priority by environmental groups, the federal government and multilateral donors alike, but is not legally protected and is threatened by deforestation (WWF, 1990). The main inhabitants of the area are Zoque indians. They have resisted invasion by *colonos* and cattle ranchers and a variety of development programmes (Vocalía Ejecutiva de los Chimalapas, 1990), and are not willing to have conservation imposed from the outside as a "plan" to protect an endangered area of biological importance. Instead, it is proposed that the area be managed as a Reserva Campesina. Under this scheme, the inhabitants of the area would be in charge of its conservation. Management of the reserve would be conducted according to a plan that includes the cultural and economic needs of the Zoques and that is accepted and followed by all parties involved. The federal government has agreed to this concept and is in the process of gazetting the new reserve.

References

Alcérreca, C., Consejo, J.J., Flores, O., Guitiérrez, D., Hentschell, E., Herzig, M., Pérez-Gill, R., Reyes, J.M. and Sánchez-Cordero (1988). *Fauna Silvestre y Areas Naturales Protegidas*. Universo Veintiuno, Mexico. 193 pp.

Almada, P. (1992). *Identificación de las Prioridades de Conservación de la Zona Costera y Marina de México para el WWF*. Internal Report, World Wildlife Fund. 21 pp.

Anaya, A.L., Consejo, J.J., Gutierrez, D. and Hentschel, E. (1992). *Las Areas Naturales Protegidas en Mexico*.

Collar, N.J., Gonzaga, L.P., Krabbe, N., Madroño Nieto, A., Naranjo, L.G., Parker III, T.A. and Wege, D.C. (1992). *Threatened Birds of the Americas. The ICBP/IUCN Red Data Book*. ICBP, Cambridge, U.K.

del Amo, S. (1991). Management of secondary vegetation for the creation of useful rain forest in Uxpanapa, Veracruz, Mexico. Pp. 343–350. In: *Rain Forest Regeneration and Management* Gómez-Pompa, A., Whitmore, T.C. and Hadley, M. (eds). UNESCO.

Dirzo, R. (1992). Diversidad florística y estado de conservación de las selvas tropicales de México. Pp. 283–290. In: *México ante los Retos de la Biodiversidad*. Sarukhán, J. and Dirzo, R (eds). Comisión Nacional para el Conocimiento y Uso de la Biodiversidad, Mexico, D.F.

Eggen-McIntosh, S.E., Borbolla Muñoz, E.B., Ornelas de Anda, J.L., Zhu, Z. and Evans, D.L. (1992). Forest cover mapping of Mexico using Advanced Very High Resolution Radiometer Imagery. In: *Mapping and Monitoring Global Change*. American Society for Photogrammetry and Remote Sensing/American Congress on Surveying and Mapping/Resource Technology '92 technical papers; 1992 August 3–8; Washington, DC.

Evans, D.L., Zhu, Z., Eggen-McIntosh, S., Mayoral, P.G. and Ornelas de Anda, J.L. (1992). *Mapping Mexico's Forest Lands with Advanced Very High Resolution Radiometer*. UDSA Forest Service Research Note SO-367. 4 pp.

Fa, J.E. and Morales, L.M. (1993). Patterns of mammalian diversity in Mexico. In: *Biological Doiversity of Mexico: Origins and Distribution*. Ramamoorthy, T.P., Bye, R., Lot, A. and Fa. J (eds). Oxford University Press, Oxford.

FAO (1988). *An Interim Report on the State of Forest Resources in the Developing Countries*. FAO, Rome, Italy.

FAO (1993) *Forest resources assessment 1990: Tropical countries*. FAO Forestry Paper 112. FAO, Rome, Italy.

FAO (1994). *FAO Yearbook: Forest Products 1981–1992*. FAO Forestry Series No. 27, FAO Statistics Series No. 116. FAO, Rome, Italy.

Flores-Villela, O. and Gerez, P. (1989). *Mexico's Living Endowment: an Overview of Biological Diversity*. Conservation International. 51 pp.

Galletti, H. and Arguelles, A. (1987). Planificación estratégica para el desarrollo rural: el caso del plan piloto forestal de Quintana Roo. Pp. 317–320. In: *Land and Resource Evaluation for National Planning in the Tropics: an international conference and workshop*. U.S. Department of Agriculture, Forest Service.

Gómez-Pompa, A. (1966). *Estudios Botánicos en la Región de Misantla, Veracruz*. Instituto Mexicano de Recursos Naturales Renovables. México, D.F. 173 pp.

Gómez-Pompa, A. (1990). El Problema de la deforestación en el trópico mexicano. Pp. 229–255. In: *Medio Ambiente y Desarrollo en México, Vol. I*. E. Leff (ed.). Centro de Investigaciones Interdisciplinarias en Humanidades, UNAM.

Gómez-Pompa, A., Kaus, A., Jiménez, J., Brainbridge D. and Rorive, V. (1993). Mexico: a case study. Pp. 483–548. In: *Sustainable Agriculture and the Environment in the Humid Tropics*. National Research Council. National Academy Press, Washington, D.C., USA.

González-Medrano, F. (1972). Bosque caducifolio. In: *Guías Botánicas de Excursiones en México*. Sociedad Botánica de México. México, D.F. 253 pp.

Groombridge, B. (Ed) (1993). *1994 IUCN Red List of Threatened Animals*. IUCN, Gland, Switzerland and Cambridge, U.K. 286 pp.

Gutierrez Palacio, A. (1989). *Conservacionismo y Desarrollo del Recurso Forestal*. Editorial Trillas, Mexico, D.F. 199 pp.

Holdridge, L.R., Grenke, W.H., Hatheway, W.H., Liang, T. and Tosi, J.A. (1971). *Forest Environment in Tropical Life Zones: A Pilot Study*. Pergamon Press, Oxford. 747 pp.

INEGI (1984). *X Censo General de Población y Vivienda, 1980*. Instituto Nacional de Estadística Geografia e Informática, México, D.F.

Jardel, P. (1985). Una revisión crítica del método Mexicano de ordenación de bosques, desde el punto de vista de la ecología de poblaciones. *Ciencia Forestal* 10(58): 3–16.

Koeppen, W. (1948). *Climatología*. Fondo de Cultura Económica. Mexico, D.F. Pp. 478.

Lara, Y. (1991). El mercado de productos maderables en México. *Hoja Informativa de Estudios Rurales y Asesoría*, No. 4. Oaxaca, Mexico. 12 pp.

Lot, A. and Novelo, A. (1990). Forested wetlands of Mexico. In: *Ecosystems of the World 15: Forested Wetlands*. Lugo, A.E., Brinson, M. and Brown, S. (eds). Elsevier, Amsterdam. Pp. 287–298.

Masera, O., Ordoñez, M.J. and Dirzo, R. (1992). *Carbon Emissions from Deforestation in Mexico: current situation and long-term scenarios*. Internal Report, Environmental Protection Agency. 38 pp.

McNeely, J.A., Miller, K.R., Reid, W.V., Mittermeier, R.A. and Werner, T.B. (1990). *Conserving the World's Biological Diversity*. IUCN, WRI, CI, WWF-US, the World Bank. 193 pp.

Merino, L. (1992). Contrastes en el sector forestal: Canadá, Estados Unidos y México. *El Cotidiano* 48: 67–73.

Miranda, F. (1952). *La Vegetación de Chiapas, Vol I and II*. Gobierno de Chiapas, Mexico.

Miranda, F. and Hernández, X. (1963). Los tipos de vegetación de México y su clasificación. *Boletin de la Sociedad de Botánica de México* 28: 29–179.

Mittermeier, R. and Goettsch, C., (1992). La importancia de la diversidad biológica de México. Pp 63–74. In: *México ante los Retos de la Biodiversidad*. Sarukhán, J. and Dirzo, R. (eds). Comisión Nacional para el Conocimiento y Uso de la Biodiversidad, Mexico, D.F.

Morales, C. (1990). La ganaderización de Tabasco: reflejo de la ineficiencia e irresponsabilidad empresarial en el aprovechamiento y manejo del trópico húmedo mexicano. *Revista de Difusión Científica/Tecnológica y Humanística 1:* 37–42.

Pennington, T. and Sarukhán, J. (1968). *Arboles Tropicales de México*. INIF-FAO. 413 pp.

Pérez-Gil, R. and Jaramillo, F. (1992). *Areas Naturales Protegidas en México*. Informe para IUCN-BID. Internal Report, IUCN. 56 pp.

PROAFT (1991). *Programa de Acción Forestal Tropical: Hacia un Programa Nacional a Largo Plazo*. Subsecretaría Forestal, SARH, Mexico, D.F. 21 pp.

Ramamoorthy, T.P., Bye, R., Lot, A. and Fa, J. (1993). *Biological Diversity of Mexico: Origins and Distribution*. Oxford University Press, Oxford. 812 pp.

Richards, E. (1992). *The Forest Ejidos of South-east Mexico: a case study of participatory natural forest management*. Rural Development Forestry Network, Overseas Development Institute. 28 pp.

Rodríguez, C. (1958). *Discusión de Fórmulas para el Cálculo de la Productividad Maderable y Exposición del Método Méxicano de Ordenación de Montes de Especies Coníferas*. Comisión Forestal del Estado de Michoacán, Morelia, Michoacán, Mexico.

Rzedowski, J. (1978). *Vegetación de México*. Limusa. 432 pp.

Rzedowski, J. (1991a). El endemismo en la flora fanerogámica Mexicana: una apreciación analítica preliminar. *Acta Botánica Mexicana 15: 47–64*.

Rzedowski, J. (1991b). Diversidad y orígenes de la flora fanerogámica de México. *Acta Botánica Mexicana 14: 3–21*.

Rzedowski, J. (1992). Diversidad del universo vegetal de México. Pp. 251–258. In: *México Ante los Retos de la Biodiversidad*. Sarukhán, J. and Dirzo, R. (eds). Comisión Nacional para el Conocimiento y Uso de la Biodiversidad, Mexico, D.F.

Rzedowski, J. (1993). Diversity and origins of the phanerogamic flora of Mexico. In: *Biological Diversity of Mexico: Origins and Distribution*. Ramamoorthy, T.P., Bye, R., Lot, A. and Fa, J. (eds). Oxford University Press, Oxford. Pp. 129–144.

SARH (1971). *Mapa de Tipos de Vegetación de la República Mexicana*. Secretaría de Agricultura y Recursos Hidráulicos, Mexico.

SARH (1991). *Inventario Nacional Forestal de Gran Visión. Reporte Principal*. Subsecretaría Forestal, Mexico, D.F.

SARH (1992a). *Mexico 1991–1992 — Inventario Nacional Forestal de Gran Vision: Reporte Principal*. Secretaria de Agricultura y Recursos Hidraulicos, Subsecretaria Forestal.

SARH (1992b). *Reforma a la Ley Forestal: Estado Actual de los Recursos Forestales de México*. Internal Document, Secretaría de Agricultura y Recursos Hidráulicos. 40 pp.

Sedjo, R. (1992). *Forestry in North America: Opportunities and Challenges in the Face of a Free Trade Agreement*. Internal Report, World Wildlife Fund. 7 pp.

SEDUE (1988). *Información Básica Sobre las Areas Protegidas de México*. Internal Report, Dirección General de Conservación Ecológica de los Recursos Naturales. 77 pp.

Snook-Cosandey, L. (1986). *La Problemática Forestal de México: Oportunidades y Limitantes para el Desarrollo*. Internal Report, CONACYT/ONUDI. 52 pp.

Snook, L. (1992). Opportunities and constraints for sustainable tropical forestry: lessons from the Plan Piloto Forestal, Quintana Roo, México. Pp. 65–84. In: *Proceedings of the Humid Tropical Lowlands Conference*. Ford, L. (ed.). Development Strategies for Fragile Lands, USAID, Washington, D.C.

The Nature Conservancy (1990). *Parks in Peril: A Conservation Partnership for the Americas*. 23 pp.

Toledo, V. (1988). La diversidad biológica de México. *Ciencia y Desarrollo 81: 19–30*.

Toledo, V. (1990). El Proceso de Ganaderización y la Destrucción Biológica y Ecológica de México. pp. 191–227. In: *Medio Ambiente y Desarrollo en México, Vol. I*. Leff, E. (ed.). Centro de Investigaciones Interdisciplinarias en Humanidades, UNAM.

Toledo, V., Carabias, J., Toledo, C. and González–Pacheco, C., (1989). *La Producción Rural en México: Alternativas Ecológicas*. Universo Veintiuno. 402 pp.

Tudela, F. (1989). Los "Hijos Tontos" de la planeación: los grandes planes en el trópico húmedo Mexicano. In: *Una Década de Planeación Urbano-Regional en México, 1978–1988*. Garza, G. (ed.). El Colegio de México, Mexico, D.F.

Vocalía Ejecutiva de los Chimalapas (1990). *Tequio por Chimalapas*. Gobierno del Estado de Oaxaca, Mexico. Pp. 243.

WWF (1990). *Environmentally-sound Community Development around Key Protected Areas in South-eastern Mexico*. Internal Report, World Wildlife Fund. 25 pp.

Yañez-Arancibia, A. and Lara, A. (1993). *Ecosistemas de manglar en América tropical: estructura, función y manejo*. EPOMEX, Serie Científica 2. Campeche, Mexico. Pp. 300.

Author: Dr Guillermo Castilleja, WWF-US, with contributions from David Evans and Susan Eggen-McIntosh, USDA/Southern Forest Experiment Station, New Orleans.

Map 21.1 Mexico

Data from the Advanced Very High Resolution Radiometer (AVHRR) were used in a programme sponsored by the US Department of Agriculture, Forest Service and FAO to help scientists from Mexico generate forest-cover maps of Mexico (Evans *et al.*, 1992; Eggen-McIntosh *et al.*, 1992).

Near-cloud-free composite images were generated from AVHRR Local Area Coverage datasets for 1990 and 1991. Supporting information from 1:1 million vegetation maps, Landsat TM prints and aerial photographs was also incoporated. Physiographic regions were stratified and classified separately to reduce spectral variance. Regional classifications were combined to produce the final map. These data were kindly made available to WCMC by David Evans and Susan Eggen-McIntosh of the Southern Forest Experiment Station of the US Forest Service. The resulting Map 21.1, however, gives only an approximation of the distribution and areas of the different forest types, as areas of disturbed and fragmented forests were included on the original dataset and were not distinguished as such. Map 21.1 cannot, therefore, be used to take measurements of the amount of forest remaining in the country.

On Map 21.1, the *temperate forest* in the original dataset is shown as pine forest; *tropical high (> 30 m in height) and medium (15 to 30 m in height) forest* is shown as lowland moist and montane forest (delimited by a 3000' contour taken from the Digital Chart of the World); *tropical low (< 15 m in height; dry) forest* is shown as dry forest; *all other nonforested land* as nonforest; and *clouds* as cloud cover. Note that the pine forest on Map 21.1 is, in reality, a mixture of conifer (*Pinus, Abies*, etc.) and broadleaved species, especially oak (*Quercus* spp.) and *Liquidambar*. Mangroves are not shown on Map 21.1.

Boundary data for the conservation areas were provided by Conservation International with additional material taken from the WCMC protected areas database.

22 Nicaragua

Country area	130,000 sq. km
Land area	118,750 sq. km
Population (mid-1994)	4.3 million
Population growth rate	2.9 per cent
Population projected to 2025	9.1 million
Gross national product per capita (1992)	US$410
Forest cover in 1990 (see Map)	57,450 sq. km
Forest cover in 1990 (FAO, 1993a)	60,130 sq. km
Annual deforestation rate (1981–1990)	1.9 per cent
Industrial roundwood production	300,000 cu. m
Industrial roundwood exports	—
Fuelwood and charcoal production	3,265,000 cu. m
Processed wood production	85,000 cu. m
Processed wood exports	1000 cu. m

Nicaragua is the largest of the countries on the Central American isthmus and has the greatest percentage and total area of intact ecosystems in the region. Its rain forest is the largest north of the Amazon.

The country has been war-torn and subjected to an international blockade until recently and during this time international assistance for conservation activities was extremely limited. However this situation has now improved and some major projects are planned.

INTRODUCTION

Nicaragua, a country of lakes, rivers and volcanoes, is located in the middle of the Central American isthmus. It is the largest of the seven countries in the region, with approximately 480 km of Caribbean coastline and 350 km of Pacific coastline. It can be divided into three main topographical regions. The Pacific region is a broad lowland belt, about 80 km in width, which runs along the Pacific coast from the Gulf of Fonesca in the north to Costa Rica in the south. This comparatively dry region contains the Central Depression and associated rift lakes and a chain of volcanoes, many of them active. The highest is Volcan Cristobal at 1806 m. The Central Highland region is dominated by three ranges, the Cordillera Segoviana, the Cordillera Isabelia and the Cordillera Dariense, all running east to west. The elevation of this area is between 600 m and 2150 m (Sutton, 1989). The third area is the Caribbean lowlands, a largely uninhabited region of humid lowland forest and pine savanna that occupies about half the country.

The west has a mean temperature of about 27°C, a rainy season between May and November and a dry season from December to April; annual rainfall is 2000 mm or less. The central highland area is cooler with a longer, but lighter, rainy season. The climate in the east is tropical, it is generally hot and humid throughout the year. Mean annual precipitation in this region is nearly 4000 mm, with a nine month rainy season and no well defined dry period (Sutton, 1989).

The estimated population of Nicaragua is 4.3 million, giving an overall population density of 36 people per sq. km. However, the Pacific region, occupying only 15 per cent of the land area, contains over 60 per cent of the population, leaving the Central and Caribbean regions with densities as low as five inhabitants per sq. km. The Central Highland area is settled chiefly by subsistence and commercial farmers. Most settlement in the Caribbean lowland is confined to coastal towns and mining areas. About 62 per cent of the population are urban inhabitants, the biggest town is the capital Managua with around 700,000

inhabitants. The people are mainly mestizo, but there are also some Afroamericans, on the Caribbean coast, and a small number of Amerindians.

The country is divided into nine politico-administrative regions. Two of them are autonomous, due to their special ethnic and socio-cultural characteristics. These are the Región Autónoma del Atlántico Norte (RAAN — the Autonomous Region of the Northern Atlantic) and the Región Autónoma del Atlántico Sur (RAAS — the Autonomous Region of the Southern Atlantic). Civil war, as well as a trade and aid embargo imposed by the U.S.A., has caused considerable disruption of the country's economy. Nicaragua's GNP per capita is one of the lowest in the Americas. Agriculture is the principal source of income for the nation. The main exports are cotton, coffee, meat, sugar and bananas.

The Forests

Nicaragua contains mostly lowland tropical broadleaved forests, but there are some patches of cloud forest, some important pine forests and a few fragments of dry forest remaining in the country, as well as areas of mangrove and some swamp forest.

Many of the forests in the moderately warm and humid zones of the lowlands, below 500 m asl, have already been exploited as access to them is easy and they have a wealth of commercial timber species. The remnants of these forests are found as isolated patches in small intermontane valleys. Some of the species that characterize the forests are guachipilín *Diphysa rabinioides*, guanacaste or ear fruit *Enterolobium cyclocarpum* and genízero or raintree *Pithecellobium saman*.

The evergreen forests at slightly higher elevations (500–1500 m) have also mostly been cleared, and replaced with coffee plantations and livestock pastures, or have suffered from exploitation. The only large extensions left are located in the most isolated areas of the departments of Matagalpa and Jinotega. Some of the species that characterize this type of forest are: kapok tree *Ceiba pentandra*, palm or giant fern *Cyathea chnoodes* and the oak *Quercus oleoides*.

Extensive areas of tall evergreen forests are found in the Caribbean lowlands in areas with the highest precipitation (2750–6000 mm). They occur at altitudes lower than 1000 m in moderately cool and humid conditions. These are a multistoried formation, the tallest trees reach or surpass 30 m and their thick foliage is sometimes entangled with gigantic lianas. Species characteristic of this wetter evergreen forest type include cedro macho *Carapa guianensis*, palo de agua *Vochysis hondurensis* and guayabón *Terminalia oblonga*.

Cloud forests occur at elevations over 1500 m. They are more or less limited to the permanently clouded tops of the volcanic cones in the Pacific coast and to the tops of the great mountain massifs such as the Mogotón, Misún, Kilambé and Peñas Blancas. These forests are home to species such as santa maría *Calophyllum brasilensis*, sangredrago *Croton panamensis* and majagua *Heliocarpus appendiculatus*.

Swamp forests are periodically or permanently flooded with fresh water. Characteristic species include *Bravaisia integerrima*, river willow *Salix humboldtiana* and the dog almond *Andira inermis*. These are found throughout the Caribbean coastal region.

The pine forests are characteristic of the high and moderately dry lands from the north of Nicaragua, mainly the department of Nueva Segovia. They typically occur between 400 and 700 m in well-drained areas. The best conserved samples of this ecosystem are the pinewoods of Dipilito, which contain species such as *Pinus oocarpa*, *P. maximinoi* and *P. patula tecunumanii*. In addition, pine savannas occur on low, flat lands such as those in the north of the Caribbean region. These are primarily grasslands with scattered *Pinus caribaea* in different associations and transitions with broadleaved species. The pine savannas is a fire-caused disclimax, whereas the true climax vegetation is evergreen rain forest of tropical lowlands (Sutton, 1989).

Tropical dry forests are medium to low forests of deciduous and semi-deciduous trees. They occur at altitudes lower than 500 m in warm and dry zones. Temperatures are over 26°C and annual rainfall ranges from 1000 to 1200 mm. The last remnants of these forests are located in isolated zones of the Pacific region. Some of the species that characterize them are escobillo *Phyllostylon brasiliensis*, lignum vitae *Guaiacum sanctum* and *Haematoxylum brasiletto*.

Mangroves

The mangroves in Nicaragua are more extensive and less degraded on the Caribbean coast than on the Pacific coast. In 1981, FAO/UNEP reported that they covered an area of 600 sq. km and this same figure is given in Saenger *et al.* (1983). On Map 22.1, the mangroves are shown covering the much larger area of 1718 sq. km, though 772 sq. km of these are degraded.

These forests contain *Rhizophora mangle*, *Laguncularia racemosa* and *Avicennia germinans*. The estuaries and marshes of the Caribbean coast are the northern boundary of the natural distribution of the mangrove species *Pelliciera rhizophorae* in the Caribbean slope.

Forest Resources and Management

In 1950, there were 70,000 sq. km of forest in Nicaragua. However, the rapid deforestation of the past four decades has reduced this area considerably to 43,000 sq. km. Broadleaved forests cover 38,000 sq. km, while conifer forests occupy the remaining 5000 sq. km (IRENA, 1992). More than 10,000 sq.

Table 22.1 Estimates of forest extent in Nicaragua

Forest type	Area (sq. km)	% land area
Lowland moist°	30,086	25.3
Montane	6,289	5.3
Pine+	11,284	9.5
Dry	2,509	2.1
Swamp	5,564	4.9
Mangrove*	1,718	1.4
Total	57,450	48.4

°   includes 1,645 sq. km affected by Hurricane Joan in 1988
+   includes areas of pine savanna
*   includes 772 sq. km of degraded mangrove

Based on analysis of Map 22.1. See Map legend on p. 211 for details of sources.

km of the broadleaved forests are degraded, mostly due to shifting cultivation occurring in them (IRENA, 1992). The dense broadleaved forests occur mainly in the autonomous regions of the Atlantic coast (RAAN and RAAS), while the conifer forests are principally found in the northeast of the RAAN and in Nueva Segovia. The pine forests are also mostly degraded, due both to frequent forest fires and to logging (IRENA, 1992). FAO (1993a) estimates (using a 1979 survey as a baseline) that there are 60,130 sq. km of forest in the country — none of this is considered to be dry deciduous forest. The figure given for closed broadleaved forest by FAO (1993a) is 47,380 sq. km.

The areas of the different forest types shown on Map 22.1 are given in Table 22.1. The total of 57,450 sq. km is certainly not pristine closed canopy forest; it includes 772 sq. km of degraded mangrove as well as an unknown area of pine savanna. The source for Map 22.1 was a dye-line map produced by the Nicaraguan Institute of Natural Resources and the Environment (IRENA) in 1991, which was based on a 1983 land-use map (see Map Legend).

The forestry sector does not have a specific governing institution. Forest activities are carried out by two units of IRENA, the National Forest Service (regulation and control) and a State Forestry Administration (for State forest lands). Neither of them have regional branches (FAO, 1993b). Other institutions involved with forest activities in Nicaragua are the Forest Seeds Bank (BSF — Banco de Semillas Forestales), the National Technical Institute for Forestry (INTECFOR — Instituto Nacional Técnico Forestal) and the National Agricultural University (UNA — Universidad Nacional Agraria). Implementation of the existing laws and regulations concerning forests has been inefficient.

Nicaragua has around 25,000 sq. km of tree-less land which is potentially suitable for forestry. About half of this area (12,000 sq. km) is considered to be highly productive and all of it could be reforested for the production of goods and services for national consumption and for export.

Forestry does not play a substantial direct role in the country's economy: it represents approximately 0.2 per cent of the GNP, and its exports yielded a total of US$1.5 million in 1989, which correspond to only 0.5 per cent of the country's exports for that year. According to FAO (1994), no industrial roundwood was exported, while only 85,000 cu. m of processed wood was exported in 1992. Most tree felling is not for commercial purposes, but is a result of slash-and-burn agriculture. The

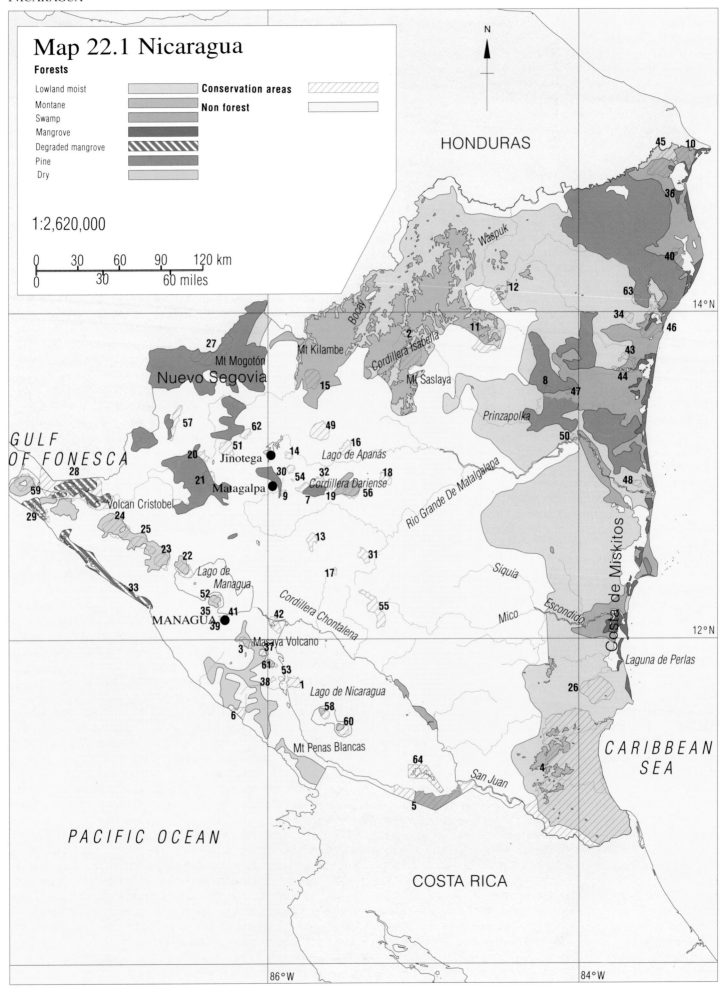

Map 22.1 Nicaragua

Forests

Lowland moist	
Montane	
Swamp	
Mangrove	
Degraded mangrove	
Pine	
Dry	

Conservation areas

Non forest

1:2,620,000

0   30   60   90   120 km

0   30   60 miles

HONDURAS

N

Waspuk

Bocay

Cordillera Isabella

Mt Kilambe

Mt Saslaya

Prinzapolka

45   10

36

40

63

34

46

43

44

47

50

48

27

Mt Mogotón

Nuevo Segovia

57

62

51

49

16

20

Jinotega

14   Lago de Apanás

30   54   32   18

21

Matagalpa

9   19   7   56

Cordillera Dariense

Río Grande De Matalgalapa

13

31

17

Siquia

Mico

Escondido

Costa de Miskitos

GULF
OF FONESCA

28

59

29

Volcan Cristobel

24

25

23

22

Lago de
Managua

52

33

35   41

MANAGUA
39

42

Masaya Volcano

Cordillera Chontalena

55

26

Laguna de Perlas

CARIBBEAN
SEA

3   37

61   53

38   1

6

58

60

Mt Penas Blancas

Lago de Nicaragua

64

5

4

San Juan

PACIFIC OCEAN

COSTA RICA

15

12

11

2

8

86°W

84°W

14°N

12°N

208

forestry sector does, however, play an important indirect role in the economy. It provides some 50,000 cu. m of wood for house building and 27,000 cu. m for the mining industry, as well as providing about 90 per cent of the fuel used for domestic purposes and 25 per cent of that used in industry. In addition, there are over 250 timber factories and furniture shops creating employment for numerous people.

The primary transformation industry has some 90 sawmills and one plywood factory. The secondary transformation industry is made up of seven medium-scale companies and 800 craft shops with capacity to process 6000 – 12,000 cu. m of sawn wood. The main products are furniture, floorboards and pre-fabricated houses. The capacity of the transformation industry is in the order of 300,000 cu. m, but the processing plants are obsolete and are not well maintained so only 60 per cent of this capacity is used.

Deforestation

Much of the deforestation in Nicaragua has occurred over the last few decades; most of it the result of clearing the forests to use the land for other purposes, rather than as result of the commercial or noncommercial demand for timber (Leonard, 1987). In the 1950s and 1960s, the land area planted with cotton quadrupled and forests were cleared to make way for this expansion (Nietschmann, 1990). In the 1960s and 1970s, clearing for cattle ranches was the main cause of deforestation.

Between the years of 1952 and 1984, annual deforestation in Nicaragua varied between 950 sq. km and 1250 sq. km. It decreased during the period of the war (1985–1990), but it increased again in 1991, as a consequence of the thousands of returning refugees clearing and colonising areas of the forest. Today, it is estimated that the annual rate is between 1500 and 2000 sq. km (IRENA, 1992). FAO (1993a) estimates that, between 1981 and 1990, 1240 sq. km of forest were cleared each year, an annual rate of 1.9 per cent.

The direct and indirect causes of deforestation are numerous, complex and interrelated. The main direct cause is the conversion of forest land to agricultural land. This occurs because of the lack of options for the economic use of the forest resources, the low productivity of the land farmed by the campesinos, the absence of appropriate technology to increase productivity and the unstable land tenure situation. In addition, production systems which are unsuitable for the country's tropical soils are used; there are few or no well managed credit programmes for campesinos, there is a lack of coordination between the institutions controlling agricultural and forestry matters, an absence of operating capacity within these institutions and inappropriate economic and financial policies are applied to the problems.

Problems are also caused by the general lack of awareness for the need to use the forest in a sustainable manner, the lack of interest in medium and long-term investments (as opposed to short-term ones) and the fact that little value is attached to the social and economic advantages of good forest management.

As well as the deforestation caused by the conversion to agricultural land, a considerable degree of degradation of the forests is caused by the amount of wood cut for fuel. Every year, 3.5 million cu. m of firewood are cut to be used in homes, industries and commerce; wood provides 49 per cent of Nicaragua's energy requirements.

IRENA estimate that the 170 mph winds of Hurricane Joan in 1988 damaged one fifth of the country's forest wealth, with losses in timber alone amounting to US$1.6 billion.

Biodiversity

Nicaragua is part of the Biological Province of Central America, where South American and North American elements intermingle. The flora is characterized by a large number of Cactaceae and Bromelaceae and there are also over 800 species from the Orchidaceae family. In a recent publication, IRENA (1992) reports that more than 9000 plant species have been identified in Nicaragua and that there are probably an additional 4000 to 5000 species not yet discovered.

In spite of being the largest country on the Central American isthmus, Nicaragua has a somewhat lower biological diversity than its neighbouring countries. This is due primarily to its lack of altitudinal diversity and absence of high isolated mountain ranges (Cedeño et al., 1992). For the same reasons, endemism rates are also lower. Only two per cent of the vertebrate fauna and 0.6 per cent of the flora are endemic.

There are reported to be 750 bird species and 200 mammal species in the country. Numbers of amphibians and reptiles are 59 and 161 respectively (WCMC, 1992).

Nicaragua contains only two bird species listed as threatened by Collar et al. (1992). These are the golden-cheeked warbler Dendroica chrysoparia, which over-winters in the country's forests, and the keel-billed motmot Electron carinatum, a lowland forest species with a very patchy distribution throughout most of Central America.

Globally threatened mammal species that occur in the country include the olingos Bassaricyon gabbii and B. sumichrasti, the tiger cat Leopardus tigrinus, the margay L. wiedii, the tapir Tapirus bairdii, Geoffroy's spider monkey Ateles geoffroyi and the giant anteater Myrmecophaga tridactyla (Groombridge, 1993). Most of these are forest dwellers. Other than the five marine turtles, the only threatened reptiles reported to occur in Nicaragua are the American crocodile Crocodylus acutus and the narrow-bridged mud turtle Kinosternon angusipons (Groombridge, 1993).

The country's most important areas for biodiversity are: the San Cristóbal-Casita volcanic complex, the Masaya Volcano National Park, the Zapatera Archipelago, the Río Escalante-Chococente, the BOSAWAS, the Saslaya hill, the Solentiname Archipelago, the Río Indio Maíz, the Cayos Miskitos and Los Guatusos. All of these sites are conservation areas.

Conservation Areas

Nicaragua's first protected area, a wildlife refuge, was established in 1958 and its first national park (Saslaya) was declared in 1971. However, with no national policy to support their protection, these areas were largely ineffectual (Cedeño et al., 1992). It was only when the Sandinista government came to power in 1979 that IRENA was formed. This was the first Nicaraguan institute concerned with the protection of the environment to be created. Also in 1979, a National Parks Service (SPN) was formed within IRENA which was specifically responsible for establishing and managing protected areas. The intensification of the civil war and the economic crisis after 1983 meant that IRENA could barely function and it was further weakened in 1988 when it lost its ministerial status and became a department within the Ministry of Agricultural Development and Agrarian Reform. It regained its status after the change of government in 1990 but its activities are still constrained by lack of money (Utting, 1993).

In 1983, 17 new conservation areas were created and a further 45 in 1991, most designated as nature reserves. In 1990, a decree formalised the creation of a network of protected areas

Table 22.2 Conservation areas in Nicaragua

Existing conservation areas in IUCN's categories I–IV. For information on World Heritage Sites see Chapter 8.

Map Ref	National Parks	Area (sq. km)
1	Archipélago Zapatera	52
2	Saslaya*	150
3	Volcán Masaya*	51
	Biological Reserves	
	Cayos Miskitos+	500
4	Río Indio Maíz*	2,950
	Wildlife Refuges	
5	Los Guatusos*	438
6	Río Escalantes-Chococente*	48
	Genetic Reserve	
7	Yucul*	48
	Natural Reserves	
8	Alamikamba*	21
9	Apante	12
10	Cabo Viejo*	58
11	Cerro Bana Cruz*	101
12	Cerro Cola Blanca*	222
13	Cerro Cumaica - Cerro Alegre	50
14	Cerro Datanli - El Diablo	22
15	Cerro Kliambé*	101
16	Cerro Kuskawas*	48
17	Cerro Mambachito La Vieja	9
18	Cerro Musún*	41
19	Cerro Paucasan	3
20	Cerro Qulabuc (Las Brisas)	36
21	Cerro Tisey - Estanzuela*	64
22	Complejo Volcánico Momotombo y Momotombito*	85
23	Complejo Volcánico Pilas - El Hoyo*	74
24	Complejo Volcánico San Cristóbal*	180
25	Complejo Volcánico Telica - Rota*	91
26	Cordillera de Yolaina*	400
27	Cordillera Dipilto y Jalapa*	412
28	Delta del Estero Real*	550
29	Estero Padre Ramos*	88

Map Ref		Area (sq. km)
30	Fila Cerro Frío - La Cumpilda	18
31	Fila Masigüe	46
32	Guabule	11
33	Isla Juan Venado*	46
34	Kligna*	10
35	Laguna de Asosoca	1
36	Laguna Bismuna-Raya*	118
37	Laguna de Apoyo	35
38	Laguna de Mecatepe	12
39	Laguna de Nejapa	2
40	Laguna de Pahara*	102
41	Laguna de Tiscapa	0.4
42	Laguna de Tisma	103
43	Laguna Kukalaya*	35
44	Laguna Layasica*	18
45	Laguna Tala - Sulamas*	314
46	Laguna Yulu Karata*	253
47	Limbaika*	18
48	Llanos de Karawala*	20
49	Macizos de Peñas Blancas	113
50	Makantaka*	20
51	Mesas de Monopotente	75
52	Península de Chiltepe*	18
53	Río Manares	11
54	Salto Río Yasica	0.4
55	Sierra Amerrisque	121
56	Sierra Kiragua*	91
57	Tepesomoto/Pataste*	87
58	Volcán Concepción*	22
59	Volcán Cosigüina*	124
60	Volcán Madera*	41
61	Volcán Mombacho*	25
62	Volcán Yali*	35
63	Yulu*	10
	National Monument	
64	Archipiélago de Solentiname	189
Total		9,049.8

* area with forest within its boundaries as shown on Map 22.1
+ not mapped

Source: WCMC (unpublished data)

in the south-eastern region on the border with Costa Rica. These comprise the Nicaraguan component of the International System of Protected Areas for Peace (Sistema Internacional de Areas Protegidas para la Paz) known as SI-A-PAZ which was first proposed in 1974 (Castiglione, 1990). This system is about 3370 sq. km in extent. Several other areas have been designated since then, the largest (7300 sq. km) being BOSAWAS, a national natural resource reserve in the north of the country (IUCN category VIII). Overall, many significant protected area policies and programmes are being initiated in the country.

There is no single unifying law that gives definitions of the management categories of protected areas used in Nicaragua (IUCN, 1992). Table 22.2 shows the country's protected areas in IUCN categories I–IV.

Conservation Initiatives

The problems faced by Nicaragua's forest sector are worsening, and this has motivated the Government to support the implementation of the Tropical Forestry Plan. In Nicaragua, the latter received the name of ECOT-PAF (Estrategia Nacional de Desarrollo Sostenible, Ordenamiento Territorial y Plan de Acción Forestal) (National Strategy for the Sustainable Development, Territorial Zoning and Action Plan for Forestry). This plan was financed by the Swedish Authority for International Development, under the supervision of IRENA, with the collaboration of several governmental institutions, especially the Ministry of Economy and Development (MEDE) and the Nicaraguan Institute for Territorial Studies (INETER).

The National Forestry Action Plan, completed in June 1992, includes a detailed analysis of the forestry sector, an identification of the main issues and basic conditions needed for the development of the forestry sector (FAO, 1993b). The second part of the plan includes a set of policies, objectives and strategies for the sector, followed by a short-term action plan, details of financial arrangements and the expected results and benefits.

A regional forestry action plan has been prepared for two regions of the country — RAAS and Región V. This was part of an effort to develop these two areas which had been particularly badly affected by the civil war and by Hurricane Joan (FAO, 1993b).

The National Forestry Action Plan was inserted in the National Strategy for Conservation and Sustainable Development and the Environmental Action Plan for Nicaragua, which was completed in June 1993.

References

Castiglione, J. (1990). *SI-A-PAZ en 1990, Recursos suplemento especial: SI-A-PAZ.* IUCN, Gland, Switzerland.

Cedeño, V., Cedeño J. and Barborak, J. (1992). *Country Report on Nicaragua.* Unpublished draft.

Collar, N.J., Gonzaga, L.P., Krabbe, N., Madroño Nieto, A., Naranjo, L.G., Parker III, T.A. and Wege, D.C. (1992). *Threatened Birds of the Americas. The ICBP/IUCN Red Data Book.* ICBP, Cambridge, U.K.

FAO (1993a). *Forest resource assessment 1990: tropical countries.* FAO Forestry Paper 112. FAO, Rome, Italy.

FAO (1993b). *TFAP Update 30.* FAO, Rome, Italy.

FAO (1994). *FAO Yearbook: Forest Products 1981–1992.* FAO Forestry Series No. 27, FAO Statistics Series No. 116. FAO, Rome, Italy.

FAO/UNEP (1981). *Proyecto de Evaluacion de los Recursos Forestales Tropicales: Los Recursos Forestales de la America Tropical.* FAO, Rome, Italy.

Groombridge, B. (Ed) (1993). *1994 IUCN Red List of Threatened Animals.* IUCN, Gland, Switzerland and Cambridge, U.K. 286 pp.

IRENA (1992). *Plan de Accion Forestal: Documento Base.* IRENA-ECOT-PAF, Managua, Nicaragua.

IUCN (1992). *Protected Areas of the World: A review of national systems. Volume 4: Nearctic and Neotropical.* IUCN, Gland, Switzerland and Cambridge, U.K.

Leonard, H.J. (1987). *Natural Resources and Economic Development in Central America. A Regional Environmental Profile.* International Institute for Environment and Development. Transaction Books, Oxford, U.K.

Nietschmann, B. (1990). Conservation by conflict in Nicaragua. *Natural History* 11: 42–48.

Saenger, P., Hegerl, E.J. and Davie, J.D.S. (1983). (eds). *Global Status of Mangrove Ecosystems.* Commission on Ecology Papers No. 3. IUCN, Gland, Switzerland.

Sutton, S.Y. (1989). Nicaragua. In: *Floristic Inventory of Tropical Countries: the status of plant systematics, collections, and vegetation plus recommendations for the Future.* Campbell, D.G. and Hammond, D. (eds). New York Botanical Garden, New York. Pp. 299–304.

Utting, P. (1993). *Trees, people and power.* Earthscan Publications Ltd, London.

WCMC (1992). *Global Biodiversity: Status of the Earth's Living Resources.* Chapman and Hall, London xx + 594 pp.

Author: Roberto Araquistain, Director Forestal SFN-IRENA, Managua, Nicaragua.

Map 22.1 Nicaragua

The forest cover data shown on Map 22.1 have been digitised from a dyeline map entitled *Estado Actual de la Vegetacion Forestal de Nicaragua*. The source map, dated 1991, is based on an earlier land-use map of 1983, and has been prepared at a scale of 1:1 million by the Instituto Nicaraguense de Recursos Naturales y del Ambiente, Direccion de Administracion de Bosques Nacionales.

The source data are grouped into five broad categories: *Bosque Denso, Bosque Claro, Matorral, Uso Agropecuario* and *Otros*. These are further sub-divided into more specifically defined vegetation types.

The source data have been harmonised for this atlas in the following way: *Bosque denso tropical ombrofilo (pluvial) de baja altitud, Zona afectada por el Huracan Juana,* and *Bosque claro latifoliado sempervirente* are shown as lowland and montane rain forest (delimited by 3000' contour taken from the Digital Chart of the World) — *Bosque claro latifoliado sempervirente,* which occurs in the previous northern 'war zone', has been included on the advice of J. Castiglione (pers. comm., 1991); *Bosque denso tropical ombrofilo (pluvial) de pantano* is shown as inland swamp forest; *Bosque claro de pino de tierras altas* and *Bosque claro de pino de tierras bajas* as pine forest; *Bosque de manglares* as mangroves; *Bosque claro sempervirente de manglares y tierras pantanosas de manglares sin vegetacion arborescente* is shown as degraded mangrove; and *Bosque claro mayormente deciduo por la sequía* as dry forest.

Conservation areas have been extracted from a dyeline map: *Nicaragua — Sistema Nacional de Areas Silvestres Protegidas,* compiled by the Servicio de Parques Nacionales, Managua, Nicaragua, and published in 1992 by the Instituto de Ambiente y los Recursos Naturales (IRENA) at a scale of 1:500,000.

23 Panama

Country area 77,080 sq. km
Land area 75,990 sq. km
Population (mid-1994) 2.5 million
Population growth rate 1.8 per cent
Population projected to 2025 3.9 million
Gross national product per capita (1992) US$2440
Forest cover for 1990 (FAO, 1993) 31,170 sq. km
Annual deforestation rate (1981–1990) 1.9 per cent
Industrial roundwood production 118,000 cu. m
Industrial roundwood exports 1000 cu. m
Fuelwood and charcoal production 910,000 cu. m
Processed wood production 58,000 cu. m
Processed wood exports —

Panama has a greater number of vertebrate species than any other country in Central America. However, forest cover in the country has declined from around 70 per cent to 40 per cent over the last 44 years and there is bound to be a concurrent reduction in the country's biodiversity. Preoccupation at all levels of government with economic issues and the need for development have, until recently, made conservation a low priority in the country.

INTRODUCTION

Topographically the country comprises four regions: western Panama, which is dominated by the Cordillera de Talamanca that extends down from Costa Rica in a southeasterly direction; the central lowlands, bisected by the Panama Canal; the eastern region, characterised by a series of coastal ranges; and the narrow lowlands on the Caribbean coast. Elevations range from sea level to 3427 m, but most of the isthmus has an elevation of less than 500 m, and nearly 90 per cent is less than 1000 m high (Porter, 1973).

Mean monthly temperature is about 27°C, with little change throughout the year. The Pacific rainfall regime consists of a seven month rainy season with a five month dry season from December to April. In contrast, the narrow Caribbean slope and lowlands have two wet seasons — in June/July and November/December and two less wet periods in September/October and February/March. Rainfall is higher on the north side of the isthmus so that, for instance, Panama City receives an annual precipitation of 1770 mm while Colón has 3175 mm.

Overall population density in Panama is around 33 people per sq. km. However, 50 per cent of the inhabitants are concentrated in the cities of Panama and Colón and along the length of the Canal route, while other areas of the country are much less densely populated (INRENARE, 1990). The official language is Spanish and this is spoken by about 80 per cent of the population, about 14 per cent speak Creole English. About 60 per cent of the people are mestizo or mulatto, only eight per cent are Amerindians.

The principal agricultural exports are coffee, bananas and sugar. Agriculture produces 10 per cent of GNP while the forestry sector represents only one per cent of GNP (INRENARE, 1990).

The Forests

There are lowland forests, with high rainfall, along the Caribbean side of Panama and more seasonal, deciduous forests along the Pacific side of the country. Some swamp forest occurs in the Darien lowlands and there is montane forest in the uplands.

The Darien lowlands in eastern Panama, which are in Holdridge's tropical moist life zone, are dominated by cuipo *Caivanillesia plantifolia* trees which may reach 40 m in height (Harsthorn, 1981). Other dominant emergent trees are *Anacardium excelsum* and *Ceiba pentandra*, with *Bombacopsis quinata, B. sessilis, Enterolobium cyclocarpum, Licania hypoleuca, Platypodium elegans, Terminalia amazonia* and *Vitex cymosa* occurring frequently in the canopy. Palms such as *Sabal allenii* are commonly found in the subcanopy. Epiphytes are scarce, but lianes are abundant. In the slightly higher or wetter areas of the Darien, tropical wet forest occurs, extending into the Choco of neighbouring Colombia. *Anacardium excelsum* is dominant in this forest type, with *B. quinata, B. sessilis, Brosimum quianense, Ceiba pentandra, Cochlospermum williamsii, Myroxylon balsamum* and *Oleiocarpon panamense* occurring commonly in the canopy.

Cativo forests, which are pure or very nearly pure stands of *Prioria copaifera* trees, occur on well-drained alluvial flats that are occasionally inundated with fresh water and have a canopy of 20–25 m in height. They are mostly found along rivers and occur, for instance, in broad stands along the Chucunaque, Tuira and Balsas rivers in the Darien lowlands. Other prominent canopy trees include *Pterocarpus officinalis, Swartzia panamensis* and *Tabebuia pentaphylla*.

Orey *Campnosperma panamensis* forests occur on badly drained lands on the Western Atlantic coast. They are found in pure stands in flooded areas such as around Laguna de Chiriquí, where they are high and dense with a single canopy. In areas with better drainage they are mixed with other species, sometimes with mangroves, and palm species may be common in the understorey.

The montane forests in Panama are generally lower and less dense than the cativo or cuipo forests and they are not clearly stratified. The canopy is dominated by berba *Brosimum* sp., guayabillo *Terminalia lucida*, olivo *Sapium* sp., cuajado *Vitex cooperi* and cedro macho *Carapa guianensis. Anacardium excelsum* is rare. Palms are common in the lower vegetation layer and there is a thick undergrowth.

Quercus forests occur in hilly areas, particularly in the Western Cordillera. Very large specimens of *Q. costaricensis* are present in the montane forests on Volcan Barú (Hartshorn, 1981), while *Q. humboldtiana* ia a major tree in the oak forests of Cerro Tacarcuna.

Mangroves

Mangroves are found mainly on the Pacific coast of Panama. FAO/UNEP (1981) estimated that they covered 4860 sq. km in the early 1980s, but the estimate in Dirección Nacional de Recursos Naturales Renovables (1982) is considerably less at 1760 sq. km (Table 23.2); D'Croz (1993) estimates 1710 sq. km. Map 23.1 shows a coverage of 1819 sq. km for an undetermined date between 1970 and 1980. The red mangroves *Rhizophora brevistyla* and *R. mangle* are overwhelming dominants of the mangrove forests, generally forming pure stands with an average height of 25 m. The black mangrove *Avicennia germinans* and *Pelliciera rhizophorae* are only occasional associates (Harsthorn, 1981).

The area of mangroves has been systematically reduced by reclamation of the land for agriculture and cattle pastures and the establishment of shrimp farms. The mangroves have also been degraded by collection of wood for fuel and construction poles and the use of their bark for tannins (INRENARE, 1990).

Forest Resources and Management

In a 1982 publication, the Dirección Nacional de Recursos Naturales Renovables reported that 35,497 sq. km of forest remained in 1980 and this is broken down into forest types as shown in Table 23.1. This agrees with the figure in the report by INRENARE (1990) given in Table 23.2. By 1987, a further three per cent of Panama had been deforested leaving 33,053 sq. km of forest in the country. This is a reduction of over 10,000 sq. km from 1970 (Table 23.2). FAO (1993) reports 31,170 sq. km remaining in 1990 — all of this is considered to be closed broadleaved forest.

The source map used for Map 23.1 is very generalised and based on a mixture of data some of which are now 25 years old (see Map Legend). As a result, no figure for forest cover has been quoted at the head of the chapter or given in the usual table as it is considered that it would be too misleading. The forest area shown on this Map is 35,486 sq. km of lowland forest, 1723 sq. km of submontane forest, 235 sq. km of montane forest and 1819 sq. km of mangrove, giving a total of 39,263 sq. km for some undetermined date between the years of 1970 and 1980.

Table 23.1 Area of the main forest types in Panama in 1980

Forest Types	Area (sq. km)	percent
Orey forests	450	1.3
Orey and other species	170	0.5
Cativo forests	300	0.8
Cativo and other species	194	0.5
Mixed forests	17,880	50.4
Mangroves	1,760	5.0
Protection forests	14,743	41.5
Total	35,497	100

Source: Dirección Nacional de Recursos Naturales Renovables (1982) in INRENARE (1990)

Table 23.2 Forest Area in Panama 1970–1987

Province	1970 Area	%*	1980 Area	%*	1987 Area	%*
Bocas del Tora	8,569	96	8,369	93	7,975	89
Coclé	1,755	34	1,263	25	1,090	22
Colón/San Blas	4,352	53	3,355	41	4,385	53
Darién	15,893	94	12,652	75	11,397	68
Chiriqui	1,553	17	1,101	12	1,103	13
Herrera	182	7	126	5	372	10
Los Santos	407	10	347	9	84	2
Panamá	7,401	61	5,813	48	3,904	32
Veraguas	3,333	30	2,465	22	2,766	25
Total+	43,445	56	35,491	46	33,076	43

* Per cent of the province covered in forest

+ The country area, rather than land area, of Panama appears to have been used in calculating per cent cover in the total row. These totals have been recalculated, slightly different figures are in the source material.

Source: INRENARE (1990)

The cativo forests are the only ones that are currently being commercially exploited (INRENARE, 1990). They have been reduced from 700 sq. km to 300 sq. km in the past 19 years and are in danger of disappearing altogether (INRENARE, 1990). The orey forests are not being managed at present (INRENARE, 1990). They probably have the highest stocking of timber in the tropics with average volumes of 383 cu. m/ha for boles greater than 40 cm in diameter and 716 cu. m/ha for all boles larger than 10 cm in diameter (Falla, 1978).

The forest industry consisted of 50 mills, 600 furniture shops and three plywood factories in 1990 (INRENARE, 1990). At that time the mills were working at only 50 per cent of their capacity. There is little growth in the industry.

An area of over 20,000 sq. km is potentially available for reforestation, but only 100 sq. km have been planted in the past twenty years (INRENARE, 1990).

In 1972, Heckadon estimated that 17 per cent of Panama was occupied or regularly used by indigenous people. Wildlife, as both a source of protein and income, plays an important part in the life of these people. Hunting is particularly important to the Choco indians and the Cuna indians of the interior. Some of the most frequently hunted species are agouti *Dasyprocta punctata*, collared peccary *Tayassu tajacu*, the Central American tapir *Tapirus bairdii*, crested guan *Penelope purpurascens* and iguana *Iguana iguana*. The use of firearms instead of conventional weapons means that there is now excessive killing of many species.

Deforestation

Hartshorn (1981) has found no evidence of extensive natural savannas in Panama and he assumes that practically all of the country was forested at least until the 17th century. However, the first estimate of forest cover in Panama was not made until 1947 (Garver, 1947). At that time, 70 per cent of the country, excluding the Canal Zone, was forested. The provinces of Coclé, Los Santos and Herrera had already lost a considerable extent of their forest, 70 per cent in the case of the first two provinces and 85 per cent in the last. Darien, Bocas del Toro, Colón/San Blas, and Panamá all had 90 per cent or more forest cover at that time.

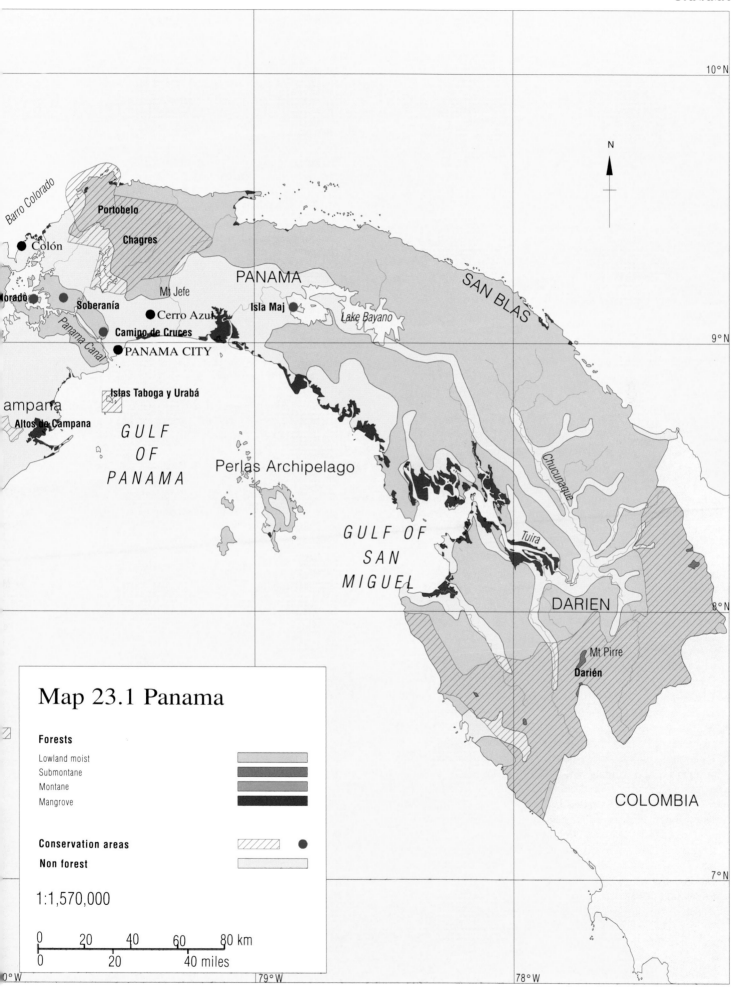

10°N

N

Barro Colorado

Portobelo

Chagres

● Colón

orado

Soberanía

Mt Jefe

● Cerro Azul

Isla Maj

PANAMA

SAN BLAS

Lake Bayano

9°N

Camino de Cruces

● PANAMA CITY

Panama Canal

Islas Taboga y Urabá

ampana

Altos de Campana

GULF
OF
PANAMA

Perlas Archipelago

GULF OF
SAN
MIGUEL

Chucunaque

Tuira

DARIEN

8°N

Mt Pirre

Darién

Map 23.1 Panama

Forests

Lowland moist

Submontane

Montane

Mangrove

Conservation areas   ●

Non forest

1:1,570,000

0   20   40   60   80 km

0   20   40 miles

COLOMBIA

7°N

0°W

79°W

78°W

Table 23.3 Estimates of forest cover in Panama between 1947 and 1987

Year	Area (sq. km)	Per cent	Source
1947	52,540	70	1
1950	52,445	68	2
1960	45,000	58	2
1970	40,816	53	2
1974	39,000	50	2
1980	35,497	46	3
1987	33,053	43	3
1990	31,170	40	4

Sources: 1 Garver (1947) and 2 Falla (1978) both reported in Hartshorn (1981); 3 INRENARE (1990) (as in Table 23.1 above); 4 FAO (1993)

Table 23.3 shows the estimated forest cover between the years of 1947 and 1990 from a number of sources. This table indicates a total deforestation between these years of 21,370 sq. km, a mean rate of 486 sq. km each year. Annual deforestation was estimated at 700 sq. km by the National Institute of Renewable Natural Resources (INRENARE, 1990), while FAO (1993) estimated the slightly lower figure of 644 sq. km between the years of 1981 and 1990. The latter figure gives a rate of 2.1 per cent per year.

In Panama, government assisted colonisation, and spontaneous colonisation facilitated by extensive road construction, is a major force putting pressure on the forests of the highlands of Panama, especially along the Caribbean slope and in the Darien province. Much of the migration is of peasants from heavily populated and overexploited areas of Los Santos, Herrera and Chiriquí (Leonard, 1987). Agriculture is advancing rapidly into lands unsuitable for traditional farming, and there is considerable clearing for cattle pasture.

Biodiversity

Panama has a high biological diversity for its size. Its 218 mammal species, 929 birds (Ridgely and Gwynne, 1989), 226 reptiles and 164 amphibians constitute more vertebrate species than are found in any of the other Central American countries (WCMC, 1992).

The total number of vascular plants in Panama is estimated to be around 9000 (D'Arcy, 1980; Gentry 1982), with 1226 endemics already recorded (Davis *et al.*, 1986). Areas high in endemics are Santa Rita Ridge, El Valle de Anton and Cerros Azul, Pirre, Campana, Jefe and Pilon (Davis *et al.*, 1986). The largest and most species rich forest is in Darién Province.

Panama is one of the best known countries of the Neotropics with regard to the animals within it. For instance, the birds have been systematically studied for over a century (Ridgely, 1976; see also Karr, 1985). Detailed behavioural and ecological studies have been greatly enhanced by the establishment of the Barro Colorado Research station in 1923.

Three primates, the brown-headed and Geoffroy's spider monkeys *Ateles fusciceps* and *A. geoffroyi* and the Central American squirrel monkey *Saimiri oerstedi* are listed by IUCN as threatened in Panama (Groombridge, 1993). Other threatened forest mammals are the Central American tapir *Tapirus bairdii*, the margay *Leopardus wiedii*, the bush dog *Speothos venaticus*, the spectacled bear *Tremarctos ornatus* and the olingo *Bassaricyon* spp.

There are five bird species listed as threatened by Collar *et al.* (1992). Four of these species are forest inhabitants and are shared only with either Costa Rica or Colombia, while the fifth is the endemic glow-throated hummingbird *Selasphorus ardens* and little is known of its ecology. Panama is an important staging post for migrating birds with 184 species of them reported in the country (Ridgely and Gwynne, 1989). Three of the four major bird migration routes between the two Americas converge in the country.

None of the amphibians is known to be threatened. The reptiles listed by IUCN (Groombridge, 1993) are the narrow-bridged mud turtle *Kinosternon angustipons*, the American crocodile *Crocodylus acutus* and five marine turtles.

Little is known about the invertebrates in Panama. The threatened dragonfly *Thaumatoneura inopinata* and butterfly *Dalla octomaculata* occur in the country, and otherwise only in Costa Rica.

Conservation Areas

The development of parks in Panama began in 1966 with the establishment of Altos de Campana National Park; the Department of Wildlife and National Parks was created two years later, primarily to administer this park (IUCN, 1992). It was not until 1975 that a second park was gazetted. There are now 18 conservation areas within IUCN's categories I–IV (Table 23.4).

There are also five forest reserves covering 2127 sq. km, two large protection forests totalling 4550 sq. km, a water produc-

Table 23.4 Conservation Areas in Panama

Existing conservation areas in IUCN's categories I–IV are listed below. For information on World Heritage Sites, Ramsar Sites and Biosphere Reserves see Chapter 8.

National Parks

Altos de Campana	48
Camino de Cruces*	40
Cerro Hoya*	326
Chagres*	1,290
Coiba (includes a marine section)*	2,701
Darién*	5,790
Gral. División Omar Torrijos H. (El Cope)*	nd
La Amistad*	2,070
Isla Bastimentos (includes a marine section)*	132
Portobelo*	348
Sarigua*	80
Soberanía*	221
Volcán Barú*	140

Wildlife Refuges

Ciénega del Mangle*	8
Isla Iguana	<1
Islas Taboga y Urabá	3
Peñón de la Onda	20

Natural Monument

Barro Colorado*	54

Total	13,272

* Area with forest within its boundaries according to Map 23.1.

Source: WCMC (unpublished data)

View towards Bocas del Toro from the interior of La Amistad National Park.　　　　　　　　(Jim Thorsell)

tion reserve of 150 sq. km and two indigenous reserves covering 7526 sq. km; one of these, Comarca Kuna Yala, was set up as long ago as 1938.

In 1986, the private, nonprofit-making organisation, ANCON (Asociación Nacional para la Conservación de la Naturaleza), founded in 1985, and INRENARE signed a ten year cooperative agreement that includes plans for protecting top priority natural lands. Their first joint project was in Soberanía National Park. They have begun marking the boundary of this park and there are plans to halt deforestation, farming and illegal hunting within it (Navarro and Fletcher, 1988). Other national parks ANCON is involved with include Chagres, Darién, La Amistad, Coiba and Isla Bastimentos.

Initiatives for Conservation

There are some 50 agencies in Panama actively concerned with conservation. They are involved in environmental educa-tion, protection of conservation areas, reforestation, scientific investigation and technological development amongst other things.

The Smithsonian Institution has developed several projects in the country, probably best known is their considerable scientific investigation on the island of Barro Colorado.

As well as being involved with the development of conservation areas, ANCON promotes programmes of environmental education, sustainable development, conservation and scientific research. ANCON has, for instance, collaborated with USAID to reforest 64 hectares in the Finca Rio Cabuya in the basin of the Panama Canal; this project was the catalyst for similar projects in Finca Peresénico in Darien, Finca La Pintada in Coclé and Bocas del Tora. Programmes in these areas include planting native tree species, the establishment of an agroforestry system and the breeding of *Agouti paca* and *Iguana iguana* for food.

References

Collar, N.J., Gonzaga, L.P., Krabbe, N., Madroño Nieto, A., Naranjo, L.G., Parker III, T.A. and Wege, D.C. (1992). *Threatened Birds of the Americas. The ICBP/IUCN Red Data Book.* ICBP, Cambridge, U.K.

D'Arcy, W.G. (1980). The flora of Panama: historical outline and selected bibliography. *Annals Missouri Botanical Garden* 67(4): v–viii.

Davis, S.D., Droop, S.J.M., Gregerson, P., Henson, L., Leon, C.J., Villa-Lobos, J.L., Synge, H. and Zantovska, J. (1986). *Plants in Danger. What do we know?* IUCN, Gland, Switzerland and Cambridge, U.K.

D'Croz, L. (1993). Status and uses of manroves in the Republic of Panamá. In: *Conservation and Sustainable Utilization of Mangrove Forests in Latin America and Africa Regions. Part 1: Latin America.* ITTO/ISME Project PD114/90(F). Pp. 115–137.

Falla, A. (1978). *Plan de Desarrollo Forestal: estudio actual del subsector.* FAO/PCT/6/01/I, Panama, Informe tecnico No. 1. Pp. 107.

FAO (1993). *Forest resource assessment 1990: tropical countries.* FAO Forestry Paper 112. FAO, Rome, Italy.

FAO/UNEP (1981). *Proyecto de Evaluacion de los Recursos*

Forestales Tropicales: Los Recursos Forestales de la America Tropical. FAO, Rome, Italy.

Garver, R.D. (1947). *National Survey of the Forest Resources of the Republic of Panama.* State Department, Washington. 28 pp.

Gentry, A.H. (1982). Phytogeographic patterns as evidence for a Chocó refuge. In: *Biological Diversification in the Tropics.* Prance, G.T. (ed). Pp. 112–136. Columbia University Press, New York.

Groombridge, B. (Ed) (1993). *1994 IUCN Red List of Threatened Animals.* IUCN, Gland, Switzerland and Cambridge, U.K. 286 pp.

Hartshorn, G.S. (1981). *Forests and Forestry in Panama.* Institute of Current World Affairs. 16 pp.

INRENARE (1990). *Plan de Accion Forestal de Panama. Documento Principal.* Instituto Nacional de Recursos Naturales Renovables.

IUCN (1992). *Protected Areas of the World: A review of national systems. Volume 4: Nearctic and Neotropical.* IUCN, Gland, Switzerland and Cambridge, U.K.

Karr, J.R. (1985). Birds of Panama: biogeography and ecological dynamics. In: *The Botany and Natural History of Panama: La Botánica e Historia Natural de Panamá.* D'Arcy, W.G. and Correa, M.D. (Eds). Pp. 77–93.

Leonard, H.J. (1987). *Natural Resources and Economic Development in Central America: A Regional Environmental Profile.* International Institute for Environment and Development. Transaction books, Oxford, U.K.

Navarro, J.C. and Fletcher, R. (1988). Preserving Panama's parks. *The Nature Conservancy Magazine* January/February: 20–24.

Ridgely, R.S. (1976). *A Guide to the Birds of Panama.* Princeton University Press.

Ridgely, R.S. and Gwynne, J. (1989). *A Guide to the Birds of Panama with Costa Rica, Nicaragua and Honduras.* Princeton University Press, U.S.A. Pp. 543.

WCMC (1992). *Global Biodiversity: the Status of the Earth's Living Resources.* Chapman and Hall, London. xx+594 pp.

Author: Caroline Harcourt with contributions from Graciela Palacios, ANCON, Panama and Julio Ruiz Murrieta, IUCN, Switzerland.

Map 23.1   Panama

Forest cover data were obtained from the *Atlas Nacional de Panamá: 8.1 Vegetacion Actual* (1980) at a 1:1,000,000 scale. These data are very generalised and based on three main sources: FAO (1970/71) *Inventario Forestal Nacional*; *Atlas Nacional de Panamá* (1975) and Dirección de Desarrollo Forestal, Instituto de Recursos Naturales Renovables (INRENARE). Neither more recent nor more accurate information was able to be found for this project.

The following categories have been combined to produce an estimation of the moist forest cover of Panama: *Bosques perennifolios tropicales, Bosques perennifolios subtropicales, Bosques perennifolios de tierras altas, Bosques subperennifolios tropicales.* To present forest 'type' information, Holdridge's Life Zones have been overlaid onto this forest cover. The following Life Zones were combined to generate the forest types shown on Map 23.1. *Bosque húmedo tropical, Bosque muy húmedo tropical, Bosque húmedo premontano, Bosques muy húmedo premontano,* and *Bosque pluvial premontano* — lowland rain forest; *Bosque húmedo montano bajo, Bosque muy húmedo montano bajo* and *Bosque pluvial montano bajo* — submontane rain forests; *Bosque muy húmedo montano* and *Bosque pluvial montano* — montane rain forests. Mangrove data shown in the *Atlas Nacional de Panamá* appear to be incomplete. Larger scale (1: 250,000) information has therefore been added from a dyeline map, *Republica de Panama — Inventario de Manglares,* produced in five sheets by the Instituto Geografico Nacional "Tommy Guardia" (1988).

Data for the protected areas of Panama have been digitised from a dyeline map which accompanies a report *La Cobertura Boscosa de Panamá* (1990), *Instituto Nacional de Recursos Naturales Renovables* (INRENARE). The map, showing *'Reservas Forestales'* and *'Areas Silvestres Protegidas',* has been prepared by the *Oficina de Cartografía del Instituto Nacional de Recursos* at a scale of 1:1 million.

24 Bolivia

Country area   1,098,580 sq. km
Land area   1,084,390 sq. km
Population (mid-1994)   8.2 million
Population growth rate   2.7 per cent
Population projected to 2025   14.3 million
GNP per capita (1992)   US$680
Forest cover for 1992 (see Map)   451,426 sq. km
Forest cover for 1990 (FAO, 1993)*   419,670 sq. km
Annual deforestation rate (1981–1990)*   1.2 per cent
Industrial roundwood production   256,000 cu. m
Industrial roundwood exports   —
Fuelwood and charcoal production   1,377,000 cu. m
Processed wood production   114,000 cu. m
Processed wood exports   93,000 cu. m
* excluding the dry deciduous formation

Bolivia's forests rank twelfth in the world in terms of area. They contain important reserves of valuable wood, but logging is very selective and timber contributes little to the country's economy. Exports of unprocessed timber are banned. As in most Latin American countries, expansion of agriculture and colonisation are the main causes of deforestation in Bolivia.

The system of protected areas is far from adequate, but there are proposals to remedy this. Conservation of the country's biodiversity is becoming an increasingly important concern to Bolivians.

INTRODUCTION

Bolivia is a landlocked state situated in the central western part of South America. A wide range of geographical, physiographical and climatic factors, linked to its intertropical position and the presence of the Andes, gives rise to a great variety of landscapes. These range from tropical lowland forests to high, permanently snow-covered mountains and from semiarid, deserts to forests with an annual rainfall up to 6000 mm.

The country forms part of two of the largest South American basins, those of the Paraná and Amazon, and includes an extensive area of the High Andean Plateau, the Altiplano. The Amazon Basin covers two thirds of Bolivia (724,000 sq. km); the Paraná Basin, covers 229,500 sq. km or 21 per cent of the country; and the Altiplano accounts for the remaining 145,080 sq. km (Montes de Oca, 1989). The Altiplano Intercordillera is a broad expanse of interior basins and valleys with a mean elevation of 3800 m. It is bordered on one side by the Western Cordillera and on the other by the Eastern Cordillera and Sub-Andean ranges. Approximately one third of the country is mountainous; the highest peak, Volcán Sajama at 6520 m, is in the Western Cordillera on the border with Chile. The other two thirds of Bolivia are relatively level or with low relief, mostly less than 500 m in elevation and sloping gently from south to north. A few isolated mountains occur in the eastern portion of Santa Cruz Department.

The latitudinal variations produce wide north-south climatological differences. There is a typical tropical region in the northernmost part of the country, a subtropical-temperate region in the south and a wide transitional zone between them. In the subtropical-temperate region, summers are very hot and winters are relatively cold (Ribera, 1992). The low-lying areas of the Amazon Basin are warm and damp throughout the year, with heavy rainfall from November to March. The altiplano is generally dry between May and November and the nights are coldest in June and July. Annual rainfall in the driest areas is less than 100 mm, while the wettest areas receive up to 6000 mm (Solomon, 1989).

According to the preliminary results of the 1992 Population and Housing Census, Bolivia has a population of 6,300,000, giving a population density of 5.7 inhabitants per sq. km, one of the lowest in Latin America (INE, 1992). The higher figure for Bolivia's population given at the head of this chapter is an estimate from the Population Reference Bureau (1994), but even this gives a population density of only 7.6 people per sq. km.

The growth rate of Bolivia's population is 2.7 per cent per year, with annual urban population growth averaging 4.1 per cent and rural populations decreasing at a rate of −0.01 per cent each year. The increasing rural to urban migration is a result of economic problems, which are particularly affecting the Altiplano and Andean valleys (INE, 1992). Donoso (1992) indicates that around 42 per cent of the population live in rural areas, while PRB (1994) gives the higher figure of 58 per cent. The urban population is concentrated in three cities: La Paz, Santa Cruz and Cochabamba.

Bolivia is a multiethnic and pluricultural country. The native Andean inhabitants are the Quechuas (1.5 million) and the Aymaras (1 million); these two groups have been most exposed to Hispanic and Creole cultures. There are, in addition, other, less numerous indigenous peoples such as the Urus, Chipayas, Jruhitos and Muratos (Marconi and Donoso, 1992; Martínez and Carvajac, 1985).

Indigenous forest peoples live in eastern Bolivia. There are between 130,000 and 200,000 of them, grouped into 38 ethnic groups belonging to 10 linguistic families. The most numerous are the Ava Izoceños (38,500) and the Chiquitanos (28,300). The Tacanas, Guarayos, Ignacianos, Trinitario Arawaks, Itonamas and Chimanes, each consist of 5000 to 8000 individuals. Many of these people are nomadic or semi-nomadic and depend on harvesting, hunting, fishing and itinerant agriculture for their livelihood (Arango, 1989).

Bolivia's main exports are minerals and hydrocarbons, the latter have been important since the 1970s. In 1991, these two accounted for 69 per cent of total exports and earned US$652 million for the country. Coffee and sugar are the main agricultural exports.

The Forests

Bolivia's forests are characterised by a great structural complexity and an enormous diversity of flora, much of which has not yet been scientifically described. However, Tim Kelleen and collaborators at the Herbario National are working on a book about the genera of trees in Bolivia and this should provide much valuable information. The forests cover mountain areas, known as "Yungas" and sub-andean regions, as well as vast lowland regions.

Brockmann's (1978) *Mapa de Cobertura y Uso de la Tierra* (Map of Forest Cover and Land Use), prepared on the basis of LANDSAT imagery, is the most accurate cartographic representation of Bolivia's forest cover. Brockmann classified the forests according to their distribution across highlands (over 3000 m), lands of intermediate heights (between 500 and 3000 m) and lowlands (below 500 m). He distinguished between evergreen and semi-evergreen dense moist forests. The description below of the forests in the country is based on the work of Ribera (1992) who combines and integrates the maps and classification systems developed by different authors, including Brockmann.

EVERGREEN FORESTS

a. Highland forests

Situated in the Yungas region, these forests make up the upper layer of the very moist cloud forest and Yungas montane semi-moist forest. The trees, of medium height and with twisted branches, are covered with epiphytes. There are many species with small, leathery leaves (Ericaceae and Myrtaceae) as well species from the Lauraceae family. Trees of *Brunellia*, *Clusia* and *Weinmannia* occur.

b. Forests at intermediate elevations

These forests, rich in species, are in a very advanced state of degradation. They include the intermediate and lower layers of the Yungas forests: cloud forest, semi-moist Yungas forest and moist Yungas forest. The trees do not exceed 20 metres in height. The undergrowth is dominated by Gramineae in the genus *Chusquea*. At lower elevations, these forests resemble lowland formations, but have a greater number of palm trees, treelike ferns (*Alsophila* sp.) and Moraceae in the genus *Cecropia*.

The sub-andean rain forest is a dense multi-strata formation. It is taller than the Yungas forests and is more diverse. Palms and species with buttressed roots are common. Dominant species include *Ceiba pentandra*, *Clarisia racemosa*, *Dipteryx alata*, *Gallesia integrifolia*, *Hura crepitans*, *Sloanea fragrans*, *Spondias mombin* and *Iriartea deltoidea*.

c. Lowland forests

These are dense, multi-layered forests containing a great variety of species; buttress roots are a typical structural characteristic. The canopy is around 30 m high with emergent trees of more than 40 m in height. Palm trees are often found in the intermediate layer.

In the Amazonian moist forest there are two tree species of great regional economic importance: the rubber tree *Hevea brasiliensis* and the Brazil nut *Bertholletia excelsa*. The flora of the Beni plain moist forest includes a large number of species that are widely distributed in the Amazon, as well as others of importance from the Chaco-cerrado region. Those formations which are subject to extended periods of flooding have relatively low biological diversity, tending to have fewer plants and little variety in their flora and structure.

SEMI-EVERGREEN FORESTS

a. Forests at intermediate elevations

The canopy exceeds 20 m in height; there are emergent trees reaching above 30 m in height. The composition of the semi-moist forest of the Chiquitan mountain area gives evidence of its highly intermediate nature, with species from the Amazon, the Chaco and the cerrado.

The semi-moist forest of the Sub-Andean strip, which constitutes the lower layer of the Tucumán-Bolivian forest, contains species from the Lauraceae and Myrtaceae family; the family Bignoniaceae is common. Epiphytes, especially Bromeliaceae, are abundant.

b. Lowland forests

The semi-evergreen lowland forests are tall and very diverse, the canopy has an average height of 30 m, with emergents often exceeding 40 m in height. Buttress roots are common on large trees. Brazilian mahogany *Swietenia macrophylla* occurs in many of these forests.

The semi-moist forest of the Beni plain has only relict areas of precious woods. The palm *Orbignya phalerata* dominates some forests. Bolivia's lowland forest also include the very humid foothill forest and the Amazonian semi-moist forest. Not much is known about the floristic composition of the latter. Its structure seems to resemble that of the moister forest in the northern region, but it has a greater number of deciduous species.

DRY FORESTS

Bolivia's dry, open forests are continuous with the xerophytic Chaco formation of western Paraguay and northern Argentina (Solomon, 1989) and, as such, they have not been shown on Map 24.1 nor included in the statistics. However, their position is shown on Figure 24.1. Common genera include *Aspidosperma*, *Bulnesia*, *Celtis*, *Prosopis*, *Schinus* and *Schinopsis*. The dry forest zone covers an area of 230,000 sq. km but the vegetation is generally very degraded and altered so that forest covers only 50 per cent, or thereabouts, of the zone.

Forest Resources and Management

According to Brockmann's (1978) map, Bolivia's total forest cover in 1978 was 564,684 sq. km, that is, 51.4 per cent of the nation's land area. On the basis of this map and using the work of Ribera (1992) and others, Bolivia's Conservation Data Centre (CDC) has estimated the area of dense moist forest to be 454,197 sq. km (Table 24.1). FAO (1993) estimates the slightly lower total of 419,670 sq. km, with 355,820 sq. km of this in the moist deciduous forest zone and 63,850 sq. km in the hill and montane forest zone. In addition FAO (1993) reports 73,460 sq. km of forest in the dry deciduous zone, this is the the chaco-type formation so has not been included in the statistics at the top of the chapter. The area of closed broadleaved forest in Bolivia is given by FAO (1993) as 407,850 sq. km.

Figure 24.1 shows the forest types as distinguished by CDC-Bolivia, including the dry open forests, and Table 24.1 gives CDC's figures for the areas of the different dense moist forest

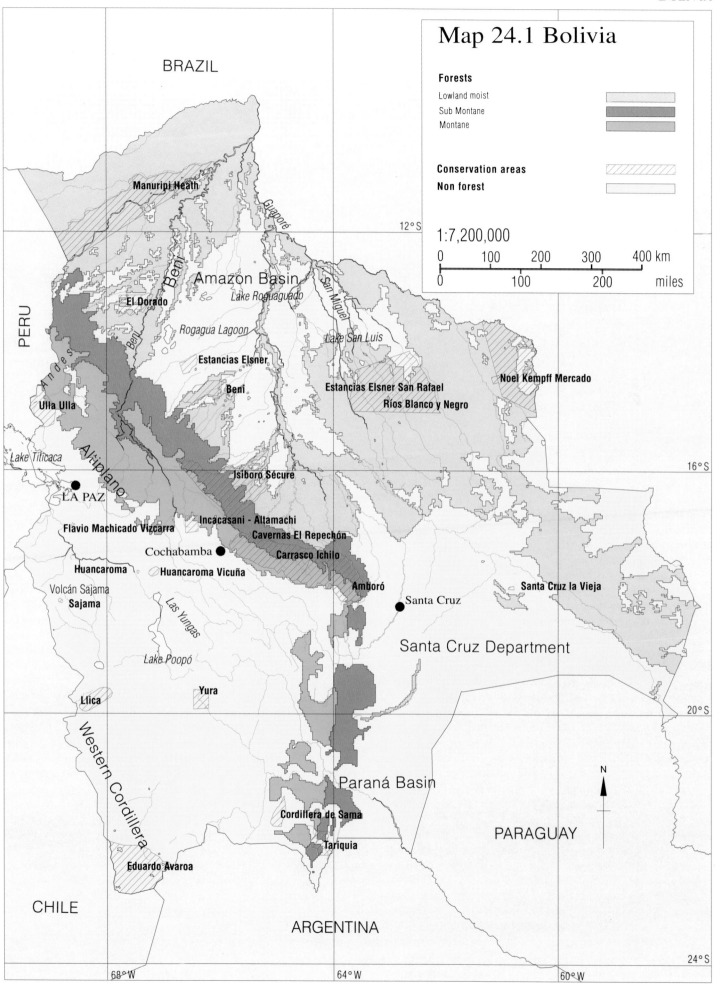

Map 24.1 Bolivia

Forests
Lowland moist
Sub Montane
Montane

Conservation areas
Non forest

1:7,200,000

0   100   200   300   400 km

0   100   200   miles

BRAZIL

Manuripi Heath

Guaporé

Beni

Amazon Basin

El Dorado

Lake Roguaguado

PERU

Rogagua Lagoon

San Miguel

12°S

Estancias Elsner

Lake San Luis

Andes

Beni

Estancias Elsner San Rafael

Noel Kempff Mercado

Ulla Ulla

Ríos Blanco y Negro

Lake Titicaca

Altiplano

16°S

Isiboro Sécure

LA PAZ

Flavio Machicado Vizcarra

Incacasani - Altamachi

Cavernas El Repechón

Cochabamba

Carrasco Ichilo

Huancaroma

Huancaroma Vicuña

Amboró

Santa Cruz la Vieja

Volcán Sajama

Santa Cruz

Sajama

Las Yungas

Santa Cruz Department

Lake Poopó

Yura

20°S

Llica

Western Cordillera

Paraná Basin

N

Cordillera de Sama

PARAGUAY

Tariquia

Eduardo Avaroa

CHILE

ARGENTINA

24°S

68°W   64°W   60°W

BOLIVIA

Table 24.1 Area of Dense Moist Forests in Bolivia as shown on Figure 24.1

Forest Type	Area (sq. km)
EVERGREEN FOREST	320,705
Cloud forest	11,567~
Yungas semi-moist forest	16,525~
Yungas moist forest	41,264~
Subandean rain forest	31,332+
Amazonian moist forest	97,327*
Beni plain moist forest	99,867*
Riverine forest	19,741*
Brazilian Shield moist forest	3,082*
SEMI-EVERGREEN FOREST	133,492
Chiquitano semi-moist forest	10,432*
Subandean semi-moist forest	15,837+
Beni plain semi-moist forest	90,698*
Very moist foothill forest	13,890+
Amazonian semi-moist forest	2,635*
Total	454,197

* Lowland forest 323,782
\+ Sub-montane forest 61,059
~ Montane forest 69,356

Source: CDC-Bolivia (unpublished)

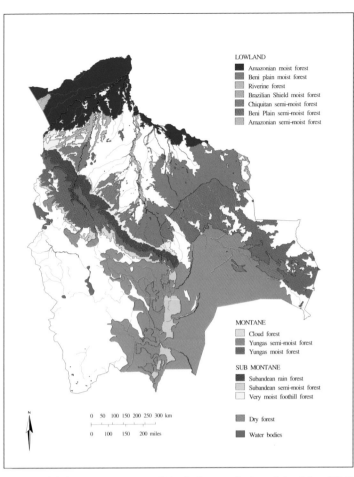

Figure 24.1 Forest types of Bolivia, as distinguished by CDC Bolivia — including the dry open forest formations

types. The forest types in Table 24.1 have been amalgamated into the categories used in this atlas, i.e. into lowland, sub-montane and montane forest and are shown in this form on Map 24.1. Table 24.2 shows the areas of these three forest types as measured from Map 24.1. The slight variation between the figures for forest area in Tables 24.1 and 24.2 are caused by differences in measuring techniques.

The use and management of forest resources are regulated by Bolivia's General Forest Act (D.L. 11686 of 1974), with some additional regulations imposed by the more recent "Pausa Ecológica Histórica" (S.D. 22407 of 1990). The Forest Act established the Centre for Forest Development (CDF) as a decentralized unit, dependent on the Ministry of Rural and Agricultural Affairs (MACA), with full power to protect and manage the forest system. It was to be involved in "*all rules governing the use, marketing, industrialization, management, monitoring and control, research, protection and conservation of forests or equivalent vegetation cover*". Most forests are currently placed in one of five categories — permanent production, permanent protection, closed forest reserve, special forest or multiple-use forest, although some remain unclassified.

According to the prevailing legislation, forest use must be based on management plans and take place in the permanent production forests (Table 24.3). In reality, these production areas are not being appropriately managed and there have been cases of irregular and unsustainable extractive activities. In addition, 70 per cent of the areas under forestry concession, allocated by the State for timber extraction, are situated outside these production forests. The concessions cover approximately 205,000 sq. km (MACA-CDF-SEGMA, 1990).

Forests with the greatest potential productivity are distributed across the moist, very moist and supermoist areas of the tropical and subtropical regions, covering approximately

290,000 sq. km. In addition to their high species diversity, these forests have a large biomass, the commercial timber volume of which is estimated at between 50 and 200 cu. m per hectare. Some especially rich stands contain double this volume (Tosi, 1987).

Despite their great potential, the contribution of forests to the national economy is slight. In terms of Gross National Product, their contribution has always been less than 3 per cent. Nevertheless, there are some regions where the forests are relatively more important.

Logging is selective, focusing on only very few species. Indeed, less than 20 per cent of Bolivia's native species are marketable either nationally or internationally. In the last 10 years, the greatest volume of trade has been in mara *Swietenia macrophylla*, ochoó *Hura crepitans*, roble *Amburana cearensis*, cedro *Cedrela* spp., palo maría *Calophyllum* spp., yesquero *Cariniana* spp., bibosi *Ficus* spp. and tajibo *Tabebuia* spp.

Table 24.2 Estimates of forest extent in Bolivia

Forest types	Area (sq. km)	% of land area
Lowland moist	321,013	29.6
Sub Montane	61,165	5.6
Montane	69,248	6.4
Total	451,426	41.6

Based on analysis of Map 24.1. See Map Legend on p. 228 for details of sources.

Table 24.3 Permanent Production Forests in Bolivia

Name	Year of Creation	Location (Dept.)	Area (sq. km)
Quinera del Atén	1977	La Paz	200
Chimanes	1986	Beni	4200
Bajo Paraguá	1988	Santa Cruz	33882
El Chore	1966	Santa Cruz	8000
Guarayos	1969	Santa Cruz, Beni 1	4000
Total			60282

The technology used by the Bolivian timber industry is relatively simple. The sawmill industry has a capacity for approximately 1.3 million cu. m of logs, but at present only 30 per cent of this capacity is used. More than half of the wood sawn in the country is Brazilian mahogany. This together with *Amburana cearensis* and *Hura crepitans* represent 90 per cent of the total. Sawn timber accounts for 90 per cent of processed wood exports.

There is only limited manufacture of finished products such as parquet, panels, plywood and furniture. The annual capacity for the production of panels is 300,000 cu. m and for plywood 45,000 cu. m, however only 20 per cent of this capacity is used. In addition, there are two recycling plants, which manufacture lavatory paper, and one plant for processing pulp for writing paper.

There has been a substantial increase in the use and export of non-timber forest products in the last few years. In 1990, Brazil nuts accounted for 75 per cent of the exports; other important products were the cochineal bug *Dactylopius coccus* and rubber from *Hevea brasiliensis*. These three products accounted for about 32 per cent of total exports in the forest sector.

Bolivia's forest products compete poorly in international markets because the country lacks access to the sea and consequently high transportation costs are incurred. The production of sawn timber is not subsidised and only minor incentives exist for manufactured products (MACA-CDF-FAO, 1989). The number of firms involved in the forest industry is decreasing due to the depressed and limited markets for their products and to the high cost of raw materials (MACA-CDF-FAO, 1989).

Although the Forest Act is one of the most complete in Latin America, there is little enforcement capacity and its effectiveness has been limited by lack of funds and qualified personnel. In general, the forest industries lack management and do not use resources sustainably. Indeed, as the main source of finance for the Centre for Forest Development is the collection of forest dues, there is a tendency to encourage over-exploitation of the forest. In addition, forests which are part of conservation units or protected areas are frequently subject to officially approved colonization and logging schemes.

There is little coordination between the Instituto Nacional de Colonización (INC), the Instituto de Reforma Agraria (IRA) and other land use agencies. This results in duplication and conflict, which is detrimental to forest conservation. In addition, the CDF is not the only body concerned with forestry. The Regional Development Corporations (CORDES) are also involved and they too earn some of their income from forest dues. Several other bodies, such as the National Forest Chamber (CNF — Cámara Nacional Forestal), universities and a few NGOs are also involved with forest sector development.

The Economic and Social Development Strategy (1989–2000) aims to generate foreign currency through an increase in sawn timber exports. It provides for improved resource use and increased domestic processing foreign markets. The recently promulgated General Environment Act (Law 1333 of 1992) established the National Environment Secretariat (SENMA) to coordinate and monitor all environment-related activities, including forestry. The sustainable use of forests is a national priority in the General Environment Act.

Deforestation

Estimates of deforestation in Bolivia vary considerably. The study carried out by Stolz (1986) quotes figures of 460 sq. km from Stolz (1978), 850 sq. km from Lanly (1980) and 890 sq. km from FAO (1983) cleared annually. Many authors, without mentioning sources, refer to an annual deforestation rate of 0.35 per cent, which gives the much higher area of almost 2000 sq. km cleared in a year. Using the figure of 0.35 per cent, would mean that approximately 28,000 sq. km or 4.9 per cent of the 564,684 sq. km of forest land estimated by Brockmann in 1978 would have been lost by 1992. FAO (1993) reports an enormous annual deforestation between the years of 1981 and 1990; in the moist deciduous zone 4411 sq. km are cleared each year, while in the hill and montane zone, 920 sq. km are deforested. This gives an annual total of 5331 sq. km and a rate of 1.2 per cent. The estimate of annual deforestation in the dry deciduous forest zone is 916 sq. km (FAO, 1993).

Studies carried out within the framework of the Cooperative Agreement between the Instituto Nacional de Investigaciones Espaciales del Brasil (INPE) and the Centro de Investigaciones y Estudio de la Capacidad de Uso Mayor de la Tierra de Bolivia (CUMAT), on the basis of Landsat-TM imagery and topographic maps, using high technology scientific instruments, show a mean annual deforestation rate of 801 sq. km for the Bolivian Amazon over the period 1985–1990 (CUMAT, 1992).

The main causes of the deforestation are agricultural expansion, colonisation and logging. Conversion of forest to agriculture is likely to increase still further as the country's Development Strategy includes the allocation of new land for crops. In addition, Bolivia's agricultural development policies require the conversion of natural forests for land ownership rights to be maintained.

Official colonisation schemes have encouraged many people to migrate from the highlands into forested areas (see Chapter 7). These people are not familiar with the ecological conditions

Tree ferns in Bolivian rain forest. (WWF/U. Hirsch)

COMMUNITY FORESTRY DEVELOPMENT IN THE ANDES

Despite the ecological and socio-economic diversity of the Andean countries, the problems of small farmers throughout the region are quite similar. Over-exploitation of forests and soils have caused erosion, a steady decline in incomes, a deterioration in nutrition and health and social upheaval within the family and the community.

Community forestry promises to improve the situation throughout the Andes. Community forestry refers to all forestry activities that are planned and carried out with and by the rural population for their own benefit. Several aid organisations execute field projects in the highlands of Peru, Ecuador and Bolivia and in the coffee producing zone in Colombia. FAO is operating two projects at the regional level to promote and consolidate these community forestry initiatives.

Farmers are motivated and trained to incorporate trees into their farming systems. Contrary to the belief that trees compete with crops and pasture, farmers are shown that with simple techniques like wind breaks and with the right selection of species, the yields actually increase. The trees protect the animals and crops against harsh climatic conditions (sun, frost, wind) and maintain hydrological functions. Trees are also used to stop erosion of terraces, ditches and drainage canals.

Some common and useful native woody species in the Andes

Species (local name)	Family	Altitudinal range and characteristics	Major uses
*Alnus jorullensis** (aliso)	Betulacea	2600–3800 m asl; fast–growing, 15–20 m high nitrogen–fixing trees	timber, firewood, charcoal, windbreak, soil improvement, silvo–pasture, river stabilization, medicine
Baccharis spp. (chilca)	Asteraceae	up to 4200 m asl; up to 2 m high, frost-resistant bushes	firewood, homestead plantations, frost protection, soil protection, compost
Buddleja spp.* (quishar, c'olle)	Buddlejacea	2500–4200 m asl; 20 m high, frost-resistant trees	timber, firewood, windbreaks, frost protection, soil protection, compost
Erythrina spp. (guato, pajuro)	Fabaceae	900–3400 m asl; to 6 m high, nitrogen-fixing bushes or trees	timber, forage, fruits, homestead plantation, soil improvement
Juglans neotropica (nogal)	Juglandaceae	1000–3000 m asl; trees up to 30 m in height	timber, fruits, homestead plantation, soil improvement
Podocarpus spp. (romerillo)	Podocarpaceae	1000–3000 m asl; trees up to 30 m in height	timber, homestead plantations, ornamental
Polylepis spp.* (qenua' q'eñua)	Rosaceae	2800–4800 m asl; frost-resistant trees, up to 25 m high	timber, firewood, charcoal, frost protection, soil protection, silvo–pasture, medicine
Prunus serotina (capulí)	Rosaceae	2100–3900 m asl; trees up to 15 m in height	timber, firewood, charcoal, fruits, windbreak
Sambucus peruviana (sauco)	Caprifoliaceae	2800–3900 m asl; trees or bushes up to 12 m in height	timber, fruits, windbreak, erosion control along rivers and slopes, medicine
Schinus molle (molle)	Anarcardiceae	2100–3900 m asl; trees up to 15 m in height	firewood, charcoal, medicine, soil improvement, river stabilization, ornamental, insect repellant, perfume
Vallea stipularis (sacha capulí)	Elaecorpaceae	2200–3900 m asl; trees up to 18 m in height	timber, firewood, dyes, forest & homestead plantations, medicine

* The most important native species used in agroforestry above 300 m

Source: Henk Remme and Charles Kenny Jordon

The farmers, whose time and labour is precious, like to see quick results. Therefore not only is the choice of techniques crucial, but also the selection of tree species. These should be well adapted to the environment, grow fast, help improve soil fertility and provide products such as firewood, wood for construction, fruits, forage and medicines. The most used and successful native species that have these characteristics are *Buddleja incana* and *B. coriacea*, *Alnus jorullensis* and *Polylepis incanca* and *P. racemosa* (see Table).

Economic benefits are a crucial factor in motivating the small farmers to produce trees. Besides the direct sale of tree products, communities are helped to establish small forestry industries for the production of charcoal, furniture, construction materials, handicrafts and household utensils. To launch the process, farmers are helped to set up their own nurseries and plantations and taught how to propagate plants.

Projects use different strategies. Some work with communities, others with families, women's groups or farmers' organizations. The extension methods, used to promote community forestry, are of crucial importance. Contrary to the more conventional approaches that try to transfer knowledge by showing the people "how to do it" in an often top-down manner, community forestry projects involve the farmers in most aspects of the planning and implementation process. This dialogue between the extension workers and the farmers, ensures the promotion of appropriate techniques and species that meet the needs of the people.

From the highlands of Peru to the coffee-producing areas of Colombia, many small farmers are now growing trees, benefiting from their products and increasing their agricultural production and household income. However, progress is not easy. During the years important lessons have been learnt:

- do not promote tree production as an end in itself, but integrate trees into the small farmer's land-use and farming system, supporting soil conservation practices and agricultural production;

- use multi-purpose tree species that grow fast, can easily be propagated, are well adapted to the environment and provide products valued by the local people;

- use a flexible approach that takes into consideration the diversity of farmer's interests, organizations and changing conditions;

- do not use financial or food incentives but try to motivate farmers by linking project activities to their priorities and pursue self-reliance.

The execution of these projects by foreign aid agencies is an important first step. However, it is necessary that national organizations become more involved. In most countries forestry networks, such as FAO's Andean initiative, are now being established to exchange information, upgrade knowledge and coordinate forestry activities.

in their new surroundings and the schemes offer no technical support to assist them. The settlers fell and burn trees and then, when the crop yields drop in two or three years time, they move on to clear another area. Spontaneous colonisation follows the same pattern.

According to figures recently published by the World Bank, colonisation and agricultural expansion are responsible for 70 per cent of deforestation in Bolivia. Goitia and Gutiérrez (1992) believe that these two factors cause as much as 90 per cent of the deforestation.

Timber exploitation also causes a significant amount of forest degradation. Although the impact of selective cutting is not as great as that of forest clearance, poor logging practices cause serious damage to the soil and residual vegetation and reduce the economic value of the remaining forest. In addition, there is considerable illegal, uncontrolled hunting of wildlife to provide food for the timber workers and settlers. The logging roads also open access to colonisers who increase deforestation.

Firewood for domestic and industrial purposes accounts for 80 per cent of the total timber used in the country. This makes a significant contribution to forest degradation, especially in the Andes and Altiplano. An increase in the consumption of fuelwood is anticipated as a result of the rise in price of electricity and oil. Even disregarding the cost, poor roads make it difficult to supply remote rural communities with other forms of energy.

Biodiversity

Bolivia is situated at the confluence of four important South American biomes: Amazonia, chaco, cerrado and Andes. The resulting mix of species and habitats gives rise to a wide variety of ecosystems and great biological diversity in Bolivia. There is particularly high diversity in the areas of Beni, Yungas, Inambari and Guaporé; these are thought by some to be Pleistocene refuge areas (Stolz, 1986).

The country has an exceedingly rich and varied flora: there are 17,000 known species of Angiospermae, 16 of Gymnospermae, 1300 of Pteridophyta, and 1200 of Bryophyta (Moraes and Beck, 1992). As comparatively little collecting has taken place within the country, it is likely that many more species remain to be discovered (Solomon, 1989).

The richest concentration of flowering plants is found in the very moist, subandean and montane cloud forests. Approximately 4000 species of Angiospermae are found in the rain forests of the Andean foothills. The richness decreases as one descends towards the seasonal moist forests of the plain and as one rises to the upper Andean levels (Moraes and Beck, 1992). Local endemics are more common among herbaceous species and shrubs than among trees and lianas, and they occur mainly in the subandean region and foothills.

In the submontane and lowland forests, the families with the greatest number of species are: Leguminosae, Lauraceae, Annonaceae, Rubiaceae, Moraceae, Myristicaceae, Sapotaceae, Meliaceae, Palmae, Euphorbiaceae and Bignoniaceae (Moraes and Beck, 1992). Pteridophytes are more important in the montane moist forests (Yungas), while the 16 species of Gymnospermae are concentrated mainly in the interandean valleys and the Tucumán-Bolivian forest.

One of the most threatened forest species in the country is the Brazilian mahogany; its numbers in lowland forests have been drastically reduced by over exploitation.

Bolivia also has a great diversity of fauna. Potess (1991) ranks it among the twelve richest countries in the world in this

Table 24.4   Conservation Areas in Bolivia

Existing protected areas in IUCN's categories I–IV are listed below. For data on Ramsar sites and Biosphere reserves see Chapter 8.

National Parks

Amboró*	1,800
Carrasco Ichilo*	13,000
Isiboro Sécure*	11,000
Las Barrancas+	3
Llica	975
Noel Kempff Mercado*	9,140
Sajama	299
Santa Cruz la Vieja*	171

Biological Station

Beni*	1,350

National Reserves

Cordillera de Sama	1,085
Eduardo Avaroa*	7,140
Incacasani – Altamachi*	230
Lagunas del beni y Pando+	2,750
Manuripi Heath*	18,840
Noel Kempff Mercado+	219
Ríos Blanco y Negro*	14,000
Tariquia*	2,469
Ulla Ulla*	2,500
Yura	nd

Wildlife Refuges

El Dorado*	1,800
Estancias Elsner Espíritu	700
Estancias Elsner San Rafael*	200
Huancaroma	110

Wildlife Sanctuary

Cavernas El Repechón*	15
Flavio Machicado Vizcarra	0.4

Reserves

Altamachi Vicuña+	1,000
Huancaroma Vicuña	1,404

Total	92,200

*   Area with forest within its boundaries as depicted on Map 24.1.
+   Not mapped
Source: WCMC (unpublished).

respect. Approximately 316 mammal species, 1274 bird species, 208 reptile species, 112 amphibian species and 389 fish species have been identified (Ergueta and Sarmiento, 1992). However, many vertebrate species are endangered or threatened with extinction. Current Bolivian legislation refers to approximately 100 species and CITES lists close to 200 species. The ICBP/IUCN Red Data Book lists 23 globally threatened bird species which occur in Bolivia, of which eight are endemic (Collar *et al.*, 1992). IUCN names an additional 27 mammals, five reptiles, one amphibian, one fish and two butterflies in the list of threatened species occurring in Bolivia (Groombridge, 1993). At least one vertebrate species is known to be extinct in

the country: the chinchilla *Chinchilla lanigera* and it is possible that the endemic fish *Orestias cuvieri* from Lake Titicaca no longer occurs.

Bolivia has 39 per cent of South America's known mammal species. Bats constitute the most numerous group with a total of 100 species. Approximately 10 endemic mammal species are known, mainly Didelphidae (opossums) and rodents (Ergueta and Sarmiento, 1992). Among the mammals requiring conservation action are several primates, including Goeldi's marmoset *Callimico goeldii*, spider monkey *Ateles paniscus*, common woolly monkey *Lagothrix lagothricha* and the howler monkey *Alouatta fusca*; species of Cervidae, such as the marsh deer *Odocoileus dichotomus* and North Andean huemul *Hippocamelus antisiensis*; and species of Mustelidae, such as the threatened giant otter *Pteronura brasiliensis*. Other important mammals for conservation are the spectacled bear *Tremarctos ornatus*, a number of cat species (Andean cat *Felis jacobita*, jaguar *Panthera onca* and margay *Leopardus wiedii*) and the vicuña *Vicugna vicugna*.

Birds are one of the best known faunal groups in the country. Bolivia contains 40 per cent of South America's avifauna and ranks sixth in the Neotropics and seventh in the world (Potess, 1991). The greatest variety of birds, over 600 species, is found in very moist and moist forests, between 400 and 1000 m above sea level. However, most endemics (11 species out of a total of 16 in Bolivia) are found in dry intermontane valleys (Ergueta and Sarmiento, 1992). Priority bird species include the lesser rhea *Pterocnemia pennata*, the horned coot *Fulica cornuta*, the endemic blue-throated macaw *Ara glaucogularis* and the hyacinth macaw *Anodorhynchus hyacinthinus*.

Among the reptiles, snakes are most numerous, with 125 species found mainly in very moist montane forests and moist lowland forests. Eight species of tortoises and five Crocodylia are known to occur in the country. The most endangered reptiles are the black cayman *Melanosuchus niger* and turtles of the *Podocnemis* genus.

The comparatively small number of amphibian species is probably a reflection of the limited number of collections. To date, seven endemic species have been identified, most notably *Epipedobates bolivianus* (Dendrobatidae). The one species listed as threatened by IUCN is the Lake Junin giant frog *Batrachophrynus macrostomus*, which occurs also in Peru.

Conservation Areas

Bolivia's first national park was declared in 1939, although it was not until 1953 that legal protection was instituted (Marconi, 1989), and only recently has this been made more than paper protection. A 1975 law provides for five categories of protected area (national park, wildlife reserve, wildlife refuge, wildlife sanctuary and hunting reserve), but there are no clear definitions of these categories. Indeed, Marconi's study (1989) of the legal foundation for the protected areas showed that it is incomplete, it lacks a clear conceptual framework, has no definitions and no specific objectives. This applies to both the system in general and to the specific management categories. In addition, the regulations are dispersed in a variety of legal texts, which causes confusion in their application.

A proposal to establish A General Law of the Environment is currently being studied in the National Senate. The law will legally establish SENMA, the National Secretariat for the Environment. SENMA will be responsible for managing protected areas, forming a coordinated national system and unifying administration of the protected areas into one organisation.

At present, the Wildlife, National Parks, Hunting and Fishing Department manages national parks and the various wildlife areas, while the Forest Department is responsible for the forest reserves.

Measures are being taken to establish a National Protected Areas System (NPAS), but at present Bolivia does not have an official list of protected areas. The 27 areas listed in Table 24.4 are those listed in IUCN's categories I–IV in the database at WCMC. At present many of the ecosystems and species within the country are not under any form of protection. Moreover, all existing protected areas are disturbed to some degree. If the country's biological diversity is to be conserved, protection of existing conservation areas must be strengthened and new areas need to be established.

Initiatives for Conservation

The rate of degradation and loss of forests, land and water resources, and the consequent loss of biological diversity, is alarming in Bolivia. However, conservation of nature became a truly and increasingly important concern at the beginning of the 1980s.

Programmes for conservation and sustainable development have mostly been initiated by non-governmental organizations. These raised political awareness of the need for improved natural resource management. The Bolivian Conservation Data Centre was established in 1986 to collect and analyse information on the environment and on protected areas and provide this information to the government and relevant national and international organisations (Sandoval *et al.*, 1989).

The recently promulgated General Environment Act recognizes the need for sustainable development practices and has the conservation of biological diversity as one of its fundamental components. This new law initiated an important legislative process which aimed at updating and adapting the country's legal framework. A new Biological Diversity Conservation Bill has been drafted and the Forest Act has been revised.

Several new institutions have been established to manage the environment in Bolivia, of which SENMA is the most important. It is in charge of regulating and monitoring environment-related activities as well as managing the National Protected Area System. SENMA is also coordinating the devel-

opment of Bolivia's Environmental Action Plan, which provides for public consultation and participation in environmental issues. Other organisation include MACA, which is responsible for the management of renewable natural resources, and the National Environment Fund (FONAMA), which coordinates national and international funds for environmental conservation.

A Strategy for the Conservation of Biodiversity and Ecosystems in Protected Areas (FONAMA, 1991) has been developed, with finance from the World Bank's Global Environment Facility. This Strategy serves as a guide for the coordination of other actions regarding the development of protected areas, undertaken by national and international institutions.

Bolivian has a Forestry Action Plan, published in 1989 in cooperation with FAO and other multilateral and bilateral aid agencies. The Plan recognizes the *"need to plan the development of this sector, so that forests may play their part in conserving genetic biodiversity, providing forest products, protecting soils and stabilizing watersheds, in addition to contributing to recreation and tourism"*.

The Plan raises important issues but is not always consistent in addressing them. For example, it identifies the lack of firewood as one of the main priorities for action, but the projects included under the section *Firewood and Energy Action* account for only four per cent of the Plan's total proposed investment. Moreover, as of 1992, approximately half of the projects included have not been funded.

A major attempt to develop sustainable natural forest management was supported by the International Tropical Timber Organization (ITTO) in the Chimanes area. Although important lessons have been learned, the project has been hampered by the limitations of a weak executive body. In addition, economic and social conflicts threaten the future of the programme.

United States Agency for International Development (USAID) has plans to implement a Sustainable Forestry Management Project in Bolivia.

In conclusion, the government's capacity to plan, monitor and regulate the current environmental situation in general, and more specifically that of forests, is still inadequate. The direct and indirect strengthening of government institutions, through cooperative work with the non-governmental sector, is therefore of utmost importance.

References

Arango, R. (1989). *Los Pueblos Indigenas del Oriente Boliviano*. La Paz. 85 pp and annexes. (Policopiado).

Brockmann, C. (Ed.) (1978). *Memoria del Mapa de Cobertura y Uso de la Tierra*. ERTS-GEOBOL, La Paz, Bolivia. Pp. 116.

Collar, N.J., Gonzaga, L.P., Krabbe, N., Madroño Nieto, A., Naranjo, L.G., Parker III, T.A. and Wege, D.C. (1992). *Threatened Birds of the Americas. The ICBP/IUCN Red Data Book*. ICBP, Cambridge, U.K.

CUMAT (1992). *Desbosque de la Amazonia Boliviana, Bolivia*. 13 pp. (Policopiado).

Donoso, S. (1992). La Población Rural en Bolivia. In: *Conservación de la Diversidad Biológica en Bolivia*. Marconi, M. (ed.). Cap. VII: 181–196. CDC-Bolivia.

Ergueta, P. and Sarmiento, J. (1992). Fauna Silvestre de Bolivia: Diversidad y Conservación. En: In: *Conservación de la Diversidad Biológica en Bolivia*. Marconi, M. (ed.). Cap. IV: 113–163. CDC-Bolivia.

FAO (1993). *Forest resource assessment 1990: tropical countries*. FAO Forestry Paper 112. FAO, Rome, Italy.

FONAMA (1991). *Proyecto: Conservación de la Biodiversidad y los ecosistemas en las áreas protegidas de Bolivia*. Fondo Nacional para el Medio Ambiente, La Paz.

Groombridge, B. (Ed) (1993). *1994 IUCN Red List of Threatened Animals*. IUCN, Gland, Switzerland and Cambridge, U.K. 286 pp.

Goitia, L. and Gutiérrez, M. (1992). *El Desarrollo Forestal en Bolivia (1972–1990)*. SEGMA-LIDEMA. 44 pp. and annexes. (Policopiado).

INE (1992). *Censo Nacional de Población y Vivienda, Resultados Preliminares, Bolivia*. Instituto Nacional de Estadistica, La Paz, Bolivia.

MACA-SDF-SEGMA (1990). *Diagnóstico Forestal 1990*. Ministerio de Asuntos Campesinos y Agropecuarios. La Paz, Bolivia. 168 pp.

MACA-CDF-FAO (1989). *Plan de Acción para el Desarrollo Forestal en Bolivia 1990–1995*. 99 pp.

Marconi, M. (1989). *Base Legal del Sistema Nacional de Areas Protegidas. Presentado en el Segundo Taller de la Red*

Boliviana de Parques Nacionales, Otras Areas Protegidas, Flora y Fauna Silvestres. CDC/IT/019/89. La Paz, Bolivia. 44 pp.

Marconi, M. and Donoso, S. (1992). Habitantes en las areas protegidas. In: *Espacios sin Habitantes, Parques Nacionales de América del Sur.* Amend, S. and Amend, T. (eds). IUCN. 497 pp.

Martínez, P. and Carvajac, J. (1985). *Etnias y Lenguas de Bolivia.* Instituto Boliviano de Cultura. 228 pp.

Montes de Oca, I. (1989). *Geografiá y Recursos Naturales de Bolivia.* La Paz. BCB. 628 pp.

Moraes, M. and Beck, S. (1992). Diversidad floristica de Bolivia. In: *Conservación de la Diversidad Biológica en Bolivia.* Marconi, M. (ed.). Cap. III: 73–111. CDC-Bolivia.

Potess, L.F. (1991). (ed.) *Países Neotropicales con "Megadiversidad".* Conservation International, Washington, DC, USA.

PRB (1994). *1994 World Population Datasheet.* Population Reference Bureau Inc., Washington, D.C., U.S.A.

Ribera, M.O. (1992). Regiones Naturales de Bolivia. In: *Conservación de la Diversidad Biológica en Bolivia.* Marconi, M. (ed.). Cap. II: 9–71 CDC-Bolivia.

Sandoval, G.J., Reyes, J.M. and Soria, J.L. (1989). *Plan de Acción para el Desarrollo Forestal 1990–1995.* Ministerio de Asuntos Campesinos y Agropecuarios, Subsecretaria de Recursos Naturales Renovables y Centro de Desarrollo Forestal, La Paz, Bolivia. Pp. 98.

Solomon, J.C. (1989). Bolivia. In: *Floristic Inventory of Tropical Countries: The Status of Plant Systematics, Collections, and Vegetation, plus Recommendations for the Future.* Campbell, D.G. and Hammond, H.D. (eds). The New York Botanical Garden, New York, U.S.A.

Stolz, R. (1986). *Posibilidades de Utilización de los Recursos Forestales Tropicales del Norte y Este de Bolivia Considerando Aspectos Ecológicos.* Unpublished report 310 pp.

Tosi. J. (1987). *Sugerencias para el Desarrollo Racional de los Bosques Naturales Tropicales y Subtropicales de Bolivia.* CUMAT, La Paz, Bolivia. 60 pp.

Authors: Namiko Nagashiro and María Marconi, CDC-Bolivia, La Paz, Bolivia with contributions from James Solomon, Curator of the Herbarium, Missouri Botanical Garden, U.S.A.; Henk Remme and Charles Kenny-Jordon, Desarollo Forestal Participativa en los Andes, FAO, Quito, Ecuador.

Map 24.1   Bolivia

A digital map, entitled *Bolivia-Bosques Humedos Densos*, was kindly made available to WCMC by the Centro de Datos para la Conservacion (CDC)-Bolivia (1992). These data are based on an earlier map, *Mapa de Cobertura y Uso Actual de la Tierra* (Brockmann, 1978), compiled from 1973–1976 LANDSAT images.

The forest types on the source map have been grouped into two main types: 'siempreverde' (evergreen) and 'semi-siempreverde' (semi-evergreen). The following source forest classes have been categorised into the broader forest categories which are being used for this atlas: lowland rain forest comprises *Humedo Amazonico, Humedo Llanura Beniana, Ribereno, Humedo Escudo Brasileno, Semihumedo Chiquitano, Semihumedo Llanura Beni* and *Semihumedo Amazonico*; montane rain forest contains *Nublado de Ceja, Semihumedo Yungas, Humedo Yungas*; submontane rain forest includes *Pluvial Subandino, Semihumedo Subandino* and *Muy Humedo Pie de Monte*. Dry forests (open, xerophytic formations) are not shown on this map but are illustrated in Figure 24.1 and have been obtained from the same data source as the moist forests.

The protected areas spatial data shown on Map 24.1 originate from a digital dataset covering several countries in Latin America, *Latin America Protected Areas Dataset — Version 2*, compiled and provided by the Centro Internacional de Agricultura Tropical, Colombia, in 1992.

25 Brazil

Country area	8,511,970 sq. km
Land area	8,456,510 sq. km
Population (mid-1994)	155.3 million
Population growth rate	1.7 per cent
Population projected to 2025	199.9 million
Gross national product per capita (1992)	US$2770
Forest cover in 1993 (see Maps)	3,415,308 sq. km
Forest cover in 1990 (FAO, 1993)*	5,322,440 sq. km
Annual deforestation rate (1981–1990)	0.6 per cent
Industrial roundwood production	77,714,000 cu. m
Industrial roundwood exports	262,000 cu. m
Fuelwood and charcoal	191,191,000 cu. m
Processed wood production	21,180,000 cu. m
Processed wood exports	1,226,000 cu. m

* excluding forest in the dry deciduous zone

Brazil is the world's fifth largest country and it contains by far the greatest extent of forest in the tropics. Until recently, the country's economy has been rooted firmly along the coastal belt and in the south of the country, while the vast forests of the interior have been of minor importance to the mainstream of society. The clearance of the Atlantic forests on Brazil's coast began almost as soon as Europeans arrived there in the 16th century, but it is only in recent decades that there has been extensive clearance of Brazil's Amazonian forest, much of it for cattle ranches. Virtually all of the development in Amazonia is unsustainable as a source of support for the region's human population, and is also devastating for the biological diversity of the converted areas.

Although the rate of deforestation in Amazonia has fallen since 1988, this is mostly due to the deepening economic recession in the country rather than to any of the changes in government policy. Indeed, the history of government attitudes to its Amazon hinterland has been dominated by the pursuit of self-interest by ruling elites and a persistent failure to recognise economic realities. Now, the country is torn between the conflicting perspectives of the government and those of an increasingly ecologically and socially aware population. As a result, the future of the forests remains unclear.

INTRODUCTION

Brazil is the largest of the tropical countries and the fifth largest in the world. Its coastline covers 7,500 km, from 4°25'N to 33°45'S, along the Atlantic Ocean. The country lacks high mountain ranges: its topography is generally relatively smooth, with 93 per cent of the land below 800 m (FAO/UNEP, 1981). The highest peaks, above 2500 m, are confined to two regions: the northern border with Venezuela (the Guyanas range with the highest peak in the country at 2875 m) and the southeast Atlantic coast. Ab'Saber (1973) recognizes six geographic and macroecologic domains in the country. These are: the forested lowlands of Amazonia (a zone of labyrinthic and meandering flood plains, much of it dissected into valleys); the central plains or *chapadões* (a region of upland massifs, mostly covered with cerrado); the tropical Atlantic area (a hilly region that used to be almost entirely covered with forest); the caatinga (semi-arid, interplateau depressions in the northeast); the araucaria plateaus (between 850 and 1300 m in the southeast); and the domain of mixed subtropical gaucho grasslands (hills and plains, with extensive marshy areas around lakes and lagoons in the southern state of Rio Grande de Sul). More details of these domains can be found in Sick (1993).

Prior to the uplift of the Andes mountains during the Cretaceous, 60 million years ago, the Amazon River flowed west into the Pacific Ocean. With the uplift, the exit to the Pacific was blocked and a large shallow sea formed covering much of the river basin. This then overflowed into the Atlantic, and cut a gorge at the natural barrier at Óbidos — the narrowest point on the river and the only one in the lower Amazon where the entire river flows through a single channel. The landscape rose, and steep river channels were eroded. The land subsequently subsided, creating the characteristic "flooded valleys" of the Amazon today, with each tributary having a wide, deep mouth for several hundred kilometres at its confluence with the Amazon.

The climate in Amazonia is characterized by heavy rainfall, but most of the region has at least some dry period. The majority of the rain is concentrated in a few months, but the rainy season begins and ends relatively gradually (in contrast to the monsoon climates of Asia). The Central Brazilian plateau is much drier than Amazonia, giving rise to the xerophytic vegetation of the cerrado. Heavy rains, often in storms of several hundred millimetres per day, fall along the seaward faces of the coastal mountains in Rio de Janeiro and São Paulo states, where the Atlantic forest used to flourish. In northeastern Brazil the climate is semi-arid, with very severe droughts posing the major limitation to natural vegetation and to agriculture. Rainfall is highly variable from one year to the next, both in Amazonia and in northeastern Brazil. It is the extreme climatic events, rather than the long-term averages, which impose limits on the vegetation and on human use of the areas.

Brazil's human population is very unevenly distributed: most people live along the coast and in the central-south region, while the Legal Amazon (a five million sq. km administrative area encompassing all or part of nine states) covers 60 per cent of the country's land area but has only 10 per cent of its population. However, migration has made Amazonia the fastest growing part of the country, dwarfing the effect of population increase through reproduction. People from northeastern Brazil have been entering the eastern Amazon, especially the Carajás area. Northeasterners fleeing droughts have also gone to south-central Brazil, and the people from that region, especially the state of Paraná, have been moving to the Amazonian state of Rondônia in great numbers since the early 1980s. The best agricultural areas in Rondônia are now fully occupied (Fearnside, 1986a) and population overflow has been moving to Roraima.

About 76 per cent of the population live in cities; the largest in Amazonia are Belém (1992 population of 1.3 million) and Manaus (1 million). The creation of a tax free zone in Manaus in 1967 caused the city to grow at an astounding rate until about 1990, doubling in size every eight years. Brazil's economic crisis has since reduced subsidies to the free zone, resulting in a reduction in employment levels and the return of some of the population to the Amazonian interior. Other cities in the Amazon have grown mainly through migration from outside of the region. In the case of Rondônia, migration has been increasingly from city to city, rather than the countryside to city pattern that predominated in the past.

The economy of Amazonia has long been based on different forms of resource mining, with little concern for sustainability of production (see Fearnside, 1990a). Since the late 1960s, cattle ranching has been a major activity in Amazonia. This is a result of major road construction improving access to the area and the introduction of African grasses to the region. The principal source of income from ranching is often land speculation rather than the sale of beef. Foot and mouth disease prevents beef export in frozen form to Europe, North America and Japan, leaving only the much smaller export markets for canned products to these major consuming areas. The infamous "hamburger connection", which creates devastating commercial pressure for beef production in Central America, has not been a factor in the Amazon. Speculation, combined with a variety of government tax and financial incentives and additional income from sale of timber, has made ownership of large ranches a source of vast fortunes for the few who benefit from this system. In Brazil's Legal Amazon region, 62 per cent of the private land was in properties over 10 sq. km in area at the time of Brazil's last agricultural census in 1985 (Brazil, IBGE, 1989). The predominance of large ranches varies greatly by state; in Mato Grosso 84 per cent of the private land is in ranches of 10 sq. km or more. In general, the distribution of land holdings and other forms of wealth is extremely uneven in the population.

Amazonia has served as a safety valve for social problems in the rest of Brazil, with highway construction and settlement projects being the response to such problems as the 1970 drought in northeastern Brazil (the official justification for building the Transamazon Highway) and the absorption of population outflow from Paraná for paving the BR-364 highway to Rondônia in 1982 with financing from the World Bank's POLONOROESTE Project (see Chapter 7).

Indigenous peoples have inhabited the forest for millennia, and have profoundly influenced the forest itself. Charcoal is found scattered in the soil under supposedly "virgin" forest throughout the Amazon, probably the result of fires set by indigenous shifting agriculturalists. Planted trees influence the composition of the forest, this explains the frequent even-aged concentrations of useful trees such as Brazilnuts *Bertholletia excelsa*. Indigenous occupation has also resulted in patches of anthropogenic black soils ("terra preta do indio") scattered throughout the forest (Smith, 1980).

THE FORESTS

Topography, soils, climate and flood regimes have led to the development of a complex pattern of vegetation types in Brazil. Figure 25.1 shows the country's main forest types, in a less generalised form than on Map 25.1, as well as the drier *cerrado* and *caatinga* formations and other woody vegetation as of the early 1980s.

There are three major forest classes in the country: *Araucaria* forest, Atlantic forest and Amazon forest and these occupy climatically distinct regions.

Araucaria forest

The araucaria or Paraná pine forests, which are (or were, prior to their recent devastation) dominated by the valuable timber tree *A. angustifolia*, occupied the sub-tropical portions of the southern part of Brazil, grading into the "pampas" grasslands in the south and the Atlantic forest in the north. The understorey of the pines contains an abundance of bamboos of the genera *Merostachys* and *Chusquea*, as well as tree ferns. *Podocarpus lambertii* is also common (Sick, 1993).

Atlantic forest

The Atlantic forest, or "Mata Atlântica," occupied not only the coast but also the interior of the state of São Paulo, Espírito Santo and part of Minas Gerais. The forests range in altitude from the coast to around 2000 m and include tropical and sub-tropical formations. As a result, composition of the forests within this area is very variable. In the montane formations, trees may reach 30–40 m high. In the understorey, palmito (*Euterpe edulis*) and tall bamboos occur in great numbers, as do tree ferns (Sick, 1993). Epiphytes are common. The lowland moist forests of eastern Brazil are related both structurally and in species composition to those in Amazonia (Mori, 1989). In the wet lowland forest in southern Bahia, dominant families are Myrtaceae and Lauraceae, followed by Sapotaceae, Leguminosae, Lecythidaceae and Bombacaceae (Mori *et al.*, 1981).

Forest clearance for domestic agriculture in the Una Reserve, Atlantic Coastal forest. (WWF/Juan Pratginestos)

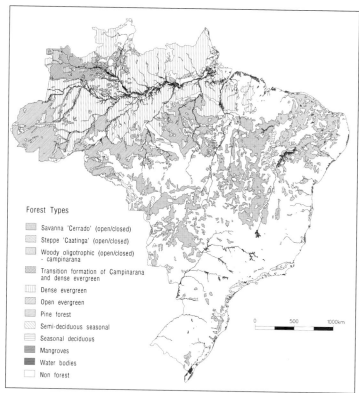

Figure 25.1 Map showing the main forest types in Brazil, as well as the cerrado, caatinga and other woody formations.

Source: IBGE (1988)

Forest Types

- Savanna 'Cerrado' (open/closed)
- Steppe 'Caatinga' (open/closed)
- Woody oligotrophic (open/closed) - campinarana
- Transition formation of Campinarana and dense evergreen
- Dense evergreen
- Open evergreen
- Pine forest
- Semi-deciduous seasonal
- Seasonal deciduous
- Mangroves
- Water bodies
- Non forest

Amazon forest

The vegetation types in Brazilian Amazonia are numerous and complex. They include a wide variety of different forests, with varying appearance in terms of readily apparent features such as the prevalence of vines and palms, as well as more subtle differences in terms of tree species composition. Liana forests can be choked with virtually impenetrable walls of vines, but most forests have more open understoreys. Descriptions of the diverse forest types can be found in Aubreville (1961), Veloso (1966), Brazil, Projeto RADAMBRASIL (1973–83), Pires and Prance (1985) and Daly and Prance (1989), amongst others. The forests are generally divided into two major categories, the *terra-firme*, or dry land forests, and the inundated or flood plain forests. In addition, there are a number of specialised forest types covering more restricted areas. The following, based on Pires and Prance (1985), is a summary of the forest types:

TERRA-FIRME FORESTS

1. **Dense Forests:** These are high biomass forests with a clear understorey. They exist in areas which do not suffer extremes of waterlogging or drought. A very wide variety of plant families are represented and no single group predominates.
2. **Open forests without palms:** These are forests that suffer occasional water stress because of more seasonal climates or special soil conditions. They may also occur in response to poor soil drainage. In general, the upper storeys of the forest are open, while the ground layers are very dense. Scattered individuals of very large trees may occur. No plant species or families predominate.
3. **Open forests with palms:** These are open forest formations frequently having high densities of one or more of the palms babaçu *Orbignya barbosiana*, bacaba *Oenocarpus* spp., pataua *Jessenia bataua*, açai da mata *Euterpe precatoria* and

inaja *Maximiliana regia*. Brazil nuts *Bertholletia excelsa* are often common. In other respects this formation resembles the previous one.

4. **Liana forests:** Extensive areas of these forests, with abundant lianas, occur in southern Amazonia and smaller patches occur elsewhere. They are usually intermixed with other *terra-firme* formations and probably owe their existence to special soil characteristics. The lianas belong mainly to the families Leguminosae Bignoniaceae, Malpighiaceae, Dilleniaceae and Menispermaceae. Large emergent trees often occur, principally *Bertholletia excelsa*, *Hymenaea parvifolia*, *Bagassa guianensis*, *Tetragastris altissima*, *Astronium gracile* and *Apuleia molaris*. Mahogany *Swietenia macrophylla* also occurs, mainly in lower areas along streams.
5. **Dry forests:** These semi-deciduous formations occur in areas with seasonal climates in southeast Brazil and Roraima. In the southeast common trees include *Geissospermum sericeum*, *Cenostigma macrophyllum*, *Physocalymma scaberrima*, *Lafoensia pacari*, *Magonia glabrescens*, *Sterculia striata*, *Erythrina ulei*, *Vochysia haenkeana* and *Orbignya barbosiana*. In Roraima, *Centrolobium paraense*, *Mimosa schomburgkii* and *Richardella surumuensis* are more common.
6. **Montane forests:** In Brazil, this term is used to describe forests growing on rocky soils and steep slopes at quite low elevations. The only true Amazonian "montane" formations in the sense that the term is used in this Atlas, are on the Guayana highlands on the frontier with Venezuela and Guyana. The highest forests in Brazil are found at an altitude of 2600 m in the Sierra Neblina in Roraima. The families Theaceae, Guttiferae and Bromeliaceae are common in these forests. Families such as the Ericaceae, Cunoniaceae, Cyrillaceae, Winteraceae and Podocarpaceae occur in montane formations, but are rare or absent in lowland forests.

INUNDATED FORESTS

7. **Várzea forests:** These are found on sediments that are deposited during annual flooding by the muddy waters originating in the rapidly eroding uplands of the Andes. The soils are therefore more fertile than elsewhere in the Amazon. Scitamineae (gingers, Marantas and heliconias) are abundant. Common trees include *Sclerolobium aureum*, *Couma utilis*, *Exellodendron coriaceum*, *Parinari campestris* and *Euphronia hirtelloides*.

   In the lower Amazon *várzea* soils are heavier clays and support extensive canarana grasslands. Common tree species include *Crataeva benthamii*, *Cordia tetrandra*, *Trichilia singularis*, *Pithecellobium multiflorum*, *Bombax munguba*, *Cecropia* spp. and *Salix martiana*.

   In the estuary of the Amazon below the confluence with the Xingu River, várzeas occur in areas flooded with water backed-up by daily tidal effects, rather than by seasonal rainfall patterns. These várzeas are dominated by a few species of palms, some of which are of great economic importance. Abundant species include *Astrocaryum murumuru*, *Raphia taedigera*, *Euterpe oleracea* (açai) *Maximiliana regia*, *Oenocarpus distichus*, *Jessenia bataua* and *Mauritia* spp.

   Várzeas dominated by pure stands of *Mauritia flexuosa* are found in the estuary of the Amazon River. These formations are known as buritizal.

8. **Igapó forests:** These formations are found in white sands flooded seasonally by mineral-poor black waters originating

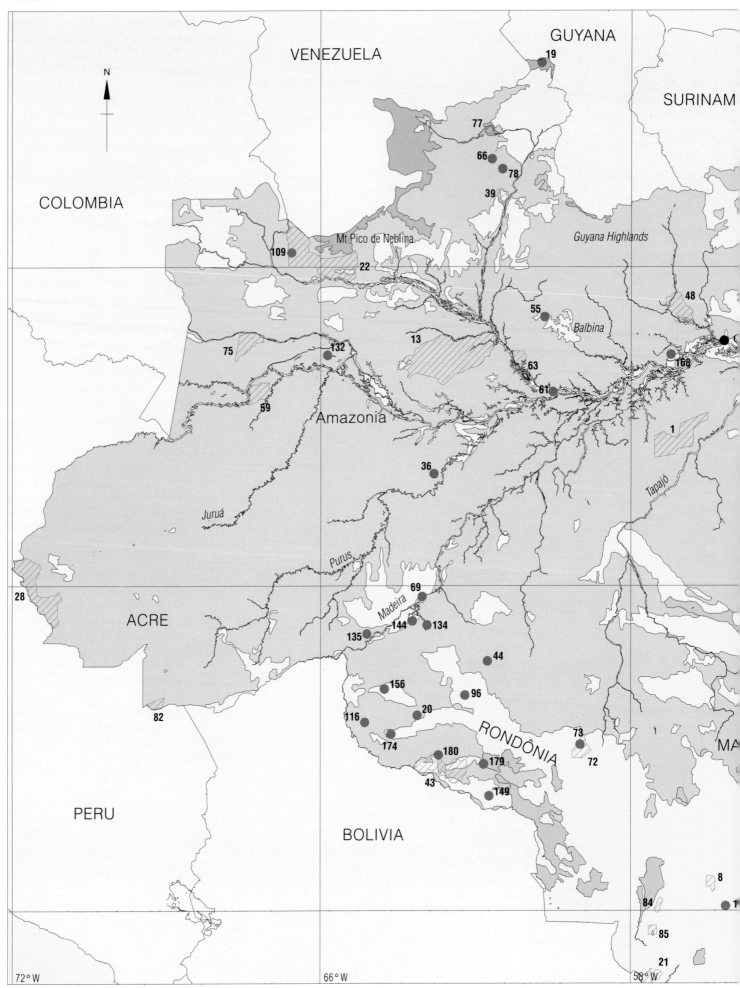

VENEZUELA

GUYANA

19

SURINAM

77

COLOMBIA

66

78

39

Mt Pico de Neblina

Guyana Highlands

48

109

55

Balbina

22

13

75

132

63

168

59

Amazonía

61

1

36

Tapajó

Juruá

Purus

69

Madeira

28

144

134

ACRE

135

44

156

96

20

116

RONDÔNIA

73

174

180

179

72

MA

43

149

PERU

8

84

1

BOLIVIA

85

21

72° W

66° W

58° W

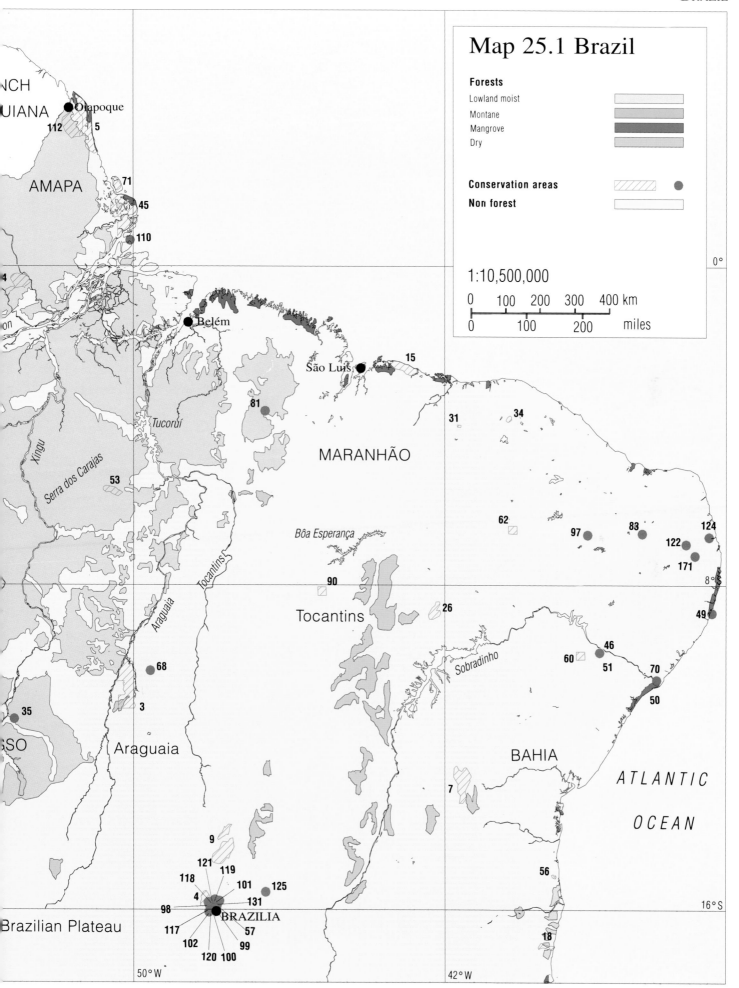

Map 25.1 Brazil

Forests

Lowland moist

Montane

Mangrove

Dry

Conservation areas

Non forest

1:10,500,000

0   100   200   300   400 km

0   100   200   miles

NCH

UIANA

112   5   Oiapoque

AMAPA

71

45

110

Belém

São Luís   15

81

Tucuruí

MARANHÃO

31   34

Xingu

Serra dos Carajás

53

62   97   83   124   122   171

Bôa Esperança

90

Tocantins   26   49

Araguaia

68   46   60   51

Sobradinho   70   50

35

SSO

Araguaia

BAHIA

7

ATLANTIC

OCEAN

9

121   119

118   101   125

4   131

98   BRAZILIA   56

Brazilian Plateau   117   57

102   99

120 100   18

50°W   42°W   16°S

0°

8°S

233

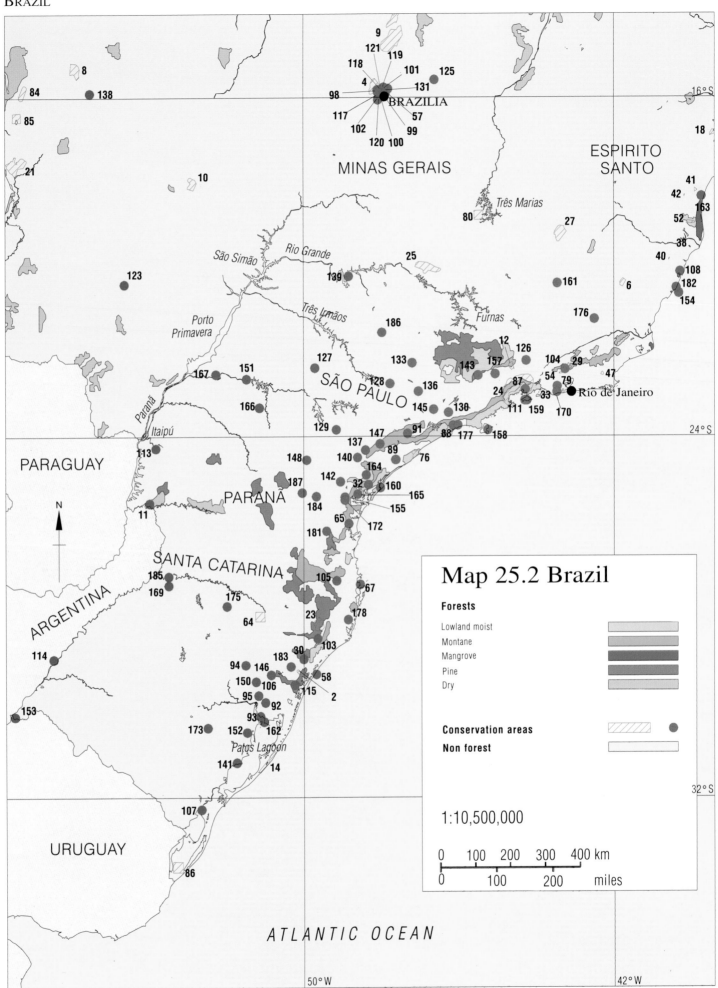

ESPIRITO
SANTO

MINAS GERAIS

Três Marias

São Simão

Rio Grande

Três Irmãos

Furnas

Porto
Primavera

SÃO PAULO

Rio de Janeiro

PARAGUAY

Paraná

Itaipú

PARANÁ

N

SANTA CATARINA

ARGENTINA

Patos Lagoon

URUGUAY

ATLANTIC OCEAN

BRAZILIA

Map 25.2 Brazil

Forests

Lowland moist	
Montane	
Mangrove	
Pine	
Dry	

Conservation areas		●
Non forest		

1:10,500,000

0	100	200	300	400 km

0	100	200	miles

16° S

24° S

32° S

50° W

42° W

in the terra-firme forests, from, for instance, the Guayana Shield. Common trees are members of the Myrtaceae, *Triplaris surinamensis, Piranhea trifoliata, Copaifera martii* and *Alchornea castaniifolia*.

There are two other major woody formations in Brazil — the cerrado and caatinga. Although, in this Atlas, these are not considered to be forest formations a brief description of them is given here.

Cerrado

Cerrado, or central Brazilian scrubland, is a complex of vegetation types characterised by trees with contorted growth forms, thick barks, deep root systems or underground stems (Mori, 1989). This term is now used to refer to a diverse array of savanna-like vegetation (Mori, 1989).

Caatinga

In Amazonia, these occur on nutrient poor white sands where forest development is limited by lack of oxygen in the soil during flood periods and/or lack of water during dry periods. The biomass and stature of the vegetation vary according to local conditions, but caatinga tends to be rather scrubby with a xeromorphic aspect and lack large trees. Characteristic genera include *Barcella, Byrsonima, Clusia, Lissocarpa, Pagamea, Retiniphyllum, Sipapoa, Tovomita* and *Zamia*. The terms *campina, campinarana, charascal* and *charravascal* are used locally for different types of caatingas. The term caatinga is used in northeastern Brazil for a completely different type of arid vegetation.

Mangroves

Mangrove forests are distributed in a patchy fashion along most of Brazil's coast. They extend from Oiapoque in Amapá to Praia do Sonho in Santa Catarina (Kjerfve and Lacerda, 1993; Mori, 1989). Saenger *et al.* (1983) reported that the total area of mangroves in Brazil was 25,000 sq. km, greater than in any other country in the world. However, Kjerfve and Lacerda (1993) consider this a gross overestimate. They regard the area

of 10,124 sq. km, given in Herz (1991), to be more accurate, but possibly a slight underestimate. The figure they propose for the total area of mangrove is 13,800 sq. km (Kjerfve and Lacerda, 1993). Map 25.1 indicates the somewhat higher total of 16,459 sq. km of mangrove remaining in 1992. The principal species are *Avicennia schaueriana, A. germinans, Conocarpus erectus, Laguncularia racemosa* and *Rhizophora mangle*.

In Maranhão, charcoal and firewood demand from the city of São Luis has made steady inroads into the mangrove ecosystem. In both Maranhão and Pará urban development has caused clearance of mangroves. This has been the major destroyer of mangroves elsewhere in Brazil, as in the states of Rio de Janeiro and São Paulo. Frequent oil spills near ports have also devastated many mangroves in São Paulo.

Forest Resources and Management

Of Brazil's 8.5 million sq. km, approximately 5.6 million sq. km (66 per cent) were forested at the time Europeans arrived in the country in 1500; of this, approximately 4 million sq. km still remain as a forest roughly similar to the original. By 1992, the Atlantic forest had shrunk to only 9.2 per cent of its original 1,090,000 sq. km area (Figure 25.2), while Brazil's Amazonian forests still had 90 per cent of their original 4.3 million sq. km area (Table 25.1). The *Araucaria* forests virtually disappeared in the space of a few decades under pressure from logging and conversion to agriculture: of the area present in 1900, less than half remained by 1950 and less than 20 per cent by 1991 (Table 25.1). Table 25.1 also gives estimates of the original and present extent of the cerrado and caatinga formations in Brazil.

FAO (1993) estimates that there is as much as 5,322,440 sq. km of forest in Brazil — this is excluding the 288,630 sq. km of forest reported to occur in the dry deciduous zone. However, only 3,871,210 sq. km of this is closed broadleaved forest. Measurements from Map 25.1 indicate that there is total of 3,227,210 sq. km of forest in the country as of 1992 (see Map Legend), rather less than that reported by FAO or that given in Table 25.1.

Table 25.1 Status of major vegetation types in Brazil

Class	Vegetation type	Original area (sq. km)	Estimate of recent area (sq. km)	Per cent remaining	Year of estimate	Source
Forest	Amazonian	4,300,000	3,870,000	90.0	1991	1
	Atlantic	1,090,000	100,000	9.2	1992	2
	Araucaria	160,000	30,000	18.8	1991	3
Non-forest	Cerrado	2,010,000	1,260,000	62.7	1985	3
	Caatinga and other semi arid	1,550,000	730,000	47.1	1991	3
	Pantanal	140,000	?	?		4

Sources: 1. Fearnside *et al.* (nd); 2. Fundaçion S.O.S. Mata Atlantica (1992); 3. Brazil, CIMA, (1991a); 4. Brazil, CIMA (1991b).

NOTES

There are some inconsistencies in the definition of original forest area used here (Table 25.1), and that used in the deforestation estimate (Tables 25.3 and 25.4). The deforestation estimate used a line between forest and non-forest drawn by INPE from LANDSAT-TM 1:250,000 scale images with some reference to the RADAMBRASIL vegetation maps (but without a list of the vegetation types classified as forest and non-forest). The area so defined has not yet been measured by INPE, but a compilation by map sheet (using IBGE 1:250,000 scale maps as a geographical base) was made of the approximate proportions of forest and non-forest in each sheet. The total from this compilation is 4,000,000 sq. km, lower than the 4,300,000 sq. km measured from the IBDF/IBGE 1.5,000,000 scale map.

The "present" vegetation is also inconsistent: the IBDF/IBGE mapping totals 3,700,000 sq. km of forest (circa 1988), whereas the original forest area from the same map, less the area deforested by 1988, yields a total of 3,900,000 sq. km.

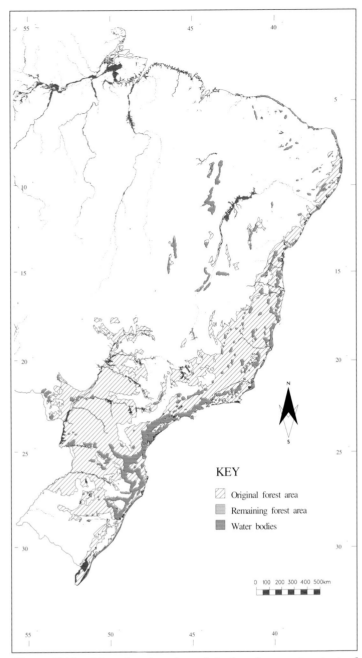

Figure 25.2 Map showing the original and present extent of Atlantic forest

Source: Information derived from an Atlantic Forest Atlas compiled by INPE, IBAMA and SOS Atlantic Forest Foundations (no reference)

KEY

▨ Original forest area
▨ Remaining forest area
■ Water bodies

0 100 200 300 400 500km

"forestry management plans" as a condition for granting logging permits. However, effectiveness of the programme is hindered by lack of guidelines as to what constitutes sustainable management and by frequent differences between stated plans and field practices. Insufficient as they are, the management plans are better than the unfettered exploitation that would result from the proposals of logging interests intent on abolishing the requirements.

It should be mentioned that the underlying logic of increasing profits to loggers as a tool to encourage sustainable management is not supported by observed behaviour. Rather than restraining harvest intensity with a view to long-term returns, cutting is increased to capture short-term profits. The explanation of the lack of interest in commercial application of sustainable management systems lies mainly in the existence of alternative investment opportunities that pay higher returns on money invested than does waiting for future cycles of a long-term management system. The key comparison is between forest management and other possible uses of **money**, not between forest management and other uses of **land**. This is because money obtained by cutting all saleable timber from the forest as quickly as possible can be freely invested anywhere in the wider economy (Fearnside, 1989a).

What is known in Brazil as "extractivism," or the harvesting of non-wood forest products without cutting down the trees, has been practised in the Amazonian interior since the rubber boom (1888–1913). These systems now form the basis for proposals for "extractive reserves" as a means of maintaining forest (Allegretti, 1990; Fearnside, 1989b). The major justification for promoting the system is its potential for safeguarding environmental services of the forest, as the resident extractivists have a greater stake in defending the forest against ranchers, squatters and loggers than do hired guards (see box in Chapter 8).

The number of sawmills and level of timber extraction activity in Brazil has increased dramatically in recent years, but is still much less than in Asia. This is because southeast Asian forests are characterized by a higher density of commercially valuable trees. They are dominated by a single plant family, the Dipterocarpaceae, making it possible to group the vast number of individual tree species into only a few categories for the purposes of sawing and marketing. In addition, most Asian woods are light in colour, making them more valuable in Europe and North America where consumers are accustomed to light woods such as oak and maple. Asian woods are also usually of lower density than Amazonian ones, making them more suitable for peeled veneer (Whitmore and da Silva, 1990). Amazonia's generally dark-coloured, hard-to-saw and extremely heterogeneous

These forests represent valuable resources, not only for timber but also for a wide variety of non-wood products and, most importantly, for the environmental services that the forest currently performs at no cost. The potential value of all of these roles is tremendous. At present, however, institutional arrangements are completely lacking to turn many of these forms of value, such as environmental services, into a means of supporting the region's human population.

Brazil has been an active participant in the International Tropical Timber Organization (ITTO), and, like ITTO, its national policies have emphasized plans for sustainable management of tropical forests. The Brazilian Institute for the Environment and Renewable Natural Resources (Instituto Brasileiro de Meio Ambiente e dos Recursos Naturais Renováveis — IBAMA), which was created in 1989, requires

Table 25.2 Estimates of forest extent in Brazil

Forest type	Area (sq. km)	% of land area
Lowland moist	3,202,973	37.9
Montane	60,345	0.7
Mangrove	16,459	0.2
Dry	110,074	1.3
Pine*	25,457	0.3
Total	3,415,308	40.4

* This is the araucaria forest

Based on analysis of Map 25.1. See Map Legend on p. 248 for details of sources.

Table 25.3   Extent of deforestation in the Brazilian Legal Amazon

Political unit	Original forest area* (a)	Deforested area*					Deforested area (% of original forest area)				
		Jan 1978	Apr 1988	Aug 1989	Aug 1990	Aug 1991	Jan 1978	Apr 1988	Aug 1989	Aug 1990	Aug 1991
1	3	4	5	6	7	8	9	10	11	12	13

DEFORESTATION EXCLUSIVE OF HYDROELECTRIC DAMS											
Acre	154	2.5	8.9	9.8	10.3	10.7	1.6	5.8	6.4	6.7	7.0
Amapá	132	0.2	0.8	1.0	1.3	1.7	0.1	0.6	0.8	1.0	1.3
Amazonas	1,561	1.7 (b)	17.3 (b)	19.3 (b)	19.8 (b)	20.8 (b)	0.1	1.1	1.2	1.3	1.3
Maranhão	155	63.9	90.8	92.3	93.4	94.1	41.2	58.5	59.5	60.2	60.6
Mato Grosso	585	20.0 (b)	71.5 (b)	79.6 (b)	83.6 (b)	86.5 (b)	3.4	12.2	13.6	14.3	14.8
Pará	1,218	56.3	129.5	137.3	142.2	146.0	4.6	10.6	11.3	11.7	12.0
Rondônia	224	4.2	29.6	31.4	33.1	34.2	1.9	13.2	14.0	14.8	15.3
Roraima	188	0.1	2.7	3.6	3.8	4.2	0.1	1.5	1.9	2.0	2.3
Tocantins	58	3.2	21.6	22.3	22.9	23.4	5.4	37.0	38.3	39.3	40.0
Legal Amazon	4,275	152.1	372.8	396.6	410.4	421.6	3.6	8.7	9.3	9.6	9.9
FOREST FLOODED BY HYDROELECTRIC DAMS											
		0.1	3.9	4.8	4.8	4.8	0.0	0.1	0.1	0.1	0.1
DEFORESTATION FROM ALL SOURCES											
		152.2	376.7	401.4	415.2	426.4	3.6	8.8	9.4	9.7	10.0

(a) These original forest areas are measured from the IBAMA map (Brazil, IBDF/IBGE, 1988). The forest areas in the deforestation estimate were defined by appearance on LANDSAT™ images, giving an original forest area of 4×10^6 sq. km. The percentages deforested in each state are therefore larger than the numbers in this table indicate, the total deforested from all sources by 1991 being 10.5 per cent

(b) Maranhao values include 57.8×10^3 sq. km, and Pará values include 39.8×10^3 sq. km, of "old" (approximately pre-1960) deforestation now largely under secondary forest.

timber has therefore been spared the pressure of large multinational timber corporations. Indeed, FAO data indicate that, as of 1985, only two per cent of internationally traded hardwood come from Latin America, versus 57 per cent from Asia. However, the approaching end to commercially significant stocks of tropical hardwoods in Asia can be expected to change this situation radically. It is estimated that, before the year 2000, Asian forests will be depleted to the point where they can no longer supply global markets. It seems likely, therefore, that technologies will be developed to use Amazonian woods — whether consumers like them or not. A more optimistic alternative view holds that world demand for tropical hardwoods from natural forests may decline due to substitution from plantations (Vincent, 1992).

Deforestation

The extent and rate of deforestation in Brazil have been the subject of considerable controversy. The figures presented here for Amazonia (Tables 25.3 and 25.4) are based on LANDSAT satellite imagery from 1978, 1988, 1989, 1990 and 1991, with re-analysis of earlier years to achieve consistent definitions of forest. Several Brazilian government estimates using LANDSAT in the 1980s gave values much lower than these, while others based on estimates of burning (as opposed to deforestation) produced much higher numbers from the US National Oceanic and Atmospheric Administration's (NOAA) Advanced Very High Resolution Radiometer (AVHRR) satellite. Another source of discrepancy is that cerrado is not considered to be forest in this atlas, but Brazilian deforestation estimates prior to 1988 included it. The controversies surrounding these estimates are reviewed by Fearnside (1990b).

The rate of deforestation in the 5 million sq. km of the administrative region of the Legal Amazon declined significantly between 1987 and 1991. The annual rate of 11,100 sq. km in 1991 was only half the 22,000 sq. km per year average rate between 1978 and 1988 (Table 25.4). It should never be forgotten, however, that the lower deforestation rate of 11,100 sq. km each year is still a huge area destroyed annually, virtually

237

Table 25.4   Rate of deforestation in the Brazilian Legal Amazon

Political unit	Deforestation rate (sq. km x 10³ per year)			
	1978-1988 (a)	1988-1989 (b)	1989-1990	1990-1991
Acre	0.6	0.6	0.6	0.4
Amapá	0.1	0.2	0.3	0.4
Amazonas	1.6	1.3	0.5	1.0
Maranhao	2.7	1.4	1.1	0.7
Mato Grosso	5.1	6.0	4.0	2.8
Pará	7.3	5.8	4.9	3.8
Rondônia	2.3	1.4	1.7	1.1
Roraima	0.2	0.7	0.2	0.4
Tocantins	1.7	0.7	0.6	0.4
Legal Amazon	21.6	18.1	13.8	11.1
Hydroelectric dams	0.4	1.0	0.0	0.0
Total from all sources	22.0	19.0	13.8	11.1

(a) Uses intervals of ten years for all political units except Rondonia, Roraima and Tocantins, for which the interval is 11 years. Intervals are rounded to the nearest year based on the state average image date for 1988 and the legal Amazon average image date for 1978

(b) Time interval calculated by individual LANDSAT scene.

Figure 25.3   Deforested area and deforestation rate in Brazilian Legal Amazon 1978–1991

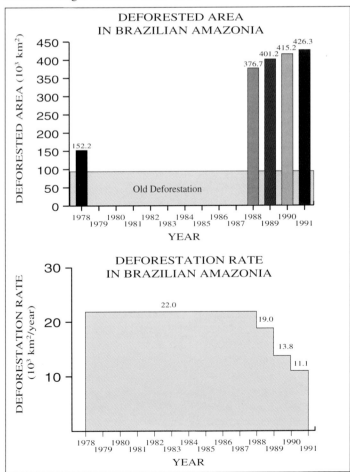

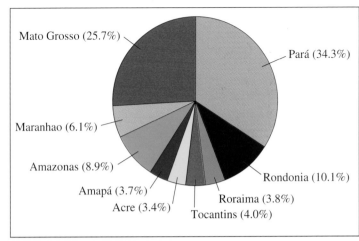

Figure 25.4   Distribution of deforestation activity by state in 1990/1991

all for unsustainable uses such as cattle pasture and with very little benefit for the people of the region. At the 1991 "reduced" rate of deforestation, the area destroyed per day is over 30 sq. km.

The decline in deforestation rates from 1987 to 1991 does not represent a trend that can be extrapolated into the future until the deforestation problem simply disappears, as some officials have claimed. The lower rates are mainly explained by Brazil's deepening economic recession over this period. Ranchers simply do not have money to invest in expanding their clearings as quickly as they have in the past. In addition, the government has lacked funds to continue building highways and establish settlement projects. Probably very little of the decline can be attributed to Brazil's repression of deforestation through inspection from helicopters, confiscating chainsaws and fining landowners caught burning without the required permission from IBAMA. Despite bitter complaints, most people continued to clear anyway. Changes in policies on granting fiscal incentives also do not explain the decline. The decree suspending the granting of incentives (Decree No. 151) was issued on 25 June 1991 — after almost all of the observed decline in deforestation rate had already occurred (Figure 25.3). Even for the last year (1991), the effect would be minimal, as the average date for the LANDSAT images for the 1991 data set was August of that year.

The distribution of 1990–1991 clearing among the region's nine states (Figure 25.4) indicates that most of the clearing is in states that are dominated by ranchers: the state of Mato Grosso alone accounts for 26 per cent of the 11,100 sq. km total. Mato Grosso has the highest percentage of its privately held land in ranches of 10 sq. km or more: 84 per cent at the time of the 1985 agricultural census, with only three per cent in small farms (Brazil, IBGE, 1989). By contrast, Rondônia, a state that has become famous for its deforestation by small farmers, had only 10 per cent of the 1991 deforestation total, and Acre had three per cent. Considering all nine states, calculations indicate that in both 1990 and 1991 the small farmers accounted for about 30 per cent of the deforestation activity, with 70 per cent being done by ranchers (Fearnside, 1993).

Relatively little deforestation in Brazil is due to subsistence agriculture; established cattle ranching projects continue to receive government subsidies, and ranches (many of which never had incentives) continue to account for most deforestation. This means that the social cost of substantially reducing deforestation rate from its current levels would be much less than is implied by frequent pronouncements that blame "poverty"

Amazonian dams goes to making aluminum for export, using energy supplied at a small fraction of its true cost. Two-thirds of the energy produced by the Tucuruí Dam in Pará is used for aluminium production in two smelters that sustain less than 2000 employees in all. Brazil's 2010 plan for a series of dams (the expected time of construction of these has been temporarily postponed due to the country's financial difficulties) would result in flooding of 100,000 sq. km in Amazonia, or three per cent of the forest (Brazil, ELETROBRÁS, 1987).

The principal danger of the spreading deforestation comes from its spatial distribution. Although most of the clearing is concentrated along the southern and eastern edges of the forest, a smaller but more threatening area is spread out along highways that now penetrate much of the region. This proliferation increases the danger that deforestation can spread quickly into relatively untouched areas. Plans for future highway construction would open up much wider areas, including the vast areas now accessible only by river in the western part of the state of Amazonas. Once road access is opened up, much of the deforestation process passes outside the control of government decision-makers (Fearnside, 1987a).

The area deforested in Amazonia is already large: the 426,000 sq. km cleared as of 1991 is almost the size of the US state of California. It has almost all been converted to non-sustainable cattle pasture, which degrades after about a decade of use (Fearnside, 1980; Uhl et al., 1988). The cleared area has already passed the limits of Brazil's financial and physical resources (such as phosphates) for maintaining permanent agriculture, ranching or silviculture (See Fearnside, 1987b, in press).

The *cerrado* has been destroyed faster than the Amazonian forests because of its proximity to the densely populated areas in Brazil's central-south region, the demand for charcoal for steel production in the state of Minas Gerais and the relative ease of clearing *cerrado* using bulldozers and converting it to mechanized agriculture for crops such as soybeans. The seasonal climate of the *cerrado* makes it more suitable than Amazonia for agriculture. The *cerrado* has been buffering the Amazonian forest from the full force of economic pressures and population migrations coming from the south-central part of Brazil. This partial protection cannot be expected to endure long, as *cerrado* areas dwindle and as transportation improves to more distant frontiers in Amazonia.

Destruction of the Atlantic forests began almost as soon as Europeans arrived in Brazil. They were first exploited for timber. Indeed, "Pau-brasil" (Brazilwood: *Caesalpinia echinata*), the commercially prized Atlantic forest tree after which the country is believed to have been named, was logged almost to extinction by the early colonists. The fertile lands of the coastal plains were converted to agriculture, for the cultivation of sugar cane in particular. Deforestation for mining, coffee, banana and rubber plantations also occurred as the settlers moved inland. This region is now the major agricultural and industrial area in Brazil, with two of the country's largest cities within its boundaries and, as a result, destruction of the forest is still occurring. For instance, LANDSAT satellite images indicate that between 1985 and 1990, the area of Atlantic forest cleared in the states of Bahia, Rio de Janeiro and São Paulo totalled 1895 sq. km (*Jornal do Brasil*, 1993). The last vestiges of Atlantic forest (Figure 25.2) are now considered to be one of the most threatened of the world's "rain forests," sharing this distinction with the remains of the tropical forest in Madagascar.

Most of the destruction of the *Araucaria* forests has taken place in the last 100 years. Logging has reduced them to scattered remnants.

Tin ore mining in Amazonia.   (WWF/Mark Edwards)

for environmental problems in the region. Halting the current pattern of deforestation for non-sustainable cattle pasture should be the first priority in any strategy for sustainable development in the region.

Land speculation has been a key factor in making unproductive cattle pastures attractive to their owners (Fearnside, 1983; Hecht et al., 1988). Profits from logging have also been a critical income source to these operations (Mattos et al., in press) as well as to small colonists (Uhl et al., 1991). For small farmers, the traditional system of gaining access to land through squatting leads to deforestation as a means of obtaining land titles: clearing for cattle pasture is still considered an "improvement" of the land by state and federal government land agencies.

Mining, while it destroys relatively little forest directly, is a significant influence in other ways. These include the building of highways to mineral-rich areas and the processing of ores in the region in ways that consume forest. Carajás, with the world's largest high-grade iron ore deposit, is coupled to a regional development plan that produces pig-iron from some of the ore. Charcoal, used both as a reducing agent and as an energy source, comes largely from native forest wood, contrary to the claims of the mill owners (Fearnside, 1989c). If fully implemented, supplying charcoal to the scheme would require deforesting as much as 1500 sq. km each year (Anderson, 1990).

Hydroelectric schemes are another potentially large source of forest loss (Table 25.3). Much of the energy produced from

Biodiversity

The biodiversity of Brazil, and Amazonia in particular, is legendary, although little reliable information exists on the numbers of species present. Trees dominate the physical structure of the Amazon forest, but make up a relatively small share of the total number of species of organisms present. Brazil as a whole has an estimated 55,000 angiosperm plant species, more than any other country (Prance, 1979).

Brazil as a whole has 428 species of mammals, placing it third in the world. However, mammals are significantly less numerous in the Brazilian portion of Amazonia than in Peru or Ecuador (Emmons, 1984; Malcolm, 1990). There are 1622 bird species in the country, a number exceeded only by Colombia and Peru, while Brazil's 516 species of amphibians (McNeely *et al.*, 1990) is the world's second largest, exceeded only by Colombia. Similarly, Brazil's reptiles and swallowtail butterflies place the country in fourth place with 467 and 74 species respectively. In Amazonia, there were 1300 fresh water fish species described by 1967 (Roberts, 1972, cited by Goulding, 1980); the total number present is estimated to be from 2000 (Geisler *et al.*, 1975) to 3000 (Goulding, 1980). The most important species economically include tambaqui *Colossoma macropomum*, tucunaré *Cichla ocellaris* and pirarucu *Arapaima gigas*.

The golden lion tamarin Leontopithecus roasalia *is one of Brazil's rarest primates, endemic to the Atlantic Coastal forest.*
(WWF/Juan Pratginestos)

Invertebrates, especially beetles (Coleoptera) make up by far the largest share of the total biodiversity. Fumigation of the canopy in four forest types near Manaus yielded 1080 species of adult beetles (Coleoptera), 83 per cent of them endemic to a single forest type (Erwin, 1983). Similar studies carried out on a larger scale in Peru and Panama have more than tripled the total number of species estimated to exist on Earth (Erwin, 1988). With extrapolations from single trees to the globe, however, the sample sizes are so small that little confidence can be attached to these numbers. The fact that the arthropod fauna is tremendously diverse is incontestable, however.

The number of threatened species in Brazil is high. For instance Collar *et al.* (1992) list more birds at risk in Brazil than in any other country in the Americas; they name 97 species, of which 64 are endemic. There are 18 endemic and two non-endemic species listed as endangered. The Atlantic forest contains most of the endangered humid forest bird species (see Chapter 4).

IUCN lists a total of 54 threatened mammal species in Brazil (Groombridge, 1993). These are: 23 primate species, four species in the order Xenarthra, 11 carnivores, eight rodents, two deer, four cetaceans and two manatees. As for the birds, it is the Atlantic forest that harbours many of the threatened mammal species. These include the maned sloth *Bradypus torquatus*, the golden lion tamarin *Leontopithecus rosalia*, one of Brazil's rarest primates, found only in the southern part of Bahia state, and the muriqui or woolly spider monkey *Brachyteles arachnoides*, probably the most endangered primate in the Americas, which is also endemic to the Atlantic forest.

The lists of threatened species in other groups occurring in Brazil are also longer than for other countries. There are 16 reptiles, eight amphibians, nine fish and seventeen invertebrates (Groombridge, 1993).

Amazonia has a number of "centres of endemism," where unique species of a variety of taxa are concentrated in certain geographical locations (see Chapters 3 and 4). For instance, the mountains in the Guyana highlands and Pico de Neblina have great numbers of unique species as a result of their isolation and topographic gradients.

Conservation Areas

Brazil's first national park, Itatiaia, was established in 1937 and the first modern legal measures relating to protected areas were also taken in the 1930s (IUCN, 1992). The country does not have specific legislation for a protected area system, but work has begun to establish one. The history of the Brazilian reserve system is reviewed by Foresta (1991).

Brazil's conservation areas are continually changing; those in IUCN's categories I–IV are shown on Maps 25.1 and 25.2 and listed in Table 25.5. Most of the changes in recent years have been additions to the list, but some have been reversals with existing areas being repealed or reduced. Many conservation areas existing on paper have minimal infrastructure and staff to protect them from disturbance.

In Amazonia, the refugia theory provided a theoretical basis for selection of the first conservation units established there (Pádua and Quintão, 1982). Giving priority to protecting centres of endemism is a logical strategy, whether or not the refugia theory is the correct explanation for their existence. A workshop held in Manaus in 1990 has more recently synthesized a much wider base of information for helping to guide future priorities (see Chapter 3).

Parks and equivalent reserves covered only 2.7 per cent of Brazil's Legal Amazon by 1992. This represents three per cent

THE BIOLOGICAL DYNAMICS OF FOREST FRAGMENTS PROJECT

Around the world, growing human populations and economic pressures are inexorably leading to widespread conversion of tropical rain forests into a mixture of human-altered habitat and isolated forest remnants. The Biological Dynamics of Forest Fragments Project (BDFFP), a bi-national research effort of Brazil's National Institute for Amazonian Research (INPA) and the Smithsonian Institution, measures ecosystem changes that occur as continuous rain forest is transformed by human development into a habitat mosaic.

The BDFFP is the only long-term, integrated study of the interface between continuous Amazonian rain forest and human encroachment. Initiated by INPA and WWF-US in 1979, north of Manaus in Brazil's Amazon rain forest, the Project is now managed by the Smithsonian Institution. It has become a critical component of the Institution's Biodiversity Program, administered by the National Museum of Natural History.

The BDFFP began as the Minimum Critical Size of Ecosystems Project, designed to identify a minimum size of tropical forest habitat that would maintain most of the biotic diversity represented in an intact ecosystem. The research design entails studies of plant and animal communities in forest plots before and after their isolation by cattle ranchers opening new pastures. Additionally, post-isolation communities in the plots are compared through time to control studies in adjacent, continuous forest.

By isolating a replicated series of different sized forest patches and studying the presence and absence patterns of biota before and after isolation, predictions can be generated as to what size forest patches are needed to maintain given percentages of the original diversity. One of the specific predictions, which would allow the correlation of the size of a forest fragment with retention of diversity, was that the rate of extinction in isolated fragments would be area dependent —extinction would proceed faster in smaller fragments.

From 1980 to 1984, ten one ha, 10 ha and 100 ha fragments were isolated. In 1990, a second 100 ha fragment was isolated, and an approximately 200 ha remnant, isolated on a neighbouring ranch in 1979, was included in the sampling regime. Twelve years of observations by BDFFP researchers indicate that the forest reserves are highly dynamic ecological entities and that it is an over simplification to expect to be able to predict "species carrying capacity" from the size of a reserve alone.

Species/area relations are insufficient to understand all of the processes that determine how many and which species will be present in a given reserve. Rather, species-specific habitat requirements, structural changes in the reserves originating from the creation of a forest edge, and changes in the vegetation surrounding the reserves as pastures are abandoned, interact with the size of the forest fragment in determining ecosystem structure in the habitat fragments.

Data have confirmed that extinction proceeds faster in smaller fragments for some taxonomic groups, whereas other groups behave in ways not predicted by simple species/area relationships. The Project is now beginning to address the next generation of related questions. For those groups which do show declines in numbers in small reserves, it is appropriate to focus on the process of extinction:

- What are the factors that lead some taxa to extinction?
- What are the factors that permit other (often closely related) species to survive?
- Why, for example, do birds, butterflies and mammals apparently respond in very different ways to habitat fragmentation?
- How do other taxa respond to fragmentation?

Answers to these questions require an in-depth understanding of the natural history and ecological and environmental interactions of the taxa involved.

Results demonstrating that a complex suite of factors affects habitat fragments led to an expansion of the research activities supported by the BDFFP. While studies of the relationships of forest fragment size and species number continue, the dynamics of forest edges, both biotic and physical, as well as the interactions between the forest islands and the sea of vegetation around them are now central issues in the Project's mission.

The BDFFP provides unique research opportunities to study the processes involved in forest regeneration. Because the history of forest clearing and secondary growth in the pastures surrounding the BDFFP forest isolates is known, researchers have a perhaps unparalleled laboratory in which to investigate, through observation and manipulation, the basic biology of succession. What, for instance, will be the role of forest remnants as seed sources for surrounding fallow lands? Applied questions, such as how manipulation of abandoned pastures might turn them into landscapes capable of supporting colonists, are also being addressed.

Studies of habitat fragmentation have taken on an undeniable urgency. Our ability to strike a balance between the need of tropical countries to use their forested land and the need to preserve their forests will depend in no small part upon our understanding of forest fragments. As the Project moves through its second decade, it will make major contributions to the relatively new field of conservation science, providing data vital to integrating the preservation of biodiversity with human development.

Field work currently underway deals with a broad range of organisms and ecological questions. Birds, primates and insects are the focus of several projects. Frogs, well-studied in the Project's continuous forest study areas, will be monitored in second growth and forest fragments later this year. Botanists continue the daunting task of identifying over 80,000 herbarium specimens, collected in the largest vouchered forest inventory ever conducted in the Amazon. Doctoral candidates are monitoring the physical and biological changes that take place at the forest edge. Manipulative experiments are underway in the abandoned pastures that surround some of the forest remnants.

Participation is open to all scientists on a competitive basis; their projects have to be approved by a standing Scientific Advisory Committee. Student training is a very important aspect of the BDFFP. Graduate students, both Brazilian nationals and foreigners, constitute a major portion of the researchers. Since the inception of the project, over 175 students have worked in Manaus.

Source: Richard O. Bierregaard, Jr.

Table 25.5   Conservation areas of Brazil

Existing conservation areas in IUCN's categories I–IV. For information on World Heritage Sites, Biosphere Reserves and Ramsar Sites see Chapter 8.

Map Ref	National Parks	Area (sq. km)	Map Ref		Area (sq. km)	Map Ref		Area (sq. km)
1	Amazonia*	9,940	48	Rio Trombetas*	3,850	90	Urucui-Una1	350
2	Aparados da Serra*	103	49	Saltinho*	5			
3	Araguaia*	5,623	50	Santa Isabel*	28		*Federal Area of Outstanding*	
4	Brasilia	280	51	Serra Negra	11		*Ecological Interest*	
5	Cabo Orange*	6,190	52	Sooretama*	240		Manguezais da Foz do	
6	Caparao	260	53	Tapirape*	1,030		Rio Mamanguape+	57
7	Chapada Diamantina	1,520	54	Tingua*	260			
8	Chapada dos Guimaraes	330	55	Uatuma*	5,600		*Area of Relevant Historical Interest*	
9	Chapada dos Veadeiros	600	56	Una1	14		Ferrabraz+	10
10	Emas	1,319						
	Grande Sertao Veredas+	840		*Federal Ecological Reserves*			*Ecological Station*	
11	Iguaçu*	1,700		Alcobaca+	2		Pau-Brasil+	11
12	Itatiaia*	300	57	IBGE	1			
13	Jaú*	22,720	58	Ilha dos Lobos	0.02		*Faunal Reserve*	
14	Lagoa do Peixe	344	59	Jutai-Solimoes*	2,882		Crubixas+	7
15	Lencois Maranhenses	1,550	60	Raso da Catarina	2000	91	Secundario Perimetro	
16	Marinho Fernando		61	Sauim-Castanheira*	1		de Sao Roque*	239
	de Noronha	113						
17	Marinho dos Abrolhos	913		*Federal Ecological Stations*			*Municipal Biological Reserve*	
18	Monte Pascoal*	225	62	Aiuaba1	20	92	Banhado Grande	73
19	Monte Roraima*	1,160	63	Anavilhanas*	3,300	93	Lami	1
20	Pacaas Novos*	7,648	64	Aracuri-Esmeralda	3	94	Planalto	<0.1
21	Pantanal Matogrossense	1,350	65	Babitonga*	78		Santa Clara+	15
22	Pico da Neblina*	22,000	66	Caracarai*	3,946	95	Scharlau	0.2
23	Sao Joaquim*	493	67	Carijós1	13			
24	Serra da Bocaina*	1,000	68	Coco-Javaes	370		*Municipal Park*	
25	Serra da Canastra	715	69	Cunia*	1,040		Barreiras+	0.5
26	Serra da Capivara	979	70	Foz do Sao Francisco/			Lagoa do Peri+	20
27	Serra do Cipo	338		Praia do Peba*	53		Lagoas e Dunas do Abaeté+	15
28	Serra do Divisor*	6,050		Guaraqueçaba+	136	96	Ouro Preto	2,221
29	Serra dos Orgaos*	110	71	Ilha Maracá-Jipioca	720		Pituaçú+	7
30	Serra Geral*	173		Ilhas das Marias+	10		Saint-Hilaire+	12
31	Sete Cidades	62		Ique+	2,000			
32	Superagui*	210	72	Ique Juruena	1,600		*Natural Monument*	
33	Tijuca	32	73	Ique Aripuana	2,260	97	Vale de Dinossauros	0.4
34	Ubajara	6	74	Jari*	2,271			
35	Xingu*	22,000	75	Juami-Japura*	5,727		*Metropolitan Park*	
			76	Jureia*	241		Sitio Histórico Municipal	
	Federal Biological Reserves			Mambucaba+	nd		de Pirajá+	16
36	Abufari*	2,880	77	Maracá*	1,013			
37	Atol das Rocas	362	78	Niquia*	2,866		*State Area of Outstanding Biological*	
38	Augusto Ruschi	40	79	Pirai	40		*Interest*	
	(Nova Lombardia)		80	Pirapitinga	11	98	Córrego Cortado	2
39	Caracara*	611	81	Piria-Gurupi*	3,417	99	Córregos Taquara	
40	Comboios	8	82	Rio Acre*	775		e Capetinga (A)	4
41	Corrego Grande	15	83	Serido	11	100	Córregos Taquara	
42	Corrego do Veado	24	84	Serra das Araras	1,150		e Capetinga (B)	17
43	Guapore*	6,000		Serra de Itabaiana+	18	101	Paranoá	1
	Guaribas+	43	85	Taiama	120	102	Riacho Fundo	4
44	Jaru*	2,682	86	Taim	340			
45	Lago Piratuba*	3,570	87	Tamoios*	41		*State Biological Reserves*	
	Marinha do Arvoredo+	176		Tapacurá+	4		Acaua+	52
46	Pedra Talhada	45	88	Tupinambas	46	103	Aguaí*	77
47	Poco das Antas	50	89	Tupiniquins	0.4	104	Araras*	21
						105	Canela Preta	184

Map Ref		Area (sq. km)	Map Ref		Area (sq. km)	Map Ref		Area (sq. km)
	Carmo da Mata+	1		Chauas+	27	156	Guajara-Mirim	2,588
	Colonia 31 de Março+	50		Guaraguaçú+	8		Ibitipoca+	15
	Corumba+	6	128	Ibicatu	1		Ibitiria+	5
	Córrego de Sao Jorge+	3		Ilha do Mel+	22	157	Ilha Anchieta	8
	Duas Bocas+	29	129	Itabera	2	158	Ilha Bela	270
	Fazenda da Cascata+	1	130	Itapeti	1		Ilha de Itaparica+	22
	Fazenda da Lapinha+	4		Itapewa+	1	159	Ilha Grande	150
106	Ilha da Polvora e das Pombas	172		Itirapina+	23	160	Ilha do Cardoso*	225
	Jacaranda+	27	131	Jardim Botânico	40	161	Itacolomi	75
	Mar de Espanha+	2		Jatai+	45	162	Itapuá	55
	Massambara+	17		Jureia-Itatins+	800	163	Itaunas*	32
	Mata Acaua+	50	132	Mamirauá*	11,240	164	Jacupiranga*	1,500
	Mata do Jambreiro+	9	133	Mogi-Guacu	10		Jaiba+	64
	Mata dos Ausentes+	7		Nhumirim+	7		Jaragua+	5
107	Mato Grande	52		Paraiso+	49	165	Lauráceas*	239
108	Mestre Alvaro	35		Paulo de Faria+	4	166	Mata dos Godoy	7
109	Morro dos Seis Lagos	369		Ribeirao Preto+	2		Mina Velha e Arco da Gruta+	0.5
	Nova Baden+	4	134	Samuel*	209		Mirador+	3,850
	Parauna+	35		Santa Barbara+	27		Morro do Chapéu+	60
110	Parazinho	1		Santa Maria+	1	167	Morro do Diabo	344
	Pedra Azul+	12		Sao Carlos+	1	168	Nhamundá*	284
111	Praia do Sul	36	135	Serra dos Tres Irmaos*	998	169	Nonoai	175
112	Rio Ouro Preto*	464	136	Valinhos	0.2	170	Pedra Branca	125
	Santa Rita+	6	137	Xitue*	31	171	Pico de Jabre	5
113	Sao Camilo	4				172	Pico do Marumbi*	20
114	Sao Donata	44		*State Forest Parks*		173	Podocarpus	36
	Sao Sebastiao do Paraiso+	2		Rio Doce+	360		Porto Ferreira+	6
	Sassafraz+	54		*State Parks*			Quartelá+	44
115	Serra Geral*	17	138	Aguas Quentes	15		Rio Capivara+	11
	Sertaozinho+	7	139	Agudo da Cotia	10	174	Rio Cautario	1,212
116	Tracadal*	225	140	Alto Ribeira	377	175	Rondinha	10
	Vilafacchina+	1		Anhumas+	0.2		Sao Carlos+	1
				Ara+	0.6		Serra Caldas Novas+	123
	State Ecological Park			Bacanga+	31		Serra do Araçá+	18,187
117	Boca da Mata	3		Baleia+	1	176	Serra do Brigadeiro	325
118	Guara	2		Cachoeira da Fumaca+	0.3	177	Serra do Mar	3,148
119	Norte Brasilia	2	141	Camaqua	80	178	Serra do Tabuleiro	874
			142	Campinhos	2	179	Serra dos Parecis*	390
	State Ecological Reserves		143	Campos do Jordao*	83	180	Serra dos Reis*	1,009
	Culuente+	30	144	Candeias*	90	181	Serra Furada	13
120	Gama	1		Cantareira+	70	182	Setibal	5
121	Guara	1	145	Capital	2		Sumidouro+	13
122	Mata do Pau Ferro	6	146	Caracol	1	183	Tainhas	49
123	Parque dos Poderes	134	147	Carlos Botelho*	378		Terra Ronca+	145
124	Rio Vermelho	15	148	Caxambu	10	184	Torres	15
	Sistema Gurjaú+	14		Cerrado+	4	185	Turvo	175
			149	Corumbiara	5,860	186	Vascununca	15
	State Ecological Stations		150	Delta do Jacui	43	187	Vila Velha	32
125	Aguas Emendadas	105	151	Diamante do Norte	14			
	Angatuba+	14		Dunas de Natal+	12	Total		249,131.4
126	Bananal	9	152	Espigao Alto	13			
	Bauru+	3	153	Espinilho	3	+ Not mapped		
	Bracinho+	46	154	Fonte Grande	2	* Area with forest within its boundaries according to Maps 25.1 and 25.2.		
127	Caetetus	22	155	Graciosa*	12			

Source: WCMC (unpublished data)

INFORMAL SECTOR MINING IN THE BRAZILIAN AMAZON

Small-scale mining can be traced back to the eighteenth century in all Amazon Basin countries although its importance was not so much in the value of production, which was minimal before the twentieth century, as in bewitching European explorers and settlers with the notion that the deep interior of South America contained fabulous mineral wealth. The Brazilian Amazon does in fact contain large areas of diffuse mineralisation, but given the distances, high overheads and lack of local labour, it is a difficult region for formal sector mining companies to operate in. They have in practice been restricted to working exceptionally rich deposits, such as the Carajás project area in Pará state, leaving the mining of most gold, cassiterite, diamonds, emeralds, rock crystal and a range of semi-precious stones to hundreds of thousands of informal sector miners scattered throughout the Amazon basin.

Although informal sector mining is now an important part of the economy of all Amazonian countries, it is only in Brazil that the scale of activity can be compared to the great nineteenth-century gold rushes. The current Amazon gold rush began in 1979, when the price of gold on the London Metal Exchange climbed to an unprecedented US$850 per troy ounce: although it fell back and fluctuated wildly during the 1980s, it has remained at what in historical terms, is an extremely high level. Although all statistics on informal sector mining in Brazil are by definition approximate, reliable production estimates by the federal National Department of Mineral Production (DNPM) estimate informal sector production in 1992 at 80 metric tonnes, down from a peak of over 100 metric tonnes annually in the late 1980s (see Table 1). This level of production puts Brazil around third or fourth in a league of world gold exporters, and means the value of gold production by the

informal sector in the Brazilian Amazon has been over a billion dollars annually since the early 1980s. Accurate estimates for the number of people involved directly in informal sector mining in the Brazilian Amazon do not exist. The best guess is that somewhere around 300,000 miners are involved directly in gold extraction alone, and a further 50,000 in mining other minerals, mainly cassiterite. It is probable that an additional 350,000 people make all or part of their living supplying miners and trading and processing the gold they produce.

Clusters of mining camps are found throughout much of Brazil (Figure 1), and the economy of large parts of the Amazon interior revolves around their exploitation. The social and economic importance of informal sector mining has made it politically difficult for Brazilian governments to intervene in the mining areas. Despite the existence of an elaborate body of mining law, which, for example, prohibits the use of mercury, the state has proved incapable of enforcing any form of regulation on miners.

The technologies used in the informal sector, although often simple, are cheap, portable and well adapted to Amazonian conditions. They range from sluices, pans and rockers, similar to those used in the nineteenth century, to large floating dredges requiring an initial investment of US$50,000. Portable mechanical crushers allow miners to exploit primary as well as alluvial deposits. Since 1979, water supply has been mechanised in most mining camps, and motorised suction pumps, once used only on dry land, have been adapted to rafts which now scour river beds. All manual and mechanised technologies use mercury in the extraction process: they all have in common a sluice over which water mixed with alluvium or crushed ore is passed. Mercury is placed in a box at the top of the sluice, and behind horizontal riffles. Mercury amalgamates with gold on a 1:1 ratio, making it more likely the gold will lodge in the lining of the sluice. The amalgam is then burnt to vaporise the mercury. The two contamination pathways are the inhalation of mercury vapour, and spillage directly into watercourses from machinery in operation.

The environmental consequences of informal sector gold mining are a subject of intense controversy, where much basic research remains to be done. It is clear that it is a relatively unimportant factor in Amazonian deforestation, compared to ranching, smallholder agriculture and timber extraction. In the Tapajós valley, the largest and longest established goldfield in the Brazilian Amazon, deforestation is minimal by Amazonian standards. Primary forest still overlooks mining camps which are more than three decades old. The effect of mining on aquatic ecosystems in Amazonia, in contrast, are often dramatic. Many smaller streams and rivers have had their courses altered by intensive dredging, while sedimentation linked to mining has turned clear rivers brown, altered ph. levels and reduced fish life. The fact that mining leaves innumerable holes which fill with water during the rains has made malaria control more difficult in goldfields. Miners have also been responsible for bringing new disease strains into contact with vulnerable indigenous populations.

Table 1: Informal sector gold production in Brazil

Year	Metric Tonnes
1980	35
1981	35
1982	35
1983	59
1984	61
1985	72
1986	67
1987	84
1988	100
1989	110
1990	90
1991	82
1992*	80

* Author's estimate
  Data for other years are from annual reports of the Departamento Nacional da
  Produção Mineral.

Source: David Cleary.

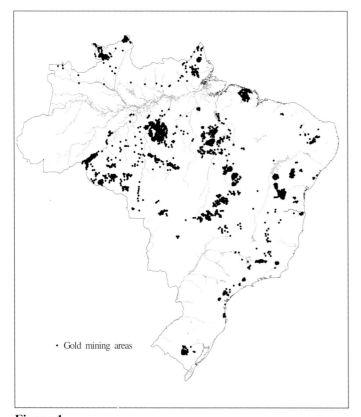

Figure 1

Most concern has been expressed about the long-term implications of the unregulated mercury use in mining camps. Gold production levels are a rough guide to the order of magnitude of mercury use: if 100 metric tonnes are produced annually, an equal amount of mercury will have been vaporised in the production process. A further 200–300 metric tonnes can be assumed to have escaped in spillages from machinery. There is a growing body of information about mercury levels in sediments, soils and river water, based on field sampling in all major goldfields. There is some information on mercury levels in fish, and only fragmentary data on human contamination. Fish with mercury levels up to 8 times higher than the EEC Environmental Quality Standard have been recorded in the Tapajós and Madeira Rivers. The most comprehensive sampling of mercury levels in human populations so far carried out, by an Anglo-Brazilian research team in the Tapajós valley in 1990, found blood mercury levels were significantly higher among riverine fish-eating communities some way from mining areas than among the miners themselves. No generalised contamination was found among the population of a major gold trading centre. This suggests that fish-eating is a more important contamination pathway than inhaling vapour, and, paradoxically, that it is not the miners themselves who are most at risk. It is likely that the first cases of Minanata disease, caused by acute methyl mercury poisoning, will be recorded in the Brazilian Amazon before the turn of the century.

of the natural vegetation. Current plans identify a target of 170,000 sq. km, or 3.3 per cent of the region. In contrast, preservation of 25 per cent of the original vegetation of the region was recommended in 1979 by the Interministerial Commission on Forest Policy in the original version of the draft law drawn up by the commission (see Fearnside, 1986b). These areas cover all types of vegetation, not only forests.

In addition to the conservation areas listed in Table 25.5, Brazil has a variety of types of semi-protected areas, such as national forests (for timber production), indigenous reserves, and extractive reserves. These have the effect of impeding deforestation, but, if the environmental benefits are to be guaranteed over the long term, negotiations need to be undertaken; in the case of the extractive and indigenous reserves these must be with forest peoples who live in the areas (Fearnside and Ferraz, in press). These semi-protected areas lack legal requirements to prevent future exploitation and perturbation. Including semi-protected areas would increase the fraction protected in the Legal Amazon from 2.7 per cent to 19.0 per cent (Fearnside and Ferraz, in press). Incorporating indigenous and other semi-protected areas into a system of conservation units does not imply expelling the forest dwellers. On the contrary, not only do they have the right to inhabit their traditional homes, but their presence can potentially offer a better guarantee that the forest will remain standing than would the transformation of these areas into parks empty of people, with protection against encroachment entrusted to IBAMA guards (but see Chapter 5).

Only one-third of the terrestrial ecosystem types present in the Brazilian Legal Amazon are protected, considering as "ecosystems" the area within each of the region's nine states that is covered by one of the region's 28 types of natural vegetation mapped by IBAMA at a scale of 1:5,000,000. To protect all of the 111 terrestrial ecosystems present in the region it would not be necessary to have a separate reserve for each of these ecosystems because it is often possible to encompass several types in a single reserve. At present, only 38 (33 per cent) of the ecosystems have some area protected, which leaves 74 (67 per cent) without protection. The situation is most critical in the

Figure 25.5 Number of protected and unprotected terrestrial ecosystems in each state and overall in Brazilian Legal Amazon.

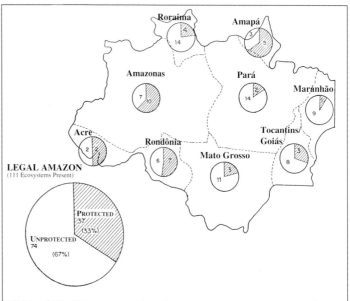

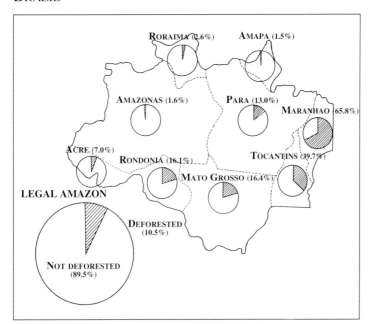

Figure 25.6 Percentage of original forest lost in each state and overall in Brazilian Legal Amazonia by 1991.

Isolated forest reserves of the BDFF Project, near Manaus, Brazil.
(Rob Bierregaard)

contact areas between the forest and the *cerrado* in Maranhão, Tocantins and Mato Grosso. In Maranhão, only one of ten vegetation types presently has protection. The states with the fewest of their ecosystems protected (Figure 25.5) are generally those that have already lost the largest percentages of their forest cover (Figure 25.6).

Although there are a considerable number of conservation areas in the Atlantic forest, the total area covered by parks, reserves and ecological stations amounts to only about 3000 sq. km, although a larger area is protected in other categories of conservation area (Sick, 1993). Several conservation areas, including the 1700 sq. km Iguaçu National Park, protect the remains of the *Araucaria* forest.

Brazil's record of sacrificing protected areas does not lead to confidence that all areas protected will survive indefinitely (see Fearnside and de Lima Ferreira, 1985; Foresta, 1991). Examples include the flooding of Sete Quedas National Park by the Itaipú Dam in 1982, building a road through the Araguaia National Park (also in 1982), and the current plans to sacrifice the turtle protection functions of the Trombetas Biological Reserve when the Cachoeira Porteira Dam is built. A number of protected areas have illegal logging and gold-mining activities within them.

Initiatives for Conservation

Brazil's national conservation institutions have changed frequently since the first such agency was established. In October 1992, a Ministry of the Environment was created, which took over control of IBAMA. This institute was formed by merging three previous agencies.

Many states also have environmental departments or secretariats. The national and state governments frequently differ over protecting natural habitats and over what forms of use are "conservation" or "sustainable development." Particularly in Amazonia, state agencies argue for smaller reserves and for permitting more disturbances for economic exploitation. One such proposal (by the governor of the state of Amazonas) calls for "sustainable management" by cutting trees so as to leave 60 cm high stumps, which are supposed to resprout to regenerate the forest. To this author's knowledge, the proposal has not been endorsed by anyone in the forestry profession.

Brazil has been slow to join many international conservation efforts, which are frequently denounced in political rhetoric as conspiracies threatening national sovereignty. In spite of this, Brazil hosted the United Nations Conference on Environment and Development (UNCED) in June 1992. In 1991, Brazil allowed two UNESCO biosphere reserves to be declared in the country (see Chapter 8). Brazil has not yet entered the Tropical Forestry Action Program (TFAP) process, but this is expected to occur shortly. Security concerns dominate any discussion of conservation initiatives: in 1992 adjoining UNESCO World Heritage Sites at Iguaçu had to be listed separately for Brazil and Argentina.

The principal research institutions in Amazonia are the National Institute for Research in the Amazon (INPA) in Manaus and the Museu Paraense Emílio Goeldi (MPEG) in Belém. Knowledge of Amazonia is scant considering the scale of the region. The largest herbarium is that of INPA, with 200,000 specimens. For comparison, this is one-tenth the size of Indonesia's herbarium at Bogor. On a per-area basis, indices of knowledge such as herbarium specimens per hectare of forest, or scientific publications per hectare are hundreds or thousands of times lower than in relatively well-studied tropical forests such as those of Costa Rica, Panama or Puerto Rico. The importance of events in Amazonia for global change makes increasing the base of scientific information a high priority.

References

Ab'Saber, A.N. (1973). A organização natural das paisagens inter e subtropicais brasileiras. *Geomorfologia* 41. São Paulo: IGEOB-USP.

Allegretti, M.H. (1990). Extractive reserves: An alternative for reconciling development and environmental conservation in Amazonia. pp. 252–264 In: A.B. Anderson (ed.) *Alternatives to Deforestation: Steps toward Sustainable Use of Amazonian*

Rain Forest. Columbia University Press, New York. 281 pp.

Anderson, A.B. (1990). Smokestacks in the rainforest: Industrial development and deforestation in the Amazon Basin. *World Development* 18(9): 1556–1570.

Aubreville, A. (1961). *Etude écologique des principales formations végétales du Brésil*. Centre Technique Forestiers Tropicale. Nogent-sur-Mer, France. 268 pp.

Brazil, CIMA (1991a). *O Desafio do Desenvolvimento Sustentável: Relatório do Brasil para a Conferência das Nações Unidas sobre Meio Ambiente e Desenvolvimento*. Presidência da República, Comissão Interministerial para Preparação da Conferência das Nações Unidas sobre Meio Ambiente e Desenvolvimento (CIMA), Brasília. 204 pp.

Brazil, CIMA (1991b). *Subsídio Técnicos para Elaboração do Relatorio Nacional do Brasil para a Conferência das Nações Unidas sobre Meio Ambiente e Desenvolvimento*. Presidência da República, Comissão Interministerial para Preparação da Conferência das Nações Unidas sobre Meio Ambiente e Desenvolvimento (CIMA), Brasília. 172 pp.

Brazil, ELETROBRÁS (1987). *Plano 2010: Relatório Geral. Plano Nacional de Energia Electrica 1987/2010 (Dezembro 1987)*. Centrais Electricas do Brasil (ELETROBRAS). Brasilia, Brasil. 269 pp.

Brazil, IBGE (1989). *Anuário Estatístico do Brasil 1989. Vol. 49*. Presidência da República, Instituto Brasileiro de Geografia e Estatística (IBGE), Rio de Janeiro. 716 pp.

Brazil, IBDF/IBGE (1988). *Mapa de Vegetação do Brasil. Map Scale 1:5,000,000*. Instituto Brasileiro de Desenvolvimento Florestal and Instituto Brasileiro de Geografia e Estatística, Brasília.

Brazil, Projeto RADAMBRASIL (1973–83). *Levantamento de Recursos Naturais Vols 1–23*. Ministério das Minas e Energia, Departamneto Nacional de Perdação Mineral, Rio de Janeiro, Brasil.

Collar, N.J., Gonzaga, L.P., Krabbe, N., Madroño Nieto, A., Naranjo, L.G., Parker III, T.A. and Wege, D.C. (1992). *Threatened Birds of the Americas. The ICBP/IUCN Red Data Book*. ICBP, Cambridge, U.K.

Daly, D.C. and Prance, G.T. (1989). Brazilian Amazon. In: *Floristic Inventory of Tropical Countries: The Status of Plant Systematics, Collections and Vegetation, plus Recommendations for the Future*. Pp. 401–426. Campbell, D.G. and Hammond, H.D. (eds). The New York Botanical Garden, New York, U.S.A.

Emmons, L.H. (1984). Geographic variation in densities and diversities of non-flying mammals in Amazonia. *Biotropica* 16: 210–222.

Erwin, T.L. (1983). Beetles and other arthropods of the tropical forest canopies at Manaus, Brazil, sampled with insecticidal fogging techniques. In: *Tropical Rain Forests: Ecology and Management*. Pp. 59–75. Sutton, S.L., Whitmore, T.C. and Chadwick, A.C. (eds). Blackwell Scientific Publications, Oxford, U.K.

Erwin, T.L. (1988). The tropical forest canopy: heart of biotic diversity. In: *Biodiversity*. Pp. 123–129. Wilson, E.O. (ed.). Natural Academy Press, Washington, D.C. USA. 521 pp.

FAO (1993). *Forest resource assessment 1990: tropical countries*. FAO Forestry Paper 112. FAO, Rome, Italy.

FAO/UNEP (1981). *Proyecto de Evaluacion de los Recursos Forestales Tropicales: Los Recursos Forestales de la America Tropical*. FAO, Rome, Italy.

Fearnside, P.M. (1980). The effects of cattle pasture on soil fertility in the Brazilian Amazon: Consequences for beef production sustainability. *Tropical Ecology* 21(1): 125–137.

Fearnside, P.M. (1983). Land use trends in the Brazilian Amazon region as factors in accelerating deforestation. *Environmental Conservation* 10(2): 141–148.

Fearnside, P.M. (1986a). Settlement in Rondônia and the token role of science and technology in Brazil's Amazonian development planning. *Interciencia* 11(5): 229–236.

Fearnside, P.M. (1986b). *Human Carrying Capacity of the Brazilian Rainforest*. Columbia University Press, New York, E.U.A. 293 pp.

Fearnside, P.M. (1987a). Causes of Deforestation in the Brazilian Amazon. In: *The Geophysiology of Amazonia: Vegetation and Climate Interactions* pp. 37–61. Dickinson, R.F. (ed.). John Wiley & Sons, New York. 526 pp.

Fearnside, P.M. (1987b). Rethinking continuous cultivation in Amazonia. *BioScience* 37(3): 209–214.

Fearnside, P.M. (1989a). Forest management in Amazonia: The need for new criteria in evaluating development options. *Forest Ecology and Management* 27: 61–79.

Fearnside, P.M. (1989b). Extractive reserves in Brazilian Amazonia: An opportunity to maintain tropical rain forest under sustainable use. *BioScience* 39(6): 387–393.

Fearnside, P.M. (1989c). The Charcoal of Carajás: Pig-iron smelting threatens the forests of Brazil's Eastern Amazon Region. *Ambio* 18(2): 141–143.

Fearnside, P.M. (1990a). Predominant land uses in the Brazilian Amazon. In: *Alternatives to Deforestation: Towards Sustainable Use of the Amazon Rain Forest*. pp. 235–251. Anderson, A.B. (ed.). Columbia University Press, New York. 281 pp.

Fearnside, P.M. (1990b). The rate and extent of deforestation in Brazilian Amazonia. *Environmental Conservation* 17(3): 213–226.

Fearnside, P.M. (1993). Deforestation in Brazilian Amazonia: The effect of population and land tenure. *Ambio* 22 (8): 537–545.

Fearnside, P.M. (in press). Agroforestry in Brazil's Amazonian development policy: The role and limits of a potential use for degraded lands. In: *Ecologically, Socially and Economically Sustainable Resource Use Patterns in the Humid Tropics*. Sachs, I. (ed.). UNESCO, Paris. (forthcoming).

Fearnside, P.M. and de Lima Ferreira, G. (1985). Roads in Rondonia: Highway construction and the farce of unprotected reserves in Brazil's Amazonian forest. *Environmental Conservation* 11(4): 358–360.

Fearnside, P.M. and J. Ferraz. (in press). Identifying areas of biological importance in Brazilian Amazonia. In: *Priority Areas for Conservation in Amazonian Rainforest*. Prance, G.T., Lovejoy, T.E. Rylands, A.B., dos Santos, A.A. and Miller, C. (eds.). Smithsonian Institution Press, Washington, DC, U.S.A. (forthcoming).

Fearnside, P.M., Tardin, A.T. and Meira Filho, L.G. (nd) *Deforestation rate in Brazilian Amazonia*. Unpublished manuscript.

Foresta, R. (1991). *Amazon Conservation in the Age of Development: The Limits of Providence*. University Presses of Florida, Gainesville, Florida. 366 pp.

Fundação S.O.S. Mata Atlântica (1992). *Mata Atlântica*. Fundação S.O.S. Mata Atlântica, São Paulo.

Geisler, R., Knöppel, H.A. and Sioli, H. (1975). The ecology of freshwater fishes in Amazonia — present status and future tasks for research. *Animal Research and Development* (Tübingen) 1: 102–119.

Goulding, M. (1980). *The Fishes and the Forest*. University of California Press, Berkeley, California, U.S.A., 280 pp.

Groombridge, B. (Ed) (1993). *1994 IUCN Red List of Threatened Animals*. IUCN, Gland, Switzerland and Cambridge, U.K. 286 pp.

Hecht, S.B., Norgaard, R.B. and Possio, C. (1988). The economics of cattle ranching in eastern Amazônia. *Interciencia* 13(5): 233–240.

Herz, R. (1991). *Manguezais do Brasil*. Instituto Oceanográfico, Universidade de São Paulo, São Paulo, Brazil. Pp. 277.

IUCN (1992). *Protected Areas of the World: A review of national systems. Volume 4: Nearctic and Neotropical*. IUCN, Gland, Switzerland and Cambridge, U.K.

Jornal do Brasil (1993). Mata Atlântica é devastada na Bahía *Jornal do Brasil*, May 11, p. 12.

Kjerfve, B. and Lacerda, L.D. (1993). Mangroves of Brazil. In: *Conservation and Sustainable Utilization of Mangrove Forests in Latin America and Africa Regions. Part 1: Latin America*. ITTO/ISME Project PD114/90(F). Pp. 245–272.

Malcolm, J.R. (1990). Estimation of mammalian densities in continuous forest north of Manaus. In: *Four Neotropical Rainforests*. Pp. 339–357. Gentry, A.H. (ed.). Yale University Press, New Haven, Connecticut, U.S.A. 627 pp.

Mattos, M., Uhl, C. and Gonçalves, D. (in press). Perspectives econômicas e ecolôgicas de pecuária na Amazônia oriental nos anos 90. *Pará Desenvolvimento*.

McNeely, J.A., Miller, K.R., Reid, W.V., Mittermeier, R.A. and Verner, T.B.. (1990). *Conserving the World's Biodiversity*. IUCN, Gland, Switzerland; WRI, CI, WWF-US and the World Bank, Washington, D.C.

Mori, S.A. (1989). Eastern, extra-Amazonian Brazil. In: *Floristic Inventory of Tropical Countries: The Status of Plant Systematics, Collections, and Vegetation, plus Recommendations for the Future*. Campbell, D.G. and Hammond, D. (eds). The New York Botanical Garden, New York, U.S.A.

Mori, S.A., Boom, B.M. and Prance, G.T. (1981). Distribution patterns and conservation of eastern Brazilian coastal forest tree species. *Brittonia* 33: 233–245.

Pádua, M.T.J. & Quintão, A.T.B. (1982). Parks and biological reserves in the Brazilian Amazon. *Ambio* 11(5): 309–314.

Pires, J.M. and Prance, G.T. (1985). The vegetation types of the Brazilian Amazon. In: *Amazonia*. Key Environments. Pp. 109–145. Prance, G.T. and Lovejoy, T.E. (eds). Pergamon Press, Oxford. 442 pp.

Prance, G.T. (1979). The present state of botanical exploration: South America. In: *Systematic Botany, Plant Utilization and Biosphere Conservation*. Hedberg, I.(ed). Almqvist and Wiskell International, Stockholm, Sweden. Pp. 55–70.

Roberts, T.R. (1972). Ecology of fishes in the Amazon and Congo basins. *Bulletin of the Museum of Comparative Zoology of Harvard University* 143(2): 117–147.

Saenger, P., Hegerl, E.J. and Davie, J.D.S. (1983). (eds). *Global Status of Mangrove Ecosystems*. Commission on Ecology Papers No. 3. IUCN, Gland, Switzerland.

Sick, H. (1993). *Birds in Brazil: a Natural History*. Princeton University Press, New Jersey.

Smith, N.J.H. (1980). Anthrosols and human carrying capacity in Amazonia. *Annals of the Association of American Geographers* 70(4): 553–566.

Uhl, C., Buschbacher, R. and Serrão, E.A.S. (1988). Abandoned pastures in Eastern Amazonia. I. Patterns of plant succession. *Journal of Ecology* 76: 663–681.

Uhl, C., Verissimo, A., Mattos, M.M., Brandino, Z. and Vieira, I.C.G. (1991). Social, economic, and ecological consequences of selective logging in an Amazon frontier; The case of Tailândia. *Forest Ecology and Management* 46: 243–273.

Veloso, E. (1966). Tipos de vegetaçao. In: *Atlas Florestal do Brasil*. Ministério da Agricultura, Conselho Florestal Federal, Rio de Janeiro.

Vincent, J.R. (1992). The tropical timber trade and sustainable development. *Science* 256: 1651–1655.

Whitmore, T.C. and da Silva, J.N.M. (1990). Brazil rain forest timbers are mostly very dense. *Commonwealth Forestry Review* 69(1): 87–90.

Author: Philip Fearnside, INPA, Manaus, Brazil; with contributions from Jeff Sayer, IUCN; David Cleary, Centre of Latin American Studies, Cambridge University; Richard O. Bierregaard, Jr., Smithsonian Institution, Washington, U.S.A., and Ghillean Prance, Royal Botanic Gardens, Kew.

Maps 25.1 and 25.2 Brazil

Forest data for Brazil have been digitised from a map published by IBAMA and compiled by the Fundacao Instituto Brasileriro de Geografia e Estatistica (IBGE). The source map — *Mapa de Vegetacao do Brasil* — based on the RADAMBRAZIL project (a radar and aerial survey of Amazonia carried out between 1973–83), was originally published at 1:5 million in 1988 and updated and reprinted in 1993. The differences between the 1988 version and 1993 update mostly seem to account for changes in the classification and nomenclature, rather than significant changes in the vegetation cover.

Fifty-two vegetation/land use classes are shown on the source map. Of these, sixteen forest classes have been selected to depict forest cover in Brazil; the remainder have been grouped under non-forest.

Lowland moist forest:

Floresta ombrofila densa (Floresta tropical pluvial): Aluvial; Terras baixas; Submontana

Floresta ombrofila aberta (Faciaçóes da floresta ombrofila densa): Terras baixas; Submontana

Areas de tensão ecológica: ON - Floresta ombrofila-Floresta estacional; OM - Floresta ombrofila densa-Floresta ombrofila mista

Montane forest:

Floresta ombrofila densa (Floresta tropical pluvial): Montana

Pine forest:

Floresta ombrofila mista (Floresta de Araucaria): Montana; Alto-montana

Areas de tensão ecológica: NM - Floresta estacional-Floresta ombrofila mista

Dry forest:

Floresta estacional semidecidual (Floresta tropical subcaducifolia): Aluvial; Terras baixas; Submontana; Montana

Floresta estacional decidual (Floresta tropical caducifolia): Terras baixas; Submontana; Montana

Mangroves:

Vegetaçáo com influência fluviomarinha (Manguezal e Campo salino)

Note:

1. secondary vegetation types showing agricultural activity are not mapped as forest here;

2. savanna woodland and scrub formations, such as the cerrado and caatinga respectively, are also not included here. However, the arboreal formations as opposed to the open wooded grassland associations of cerrado and caatinga are illustrated in Figure 25.1;

3. seasonal semi-deciduous and deciduous forests in central Brazil and on the southern fringes of the Amazon are mapped as dry forests;

4. open forest types 'Floresta ombrofila aberta' to the west and east of the dense forests of the Brazilian Amazon, which are more open than typical Amazon rain forest but which are taller and/or with a more closed canopy than the cerrado in the east, have been mapped with the lowland moist forest types;

5. in the majority of cases, the transitional vegetation formations have not been mapped, especially when the transition is from savanna, scrub or grassland formations. However, where the transitional forest type is from broadleaved, mixed and seasonal deciduous or semidecidous, they have been mapped (see above for details concerning data harmonisation); and

6. submontane forest formations (*submontana*) have been incorporated into the lowland forest category as these forests fall below 700 m.

Conservation areas data are derived from numerous sources held within WCMC.

26 Colombia

Country area 1,138,910 sq. km
Land area 1,038,700 sq. km
Population (mid-1994) 35.6 million
Population growth rate 2.0 per cent
Population projected to 2025 51.3 million
Gross national product per capita (1992) US$1290
Forest cover for 1985 (see Map) 510,935 sq. km
Forest cover for 1990 (FAO, 1993)* 540,460 sq. km
Annual deforestation rate 1981–1990 0.7 per cent
Industrial roundwood production 3,683,000 cu. m
Industrial roundwood exports —
Fuelwood and charcoal production 16,936,000 cu. m
Processed wood production 990,000 cu. m
Processed wood exports 13,000 cu. m
* excludes dry deciduous forest

Colombia lies at the junction of the continental land masses of North and South America. Its rich diversity of landscapes extend from snow covered summits reaching almost 6000 m to tropical beaches and from deserts to rain forests. The country has a rich cultural heritage, a well educated population and efficient agriculture and industries.

Only half of Colombia is now forested and most of the clearing has taken place over the last fifty years. Shifting cultivation and colonisation are the main causes of deforestation. There are many other problems contributing to the disappearance of the forests including lack of awareness of the need for sustainable management of the forests, poor functioning of state institutions involved with conservation and lack of participation of the commercial forestry sector in the national economy and in the socioeconomic development of the rural communities. Nevertheless, the country has vast areas of pristine forest, some of the most spectacular protected areas on the continent and some highly innovative forest conservation programmes.

INTRODUCTION

The Republic of Colombia, situated in the north-west corner of the South American continent, is the only country in the region with both Pacific and Caribbean coastlines.

The country can be divided into four main topographical regions (Forero, 1989). The Pacific coastal region is an irregular strip, narrow near Panama but extending inland as far as 100 km in places near the border with Ecuador. Although mostly flat, it is interrupted by spurs of the Cordillera Occidental and by isolated peaks separated by a network of rivers and creeks. The area extending along the Pacific watershed is the biogeographic region of the Chocó.

The Caribbean coastal plain stretches east from the Río Sinú to the Guajira Peninsula. It is a level or moderately hilly region, generally semi-arid and open, but partly marshy along rivers. Although much of the Guajira Peninsula is arid, the Serranía de Macuira in the north is an "island" of dense vegetation, completely different from the surrounding desert (Forero, 1989).

The Andes forms three cordilleras in Colombia; with their axes running parallel south to north, they are separated by the long, deep, longitudinal valleys of the rivers Magdalena and Cauca. Although considered to be part of the Central Cordillera, the Sierra Nevada de Santa Marta appears like an island in northern Colombia, rising to almost 6000 m within a very short distance from the sea and having no connection with any of the three cordilleras. The country's highest peak, Pico Colón at 5800 m, is found in this Sierra.

East of the Andes is a mostly low altitude region which, in the southeast, includes the Amazon forest. Also in the area is the Sierra de la Macarena, this, along with other isolated hills, is considered to be the western extreme of the Guyana highlands. Emergent rock formations, or tepuis, covered with sclerophyllous forests occur in this region. Most of the lowlands of the Orinoco River drainage system are covered with natural grassland; there are also gallery forests and dispersed wetlands in the region.

Annual precipitation varies from 150 to 200 mm in the north of the Guajira Peninsula to more than 11,700 mm in the hot south-central region of the Department of Chocó; the latter is one of the wettest places in the world (Hernández, 1990). Temperatures vary very little over the year, the differences between average temperatures for the coldest month and those for the hottest month in any particular place are less than 5°C. However the difference between night and daytime temperatures can be as much as 20°C.

After the Spanish conquest in the 16th century, Colombia's overall population density was quite low; areas of relatively high density were restricted to the Interandean valleys, some coastal regions and some areas on the flanks of the cordilleras along the rivers Cauca and Magdalena. However, the population has doubled in the last 35 years and now stands at almost 35 million. In the 1960s, the rate of population growth reached 3.4 per cent per year, though this has now dropped to two per cent. Between 1950 and 1985, the proportion of rural to urban population inverted, becoming 32 per cent to 68 per cent respectively. The largest city is the capital, Bogotá, with almost 5 million inhabitants. Less than one per cent of the population is Amerindian, most are of mixed Spanish and Indian descent.

The contribution of agriculture to GDP is declining. The

country is, however, the world's second largest exporter of coffee; the cut-flower industry is also important. It has substantial reserves of oil, coal and natural gas.

The Forests

The humid lowland forests have extraordinarily diverse floras, with between 100 and 240 woody species per hectare; only in rare instances are communities dominated by a single tree species (Sánchez Páez et al., 1990). The lowland forests have a canopy of between 35 and 55 m in height and a relatively open understorey. The most diverse woody plant families of the lowland rain forest are Leguminosae, Rubiaceae, Palmae, Annonaceae, Melastomataceae, Sapotaceae and Guttiferae (Gentry, 1990a). Other woody families found in this habitat include Moraceae, Lauraceae, Lecythidaceae, Myristicaceae, Euphorbiaceae, Chrysobalanaceae and Myrtaceae. A characteristic of these forests is the abundance of both large and small palms such as *Jessenia*, *Socratea*, *Iriartea* and *Wettinia*. Indeed, the forests of the Chocó have a larger proportion of palms than any other forest in the world (Gentry, 1990b).

In the Chocó, there are areas of swamp or alluvial forest which are subject to periodic or permanent flooding. These include "Cativales", named after the cativo *Prioria copaifera*, located in the extreme north, which were once the region's greatest timber producers. "Sajales" are found in the south, these are forests of sajo *Campnosperma panamensis*, a species which dominates the freshwater swamps and is also exploited for timber. In the wetter areas, "naidizales" are also found, with an abundance of the palm *Euterpe cuatrecasana*.

Colombia is the only country which possesses in its Amazon region both the species-poor vegetation of the white sand soils of the Guyanan Shield and the species-rich communities of the relatively fertile soils of the Andean foothills. The forests on these foothills are very rich in endemics, more so than any other forests in the Amazon Basin, and are among the most diverse forests on the planet (Gentry, 1990a). Preliminary collections indicate that it is the southern part of Colombian Amazonia and the adjacent northern area of Peru which are the world's most diverse forest. Ten families (Leguminosae, Moraceae, Annonaceae, Rubiaceae, Myristicaceae, Zapotaceae, Meliaceae, Palmae, Euphorbiaceae and Bignoniaceae) dominate the flora of most of the forests of Upper Amazonia and eight of these are amongst the ten most species-rich families in the world.

The species-rich forests of the more accessible hills of the Pacific are characterised by *Brosimun utile* and by tree species from the genera *Virola*, *Sapium*, *Pouteria* and *Eschweilera* in the north; by *Brosimun utile*, *Clarisia racemosa*, *Virola reidii* and *Protium* sp. in the centre; and by *Saccoglottis procera*, *Apeiba aspera*, *Goupia glabra*, *Laetia procera* and species of the genera *Pouteria*, *Eschweilera*, *Inga* and *Aspidosperma* in the south of the Chocó.

On the Chiribiquete plateau, the bushy dwarf forest is dominated by *Bonnetia martiana*, while *Hevea nitida* var. *toxicodendroides*, *Graffenrieda fantastica*, *Calliandra vaupesiana* and *Senefelderopsis chiribiquetensis* are amongst the smaller trees found on this plateau and on other hills in Amazonia.

Sub-andean forests occur on the lower slopes and foothills of the cordilleras and mountain chains (1000–2000 m). Their physiognomy is somewhat similar to that of the hot lowland forests, but with fewer large palms, fewer species with buttress roots and fewer lianas and woody epiphytes. The frequent mists increase atmospheric humidity and decrease evapotranspiration. The species here are a mixture of those characteristic of lowlands and ones which are associated with the cooler conditions of higher altitudes, such as those in the genera *Weinmannia* and *Clusia*. The canopy of these forests is 20–30 m tall, common trees include species of *Cedrela*, *Juglans* and *Quercus*, while *Cecropia* appears sporadically. Other principal tree species are *Billia colombiana*, *Brosimum utile*, *Hyeronima macrocarpa*, *Anacardium excelsum*, *Dendropanax* sp., *Sloanea robusta*, *Panopsis mucronata* and species of the genera *Protium*, *Virola*, *Guarea*, *Ocotea*, *Meliosma*, *Eugenia* and *Tabebuia*. Palms such as *Socratea exhorriza*, *Iriartea gigantea* and *Jessenia bataua* are also present.

The montane forests of the Andes are found on steep areas of the cordilleras and at altitudes over 2000 m up to where the páramo begins, this varies from 3200 to 3800 m depending on location. As the altitude increases, the trees and their leaves get smaller and epiphytes become more abundant. The latter include algae, mosses, lichens, ferns and liverworts, as well as Angiosperms such as bushy Ericaceae, Bromeliaceae, Gesneriaceae, Orchidaceae, Begoniaceae and *Anthurium*, which almost completely cover the trunk and main branches of the trees. Mist is frequent and the temperature varies from 14–16°C to 5–6°C.

Palms of the genera *Aiphanes* and *Euterpe* are found in the forests up to 2500 m, while between 2200 and 3200 m wax palms *Ceroxylon* spp. occur; amongst these the most important is *Ceroxylon quindiuense*, Colombia's national tree. Small palms of the genus *Geonoma*, in particular *Geonoma weberbaueri*, are important in some areas where there is more light. Tree ferns are common in such areas. The rhizomatose bamboos of the genera *Swallenochloa* and *Chusquea* are also common.

The floristic composition of the Andean forests is very varied. The more common species include *Bocconia intergrifolia*, *Vallea stipularis*, *Drimys granadensis*, *Alnus acuminata*, *Cedrela subandina* as well as some from the genera *Weinmannia*, *Clethra*, *Brunellia*, *Juglans*, *Clusia*, *Hedyosmun*, *Hyeronima*, *Hesperomeles*, *Escallonia*, *Oreopanax*, *Dendropanax*, *Schefflera*, *Podocarpus*, *Ocotea*, *Nectandra*, *Persea*, *Cavendishia*, *Macleania*, *Piper*, *Cinchona* and *Tibouchina*. Several composites from such genera as *Baccharis*, *Paragynoxys* and *Diplostephium* are also present in the Andean forests (Hernández, 1990).

Mangroves

Colombia's mangroves were estimated by Escallón and Rodriguez (1986) to cover an area of approximately 3463 sq. km, of which 650 sq. km are on the Caribbean coast and 2813 sq. km on the Pacific coast; Alvarez-León (1993) reports an area of 3580 sq. km. Map 26.1 shows the slightly higher area of 3680 sq. km (Table 26.2). The mangroves attain their maximum biomass in the Pacific departments of Valle and Chocó where annual rainfall is between 2000 and 6000 mm. They also occur in areas where rainfall is only 150 to 200 mm annually.

On the Caribbean coast, the mangrove canopy is 20–25 m high and consists of red mangrove *Rhizophora mangle* in the intertidal zone, followed by a band of mainly black mangrove *Avicennia germinans*, button mangrove *Conocarpus erecta* and white mangrove *Laguncularia racemosa*. In intermediate areas, the fern *Acrostichum aureum* is found. *Pelliciera rhizophorae* has been recently reported to occur on this coast (Calderón, 1992). Most of the mangroves on the Caribbean coast have a disjunct distribution, being restricted to certain small protected bays, but greater areas are found in places such as Isla Salamanca, La Ciénaga Grande de Santa Marta and the deltas of the Sinú and Atrato rivers.

Table 26.1   Area (sq. km) of forest in each biogeographic region of Colombia

Region	Unexploited commercial	Exploited commercial	Not commercial	Total forest	Total unexploited
Pacific	25,487	6,897	21,843	54,227	47,330
Andes	49,542	7,612	20,114	77,267	69,655
Caribbean	2,228	1,856	1,219	5,303	3,447
Orinoco	40,466	29,298	1,745	71,508	42,210
Amazon	274,094	–	49,398	323,493	323,493
Total	391,817	45,663	94,319	531,797	486,135

Totals may not tally due to rounding.

Source: IGAC-INDERENA-CONIF (1984)

The mangroves of the Pacific coast are found in an almost continuous belt of variable width from the Mataje River in the south to Cabo Corrientes in the north; from there to Punta Ardita the presence of cliffs means that the belt is reduced to small patches. The canopy reaches 25–30 m high, although the button mangrove does not grow taller than 10 m. The composition of the mangroves is more heterogenous and includes *Rhizophora harrisonii* and *R. brevistyla*, as well as the red, white, black and button mangroves of the Caribbean coast. *Pelliciera rhizophorae* is also found in this association. The Pacific mangroves have a spatial and successional relationship with *Mora megistosperma* which can tolerate slight salinity, and with a complex of swamp forest species which cannot tolerate saline conditions, amongst which are found *Pachira acuatica* and *Euterpe cuatrecasana*. The fern *Acrostichum aureum* also forms vast associations here.

The principal causes of the degradation of mangroves are their overexploitation for timber, firewood and poles and use of the bark. Another problem is hypersalinity or prolonged stagnation brought about through human action, such as the obstruction of the flow of fresh, salt or brackish water, which causes the mangroves to degrade or die. Mangroves have also been cleared for the construction of shrimp farms and for developments such as roads, hotels, urban, industrial and recreational areas and for the improvement of harbours and jetties.

Projects to restore mangroves include one in the Ciénaga Grande de Santa Marta which aims to restore the flow of fresh and salt water into the mangrove areas.

Forest Resources and Management
In 1982, Colombia's forest cover was estimated to be about 532,000 sq. km (IGAC-INDERENA-CONIF, 1984). This was made up of approximately 392,000 sq. km of commercially unexploited forest, 46,000 sq. km of commercially exploited forest and 94,000 sq. km of forest that was not considered commercially exploitable for various physical reasons. The areas of these different forest categories in each biogeographic region of Colombia (Figure 26.1) are shown in Table 26.1. The same source indicates that lowland forests (including mangrove) covered 473,870 sq. km, submontane forests (between 1000 and 2000 m) covered 27,447 sq. km and montane forests covered 30,481 sq. km of Colombia.

Map 26.1 was digitised from a source map published in 1985 and it shows a total of 510,935 sq. km (Table 26.2) of forest in the country, this includes exploited forests but they have not been distinguished from the unexploited ones (see Map Legend). FAO (1993) estimates the somewhat higher figure of 540,460 sq. km of forest in the rain, moist deciduous, hill and montane zone in the country as of 1990. FAO also reports an additional 180 sq. km of forest in the dry deciduous zone, but

Table 26.2   Estimates of forest extent in Colombia

Forest Type	Area (sq. km)	% land area
Lowland moist	446,134	43.0
Submontane	29,630	2.9
Montane	31,491	3.0
Mangrove	3,680	0.4
Total	510,935	49.2

Based on analysis of Map 26.1. See Map Legend on pp. 258/259 for details of sources.

Figure 26.1   Biogeographic regions of Colombia

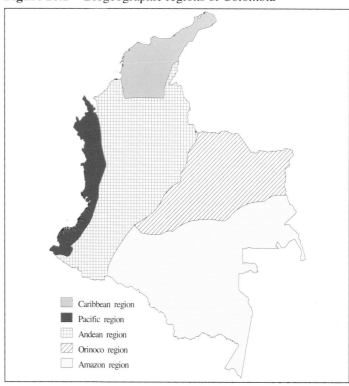

Caribbean region
Pacific region
Andean region
Orinoco region
Amazon region

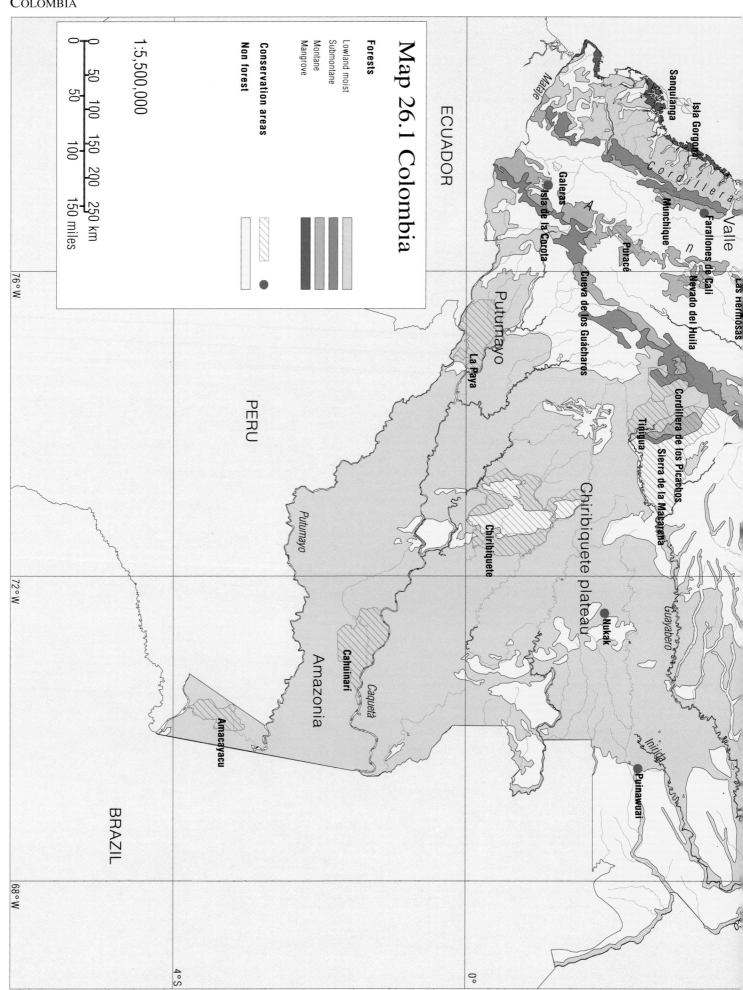

Map 26.1 Colombia

1:5,500,000

Forests

Lowland moist
Submontane
Montane
Mangrove

Conservation areas

Non forest

0	50	100	150	200	250 km
0	50	100	150 miles

ECUADOR

PERU

BRAZIL

76°W

72°W

68°W

0°

4°S

Valle

Cordillera

A n

Isla Gorgona

Sanquianga

Isla de la Corota

Galeras

Munchique

Farallones de Cali

Nevado del Huila

Puracé

Las hermosas

Cueva de los Guácharos

Cordillera de los Picachos

Tinigua

Sierra de la Macarena

Matate

Putumayo

La Paya

Chiribiquete

Chiribiquete plateau

Guayabero

Nukak

Inírida

Puinawai

Putumayo

Amazonia

Cahuinarí

Caquetá

Amacayacu

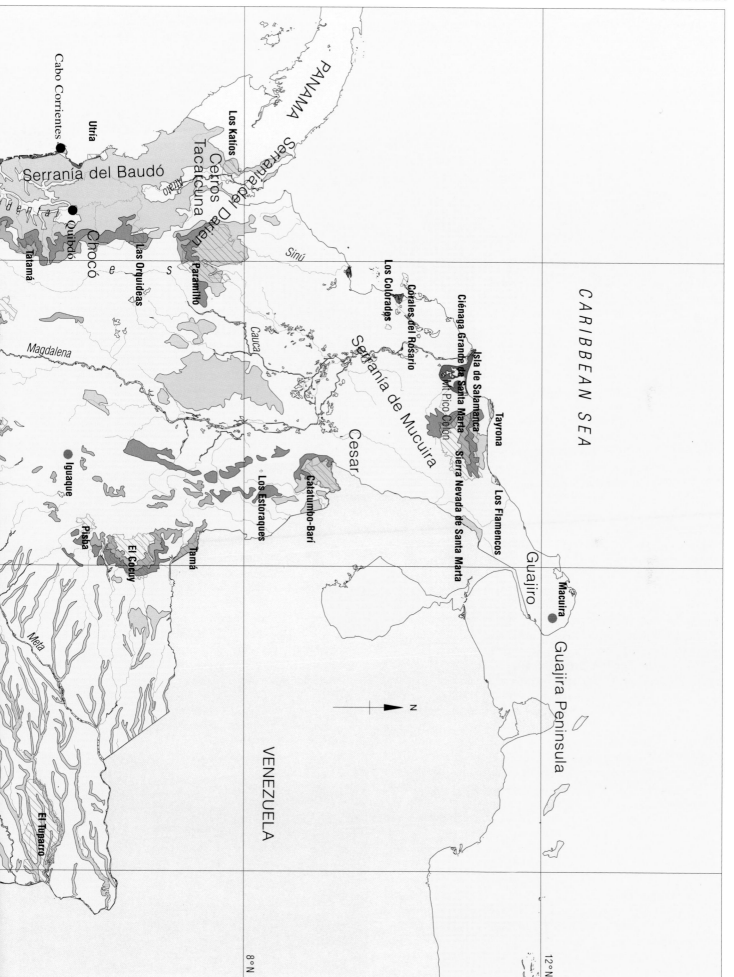

Cabo Corrientes

Utría

Serranía del Baudó

Occidental

Talamá

Quibdó

Chocó

Las Orquídeas

Los Katíos

Cerros Tacarcuna

Serranía del Darien

Atrato

Paramillo

PANAMA

Sinú

Los Colorados

Corales del Rosario

Cauca

Ciénaga Grande de Santa Marta

Isla de Salamanca

Mt Pico Colón

Tayrona

Los Flamencos

Sierra Nevada de Santa Marta

Serranía de Mucuira

Cesar

Macuira

Guajiro

Guajira Peninsula

CARIBBEAN SEA

Magdalena

Iguaque

Catatumbo-Barí

Los Estoraques

Pisba

El Cocuy

Tamá

Meta

El Tuparro

VENEZUELA

N

this forest is a drier formation than any considered in this Atlas and has not been included in the statistics at the head of the chapter.

There are 780,000 sq. km of land calculated to be suitable for some sort of forestry by the Departamento Nacional de Planeación (1992), a considerably higher area than that actually covered in forest at present.

In 1986, the forestry industry (timber, wood products and cork, furniture and accessories, and paper-making and its products) in Colombia had a gross production worth US$666.3 million, with an additional processed value of US$256.7 million. The sector covering paper and its products makes up the highest proportion of the value of forest production with more than 82 per cent; timber contributes 11 per cent and the furniture industry 6.9 per cent. National wood consumption is low (4 cu.m of wood panels per thousand people in 1983; 19.25 kg of paper and cardboard per person in 1987), but it is increasing. In total, 3.4 million cu. m of timber is used nationally per year and this supplies 94 per cent of the primary material needed by the secondary forestry industry. To this consumption must be added between 9.8 and 12.7 million tonnes of fuelwood per year and one million tonnes of charcoal per year (Departamento Nacional de Planeación 1992; PAFC/BID (1991).

The consumption of wood by the forestry industry has grown at an average rate of 3.5 per cent per year over the last decade. The increase is a consequence firstly of a rise in consumption by sawmills and higher wastage levels in the industry and secondly of the expansion in the pulp industry.

The value of forest sector exports has been about US$54 million per year and imports about US$55 million per year. The contribution of the sector to Gross National Product was, on average, 1.7 per cent between 1980 and 1990 and the sector employs approximately 54,000 people of which 24,000 have permanent jobs in forest industries.

More than two hundred non-timber tree species are known to have potential for exploitation. These species produce rubber, resins, tannins, tanning substances, oils, spices, condiments, foods, medicines, dyes, food colours, etc. These non-timber forest products have rarely been taken into account in government programmes for the management and exploitation of the country's forests. However, the market demand and the potential of the forests suggest that this will change in the future.

The legal framework for the management of Colombia's forests is given in the National Code of Renewable Natural Resources and Protection of the Environment (Código Nacional de los Recursos Naturales Renovables y Protección al Medio Ambiente), Decree 2811 of 1974. The national institution charged with formulating forest policy for the government is INDERENA, the National Institute of Renewable Natural Resources and Environment. Created in 1968 under the Ministry of Agriculture, INDERENA is responsible at the national level for administration, control, regulation, promotion, protection and management of the forests. It shares this responsibility with 18 Autonomous Corporations for Regional Development. The corporations are decentralised bodies under the National Planning Department which operate at regional level.

INDERENA is responsible for 72 per cent of the country while the corporations cover the remaining 28 per cent. In general, however, the state institutions' mechanisms for conservation and for effectively controlling the forms of forest exploitation function only poorly and there is also a lack of awareness of the need for sustainable management of forests on the part of the various sectors which make use of the resource.

At present, the National Planning Department, through the agrarian development unit, is responsible for the Colombian Forestry Action Plan (PAFC). The possibility of establishing a Ministry of the Environment to take responsibility for all natural resource management issues is under discussion.

Deforestation

More natural areas have been destroyed in the last fifty years than in the country's entire preceding history. During the Prehispanic period, there was only moderate use of natural resources for subsistence and bartering between tribes. During the colonial period, although the Spanish increased exploitation of the forests, the pressure on them was not significant because population density was low. This is no longer the case and population pressure combined with social and economic problems and grossly unequal distribution of wealth and land, means that the rate of deforestation continues to increase. Other factors including the lack of basic health services, education, drinking water and communications all exacerbate the problems.

There have been several estimates of the area deforested each year. Comparing maps of forest cover published in 1966 and 1984 gives the figure of 8750 sq. km of forest cleared each year (an annual rate of 1.6 per cent). The National Planning Department's estimate is 6000 sq. km per year. FAO (1993) estimates that for the years from 1981 to 1990, 3666 sq. km have been lost annually, an area which is in agreement with INDERENA's own evaluation carried out over the last four years. This gives an annual rate of 0.7 per cent.

It is estimated that shifting cultivation and human settlements are responsible for 76.3 per cent of the deforestation in Colombia; cutting of wood for fuel accounts for 12.7 per cent and extraction of timber for the remaining 11 per cent (Departamento Nacional de Planeacíon, 1989). A relatively minor contribution to forest clearance is the growing of opium poppies — estimated in El Tiempo (1993) to have resulted in 15 sq. km of forest being cleared between 1991 and 1992, and this is decreasing as a result of action taken by the National Guard to eradicate the crop.

There are numerous other problems contributing to the deforestation of Colombia. There has, for instance, been an imbalance in the use of forests, over-exploitation of some species and resources and under-exploitation and even waste of others. The commercial forestry sector does not participate in the national economy, nor does it contribute to the socio-economic develop-

Shifting cultivation and colonization are the main causes of deforestation in Colombia. Here, in Amazonia, slash and burn is being practised to clear the forest. (WWF/Fernando Urbina)

ment of rural communities. In addition, there is no fair distribution of profits accruing from forest exploitation amongst the people living in the areas being exploited. On the whole, the state institutes concerned with conservation do not function well and they do not effectively control forest exploitation. Indeed, there is little awareness of the need for sustainable management of the forests on the part of the various sectors that use them. Another very significant factor is the concentration of land in the hands of a small number of land-owners. Overall, this indiscriminate destruction of ecosystems of great biological value has contributed to the disappearance of several species of plants and animals.

Biodiversity

Colombia, because of its complex geological, climatic, palaeo-geographical and ecological history, is incredibly rich in species, habitats and ecosystems. This is nowhere better illustrated than in its dense humid forests, a biome of great structural complexity which once covered most of the country's surface.

Complete taxonomic inventories of the country's biota are not yet available, but it is estimated that Colombia's flora and fauna (excluding marine taxa) make up about 10 per cent of the world's biota (Hernández and Sánchez, 1988). The enormous biotic diversity in Colombia has led to its recognition as one of the dozen "megadiversity" countries, along with Brazil, Ecuador, Peru, Mexico, Zaire, Madagascar, Australia, China, India, Indonesia and Malaysia (McNeely et al., 1990). The greatest floristic and faunal diversity within Colombia's biomes is found in the forests.

There are some 45,000–50,000 flowering plants in the country, with 1500 endemics recorded and many new species being discovered (Davis et al., 1986, Prance, 1977). Some groups, such as the palms of the Arecaceae and Palmae families, have their greatest diversities in Colombia; in the Araracuara area of Amazonia, 64 species of palm of 24 genera are found, an astonishing figure given the relatively small size (10,000 sq. km) of the study area (Galeano, 1992). There are 3500 species of orchid in the country — that is 15 per cent of those found in the whole world.

The richest area in Colombia for biodiversity is the Chocó Region. Indeed it is considered to be the richest in the world in terms of plant species (Gentry, 1982). This is illustrated by Gentry's (1990b) study where plants with a diameter of more than 2.5 cm were sampled in two 0.1 ha plots in the Chocó; one plot was in Bajo Calima near Buenaventura and the other was located in the vicinity of Tutunendó, to the east of Quibdó. It was found that these plots held the greatest number of species ever recorded in any forest on the planet. The most diverse plot, with 265 species was that in Bajo Calima.

One of Colombia's greatest biological treasures are its birds. There are 1721 recorded, more than in any other country in the world, of which 73 are endemic (WCMC, 1992). Collar et al. (1992) list 55 threatened species, of these 46 are moist forest species and 30 are endemic. Moist forest species that are listed as endangered by Collar et al. (1992) are the northern helmeted curassow Pauxi pauxi and the endemic blue-billed curassow Crax alberti, both of which are hunted, the yellow-eared parrot Ognorhynchus icterotis, the endemic Fuertes's parrot Hapalopsittaca fuertesi, the endemic moustached and brown-banded antpittas Grallaria gigantea and G. milleri, the recurve-billed bushbird Clytoctantes alixii and the ochraceous attila Attila torridus. Habitat destruction is a major factor in the decline of all these species.

More than 359 species of mammals are known from Colombia, of which its 27 primates represent 15 per cent of the world's living primates. Three of these are listed as endangered by IUCN (Groombridge, 1993): the white-footed tamarin Saguinus leucopus and the cottontop tamarin S. oedipus, which are endemic, and the black uakari Cacajao melanocephalus. A further six primates are threatened, although to a lesser extent. Of the 900 species of known Chiroptera, 155 are found in Colombia. One of these, Leptonycteris curasoae, is listed as threatened (Groombridge, 1993). A total of thirty threatened mammal species are found in Colombia.

According to INDERENA's herpetologist José Vicente Rueda, there are 585 amphibian species (543 anurans, 22 urodelans or salamanders and 20 apodans or caecilians) and 590 reptiles (310 snakes, 33 turtles, 240 saurians and seven crocodiles) in the country. Fifteen threatened reptiles, including the endangered Crocodylus intermedius and Podocnemis expansa, are found in Colombia.

There are no figures for the number of freshwater fish species in the country. They are, however, of great importance as a source of food, particularly for the residents of the Amazon for whom they make up a considerable percentage of the animal protein eaten. Three species (Eremophilus mutisii, Gambusia aestiputeus and Poecilia vetiprovidentiae) are listed as threatened by IUCN, they are all endemic.

Hernández et al. (1992) have identified 58 centres of endemism for Colombia. These are of key importance in determining the location of conservation areas. Amongst these centres are Centro de la Gloria, Cesar which corresponds to a system of Pleistocene terraces with natural savannas surrounded by moist forests; Cerros Tacarcuna and Serranías del Darién and Baudó; Centro Guajiro; Catatumbo; Chocó Biogeográfico and a region of the Upper Putumayo.

Conservation Areas

Colombian protected areas within IUCN's categories I–IV are listed in Table 26.3. These cover about 90,200 sq. km, or 8.7 per cent of the country's land area. Areas allocated as forest reserves (454,158 sq. km), protection forest reserves (3462 sq. km), special management areas (more than 36680 sq. km), resguardos and indigenous reserves also have conservation value.

There are 267 resguardos and 28 indigenous areas in the country, covering respectively approximately 175,640 sq. km and 79,546 sq. km (Figure 26.2). Resguardos are lands communally owned by indigenous peoples through a legal title, while the indigenous reserves are territories provisionally assigned to a particular indigenous community for their own use but the actual land remains in the hands of the state (IUCN, 1992). Local people determine the management of these areas subject to specific restrictions to safeguard ecological values. Subsistence hunting is allowed in these areas, as is the exploitation of forest products, including timber provided a permit is obtained. Mostly the reserves are used only in a traditional, non-destructive fashion and are not exploited commercially.

Colombia's first conservation area, declared in 1961, was Cueva de los Guácharos National Park. However, protected areas showing some affinity in terms of conservation criteria with those of the current national parks system (according to the definitions given in the National Code of Renewable Natural Resources and its Regulating Decree No. 622 of 1977) were in existence long before this. Examples are La Macarena Biological Reserve created in 1948, and several areas at high altitudes which were declared to be national parks under the Second Law of 1959.

Although there is legislation detailing national conservation objectives, there is no strategy providing for its implementation.

Table 26.3 Conservation areas in Colombia

Existing conservation areas in IUCN's categories I–IV are listed below. For information on Biosphere Reserves see Chapter 8.

Natural National Parks	Area (sq. km)
Amacayacu*	2,930
Cahuinarí*	5,755
Catatumbo-Barí*	1,581
Chingaza*	504
Chiribiquete*	12,800
Corales del Rosario	195
Cordillera de los Picachos*	4,390
Cueva de los Guácharos*	90
El Cocuy*	3,060
El Tuparro*	5,480
Farallones de Cali*	1,500
Isla Gorgona*	492
Isla de Salamanca*	210
La Paya*	4,220
Las Hermosas*	1,250
Las Orquideas*	320
Los Katíos*	720
Los Nevados*	380
Macuira	250
Munchique*	440
Nevado del Huila*	1,580
Paramillo*	4,600
Pisba	450
Puracé*	830
Sanquianga*	800
Sierra Nevada de Santa Marta*	3,830
Sierra de la Macarena*	6,300
Sumapaz*	1,540
Tamá*	480
Tatamá*	519
Tayrona*	150
Tinigua*	2,018
Utría	543

Natural Reserve	
Laguna de Sonso+	20

Fauna and Flora Sanctuaries	
Ciénaga Grande de Santa Marta*	230
Galeras	76
Iguaque	68
Isla de la Corota*	<0.1
Los Colorados	10
Los Flamencos	70

Natural National Reserves	
Nukak*	8,550
Puinawuai*	10,920

Natural Unique Area	
Los Estoraques	6

| Total | 90,157 |

* Area with forest within its boundaries as depicted on Map 26.1.

+ Not mapped — data not available for this project.

Source: WCMC (unpublished)

Figure 26.2 Resguardos and indigenous areas of Colombia
Source: WCMC (unpublished data, 1994)

This gives rise to conflict between government institutions over land use and ownership rights (INDERENA-DPN, 1991). Land-rights conflicts are one of the most serious threats to the protected areas system.

There is a proposal to create a National Parks Directorate as part of a new Ministry for the Environment in order to introduce a better system for administration and management of the parks. The Directorate could generate its own funds through ecotourism and thereby achieve a degree of self sufficiency. It is hoped that, through extension and development programmes as well as environmental education, local communities will participate in park management and conservation of biodiversity.

Currently 80 per cent of the government's conservation budget is used to support INDERENA. Funds have also been obtained for some parks through the AID-TNC programme "Parks in Peril" and through the Colombian Forestry Action Plan. It is hoped that the World Bank will support a programme for Biodiversity Conservation in the Colombian Pacific.

Conservation Initiatives

The recent promulgation of a new National Constitution, which has been termed the "Green Constitution" is an important step for conservation (Sarmiento, 1994). It covers vital subjects of environmental law, biogenetic heritage, the citizen's responsibility for the conservation of natural resources and the environment, the process of municipal decentralisation and its role in the management and administration of natural resources, national parks, indigenous reserves and other protected areas.

Over the last three years, the National Government has been negotiating funding for environmental management through a project called the "Colombia Programme: International Cooperation for the Environment". This is being coordinated by INDERENA and the National Planning Department and was, in 1992, presented at the United Nations World Conference on Environment and Development in Rio de Janeiro. An ECO-

FUND is also being set up in order to strengthen NGOs working in conservation, research and sustainable use and management of natural resources.

Negotiations are under way for several projects requiring considerable economic inputs. These include biodiversity conservation in the Chocó Biogeográfico for more than 30 million dollars (World Bank and GEF); Amazonia for more than 10

THE SIERRA NEVADA DE SANTA MARTA

The Sierra Nevada de Santa Marta is a 17,000 sq. km massif that arises from the Caribbean coast of Colombia to snow covered summits, the highest of which reaches 5575 m. Examples of virtually all Colombia's ecosystems are found in this region, even though it covers only 1.4 per cent of the country's area.

The diversity and isolation of the Sierra Nevada de Santa Marta have resulted in the evolution of a remarkable degree of endemism in its fauna and flora throughout all the vegetation zones on the mountain; these include lowland rain forests, dry forests, montane forests and alpine paramo. The diversity and endemism is increased due to the fact that different aspects of the mountain are effectively isolated from one another so that new sub-species and species have evolved in forested valleys separated by high alpine ridges. There are, for instance, five endemic plant genera — *Cabreriella, Castenedia, Raouliopsis, Micropleura* and *Perissocoeleum*, a total of 15 species of endemic birds (Table 26.4) and at least nine endemic species or sub-species of mammals (Table 26.5), while in the amphibians, the genus *Eleutherodactylus* alone has eight endemic species.

The Sierra Nevada de Santa Marta is perhaps even more interesting for its cultural history. It was the site of the amazing pre-Colombian Tayrona civilisation. These people had a very advanced society on the mountain several hundred years before Europeans arrived in the Americas. They were masters of the use of stone for buildings, construction of terraces and for irrigation systems. The stone stairways that linked their communities can still be traced for hundreds of kilometres over the mountain slopes. Magnificent gold and ceramic artwork and elaborate stone carvings are still being discovered in excavations on the mountain. The most notable relict of the Tayrona civilisation is the so-called Ciudad Perdida (Lost City), the stone streets and buildings of which have been excavated and restored. The Tayronas succumbed to disease and conflicts with the European settlers, and now only small numbers of Koghi, Ijka and Wiwa indians live on the higher slopes of the mountain.

The Sierra was largely unaffected by developments during the first 300 years of colonisation. However, in this century it has become a refuge area for campesino farmers fleeing violence elsewhere in the country. The campesinos inflicted a great deal of damage on the forest and forced the Indian communities to move to even higher and remoter areas. In the 1970s, marijuana cultivation and the robbing of archaeological sites further destabilised the situation. Armed guerilla groups moved in and the Sierra became a "no-go" area for government officials. The mountain became notorious for violence and banditry.

Although the massif still shows signs of the 70 per cent

Table 26.4   Endemic bird species in Santa Marta

Species	English name
Acestrura astreans	Santa Marta woodstar
Anisognathus melanogenys	Santa Marta mountain tanager
Atlapetes melanocephalus	Santa Marta brush-finch
Basileuterus conspicillatus	White-lored warbler
Basileuterus basilicus	Santa Marta warbler
Campylopterus phainopeplus	Santa Marta sabrewing
Coeligena phaleraia	White-tailed starfrontlet
Cranioleuca hellmayri	Streak-capped spinetail
Grallaria bangsi	Santa Marta antpita
Myioborus flavivertex	Yellow-crowned redstart
Myiotheretes pernix	Santa Marta bush-tyrant
Pyrrhura viridicata	Santa Marta parakeet
Ramphomicron dorsale	Black-backed thorntail
Synallaxis fuscorufa	Rusty-headed spinetail
Troglodytes monticola	Santa Marta wren

deforestation that afflicted it during the troubled years of marijuana cultivation, the situation is now stabilising. There are two national parks and two indigenous reserves in the area and major programmes are under way to support the local people in charting their own future management of the environment.

Most importantly, in 1986 the Sierra Nevada de Santa Marta Foundation was established to conserve the natural and cultural resources of the area and promote the welfare of all sectors of its population. The foundation has health programmes, it is promoting reforestation and kitchen-gardens, helping construct fish tanks and excavating and preserving archaeological remains. It also has a programme to encourage the use of traditional Tayrona and Koghi architectural techniques for local buildings.

Table 26.5   Endemic species and sub-species of mammals in Santa Marta

English name	Latin name
Bay or white-faced monkey	*Cebus albifrons malitious*
Brocket deer	*Mazama americana carrikeri*
Tree squirrel	*Sciurus granatensis bondae*
Tree squirrel	*Sciurus g. saltuensis*
Tree squirrel	*Sciurus g. agricolae*
A paramo mouse	*Thomasomys monochromos*
A rice rat	*Oryzomys narus*
A spiny rat	*Proechimys mincae*
A rodent	*Diplomys rufodorsalis*

Source: Maria Jose Duran and Rosario Ortiz Quijano.

million dollars (EC and the Netherlands) and many other smaller projects such as those of GTZ/IUCN in the Sierra Nevada de Santa Marta (see box) and Ciénaga Grande, ITTO for mangrove ecosystems and USAID for the "Parks in Peril" programme.

The Colombian Forestry Action Plan has identified priority actions for encouraging the development of forest-based industry. These include improving yields, beginning planned, rational, sustainable use of natural forests, promoting the gradual substitution of natural forest exploitation by that of plantations and developing markets for forest products. Land-use zoning is already under way and this will identify which areas

are suitable for which particular forestry functions. Forest-based social development, with emphasis on improving the quality of life for peasant communities, colonisers and indigenous people dependent on the forest, is also included in the Forestry Action Plan.

Thus the efforts launched by government, through the Colombian Forestry Action Plan and with the help of international and government donors, are of the greatest importance in solving as far as possible the growing imbalance in the use of forests and forest resources, their under-utilization and the indiscriminate destruction of biologically valuable ecosystems.

References

Alvarez-León, R. (1993). Mangrove ecosystems of Colombia. In: *Conservation and Sustainable Utilization of Mangrove Forests in Latin America and Africa Regions. Part 1: Latin America.* ITTO/ISME Project PD114/90(F). Pp. 75–113.

Calderón, S.E. (1992). Hallazgo de *Pelliciera rhizophorae* Triana and Planchón, en la costa del Atlántica con observaciones taxonomicas y biogeográficas preliminareas. *Acta Biológica Colombiana* 1(1): 89–110.

Collar, N.J., Gonzaga, L.P., Krabbe, N., Madroño Nieto, A., Naranjo, L.G., Parker III, T.A. and Wege, D.C. (1992). *Threatened Birds of the Americas. The ICBP/IUCN Red Data Book.* ICBP, Cambridge, U.K.

Davis, S.D., Droop, S.J.M., Gregerson, P., Henson, L., Leon, C.J., Villa-Lobos, J.L, Synge, H. and Zantovska, J. (1986). *Plants in Danger. What do we know?* IUCN, Gland, Switzerland and Cambridge, U.K.

Departamento Nacional de Planeación (1989). *Plan de Acción Forestal para Colombia.* Bogatá. Pp. 64.

Departamento Nacional de Planeación (1992). *Plan de Acción Forestal para Colombia. Gestión 1989–1992.* Bogatá. Pp. 48.

El Tiempo (1993). *Amapola.* Newspaper report on Tuesday May 25 1993, pages 1A and 16A.

Escallón, C. and Rodriquez, M. (1986). Aspectos geográficos e importancia ecológica de los manglares con especial referencia a Colombia. *Revista Perez-Arbelaezia* 1(2): 225–241, Bogota.

FAO (1993). *Forest resource assessment 1990: tropical countries.* FAO Forestry Paper 112. FAO, Rome, Italy.

Forero, E. (1989). Colombia. In: *Floristic Inventory of Tropical Countries: The Status of Plant Systematics, Collections, and Vegetation, plus Recommendations for the Future.* Campbell, D.G. and Hammond, D. (eds). The New York Botanical Garden, New York. Pp. 353–361.

Galeano, G. (1992). *Las Palmas de la Región de Araracuara Colombia.* Tropenbos, Bogota, Colombia. Pp. 180.

Gentry, A.H. (1982). Phytogeographic patterns as evidence for a Chocó refuge. In: *Biological Diversification in the Tropics.* Prance, G.T. (ed.). Columbia University Press, New York. Pp. 112–136.

Gentry, A. (1990a). La región Amazónica. In: *Selva Húmeda de Colombia.* Villegas Editores, Bogotá. Pp. 53–68.

Gentry, A. (1990b). La región del Chocó. In: *Selva Húmeda de Colombia.* Villegas Editores, Bogotá. Pp. 41–48.

Groombridge, B. (Ed) (1993). *1994 IUCN Red List of Threatened Animals.* IUCN, Gland, Switzerland and Cambridge, U.K. 286 pp.

Hernández, J. (1990). La selva en Colombia. In: *Selva y Futuro Colombia.* Carrizosa, J. and Hernández, J. (Eds). El Sello Editorial, Bogotá, Colombia. Pp. 13–40.

Hernández, C.J.I. and Sanchez, H. (1988). *Proyecto de Formulación No. 3 Determinación de Programmas para fortalecer la Red de Areas de Manejo Especial. Informe final.* Plan de Acción Forestal Para Colombia, Bogatá. Pp. 130.

Hernández, C.J.I. Hurtado, A., Ortiz, R. and Walschburger, T. (1992). Centros de endemismos en Colombia. In: *La Diversidad Biológica de Iberoamérica.* Halffter, G. (Ed). Acta Žoológica Mexicana, Volumen Especial 1992. Instituto de Ecología, Xalapa, Mexico.

IGAC-INDERENA-CONIF (1984). *Mapa de Bosques de Colombia. Memoria Explicativa.* Bogotá, Colombia. Pp. 206.

INDERENA-DPN (1991). Colombia — proyecto de manejo forestal y protección del media ambiente. Conservación de la diversidad biológica a través de parques nacionales naturales del Pacífico. División de Parques Nacionales. Draft. Pp. 84.

IUCN (1992). *Protected Areas of the World: A review of national systems. Volume 4: Nearctic and Neotropical.* IUCN, Gland, Switzerland and Cambridge, U.K.

McNeely, J.A., Miller, K.R., Reid, W.V., Mittermeier, R.A. and Werner, T.B. (1990). *Conserving the World's Biological Diversity.* IUCN, Gland, Switzerland; WRI, CI, WWF-US and the World Bank, Washington, D.C.

PAFC/BID (1991). *Programa de Acción Forestal.* Departamento Nacional de Planeación — Secretaria PAFC y Banco Interamericano de Desarrollo, Bogatá. Pp. 77.

Prance, G.T. (1977). Floristic inventory of the tropics: where do we stand? *Annals Missouri Botanical Garden* 64(4): 659–684.

Sanchez Páez, H., Hernández, J.C., Castaño, U. and Rodriguez, M. (1990). *Nuevos Parques Nacionales de Colombia.* INDERENA, Bogatá. Pp. 238.

Sarmiento, G. (1994). The new constitution of Colombia: environmental and indigenous people's issues. In: *Widening Perspectives on Biodiversity.* Krattiger, A.F., McNeely, J.A., Lesser, K.R., St. Hill, Y. and Senanayake, R. (Eds). IUCN and the International Academy of the Environment.

WCMC (1992). *Global Biodiversity: Status of the Earth's Living Resources.* Chapman and Hall, London. Pp. 594.

Authors: Heliodoro Sanchez Paez and Carlos Castaño Uribe, INDERENA, Bogotá, Colombia, with contributions from Maria Jose Duran and Rosario Ortiz Quijano, Fundacion Pro-Sierra Nevada de Sante Marte, Colombia.

Map 26.1 Colombia

The forest cover shown on Map 26.1 has been taken from a map produced by the Ministerio de Hacienda and Instituto Geografico "Agustin Codazzi", *Republica de Colombia: Mapa de Bosques* and has been elaborated from and based on an earlier (1984), large scale map (1: 500,000) map, *Mapa de Bosques de Colombia,* compiled by IGAC-INDERENA. The source map was published in 1985 at a 1:1,500,000 scale. The 24 vegetation categories shown on the source map have been amalgamated into the forest types illustrated in this atlas, following the advice of Heliodoro Sánchez, Carlos Castaño Uribe and Cesar Barbosa of INDERENA. The source vegetation categories have been amalgamated into broader forest types in the following way:

Mangrove:

BM — *Bosque de mangle, homogéneo en fisonomía sobre áreas de inundación por mareas y llanuras fluvio-marinas*

Lowland rain forest: ***Bosques Densos y Heterogeneos***

BAa — *Bosque con marcada tendencia a la homogeneidad de especies en paisajes aluviales. En la Amazonia la vegetación presenta un dosel superior de árboles poco desarrollados y abundancia de palmas y herbáceas*

BOa — *Bosque, con marcada tendencia a la homogeneidad de especies en paisajes aluviales de la Orinoquia*

BPa — *Bosque con marcada tendencia a la homogeneidad de especies en paisajes aluviales del Pacífico*

BA1 — *Bosque bajo poco desarrollado sobre terrazas mal drenadas y superficies de erosión planas de la Amazonia*

BA2 — *Bosque alto bien desarrollado sobre superficies disectadas de la Amazonia*

BA3 — *Bosque alto bien desarrollado sobre superficie de erosión profundamente disectada de la Amazonia*

BP1 — *Bosque de terrazas en condiciones muy severas de alta pluviosidad del Pacífico*

BO1 — *Bosque de terrazas y altillanuras de la Orinoquia*

BC2 — *Bosque muy heterogéneo en especies sobre colinas accesibles*

BC3 — *Bosque muy heterogéneo en especies sobre bolinas de relieve abrupto*

Submontane forest: ***Piso Subandino*** (1000–2000 m) (IGAC-INDERENA-CONIF, 1984)

BQ2 — *Bosque sobre el piedemonte cordillerano y serranías*

Montane forest: ***Piso Andino*** (2000 m +) (IGAC-INDERENA-CONIF, 1984)

BQ3 — *Bosque de zonas escarpadas de cordillera*

Non forest: Sg1,Sg2,Sa,BAs,BAc,Vpa,Vpt,Wa,Wi,H1,H2

The 'non forest' category comprises the savanna formations, scrub forest, drier arid vegetation, grassland formations, heath land, marshland and agricultural land.

The *Bosques Intervenidos* category has not been distinguished from 'undisturbed' forests; these exploited forests mainly occur in the mangrove and lowland rain forests in the south-west of the country. Also, please note, that in addition to the forest cover indicated on the source map, a corridor of lowland rain forest has been added in central Colombia, following the advice of Cesar Barbosa of INDERENA. This additional forest cover substitutes c. 7,341 sq. km of savanna marked as Sg2 on the source map.

Conservation areas were extracted from a digital dataset covering several countries. The *Latin American Protected Areas Dataset — Version 2* was provided by the Centro Internacional de Agricultural Tropical (1992), Colombia. Reference was also made to a dyeline 1:1.5 million scale map, *Republica de Colombia -Areas del Sistema de Parques Nacionales* (nd) prepared by INDERENA, illustrating national parks and wildlife sanctuaries.

27 Ecuador

Country area   283,560 sq. km
Land area   276,840 sq. km
Population (mid-1994)   10.6 million
Population growth rate   2.5 per cent
Population projected to 2025   16.8 million
Gross national product per capita (1992)   US$1070
Forest cover for 1987 (see Map)   142,370 sq. km
Forest cover for 1990 (FAO, 1993)*   119,190 sq. km*
Annual deforestation rate (1981–1990)   1.8 per cent
Industrial roundwood productions   3,268,000 cu.m
Industrial roundwood exports   —
Fuelwood and charcoal production   4,231,000 cu.m
Processed wood production   1,087,000 cu.m
Processed wood exports   58,000 cu.m
* excludes FAO's category of dry deciduous forest

Ecuador's remarkable geography, extending from the coast of the Pacific through the two mountain chains of the Andes to the western Amazonian lowlands, results in an extraordinary biological diversity. Much of this diversity is not yet documented and it may remain unknown and be lost forever if the tropical forests continue to be destroyed at the present rate. The rapidly increasing population in the high Andean valleys, which are already densely settled, is producing a mobile population of landless farmers who seize every opportunity to colonise new forest areas. Government policies still favour this extension of the agricultural frontier and most of the forested areas of the country are being threatened as a result. A system of protected areas has been created, but this has already proved vulnerable to intensive pressure from private and government owned industry, agriculture and mineral extraction.

INTRODUCTION

Mainland Ecuador divides naturally into three regions: the coastal plain, the Andean highlands (or Sierra) and the eastern Amazonian lowlands. The country also includes the Galapagos Islands, in the Pacific Ocean, about 1000 km west of the mainland.

The coastal plain is 100–200 km wide and is flat, except for a row of coastal hills seldom exceeding 800 m in elevation. The soils of the region are very productive and most of Ecuador's agricultural exports are grown there, in Guayas Valley. The original vegetation in the southern half of the region was tropical dry forest. This area has an unusually high level of plant endemism, but has been devastated by lumbering, fuelwood gathering and overgrazing as well as droughts. The northern half of the coastal plain was originally covered by moist tropical forests. Now, extensive areas have been converted to banana and African oil-palm plantations and pastures. Some biologically important forested areas still exist in north-western Ecuador near the Colombian border.

The Andean region consists of a 100–200 km wide cordillera. In northern and central Ecuador the mountains are arranged in two parallel rows of peaks and ridges, separated by the Interandean Valley. Many of the higher peaks reach almost 6000 m, with Chimborazo the highest at 6310 m. The ridges connecting the mountains typically lie about 4000 m above sea level. The main Interandean Valley at 2600–2700 m elevation, is interrupted by low transverse ridges connecting the two parallel rows. In southern Ecuador the mountains usually do not reach above 4000 m, they form a complex pattern of differently oriented ridges. Volcanic activity has shaped the Andean region, and the fertile soils there are derived from volcanic ash. The Interandean valleys provide the most hospitable environment for humans in the country and these areas were already densely settled in pre-Columbian times. The natural vegetation of the upland Andean region has been largely replaced by farms and pastures. On the inner slopes on either side of the central valley, only a few, highly disturbed, cloud forest patches still exist. On the Pacific slopes of the Andes, between approximately 1300 m or 1500 m and 3500 m, montane cloud forest still occurs, especially in the extreme north. The páramo vegetation, above 3500 m, has been extensively modified, particularly by seasonal burning and grazing. The eastern slopes are relatively undisturbed, but colonists are now moving into these areas along the expanding network of roads which are being constructed to give access to the Amazon Basin.

The eastern lowlands of Ecuador extend into the western edge of the Amazon Basin. The flat plain is traversed by several rivers that drain the Andean slopes and flow east to the Amazon River. This is one of the wettest parts of the whole Amazon Basin and has an extraordinary biological and cultural diversity. However, migration out of the Andean and coastal regions is creating tremendous pressures on the evergreen rain forests of the region. Following the discovery of oil in the late 1960s, there has been intensive road-building, which has been accompanied by increasing colonization and deforestation.

Ecuador's climate varies with region and altitude, indeed there are 25 of Holdridge's life zones within the country (Cañadas, 1983). In the northern coastal zone there is no real dry season and rainfall is over 2000 mm annually, while in the south there is as little as 355 mm of rain in a year. The mean monthly temperature is between 24° and 27°C with little seasonal variation. In the Sierra, the rainy season is from October through May, with Quito receiving about 1500 mm of rain in a year. Here too there is little seasonal change in temperature but diurnal changes can be considerable. Rainfall in the eastern lowlands (the Oriente) ranges from around 2000 mm to about 5000 mm annually and, as on the coast, there is no dry season. Temperatures here are fairly uniform, but somewhat lower than on the coast.

Population growth across the country is estimated to be 2.5 per cent. However, growth rates are different regionally, with 2.2 per cent estimated in the Sierra, 2.5 per cent for the coastal plain and as much as 4.9 per cent for the period 1974–1982 in the Oriente, due to a major influx of young colonists (Cabarle et al., 1989). Fifty-seven per cent of the population are urban dwellers, concentrated in the capital city of Quito, in the port of Guayaquil and in Cuenca. This urban population has grown fourfold between 1950 and 1990. Ecuador's population is made up of two major groups: Amerindians (40 per cent) and the mestizos, who are descended from the intermarriage of Spaniards and Amerindians. The former are represented by both Quichua-speaking farmers in the highlands and groups living in the Amazon. There are also some Caucasians (10 per cent) and Negroes in the country. The ancestors of the latter were slaves, brought by the Spanish to work on the coastal plantations.

The economy of the country is essentially dependent on petroleum and agriculture (including shrimp farming). Agricultural exports account for nearly one fourth of foreign exchange earnings. The main export crops are shrimps, bananas, coffee, cacao and sugar cane. Forestry plays a fairly minor role in the economy at present. Tourism is an increasingly important source of foreign earnings.

The Forests

Ecuador's forests are still not well known botanically. They can be classified using the Holdridge Life Zone system (shown in a modified form in Figure 27.1), but a variety of other descriptions are also used (e.g. Cifuentes et al., 1989; Cabarle et al., 1989).

Humid lowland forests cover most of the tropical moist and wet forests of western Ecuador and almost the entire Amazonian region (Balslev, 1988). Although there are some differences in the floristic composition of the western and eastern rain forests, in both cases the vegetation is dominated by trees with a dense canopy about 30 m high and it is rich in lianas and epiphytes. The forest physiognomy is uniform without dominant species and with a very high diversity. The most important tree families are Leguminosae, Moraceae, Lauraceae, Myristicaceae and Meliaceae.

Most of the rain forest in eastern Ecuador is unflooded (terra firme) forest, but along the rivers in large areas of the upper Amazonia the forests are seasonally inundated (Gentry, 1977). These floodplain forests include those inundated by white waters (várzea) and by black waters (igapó). At present 1200 trees are known from the eastern lowlands (Balslev and Renner, 1989) but, with further work, it is thought that as many as 3000 may be found to occur there (Neill and Palacios, 1987).

Both wet and moist forests are found in western Ecuador, the former appear to be particularly rich in endemics. For instance, at least thirty species of plant are known only from Rio Palenque Field Station, a mere 1.7 sq. km area of wet forest. These include *Quararibea palenquiana, Persea theobromifolia, Dalbergaria rubriacuta* and *Dichaea riopalenquensis* (Gentry, 1977).

Montane forests gradually replace lowland forests at a height of about 600–900 m on both sides of the Andes (Balslev and Renner, 1989). They are very rich in species, particularly in orchids, bromeliads, ferns and mosses. The lower montane forests have a canopy layer about 30 m above the ground. With increasing elevation, the forests' stature decreases and at about

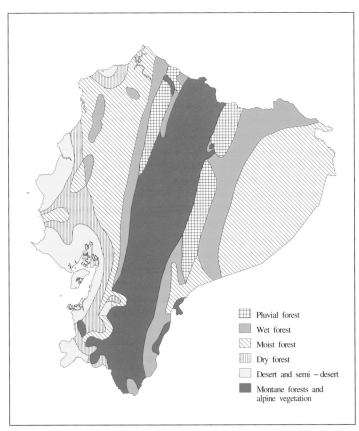

Figure 27.1   Holdridge's Life Zones of Ecuador
Source: Gentry (1977)

3000 m above sea level the canopy is often only 10 m high. Typical lowland families, such as Myristicaceae and Lecythidaceae are replaced by, among others, Melastomataceae and Cuoniaceae (Harling, 1979). The upper montane or cloud forest, found between 2500 and 3400 m asl, is a dense microphyllous forest with trees heavily loaded with mosses, ferns and lycopods. Some of the many characteristic genera of the cloud forest trees are *Podocarpus, Cinchona, Oreopanax* and *Miconia*. Páramo vegetation (dominated by bunch grasses, generally mixed with herbs, small shrubs and cushion plants) occurs on the high mountains above about 3500 m, but the altitude at which it replaces forest is not clear cut; patches of quite large *Polylepis* trees may occur as high as 4000 m. Burning and grazing drives back the forest line and where this influence is strong, a very sharp line between woody and herbaceous vegetation may be observed. Cold mountain deserts generally begin at about 4500 m and extend up to the snow limit.

The coastal dry forests in Ecuador (and Peru) contain many species that are endemic, some at the generic level. For instance *Macranthisiphon*, one of the most distinctive genera of the family Bignoniaceae, is found only in these coastal formations, as are *Ceiba trichistandra, Hymenocallis quitoensis, Carica paniculata* and *Eriotheca ruiziana* (Gentry, 1977). The most important timber tree in the region is *Tabebuia chrysantha*.

Mangroves

Discontinuous mangrove communities occur along the coastline, at the mouth of the major river systems, especially in the Gulf of Guayaquil and between Limones and the Colombian border. There are a variety of different estimates for mangrove cover in Ecuador. Jordon (1988) estimates an area of 2603 sq. km; on Map 27.1, the mangroves on the mainland are shown covering an area of 2377 sq. km in 1987; while, more recently,

261

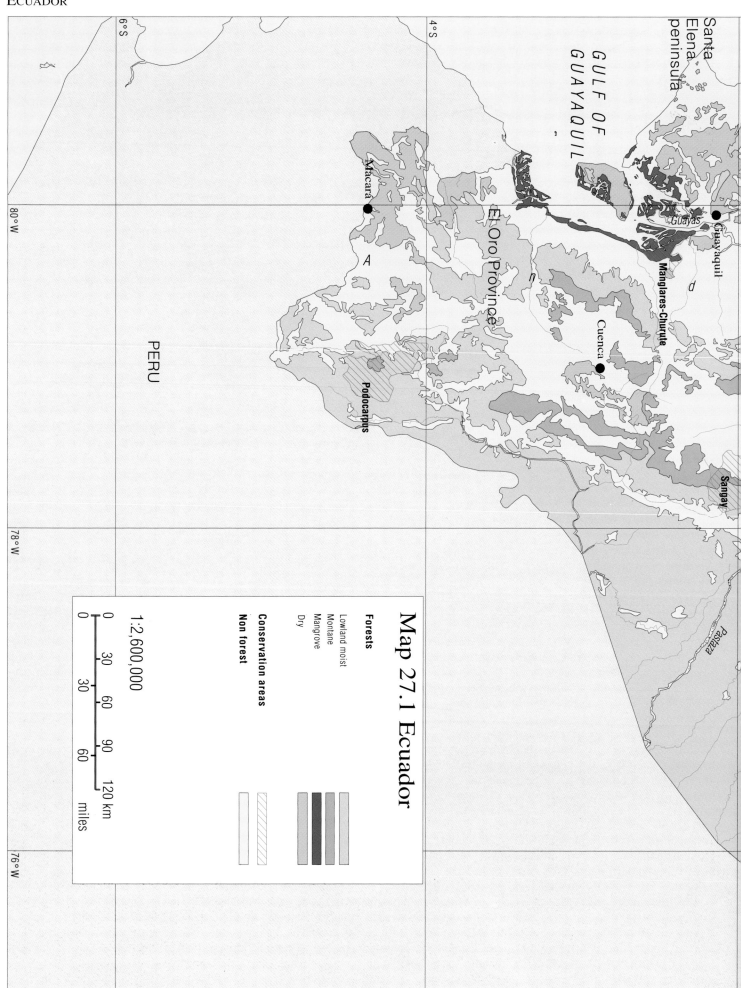

Map 27.1 Ecuador

Forests

Lowland moist
Montane
Mangrove
Dry

Conservation areas

Non forest

1:2,600,000

0   30   60   90   120 km
0   30   60   miles

6°S
4°S

80°W
78°W
76°W

Santa
Elena
peninsula

GULF OF
GUAYAQUIL

Guayaquil

Guayas

Manglares-Churute

Macará

El Oro Province

Cuenca

Podocarpus

Sangay

Pastaza

PERU

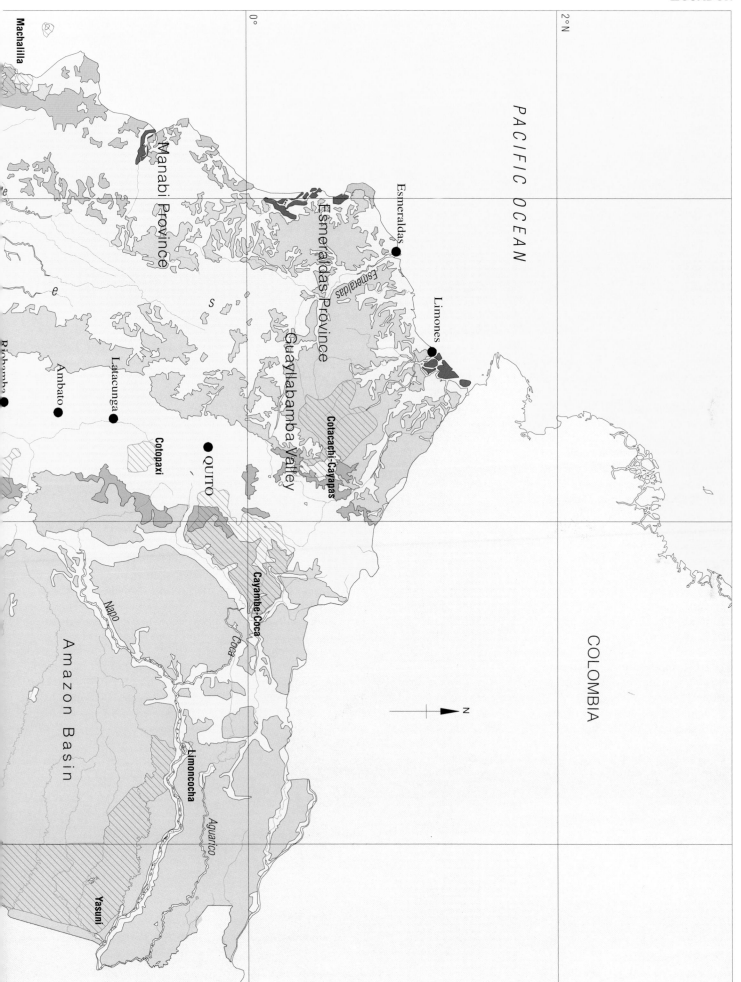

PACIFIC OCEAN

2°N

0°

COLOMBIA

N

Machalilla

Manabi Province

Esmeraldas

Esmeraldas Province

Esmeraldas

Limones

Cotacachi-Cayapas

Guayllabamba Valley

Riobamba

Ambato

Latacunga

Cotopaxi

QUITO

Cayambe-Coca

Amazon Basin

Napo

Coca

Limoncocha

Aguarico

Yasuní

263

Table 27.1 The extent of mangroves, salt flats and shrimp ponds (areas in sq. km) in western Ecuador 1969–1987.

Province	Mangroves			Salt Flats			Shrimp ponds	
	1969	1984	1987	1969	1984	1987	1984	1987
Guayas	1,256	1,195	1,130	409	173	100	529	700
El Oro	336	245	230	98	25	25	265	300
Manabí	124	80	60	8	2	2	84	100
Esmeraldas	320	301	280	–	–	–	16	35
Totals	2,036	1,821	1,700	515	200	127	894	1,135

Source: CLIRSEN (1986) and 1987 preliminary data by CLIRSEN reported in Cabarle *et al.* (1989).

SUFOREN (1991) and MAG (1991) estimated that they cover respectively only 1776 sq. km and 1618 sq. km. These forests provide critical habitat for a large number of crustaceans, molluscs and fish that are important commercially and for the local people. Several thousand fishermen are employed in the exploitation of these resources.

The mangroves have been exploited for more than 100 years, the wood being used for construction in Guayaquil and other coastal cities, the trees cut to make charcoal and the bark peeled off to provide tannin for the leather industry. Currently, urban development, road building, drainage works, port construction and pollution from petroleum spills, mine discharges and waste disposal are all having adverse effects on the mangroves. They are, in addition, being affected by overgrazing in upland catchment areas. The overgrazing leads to soil erosion and consequent sedimentation in the mangroves.

Most destructive though has been the construction, in the last two decades, of over 1200 sq. km of shrimp ponds, which has brought about almost complete eradication of the mangroves in many estuaries. About half of the ponds are now unproductive due to salinisation and acidification. This industry has been an extremely profitable one, second to petroleum as a foreign exchange earner, but it reached its peak in 1988 and is now declining. The 1987 extent of the mangrove forests, salt flats and shrimp ponds in western Ecuador is shown in Table 27.1.

Forest Resources and Management
Official statistics estimate that natural forests cover approximately 115,000 sq. km (Table 27.2) or 42.3 per cent of Ecuador (Cifuentes *et al.*, 1989). However, Cabarle *et al.* (1989) estimated that only 26 per cent or 72,000 sq. km of primary forest

remains, with more than half (41,000 sq. km) occurring in the eastern lowlands.

The latest estimate by FAO (1993) indicates a somewhat greater forest cover. Using a 1987 survey as a baseline, FAO estimates that, in 1990, there were a total of 119,190 sq. km of forest in the rain, moist deciduous and hill and montane zones in the country. FAO estimates an additional 440 sq. km of forest in the dry deciduous zone, but, as in other chapters, this forest type, has been excluded from the statistics at the head of the chapter. Closed broadleaved forests cover 117,710 sq. km (FAO, 1993). Measurements taken from Map 27.1 (from data that were collected between 1977 and 1987 — see Map Legend) give the even higher estimate of forest cover of 142,370 sq. km (See Table 27.3).

Currently, the legal basis for forest conservation and management in Ecuador is provided by the Forestry and Conservation of Natural Areas and Wildlife Law (Ley Forestal y de Conservación de Areas Naturales y Vida Silvestre), passed by the Ecuadorian House of Representatives in 1981. Detailed regulation of forest resource management and activities permitted within protected areas is provided by Decree No. 1529 of 1983.

The Subsecretariat of Forestry and Renewable Resources (SUFOREN), under the Minister of Agriculture and Livestock (MAG), was responsible for the administration of forest resources and protected areas. In 1992, this organisation was replaced by the INEFAN (Instituto Ecuatoriano Forestal y de Areas Naturales y de Vida Silvestre) an autonomous institute attached to MAG. Operational responsibility rests with the Ecuadorian Forestry Directorate (DINAF), within which are divisions for: reforestation, investigation and training; management and utilization; natural areas and wildlife.

The government theoretically controls all forested lands, however forestry exploitation is carried out without management or technical support and with little control by the State. Timber concessions were banned in 1982 because loggers did not abide by the terms of their contracts and because of practical and political difficulties associated with protecting production forests from colonization. Currently most of the timber comes from unreserved forest lands ("tierras baldías") which are converted to agriculture by colonists. Some timber is extracted from unreserved forests using a system of short-term licences.

Destructive logging practices and the lack of incentives for sustainable forest management have been important factors contributing to deforestation in Ecuador. Felling, skidding and landing techniques are inefficient and cause great damage to the residual stand. Logging crews strip the area of the most valuable species, although rarely removing trees of less than 40 cm in

Table 27.2 The extent of natural forest in Ecuador in 1988

Forest Type	Area (sq. km)	% of forested area	% of land area*
Tropical humid	81,250	70.8	30
Subtropical humid	27,540	24.0	10.2
Tropical dry	4,200	3.7	1.5
Mangroves	1,740	1.5	0.6
Total	114,730	100	42.3

* This column was added by the editor using a land area of 271,230 sq. km as appears to have been used in Cifuentes *et al.* (1989).

Source: Based on Cifuentes *et al.* (1989)

Table 27.3 Estimates of forest extent in Ecuador

Forest type	Area (sq. km)	% of land area
Lowland moist*	121,546	43.9
Montane	7,634	2.8
Dry	10,813	3.9
Mangrove	2,377	0.9
Total	142,370	51.4

* includes seasonally inundated areas which are marked as dominated by palm on the source map.

Based on analysis of Map 27.1. See Map Legend on p. 269 for details of sources.

diameter, and quickly move on to the next forest tract. As a result, only 25–30 per cent of wood is recovered from timber harvesting operations. Timber fees are extremely low and royalties are based on the amount of wood removed from forest tracts, rather than the true harvestable volume (Cabarle et al., 1989), which encourages the high-grading and wasteful harvesting methods. The extraction trails and roads often penetrate protected areas and lands occupied by forest-dwelling Amerindians, opening the forests to landless settlers and land speculators.

The forestry sector (timber production, primary and secondary manufacturing) contributed 3.2 per cent to the 1988 Gross National Product (SUFOREN, 1991). Eighty per cent of the forest industry's wood supply comes equally from the western and eastern lowlands, with the remaining 20 per cent from the Andean region (Cabarle et al., 1989). Forests also provide some four to six million cu. m of firewood, the main energy source for almost half of the rural population as well as for small local industries (FAO, 1994; SUFOREN, 1991).

Reforestation in Ecuador is largely oriented towards *Pinus* and *Eucalyptus* plantations in the Andean region, in other words not in the areas where the deforestation is mainly occurring. Official statistics reported that approximately 601 sq. km of forest plantations were established in Ecuador from 1962 to 1985, with 93 per cent of the plantation area in the Andean region, six per cent in the western region and one percent in the Amazonian region (SUFOREN, 1991). According to the Ecuadorian Forestry Action Plan the annual reforestation rate is around 33 sq. km. The plan proposes increasing this rate to 152 sq. km. This, though, would still be less than a twentieth of the area being deforested each year.

Deforestation

According to a WRI/UNEP/UNDP (1990) report, the annual deforestation rate in Ecuador is an alarming 2.3 per cent, equivalent to the loss of 3400 sq. km per year. If this continues, the country will be almost entirely deforested by the year 2025. Other estimates place the deforestation rate between 750 to 3000 sq. km per year (see Cabarle et al., 1989). FAO (1993) estimates that, excluding forest in the dry deciduous zone, 2372 sq. km was cleared each year between 1981 and 1990, an annual rate of 1.8 per cent.

The direct causes of deforestation are land clearance for colonisation and the production of fuelwood and charcoal. IUCN (1988) estimated that these accounted for the annual destruction of 2,300,000 cu. m of timber, but FAO (1994) estimates that, in 1992, 4,231,000 cu. m of timber were used for fuelwood and charcoal alone. Indirect causes include problems with land ownership, less than three per cent of the population own 66 per cent of the country's arable land. In addition, Ecuador's colonization policies promote deforestation. The government encourages individuals and private companies to acquire public lands, but clearance is a prerequisite for acquiring title to the land. Until recently, the Institute of Agrarian Reform and Colonization (IERAC) approved a claim for private tenure only if at least half of a plot had been cleared and converted into cropland or pasture. Southgate et al. (1991) claim that the authorities do not recognise indigenous common property regimes, which traditionally promoted forest conservation.

The central Andean highlands are practically devoid of natural forest cover, while the few remaining areas of primary forest in western Ecuador and forested areas in Amazonia are under increasing pressure from industrial agriculture, cattle grazing,

subsistence farming, logging, mining and the exploration for and extraction of oil. Table 27.4 gives estimates of the areas of the different types of forest over time, from original extent to area present in 1988 (Cabarle et al., 1989).

The forests of western Ecuador are amongst the most threatened on earth (Myers, 1988). Dodson and Gentry (1991) have documented the extent of the deforestation in the area. Only 200 sq. km of the western dry forests remain in an undisturbed condition, most have been severely altered by humans and their domestic animals. The moist forest was once the most extensive forest vegetation in western Ecuador (Table 27.4). Now less than 1500 sq. km remain in the remote northern part of the region. The coastal wet forest, a narrow strip extending along the base of the Andes, is the fastest-disappearing habitat in Ecuador. Before the area was penetrated by the first road in 1960, it was almost completely covered with undisturbed vegetation; but within 10 years this wet forest had been more or less totally converted to banana, African oil-palm and rubber plantations. Less than 90 sq. km now survive. The pluvial forest was never very extensive, but it is now the only substantial forest type left in western Ecuador (Table 27.4).

In the Andean region, much of the lower land is used for agriculture, while the intermediate levels are used for pasture (Gentry, 1977). In the higher regions, above the 3000 m contour, the forests are less diverse. The extensive forests that once existed on the inner flanks of the Andes and in the Interandean valleys were mostly cleared by indigenous populations prior to the Spanish conquest. By 1989, only about 25,468 sq. km of the Andean region was still covered by natural vegetation (this is, however, not all forest), mostly on the very wet and steep eastern flanks of the mountains (Cabarle et al., 1989).

Lack of roads and poor river communications restricted human incursions into the Amazonian forests until recently. However, the easy access provided by the road networks built for oil exploration and exploitation and a massive government colonization effort have resulted in a significant reduction of

Table 27.4 Areas of the different forest types in Ecuador over time

Forest Categories	Original (sq. km)	Aboriginal (sq. km)	1958 (sq. km)	1988 (sq. km)
Western Ecuador				
Dry	20,000	15,000	12,000	200
Moist	40,000	30,000	24,000	1,500
Wet	12,000	10,000	7,000	<100
Pluvial	8,000	8,000	6,000	3,200
Subtotal	80,000	63,000	49,000	5,000
The Sierra or Andean Highlands				
Flanks	61,000	45,000	40,000	18,000
Highlands	40,000	12,000	10,000	8,000
Subtotal	101,000	57,000	50,000	26,000
The Oriente				
Andes' Base	39,000	39,000	35,000	11,700
Amazon Basin	42,000	42,000	41,000	30,000
Subtotal	81,000	81,000	76,000	41,700
Totals	262,000	201,000	175,000	72,700

Source: Cabarle et al. (1989)

Virgin rain forest along the Rio Napo of the Ecuadorian Amazon   (WWF/Anna Zuckerman)

forest cover in the last 20 years. The population expanded very fast during the 1970s, especially in the Napo area where the rain forest is being rapidly converted to oil-palm plantations, pastures and small-scale farming. Now only half, or thereabouts, of the eastern region remains forested.

Biodiversity

Ecuador contains two of Myers' (1988) ten "hotspots". These are areas characterized by exceptional numbers of species with high levels of endemism and ones that are experiencing unusually rapid rates of depletion. The hotspots in Ecuador are the western lowland wet forests and the upland forests of western Amazonia. The western wet forests are one of the richest areas in the world, as demonstrated by the over 1250 plant species from 136 families recorded in less than 1 sq. km at Río Palenque Science Center. As many as 100 of these species have proved to be new to science; 43 are known only from this site (Dodson and Gentry, 1978). This forest shows some floristic affinity with the Colombian Choco, but because of its many unique features, such as the abundant endemic epiphytes, it is considered to be a distinct phytogeographic zone (Myers, 1988). It is estimated that the lowland wet forests of western Ecuador once contained some 10,000 plant species, around 2500 of them endemic to the region (Dodson and Gentry, 1978).

The upland forests of western Amazonia, which lie nearest to the base of the Andes, have a distinctive and highly diverse flora. They include the large Napo centre of biodiversity where, in a relatively small area, some 4000 species are reputed to occur (Balslev, 1988). During recent research by the Missouri Botanical Garden in this area, it was found that 70 per cent of the tree species collected had not been previously recorded from Amazonian Ecuador and 10 per cent were species new to science (Marles and Neill, 1988).

Other vegetation types of Ecuador also have a highly diverse flora, especially the tropical dry forests of the coastal region, the montane forests and the Galapagos. The tropical dry forests have several endemic species, such as the grotesque-trunked "ceibo" *Ceiba trischistandra* and the conspicuous *Hymenocallis quitoensis* (Gentry, 1977). According to Balslev (1988) the montane forests, between 900 m and 3000 m, house about half of the country's species although they constitute only 10 per cent of the area. Thirty-nine per cent of the species in these forests do not occur outside Ecuador. The western slopes in particular are rich in endemics, with 10 per cent of the total

Ecuadorian flora restricted to them. These montane forests are one of the world's richest areas for bromeliad and orchid species. They are also botanically famous as the home of *Cinchona officinalis*, the bark of which is the source of quinine, the anti-malaria drug (Gentry, 1977). The Galapagos Islands house 543 indigenous vascular taxa, of which 229 are endemic (Davis *et al.*, 1986).

Ecuador's forests contain a wealth of wild relatives of crops. These include relatives of millets (*Eleusine*, *Panicum*, *Pennisetum*), pseudocereals (*Amaranthus*, *Chenopodium*), legumes (*Lupinus*), rootcrops (yam *Dioscorea*, *Ipomoea*, *Oxalis*), caffeine-containing beverage plants (*Ilex*, *Theobroma*), spices (*Capparis*, *Capsicum*, *Piper*), numerous oilseeds (*Euterpe*, *Jessenia*, *Oenocarpus*) and fruits (custard apple *Annona*, passion fruit *Passiflora*, *Prunus*, guava *Psidium*, avocado *Persea*, papaya *Carica*). Genetic material from Ecuador's wild tomatoes *Lycopersicon esculentum carasiforme* and *L. hirsutum* have improved the domesticated crop by increasing the vitamin C content and amount of soluble solids in tomatoes (Cabarle *et al.*, 1989). Hundreds of other plants are used for medicinal purposes by the local inhabitants and may prove to be useful outside Ecuador.

Several plant species are endangered, especially through habitat destruction, such as the vine *Dicliptera dodsoni*, an Acanthaceae known only by a single individual from Rio Palenque Science Center; its habitat has been almost entirely converted to plantations of bananas and African oil-palms (IUCN, 1978). Some of the 3276 recorded species of orchids are also particularly susceptible to selective extinction through over-collecting and habitat loss. Other species have declined as a result of over exploitation, such as guayacan *Tabebuia chrysantha*, the most important timber of the coastal tropical dry forests of Ecuador (Gentry, 1977).

In total, Ecuador has 20,000 to 25,000 species of vascular plants and, based on distribution patterns of local floras, it is estimated that 20 per cent of these are endemic (Gentry, 1982).

While the data base on wildlife in Ecuador is extremely poor, it is known that the country is exceptionally rich in endemic species. Of the 2436 species of terrestrial vertebrates reported in 1989, 307 (37 bird species, 26 mammals, 106 reptiles and 138 amphibians) are found nowhere else in the world (Cabarle *et al.*, 1989).

Birds are the best-known group of Ecuadorian fauna, and their species count continues to grow. Over 1500 bird species have been reported by Ortiz *et al.* (1990). At least 324 species of mammals (Albuja, 1991), 402 amphibians and 379 reptiles (Almendáriz, 1991) and 706 species of freshwater fishes (Barriga, 1991) have been recorded in the country, but as with the avian fauna, the exact ranges of the species are known only generally. A recent inventory in northwestern Ecuador found five species of mammals new to science and eight species that had not been previously recorded in the country (Albuja, 1988).

Sixty four species of birds are thought to be threatened in Ecuador, especially through forest destruction and hunting, including two rare birds of prey of the tropical lowland forests: the harpy eagle *Harpia harpyja* and the crested eagle *Morphnus guianensis* and three frugivores of the Andean cloud forests: the yellow-eared conure *Ognorhynchus icterotis*, the toucan barbet *Semnornis ramphastinus* and the long-wattled umbrella bird *Cephalopterus penduliger* (Suarez and Garcia, 1986). Collar *et al.* (1992) list 40 globally threatened species in the country, seven of which are endemic. These include the endangered black-breasted puffleg *Eriocnemis nigrivestis* from montane forest and the Esmeraldas woodstar *Acestrura berlepschi*, also endangered but found in lowland forest.

Similarly, several mammals are threatened due to habitat loss and hunting, including the spectacled bear *Tremarctos ornatus* and the mountain tapir *Tapirus pinchaque* in the Andean cloud forests, and the jaguar *Panthera onca* in the western and eastern tropical forests. IUCN lists a total of 27 threatened mammal species in Ecuador (Groombridge, 1993). Populations of some commercially valuable reptiles have declined due to over exploitation, such as the black caiman *Melanosuchus niger* in the Amazonian lowlands and the American crocodile *Crocodylus acutus* in the coastal region (Suarez and Garcia, 1986), both are listed as vulnerable by IUCN. Nine other threatened reptile species are found in the country. These are three iguana species and the giant tortoise *Geochelone elephantopus* on the Galapagos islands, three marine turtles and two river turtles.

In the Galapagos Islands, introduced species such as rats, cats, goats, dogs, pigs and donkeys are a major threat to the survival of whole communities and habitats as well as to individual species. Feral animals threaten endemic birds such as the flightless cormorant *Nannopterum harrisi* and dark-rumped petrel *Pterodroma phaeopygia phaeopygia*. The endemic giant tortoises and land iguanas *Conolophus subcristatus* and *C. pallidus* are also at risk. Introduced plants, such as *Lantana* and *Cinchona*, are another threat on these islands.

Conservation Areas

Actions to protect Ecuador's wildlands started in 1936 when the government set aside several islands of the Galapagos Archipelago as the first national park. A few other areas were declared between then and the mid 1970s. The *Strategy for the Conservation of Outstanding Natural Areas* was completed in 1976. It identified priority areas and provided guidelines for their management (Putney, 1976). Ecuador now has 12 protected areas in IUCN's categories I–IV: six national parks, four ecological reserves, one biological reserve and one marine resources reserve (Table 27.5). The practical distinctions between these categories are not clear, but their primary function is the protection of the natural environment. The National System of Protected Areas was managed by SUFOREN's Division of Natural Areas and Wildlife. However, INEFAN has now taken over the administration of these areas. The 31,254 sq. km of protected land represents 11.3 per cent of the national territory. There is, in addition, a marine resource reserve covering 79,900 sq. km around the Galapagos islands.

The western region has only three protected areas. The Manglares-Churute Ecological Reserve protects a small sample of the coastal mangroves and some disturbed dry forests. The Machalilla National Park conserves an important area of the coastal dry forest. The park boundaries extend two nautical miles into marine environment and include beautiful beaches, bays and inlets. The Cotacachi-Cayapas Ecological Reserve is the only large conservation area protecting wet and moist tropical forests in western Ecuador.

The Andean vegetation is well represented in several protected areas in the mountains. The Cotopaxi National Park includes the Cotopaxi volcano and areas of páramo vegetation. The Cajas National Recreation Area (IUCN category V — 288 sq. km) protects páramo vegetation and several high mountain lakes. The Sangay National Park and the Cayambe-Coca Ecological Reserve protect large samples of páramo vegetation and eastern cloud forests. The Podocarpus National Park protects the highly endemic cloud forests of southern Ecuador. However, there are

Table 27.5   Conservation areas of Ecuador

Existing conservation areas in IUCN's categories I–IV are listed below. The marine resource reserve and private reserves have not been included. For information on World Heritage Sites, Biosphere Reserves and Ramsar Sites see Chapter 8.

National Parks	*Area (sq. km)*
Cotopaxi	334
Galapagos°	7,278
Machalilla*	551
Podocarpus*	1,463
Sangay*	5,177
Yasuni*	9,823
Ecological Reserves	
Cayambe-Coca*	4,031
Cotacachi-Cayapas*	2,044
El Angel+	157
Manglares-Churute*	350
Biological Reserve	
Limoncocha*	46
Total	31,254

°   not shown on Map 27.1
+   not mapped, data not available to this project
*   area with forest within its boundary as shown on Map 27.1

Source: WCMC

gold mining concession covering 80 per cent of this park.

Important parts of the Amazonian rain forests are protected in the Yasuni National Park, the Limoncocha Biological Reserve and the Cuyabeno Faunal Production Reserve, but these three areas are threatened by oil exploitation. Indeed, Limoncocha has now been virtually destroyed.

As is apart, the National System of Protected Areas is far from perfect. While large areas in the Andean and Amazonian regions are protected, the coastal/marine areas and the western forests are under-represented. There is a need for additional reserves to protect the enormous biological diversity found in this small country. Only the Galapagos National Park has a reasonable number of staff and an active management programme. The other conservation areas are poorly managed. Although the parks and reserves are legally protected, the law conflicts directly with other Ecuadorian legislation, such as the mining and hydrocarbon laws under which mining and oil concessions have been granted inside national parks and other protected areas. Other government institutions have developed infrastructure inside parks and reserves without consulting the Division of Natural Areas and Wildlife. The problems are compounded by the invasion of protected areas by colonists, the extraction of wood and fauna, the pasturing of livestock and deliberate burning. These conflicts are the result of inadequate protection and management, poorly conceived and contradictory legislation, minimal coordination between public and private institutions, a lack of clear government policies, inadequate funding and lack of trained park personnel and suitable infrastructure (Cifuentes *et al.*, 1989). Fiscal reforms are also badly needed.

In addition to the areas included in the national system, there are several areas which are owned by foundations, institutions or privately. In many cases, they are better protected than the national conservation areas. These include the Rio Palenque Science Center, Capeira Science Center, Jauneche Science Center, Jatun Sacha Reserve and San Carlos Forest (Cabarle *et al.*, 1989). Other conservation units, both publicly and privately owned, have been designated as "Forest and Vegetation Protection Areas" to conserve watersheds and maintain important biological resources for the local communities.

In 1988, the Ecuadorian government established the Awa Ethnic and Forest Reserve, with the participation of the Awa Indian communities in an inter-institutional commission responsible for the reserve management. Although this reserve is not part of the national system of protected areas, it represents the largest tract of primary rain forest (approximately 1000 sq. km) in western Ecuador and contains a wide variety of species whose distribution is limited to this particular area.

The Division of Natural Areas and Wildlife wishes to expand the protected areas network in line with the recommendations of a national strategy for conserving the outstanding natural areas of the country (Cifuentes *et al.*, 1989). The new strategy, developed in 1989 by the government of Ecuador and the national NGO, Fundación Natura, identifies 17 additional areas for inclusion in the National System of Protected Areas. The establishment of a wildlife refuge to protect a good sample of the mangrove forests and other wetlands in northeastern Ecuador is a priority.

Ecuador signed the Convention on Nature Protection and Wildlife Preservation in the Western Hemisphere in 1940 and ratified the Convention Concerning the Protection of the World Cultural and Natural Heritage Sites in 1975. Two natural sites, the Galapagos and Sangay national parks, have been inscribed on the World Heritage list. Ecuador signed the Amazon Cooperation Treaty in 1978, an agreement between the eight countries with territory in the Amazon region to establish regulations for managing natural resources and to propose conservation directed alternatives to the management of multinational projects. The country also participates in the UNESCO Man and Biosphere Program, with two sites, the Galapagos and Yasuni national parks, inscribed as Biosphere Reserves. Ecuador ratified the Ramsar Convention in 1990 and two sites, the Manglares-Churute Ecological Reserve and the Machalilla National Park, have been listed.

Initiatives for Conservation

A government project was initiated in 1986 to develop management strategies for Ecuador's coastal region, including its mangrove forests and associated ecosystems.

A Conservation Data Center was established in 1990 by the Nature Conservancy in the National Council of Science and Technology (CONACYT) with support from the US. It maintains a database on natural areas and endangered species.

Several international initiatives are underway which aim to support the conservation of natural resources in Ecuador. A 10 year USAID project (Sustainable Uses for Biological Resources or SUBIR) is being implemented by a consortium of three international conservation organizations: CARE, The Nature Conservancy (TNC) and Wildlife Conservation International. The SUBIR project is a unique, long-term attempt to develop positive links between conservation and sustainable development in Ecuador through coordinated actions in protected areas management, buffer zone development, research, policy analysis and training.

The Ecuadorian government has developed a National Forestry Action Plan (PAFE). The plan aims to increase the participation of the forestry sector in the national economy, increase the use of agroforestry systems, improve watershed management, promote the rational use and conservation of forest resources, increase the benefits of forest utilization to native people and local farmers, and promote higher awareness of conservation issues. However, the plan has been criticized by some conservation groups for its emphasis on exploitative activities.

A number of local non-governmental organizations are actively campaigning for forest conservation, Cabarle *et al.* (1989) list 26 of these. Fundación Natura is the most active national-level organization in public education and lobbying. Through a debt-for-nature swap, sponsored by the World Wildlife Fund-US and TNC, Fundación Natura is supporting the Ministry of Agriculture's Division of Natural Areas and Wildlife and is assisting with the establishment of boundaries and provision of critical infrastructure and equipment for several protected areas. EcoCiencia, the Ecuadorian Foundation for Ecological Studies, is developing research and training projects in many parks and reserves in collaboration with Wildlife Conservation International.

References

Albuja, L. (1988). La Fauna en Cotacachi-Cayapas. Fundación Natura. *Revista Colibri* 4: 58–63.

Albuja, L. (1991). Lista de mamíferos del Ecuador. *Politécnica* 16(3): 163–203.

Almendáriz, A. (1991). Lista de anfibios y reptiles del Ecuador. *Politécnica* 16(3): 89–162.

Balslev, H. (1988). Distribution patterns of Ecuadorean plant species. *Taxon* 37(3): 567–577.

Balslev, H. and Renner, S.S. (1989). Diversity of east Ecuadorean lowland forests. In: *Tropical Forests: Botanical Dynamics, Speciation and Diversity*. Holm-Nielsen, L.B., Nielsen, I.C. and Balslev, H. (eds). Academic Press, London. Pp. 287–295.

Barriga, R. (1991). Lista de peces de aqua dulce del Ecuador. *Politécnica* 16(3): 7–88.

Cabarle, B.J., Crespi, M., Dodson, C.H., Luzuriaga, C., Rose, D and Shores, J.N. (1989). *An Assessment of Biological Diversity and Tropical Forests of Ecuador*. A World Resources Institute Report to USAID/Ecuador, 105 pp. + 9 maps.

Cañadas, L. (1983). *El Mapa Bioclimatico y Ecologico del Ecuador*. Banco Central del Ecuador, Quito, Ecuador.

Cifuentes, M., Ponce, A., Albán, F., Mena, P., Mosquera, G., Rodriguez, J., Silva, D., Suárez, L., Tobar, A., y Torres, J. (1989). *Estrategia para el Sistema Nacional de Areas Protegidas, II Fase*. Ministerio de Agricultura y Ganaderia y Fundación Natura. Quito, Ecuador.

CLIRSEN (1986) *Estudio multitemporal de manglares, camaroneras, y àreas salinas de la costa ecuatoriana mediante información de sensores remotos 1969–1984*. Instituto Geográfico Militar, Quito, Ecuador.

Collar, N.J., Gonzaga, L.P., Krabbe, N., Madroño Nieto, A., Naranjo, L.G., Parker III, T.A. and Wege, D.C. (1992). *Threatened Birds of the Americas. The ICBP/IUCN Red Data Book*. ICBP, Cambridge, U.K.

Davis, S.D., Droop, S.J.M., Gregerson, P., Henson, L., Leon, C.J., Villa-Lobos, J.L, Synge, H. and Zantovska, J. (1986). *Plants in Danger. What do we know?* IUCN, Gland, Switzerland and Cambridge, U.K.

Dodson, C.H. and Gentry, A.H. (1978). Flora of the Río Palenque Science Center. *Selbyana* 4 (1–6): 1–628.

Dodson, C.H. and Gentry, A.H. (1991). Biological Extinction in Western Ecuador. *Annals Missouri Botanical Garden* 78: 273–295.

FAO (1993). *Forest resource assessment 1990: tropical countries*. FAO Forestry Paper 112. FAO, Rome, Italy.

FAO (1994). *FAO Yearbook: Forest Products 1981–1992*. FAO Forestry Series No. 27, FAO Statistics Series No. 116. FAO, Rome, Italy.

Gentry, A.H. (1977). Endangered Plant Species and Habitats of Ecuador and Amazonian Peru. In: *Extinction is Forever*, pp.136–149. Prance, G.T. and Elias, T.S. (eds). New York Botanical Garden, New York.

Gentry, A.H. (1982). Patterns of neotropical plant species diversity. *Evolutionary Biology* 15: 1–84.

Groombridge, B. (1993). *1994 IUCN Red List of Threatened Animals*. IUCN, Gland, Switzerland and Cambridge, U.K.

Harling, G. (1979). The vegetation types of Ecuador; a brief survey. In: *Tropical Botany*. Larsen, K. and Holm Nielson, L. (eds). Academic Press, London, U.K. Pp. 165–175.

IUCN (1978). *The IUCN Plant Red Data Book*. IUCN, Gland, Switzerland.

IUCN (1988) *Ecuador (with emphasis on western Ecuador): Conservation of Biological Diversity and Forest Ecosystems*. Document number 103IJ, prepared by IUCN Tropical Forest Programme. IUCN Gland, Switzerland and Cambridge, U.K.

Jordon, E. (1988). Die mangrovenwälder Ecuadors in spannungsfeld zwischen ökologie and ökonomie. *Geographischen Gesellschaft zu Hannover* 1988: 97–138.

MAG (1991). *Inventario de los Manglares del Ecuador Continental*. Ministerio de Agricultura y Granaderia, Quito. Pp. 438.

Marles, R.J. and Neill, D.A. (1988). A contribution to the Ethnopharmacology of the lowland Quicha people of Amazonian Ecuador. *Revista de la Academia Colombiana de Ciencias Exactas, Físicas y Naturales* 16(63): 111–120.

Myers, N. (1988). Threatened biotas: "hotspots" in tropical forests. *Environmentalist* 8: 1–20.

Neill, D. and Palacios, W. (1987). *Proyecto Arboles de la Amazonia Ecuatoriana — Informe interno de los avances del proyecto*. USAID and MAG, Quito. Pp. 1–24.

Ortiz, F., Greenfiel, P. and Matheus, J.C. (1990). *Aves del Ecuador*. FEPROTUR. Quito, Ecuador.

Putney, A. (1976). *Estrategia preliminar para la conservacion de areas silvestres sobresalientes del Ecuador*. Ministerio de Agricultura y Ganaderia, Quito, Ecuador.

Southgate, D., Sierra, R. and Brown, L. (1991). The Causes of Tropical Deforestation in Ecuador: A Statistical Analysis. *World Development* 19(9): 1145–1151.

Suárez, L. and Garcia, M. (1986). *Extinción de Animales en el Ecuador*. Fundación Natura, Quito, Ecuador.

SUFOREN (1991). *Plan de Accion Forestal. Diagnostico 1991–1995*. Subsecretaria Forestal y de Recursos Naturales Renovables, Ministerio de Agricultura y Ganaderia. Quito, Ecuador.

WRI/UNEP/UNDP (1990). *World Resources 1990–1991. A Guide to the Global Environment*. Oxford University Press, New York.

Authors: Luis Suárez, EcoCiencia/WCI-NYZS and Paola Sylva, Directora Area de Investigación, Centro de Educacion y Promocion Popular; with contributions from Bruce Cabarle, WRI, Washington, D.C.; Craig McFarland, President, Charles Darwin Foundation; Pádraig Whelan, Investigator, Charles Darwin Research Station; and Sylvia Harcourt Carrasco, Charles Darwin Foundation, Quito.

Map 27.1 Ecuador

The source for the forest cover data for Ecuador is a published map, *Republica del Ecuador — Mapa Forestal*. This map produced by the Centro de Levantamientos Integrados de Recursos Naturales por Sensores Remotos (CLIRSEN) and Direccion Nacional Forestal (DINAF) was published in 1991, at a scale of 1:1 million. The Galapagos islands are also shown, but they have not been mapped in this Atlas.

The CLIRSEN/DINAF map has been compiled from various information sources of different dates. The forest information is based on satellite data, radar and aerial photographs from 1977–1983; mangrove data are based on a 1987 map *Mapa Forestal de Manglares* compiled by CLIRSEN-DINAF; and land use information is derived from 1971–1983 satellite imagery, radar and aerial photographs. Some 1987 Landsat imagery has also been used.

Twelve vegetation/land use types are shown on the source map. From these, eight forest types have been digitised to produce the forest cover shown in Map 27.1. *Bh — Bosque Higrofítico, Bp — Bosque y Palmas* and *Pp — Palmas* have been mapped as lowland moist forest; *Bm — Bosque Mesofítico* and *Bx — Bosque Xerofítico* as dry forest, *Ma — Manglares* as mangrove forest, and *Pd — Podocarpus* and *Mh — Matorral Higromorfo* as montane forest. Submontane forest has not been depicted as there were no source data available for this formation. The following vegetation classes have been amalgamated into the non-forest category: *Matorral mesomorfo, Matorral xeromorfo, Chaparro, Vegetación de Páramo* and *Areas antrópicas*.

The protected areas information is available from the same CLIRSEN/DINAF map and have been digitised from categories *Parques nacionales* and *Reservas*.

28 French Guiana

Country area 90,000 sq. km
Land area 88,150 sq. km
Population (mid-1994) 139,000
Population growth rate 2.4 per cent
Population projected to 2025 267,000
Gross national product per capita (1991) US$1794
Forest cover in 1979 (see Map) 81,490 sq. km
Forest cover in 1990 (FAO, 1993) 79,970 sq. km
Annual deforestation rate (1981–1990) —
Industrial roundwood production 188,000 cu. m
Industrial roundwood exports 14,000 cu. m
Fuelwood and charcoal production 66,000 cu. m
Processed wood production 19,000 cu. m
Processed wood exports 4000 cu. m

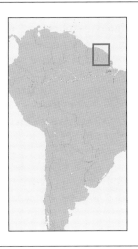

French Guiana, located between Brazil and Surinam in the northeast of South America, has been an overseas department of France since 1946. It has elected representatives in Paris and there are no plans for any weakening of links with France. Since the creation of the Guianan Space Centre, the country has become the "space port of Europe". In addition to providing the launch pad for the Ariane rockets, the Centre has done much to stimulate the country's economy.

Tropical rain forest covers more than 90 per cent of the country. There is, however, little endemism, as much of the flora and fauna of French Guiana extends throughout the Guayana Shield.

The country has always been sparsely populated, therefore until very recently, there was little human impact on forests other than those near the coast. Along the coast, population density is high and deforestation has accordingly been more permanent and extensive than in the interior.

However, the overall picture of this small territory, blessed with a high animal and plant diversity and very representative of the vast Guayanan-Amazonian zone, is of a scarcely altered environment. This is not because of effective conservation programmes but because human influence is still slight. The future conservation of the country's natural heritage will require a much more active process.

INTRODUCTION

French Guiana, 400 km long and 300 km wide on its longest axes, is the smallest of the three Guianas (Guyana, Surinam and French Guiana). The country stretches between the Oyapock and the Maroni Rivers, two of the five great rivers which drain the Guayana Shield to the Atlantic. This vast zone of Precambrian origin, extending from the Amapa River (in Brazil) to the Orinoco (in Venezuela), is geologically highly diverse (Choubert, 1979).

The relief is generally monotonous, rarely exceeding 300 m and attaining 850 m only at certain points of the Inini-Camopi chain, which lies almost parallel to the coast in the central region. The mountains are isolated from one another by large hilly areas. An extensive hilly area also spreads to the north of the Inini-Camopi chain, ranging from 50 to 200 m in altitude, with some scattered mountains exceeding 300 m in the subcoastal regions. There is a peneplain in the south with many floodplains.

Where lateritic layers protect the mountain tops against erosion, the summits have a tabular shape. In the granitic areas, especially in the southern half of the country, some of these form bare domes (inselbergs). To the north, between 10 and 40 km from the coast, the Precambrian basement sinks below the marine and estuarine Quaternary deposits of clay or sand which form the coastal plain. It is here that the principal non-forested areas and urban centres are located. Leached basement areas in the northwest form slightly elevated sandy plateaux. At the heart of these, fairly large expanses of white sand are develop-

ing as a result of the leaching. The plateaux are crossed by large rivers and streams flowing in a north-south direction. Narrow alluvial plains are associated with these.

French Guiana has a tropical moist climate. Rainfall is seasonal and annual averages range from 4000 mm in the northeast to under 2000 mm in the south. The rainy season lasts from seven to nine months; the main dry season is between August and November. The mean temperature during the day varies between 26° and 30°C, while at night it is between 18° and 28°C (Sanite, 1992).

The country has always been sparsely populated, although population distribution fluctuated significantly both before and after the arrival—at the end of the 16th century—of Europeans (Grenand, 1979; Brasseur, 1979). Population growth is now quite high with a predominantly young population and high immigration levels. The country's 1990 census indicated 114,700 inhabitants, 93.4 per cent of whom live in the northern coastal districts. The population estimate given at the head of the chapter is an unpublished figure from the Population Reference Bureau for mid-1994. The largest town is the capital, Cayenne, with over 40,000 inhabitants, followed by Saint-Laurent-du-Maroni and Kourou. The small percentage of the population inhabiting the interior live mostly along the Maroni and Oyapock Rivers; 5.8 per cent live along the former, they are dominated by people of African origin, while 0.7 per cent live along the Oyapock River. There are diverse ethnic groups in the country including

Creoles, who make up around 43 per cent of the population, Chinese (14 per cent), West Indian (14 per cent), French (11 per cent), the Amerindians (4 per cent) and several other small groups. There is a clear distinction between the virtually self-sufficient inhabitants of the interior, who hunt, fish and practice slash and burn cultivation, and the populations of the coastal and subcoastal regions who, with the exception of many Amerindians, are fully integrated into the market economy and administration.

In 1985, shrimps formed 53 per cent of French Guiana's exports and timber made up 9 per cent. The main crops are rice, manioc and sugar cane, much of which is consumed locally. There is a limited amount of gold mined in the country—800 kg in 1990 (Sanite, 1992).

The Forests

The rain forest in French Guiana displays notable differences in structure and species from one region to another (Sabatier and Prévost, 1989; Sabatier, in press). Edaphic, paleohistoric and historic factors and the climatic gradient account for this diversity (Granville, 1982, 1988; Prance, 1982, 1987; Sabatier and Prévost, 1989). Geographic variation occurs at the family level also. For example, in the north, among trees greater than 10 cm in diameter, the three most important families are Lecythidaceae, Caesalpiniaceae and Chrysobalanaceae; in the central north-east they are Lecythidaceae, Sapotaceae and Caesalpiniaceae; in the centre Burseraceae, Sapotaceae and Lecythidaceae dominate, while Burseraceae, Lecythidaceae and Meliaceae are most important in the south (Sabatier, in press; Mori and Boom, 1987).

Where Caesalpiniaceae prevail, the dominant canopy trees often include *Dicorynia guianensis*, *Eperua falcata*, *E. grandiflora*, *Peltogyne venosa* and *Vouacapoua americana*, together with Lauraceae (*Ocotea rubra*, *Ocotea* spp.) and some Vochysiaceae (*Qualea rosea*, *Erisma uncinatum*, *Vochysia* spp.). Many of these species are exploitable for timber. The Burseraceae (*Tetragastris altissima* and *Protium* spp.), on the other hand, although performing the same canopy role as the Caesalpiniaceae, are of little value for timber.

There are great local differences in species richness. For example, there are up to 3.5 times as many species of Lecythidaceae (Mori and Boom, 1987), Sapotaceae and Chrysobalanaceae (Sabatier, in press) in the central region than in the north or south. Physiognomic differences are equally important. The forests attain their most impressive stature in the central region, on "green rocks" of the paramaca geological series. Here they have a canopy of around 45 m with emergents at 60 m. Elsewhere, the forest canopy is around 30–35 m. Edaphic conditions limit development in some areas. For example, on hydromorphic soils, forest structure may be simplified (Oldeman, 1974); in areas where drainage is shallow, large diameter trees are rare (Lescure and Boulet, 1985); and on lateritic plateaux or granite outcrops, forests tend to be less tall and liane rich (Granville, 1979). Elfin, cloud forests occur on the highest mountains.

Forests on acid, sandy soils and swamp forests cover quite extensive areas. Several specialised formations exist on sandy, podzolized soil in the northwest and on the coastal plain. Of these, *Dimorphandra* forests are extensively exploited and are therefore the most threatened forest type. *Humira balsamifera* and *Clusia fockeana*, widely represented in Surinam, are found on the most leached white sands. These are less disturbed because neither the timber nor the soil has much financial value. Flooded forests are well represented in the northeast and on the southern peneplain. Where submergence is almost permanent, *Euterpe*

Table 28.1 Estimates of forest extent in French Guiana

Forest type	Area (sq. km)	% of land area
Lowland moist	73,293	83.1
Degraded lowland moist	505	0.6
Sub-montane	420	0.5
Inland swamp	6,325	7.2
Mangrove	947	1.1
Total	81,490	92.4

Based on analysis of Map 28.1. See Map Legend on p. 277 for details.

oleracea and trees such as *Symphonia globulifera*, *Triplaris weigeltiana* and *Virola surinamensis* dominate the relatively impoverished flora. The temporarily flooded zones, on the other hand, are characterized by a rich flora of edaphic specialists.

Mangroves

Estimates of the area of mangrove in the country vary. FAO/UNEP (1981) give a figure of 550 sq. km; Lescure and Tostain (1989) indicate that they cover around 700 sq km, occupying virtually the whole of the coast with the exception of some sandy beaches and rocky outcrops; while Map 28.1 shows 947 sq. km of mangrove in the country. However, this map portrays the state of the mangroves in 1979 (see Table 28.1 and Map Legend) and these formations change considerably over time.

The coast is accreting and there is typical succession, from the sea towards the interior, of *Laguncularia racemosa* being replaced by *Avicennia germinans* and then *Rhizophora racemosa* becoming dominant (Lescure and Tostain, 1989). Inland, the mangroves are frequently replaced by either swamp forest of *Euterpe* and *Symphonia* or herbaceous swamps. Tostain (1986) found five bird species in the younger mangroves as opposed to 61 for older stages enriched by *Euterpe* palms.

The shore features many mudbanks. These are gradually moving from east to west under the effect of longshore drift and the north Amazonian current. In front of them there are young mangroves, while behind them the mangroves are eroded away before they are 10 years old.

The mangroves are economically important for the shrimp industry in particular (Martosubro and Naanin, 1977) as they act as a nursery for Peneide larvae (Rojas-Beltran, 1986). The annual shrimp catch of 3,000 to 4,000 tonnes is the country's main export, it is worth US$40–60 million. The industry provides fishing for 70 boats and employment for around a thousand people (Dintheer *et al.*, 1989).

Forest Resources and Management

Except for the open formations, savanna and swamps of the coastal plain (Granville, 1986), French Guiana is covered with tropical rain forest. In 1991, in a report by the National Office of Forests (Office National des Forêts—ONF) and the Direction Departementale de l'Equipement, it was estimated that forest covered 74,500 sq. km (ONF/DDE, 1991). FAO's most recent estimate (FAO, 1993) of forest cover in French Guiana is 79,970 sq. km. This, though, includes all "ecosystems with a minimum of 10 percent crown cover of trees and/or bamboos". However, the figure given for closed broadleaved forest is only slightly lower at 79,250 sq. km. The FAO (1993) estimate of forest cover in French Guiana may not be very accurate as a 1973 survey was used as a

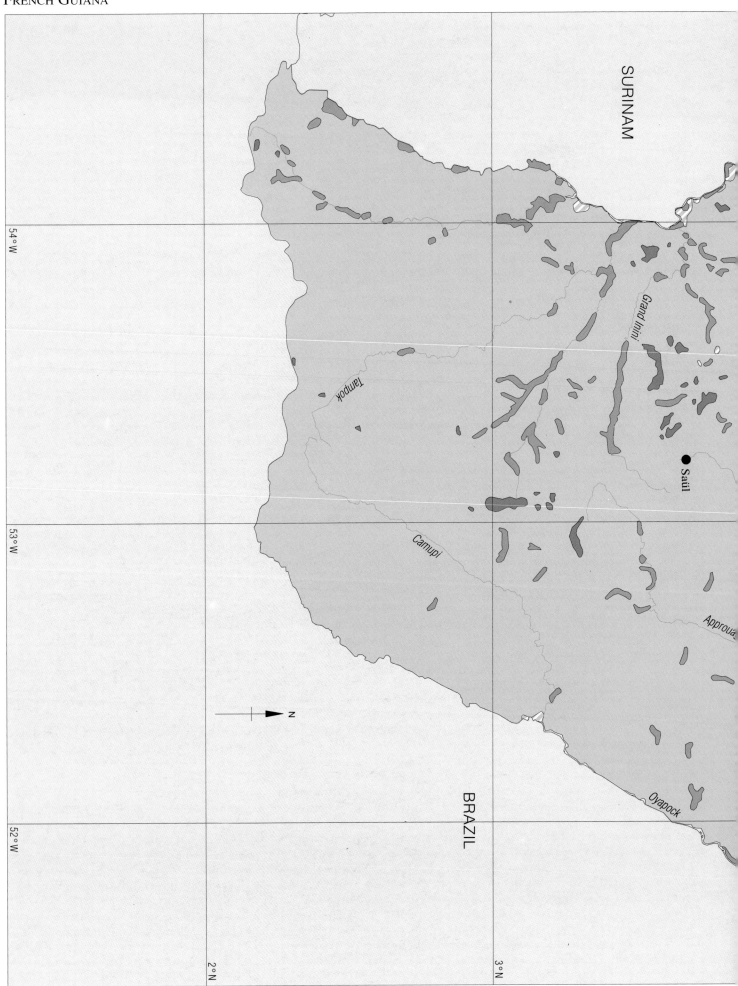

SURINAM

54°W

53°W

52°W

Grand Inini

Saül

Tampok

Camupi

Approua

Oyapock

BRAZIL

N

2°N

3°N

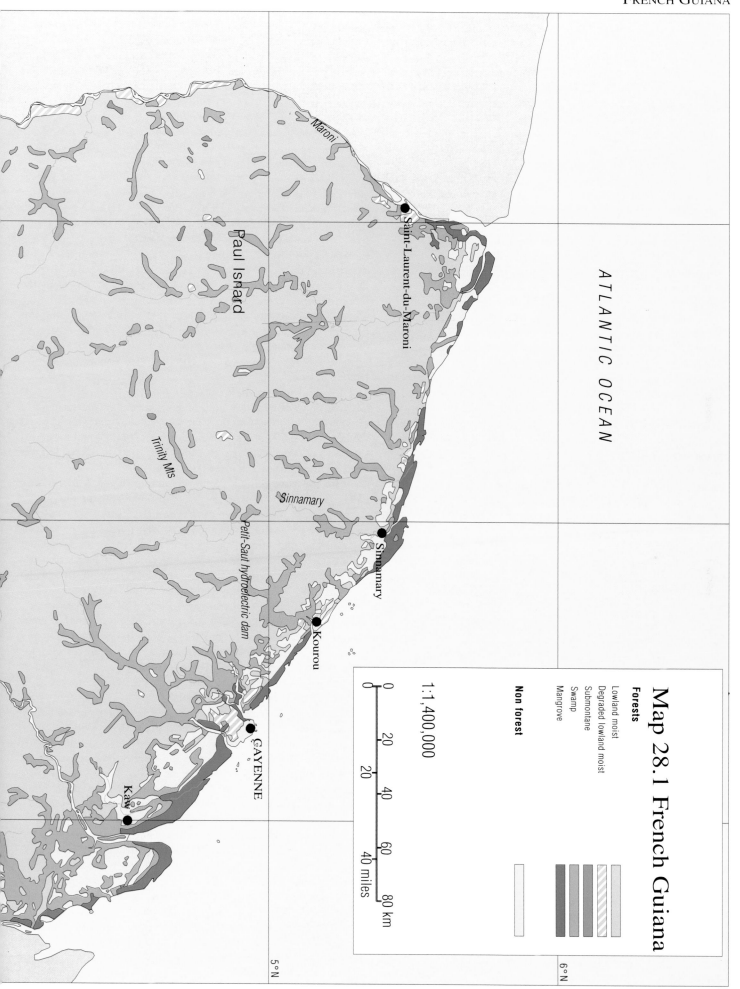

ATLANTIC OCEAN

Maroni

Saint-Laurent-du-Maroni

Paul Isnard

Trinity Mts

Sinnamary

Petit-Saut hydroelectric dam

Sinnamary

Kourou

GAYENNE

Kaw

Map 28.1 French Guiana

Forests

Lowland moist
Degraded lowland moist
Submontane
Swamp
Mangrove

Non forest

1:1,400,000

0   20   40   60   80 km
0   20   40   40 miles

6°N

5°N

baseline and the estimate of change is based only on a model.

The figure of 81,490 sq. km for total forest cover given in Table 28.1, measured from Map 28.1, is somewhat higher than the areas estimated by either ONF/DDE or FAO. This is probably because the source map used here (see Map Legend) was published 15 years ago and it is highly likely that the information shown on it is even older.

The forests belong to the French State and are managed by ONF, which was established in French Guiana in 1966 (see Valeix and Mauperain (1989) for history). ONF carries out forest inventories, undertakes construction of forest roads and other management tasks, allocates logging permits and collects a minor stumpage fee.

The various public subsidies for forest exploitation provide about 15 per cent of the income of the forest enterprises (ONF/DDE, 1991). Local subsidies promote the use of wood for construction. In spite of this, the majority of these enterprises are in financial difficulties.

Subsidies are provided in order to develop the economy by supporting the timber processing industry, one of the few local economic activities. Logging permits are given only to enterprises that are able to undertake at least a minimal degree of processing. Virtually no raw logs have been exported since 1983. Local sales of sawn timber are increasing, while sawlog exports are declining. Without government subsidies, exploitation of forest resources would doubtless have evolved differently.

Between 1986 and 1990, timber exports ranged from 9978 to 17,709 tonnes with a value of US$3.7 to 7.4 million, while imports varied from 692 to 3761 tonnes, worth between US$1.0 and 4.9 million (ONF/DDE, 1991). Exports have therefore exceeded imports by between 80 per cent and 412 per cent. Nevertheless, during this period, the quantity of sawn timber exported was always less than that consumed locally.

Figure 28.1 Map showing the extent of forest exploitation and other activities affecting the forest environment as of December 1990　　*Source:* ONF (1990)

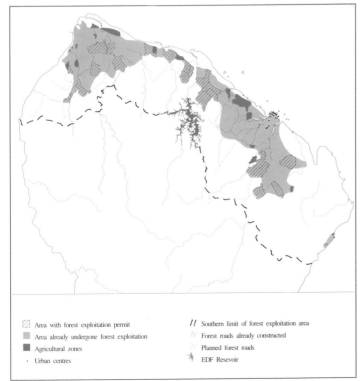

Area with forest exploitation permit

Area already undergone forest exploitation

Agricultural zones

Urban centres

// Southern limit of forest exploitation area

Forest roads already constructed

Planned forest roads

EDF Reservoir

ONF limits the area of forest which may be logged (see Figure 28.1). In the subcoastal region, 21,500 sq. km are allocated for logging. Management is based upon 40 year cycles (ONF/DDE, 1991). Forest policy aims to encourage better use of infrastructure and protect remaining intact forests.

There is a small amount of illegal logging to supply the local markets with such species as *Cedrela odorata* (used for wood carvings) and *Dicorynia guianensis* and *Ocotea rubra* (used in making dug-out canoes). The logging is restricted to areas accessible from waterways and roads.

Exploitation of rosewood *Aniba rosaeodora* for its oil (linalool) and of balata or bully-tree *Manilkara bidentata* for gum, reached its maximum between 1910 and 1930. Extraction was on a remarkably large scale—maximum registered exports amounted to 107 tonnes of oil in 1926 and 1095 tonnes of gum in 1920 (after Bruleaux, 1989)—and led to the disappearance of these species over very large areas. Distilleries for processing rosewood were even set up in the interior. Extractive activities such as these no longer take place. There have been recent attempts at industrial exploitation of palm hearts *Euterpe oleracea* in the swamp forests of the northeast, but these have failed.

Deforestation

The lowland forests of French Guiana, together with those of Guyana and Surinam, are unique among South American countries in that deforestation pressures have so far scarcely affected them. FAO (1993) gives French Guiana's average annual deforestation between the years of 1981 and 1990 as 30 sq. km per year, an annual rate of a mere 0.004 per cent.

From the 18th century to the beginning of the 20th century, industrial production of sugar-cane, cacao and annatto, the orange colouring from the fruit pulp of *Bixa orellana*, was responsible for some forest clearance along the coast. The forests of the interior were mostly undisturbed, except in areas where the rosewood and bully trees had been extracted. More recent disturbance has meant that there are some small areas of secondary growth around the sites of former villages, frequently those of gold diggers.

Some deforestation occurred following the "green plan". This came into effect in 1975 and consisted of a number of measures aimed at strengthening the country's economy. During 1976 and 1977, 11.5 sq. km of forest were cleared for agricultural purposes. During the 1980s, incentives for clearance led to deforestation of 112 sq. km with 88. sq km of this converted to pasture, 12 sq. km to orchards and 12 sq. km to non-permanent cultivation. These incentives no longer exist and now around 10 sq. km of pasture are abandoned each year (DAF, 1990).

Over the last five years, expansion of urban areas and of the space centre, together with extension of the road network, has entailed clearance of a further 25 sq. km of forest, of which 2 sq. km were mangrove. In 1990, there were 410 km of major forest roads and this network of roads, both major and secondary, is expanding at a rate of 75 km a year. The road-building, financed entirely with public funds to support forest exploitation, has favoured slash and burn agriculturalists. However, the extent of cleared areas actually in use did not exceed 50 sq. km in 1989 (DAF, 1990). In 1994, 300 sq. km of forest land will be flooded by the Petit-Saut hydroelectric dam on the Sinnamary River.

In the decades to come the pace of destruction will doubtless increase since several road projects are currently being considered and, if population growth continues, other hydroelectric schemes may be initiated.

Biodiversity

French Guiana's fauna and flora are representative of the Guayanan-Amazonian zone and especially of the Guayana Shield. Mori and Prance (1987) estimate that 30 per cent of the plant species collected around Saül, in the central region, have an extensive distribution, often reaching as far as Central America and the coastal forest of east Brazil. There is, therefore, little endemism in the territory. Species presumed to be endemic are often those described recently which may have passed unnoticed elsewhere due to their low population densities (Granville, 1982; Mori and Prance, 1987).

Several authors (Descamps *et al.*, 1978; Granville, 1982; Prance, 1987) note the existence of a centre of endemism in the Guianas (Surinam, French Guiana and Amapa in Brazil). This could be evidence of a Pleistocene refugium and would account for the high plant species diversity in the central region. Others emphasize the connection between species richness and local environmental conditions. Feuillet (1989), for instance, shows that the *Passiflora* genus is richest in the northeast, which is the region of maximum rainfall. Here 29 out of 37 known species are present and 12 of these are found exclusively in the area receiving over 3500 mm of rainfall. Brown (1982) has summated data from geomorphology, paleoclimate, soils and vegetation types to produce a map showing several proposed forest refuge areas in the Guianas. However, Granville (1988) warns that these centres of species diversity and endemism may simply coincide with well prospected regions.

There is no complete inventory of the flora in the country and estimates of the number of vascular plants range from 5000 (Cremers, 1984) to 8000 (Granville, 1982). Sabatier and Prévost (1989) consider that 10 per cent of tree species remain to be described, which will bring the total to 1200. There are more than 300 orchids and around 300 fern species within the forest. Many of the orchids are over-collected for trade.

Similarly, complete inventories for some faunal groups are lacking. One hundred and fifty mammal species are recorded in the country, of which 80 are bats. One hundred and thirty six reptile species, 89 amphibians and 700 birds are reported to occur there.

Few bird species in French Guiana have restricted ranges although around one per cent are endemic to the Guayana plateau (Cracraft, 1985; Haffer, 1974; Tostain *et al.*, 1992). Populations of forest birds are often irregularly distributed with both gaps and pockets of abundance. These pockets can sometimes be accounted for by the presence of a microhabitat essential for the species as is the case with the cock of the rock *Rupicola rupicola*. Several large raptors, including the harpy eagle *Harpia harpyja* and crested eagle *Morphnus guianensis*, occur locally in the forest zone (Thiollay, 1989). Only one species, the endemic Cayenne nightjar *Caprimulgus maculosus*, is listed as threatened by Collar *et al.* (1992), but as only one specimen has been taken and it is otherwise unknown, the validity of this species is in doubt.

Bird species in the northern coastal area are subject to pressure from human activities. Population levels of species in this area are far below their potential and the long-term survival of some may be in jeopardy. The hoatzin *Opisthocomus hoazin* and toco toucan *Ramphastos toco*, two species restricted to swamp forests and rocky areas, are especially at risk.

Terrestrial mammals listed by IUCN (Groombridge, 1993) as threatened which occur in French Guiana are the giant anteater *Myrmecophaga tridactyla*, the giant armadillo *Priodontes maximus*, the black spider monkey *Ateles paniscus*, the bush dog

The giant otter Pteronura brasiliensis *is listed as threatened by IUCN.*   (Caroline Harcourt)

Speothos venaticus, the little spotted cat *Leopardus tigrinus*, the margay *Leopardus wiedii* (possibly occurring) and the giant otter *Pteronura brasiliensis*, most of which are forest species. There is severe hunting pressure on some of the monkey species in particular, they are shot for food and sport and some are kept or sold as pets. The white-lipped peccary *Tayassu pecari* is locally threatened by hunting. Uncontrolled hunting is a complex and serious problem in French Guiana. Licences are not required and the use of any weapon is permitted. French regulations for the protection of wildlife are rarely enforced.

Threatened reptiles include the black caiman *Melanosuchus niger* and the yellow-headed sideneck turtle *Podocnemis unifilis* and four marine turtles (Groombridge, 1993).

There is little information on invertebrates in the country. IUCN lists three threatened swallowtail butterflies: *Parides coelus, Papilio garleppi* and *P. maroni*.

Conservation measures are needed to protect a variety of specialised habitats of the coastal and subcoastal regions. Additionally there is a need to protect extensive areas in the central and southern regions for the sake of species whose survival depends on large continuous tracts of forest.

Conservation Areas

French Guiana has few protected areas or reserves of any sort —none is listed in IUCN's categories I–IV. La Mirande, a forest islet of only 1.6 sq. km, was designated as a nature reserve in 1942, but 25 years later this was transferred to the forest domain (Granville and Sanité, 1992). In 1967 and 1975, plans for nature reserves were drawn up by ORSTOM, but these were not implemented. In 1983, some areas of the North Zone were proposed as state biological reserves, but were not gazetted because of lack of agreement among local elected representatives. As of 1993, one area of dryland and swamp forest at Kaw, in the northeast of the country, has been made a protected biotope. This designation provides for administrative measures to prohibit activities which are harmful to the continuing integrity of the area. Hunting, however, is still permitted. The only other existing conservation area is Grand Connétable Island which was declared in 1992. There is discussion of some of the proposed areas in the section on Conservation Initiatives.

Currently, two bodies are responsible for protected areas. One of them, the Regional Environmental Office (DIREN) was set up in 1990. It reports to the French Minister of the Environment and is responsible for protected landscapes and nature reserves. The other institution, the National Forest Office (ONF), reports to the French Minister of Agriculture and is responsible for biological reserves.

DIREN and ONF are responsible for negotiating protected area management plans with local and national authorities. The process usually starts with proposals emanating from the scientific community. Notable examples include the 14 proposals put forward in 1975 by J.J. de Granville of the ORSTOM centre in Cayenne (see Granville, 1975, in press) and that of J. M. Thiollay of CNRS, in 1987, for a large national park in the south (see SRETIE report; — Ministry of the Environment).

Conservation Initiatives

A number of protected areas are planned (Figure 28.2). These include a 600 sq. km primary forest protected biotope at Saül, (which will ultimately become a natural reserve) and some nature reserves intended to protect the undisturbed forest at Trinity Mountains and Nouragues. Included amongst these will be the ecological research station at Nouragues which was set up in 1986. Three state biological reserves are also planned. These are Lucifer and Dékou-Dékou (in the Paul Isnard region), Atachi-Bakka Mountains and Grand Croissant. The status of other areas currently proposed for protection is uncertain. These include about 25 sq. km of mangrove and coastal forest around the space centre at Kourou and 150 sq. km of forest on swamp and white sand at Sinnamary, where colonies of the scarlet ibis *Eudocimus ruber* are found. In addition, plans for a regional "landscape park", comprising several separate zones in the coastal and subcoastal region, and for a large protected area to the south of the Inini-Camopi chain are being drawn up. The latter (Parc du Sud Guyanais) provides an opportunity to conserve large areas of the lower mountains where biological diversity is highest.

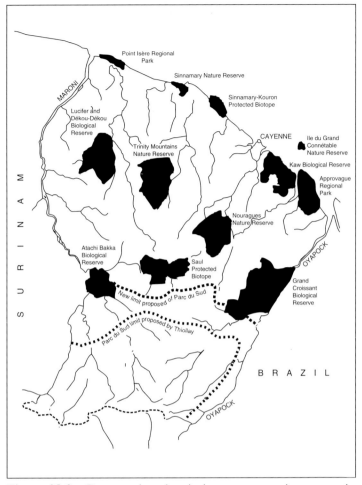

Figure 28.2 Proposed and existing conservation areas in French Guiana

Source: C. Doumerge

References

Brasseur, G. (1979). Population, Planche 21. In: *Atlas des Départements d'Outre-mer, IV La Guyane*. CNRS, ORSTOM.

Brown, K.S. Jr. (1982). Paleoecology and regional patterns of evolution in neotropical forest butterflies. In: *Biological Diversification in the Tropics*. Prance, G.T. (ed). Pp. 255–308. Columbia University Press, New York.

Bruleaux, A M. (1989). Deux productions passées de la forêt guyanaise: l'essence de bois de rose et la gomme de balata. *Bois et Forêts des Tropiques* 219: 99–113.

Choubert, B. (1979). Géologie, Planche 4. In: *Atlas des Départements d'Outre-mer, IV La Guyane*. CNRS, ORSTOM.

Collar, N.J., Gonzaga, L.P., Krabbe, N., Madroño Nieto, A., Naranjo, L.G., Parker III, T.A. and Wege, D.C. (1992). *Threatened Birds of the Americas. The ICBP/IUCN Red Data Book*. ICBP, Cambridge, U.K.

Cracraft, J. (1985). Historical biogeography and patterns of differentiations within the South American avifauna: Areas of endemism. *Ornithological Monograph* 36: 49–84.

Cremers, G. (1984). L'Herbier du Centre ORSTOM de Cayenne à 25 ans. *Taxon* 33: 428–432.

DAF (1990). *Recensement Agricole 1988–1989 Guyane principaux resultants par commune*. Ministere de la Agriculture et de la Forêt, Service Central des Enqueites et Etudies Statistiques, Paris. 55 pp.

Descamps, M., Gasc, J.P., Lescure, J. and Sastre, C. (1978). Etude des écosystèmes guyanais. II. Données biogéographiques sur la partie orientale des Guyanes. *Compte Rendu de Seance Societe Biogéographie* 467: 55–82.

Dintheer, C., Gilly, B., Legall, J.Y., Lemoine, M. and Rose, J. (1989). La recherche et la gestion de la pêcherie de crevette pénéides en Guyane Française de 1958 à 1988; 30 année de surf. *Equinoxe* 28: 21–33.

FAO/UNEP (1981). *Proyecto de Evaluacion de los Recursos Forestales Tropicales: Los Recursos Forestales de la America Tropical*. FAO, Rome, Italy.

FAO (1993). *Forest resources assessement 1990: Tropical countries*. FAO Forestry Paper 112. FAO, Rome, Italy.

Feuillet, C. (1989). Diversity and distribution of Guianan Passifloraceae. In: *Tropical Forests: Botanical Dynamics, Speciation and Diversity*. Pp. 311–318. Holm-Nielsen, L.B. (ed). Academic Press, London, San Diego, New York.

Granville, J.J. de (1975). *Projets de Reserves Botaniques et Forestiers en Guyane*. Office de la Recherche Scientifique et Technique Outre Mer, Cayenne, Fench Guiana.

Granville, J.J. de (1979). Végétation, Planche 12. In: *Atlas des Départements d'Outre-mer, IV La Guyane*. CNRS, ORSTOM.

Granville, J.J. de (1982). Rain forest and xeric flora refuges in French Guiana. In: *Biological Diversification in the Tropics*. Pp. 159–181. G. T. Prance (ed). Columbia University Press, New York.

Granville, J.J. de (1986). Les formations végétales de la bande côtière de Guyane française. In: *Le littoral guyanais*. Actes du Xéme colloque SEPANRIT, Cayenne 1985. Pp. 47–63.

Granville, J.J. de (1988). Phytogeographical characteristics of the Guianan Forests. *Taxon* 37(3): 578–594.

Granville, J.J. de (in press). Priority conservation areas in French Guiana. In: *Priority Areas for Conservation in Amazonia*. Conservation International Workshop, 1990, Manaus.

Granville, J.J. de and Sanité, L.P. (1992). Areas protegídas y actividades humanas en Guyana Francesa. In: *Espacios sin habitantes? Parques Nacionales de América del Sur*. Amend, S. and Amend, T. (eds). IUCN, Gland, Switzerland. Pp. 262–287.

Grenand, P. (1979). Histoire des Amérindiens, Planche 17. In: *Atlas des Départements d'Outre-mer, IV La Guyane*. CNRS, ORSTOM.

Groombridge, B. (Ed) (1993). *1994 IUCN Red List of Threatened Animals*. IUCN, Gland, Switzerland and Cambridge, U.K. 286 pp.

Haffer, J. (1974). Avian speciation in tropical South America. *Publications—Nuttall Ornithological Club* 14: 1–390.

Lescure, J.P. and Boulet, R. (1985). Relationships between soil and vegetation in a tropical rain forest in French Guiana. *Biotropica* 17(2): 155–164.

Lescure, J. P. and Tostain, O. (1989). Les mangroves guyanaises. *Bois et Forêts des Tropiques* 220: 35–42.

Martsobruto, P. and Naamin, N. (1977). Relationship between tidal forest (mangrove) and commercial shrimp production in Indonesia. *Marine Research in Indonesia* 18: 81–86.

Mori, S.A. and Boom, B.M. (1987). II. The forest. In: The Lecythidaceae of a lowland neotropical forest: La Fumée Mountain, French Guiana. Mori, S.A. *Memoirs of the New York Botanical Garden* 44: 9–29.

Mori, S.A. and Prance, G.T. (1987). IV. Phytogeography. In: The Lecythidaceae of a lowland neotropical forest: La Fumée Mountain, French Guiana. Mori, S.A. *Memoirs of the New York Botanical Garden* 44: 55–71.

Oldeman, R.A.A. (1974). L'architecture de la forêt guyanaise. *Mémoires ORSTOM*, No. 73. Pp. 204.

ONF/DDE (1991). *Observatoire du Bois*. Rapport annuel. Office National de Forêts/Direction Departementale de l'Equipement. Cayenne.

Prance, G.T. (1982). Forest refuges: evidence from woody angiosperms. In: *Biological Diversification in the Tropics*. Pp. 137–158. Prance, G.T. (ed.). Columbia University Press, New York.

Prance, G. T. (1987). Biogeography of neotropical plants. In: *Biogeography and Quarternary History in Tropical America*. Pp. 46–65. Whitmore, T.C. and Prance, G.T. (eds). Clarendon Press, Oxford. 46–65.

Rojas-Beltrán, R. (1986). Rôle de la mangrove comme nourricerie de crustacés et de poissons en Guyane. In: *Le littoral guyanais*. Actes du Xéme colloque SEPANRIT, Cayenne, 1985:97–110.

Sabatier, D. and Prévost, M. F. (1989). Quelques données sur la composition floristique et la diversité des peuplements forestiers de Guyane française. *Bois et Forêts des Tropiques* 219: 31–55.

Sabatier, D. (in press). *Diveristé des arbres et des peuplements forestiers en Guyane*. Actes du IIème Congrés Régional de l'Environnement. Ecosystèmes Forestiers et Aménagement de l'Espace Régional, Cayenne, 1990.

Sanite, L.P. (1992). *Propositions pour la Conservation et la Gestation du Patrimoine Naturel Guyanais*. Comité de la Culture de l'Education et de l'Environnement de la Région Guyane, Cayenne, French Guiana.

Thiollay, J. M. (1989). Area requirement for the conservation of rain forest raptors and game birds in French Guiana. *Conservation Biology* 3: 128–137.

Tostain, O. (1986). Etude d'une succession terrestre en milieu tropical: les relations entre la physionomie végétale et la structure du peuplement avien en mangrove guyanaise. *Revue d' Ecologie (La Terre et la Vie)* 41: 315–342.

Tostain, O., Dujardin, J.L., Erard, C. and Thiollay, J.M. (1992). *Les oiseaux de la Guyane française*. Société d'Etudes Ornythologiques, Paris.

Valeix and Mauperain (1989). Cinq siècles de l'histoire d'une parcelle de forêt domaniale de la terre ferme d'Amérique du Sud. *Bois et Forêts des Tropiques* 219: 13–29.

Author: Daniel Sabatier, France with contributions from Jean-Jacques de Granville, ORSTOM, Cayenne and Charles Doumenge, IUCN, Gland, Switzerland.

Map 28.1 French Guiana

Spatial data for the forests of French Guiana have been digitised from a paper map, *Vegetation— La Guyane: Planche 12*, published in 1979 by the Atlas des Departements D'Outre Mer, Centre d'Etudes de Geographie Tropicale—Office de la Recherche Scientifique et Echnique Outre-Mer, at a scale of 1:1 million. Fourteen vegetation categories are shown and from those, nine categories have been incorporated into the broad forest classes depicted in this Atlas.

The *Mangrove* has been digitised to show mangrove on Map 28.1. Forest types under the main heading of *Forêt Dense, Equatoriale Ombrophile Sempervirente* have been harmonised as follows: *Forêt fréquemment inondable et marécageuse* has been mapped as swamp forest; *Forêt de plaine et de pente douce, bien drainée, sur sol argileux, Forêt sur cuirasse lateritique (riche en lianes) et d'aspect degradé* and *Forêt à légère tendance xérique, sur sables blancs et anciens cordons littoraux* have been combined and shown as lowland moist forest (all are lower than 500 m). The forests over 500 m under the same main heading as the lowland forests (*Forêt de "montagne" sur sols argileux* and *Forêt de "montagne" sur cuirasse latérique*) have been combined and shown as submontane forest. The forest categories under the main heading of *Formations D'Origine Anthropique* (*Forêt secondaire de plaine* and *Forêt marécageuse secondaire*) have been combined into the degraded forest category. These two types (secondary forest on the plains and secondary swamp forest) and have not been distinguished because there is so little of the latter.

29 Guyana

Country area*	211,239 sq. km
Land area*	208,419 sq. km
Population (mid-1994)	0.8 million
Population growth rate	1.8 per cent
Population projected to 2025	1.1 million
Gross national product per capita (1992)	US$330
Forest cover in 1992 (see Map)	183,025 sq. km
Forest cover in 1990 (FAO, 1993)	184,160 sq. km
Annual deforestation rate (1981–1990)	0.1 per cent
Industrial roundwood production	163,000 cu. m
Industrial roundwood exports	11,000 cu. m
Fuelwood and charcoal production	14,000 cu. m
Processed wood production	10,000 cu. m
Processed wood exports	7000 cu. m

*The borders between the Guianas are disputed and in this instance we have used figures from Map 29.1 rather than FAO's figures of 214,970 and 196,850 sq. km respectively.

There has been very little deforestation in Guyana and most ecosystems represented in the country are largely intact. About 10 per cent of the land area is savanna while most of the rest is lowland tropical forest. At present, the limited exploitation of the forest appears to be sustainable. This is a result of the centralised socialist policies of the government which created an unfavourable environment for private logging enterprises. However, the government is now moving towards a market-orientated economy and foreign investors are being attracted to the forestry sector.

Within the past couple of years, the government has adopted an environmental policy and the Guyana Agency for Health Sciences Education, Environment and Food Policy (GAHEF) has been given the responsibility for environmental matters. However, this still has no legal basis. There is currently only one protected area and this lacks staff and funding, as do many of the government departments involved with environmental and forestry matters. Other protected areas have been proposed but none has been given effective protection. At present, the biodiversity of Guyana is little known and much fundamental survey work is required to provide the data needed to make decisions on land use.

Guyana is, therefore, at a turning point. The country's natural vegetation is still largely undisturbed, but unless action is taken this situation could change rapidly.

INTRODUCTION

Guyana (formerly British Guiana) is situated on the north-eastern coast of South America and together with Surinam and French Guiana forms a region known as 'The Guianas'. These, along with portions of Brazil and Venezuela, form a distinct biogeographical region known as Guiana, the area bounded by the Amazon, Orinoco and Negro Rivers (Lindeman and Mori, 1989). Included in this area is the underlying, crystalline Guayana Shield.

Guyana can be divided into four regions: a coastal plain, a white sands hinterland, a pre-Cambrian continental plateau and the Pakaraima Mountains. Along the coast is a band of land lying below sea level. It is about 25 km wide in the northwest and around 75 km wide in the east. The deposits of marine clay in this area make it much more fertile than the rest of the country. East of the Essequibo River the coastal plain is bordered by an area of infertile white sand which extends about 200 km southwards from the coast. South of this lies the pre-Cambrian plateau which covers more than half the country. Four major rivers (Essequibo, Demerara, Berbice and Courantyne) and several minor ones dissect this peneplain and empty into the Atlantic. In the south, outlying tributaries of the Amazon just reach Guyana, while in the north-west the Orinoco does likewise.

The Pakaraima Mountains, extensions of the Gran Sabana of Venezuela, are located in the mid-west of Guyana. This region is characterised by plateaus and steep table mountains. Most of it is below 1000 m with only the mesas or tepuis rising higher.

Mount Roraima, at 2772 m, is the highest point in the country. The only other significant uplands are the Kanuku Mountains in the Rupununi which rise to 1021 m and the Acarai Mountains which form the watershed between the upper tributaries of the Courantyne and the Amazon Rivers and rise to approximately 460 m.

The temperature in the capital city of Georgetown remains more or less constant year round with mean monthly maxima between 30°C and 32°C and minima between 22°C and 23°C. The interior forest region has similar temperatures throughout the year. There are, in general, two wet seasons (from May to mid-August and from December to mid-February) and two dry seasons. Average annual rainfall in the capital is about 2400 mm and increases to over 3560 mm in the forested mountain interior. In the savanna areas, especially the Rupununi, rainfall is less and the short wet season is generally absent, whereas in the upland areas such as the Pakaraimas, rainfall is higher and it is the short dry season which is frequently absent. There is, however, considerable variation in the climate from year to year. King (1968) provides further information on the climate and geography of the country.

The people in the country are of diverse racial origin; East Indians make up about 50 per cent, 30 per cent are of African origin, 10 per cent are mixed race, 5 per cent are Amerindian and the rest European or Chinese. The population is stable because of a high level of emigration over the last decade or so. This was encouraged by the government's economic and social policies. Around 90 per cent of the people live on the narrow, fertile coastal zone, consequently population density is over 750 inhabitants per sq. km in that area. In contrast large areas of the forested interior are unoccupied. The Amerindians are the main inhabitants of the interior. On the coast, most people are engaged in the cultivation of sugar and rice. These, together with bauxite and gold, are the principal foreign exchange earners.

The Forests

There have been several floristic studies within Guyana that indicate a high degree of endemicity for the Guianas (in particular within the Pakaraimas). Studies of the country's vegetation were begun many decades ago. For instance, Davis and Richards (1933, 1934) made classic studies of Moraballi Creek and Fanshawe (1952, 1954) has done considerable work on Guyana's vegetation. The following descriptions of the forests are based on work by A. M. Polak of the University of Utrecht. More complete lists of the species present in the forests are presented in a field guide to the timber trees of Guyana, published by the Dutch Tropenbos Foundation (Polak, 1992).

In the coastal plain, mangroves occur in the salt water areas and swamp and marsh forest in the fresh water regions. The mora (*Mora excelsa*) forests are also found on the coastal plain.

Figure 29.1 Major vegetation types in Guyana

Source: NFAP (1989)

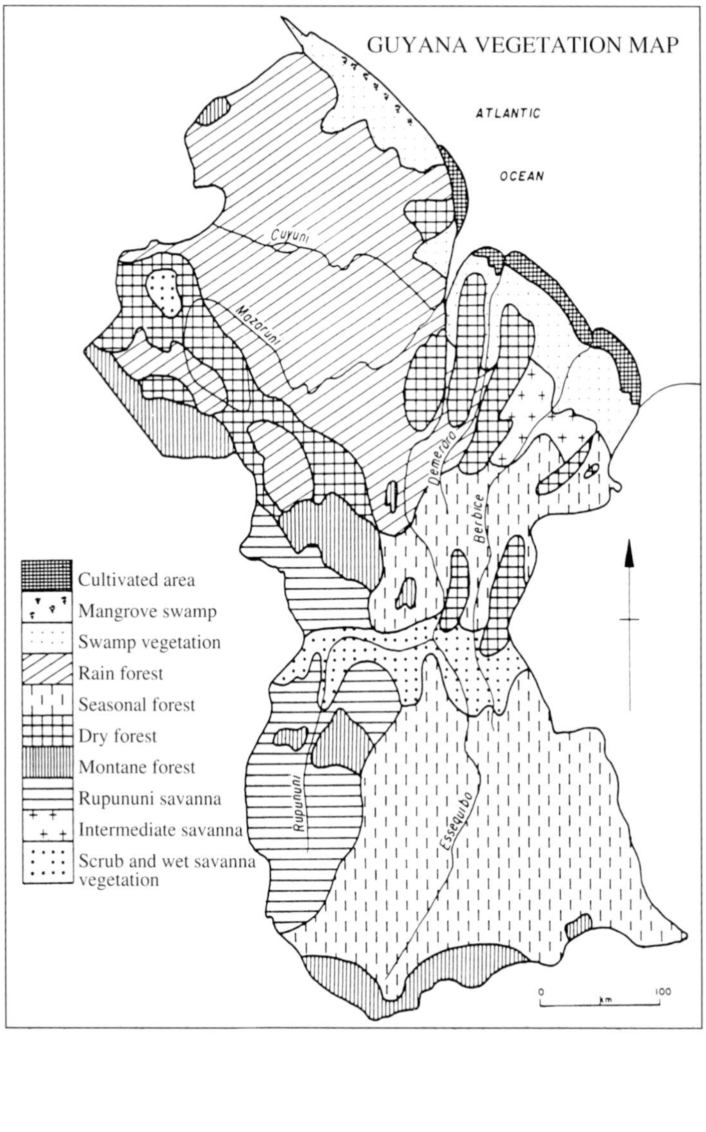

Wallaba (*Eperua* spp.) forest and seasonal evergreen forest are found on the white sands area east of the Essequibo River. Mixed forest occurs on the vast pre-Cambrian plateau and at the foot of the Pakaraima mountains. Montane forest occurs on Mt. Roraima. Figure 29.1 shows these major vegetation communities in Guyana.

Mora forests occur on alluvial silt, clay or loam along rivers and on riverine flats throughout the lowland region. The canopy height is 30–45 m, many of the trees are buttressed. Lianas are common and epiphytes are abundant. Mora is dominant in both the canopy and the lower storeys and there is also abundant regeneration of this species creating a dense sapling layer of 1.5–3 m. Other species in the canopy include *Aldina insignis, Carapa guianensis, C. procera, Couratari gloriosa, Eschweilera decolorans, Lecythis zabucajo, Symphonia globulifera, Terminalia dichotoma* and *Virola surinamensis*. Understorey species are *Anaxagorea dolichocarpa, Duguetia pycnastera* and *Hevea pauciflora*.

The marsh forests, found on alluvial silt, are inundated at least during the long rainy season from May to July. Palms are the characteristic trees of this forest. The canopy is relatively low, only 10–17 m with an emergent layer at 17–28 m. Well represented species include *Abarema jupunba, Catostemma commune, Diospyros guianensis, Macrolobium bifolium, Pterocarpus officinalis* and *Terminalia dichotoma*. The palms in the canopy layer include *Attalea regia, Euterpe edulis, Jessenia bataua, Manicaria saccifera* and *Mauritia flexuosa*. Swamp forests are found in slightly wetter areas, on soils that never completely dry out. Palm swamps of *Euterpe oleracea* are found throughout Guyana and there are also *Manicaria saccifera* palm swamps in the northwest of the country (Lindeman and Mori, 1989).

The wallaba forests have a canopy of 20–27 m high with emergents up to 33 m. The wallaba species are *Eperua falcata, E. grandiflora* and *E. jenmanii*. Also dominant in the canopy are *Catostemma fragans, Dicymbe altsonii* and *D. corymbosa*. Species in the understorey are *Tovomita* spp. and *Matayba opaca*.

The evergreen seasonal forest has a fairly open canopy between 20 and 40 m in height. Lianas may be common but epiphytes are rare. *Aspidosperma excelsum, Goupia glabra* and *Swartzia leiocalycina* dominate the canopy. Other species such as *Catostemma fragrans, Diplotropis purpurea, Emmotum fagifolium, Licaria cannella, Ocotea canaliculata* and *Vochysia surinamensis* are also present and can occur at high densities.

The mixed lowland forests are characterised by a large number of species growing together at a particular locality, although there are usually a few species that dominate the canopy. The soil can be brown sand, laterite or loam. Morabukea (*Mora gonggrijpii*) dominated forest is common on laterite and occurs on the undulating terrain where the pre-Cambrian plateau replaces the white sands. This species forms the 20–35 m high canopy, as well as a sapling layer of 1–2.5 m tall. Subdominant canopy species include *Alexa imperatricis, Catostemma commune, Clathrotropis brachypetala, Eschweilera wachenheimii, Goupia glabra, Sterculia pruriens* and *Vouacapoua macropetala*. Species in the lower storey include *Clathrotropis paradoxa, Mabea speciosa, Pausandra martinii* and *Quiina guianensis*.

Greenheart *Chlorocardium rodiei* (formerly called *Ocotea rodiaei*) forest is found particularly on the brown sand. It is known from the area east of the Pomeroon River. Canopy height is from 20–35 m and is relatively open, lianas are occasional but epiphytes are frequent. Other species common in the canopy are *Eschweilera sagotiana, Licania alba* and *Pentaclethra macroloba*. Characteristic understorey species are *Anaxagorea dolichocarpa, Duguetia neglecta, D. calycina, Sandwithia guianensis* and *Tabernaemontana undulata*. Many young specimens of the canopy tree species are also found in the understorey.

Mangroves

Mangrove forest originally covered a considerable area of the country's narrow coastal strip, but most of the mangroves have been destroyed. This area is now home to 90 per cent of Guyana's population and is the site of almost all its agriculture. Much of the land is below high spring tide level and is empoldered to keep out the sea. The mangroves that do remain are being damaged by excessive cutting for fuelwood and charcoal. It is only in the largely uninhabited stretch of coast between the Pomeroon and Waini Rivers that extensive stands of mangrove still exist. In the National Forestry Action Plan (NFAP, 1989) it is estimated that around 800 sq. km of mangroves remain along the coastal plain.

The two principal mangrove species occurring in Guyana are *Avicennia germinans* (or *A. nitida*) and *Rhizophora mangle*, the black and red mangrove respectively. Black mangrove occurs extensively on the exposed coastal mud flats with the occasional presence of *Laguncularia racemosa* or *Conocarpus erectus*, while the red mangrove tends to occur in more sheltered areas such as river and canal banks.

Avicennia germinans may grow up to 20–25 m in height. The wood is widely used as fuel and for poles, its seeds can be eaten when cooked. The flowers yield a high quality honey and bee keeping is an important activity in some areas. The wood of *R. mangle* is also used for poles, posts and fuel, it makes good quality charcoal. Its bark produces high quality tannin, very suitable for leather work and it is extensively exploited for this purpose (FAO, 1990).

Although the mangroves are located on state land, they do not form part of the state forest. There is no comprehensive assessment or inventory of them or the species they support and no management practices for their sustainable utilization. A study by FAO (1990) examined the feasibility of restoring and expanding the mangrove belt in the country so that the shoreline would be better protected. The report suggests areas where mangroves could be established, indicates the need for protection and management of existing mangrove areas and the need to educate people about the benefits of these and outlines an action plan for mangrove afforestation. Pastakia (1991) has mapped the present extent of the mangroves and he too confirms that they are badly degraded.

Forest Resources and Management

Guyana's National Forestry Action Plan is not explicit as to how much forest is found in the country. It is stated that "forests occupy more than three quarters of Guyana, or more than sixteen million hectares" (NFAP, 1989). Later in this publication, the areas of exploitable, potentially exploitable and not exploitable forest are given (see Table 29.2), and these total 165,000 sq. km. Most of them are reported to be in or near to their original state.

An analysis of maps in Fanshawe (1952), King (1968) and the NFAP (1989) suggests that only one per cent of Guyana is no longer covered with natural vegetation and that forests cover around 90 per cent of the country (Table 29.1). The savanna area of 16,100 sq. km shown in Table 29.1 occurs in the

Table 29.1 Land Use in Guyana

Land Use	Area (sq. km)	% of land area*
Lowland Forest	186,000	86.5
Montane Forest	3,000	1.4
Swamp Vegetation	7,800	3.6
Savanna	16,100	7.5
Alienated land	2,100	1.0

* In compiling this table, the author has used a figure of 215,000 sq. km for the land area of Guyana

Source: Based on maps in Fanshawe (1952), King (1968) and NFAP (1989)

Rupununi and Berbice regions. There is some debate as to whether these savannas are natural or man made, but the consensus is that they are caused by natural soil conditions, but have been expanded by human activity.

Ramdass and Hanif (1990) estimate that around 85 per cent of Guyana's forest remain undisturbed. This figure is likely to be an over-estimation, although it is undoubtably no lower than 75 per cent (Johnston 1992a; Johnston and Gillmas, 1992). FAO's (1993) estimate of forest cover in Guyana is 184,160 sq. km (93 per cent of land area), with 181,950 sq. km of this being closed broadleaved forest. Analysis of Map 29.1 indicates the slightly lower total of 183,025 sq. km of forest in the country (87.8 per cent of land area), but this is for forests with a canopy cover of more than 40 per cent, as opposed to FAO's figure which is for forests with a canopy cover of 10 per cent or more. The source for this Map was AVHRR imagery collected in 1992 compiled by the EU-Joint Research Centre TREES project (see Map Legend). Forest types were not distinguished in the source data other than by per cent canopy cover, hence Map 29.1 also does not show anything other than *forest*—this includes mangroves, seasonal forests and montane formations as well as the lowland moist forests — which make up the majority of the area.

Forests in Guyana are the responsibility of the Guyana Forestry Commission (GFC), which is a division of the Guyana Natural Resources Agency (GNRA). However, the GFC does not manage the forests, it is mainly concerned with marketing, allocation of harvesting rights and collection of revenue. In recognition of this situation and the need for proper management of the forest resource, the National Forestry Action Plan (NFAP) was prepared and published in 1989 by an interagency team comprising local representatives and international specialists under the auspices of the GFC and the Canadian International Development Agency (CIDA). The NFAP is the main policy document on all aspects of forest use, including conservation, in Guyana.

Table 29.2 Area of exploitable and unexploitable forest in Guyana

Exploitable forest*	36,000 sq. km
Allocated for harvest°	24,000 sq. km
Potentially exploitable+	104,000 sq. km
Not exploitable	25,000 sq. km

* with present infrastructure for exploitation

° i.e. this is the area of exploitable forest that has already been allocated for harvest

+ areas for which access does not presently exist

Source: NFAP (1989)

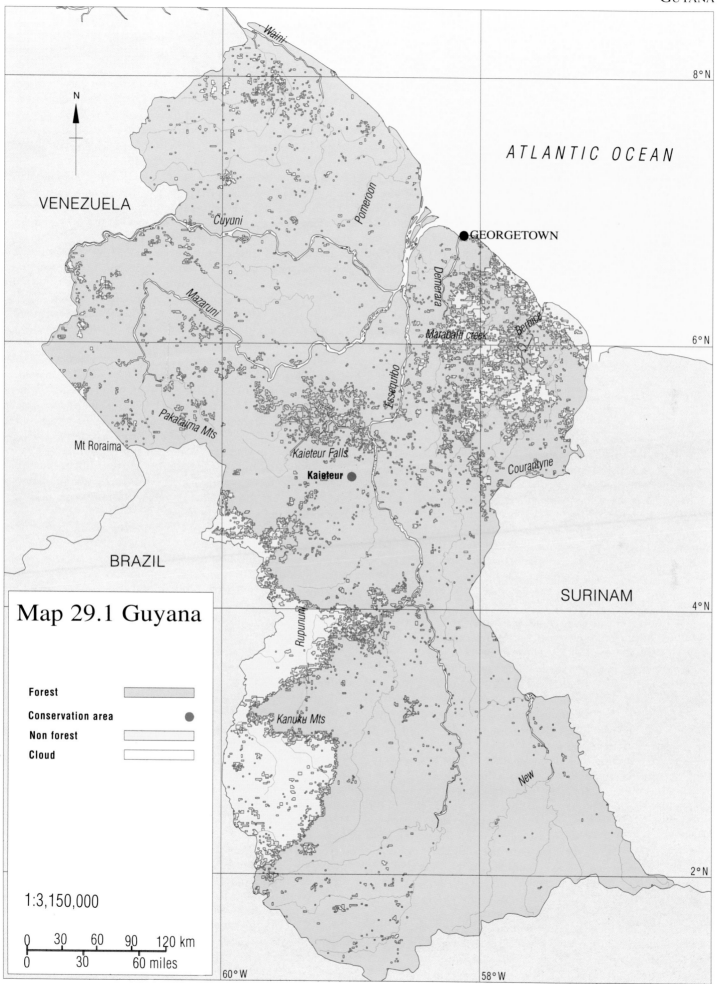

ATLANTIC OCEAN

VENEZUELA

Waini

Cuyuni

Pomeroon

●GEORGETOWN

Mazaruni

Demerara

Marabaili creek

Berbice

6°N

Essequibo

Pakaraima Mts

Courantyne

Mt Roraima

Kaieteur Falls

Kaieteur ●

BRAZIL

SURINAM

4°N

Rupununi

Map 29.1 Guyana

Kanuku Mts

New

Forest

Conservation area ●

Non forest

Cloud

1:3,150,000

0   30   60   90   120 km

0   30   60 miles

60°W

58°W

8°N

2°N

The NFAP is the only comprehensive summary available of the current status of Guyana's forests and their exploitation. However, it contains only general information on existing forest resources as little detailed information is available at present. Table 29.2, from the NFAP, gives data on forest areas presently or potentially exploitable by the timber industry.

The percentage of forest currently allocated for harvest is about 11 per cent of the existing forest and rates of extraction from this area are very low, averaging only 0.04 cu. m per hectare.

The NFAP concludes that the agencies responsible for forests do not currently have the capability to meet their responsibilities due to lack of skilled staff, infrastructure and financing. For example, only three of 13 approved professional positions and two of 106 technical and vocational positions at GFC were filled at the time the NFAP was prepared. The NFAP calls for over US$85 million in external funding to strengthen the GFC.

In the past year, the Forestry Commission has made major improvements in its ability to manage the forests. A new commissioner and several extra staff have been appointed and equipment has been purchased. The Commission has also begun organising training courses and has just started a one year Certificate of Forestry course for thirty students. Outside funding is being actively sought to support the NFAP and in the meantime the Canadian International Development Agency (CIDA) is supporting an Interim Forestry Project until 1994, after which it is hoped that other donors will have provided aid for the NFAP.

As Guyana's forest resources are still largely intact, the country is in a position to achieve sustainable forestry. The NFAP and Guyana's environmental policy and constitution commits the country to sustainable development of its natural resources, including forests.

Traditionally the logging industry in Guyana has been based almost exclusively on greenheart which is in great demand because of its tremendous resilience and resistance to marine borers. This species has accounted for over 45 per cent of fellings and 70 per cent of exports although it comprises only 1.5 per cent of the exploitable timber (NFAP, 1989). Greenheart does not occur in uniform stands but forms 'reefs' or patches where suitable conditions exist. As a result, logging was very patchy and small stands of greenheart were left uncut.

At present, the timber industry is dominated by a few locally owned family businesses. However, government policy has recently moved away from centralised socialism and opened the economy to outside investment (see Colchester, 1994). This has encouraged both local development and an influx of foreign investment in the forestry sector. Several very large projects are proposed; one of these, planned by a Korean company, would eventually result in the logging of nearly 10 per cent of the nation's forests. It is evident that the policies adopted by outside companies will have a major effect on the forests. For instance, the proposed exploitation rate of just one of the companies is approximately five times the current rate of exploitation. However, this is to be achieved mainly by greater efficiency and the use of more species of timber tree and it is possible that this increased intensity of logging could still be sustainable. Indeed, it is government policy that forestry in Guyana should be on a sustainable basis and all the new enterprises claim they will be managing the forest in this way. The major issue is whether the government is in a position to monitor the logging operations to ensure that adequate standards are maintained.

Deforestation

No detailed information is available on rates of deforestation in Guyana but it is known that they are still very low. FAO (1993) estimates that only 180 sq. km of forest is cleared each year, a annual rate of 0.1 per cent. The main causes of deforestation at present are agriculture and charcoal burning. Large scale logging could become a threat in the future. In addition, there are concerns that the road being extended from Boa Vista, Roraima in Brazil through to the coast of Guyana at Georgetown will cause increased deforestation.

Most of the natural vegetation along Guyana's coastal belt has been replaced with agricultural crops or human settlements. Although it seems unlikely that further conversion will occur in the near future, the remaining forests are threatened by felling for charcoal and fuelwood and are the most threatened in Guyana.

There is very little agriculture in the interior of Guyana, primarily because the soils are nutrient poor and unsuited to farming. The Amerindian population is sparse and concentrated mainly in savanna regions and on pockets of better soils. Although they practise shifting agriculture, many are moving into towns or working for mining or large logging companies so their farming causes little, if any, deforestation.

Collection of wood for fuel is a major cause of deforestation of the mangroves and the dry forest in the coastal belt. Recent reports suggest that 40,000 tonnes of firewood and 2000 tonnes of charcoal from State lands and State forests are used each year, but it is almost certain that these are underestimates (NFAP, 1989). In addition, fires used to produce charcoal frequently get out of control and burn large areas of forest.

There are 1040 sq. km of bauxite deposits in the white sands area and open-cast mining of these has caused some deforestation. At present, no attempt is made to use any of the forest products when the trees are cleared. Mining for gold is increasing rapidly and small areas of forest are cleared during the mining. In addition to this direct effect of the mining, some of the extraction processes used (e.g. the use of mercury) also have a deleterious effect on the environment. Exploration for other minerals is taking place and this could cause much more extensive deforestation.

Biodiversity

Maguire (1970) estimated that the Guyana Shield area contained around 8000 plant species of which perhaps 75 per cent were endemic to the Guianas. There is also considerable faunal endemicity in the region. However, as all biotypes found in Guyana are also found in its neighbouring countries, there are few species endemic to the one country. Also, as most habitats are largely intact in all three countries, virtually no species are reported to be threatened in the area. Indeed species threatened in other countries are probably fairly secure in Guyana. These include the giant river otter *Pteronura brasiliensis*, the black spider monkey *Ateles paniscus* and the black caiman *Melanosuchus niger*. IUCN (Groombridge, 1993) list eleven threatened mammal species and seven reptile species in Guyana. The only vertebrate species thought to have been lost in Guyana is the horned screamer *Anhima cornuta*, which was at the edge of its range and was probably never widespread.

There are no published lists of any major animal taxa in the country other than the birds. In an unpublished report, Johnston (1992b) estimates that there are approximately 220 mammal species in Guyana, these include over 100 bats. The Royal Ontario Museum is in the process of producing a book on Guyana's mammals.

Synder (1966) lists 720 bird species in Guyana but the total number occurring is probably in excess of 775 species. Species whose distribution is limited to the Guianan region include the caica parrot *Pionopsitta caica*, the blue-cheeked parrot *Amazona brasiliensis*, the Guianan toucanet *Selenidera culik*, the waved woodpecker *Celeus undatus undatus* and the tiny tyrant-manakin *Tyranneutes virescens*. The only threatened species listed by Collar *et al.* (1992) for Guyana is the marsh-living speckled crake *Coturnicops notata*.

Guyana is the second largest exporter of wild birds in South America; around 15,000 were exported in 1989 (Edwards, 1992). The country is also a major exporter of other wildlife. There has been considerable concern that this could be a factor in the decline of certain species. However, the Wildlife Services Division believes that, for birds at least, the established export quotas maintain trade at levels below those which would be detrimental to wild populations of the species (Edwards, 1992). This, though, is through chance rather than by design.

The Guyana Wildlife Exporters Association reported that the wild bird trade employs around 10,000 people in Guyana and that it benefits many more than that (Edwards, 1992). With proper management, it could be an important resource that would provide an incentive for local people to retain the forest intact. In order for this to be achieved, scientific surveys of the resource and a proper management structure are urgently required. Guyana has been a signatory to CITES for many years and the government is working with other groups to ensure that the surveys occur and the trade is sustainable.

Conservation Areas

At present, the only protected area in Guyana is Kaieteur National Park, which was established in 1929 to protect the famous Kaieteur Falls. The only staff allocated to the park is a caretaker for the guest house. The integrity of the park is threatened by gold and diamond mining, illegal hunting and fishing, cattle grazing and human settlements (NFAP, 1989). A detailed management

---

THE IWOKRAMA RAIN FOREST PROGRAMME IN GUYANA

In October 1989, at the Commonwealth Heads of Government meeting in Malaysia, Guyana's President offered to set aside some of his country as an area for research into conservation and sustainable development of tropical rain forests. A project site of some 3800 sq. km was identified in the interior of Guyana and a mission led by Dr M.S. Swaminathan visited the area in April 1990. The report produced as a result of the visit, entitled *Programme for Sustainable Tropical Forestry*, has four main proposals:

1. Establish and maintain a Wilderness Reserve in the project site to maintain a segment of the forest in a pristine condition. This area will be available for scientific research.
2. Maintain and manage part of the project site for yielding economic benefits to the people of Guyana in the form of forest and non-forest products and eco-tourism.
3. Establish an International Centre for Research, Training and Communication on sustainable management of tropical forests. This will be based at the University of Guyana in Georgetown, with field stations set up in the project site.
4. Promote environmental education and establish a Media Resources Centre for this purpose. The needs of the public, schools, universities and non-governmental organisations will be catered for in particular.

The Government of Guyana and the Commonwealth Secretariat have commissioned a number of reports and studies in order to ensure good management of the site. These include an environmental assessment and a study to examine the best organisational and management structures for the Programme. Very little was known about the project site and in this interim period, survey work by the Natural Resources Institute (NRI) based at Chatham, U.K. working with Guyanese and Caribbean counterparts has provided some essential information about the area.

These surveys financed by the Overseas Development Administration (ODA), U.K., are designed to build up a picture of soils, land forms, vegetation, fauna and existing human-use of the area. Some parts of the site are particularly diverse. A GIS has been created to analysis the survey data,

and will provide a tool for future survey work. The boundaries of the forest site are also being mapped as part of a training programme for survey staff.

A preliminary study on site management recommended that, until sufficient survey work had been carried out, the whole area should be protected. It also proposed checkpoints on the Lethem-Georgetown road where it enters and exits the Iwokrama district. This road, which will provide access to the Caribbean from the Brazilian state of Roraima, as well as assisting development in the Guyanese Rupununi savannas, is currently being upgraded.

At present, the site, which is largely bounded by rivers, is used by Amerindians living outside the boundaries and by small numbers of migrant miners. Draft legislation guarantees traditional Amerindian rights to hunt, fish and collect in the area. It is anticipated that this legislation will also guarantee the Amerindians intellectual property rights to any discoveries of commercial value which are based on their ethnobotanical knowledge.

The Amerindians who live near Iwokrama are largely English-speaking and eager for a modern education and access to markets. It is likely therefore that the project will, as it develops, offer employment opportunities to Amerindians which go far beyond the need for tree identifiers and forest rangers and will include administrators and scientists.

Start-up from 1992–94 has been guaranteed by a grant of US$3 million from the Global Environment Facility via the UNDP, and by the agreement of the Commonwealth Fund for Technical Cooperation to fund a core group of professionals to start work in Georgetown, Guyana. This management group is now in place.

Dr. M.S. Swaminathan has agreed to chair an interim Board of Trustees during this start-up period. It is anticipated that a Director General for the programme will be appointed in late 1994 and the DG will prepare detailed research and training activities with the management team. A business plan will be the basis for additional finance to be raised. The intention is to involve several governments and research institutions, not exclusively in the Commonwealth, so that the project is truly international. *Source:* Bryan Kerr

Table 29.3   Conservation areas of Guyana

National Parks	Area (sq. km)
Kaieteur	586

plan for the area, including a proposal to increase the size of the park to 4000 sq. km, has been drawn up by the World Wide Fund for Nature, but it has not yet been implemented.

Ramdass and Hanif (1990) have proposed areas for inclusion in a protected areas system and the possibility of establishing a number of biosphere reserves has also been investigated.

Initiatives for Conservation

There has been an almost total lack of conservation initiatives in Guyana in the past, perhaps partly because neither species nor habitats were particularly threatened, but also because foreign conservation groups were unwelcome in the country.

The Guyana Agency for Health Sciences Education, Environment and Food Policy (GAHEF) has recently been given responsibility for environmental matters. An environmental policy has been published and legislation underpinning this has been drafted by GAHEF. However, the legislation has not been passed by the government and the policy has not been implemented.

The National Forestry Action Plan contains several conservation initiatives including suggestions for a protected areas system and funding to expand and strengthen the agency responsible for the environment.

The Tropenbos Foundation has a forestry research station at Mabura Hill and their Guyana Programme is designed to provide a scientific basis for sustainable management of the forest. The Smithsonian Institute has been working in Guyana for over 20 years making detailed botanical collections, as well as collecting faunal specimens. The Smithsonian Institute, WWF and the University of Guyana have just set up the Centre for the Study of Biological Diversity, as part of a project to enhance ecological and conservation research in the country. The Centre will house the University's herbarium along with other biological material collected in Guyana.

The government has set aside 3640 sq. km of undisturbed forest as the Commonwealth-Government of Guyana Iwokrama Rain Forest Project. Part will be a wilderness preserve and part used for research into sustainable use of the forest. At present, the project area is being inventoried and a detailed plan prepared (see Box).

A bromeliad Brocchinia micrantha *found in the only established protected area in Guyana — Kaieteur*

(WWF/G. Schuerholz)

A potentially important development is the recent establishment of the Guyana Biodiversity Society which is the first NGO in Guyana with a mandate for conservation. At present, though, it is principally concerned with ecotourism and the wildlife trade.

References

Colchester, M. (1994). The New Sultans. Asian loggers move in on Guyana's forests. *The Ecologist* 24(2): 45–52.

Davis, T.A.W. and Richards, P.W. (1933). The vegetation of Moraballi Creek, British Guiana. Part I. *Journal of Ecology* 21: 350–384.

Davis, T.A.W. and Richards, P.W. (1934). The vegetation of Moraballi Creek, British Guiana. Part II. *Journal of Ecology* 22: 106–155.

Edwards, S.R. (1992). Wild bird trade: perceptions and management in the cooperative Republic of Guyana. In: *Perceptions, Conservation and Management of Wild Birds in Trade.* Thomsen, J.B., Edwards, S.R. and Mulliken, T.A. (eds). TRAFFIC International, Cambridge, U.K. Pp. 77–91.

Fanshawe, D.B. (1952). The vegetation of British Giuana. A preliminary review. *Imperial Forestry Institute Paper no. 29.*

Fanshawe, D.B. (1954). Forest types of British Guiana. *Caribbean Forester* 15; 73–111.

FAO (1990) *Restoration and Expansion of the Mangrove Belt.* Based on the work of Mohammed Zakir Hussain. Technical report No 1 TP/GUY/8953. FAO, Rome, Italy.

FAO (1993). *Forest resource assessment 1990: tropical countries.* FAO Forestry Paper 112. FAO, Rome, Italy.

Groombridge, B. (Ed) (1993). *1994 IUCN Red List of Threatened Animals.* IUCN, Gland, Switzerland and Cambridge, U.K. 286 pp.

Johnston, M.A. (1992a). *Preliminary Considerations for a Guyana Biodiversity Database.* Unpublished report. ESI/GAHEF.

Johnston, M.A. (1992b). *A Biodiversity Research Initiative.* Unpublished report. ESI/GAHEF.

Johnston, M.A. and Gillmas, M.P. (1992) *Ecology of Guyana Forests*. Unpublished expedition report.

King, K.F.S. (1968). Land and people in Guyana. *Commonwealth Forestry Institute Paper No. 39*.

Lindeman, J.C. and Mori, S.A. (1989). The Guianas. In: *Floristic Inventory of Tropical Countries: the Status of Plant Systematics, Collections and Vegetation, plus Recommendations for the Future*. Campbell, D.G. and Hammond, H.D. (eds). New York Botanical Garden, Bronx, New York, U.S.A. Pp. 375–390.

Maguire, B. (1970). On the flora of the Guayana Highland. *Biotropica* 2(2): 85–100.

NFAP (1989) *National Forestry Action Plan 1990–2000*. Guyana Forestry Commission/Canadian International Development Agency, Kingston, Georgetown, Guyana.

Pastakia, C.M.R. (1991) *A Preliminary Study of the Mangroves of Guyana*. Unpublished report to the EEC.

Polak, A.M. (1992). *Major Timber Trees of Guyana. A Field Guide*. The Tropenbos Foundation, Wageningen, The Netherlands.

Ramdass, I. and Hanif, M. (1990). *Guyana country paper*. Unpublished paper presented at Workshop 90—Biological Priorities for Conservation in Amazonia, at Manaus, Brazil.

Synder, D.E. (1966). *The Birds of Guyana*. Salem, Peabody Museum. 308 pp.

Author: Robert Brown, Georgetown, with contributions from M. Johnston, GAHEF, Georgetown; A.M. Polak, University of Utrecht; Erik M. Lammerts van Bueren, The Tropenbos Foundation; Bryan Kerr, Commonwealth Secretariat, London and Giles D'Souza, TREES, Italy.

Map 29.1 Guyana

Forest data for Guyana were provided in digital form by the EU-Joint Research Centre TREES project (Tropical Ecosystem Environment Observations by Satellite), Ispra, Italy. The TREES project is a joint initiative of the Commission of the European Communities (CEC) and the European Space Agency (ESA) and has been developed to assess the world's tropical forest cover using satellite-derived data and ancillary data from numerous other sources.

The data shown in this Atlas are derived from AVHRR imagery from the NOAA satellite, at a nominal spatial resolution of nearly 1 km. Images from several days in 1992 were used to compile a composite cloud-free image of the whole country. On NOAA-AVHRR imagery, dense vegetation areas generally appear dark and cool—these areas have been identified as densely forested areas with an estimated canopy cover of 70 per cent. Warmer and brighter responses were determined to be areas of fragmented forests with a 40–70 per cent canopy cover. Areas which yielded a generally high vegetation signal throughout the year, but with definitie seasonal fluctuation, were labelled as areas of predominantly seasonal forest. These have not, however, been demarcated in the dataset but have been included in the fragmented forest. Savanna and cultivated areas were also identified in the imagery.

The classified vegetation has been harmonised in the following way:

Forest:	*Forest — includes mangrove and any areas greater than 70% forest cover*
	Fragmented forest — includes any areas of 40–70% forest cover. This for Guyana appears to include some areas of fragmented evergreen forests, as well some areas of seasonal and dry forest with this forest cover (40–70%)
Non-forest:	*Non-forest — includes cultivated/agricultural, and other areas less than 40% forest cover, including swampy vegetation and areas of very fragmented forest (<40%)*
	Non-forest — including savannas
Cloud cover:	*Cloud/missing data*

It has not been possible to differentiate the forest cover any further. Montane forests and mangroves do occur in the country (see Figure 29.1), but accurate data have not been located to show these. The Digital Chart of the World does not show contours in Guyana, so montane formations could not be distinguished by altitude either. Map 29.1, therefore, shows only forest/non-forest.

Kaieteur National Park is shown by a centre point derived from latitude and longitude data maintained within the WCMC protected areas database.

30 Paraguay

Country area	406,750 sq. km
Land area	397,300 sq. km
Population (mid-1994)	4.8 million
Population growth rate	2.7 per cent
Population projected to 2025	9.5 million
Gross national product per capita (1992)	US$1340
Forest cover in 1985 (see Map)*+	47,488 sq. km
Forest cover in 1990 (FAO, 1993)*	60,640 sq. km
Annual deforestation rate (1981–1990)	3.4 per cent
Industrial roundwood production	3,106,000 cu. m
Industrial roundwood exports	2000 cu. m
Fuelwood and charcoal production	5,396,000 cu. m
Processed wood production	425,000 cu. m
Processed wood exports	249,000 cu.m

* In Eastern Paraguay only
+ However 1991 Landsat imagery shows only 24,030 sq. km remaining
* In the whole country, but excluding dry deciduous forest

Paraguay has the highest deforestation rate in Central and South America. The forest is generally looked on as unproductive and much has been cleared, particularly for agricultural land. However, unlike many forested areas in other countries, around two thirds of eastern Paraguay has soils suitable for crop production. Virtually all the forests in the east of the country are privately owned, which makes state-sponsored forest management problematic.

However, attitudes to conservation are changing and there is an increasing awareness of the damage caused by destruction of the forests. More protected areas are being developed and the government and an increasing number of NGOs are taking a greater interest in conserving the country's natural resources.

INTRODUCTION

Paraguay is a small landlocked country in the centre of South America, but the Paraná and Paraguay Rivers give access to the sea so that Asunción — 1600 km from the coast — is the chief port as well as the capital city. The country is divided into two large natural units by the Paraguay River; the two have very different ecological characteristics.

Covering 61 per cent of the country is the Occidental or Chaco region in the west, an alluvial plain with level topography more or less throughout; the highest point reached is 800 m. The plain is covered with savanna and xerophytic vegetation. In the centre, near the Paraguay River, is a seasonally inundated swamp, the Pantanal region. The only humid forests in the Chaco are the small areas of gallery forest. Population density in this region is only 0.2 inhabitants per sq. km.

The remaining 39 per cent (about 159,800 sq. km) of the country, the Oriental or Eastern Region, is a much more humid area. In the north there is subtropical semideciduous forest, while there is palm savanna with fertile grasslands and wooded hills in the south. On the eastern border along the Paraná River is Paraguay's only moist tropical forest, further west the vegetation changes to subtropical semideciduous lowland forest. Population density in the Eastern Region is 18.6 inhabitants per sq. km.

The average annual temperature drops as one moves from north to south, from 25°C in Bahía Negra to 21°C in Pilar. In the Chaco, absolute maximum and minimum temperatures are 48°C and –5°C respectively (Spichiger and Ramella, 1989). The south is particularly susceptible to frost, which has a profound effect on the vegetation. Average annual precipitation varies from 400 mm in the far northwest of the Chaco to 1800 mm in the southeast of the Eastern Region.

Around 98 per cent of the population live in the Eastern Region and over half of these are concentrated within a 100 km radius of the capital (IIED/USAID, 1985). Around 51 per cent of the country live in urban areas. Unlike in many other Latin American countries, there is little rural to urban migration in Paraguay, movement tends to be from one rural area to another as a result of agricultural colonisation and development programmes. The population is a more or less homogenous mixture of Spanish and Guaraní Indian descent. Indians, of other, unassimilated groups, make up only one per cent of the population.

Cattle raising is the main activity in the Chaco; agriculture is very limited in this area. The only forestry activities are extraction of quebracho (for tannin) and fuelwood collection. In eastern Paraguay, land-use capability studies classify 63 per cent of the soil suitable for crop production, while the remaining is suitable for livestock or forestry. Here, cattle raising, agriculture and forestry are all important activities and these three are the economic mainstays of the country. Chief exports are soybeans and cotton.

The Forests

Various different classification schemes have been used to describe the forests of Paraguay. In 1969, Holdridge described the country as lying within two life zones: warm temperate moist forest, corresponding to the Eastern Region and portions of the southeastern Chaco, and warm temperate dry forest, covering the remainder of the Chaco. Largely because of the annual frosts, the number of species present in the forests is much less than in true tropical or sub-tropical areas.

Hueck (1966, 1978) described most of the forests of the Eastern Region as part of the formation of "sub-tropical forests of Brazil and meridional forests". There are over 250 tree

286

species in the region. In general, species diversity increases from south to north and from west to east. Most of the tree species are found throughout the Eastern Region, but their relative proportions vary from place to place. Exceptions to this are two of Paraguay's most important commercial trees, which have a limited distribution. *Aspidosperma polyneuron* (perbol) is found in the departments of Canindeyú and Amambay (Figure 30.1), while *Amburana cearensis* (trebol), the country's most valuable species, is now threatened and is found in only a small area in the north between the Apa and Aquidabán Rivers.

Lopez *et al.* (1987) divide the forests of the Eastern Region into three major formations: high forest, low humid forest and riparian forest. The high forests are the most important from a commercial and biological perspective, they contain the largest number of commercial tree species. Dominant species include *Astronium fraxinifolium, Tabebuia heptaphylla, Cordia trichatoma, Patagonula americana, Anadenathera colubrina, Apuleia leiocarpa, Enterlobium contortisiliquum, Lonchocarpus leucanthus, Myrocarpus frondosus, Parapiptadenia rigida, Peltophorum dubium, Pterogyne nitens, Cedrela fissilis, Chlorophora tinctoria, Ficus enormis, Balfourodendron riedelianum* and *Diatenopteryx sorbifolia*. The riparian forests reach 17 m in height, they do not have any significant commercial value. Principal species include *Luehea divaricata, Sebastiana* spp., *Ruprechtia laxifolia, Cupania vernalis* and *Croton urucurana*, with the last forming almost pure stands along some rivers. The low humid forests are similar to riparian forests, but occur in patches in fields rather than along streams. They are found in the south-east of the country. The dominant species is *Peltophorum dubium*.

Other classifications are based on biogeographic divisions. These describe four forest types: the Cordilleras forest, the Paraná forests, the Central forests and gallery forests (Figure 30.2). The first three would all be included in Lopez *et al*'s high forest.

The Cordilleras forests are defined by the Mbaracayú and Amambay mountain ranges and the Carapá River, a tributary of the Paraná. The forests make up a continuous homogenous formation which merges gradually with the Paraná forests. The Cordilleras forests are the tallest and densest in the country with a canopy reaching 35–40 m. The canopy layer is made up of around 60 species, with another 20 or so emergents. Those in the northeast are characterised by large numbers of *Aspidosperma australe*, this species forms pure stands in some areas. Other valuable commercial species common in these forests include *Peltophorum dubium* and *Balfourodendron*

Flooded forest near Asuncion. (Mark Dillenbeck)

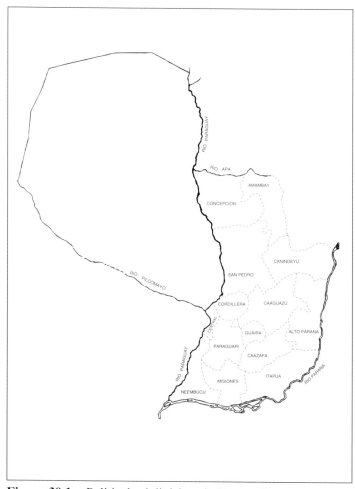

Figure 30.1   Political subdivisions in Eastern Paraguay

riedelianum (IIED/USAID, 1985). The dense understorey is characterised by an abundance of tree ferns which give the name to the "Amamabay" mountain range.

The forests of the Paraná River basin form a strip 130 km high corresponding to the western tributaries of the river. They reach 30 m or more in height in areas where there is good drainage, and are more irregular in height and density than the Cordilleras forests. The most representative trees of the canopy are *Cedrela tubiflora, Nectandra* spp., *Ocotea* spp. *Balfourodendron riedelianum, Myrocarpus frondosus, Piptadenia* sp., *Cordia trichotoma* and *Pterogyne nitens* (IIED/USAID, 1985). Species of the Lauraceae family are common in the lower strata.

The Central forests are located to the west of the Paraná forests and are separated from the Paraná watershed by discontinuous mountain chains (San Joaquin, Caaguazú, San Rafael). The northern border of this formation is defined by the Aquidabán River. These forests continue in a 200 km strip up to the Manduvirá watershed and then reappear further south associated with the Tebicuary River system.

The Central forests tend to be more open and less rich in species than those to the east. Canopy height varies from 25 to 35 m. There are more deciduous tree species and more species with spines than there are in the forests to the east. Representative species are *Tabebuia ipe* in the east, *Amburana cearensis* in the north and *Samanea saman* in the west. The forests are interspersed with natural grasslands and swamps.

The gallery forests occupy a thin strip along the Paraguay River. These forests contain species of both the Chaco and

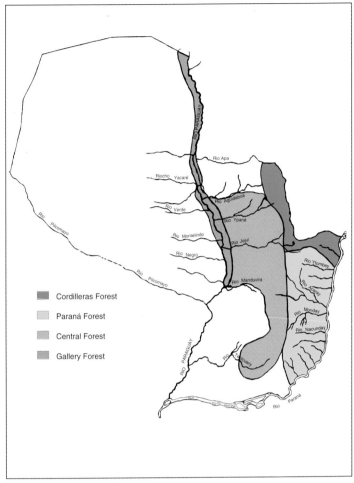

Figure 30.2   Forest types in Eastern Paraguay

Table 30.1   Original extent of forests in Paraguay

Original Area (in sq. km) of Forest, by Region

Eastern region		Chaco	
Cordilleras forests	16,200	Northern forests	30,420
Paraná forests	32,400	Pilcomayo	41,580
Central forests	44,640	Gallery forests*	8,640
Gallery forests*	648		
Total	93,888		80,640

*   along the Paraguay River

(Table 30.2 and see Map Legend). These figures compare well with those given in Kohler (1989), which were estimated from the same map. Kohler indicates that continuous forest covers 34,996 sq. km; residual forest covers 13,407 sq. km and the woody forests cover 4864 sq. km. The latter have not been mapped here as they are not considered to be forest according to the classification used in this Atlas.

The Cordilleras forests have been least exploited because of their inaccessibility. The Paraná forests, although somewhat inferior in timber yield to those further north, were subjected to exploitation early on as the logs could be extracted via the rivers.

Logging is generally done indiscriminately and marketing of the wood is uncontrolled. There are no significant public forest reserves, most of the land is in private hands and there is no policy to promote private forest management. Although there are decrees applying to the exploitation of private forest, these are seldom put into practice. Private forests are typically high-graded for a few commercial species before they are cleared for agriculture or grazing land.

The export of logs was prohibited in 1972, but some illegal export still occurs, especially from the northeast of the country (IIED/USAID, 1985). Most of the sawmills in the country are quite small and do not possess automatic equipment.

Paraguay has a huge per capita fuelwood consumption, several times higher than that in other South American countries. Around 52 per cent of the consumption is by the industrial sector (IIED/USAID, 1985).

The legal basis for the forestry sector is the Forestry Law of 1973. This law establishes, amongst other things, fiscal incentives for reafforestation, defines forest lands — as reserves, production or protection forests, created the National Forest Service (SFN), imposes a stumpage tax on the use of forests and sets up regulations and fines to protect the forest resources. However, there has been little political willingness to uphold this law and few of the restrictions are applied. For instance, forests belonging to the State are legally obliged to have man-

Eastern Region. Representative trees are *Fagara* spp. and *Crataeva tapia*.

The forests of the Chaco are mostly scrub-like, xerophytic formations. Consequently this area has not been mapped or described here. There are, however, some gallery forests in the region.

Forest Resources and Management

The original extent of the forests in the Chaco and Eastern Region is shown in Table 30.1. These have, however, been considerably depleted over the years, particularly in the Eastern region. Estimates of the area remaining vary considerably, but the most recent suggests that in 1991 only 24,030 sq. km, or 15 per cent, of the Eastern region was still forested (Bozzano and Weik, 1992 and see Table 30.3). This figure is the result of the analysis of Landsat images taken in 1991 and includes residual forests larger than 50 ha.

FAO (1993) estimates that in the whole of Paraguay, there are 60,370 sq. km of moist deciduous forest and 270 sq. km of forest in the hill and montane zone, giving the total of 60,640 sq. km quoted at the head of the chapter. FAO estimates that there are also 679,40 sq. km of dry deciduous forest in the country. However, the total area of closed broadleaved forest is estimated to be only 26,490 sq. km (FAO, 1993). Most of this must be in the Eastern Region, though the gallery forest in the Chaco may be included.

Measurements taken from Map 30.1 indicate that in 1985 there were 35,661 sq. km of continuous forest (*Bosques de masa contínua*), and 11,827 of residual forest (*Bosques residual*), which is mapped as degraded forest, in the Eastern region

Table 30.2   Estimates of forest extent in the Eastern Region of Paraguay

Forest type	Area (sq. km)	% of land area
Lowland moist	35,661	9.0
Degraded lowland moist	11,827	3.0
Total	47,488	12.0

Based on analysis of Map 30.1 See Map Legend on p. 293 for details of sources.

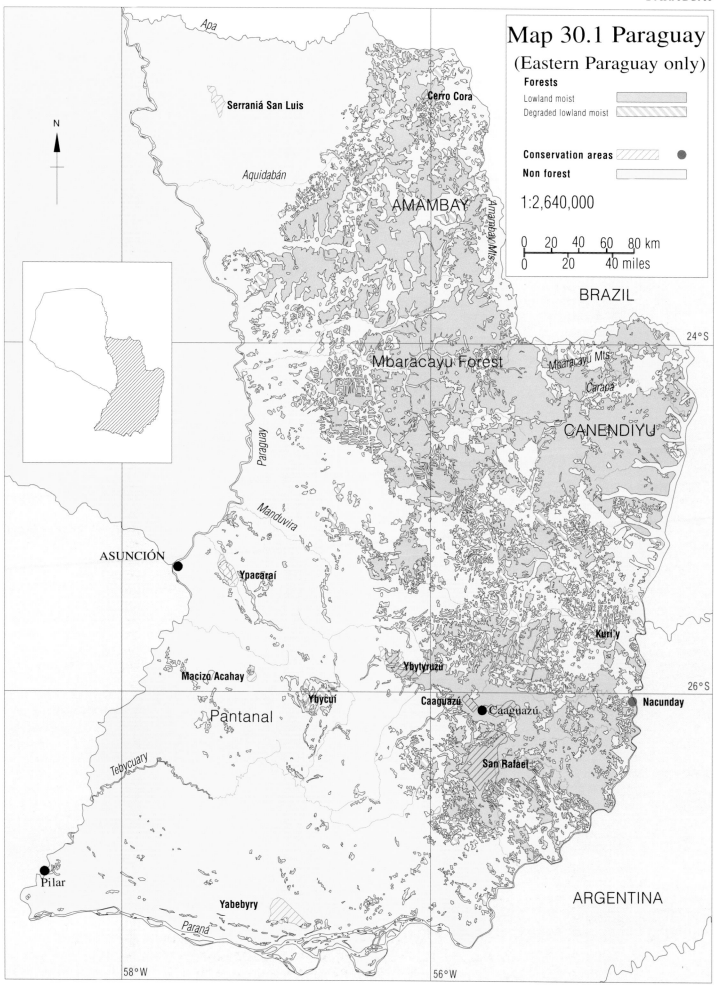

Map 30.1 Paraguay
(Eastern Paraguay only)

Forests

Lowland moist

Degraded lowland moist

Conservation areas ●

Non forest

1:2,640,000

0   20   40   60   80 km

0   20   40 miles

BRAZIL

24°S

ARGENTINA

26°S

Apa

Serraniá San Luis

Aquidabán

AMAMBAY

Cerro Cora

Amambay Mts.

Mbaracayu Forest

Mbaracayú Mts

Carapá

CANENDIYU

Paraguay

Manduvira

ASUNCIÓN

Ypacaraí

Kuri'y

Macizo Acahay

Ybytyruzú

Ybycuí

Caaguazú

Caaguazú

Nacunday

Pantanal

San Rafael

Tebycuary

Pilar

Yabebyry

Paraná

58°W

56°W

agement plans, but they rarely do; the National Forestry Service is meant to control the marketing of the wood and prepare inventories of the plants concerned with primary production and yet this does not happen. In addition, this law actually allows colonisation within the forest reserves.

Reforestation with native species is almost non-existent and there are only a few plantations of exotic species. There are a few private organisations working with small farmers to develop tree nurseries, to provide wood for fuel and construction, but they are too small and dispersed to have much effect (Sorenson, 1992).

Non-timber forest resources include the palm *Euterpe edulis*, which is intensively exploited for *palmito* or palmheart, mostly for export. Several plants, including orchids and ferns, are used in the ornamental plant trade for both domestic and export purposes. Wild fruits are of only minor commercial importance, though they are used by local people. Similarly, medicinal plants are important to the local people. *Ilex paraguariensis* supplies the raw material for a kind of tea, *yerba mate*, which can be drunk either hot or cold. It is cultivated and a limited amount is exported. *Bulnesia sarmientoi* or *palo santo*, found in the Chaco, is exploited for the essence made from its bark.

There is a large illegal trade in wildlife and wildlife products in the country, with the exported products coming both from within Paraguay and from the surrounding countries. A CITES office has been created in an attempt to remedy this problem.

Deforestation

The concept that forest lands are unproductive lands pervades the country at all levels, not only within the rural population but also in the government. As a result, there is little attempt to prevent forest clearance. Indeed, Paraguay's annual deforestation rate, at 3.4 per cent (2514 sq. km — FAO, 1993) between the years of 1981 and 1990, is higher than in any other country in South or Central America . The figure of 2514 sq. km excludes deforestation in the dry deciduous zone, which is a further 1511 sq. km, giving a total of 4025 sq. km. Inclusion of all forest types reduces the annual deforestation rate to 2.7 per cent (FAO, 1993). Bozzano and Weik (1992) reported that in 1990, approximately 1000 sq. km of forest in Eastern Paraguay were cleared, and it is in the east that most deforestation occurs.

It is estimated that the total forest area in the Eastern Region dropped from 68,364 sq. km in 1945 to 41,770 sq. km in 1976 and to less than 35,000 sq. km by 1984 (IIED/USAID, 1985). These figures are underestimates compared to those in Bozzano and Weik (1992; see Table 30.3), but either way the loss of forest is alarming, with only 15 per cent remaining in 1991.

In the 1960s and, particularly, the 1970s, indiscriminate clearing for agriculture was the main cause of forest loss, and this continues today. Another cause of deforestation in the east is the large landowners cutting their forest so that the govern-

Table 30.3 Forest cover in the Eastern Region of Paraguay between the years of 1945 and 1991.

Year(s)	Forest cover (sq. km)	Per cent of land covered
1945	88,050	55.1
1965-1968	70,420	44.1
1975-1976	54,920	34.4
1984-1985	39,290	24.6
1991	24,030	15.0

Source: Bozzano and Weik (1992)

ment will not settle landless peasants in the "unused" forest areas. This occurs in spite of the 1973 Forest Law (reaffirmed in the Decree on the Environment of 1986) which requires owners of rural properties to leave 25 per cent of their land under natural forest cover — or reforest five per cent if the land had already been cleared.

Biodiversity

Paraguay is, botanically, one of the least known countries in South America (Davis *et al.*, 1986). It is estimated to contain 7000–8000 plant species (Davis *et al.*, 1986), with 149 threatened. There have been few endemics, either flora or fauna, reported in the country. This is probably partly because its ecosystems are shared by surrounding countries, but also because it has been so little studied.

There are 156 species of mammals in the country (WCMC, 1992), only 12 of these are globally threatened, but is it estimated that 72 are threatened within Paraguay. Three species are endemic (WCMC, 1992). Forest-dwelling species in Paraguay which are listed as threatened by IUCN include the giant otter *Pteronura brasiliensis*, the margay *Leopardus wiedii* and the bush dog *Speothos venaticus* (Groombridge, 1993).

There are 650 bird species reported in the country (WCMC, 1992). Twenty-two of them are listed as threatened by Collar *et al.* (1992), but none of these is endemic and less than half are forest species. One of the most endangered species, which may even be extinct, is the purple winged ground dove *Claravis godefrida* that lives around bamboo in dense forests. Two other forest species found in Paraguay, the helmeted woodpecker *Dryocopus galeatus* and the russet-winged spadebill *Platyrinchus leucoryphus*, are listed as vulnerable by IUCN. Both appear to be rare and local, but deforestation is likely to be at least a contributory factor in their decline.

There are 120 species of reptiles in the country, of which four are endemic (WCMC, 1992). Intensive hunting of the broad-nosed caiman *Caiman latirostris* is one of the causes of its decline. Five species are listed as threatened, the black caiman, the tortoise *Geochelone chilensis* and three turtles (Groombridge, 1993).

Eighty-five species of amphibian have been recorded with four endemics (WCMC, 1992). No globally threatened species are recorded in the country.

Estimates for the number of fish in the country vary from 150–260, numbers of threatened or endemic species are not known. There is however, a considerable degree of pollution in the country's watercourses which does not bode well for their inhabitants.

Conservation Areas

The protected areas of Paraguay constitute a complex of units whose connections and objectives are weak and disjointed in the absence of a national environmental or conservation policy (Acevedo and Pinazzo, 1992). However, a National Parks Directorate was established in 1987 within the Ministry of Agriculture and Livestock and new laws for national parks and protected areas are currently being drafted. The parks had previously been administered as a department of the Forestry Service.

At present, the various conservation areas in Paraguay are controlled by either the State, private organisations or "others" (Acevedo and Pinazzo, 1992). Those that are state-run are not necessarily on state-owned land, and though production, exploitation and settlement are not legally allowed, these activities do occur in most conservation areas. Those areas in IUCN's categories I–IV are listed in Table 30.4.

Privately-owned areas include protective forests, biological reserves, national recreation parks and private natural reserves. The first three of these categories make up the network of forest reserves, covering 87 sq. km, run by the Mennonites Cooperatives of the Central Chaco. The Fundación Moisés Bertoni manages the programme for private natural reserves. These number four, currently covering 97 sq. km (Acevedo and Pinazzo, 1992).

Areas managed by other enterprises are either biological reserves, biological refuges or animal refuges. The biological reserves are the largest and are comparatively undisturbed areas; the biological refuges have generally been substantially changed by humans; while animal refuges are only 1 sq. km or there-abouts and are important for environmental education and the conservation or study of a particular species. The Itaipu Binational Entity, which runs a big hydroelectric project in the country, manages the two biological reserves and the two biological refuges covering 292 sq. km. These areas are legally designated, but are listed in IUCN's category V so are not mapped here or shown in Table 30.4. The Yacyreta Binational Entity, also part of a big hydroelectric project, manages the only animal refuge.

A new category — that of natural reserve — was adopted in 1991 for the 577 sq. km Mbaracayu Forest. This reserve (IUCN category V) was set up under an agreement between the Paraguay government, Fundación Moisés Bertoni, The Nature Conservancy (TNC) and the World Bank (See Box).

The largest area of the protected land is in the Chaco although there are a greater number of conservation units in the east. Creation of more public conservation areas in the east will be extremely expensive because most of the land is privately owned. However, private areas have the potential to become an important complementary system.

Two national parks, Defensores del Chaco and Caaguazú, and Mbaracayu Natural Reserve have been identified as candidates to receive support from USAID's Parks-in-Peril programme (TNC, 1990). Initial activities in Mbaracayu, the first

Table 30.4 Conservation areas in Paraguay

Existing conservation areas in IUCN's categories I–IV are listed below. Private reserves are not listed or mapped.

National Parks	Area (sq. km)
Caaguazú*	160
Cerro Cora*	115
Defensores del Chaco[+]	7,800
Lago Ypoá[+]	1,000
Nacunday*	20
San Rafael*	780
Serraniá San Luis	103
Teniente Enciso[+]	400
Tinfunqué[+]	2,800
Ybycuí*	50
Ybytyruzú	240
Ypacaraí	160
Natural Monument	
Macizo Acahay*	25
Wildlife Reserve	
Yabebyry	300
National Reserve	
Kuri'y*	0.6
Total	13,954

[+] not mapped, location data not available or area is located in the Western region
* area with moist forest within its boundaries according to Map 30.1

Source: WCMC (unpublished data)

MBARACAYU

Mbaracayú, Paraguay's only natural reserve, is on the country's eastern border with Brazil. It is a virtually undisturbed area that, although not actually part of the Atlantic forest, contains many of the species that are, or used to be, found there. It is one of the most important remaining examples of Alto Paraná forest and is unusually rich in endemic species.

The two parcels of land that make up Mbaracayú were owned by a branch of the World Bank (the International Finance Corporation) that gained title to them because of the bankruptcy of a timber company. IFC initially tried to sell the larger parcel (577 sq. km) for US$7 million, but finally agreed to sell it to The Nature Conservancy for just US$2 million. TNC purchased the property on behalf of the Moisés Bertoni Foundation. As part of the agreement, the Paraguay government purchased the smaller tract of 109 sq. km, with the intention of establishing agrarian reform settlements on the land.

As well as the plans to preserve the wildlife and plant communities of the area, there are programmes to allow the 1000 remaining Aché indians to hunt and gather there, and proposals to help them to make the transition to agriculture and animal husbandry.

Although most of the new reserve is high dense forest, there are also a variety of other habitats including lower transitional forest, grasslands, wetlands and rivers (Keel *et al.*, 1993). A number of large mammals such as the jaguar *Panthera onca*, ocelot *Leopardus pardalis* and howler monkey *Alouatta caraya* are relatively common in the area and there are also relict populations of others including the little-spotted cat *Leopardus tigrinus* (Brooks *et al.*, 1993) and the bush dog *Speothos venaticus*. Notable birds include the king vulture *Sarcorhamphus papa*, bare-faced currasow *Crax fasciolata*, black-fronted piping guan *Pipile jacutinga*, bare-throated bellbird *Procnias nudicollis* and russet-winged spadebill Platyrinchus leucoryphus (Brook *et al.*, 1993). Economically important plants include *Euterpe edulis*, *Ilex paraguariensis* and many timber species such as *Balfourodendron riedelianum*, *Cedrela fissilis* and *Amburana cearensis*. Many others are listed by Keel *et al.* (1993).

Public education programmes administered by the Moisés Bertoni Foundation will enlist the participation of local landowners in the overall conservation of the area. It is intended that this reserve will be a model of conservation and sustainable use that can then be replicated in other parts of the country.

to receive funds, have included hiring of a director for the reserve, training of the park guard force, clearing of the boundaries and a workshop to initiate development of the reserve's operation plan.

Initiatives for Conservation

A new constitution came into force in 1992 and this includes various Articles relating to conservation of the environment and management of natural resources. There are also several laws being passed through parliament at present that relate to forestry, wildlife and protected areas.

A Parliamentary Advisory Commission — the National Commission for the Protection of Natural Resources — has been set up to attend to the preparation of various programmes related to the environment, to supervise the execution of environmental projects, coordinate the activities of the interested bodies, to participate in the making of laws related to the environment and to advise Congress. There are some 30 NGOs with representatives on this Commission, as well as representatives from both the public and private sector.

Environmental NGOs, formerly very weak in Paraguay, are on the increase; about ten have been formed in the last five years and there are currently at least 50 NGOs with interests in the environment (Sorenson, 1992). The largest and most active of these is the Fundación Moisés Bertoni, which was set up in 1988 with strong support from TNC. This foundation is concerned with expanding and strengthening the national parks system, supporting private protected areas and promoting public awareness of and involvement with conservation in the country.

The Carlos Pfannl Institute — which provides agricultural training — has, with the financial help of USAID, introduced environmentally correct courses in sustainable agriculture and has entered into a joint programme with the Private University of the North to establish the country's first private degree programme in agricultural technology.

A Conservation Data Centre (CDC) was created in 1986 through the cooperation of the Ministry of Agriculture and Livestock (MAG), TNC and the Peace Corps. In 1991, the CDC was placed under the Direction of National Parks and Wildlife Service. A classification of the major ecoregions of the country and the natural communities within them is currently being developed by CDC-Paraguay. Study of the Chaco area is not yet complete, but the Eastern region has been divided into six ecoregions (on the basis of soils types, climate, geology, topography, natural vegetation, etc.). The six are: Aguidabán, Amambay, Alto Paraná, Selva Central, Litoral Central and Neembucú; within these are 33 distinct natural communities (CDC, 1990). Twelve mammals, 35 birds, four reptiles and 27 plants are considered to be critically endangered in the Eastern region (CDC, 1990; Sorenson, 1992). As a result of this work, 23 priority areas, covering all the representative ecosystems, are recommended for conservation (also see Keel *et al.,* 1993).

In general, the Paraguayan people are becoming increasingly concerned about deforestation in their country and its cost to the economy. Along with this, is a growing interest in environmental education (Sorenson, 1992). Mainly as a result of the rising public interest, there has been a change in the government's attitude to the environment and there is more cooperation between the government, NGOs and various international organisations to find a solution to the country's environmental problems and to develop rational, sustainable uses of the natural resources.

References

Acevedo, C. and Pinazzo, J. (1992). Areas protegidas paraguayas y su relación con la población. In: *Espacios sin Habitantes? Parques Nacionales de América del Sur.* Amend, S. and Amend, T. (eds). IUCN and Editorial Nueva Sociedad, Caracas. Pp. 291–304.

Bozzano, B.E. and Weik, J.H. (1992). *El Avance de la Deforestación y el Impacto Económico.* Proyecto de Planificación del Manejo de los Recursos Naturales (MAG/GT-GTZ), Series No. 12. Asunción, Paraguay.

Brooks, T.M., Barnes, R., Bartrina, L., Butchart, S.H.M., Clay, R.P., Esquivel, E.Z., Etcheverry, N.I., Lowen, J.C. and Vincent, J. (1993). *Bird Surveys and Conservation in the Paraguayan Atlantic Forest. Project Canopy '92: Final Report.* Birdlife International Study Report No. 57, Birdlife International, Cambridge, U.K.

CDC (1990). *Areas Prioritarias para la Conservacion en la Region Oriental del Paraguay.* Centro de Datos para la Conservacion, Asunción, Paraguay.

Collar, N.J., Gonzaga, L.P., Krabbe, N., Madroño Nieto, A., Naranjo, L.G., Parker III, T.A. and Wege, D.C. (1992). *Threatened Birds of the Americas. The ICBP/IUCN Red Data Book.* ICBP, Cambridge, U.K.

Davis, S.D., Droop, S.J.M., Gregerson, P., Henson, L., Leon, C.J., Villa-Lobos, J.L, Synge, H. and Zantovska, J. (1986). *Plants in Danger. What do we know?* IUCN, Gland, Switzerland and Cambridge, U.K.

Groombridge, B. (Ed) (1993). *1994 IUCN Red List of Threatened Animals.* IUCN, Gland, Switzerland and Cambridge, U.K.

GTZ (1986). *Republica del Paraguay Regional Oriental — Cobertura Vegetal y uso Actual de la Tierra.* Produced by CIF, SNF, MAG and GTZ, Ascuncion.

Hueck, K. (1966). Die Walder Sudamerikas: Olologie Zusammensetzung und wirtschaftliche Bedeutung. 422 pp. Stuttgart.

Hueck, K. (1978). (ed). *Los bosques de Sudamérica, ecología, composición e importancia económica.* Sociedad Alemana de Cooperación Técnica, Ltda (GTZ).

IIED/USAID (1985). *Environmental Profile of Paraguay.* IIED/Technical Planning Secretariat/USAID, Washington, D.C., U.S.A.

Keel, S., Gentry, A.H. and Spinzi, L. (1993). Using vegetation analysis to facilitate the selection of conservation sites in Eastern Paraguay. *Conservation Biology* 7(1): 66–75.

Kohler, V. (1989). Cambios en el Uso de las Tierras y sus Consecuencias Ambientales en el Paraguay. *Cuadernos Forestales* 1: 1–21.

Lopez, J.A., Little, E.L., Ritz, G.F., Rombold, J.S. and Hahn, W.J. (1987). *Arboles Comunes del Paraguay.* Cuerpo de Paz, Washington, D.C., U.S.A.

Sorenson, C. (1992). *Update of Forest and Biodiversity Assessment for Paraguay.* Prepared for USAID/Washington.

Spichiger, R. and Ramella, L. (1989). The forests of the Paraguayan Chaco. In: *Tropical Forests: Botanical Dynamics, Speciation and Diversity.* Holm-Nielsen, L.B., Nielson, I.C. and Balslev, H. (eds). Academic Press, London, U.K. Pp. 259–270.

TNC (1990). *Parks in Peril: a Conservation Partnership for the Americas.* The Nature Conservancy, Virginia.

WCMC (1992). *Global Biodiversity: Status of the Earth's Living Resources.* Chapman and Hall, London xx + 594 pp.

Authors: Marcos Sanjurjo and Raúl Gauto, Fundación Moisés Bertoni, with contributions from Celeste Acevedo, Fundación Moisés Bertoni; Mark Dillenbeck, IUCN-US; Jennifer Fox, CDC-Paraguay; Claire Sorenson, USAID; Rob Clay and James Lowen, Birdlife International, Cambridge, U.K.

Map 30.1   Paraguay

The moist forests of Eastern Paraguay have been digitised from a 1:500,000 published map, *Republica del Paraguay, Region Oriental — Uso Actual de la Tierra* and accompanying map legend (*Cobertura Vegetal y Uso Actual de la Tierra* [GTZ, 1986]), produced by the Carrera de Ingenieria Forestal, Servicio Forestal Nacional, Gabinete Tecnico, Universidad Nacional de Asuncion, Ministerio de Agricultura y Ganaderia and Mision Forestal Alemana (GTZ — the German aid agency) in 1986. Please note, that the dry Chaco formations of western Paraguay have not been included.

The source map is based on 1984–85 Landsat satellite imagery at a scale of 1:250,000. H. Huespe, F. Recalde, G. Rolon, L. Cabral, P.E. Meza, P. Florentin and N. Brítez are responsible for the compilation of the map. Seven vegetation classes are depicted on the source map and from these, two of three forest classes have been digitised.

On the original land use map, some forests are classified as *Bosques de masa contínua* or continuous forests. These are *continuous forest blocks with little human influence which, due to their geographical location, floristic composition and area, could be considered as forests manageable for timber production. . .* These are mapped here as lowland moist forest. The second forest category is *Bosques residuales* or residual forests, these *consist of those forest blocks of less than 2000 ha which have been highly modified and, because of their location, are subject to great agricultural/grazing pressure. . . The low forests of the Paraguay River basin in the centre and south of the eastern region are also included in this category.* These are mapped here as degraded forest. The third forest formation on the original map is *Bosques leñosos del litoral del Río Paraguay.* These woody forests of the edges of the River Paraguay are *the forest formations found in the littoral zone close to the middle course of the river and they are composed of low trees grouped on islets or clumps and irregular blocks alternating with natural open areas.* (Forest descriptions have been translated from GTZ [1986].) These are not considered to be "forest" as defined in this Atlas and they have not been shown on Map 30.1.

Boundary data for the conservation areas of Paraguay were derived from a published map *Republica del Paraguay — Areas Silvestres Protegidas* compiled by the Plan Maestro del Sistema Nacional de Areas Silvestres Protegidas del Paraguay (SINASIP) at a scale of 1:2 million and published in 1993. Protected areas data are organised by management agency on this source map.

NB: it has been brought to our attention that a reservoir on the Paraná River on the southern border of the country now exists. It has not been possible to obtain information on this, and therefore the reservoir has not been shown on Map 30.1.

31 Peru

Country area	1,285,220 sq. km
Land area	1,280,000 sq. km
Population (mid-1994)	22.9 million
Population growth rate	2.0 per cent
Population projected to 2025	35.6 million
Gross national product per capita (1992)	US$950
Forest cover in 1990 (FAO, 1993)*	674,340 sq. km
Annual deforestation rate (1981–1990)	0.4 per cent
Industrial roundwood production	1,013,000 cu. m
Industrial roundwood exports	1000 cu. m
Fuelwood and charcoal production	6,813,000 cu. m
Processed wood production	513,000 cu. m
Processed wood exports	4000 cu. m

* excluding forest in the dry deciduous, very dry and desert zones

Peru is a nation of dramatic contrasts. It contains coastal deserts where it never rains, the longest chain of mountains in the tropics and vast expanses of largely undisturbed rain forest in the Amazon basin. The forests of the eastern Andean foothills are probably the most biologically diverse in the world. Manu National Park has more species of plants and animals than any other protected area on earth.

Peru has a rich cultural heritage. The spectacular structures of Machu Pichu are testimony to one of South America's most advanced pre-Columbian societies. The sophisticated irrigated agriculture and communications of the Inca and other civilisations were destroyed during the savage assaults of Spanish conquistadors in search of gold and christian missionaries in search of souls. It was not until the second half of the twentieth century that Peru's population recovered its pre-Columbian density.

Peru's recent history has been dominated by civil strife as deprived rural communities, left-wing intellectuals and drug barons form alliances with corrupt branches of the military in the struggle against a succession of ineffective governments.

The nation's failed development programmes and the physical isolation imposed by the Andes and the forests of neighbouring Brazil have not only saved Peru's rain forests, the second most extensive in the world, but have also left intact much of the rich culture of the numerous forest dwelling indians.

INTRODUCTION

Peru has an enormous cultural and natural diversity. The ecosystems within the country range from deserts totally denuded of higher plants, to tropical forests which may contain up to 300 tree species per hectare. Between these two extremes, there is a variety of plant formations: mangroves, mist-induced formations (lomas) and tropical dry forests on the coast, relicts of Andean forests, small areas of uniform conifer forests, vast areas of high andean steppes (punas) and semi-arid scrub vegetation in the sierra. Biodiversity reaches its peak in the complex tropical rain forests on the slopes of the Andes and in the Amazon lowlands.

The country can be divided into three main natural regions: the arid, desertic coastal region (Costa), the mountains and plateaus of the Andes (Sierra) and the hills and lowlands of the Amazon Basin (Selva).

The Costa, comprising 11 per cent of Peru's land mass, consists of dry flat plains and sand dunes on the coastal plain and the dry foothills of the Andes up to 2000 m. Rich alluvial soils occur chiefly in the valleys of the otherwise desert Costa region. This is where most of the productive agricultural activity is situated. It is only in the north that forests are found and these are dry, seasonally deciduous forests.

The Sierra encompasses the mountain ranges of the Andes, running north-south through Peru, and the valleys and high plateau country (altiplano or puna) which run between them. There are three major Andean ranges, the Cordillera Occidental,

the Cordillera Central and the Cordillera Oriental. Many of the peaks are snow-capped, the highest is Mount Huascaran at 6768 m. The Sierra has been settled for a considerable length of time; it was the centre of the ancient Inca empire and much of Peru's Indian population now live there. The soils have been over-worked and are infertile in many areas. Most of the natural forest in the region is degraded or entirely lost as a result of many centuries of intense human activity.

The Selva, accounting for 63 per cent of the country, consists of the Low Selva, a gently rolling plain mostly covered in low-land rainforest between 200 m and 700 m in elevation and the transitional High Selva, 100–160 km in width running between the Andes and the lowland rain forest. The vegetation of the High Selva is exceptionally diverse, depending on soil, rainfall and relief. It is this region which has been most affected by migrant populations moving in and clearing the forest.

The climate in the Costa is dominated by the cold Humboldt Current, air temperatures along the coast range from 18° to 22°C, considerably colder than those at the same latitude on the other side of the continent. Annual rainfall in this region is as little as 10 mm. Temperatures in the Sierra drop quite low in winter, frosts occurring frequently in areas above 4000 m. Rainfall is much higher than in the Costa, over 1200 mm in places although rain-shadow effects mean that some valleys receive only meagre precipitation. Rainfall is heaviest in the summer months from

September to April. In the Low Selva, temperatures average 21°C throughout the year at Iquitos and annual precipitation is around 2540 mm with no completely dry season. The High Selva has more rain, around 3960 mm per year.

Overall population density is about 18 people per sq. km. However, the Sierra and Costa are very densely populated whereas very few people live in the Selva. About 70 per cent of Peruvians are urban dwellers with approximately 6.5 million living in the capital city of Lima, many of these live in conditions of absolute poverty. Indians make up about 50 per cent of Peru's population. Most of these, including the Quechua and Aymara, live in the Sierra, while others (e.g. the Pano and Tupi) are nomadic, forest-living people. One third of the population are mestizos, of mixed Indian and European descent and about 10 per cent are Europeans, principally of Spanish descent. Spanish and Quecha are the official languages of the country but there are numerous Indian languages which are of local importance.

About a third of Peru's cultivated land is found in the Costa, where much of it has to be irrigated, and a half occurs in the Sierra. Shifting cultivation is practised in the Selva, particularly on the slopes of the Andes. One third, or thereabouts, of the workforce are involved with the agricultural sector and this is the basis of the country's economy. Copper is the largest foreign exchange earner, followed by fishery products.

The Forests

Peru's National Forest Action Plan (PNAF, 1991) lists the different types of forest/woodland and scrub formations in the country and the areas they cover (Table 31.1).

Closed mixed forests of the low Selva contain most of the valuable timber species such as mahogany *Swietenia macrophylla*, cedars *Cedrella* spp., ishpingo *Amburana cearensis* and tornillo *Cedrelinga catenaeformis*. Other important species include those providing non-timber products. Examples of these are the Brazil nut or castaña *Bertholletia excelsa* and rubber (shiringa or jebe) *Hevea brasiliensis*.

Swamp forests, including the aquajales, are common. The aguajales are palm swamps characterised by species of the genus *Mauritia*. *Euterpe* (huasai) and *Jessenia* (hungurahui) are also common. The huasai yield palm hearts (known as chonta in Peru and palmito in Spanish) and the hungurahui produce an oil similar to olive oil and nuts that can be used to make soy meat.

Pacales are bamboo-dominated open forests. The bamboos, commonly *Merostachys* sp. and *Bambusa* subgenus *Guadua* spp., are rarely in pure stands. They form large clumps which reach up into the canopy at 30 m and spread over the interspersed trees (Prance, 1989). The tree genera *Schizolobium*, *Triplaris* and *Perebea* are common in this forest type.

Cloud forests occur on the eastern slopes of the Andes, at altitudes ranging from 1500 m to 3500 m. They are characterised by a high humidity and contain numerous orchids, other epiphytes and tree ferns. Some of the main tree species are also *Alnus jorullensis*, cascarilla *Cinchona* spp., carapacho *Weinmannia* sp., *Chusquea* sp. and *Gynoxys* sp.

Podocarpus is the only conifer genus native to Peru. Forests dominated by this genus have been considerably reduced in extent. Most of them occur in the north of the province of San Ignacio. Others persist in Ampay National Sanctuary in the south of the country. *Podocarpus* also occurs in other montane forests, but at lower densities. It is usually found in association with species such as the yauchi *Eugenia* sp., quinilla *Manilkara* sp., pino blanco *Alseis* sp. and tahuari *Tabebuia* sp.

Of the three regions of Peru, the Sierra has the least natural

Table 31.1 Peru's main forest, woodland and scrub ecosystems

Ecosystem	Area (sq. km)
SELVA	
Dense mixed forest	480,037
Cloud forest	139,250
Marsh forest	46,740
Aguajales	16,033
Pacales	14,933
Podocarpus forest	1,528
Sub total	698,521
SIERRA	
Evergreen matorrales*	17,582
Tolares*	6,020
Quinales forest	430
Sub total	24,032
COSTA	
Algarrobo forest	13,875
Closed deciduous forest	12,680
Lomas formation	2,000
Open deciduous forest	1,782
Hualtaco forest	1,640
Mangrove	58
Sub total	32,035
Total	810,655

* scrub/woody formations, not forest.

Source: PNAF (1991).

forest. The evergreen matorrales in Table 31.1 is not forest but a shrub formation with only a low density of trees. The tolares is also a bushy formation rather than forest. The quinuales forests occur in small scattered areas over 4000 m above sea level, where annual rainfall is only 420 mm to 660 mm. The dominant genera in these forests are *Polylepis* (quinua or qeñua), *Buddleja* (including quisuar *B. incana* and colle *B. coriacea*), *Escallonia* and *Gynoxys*. Puna grassland is found at elevations ranging from 3900 m to 4700 m.

There are several types of forest in the Costa region. Most common are the algarrobo forests where the dominant species is *Prosopis pallida*, known locally as carob or algarroba, but zapote *Capparis angulata* and bichayo *C. ovalifolia* also occur. The lomas formations, containing herbaceous plants and trees of several endemic genera and including many endemic species, are scattered in small patches throughout the central and southern Costa. They are formed against the dry coastal ridges and hills as a result of the mists which, in winter, condense out due to thermal inversion.

The dry forests are located mainly in the north of the Costa, in parts of the Marañón valley and in the department of Ica (south of Lima). The open deciduous forests contain species such as charán *Caesalpinia corymbosa*, hualtaco *Loxopterygium huasango*, algarrobo, faique *Acacia macracantha*, angolo *Pithecolobium* sp. and the cactus gigantón *Neorraimondia macrostibas*. The closed deciduous forests contain several of these open forest species, but other characteristic species include the payaso *Bombax* sp., ceibo *Chorisia* sp., palo santo *Bursera graveolens*, guayacán *Tabebuia* sp. and Fernán

Sánchez *Triplaris peruviana*. Epiphytes, especially *Tillandsia usneoides*, abound in this forest type.

Mangroves

Mangroves are found in northern Peru, in the Tumbes and Zarumilla Deltas and in a few patches, totalling 3 sq. km, in the department of Piura. They do not extend further south because of the cool Humboldt current which limits their distribution (Prance, 1989). They occur over a very small surface of only 48 sq. km (Echevarria and Sarabia (1993). However, they are a highly productive ecosystem in terms of hydrobiological resources and have great socioeconomic importance at a local level. The mangrove forests contain species such as the mangle *Rhyzophora mangle*, jeli salado *Avicennia germinans*, *Conocarpus erectus* and jeli dulce *Laguncularia racemosa*.

Forest Resources and Management

In Peru's National Action Plan for Forests (PNAF, 1991), it is estimated that forests cover 810,655 sq. km of the country (Table 31.1). However, two of the formations in the Sierra — the matorrales and tolares — are shrubby/bushy formations rather than forest, which reduces the area to 787,053 sq. km. This is still a much higher estimate than that in FAO (1993). Even including the dry formations, FAO estimates only 679,060 sq. km of forest and excluding these reduces the area to 674,340, of which 662,820 are closed broadleaved formations. Forest areas have not been measured from Map 31.1 as the source of these data was a dyeline regional map (Peru, Colombia, Venezuela) with no date and no information as to how the map was compiled and it was felt that the measurements of national forest cover would not be reliable (see Map Legend).

The Costa and Sierra regions contain little of Peru's forests (Table 31.1). Many of the dry forests on the northern coast have been cleared to make way for pastures and those remaining are under great pressure from people cutting them for firewood and charcoal production. Harvesting of living trees is not allowed in this area, only dead trees may be cut. In the Sierra, introduced species such as *Eucalyptus* and pine *Pinus* trees were initially planted for industrial purposes. Later, during the 1980s, emphasis was put on the planting of native species for social purposes. These were to supply the Andean campesinos with products such as firewood, forage and construction materials and to control erosion. This social forestry approach, based on restoring native tree species and on encouraging appropriate technologies, is yielding promising results (see Box in Chapter 24).

The Peruvian Amazon covers 59 per cent of the country and contains over 90 per cent of Peru's forest (Table 31.1). It is here that timber production is concentrated. There are at present, three laws designed to regulate the extraction of forest products for both subsistence and industrial purposes, but they have not been very effective.

There have been few attempts at establishing plantations in Peru. This is well illustrated in Table 31.2 which shows the area of land considered to be suitable for reforestation in the three regions of Peru and the areas actually planted in 1980 and 1990. In the Selva, for instance, 25,000 sq. km had been cleared of primary forest and were considered suitable for plantation forestry and yet, as of 1990, only 93 sq. km of plantation were present there.

According to current legislation, Peru's exploited forests are divided into two management categories: national forests and open-access forests (bosque de libre disponibilidad). The former are allocated for wood exploitation by the state or by private individuals, under stricter conditions than in the open-access forests. In 1975, there were 17 national forests in Amazonia covering 69,546 sq. km, but, due to the lack of state management and to the pressures exerted on them, the number of these forests has now gone down to four, covering only 33,339 sq. km. The open-access forests can be used for production of timber and other forest products. However, they have not been managed or monitored by the forestry authorities and many have been partially invaded. Today, there are 38 of these forests covering a total of 367,000 sq. km.

Combining the areas covered by the national and open-access forest, means that, in theory, the use of 402,000 sq. km of Peru's forests is regulated. In reality, in both the national and open-access forests, exploitation is virtually uncontrolled and there is little silvicultural management of them. A short-term approach prevails, as much timber as possible is removed from an area with no thought for future production. This is because the logging areas are not secure and the forestry authorities are unable to control invasions by landless people. Except for some concessions in national forests, there is a lack of technical supervision and monitoring. Within the national forests, concessions are normally granted covering areas of between 200 and 500 sq. km, though state enterprises may obtain concessions of up to 2000 sq. km. The concessions are granted for 20 years, but they may be renewed. In 1990, there were seven concessions in national forests, covering an area of only 2,650 sq. km, which is less than 10 per cent of the available land. Even in these concession areas, forest management is neglected, the forests are open to invasion by settlers and are being continuously depleted.

The concessions in the open-access forests are granted for areas of up to 1000 sq. km, for renewable periods of up to a maximum of 10 years. In 1986, there were more than 3300 concessions of less than 10 sq. km and these were scattered throughout the open-access forests. The large number and wide dispersion of small concessions hinders zoning and regulation of the forest. New forest legislation is now being drafted to address these problems. Permanent forest production areas and forest reserve zones are to be set up under the new system.

Timber is extracted by both small and large-scale operators. The small-scale extractors operate in concessions of less than 10 sq. km. They work with mechanical saws and hand tools and use the water power generated by the annual floods to cut and transport trees. This method of extraction is used to remove around 80 per cent of Peru's timber and yields between one and three cubic metres of timber per hectare. The large-scale operations, extracting the remaining 20 per cent of the country's timber, use heavy-duty machinery to transport the logs and take as much as 27 cu. m of timber from each hectare.

There are 540 sawmills in the Peruvian Amazonia, which, in 1990, produced 531,300 cu. m of timber (DGFF, 1990). They were, however, working at only 25 per cent of their full capacity.

Table 31.2 Reforested areas and lands suitable for reforestation in Peru's three natural regions

Region	Area suitable for reforestation	Area reforested (sq. km)	
		As of 1980	As of 1990
Costa	5,000	88	206
Sierra	75,000	1,240	2,331
Selva	25,000	42	93
Total	105,000	1,370	2,630

Source: DGFF (1990)

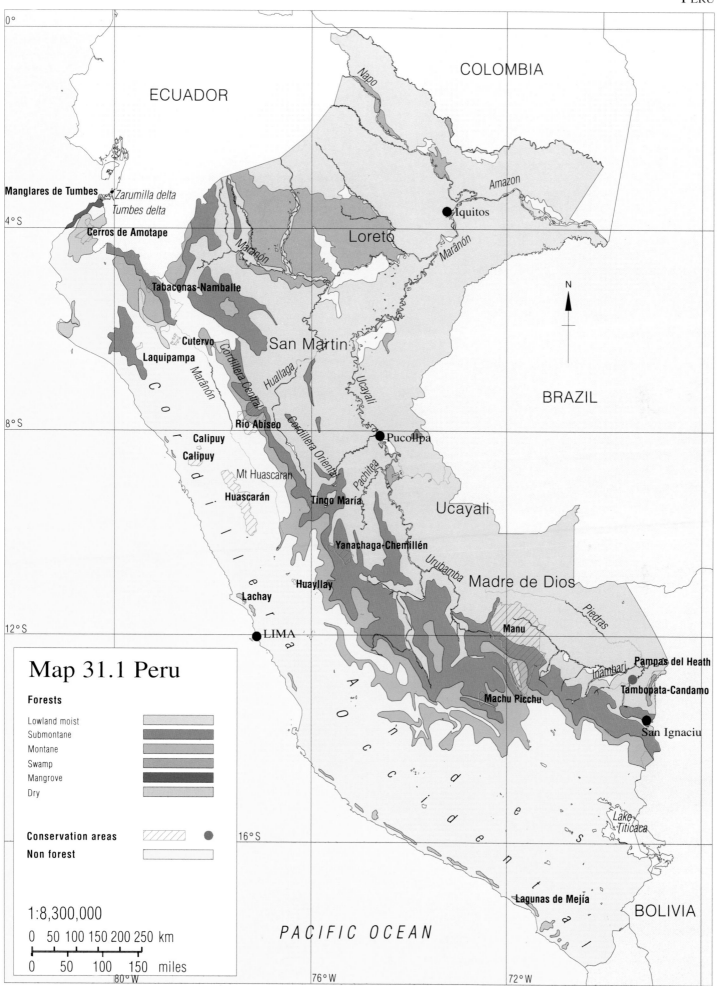

ECUADOR

COLOMBIA

Napo

Manglares de Tumbes

Zarumilla delta
Tumbes delta

Loreto

Amazon

Iquitos

4°S

Cerros de Amotape

Marañón

Marañón

N

Tabaconas-Namballe

Cutervo

San Martín

Laquipampa

Cordillera Central

Huallaga

Ucayali

BRAZIL

Marañón

8°S

Río Abiseo

Cordillera Oriental

Pucollpa

Calipuy

Calipuy

Pachitea

Mt Huascarán

Huascarán

Tingo María

Ucayali

Yanachaga-Chemillén

Urubamba

Madre de Dios

Huayllay

Piedras

Lachay

12°S

Manu

LIMA

Pampas del Heath

Inambari

Machu Picchu

Tambopata-Candamo

San Ignaciu

Map 31.1 Peru

Forests

Lowland moist	
Submontane	
Montane	
Swamp	
Mangrove	
Dry	

Conservation areas ⬤

Non forest

16°S

Lake Titicaca

1:8,300,000

0 50 100 150 200 250 km

0   50   100   150 miles

Lagunas de Mejía

BOLIVIA

PACIFIC OCEAN

80°W

76°W

72°W

Cordillera Occidental

Table 31.3 Production, imports, exports and national use of processed wood in 1990 (000 cu. m)

Item	Production	Imports	Exports	National Use
Sawn wood	489.3	0.2	1.3	488.2
Plywood	23.7	–	–	23.7
Wood in sheets	1.7	–	–	1.7
Parquet	12.6	–	0.5	12.1
Decorative boards	1.6	–	0.1	1.5
Sleepers	2.4	0.4	–	2.8
Total	531.3	0.6	1.9	530

Source: DGFF (1990)

This is because their suppliers are mainly small-scale operators with low productivity, working in small areas and depending on rivers to transport logs. This lack of raw materials is a serious problem for the wood processing industry. Most timber is consumed within Peru with only 1900 cu. m, or less than one per cent, being exported (Table 31.3).

Several forest management and silviculture systems have been studied in the Peruvian Amazon. In Jenaro Herrera, research work on improvement of forest strip systems have been carried out in collaboration with the Swiss Technical Cooperation COTESU (Cooperacion Tecnica Suiza) and the Peruvian Amazon Research Institute IIAP (Instituto de Investigaciones de la Amazonia Peruana). In the Alexander Von Humboldt National Forest, systems based on natural regeneration have been studied by FAO and the Japanese Technical Cooperation (JICA). Similar projects have taken place in the Palcazu with the cooperation of the US-AID. Here, a strip management system has been developed and is currently being used by the Yanesha Forestry Cooperative (see Box 1).

The biological complexity of the Amazonian forests is an obstacle to their sustainable management. Several agencies have carried out forest management trials to favour selected species. However, almost all of them have encountered difficulties due to lack of knowledge of the ecology of commercially valuable species, to the low rate of growth of these species and to the high cost of suppressing natural competitors. Even with low royalties, the exploitation of two to five cu. m per ha of a few valuable species does not cover the costs of managing the natural forest.

Forests play an important role in the generation of income and supply of consumable products for local communities in Peru. They provide, amongst other things, construction materials, dyes, medicinal plants, edible fruits and ornamental species, some of which are extracted for commercial purposes. Rubber from *Hevea brasiliensis* and brazil nuts are two important commercial products collected by the local communities. They both require management programmes to improve their productivity and their quality. The estimated potential production of brazil nuts is 2100 metric tons (worth US$32 million) per year and of rubber it is 500 metric tons (worth US$700,000) each year.

The dry algarrobo forests are of vital importance because they control the expansion of the desert. In addition, they yield numerous products, such as timber, firewood and charcoal and provide fruit, flowers and young leaves which are eaten by humans and cattle. The hualtaco is also a very valuable species, its wood is used for floorboards. However, it should be put

---

MANAGEMENT OF FORESTS IN PALCAZU, THE CASE OF THE YANESH FOREST COOPERATIVE IN PASCO, PERU

The Yanesha Forest Cooperative (COFYAL) was founded in February 1986, with the purpose of managing the forests of the Yanesha communities of the Palcazu Valley. The forest management carried out by COFYAL began as part of a regional development project financed by USAID in the Palcazu Valley. The Peruvian Foundation for the Conservation of Nature, through its Tropical Forests Programme and WWF-US, have supported the plan since 1989 through technical assistance and funding to develop the Cooperative's management plan. Five Yanesha native communities form COFYAL and the objectives of the Cooperative are to create jobs for its members; to manage the forests in a way that the yields obtained are sustainable; and to maintain the integrity of the Yanesha ethnic group. It was also intended to establish a local industry that would use the timber from its forests in an integrated fashion.

The management plan for Yanesha, which is a tropical wet forest with an annual rainfall of 4000 mm and a very wide diversity of species, was designed by the Centro Científico Tropical (CCT), with headquarters in Costa Rica. The system used in the management of Yanesha forest is called *de franjas o fajas a tala rasa, o fajas protectoras* (full clearing strips or protection strips). It is based on ecological observation of gap-phase dynamics of tropical forests. This replicates the process of renovation of the forest that occurs after tree falls. It takes advantage of the rapid natural regeneration from the seed bank found in the tropical forest soils and from propagules that disperse into the gaps from the surrounding forest. The small "gap" size of the strips minimises disruption of the local climate. When the trees are cut to harvest the timber, the clearing is limited to long narrow strips 30 to 40 m wide, but of different lengths depending on the land's configuration. These strips are inserted in the natural forest, keeping the surrounding forest as a source of seeds. The felling cycle for this system is expected to be 40 years.

The use of all the wood is an important component of this management plan. There is a saw mill on the site to cut up the large trees and a carpentry workshop equipped for the manufacture of furniture. Smaller trees are preserved and used for fence posts and poles for telephone and electric lines. Any residual woody material is used for making charcoal.

Although still considered to be experimental, the project has already made some major steps. For instance, hardwoods, including lesser known species, have been exported to the US and UK to ecological agencies who pay better prices than national wood companies. The hardwoods are also sold nationally, mainly in Lima, and produce some income, though not much as yet. The preserved poles, after a slow start, are at present one of the main sources of income.

Quite apart from the financial aspects of the project, the existence of the Cooperative has helped the local communities who are committed to its success and the sustainable use of the forests.

COCA AND DEFORESTATION

The illegal growing of coca *Erythroxylum coca*, for the production of cocaine, is causing deforestation, especially in the forests of Peru and Bolivia. In addition, the chemical products used in the manufacture of cocaine paste are becoming major polluters of the regions' mountain streams and rivers. The fact that the coca is grown mainly on the hillsides of the upland forests increases the problems because of erosion and consequent flooding.

Although the existing data are not reliable, estimates indicate that, in Peru, as much as 7000 sq. km has been deforested to plant coca bushes (Dourojeanni, 1989). At present, 3000 sq. km are under production. After six months of growth, it is calculated that one hectare of coca, harvested three to five times in a year, will yield 2000 kg of cocaine per year, thereby providing an annual income of US$6000.

The coca leaf was sacred to the Incas and for centuries, neither its harvesting nor its traditional use, caused any environmental or social problems. The coca is, even now, an extremely important cultural element in the Andean world, many of the local people chew the leaves as a stimulant and it is also used in nutrition, medicine and for magical-religious purposes. The present ecological and social problems are a consequence of the demand for cocaine by North Americans and Europeans.

The governments of the region have been fighting the problem for many years, but have not managed to find any solution. The campesino who grows the coca is usually poor and there is no crop as profitable as coca. He is frequently coerced into coca cultivation by the drug dealers. Police action to eradicate the coca plantations through chemical or mechanical methods merely leads to the clear cutting of a neighbouring forest and the planting of more bushes. Rather than solving the problem, the police action moves it to forested areas that were previously free from the crop. Furthermore, the chemical products used in the eradication cause pollution problems.

Any attempt to solve the problem must include serious efforts to reduce the demand for cocaine, to achieve a more effective control of its illegal trade and to offer viable crop alternatives to the campesinos. This would involve making credit plans and technical assistance available to them as well as guaranteeing the market for the alternative products. In addition, the degraded soils must be restored using leguminous plants and forest fallows.

---

under total protection as these forests are already considerably reduced in extent.

The fauna from the forests plays an important role in the protein intake of the rural population, especially in Amazonia. In 1987, wildlife was the source of 13,000 metric tons of meat; it provides 50 per cent of the animal protein consumed (PNAF, 1987). This is equivalent to 65,000 head of cattle, but wildlife does not create the environmental problems that this number of livestock would cause (but see Box on Manu in Chapter 5).

Deforestation

Due to the lack of continuous and careful monitoring of the country's forest cover, there is no universally accepted figure for the rate of deforestation in Peru. A number of estimates have been reported. In 1982, Malleaux indicated an annual deforestation rate of 2800 sq. km; a rate of 2500 sq. km per year was estimated in PNAF (1991), while recent FAO figures (1993), give the annual rate of forest depletion as 2592 sq. km (this excludes forest in the dry deciduous, very dry and desert zones) or 0.4 per cent between 1981 and 1990. Including these zones increases annual deforestation to 2712 sq. km (FAO, 1993). Dourojeanni (1989) estimated total forest loss in the Peruvian Amazon to be 75,000 sq. km.

The main cause of deforestation in Peru is the invasion of the forests in the Selva region by campesinos, migrating from the Sierra in search of land. Chronic neglect from the country's successive governments has meant that there is considerable poverty in the Sierra and it is this that the campesinos are trying to escape. In addition, an aggressive official colonization process began in the 1960s. Road construction was increased, especially in the montane forests. A road, the *marginal de la Selva*, was planned to connect all the montane forest east of the Andes, from north to south of the country and finally merge into the highways of neighbouring countries. Although an agrarian reform programme was attempted in the 1970s, it failed, and the depressed situation of the Sierra, population growth and the violence of the 1980s, led to a continuous migration into the Selva, especially into the ecologically fragile montane forest. As in other Amazonian countries (see Chapter 7), the government chose to open up Amazonia to settlers rather than to confront the agrarian reforms needed in the Sierra.

In general, pasture lands are produced as part of the cycle of shifting agriculture. After the deforested land has had crops on it for a few years it is converted to pasture land. However, by then the quality of the pasture is so low that a single head of cattle needs up to seven ha grassland. The forest has been cleared explicitly for pasture, rather than for subsistence agriculture, in only a few places. This has occurred close to Pucallpa, in Madre de Dios, in San Martín and near Iquitos.

The illegal production of coca leaves occurs mostly in areas that were opened up for colonization under official plans. The total area occupied by coca plantations at present is thought to be between 2000 and 3000 sq. km (see Box 2).

Logging is rarely a direct cause of deforestation as, in general, few trees are extracted per hectare and there is little use of heavy machinery. However, roads built by the loggers open up the forest, thereby providing easy access for the invading campesinos. The internal communication roads and work sites constructed during oil exploration and exploitation also cause some forest clearing. However, these activities have little significant impact as no penetration roads are built, air and river transport is used instead.

Biodiversity

Peru is a country with an exceptionally high biological diversity. It has eight biogeographic provinces (Udvardy, 1975) and 84 of Holdridge's Life Zones with 17 transition zones. At the world level, Peru occupies second place for diversity of birds and primates and sixth place for mammals. In the Neotropics, it is second in importance for birds and primates, third for mammals, fourth for butterflies and fifth for reptiles, amphibians and angiosperms (Mittermeier and Werner, 1990). Table 31.4 shows

Table 31.4 Number of species identified worldwide, in the Neotropics and in Peru.

	Number of Species			Percentage in Peru	
Group	Worldwide	Neotropics	Peru	Worldwide	Neotropics
Amphibians	3,500	1,926	241	7	13
Reptiles	6,500	2,406	298	5	12
Birds	9,400	3,806	1,701	18	44
Mammals	4,000	1,232	359	9	29
Plants	400,000	150,000	35,000	9	23

Source: CDC-UNALM (1991)

the number of species in some floral and faunal groups in Peru, in the Neotropics and worldwide.

Peru's endemic animal species include 35 mammals, 90 birds, 69 reptiles, 96 amphibians and 50 fish. Endemism is highest in the areas thought to be Pleistocene refuges, such as Marañón, Huallaga, Pachitea-Ucayali, Chanchamayo-Apurimac, Urubamba, Inambari, Loreto and Napo.

Peru has more than 35,000 species of vascular plants, including at least 2300 species of orchids. Near Iquitos, 300 different species of trees may be found in one hectare (Gentry, 1988). The areas with the greatest diversity of flora are, first, the eastern slopes of the Andes and second, the lower selva. The dry northwestern forests are also species rich, while the coastal Lomas are the habitat of some seriously endangered endemic plant species.

Some of the world's most important crop plants originated in Peru. These include the potato, tomato and tobacco. Several medicinal plants, for instance cinchona or Peruvian bark (for quinine) and plants for industrial use also originated there. Other Andean crops, such as the grain called quinua *Chenopodium quinoa* and tarwi *Lupinus mutabilis*, a legume, are being increasingly cultivated outside Peru.

Thirty eight threatened mammals are found in Peru (Groombridge, 1993); these include the uakari *Cacajao calvus*, the yellow-tailed woolly monkey *Lagothrix flavicauda*, the mountain tapir *Tapirus pinchaque* and the giant otter *Pteronura brasiliensis*. A number of mammals are important food sources for local people; they include the collared and white-lipped peccary (*Tayassu tajacu* and *T. pecari*), the capybara *Hydrochaeris hydrochaeris*, the coati *Nasua nasua* and the nine-banded armadillo *Dasypus novemcinctus*.

There are 64 bird species listed as threatened in Peru, of which 30 are endemic (Collar *et al.*, 1992). Manu National Park is particularly rich in species, with 554 listed within the park's boundaries (Karr *et al.*, 1990). The bearded and white-winged guan (*Penelope barbata* and *P. albipennis*) are both threatened by the destruction of the forests in the north-west of Peru. The latter is endemic and may number no more than a few hundred individuals (Collar *et al.*, 1992). The majority of Peru's threatened endemics are in dry areas such as montane scrub, grassland and *Polylepis* woodland. Only one, the Selva cacique *Cacicus koepckeae*, is found in the forests of Amazonia, although the rufous throated antthrush *Formicarius rufifrons* is present in riverine forest in Manu. Several threatened species are found in the humid montane forests including the southern helmeted curassow *Pauxi unicornis* and the spot-winged parrotlet *Touit stictoptera*.

One species of amphibian is considered threatened. This is the endemic frog *Batrachophrynus macrostomus*. Threatened reptiles include the American crocodile *Crododylus acutus*, the

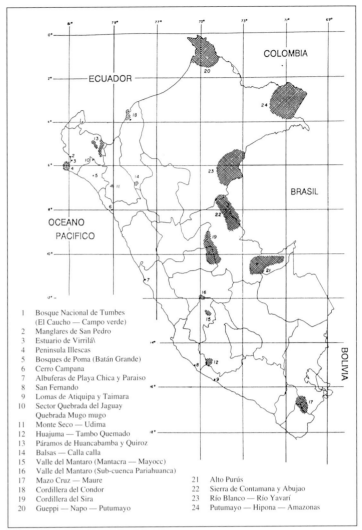

1	Bosque Nacional de Tumbes (El Caucho — Campo verde)	
2	Manglares de San Pedro	
3	Estuario de Virrilá\	
4	Peninsula Illescas	
5	Bosques de Poma (Batán Grande)	
6	Cerro Campana	
7	Albuferas de Playa Chica y Paraiso	
8	San Fernando	
9	Lomas de Atiquipa y Taimara	
10	Sector Quebrada del Jaguay Quebrada Mugo mugo	
11	Monte Seco — Udima	
12	Huajuma — Tambo Quemado	
13	Páramos de Huancabamba y Quiroz	
14	Balsas — Calla calla	
15	Valle del Mantaro (Mantacra — Mayocc)	
16	Valle del Mantaro (Sub-cuenca Pariahuanca)	
17	Mazo Cruz — Maure	21 Alto Purús
18	Cordillera del Condor	22 Sierra de Contamana y Abujao
19	Cordillera del Sira	23 Río Blanco — Río Yavarí
20	Gueppi — Napo — Putumayo	24 Putumayo — Hipona — Amazonas

Figure 31.1 Proposed protected areas of Peru
Source: CDC–UNALM (1991)

black caiman *Melanosuchus niger* and four river turtles as well as three sea turtles (Groombridge, 1993).

Number of fish and invertebrates are unknown. Only one fish *Arapaima gigas* is listed by IUCN. Invertebrates listed as threatened comprise one beetle and three butterflies — the latter includes the endemic *Styx infernalis* which is considered vulnerable to extinction (Groombridge, 1993).

Conservation Areas

Peru's National System of Conservation Units SINUC (Sistema Nacional de Unidades de Conservación) was established in 1975. It provided for the establishment of national parks, national reserves, national sanctuaries and historic sanctuaries. All exploitation is prohibited in the national parks, national sanctuaries and historic sanctuaries, but sustainable harvesting of wildlife is permitted in the national reserves. Legislation provided for other categories, but it was not until 1990 that they were incorporated in the extended system provided by the National System of State Protected Natural Areas (SINANPE — Sistema Nacional de Areas Naturales Protegidas por el Estado). The extra categories included in SINANPE are: communal reserves, hunting reserves, protection forests and national forests. In practice, the protection and national forests are not under the jurisdiction of SINANPE, but under that of the Forest Department. There is also a provisional category called a reserved zone, but this is used only until studies allow a permanent management category to be allotted to the area in question. Table 31.5 shows the protected areas in IUCN's categories I–IV.

In 1990, the Conservation Data Centre of La Molina National Agricultural University drew up a list of 24 proposed protected areas, indicating the areas that are a priority for the conservation of biodiversity at the national level (Figure 31.1).

Greater emphasis is needed on areas that allow sustainable use of resources by indigenous people. An example of these are the communal reserves, in which subsistence hunting and extraction are allowed, but logging is forbidden. The conservation of high basins, especially in the region of the yungas or high selva, will receive support through the establishment of a network of protection forests. These will contribute to the conservation of water sources, to the protection of biological diversity and will help prevent erosion in these ecologically important zones.

Three of Peru's protected areas (Manu, Huascarán and Río Abiseo) have been declared World Natural Heritage Sites, three (Manu, Huascarán and Noroeste) are Biosphere Reserves and Machu Picchu is a World Natural and Cultural Heritage Site.

Conservation Initiatives

Peru was the first South American country to begin preparing a National Forestry Action Plan. In 1988, the Plan's first draft was drawn up and it was reviewed and updated in 1991. The plan highlights the role of forestry in national development and its potential value for rural communities. The plan also gives priority to strengthening the system of protected areas and improving wildlife management in the country.

The 1975 Forestry and Wildlife Law has proved difficult to implement and has notably failed to regulate timber extraction. A team made up of representatives from the General Office for Forestry and Fauna, the Department of Forestry from La Molina National Agrarian University, the National Chamber of Forestry (CNF), the Peruvian Association of Forestry Experts (APIF), conservation NGOs and the Peruvian Society for Environmental Legislation (SPDA) have, after extensive public consultation, drafted a new law. This would divide the forests into permanent production forests and forest reserves. The earlier categories of national and open-access forests would be abandoned. The new law aims to concentrate the small scattered concessions and to zone the forests. Stumpage charges would generate income for silvicultural work in the productive forests. ITTO guidelines for sustainable management of the tropical forests are being included.

A process to prepare a national conservation strategy was ini-

Table 31.5 Conservation areas of Peru

Existing areas in IUCN's categories I–IV are included. For information on World Heritage Sites, Biosphere Reserves and Ramsar Sites, see Chapter 8.

National Parks	Area (sq. km)
Cerros de Amotape*	913
Cuervo	25
Huascarán*	3,400
Manu*	15,328
Río Abiseo*	2,745
Tingo María*	180
Yanachaga-Chemillén*	1,220
National Reserves	
Calipuy	640
Lachay*	51
National Sanctuaries	
Calipuy	5
Huayllay	68
Lagunas de Mejía	7
Manglares de Tumbes*	30
Pampas del Heath*	1,021
Tabaconas-Namballe*	295
Reserved Zones	
Laquipampa	113
Tambopata-Candamo*	14,789
Historical Sanctuaries	
Machu Picchu*	326
Total	41,156

* Area with forests within its boundaries as shown on Map 31.1.

Source: WCMC (unpublished data)

tiated in 1988. Several NGOs and two government agencies (the National Bureau for the Evaluation of Natural Resources, Oficina Nacional de Evaluacion de Recursos Naturales, and the National Institute for Planning, Institito Nacional de Planificacion) are taking the lead. In 1988, the Peruvian Foundation for the Conservation of Nature (FPCN) published a draft National Conservation Strategy (NCS). It is hoped that a presidential decree will make the NCS official by the end of 1993. The policies of the National Forestry Action Plan are based on the NCS. At least three of the country's 12 regions have been working on regional conservation strategies.

At present, several national and international NGOs (including WWF, TNC and CI) are collaborating with National Parks-Peru (the organisation responsible for directing SINANPE) in the management of the country's main parks, reserves and sanctuaries. With support from GTZ and the GEF, the master plan for SINANPE will be drawn up. A permanent fund for financing the system's management and administration has already been established. This collaborative effort guarantees long-term support for Peruvian protected areas. It strengthens their management and also favours the development of the rural communities living near the parks.

The National Conservation Strategy, the master plan for

River scenery, Manu National Park   (Caroline Harcourt)

SINANPE, the National Forestry Action Plan and the new forest legislation should provide a framework for conservation and sustainable use of forests, especially in the Amazon Region.

Parliament is examining a law to establish a National Council for the Environment. This council was provided for in the Environmental and Natural Resources Code that was adopted in 1990. The Code has represented a significant step forward for Peru in the field of conservation. Among other things, it makes environmental impact studies mandatory for all major development programmes.

There is a growing commitment to the cause of nature conservation in Peru. Both the government and the general public are increasingly aware of the environmental problems in the country. There are over 80 local, national and international NGOs in the country concerned with conservation issues. They are coordinated by the Peruvian Environmental Network. As a result, environmental legislation has improved, a more environmentally oriented planning of development occurs and more money is allocated to conservation, especially at the level of the regional governments.

References

CDC/UNALM (1991). *Plan Director del Sistema Nacional de Unidades de Conservación (SINUC), Una Aproximación Desde la Diversidad Biológica*. Centro de Datos para la Conservación, Universidad Nacional Agraria La Molina, Lima. 170 pp.

Collar, N.J., Gonzaga, L.P., Krabbe, N., Madroño Nieto, A., Naranjo, L.G., Parker III, T.A. and Wege, D.C. (1992). *Threatened Birds of the Americas. The ICBP/IUCN Red Data Book*. ICBP, Cambridge, U.K.

DGFF (1990). *Perú Forestal en Números*. Dirección General Forestal y de Fauna, Lima, Peru.

Dourojeanni, M. (1989). *Amazonia Peruana ¿Qué Hacer?*. Centro de Estudios Teológicos de la Amazonia. Iquitos. 444 pp.

Echevarría, J. and Sarabia, J. (1993). Mangroves of Peru. In: *Conservation and Sustainable Utilization of Mangrove Forests in Latin America and Africa Regions. Part 1: Latin America*. ITTO/ISME Project PD114/90(F). Pp. 43–53.

FAO (1993). *Forest resource assessment 1990: tropical countries*. FAO Forestry Paper 112. FAO, Rome, Italy.

Gentry, A. (1988). Tree species richness of Upper Amazonian forests. *Proceedings of the National Academy of Science USA* 25: 156–159.

Goombridge, B. (Ed). (1993). *1994 IUCN Red List of Threatened Animals*. IUCN Gland, Switzerland and Cambridge, U.K.

Karr, J.R., Robinson, S., Blake, J.G. and Bierregaard Jr., R.O. (1990). Birds of four Neotropical forests. In: *Four Neotropical Rainforests*. Pp. 237–269. Gentry, A.H. (ed.). Yale University Press, London

Mittermeier, R. and Werner, T.B. (1990). Wealth of plants and animals unites "megadiversity" countries. *Tropics*: 4(1): 1, 4–5.

PNAF (1987). *Plan Nacional de Acción Forestal 1988–2000*. Dirección General Forestal y de Fauna/Agencia Canadiense para el Desarrollo Internacional. Lima. 158 pp.

PNAF (1991). *Plan Nacional de Acción Forestal del Perú*. Dirección General Forestal y de Fauna/Programa Nacional de Acción Forestal. Lima. 114 pp.

Prance, G.T. (1989). American tropical forests. In: *Tropical Rain Forest Ecosystems: Biogeographical and Ecological Studies*. Pp. 99–132. Lieth, H and Werger, M.J.A. (eds). Ecosystems of the World 14B. Elsevier, Oxford, U.K.

Udvardy (1975). *A Classification of the Biogeographic Provinces of the World*. IUCN Occasional Papers 18: 1–48. IUCN, Morges, Switzerland.

Authors: Gustavo Suárez de Freitas C. Executive Director, Peruvian Foundation for the Conservation of Nature, with the collaboration of Javier Arce (FPCN) and Jaime Melo P. (UNA La Molina). Contributions from Fernando Ghersi, IUCN, Gland, Switzerland.

Map 31.1   Peru

Forest data have been digitised from a dyeline map entitled *Mapa Integrado de Ecosistemas Forestales del Peru Colombia y Venezuela* (nd), compiled under FAO project GCP/RLA/081/JPN at a scale of 1:5,000,000. This regional vegetation map covers Peru, Colombia and Venezuela. No information is available regarding the sources or dates of the data portrayed on this map.

Twenty six land use/vegetation categories are found within the boundaries of Peru. Of these, 13 have been included and harmonised into the broad forest categories shown in this Atlas. Map 31.1 shows the following forest types:

Lowland moist forest —	*Bosque Alto Denso, Bosque Bajo Denso* within the category *Vegetacion de Terrazas Altas y Superficies Denudadas*; *Bosque Alto Denso* within the category *Llanuria Aluvial no Inundable*; and *Bosques Riberenos* within the category *Llanura Aluvial Inundadble*.
Inland swamp forest —	*Pantanos Arboreas con Palmas* within *Llanura Aluvial Inundable*.
Mangrove —	*Manglares* within *Llanura Aluvial Inundable*.
Submontane forest —	*Bosque Alto Denso* and *Bosque Bajo Denso* within the category *Pie de Monte*; and *Bosque Alto Denso, Bosque Bajo Denso* within the category *Sub Montano*.
Montane forest —	*Bosque Bajo Denso* within the category *Montano*.
Dry forest —	*Sabana Arborea* and *Sabana Arborea-Arbustiva (mixta)* within the category *Selva Baja*. The *mixta* category includes the mist induced lomas formations which occur along the coast.

Inevitably, because the source map is at a regional scale, details of the smaller areas of forest and non-forest areas will have been lost. For example dry forests in the interandean valleys, such as the Maranon, are not shown. The data displayed on Map 31.1, therefore, provide only an outline of existing forest cover. It would not be realistic to measure forest areas from it and consequently forest statistics derived from Map 31.1 have not been included in this Atlas.

Spatial information of Peruvian protected areas was digitised from a dyeline map *El Perú y sus Areas Naturales Protegidas* (1991), prepared at a scale of 1:2 million by the Fundación Peruana para la Conservación de la Naturaleza, Peru. Nine different designations are listed on the source map, with locations of 44 areas, including protection forests and national forests. Only conservation areas which are classified as IUCN categories I–IV are mapped in this Atlas.

32 Surinam

Country area*	146,986 sq. km
Land area*	143,662 sq. km
Population (mid-1994)	0.4 million
Population growth rate	1.6 per cent
Population projected to 2025	0.6 million
Gross national product per capita (1992)	US$3700
Forest cover for 1978 (see Map)	133,284 sq. km+
Forest cover for 1990 (FAO, 1993)	147,680 sq. km
Annual deforestation rate 1981–1990	0.1 per cent
Industrial roundwood production	135,000 cu. m
Industrial roundwood export	1000 cu. m
Fuelwood and charcoal	19,000 cu. m
Processed wood production	51,000 cu. m
Processed wood export	3000 cu. m

* The borders between the Guianas are disputed and in this instance we have used figures from Map 32.1 rather than FAO's figures of 163,270 and 156,000 sq. km respectively.

+This figure would be increased by around 17,000 sq. km if the boundary disputes were settled in Surinam's favour.

Surinam lies in the centre of the Guayana biotic province. Forest covers around 90 per cent of the country's land area with seasonal evergreen forests making up the majority of this. The population density is very low and, with 90 per cent of the people concentrated in the coastal plain, large areas of Surinam are uninhabited.

The military came to power in 1980 and were responsible for serious violations of human rights. As a result, The Netherlands suspended development aid in 1982 and the economy began to fail. A dramatic decline in the timber industry was the result of a shortage of foreign investment. In addition, the principal timber production areas were inaccessible between 1986 and 1989 due to fighting between the military regime and revolutionary groups in the interior of the country. Democracy was restored in 1989 and economic and social prospects now appear to be much better. In principle, this might be expected to result in increased activity by the timber industry and a rise in development pressure on forest lands. As yet, however, the forests remain secure.

The natural vegetation in Surinam has been less disturbed than that in most Central and South American countries. An excellent system of protected areas exists and these cover all major ecosystems in the coastal and savanna zones, as well as several significant areas in the interior.

INTRODUCTION

Surinam was formerly a Dutch colony but has been an independent republic since 1975. The country has a typical tropical climate. The capital, Paramaribo, on the coast has an average daily temperature of 27.3°C and an annual daily range of only 2°C. Mean rainfall varies between 1500 mm on the coast to almost 3000 mm in the higher parts of the centre and south-east of Surinam. There are two rainy seasons, a major one from around the end of April to mid-August and a minor one from December to February.

Geologically, Surinam is divided into a mountainous region and a coastal region. The mountainous region, which covers more than 80 per cent of the country, consists almost entirely of a Precambrian rock formation which is part of the Guayana Shield. The highest point is Juliana Top at 1230 m above sea level in the Wilhelmina Mountain range. Some of the Guyana Shield is covered in Roraima sandstones, which form tepuis or table mountains. Tafleberg, 1026 m high in central Surinam, is one of these. Along the northern edge of the Guayana Shield lies the Savanna Belt (also known as the Zanderij formation or Cover Landscape), then the Old Coastal Plain and finally the Young Coastal Plain (Figure 32.1). The Savanna Belt, located 10–100 m above sea level, is a dissected plain lying on quartz rich sand sediments. The Old Coastal Plain is only 1–12 m above sea level and consists mostly of marine sediments that

were deposited at times of higher sea levels during the Pleistocene. The Young Coastal Plain is made up of Holocene swamp clays and sand and shell ridges; it lies at 0–4 m above sea level. It is these geomorphological features, rather than climate, that are responsible for the ecological and forest diversity in Surinam (Mittermeier *et al.*, 1990).

The average population density in Surinam is less than three inhabitants per sq. km. However, around 90 per cent of the population is concentrated in the capital city, Paramaribo, and in small communities in the coastal plain, leaving large areas of the interior uninhabited. The country's indigenous inhabitants are Amerindians, but as early as the sixteenth century different ethnic groups from Africa, Indonesia and India were brought to Surinam. As a result, nowadays the population consists of Hindustani (37 per cent), Creoles (31 per cent), Javanese (15 per cent), Afro-americans (10 per cent), Amerindians (3 per cent) and a variety of other small communities including Chinese and Europeans. The Afro-americans represent the only intact communities descended from runaway slaves remaining in the New World (Mittermeier *et al.*, 1990). The official language is Dutch, but Sranan-Tonga is the *lingua franca* of the country.

Almost all economic activity takes place in the northern part of the country, most within a radius of 30 km of the capital (Jonkers, 1987). The economy is dominated by the bauxite

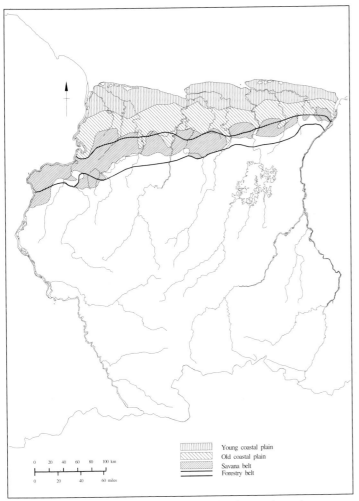

Figure 32.1 The major regions of Surinam, based on geomorphology, showing the forestry belt which is the main production area   *Source:* after M. Hermeies *et al* (1990); Boxman *et al* (1987)

industry, which accounted for 80.7 per cent of the total value of exports in 1980 (SPS, 1988). Rice, bananas, citrus, oil palm, coconuts, peanuts and vegetables are the only crops raised on a commercial scale. These are predominantly grown in the Young Coastal Plain. In the interior, most people are subsistence farmers. The forestry sector contributes only 1.5 per cent to GNP and 2.5 per cent to export figures (Jonkers, 1987).

The Forests

The most comprehensive studies of the forest vegetation of Surinam are by Lindeman (1953), Lindeman and Moolenaar (1959), Lindeman and Mori (1989) and in the *Suriname Planatlas* (SPS, 1988). The classifications of the forests in these publications are different and in this Atlas we have generally followed that given in the *Suriname Planatlas*.

The swamp forests in the country are called marsh forests by Lindeman and Mori (1989) and are defined as forests that have waterlogged soils for part of the year and are dry for the remainder of the year.

Low swamp forests are found in the Young Coastal Plain, they cover about three per cent of Surinam's land area. They are dominated by the following tree species: *Mauritia flexuosa*, *Chrysobalanus icaco, Annona glabra, Erythrina glauca, Triplaris surinamensis, Pterocarpus officinalis* and *Tabebuia insignis*. Although high swamp forests may occur in the Young Coastal Plain, along creeks and rivers of the Savanna Belt and

in the hilly/mountainous interior, they occur predominantly in the Old Coastal Plain. This forest type covers about two per cent of the country. In the shallow fresh-water swamps, the mixed *Virola surinamensis/Symphonia globulifera/Euterpe oleracea* forest forms the vegetation at the final stage of succession. In other places *Hura crepitans* may dominate. In the central part of the Old Coastal Plain, the species-poor *Crudia glaberrima-Macrolobium acaciifolium* forest is the climax vegetation.

Forests described as high seasonal swamp forests in *Suriname Planatlas* are called swamp forests by Lindeman and Mori (1989). Following Beard (1944), they consider the forests that grow on soils that never completely dry out to be swamp forests.

High seasonal swamp forests are found on poorly drained soils, low ridges, levees of rivers and plateaux of the coastal plain, as well as along creeks and rivers in the Savanna Belt and in the interior. They cover three per cent of Surinam's land area. Many of these forests are dominated by a single tree species, for instance the palm *Euterpe oleracea*. Some isolated forests are dominated by *Hura crepitans*. *Mora excelsa* trees predominate on the levees of the larger rivers in western Surinam.

Lindeman and Mori (1989) describe the high dryland forests (SPS, 1988) as seasonal evergreen forests. They have been the subject of numerous and detailed studies. Lindeman (1953), Lindeman and Moolenaar (1959), Maas (1971) and Schulz (1960) provide descriptions of this forest type, which covers about 80 per cent of Surinam. These forests thrive on the well-drained soils of the higher ridges, levees and plateaux of the coastal plain, on the loamy sands within the Savanna Belt and in the hilly/mountainous areas that do not desiccate seasonally.

Structurally similar forests often differ greatly in species composition from one area to another. Only in very small areas do single tree species predominate. In western Surinam, in the Savanna Belt, species such as *Mora gonggrijpii, Aspidosperma excelsa* and *Ocotea rodiaei* can form isolated stands. In the hilly interior, small concentrations of trees such as *Vouacapoua americana, Manilkara bidentata* or *Bertholletia excelsa* are found.

Mountains with peaks over 500 m are located in western and south-central Surinam and the forests (considered to be submontane, see Granville, 1988) on these account for about three per cent of the land area of Surinam. In general, trees are smaller, tree species diversity falls and cryptogams are more abundant (Lindeman and Mori, 1989). The vegetation of the upper reaches of Tafleberg is a mosaic of elfin woodland, montane rain forest, savanna on rocky soils and grass-edge savanna mountain. The forest on this tepuis is somewhat different to that on other high points in the country, these have not yet been the subject of detailed studies.

High and low xerophytic forests cover at least two per cent of the country. In Surinam, the forest transition from savanna to high dryland forest is usually referred to as savanna forest (Lindeman, 1953). The high xerophytic (or high savanna) forest is a two-storeyed dry evergreen formation with a closed upper canopy reaching 25–30 m in height; it commonly occurs on deep white sands (FAO/UNEP, 1981). Although high xerophytic forests are usually mixed in composition, in many places they are dominated by such trees as *Eperua falcata, Humiria balsamifera, Dimorphandra conjugata, Swartzia bannia* and others (SPS, 1988). The low xerophytic forest varies in height from 10–20 m, but does not have different storeys. It is a very dense, closed formation and generally fairly homogeneous (FAO/UNEP, 1981). The species mentioned above (with the exception of *Eperua falcata*) can dominate, while *Clusia fockeana* and *Licania incana* may also be important.

Small patches of savanna are found scattered over the whole forest area of Surinam but they cover only one per cent of the country in total.

Mangroves

The coastal area consists largely of vast tidal mudflats, the higher parts covered with black mangroves *Avicennia germinans*. The estuarine zone also comprises narrow sand and shell beaches and mangrove swamps that are bordered inland by shallow saline and brackish lagoons (Spaans and de Jong, 1982). Red mangrove *Rhizophora* spp. forests are found along the muddy, downstream riverbanks. Mangrove forests cover 1150 sq. km, according to SPS (1988), while Map 32.1 shows them as covering an area of 1088 sq. km (Table 32.2). It should be noted, however, that these estimates are for over 15 years ago (see Map Legend). The vegetation of the brackish coastal area (salt marshes, brackish lagoons, sandy beaches and coastal ridges) covers about 1600 sq. km or one per cent of Surinam.

The estuarine zone is important as a natural breeding and nursery ground for commercially valuable species of fish and shrimps. This zone is of critical importance as a nesting area for the South American endemic scarlet ibis *Eudocimus ruber* (Held, 1990). It also forms a favourite breeding area for large numbers of egrets and herons (de Jong and Spaans, 1984). The coast is by far the most important wintering area within South America for the shorebirds of boreal and arctic North America (Spaans and Baal, 1990). The coast also has internationally significant nesting beaches for three species of sea turtles, the leatherback *Dermochelys coriacea*, the green turtle *Chelonia mydas* and the olive ridley *Lepidochelys olivacea*. Surinam has been a leader in turtle research for many years (Schulz, 1975).

Except for some habitat destruction by rice cultivation, the estuarine ecosystem is undamaged (Spaans and Baal, 1990; Mittermeier *et al.*, 1990). Part of the estuarine zone, about 683 sq. km, of the coastal wetlands, has already been declared as a multiple-use management area, while legislation is pending for a further 1220 sq. km (Werkhoven and Held, 1989).

Forest Resources and Management

According to the latest FAO (1993) estimate, forest in Surinam covers 147,680 sq. km, all in the tropical rain and moist deciduous forest zones, of this 146,050 sq. km is closed broadleaved forest. The figures from *Suriname Plantatlas* indicate that 148,550 sq. km of forest is found in the country; the forest types making up this total are indicated in Table 32.1.

Although Map 32.1 has been digitised from the *Suriname Planatlas* (see Map Legend), the total forest figure measured from this map (Table 32.2) is somewhat lower than that indicated in Table 32.1. The probable reason for the differences is that the borders between the Guianas are disputed. In the *Suriname Planatlas* the area of the country is considered to be 164,000 sq. km, whereas here the boundary of the country as shown on Mundocarte (see Chapter 1) is used; this gives a country area of only 146,986 sq. km. The disputed areas, nearly 17,000 sq. km, are almost entirely covered with lowland forest and the addition of this to the total forest figure shown in Table 32.2 makes it similar to the other estimates of forest cover in the country. Calculations using FAO's figures, those in the Surinam Planatlas and Map 32.1 all lead to the same conclusion, i.e. between 90 and 91 per cent of the country (NB not land area) is clothed in forest.

A narrow band of forest, the "forestry belt" located immediately to the south of the savannas is the only area considered to have commercial timber production potential (Figure 32.1).

Table 32.1   Forest types in Surinam

Forest type	Area (sq. km)
High dryland forest	133,600
Savanna forest (xerophytic forest)	1,850
Swamp forest	7,250
Seasonal swamp forest	4,700
Mangrove forest	1,150
Total	148,550

Source: SPS (1988)

South of this belt, hilly land makes road construction very expensive, while transport of logs by water is not possible. In the *Suriname Planatlas* (SPS, 1988), the total area of the forestry belt is stated to be 22,000 sq. km, while Vink (1970) regards its total area to be about 14,000 sq. km. Vink (1970) further considers that in view of topography and stand composition only some 6000 sq. km are exploitable; this figure includes some xerophytic forests north of the actual belt.

The forestry belt consists of rain forest (70 per cent), seasonal swamp forest (13 per cent) and xerophytic forest (six per cent). The remaining 11 per cent consists of forest types which are of less economic importance. There are, in addition, some swamp forest complexes in the coastal plain, with economically valuable *Virola surinamensis* stands (for plywood), which cover an area of about 1000 sq. km. The area of timber production forest is, therefore, small in relation to the total area of Surinam.

The rain forest is rich in tree species, and patches of forest in which one species predominates are unusual (de Graaf, 1986). Inventories carried out by the Surinam Forest Service in this forest type have shown that more than 300 tree species can attain a diameter of 25 cm or more. The average timber volume is 200 cu. m per hectare. About 50 tree species have commercial value, but of these only 10 to 15 species are commonly used (Vink, 1977).

About 220 sq. km of previously exploited natural forest have been replanted with indigenous and exotic species. The indigenous species used for reforestation include *Virola surinamensis*, *Carapa procera*, *Mora excelsa*, *Cedrela odorata*, and *Simarouba amara*. Exotic species belonging to the genera *Pinus*, *Eucalyptus*, *Gmelina*, *Aucoumea*, and *Cordia* are also planted. Of the 220 sq. km, some 80 sq. km have been replanted

Table 32.2   Estimates of forest extent in Surinam

Forests	Area (sq. km)	% of land area[°]
Lowland moist	110,564	77.0
Submontane*	5,147	3.6
Dry	3,471	2.4
Swamp forest[+]	13,014	9.1
Mangrove	1,088	0.8
Total	133,284	92.8

[°]   as measured from Map 32.1

*   at greater than 500 m (see text)

[+]   includes seasonal swamp forest

Based on analysis of Map 32.1. See Map Legend on p. 311 for details of sources.

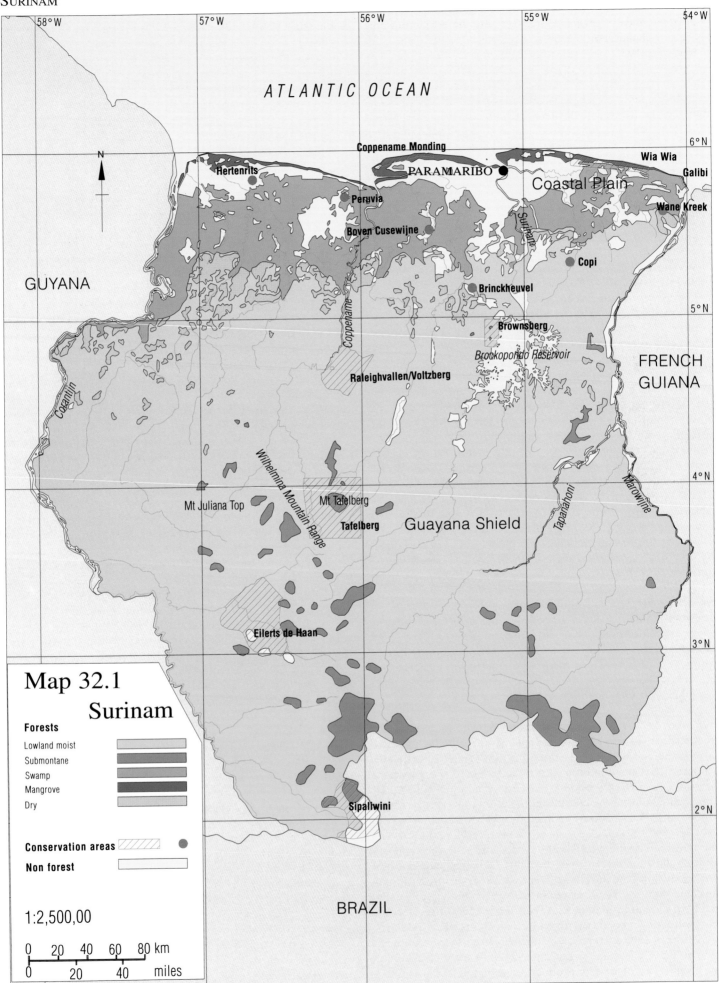

ATLANTIC OCEAN

Coppename Monding

PARAMARIBO

Wia Wia

Galibi

Coastal Plain

Hertenrits

Wane Kreek

Peruvia

Boven Cusewijne

Copi

GUYANA

Brinckheuvel

Brownsberg

Brokopondo Reservoir

FRENCH
GUIANA

Raleighvallen/Voltzberg

Mt Juliana Top

Mt Tafelberg

Tafelberg

Guayana Shield

Eilerts de Haan

Sipaliwini

Map 32.1

Surinam

Forests

Lowland moist

Submontane

Swamp

Mangrove

Dry

Conservation areas

Non forest

1:2,500,00

0   20   40   60   80 km

0   20   40
miles

BRAZIL

with pure stands of *Pinus caribaea*, while the remaining area has been replanted using line and spot planting techniques.

Since the 1950s, efforts have been made to develop a silvicultural system for the rain forest of Surinam (Boxman *et al.*, 1987). A polycyclic system for sustained timber production has been developed by a project which forms part of the UNESCO Man and the Biosphere Programme. This system is referred to as the CELOS Silvicultural System. It is based on an improved harvesting technique and post-harvest silvicultural treatments (Jonkers and Schmidt, 1984; see Box). De Graaf (1982) considers that the forests of Surinam are suitable for extensive "selection" forest management systems as there are large expanses of *terra-firma* forest and little danger of agricultural encroachment even in forests rendered accessible by logging.

SILVICULTURE IN SURINAM

Attempts to devise silvicultural methods for Surinam's native species began early this century, shortly after the formation of a forest service. These activities came to an end when the forest service was abolished in 1925, and most of the data gathered were subsequently lost. However, some of the early trial plots still existed when the forest service was reinstated after World War II, and an assessment of the results was made in 1948.

The growth rates of the indigenous species were encouraging, but *Pinus caribaea* plantations were considered more promising. Silviculture therefore focused on the establishment of plantations of exotic species until the 1970s, and management of natural forest outside nature reserves remained restricted to regulating logging operations. The Forestry Department was, nevertheless, interested in research on the ecology and silviculture of natural forest. After 1965, this research was continued by the Centre for Agricultural Research in Surinam (Celos).

In the 1980s, these efforts resulted in the Celos Management System (CMS) being devised. CMS is a polycyclic system, in which only the largest trees are harvested, while the smaller individuals of marketable species are retained for future harvests. It includes a logging method, the Celos Harvesting System, and a series of silvicultural interventions, referred to as the Celos Silvicultural System (CSS).

CMS is meant for management units of at least 250 sq. km. For each unit, a management plan is prepared based on reconnaissance mapping of forest composition and terrain characteristics. The areas allocated as production forest are divided into compartments of about 2 sq. km and a network of roads is planned to allow timber transport by truck from the compartments to the processing plant. In a standard unit of 250 sq. km, five compartments are logged annually, giving a felling cycle of 25 years.

The Celos Harvesting System was devised to reduce logging damage and to improve harvesting efficiency. Before harvesting begins, compartment boundaries are demarcated and truck roads constructed. Then, in each compartment, all harvestable trees are enumerated and mapped. These maps, which also show important terrain characteristics, are used to plan a network of main skid trails, which form the (semi)-permanent infrastructure of a compartment, and branch trails. The main trails, which are about 100 m apart, are opened up before felling.

Approximately seven large trees are felled per ha, giving a yield of around 20 cu. m in each hectare. Directional felling is applied so that the felled stems make an angle of 30 to 60 degrees to the adjacent main trail whenever possible. The stems are then winched to the main trail, or, if the stem is ill-positioned or too heavy for winching, a branch trail is opened up, forming the shortest connection between the main trail and the felled stem. The stems are subsequently skidded to the truck road and loaded on a lorry for further transport. This logging method minimizes skidding damage and reduces skidding costs. Another advantage is that the main trails can be used again during the second harvest, 20–25 years later.

Silvicultural operations start about one year after logging. Felling creates sufficient openings in the canopy for natural regeneration, therefore the main aim of CSS is to stimulate the growth of the remaining timber trees. This is done by eliminating a considerable number of trees without commercial value and cutting thick lianas.

Two different approaches have been developed to select trees to be eliminated. One is based on the assumption that the average stand density should be reduced to a predetermined level, and uses inventory data to compute a minimum diameter limit of 20 cm or more for non-commercial trees to be eradicated. The other approach tends to be less drastic and applies two fixed stem diameter limits: the lower limit of 20 cm applies for non-commercial trees in the immediate vicinity of a commercial tree, the higher one of 40 cm for other non-commercial trees.

Trees to be eliminated are to die slowly and to remain standing. This is achieved by ring-barking, supplemented by small doses of arboricide where necessary. In this way, light conditions are improved without abrupt changes in microclimate or major damage caused by falling trees. In addition, nutrients stored in the killed phytomass gradually become available to the remaining vegetation.

The silvicultural treatment leads to rapid growth of the remaining trees. After 8 to 10 years, the canopy is closed again and growth rates quickly decline. A second treatment is then required to keep increment of commercial trees at a high level. This second treatment is comparable to the first one, although less drastic and with more emphasis on selection within the commercial stand.

Application of CMS results in a threefold increase in diameter growth to about one cm per year and annual volume increment is about four cu. m/ha. After 20 to 25 years, a second yield of 20 cu. m/ha or more can be obtained, and the forest will be substantially richer in commercial trees after this second harvest than after the first one.

In the mid 1980s, guerilla groups became active in the rain forests of Surinam, and consequently logging operations had to be discontinued in virtually the whole country. This impeded the application of the Celos Management System. In 1992, the various guerilla groups signed a peace treaty with the government, and the timber industry gradually resumed its logging activities. A new forest law was gazetted at almost the same time. It provides a legal basis and a new start for sustainable forest management in Surinam.

Source: Dr. W.B.J. Jonkers

Slightly more than 19,620 sq. km of exploitable forests have been leased to private and para-statal companies in the form of timber concessions, which are renewed on a yearly basis. The Timber Ordinance of 1947 regulated exploitation of timber and forest products on state-owned land. This old timber law was replaced by new legislation — the Forestry Law — in August 1992. In addition to the industrial timber operations, some tribal inhabitants of the interior have been granted cutting licenses for an indefinite period. These cover an area of 6,600 sq. km.

Timber production has decreased dramatically since 1980. In that year, roundwood production was estimated at about 310,000 cu. m, while in 1989 it was only 120,000 cu. m. The value of wood exports dropped from US$12 million in 1980 to about US$1.42 million in 1989. The forestry sector has never contributed more than 1.5 per cent to the GNP and 2.5 per cent to export earnings.

Deforestation

FAO (1993) estimates that between the years of 1981 and 1990, Surinam lost 127 sq. km of forest each year. This is an annual rate of only 0.1 per cent, one of the lowest in the tropical world. Between 1986 and 1989, the armed struggle in the interior made timber production areas inaccessible and thereby reduced the deforestation rate to some extent.

The *Suriname Planatlas* (SPS, 1988) gives information on land use in Surinam and from this it has been possible to calculate the area of forest cleared for each purpose (Table 32.3).

In the eastern and central parts of the country, concessions were granted for the mining of bauxite in areas of 200 and 120 sq. km respectively. The mines themselves have not caused significant deforestation, but a dam constructed on the Surinam River to supply the aluminium smelter with electrical energy, inundated 1560 sq. km of forest, forming the Brokopondo Reservoir.

Plantations of indigenous and exotic trees, occupy 220 sq. km of land but the natural forest these replaced had been previously exploited. As yet, only one oilfield, covering an area of 34 sq. km, has been brought into production so this is not a major cause of deforestation.

Commercial agricultural land covers about 620 sq. km, or 0.4 per cent of the land area. Cattle raising takes place only on enclosed pastures in the coastal plain, and on one small experimental farm in the interior. Shifting cultivation occupies an estimated 1700 sq. km, about 10 per cent of which is planted at any one time (Jonkers, 1987). In total, only 3 per cent of Surinam has been brought under cultivation and, because of the inaccessibility of the interior, one may assume that deforestation for this purpose will always be low.

Table 32.3 Land-use in Surinam

Land Use	Area (sq. km)
Bauxite mining	320
Forest plantations	220
Oil exploitation	34
Agriculture and animal husbandry	650
Shifting cultivation	1,700
Built-up areas and abandoned land	2,050
Total	4,974

Source: Stichting Planbureau Suriname (1988).

Biodiversity

The botanical inventory of the Guianas, and especially of Surinam, is one of the more comprehensive in South America. Surinam is a small but important part of the larger Guayanan floristic province and possesses between 4000 and 4500 species of angiosperms (Lindeman and Mori, 1989). There are 188 endemic species of angiosperms and 550 species are considered rare, while a further 26 species are both endemic and rare (Mittermeier *et al.*, 1990). According to Kramer (1978), 290 species of ferns and fern-allies are known from Surinam. Recent data indicate that only three of these are endemic.

The cryptogams have not been well studied. About 340 species of lichens have been reported from the Guianas (Hekking and Sipman, 1988). The total number of mosses, liverworts, algae, fungi and bacteria is unknown.

Mittermeier *at al.*, (1990) give lists of the vertebrate species found in Surinam. One hundred and eighty four species of mammals are known to occur, including four introduced species. Two bats, *Tonatia schulzi* and *Molossops neglectus*, are endemic. Of the eight primates that occur, only one, the black spider monkey *Ateles paniscus*, is listed as threatened by IUCN (Groombridge, 1993) and this is mainly because of its declining status in other parts of its range (Baal *et al.*, 1988). This is probably also true for the other five terrestrial, globally threatened mammal species — the bush dog *Speothos venaticus*, the little spotted cat *Leopardus tigrinus*, the margay *Leopardus wiedii*, the giant otter *Pteronura brasiliensis*, giant anteater *Myrmecophaga tridactyla* and the giant armadillo *Priodontes maximus* — that occur in Surinam.

Six hundred and seventy bird species are known from the country, but none of these is endemic (Mittermeier *et al.*, 1990). Further species will undoubtedly be recorded when inventories of the interior are completed. The only threatened species to occur in Surinam is the rufous-sided pygmy-tyrant *Euscarthmus rufomarginatus* (Collar *et al.*, 1992), which is found in savanna regions, not forest.

The reptiles are represented by 156 species with one endemic *Amphisbaena myersi*. One threatened river turtle *Podocnemis unifilis* occurs in the country (Groombridge, 1993). Of the 95 amphibians, six are endemic, these are: *Centrolenella geijskesi*, *Dendrobates azureus*, *Hyla fuenti*, *Eleutherodactylus grandoculis*, *Caecilia albiventris* and *Microcaecilia taylori*.

There are an estimated 300 species of freshwater fish and about 50 species of brackish-water fish. The fish from the brackish waters of the estuarine zone are the best known, perhaps because large numbers of them are caught by the local people. The number of species of marine fish is unknown.

The fauna of Surinam is rich in invertebrates, but the total number of species cannot even be estimated. The Odonata are the best known, and are represented by about 280 species (Bruijning and Voorhoeve, 1977). Only one threatened invertebrate is listed as occurring in the country, the butterfly *Papilio garleppi*.

The Game Law and the Nature Conservation Law, both passed in 1954, give protection to flora, fauna, natural communities and unique landscapes. Since 1980, all exports of animals must be accompanied by permits issued by the Surinam Forest Service. Surinam has been a member of CITES since 15 February 1981. The low level export trade in wildlife which has existed in Surinam for many years is not considered to pose a serious threat to the fauna and the flora at present. The most sought after species are parrots, macaws, parakeets and song birds, as well as a variety of reptiles, amphibians and orchids. Since the deforestation rate is so low, there is little threat of extinction or even endangerment of species due to the destruction of their habitats.

Conservation Areas

The 1954 Nature Conservation Law provided for the establishment of nature reserves by state resolution. Protection of natural areas is part of the overall resource development programme of the Surinam government and the nature conservation system in the country ranks among the best in South America (Schulz, 1971). Between the years of 1961 and 1972, nine nature reserves and one nature park were established. These areas were selected for their 'diverse and scenic landscape and/or the presence of floristic, faunistic and geological objects that are important in scientific or cultural respects'.

Before independence in 1975, development programmes were drawn up to be implemented with Dutch aid. Development was to be concentrated in the north of the country and it was planned that some natural areas would be converted for agricultural land and plantations. Factory complexes, urban areas and mines would also be developed in this region. A system of 10 protected areas was, therefore, planned in this vulnerable northern region in places adjacent to development zones. The system was based on an ecosystem map prepared by Teunissen (1978). In 1986, four of the ten sites were gazetted as nature reserves and in 1987, part of the estuarine zone was put at the disposal of the Ministry of Natural Resources to be managed as a multiple use zone.

At present the conservation areas in IUCN's categories I–IV cover 7361 sq. km or 5.2 per cent of Surinam's land area (Table 32.4). They include tropical forest ecosystems and important coastal formations. Two more nature reserves, which cover ecosystems not yet represented in the established system, are proposed for protection. In addition, enlargement of the nature park is planned. Table 32.4 does not include multiple use management areas; Bigi Pan (683 sq. km — category VIII) is already established and two others are proposed. Also proposed are two small forest reserves. When all these proposed protected areas are established some seven per cent of Surinam will have protected status.

The reserves are managed by the Nature Conservation Division of the Surinam Forest Service, with the help of a NGO, the Foundation for Nature Preservation in Surinam (STINASU). The head of this Service is authorised to take any measures necessary to protect the reserves. There is a total ban on use of the resources in these areas. The Surinam Forest Service is committed to maintaining guard forces in the protected areas, but enforcement of protective legislation has been greatly hampered in recent years by lack of equipment, particularly outboard motors and jeeps. The development of eco-tourism has been limited as most of the nature reserves have not been open to the public.

The one nature park, Brownsberg, is an area obtained on long-term lease by STINASU. This park is primarily intended for use as an "educational reserve".

In addition to the conservation areas listed in Table 32.4, there are also some forest reserves in the country; their establishment is provided for under the Timber Ordinance of 1947. Although it is illegal to exploit the forest in these areas, it appears that there are no other restrictions on activities within them.

The multiple use management area is controlled by the Ministry of Natural Resources. In this area some forms of exploitation, for instance agriculture, animal husbandry or fisheries, are allowed under certain management conditions.

A management plan is being prepared for the Bigi Pan Multiple Use Area and a plan has been drafted for the Galibi

Table 32.4 Conservation areas of Surinam

Existing conservation areas in IUCN's categories I–IV are listed below. For information on Ramsar sites see Chapter 8.

Nature Reserve	Area (sq. km)
Boven Cusewijne	270
Brinckheuvel*	60
Copi*	280
Coppename Monding*	120
Eilerts de Haan*	2,200
Galibi*	40
Hertenrits	1
Peruvia*	310
Raleighvallen/Voltzberg*	782
Sipaliwini*	1,000
Tafelberg*	1,400
Wane Kreek*	454
Wia Wia*	360
Nature Park	
Brownsberg*	84
Total	7,361

* Area with forest within its boundaries as shown on Map 32.1

Source: WCMC (unpublished data)

Nature Reserve but all the other reserves lack management. Indeed, the protected areas in the interior of the country have hardly been studied. Extensive floristic and faunistic research has been restricted to the lowlands and is now urgently needed in the inland reserves.

Conservation Initiatives

STINASU was founded in 1969 to support the Nature Conservation Division of the Surinam Forest Service in its nature conservation activities. Nature tourism is under the jurisdiction of STINASU. It operates facilities for overnight visits in four nature reserves and in the nature park.

A Conservation Action Plan has been written for Surinam by Mittermeier *et al.* (1990). It outlines a number of projects proposed for 1991–1995. The plan provides for development of an ecological data base, the development of a field research and training centre in the Raleighvallen/Voltzberg Nature Reserve and research on wildlife trade, ethnobotany, key animal species and the sustainable use of forest resources. The environmental education programme includes the development of an education building and permanent exhibit at the Brownsberg Nature Park, the creation of a mobile lecture series using slides, videos and films and the provision of slide sets, videotapes, projection equipment and printed materials to schools. Proposals for technical training cover the development of a joint Forest Service and University of Surinam programme in conservation and the provision of fellowships for masters and doctoral students. Tourism is a critical component of the overall conservation plan for Surinam, but the existing facilities need renovating and new ones need developing.

WWF-Nederland has provided a grant for a technical advisor to the Surinam Forest Service and STINASU. The advisor is concerned with implementing the Action Plan and has written management plans for some of the protected areas.

Conservation International has an office in Paramaribo which is helping to document ethnobotanical information. This organisation also provides money for technical training.

Numerous national and international NGOs and governments are providing funds for conservation in Surinam. These include the Mac Arthur Foundation, WWF-US, WWF-Holland, the Canadian Wildlife Service, the Roundtable-Suriname, the Canadian International development agency, the Organisation of American States and local private foundations.

References

Baal, F.L.J., Mittermeier, R.A. and van Roosmalen, M.G.M. (1988). Primates and protected areas in Suriname. *Oryx* 22(1): 7–14.

Beard, J.S. (1944). Climax vegetation in tropical America. *Ecology* 25(2): 127–158.

Boxman, O., de Graaf, N.R., Hendrison, J., Jonkers, W.B.J., Poels, R.L.H., Schmidt, P. and Tjon Lim Sang, R. (1987). Forest Land Use in Suriname. *Tropenbos Scientific Series* 1: 119–129.

Bruijning, C.F.A. and Voorhoeve, J. (Eds.). (1977). *Encyclopedie van Suriname.* Elsevier, Amsterdam-Brussel. 716 pp.

Collar, N.J., Gonzaga, L.P., Krabbe, N., Madroño Nieto, A., Naranjo, L.G., Parker III, T.A. and Wege, D.C. (1992). *Threatened Birds of the Americas. The ICBP/IUCN Red Data Book.* ICBP, Cambridge, U.K.

FAO (1993). *Forest resources assessement 1990: Tropical countries.* FAO Forestry Paper 112. FAO, Rome, Italy.

FAO/UNEP (1981). *Proyecto de Evaluacion de los Recursos Forestales Tropicales: Los Recursos Forestales de la America Tropical.* FAO, Rome, Italy.

Graaf, N.R. de. (1982). Sustained timber production in the rainforest of Suriname. In: *Management of Low Fertility Acid Soils of the American Humid Tropics.* J.F. Wienk and H.A. de Wit (eds): Series: Ponencias, Resultados y Recomendaciones de Eventos Techicos. No.266: 175–190. San Jose, Costa Rica.

Graaf, N.R. de. (1986). *A Silvicultural System for Natural Regeneration of Tropical Rain Forest in Suriname.* Agricultural University Wageningen, The Netherlands. 250 pp.

Granville, J.J. de (1988). Phytogeographical characteristics of the Guianan forests. *Taxon* 37(3): 578–594.

Groombridge, B. (Ed) (1993). *1994 IUCN Red List of Threatened Animals.* IUCN Gland, Switzerland and Cambridge, U.K. 286 pp.

Hekking, W.H.A. and Sipman, H.J.M. (1988). The lichens reported from the Guianas before 1987. *Willdenowia* 17: 193–228.

Held, M.M. (1990). Status and conservation of the scarlet ibis in Suriname. Proceedings of the First International Scarlet Ibis Conservation Workshop, Caracas, Venezuela, 1988. *IWRB Special Publication* No.11: 100–106.

Jong, B.H.J. de and Spaans, A.L. (1984). *Waterfowl and Wetlands in Suriname. Contribution to the IWRB/ICBP Neotropical Wetlands Project.* RIN Contributions to Research on Management of Natural Resources No.1984–1. Arnhem, The Netherlands. 277 pp.

Jonkers, W.B.J. (1987). *Vegetation Structure, Logging Damage and Silviculture in a Tropical Rain Forest in Suriname.* Agricultural University Wageningen, The Netherlands. 172 pp.

Jonkers, W.B.J. and Schmidt, P. (1984). Ecology and timber production in tropical rainforest in Suriname. *Interciencia* 9 (5): 290–297.

Kramer, K.U. (1978). *The Pteridophytes of Suriname. An enumeration with keys of the ferns and fern-allies.* Natuurwetenschappelijke Studiekring voor Suriname en de Nederlandse Antillen 93. Utrecht, The Netherlands. 198 pp.

Lindeman, J.C. (1953). The vegetation of the coastal region of Suriname. *The Vegetation of Suriname 1(1).* 135 pp.

Lindeman, J.C. and Moolenaar, S.P. (1959). Preliminary survey of the vegetation types of northern Suriname. *The Vegetation of Suriname 1(2).* 145 pp.

Lindeman, J.C. and Mori, S.A. (1989). The Guianas. In: *Floristic Inventory of Tropical Countries: the Status of Plant Systematics, Collections, and Vegetation, plus Recommendations for the Future.* Campbell, D. G. and Hammond, H.D. (Eds), pp. 375–390. The New York Botanical Garden.

Maas, P.J.M. (1971). Floristic observations on forest types in western Suriname I and II. *Proceedings Koninklijke Nederlandse Akademie van Wetenschappen. Series C* 74(3): 269–284, 285–302.

Mittermeier, R.A., Malone, S.A.J., Plotkin, M.J., Baal, F., Mohadin, K., MacKnight, J., Werkhoven, M. and Werner, T.B. (1990). *Conservation Action Plan for Suriname.* World Wildlife Fund — U.S.A. 45 pp.

Schulz, J.P. (1960). Ecological studies on rain forest in northern Suriname. *Verhandelingen der Koninklijke Nederlandse Akademie van Wetenschappen Afdeling Natuurleunde, Tweede Reelis* 53(1): 1–267.

Schulz, J.P. (1971). *Nature Preservation in Surinam.* Nederlandse Commissie voor Internationale Natuurbescherming Mededelingen No. 20. 22 pp.

Schulz, J.P. (1975). *Sea turtles nesting in Surinam.* Nederlandse Commissie voor Internationale Natuurbescherming. Mededelingen No. 23. 143 pp.

Spaans, A.L. and Baal, F.L.J. (1990). The estuarine zone of Surinam: towards a symbiosis between conservation and development of a coastal wetland area. In: *Living off the Tides.* Fiselier, J.L. (Ed), pp. 75–84. Environmental Database on Wetland Interventions, Leiden, The Netherlands.

Spaans, A.L. and de Jong, B.H.J. (1982). Present status of some colonial waterbird species in Suriname, South America. *Journal of Field Ornithology* 53: 269–272.

SPS (1988). *Suriname Planatlas.* Stichting Planbureau Suriname. Department of Regional Development, O.A.S. Washington, D.C.

Teunissen, P.A. (1978). *Reconnaissance Map Suriname Lowland Ecosystems (Coastal Plain and Savanna Belt).* Scale 1:200,000. Foundation for Nature Preservation in Suriname. Paramaribo, Suriname.

Vink, A.T. (1970). *Forestry in Suriname.* Paramaribo, Suriname Forest Service. Pp. 97.

Vink, A.T. (1977). *Suriname Timbers.* 4th edition. Paramaribo, Suriname. State Forest Industries Inc. (SURTIM). 253 pp.

Werkhoven, M.C.M. and Held, M.M. (1989). *Conservation of*

Natural Ecosystems Versus Land-Use in Suriname. Workshop 90, Manaus: Priority Areas for Conservation in Amazonia. 62 pp.

Author: Marga Werkhoven, Curator, National Herbarium of Suriname, with contributions from N.R. de Graff and W.B.J. Jonkers, both from Wageningen Agricultural University.

Map 32.1   Surinam

Forest cover data for Surinam were digitised from plate B₇ *Vegetation* of the *Suriname Planatlas* (1988). The *Planatlas* was prepared by the National Planning Office of Suriname, Regional Development and Physical Planning Department, with assistance from the Organization of America States, Executive Secretariat for Economic and Social Affairs Department of Regional Development, Washington, D.C. The source map has mainly been based on 1978 data and is derived from the *Reconnaissance Map of Suriname Lowland Ecosystems* compiled by Teunissen.

Eleven vegetation types are depicted on the source map. These have been harmonised into the broader classification shown on Map 32.1. The vegetation types have been harmonised as follows: mangrove — *Mangrove forest, salt water and brackish marsh*; lowland rain forest — *High dryland forest*; inland swamp forest — *Low swamp forest, High swamp forest, High seasonal swamp forest*; sub-montane rain forest — *Mountain forest (elevations > 500m)*; dry forest — *High and low xerophytic forest*, and non-forest — *Fresh water marsh and swamp scrub, Savanna, Cultivated and abandoned land*.

Location and boundary data for Surinam's protected areas were derived from the same source as above but from plate D₁ *Land Use and Concessions*. The category *Nature reserve/park* has been digitised. Additional locational point data have been taken from the WCMC protected areas database.

33 Venezuela

Country area   912,050 sq. km
Land area   882,050 sq. km
Population (mid-1994)   21.3 million
Population growth   2.6 per cent
Population projected to 2025   34.3 million
Gross national product per capita (1992)   US$2900
Forest cover for 1982 (see Map)   542,682 sq. km
Forest cover for 1990 (FAO, 1993)*   454,570 sq. km
Annual deforestation rate (1981–1990)   1.2 per cent
Industrial roundwood production   750,000 cu. m
Industrial roundwood exports   —
Fuelwood and charcoal production   776,000 cu. m
Processed wood production   369,000 cu. m
Processed wood exports   —
* excludes dry deciduous and very dry formations

Venezuela has never been a timber-exporting country, indeed the country imports about 50 per cent of its wood-derived products. In spite of this, the country has lost a total of 60,000 sq. km of forest in the last forty years. Only the State of Amazonas, due to its inaccessibility, shows a lower rate of deforestation. Despite advances in environmental legislation and an increase in the number of protected areas in recent years, deforestation continues due to increasing social pressure and the unjust system of land tenure.

Venezuela has a reasonably good legal and institutional basis, which should enable it to achieve high levels of environmental conservation. However, conservation of the environment is not yet recognised as an integral part of the development strategy and high-level political support for protected areas is lacking. In the absence of real agrarian reform and improvements in the socio-economic conditions of rural populations, it will be impossible to enforce the legislation.

INTRODUCTION

Venezuela, the fifth largest country in South America, has 3700 km of coastline and over 100 large offshore islands. It contains all the characteristic biogeographic zones of the northern part of South America, with arid and semi-arid regions near the coast, large deltas with mangroves and swamp forests, seasonally flooded plains, mountains with cloud forest and paramo vegetation and a large area of relatively undisturbed moist forest in the south.

Geographically, the country can be divided into three regions. The first of these is the Andes and Coastal Cordilleras which cover about one third of the country's area. The Andes Cordillera crosses the west of Venezuela in a northeast-southwest direction, joins the Coastal Cordillera of the Caribbean Sea and continues along the coast from the west to the Atlantic in the east. The Andes is a young Tertiary mountain system, its highest peaks are between 4000 and 5000 m, whereas the Coastal Cordillera is lower, reaching only 2000 to 3000 m. Cloud forest still covers most of the slopes between 800 and 3000 m. However, in the foothills and flood plains of this area the natural vegetation of evergreen and semi-deciduous dense forest has mostly been converted into extensive pasture and agricultural land.

The second region is the Orinoco Llanos, a very flat alluvial region between the mountain region in the north and the Guiana Shield in the south, encompassing about one fifth of the country's area. The high Western Llanos close to the Andes were originally covered by seasonal evergreen and semi-deciduous closed forests, but much of this has now been cleared. The Central and Eastern Llanos, with a semi-arid climate, is savanna-

shrub land. It was originally partially covered by dry deciduous closed and open forest. These areas have been exploited for timber and then progressively cleared for pasture and cash crops (corn, sorghum, groundnuts and others).

Thirdly, the Guayana-Amazonas region (the States of Bolívar and Amazonas), comprising half the country's area, is located to the south of the Orinoco River. About 70 per cent of Venezuela's rain forest is found here.

There is generally a gradient of increasing rain from north to south; part of the coast is desertic with 0–600 mm rain, the central area of the Llanos has 800–2000 mm annual precipitation while the southern Amazonas receives 2500–4000 mm. However, the highest annual rainfall, up to 4300 mm, occurs in the southwestern edge of the Maracaibo basin in the north of the country. Temperatures vary with altitude, the lowlands have a mean annual range between 24°C and 28°C, while above 2000 m in elevation the mean temperatures are as low as 8°C–15°C (Huber and Frame, 1989).

About 95 per cent of the country's population live to the north of the Orinoco River, where most of the industrial and socio-economic development is also found. There is, in contrast, a very low population density in the region south of the Orinoco, only 0.5 inhabitants per sq. km in Amazonas and three per sq. km in Bolívar State. This part of the country has been divorced from the development of the north until recently. However, there is now considerable economic activity in Bolívar State. Beginning in the 1960s, this focused on hydroelectricity and the steel industry, while an aluminum industry developed in the 1980s. These activities are all concentrated near Ciudad Guayana, which has become the most important city in the State of Bolívar and the biggest centre for heavy industry in the country. The Orinoco is being opened up for exploitation of the heavy crude oil which is found along much of its lower reaches.

Eighty-four per cent of Venezuela's population live in urban areas, one of the highest percentages in any Latin American country. The capital city of Caracas has over four million inhabitants. Most Venezuelans (69 per cent) are mestizo, 20 per cent are European, nine per cent are of African origin and only two per cent are Amerindian (see Box).

Since the 1950s, the country's economy has been strongly supported by oil exports. Most of this comes from around Maracaibo, but the middle Orinoco region is likely to prove to have one of the largest reserves in the world. Main agricultural exports are coffee, cacao, tropical fruits, beverages and fish, but over 50 per cent of farmers practice subsistence agriculture rather than growing cash crops.

The dramatic Valle de las Mil Columnas, Canaima National Park, Venezuela. Canaima comprises outstanding tepuy formations.

(WWF/Bruno Pambour)

The Forests

Humid evergreen forests are found in the Amazonas-Guayana region, in the Orinoco Delta, and in the area south and south-east of Lake Maracaibo. The flora in Guayana and Amazonas is extraordinarily rich. Huber (1982) described 13 types of forest, scrub and savanna vegetation in the Venezuelan Amazonas. The most important species are *Couroupita guianensis*, *Ceiba pentandra*, *Coumarouna punctata* and *Carapa guianensis*. Canopy species include *Calophyllum brasiliense*, *Guarea trichilioides*, *Pentaclethra macroloba* and *Swartzia* sp., as well as palms of the genera *Iriartea*, *Oenocarpus*, *Scheelea* and *Socratea*. In the lower canopy, species from the genera *Brownea*, *Inga*, *Luehea*, *Protium*, *Trichilia* and *Bactris* are found. The floristic composition of these forests is, however, very variable (FAO/UNEP, 1981) and there is a very close relationship between different types of forest vegetation and soils (Franco, 1979, 1988; Franco and Dezzeo, 1992).

The Orinoco Delta is mainly covered by swamp forest. The palm *Euterpe oleracea* is abundant and produces the palmheart,

the basis of an important local industry which, in 1990, produced 6480 tons of oil, mainly for export (Finol, 1992; MARNR-SEFORVEN, 1991).

One of the most interesting vegetation types in the Amazonas-Guayana region is that found growing on the top of the table mountains, or tepuis, over 1600 m. Many of the species on the tepuis are endemic, these include *Heliamphora* spp. and other carnivorous plants.

Cloud forest is found from 3000 m down to 800 m in the Andes and in the northern coastal range. In the former, several species of *Podocarpus*, together with the families Lauraceae, Myrtaceae, Cunoniaceae and Brunelliaceae predominate, whereas in the latter *Gyranthera caribensis* is a dominant canopy species, along with trees from the genera *Sloanea*, *Ecclinusa*, *Licania* and *Graffenrieda*. Above the cloud forest in the Andes is the paramo vegetation, with its specialized flora characterized by species of the genus *Espeletia*.

ETHNO-CULTURAL DIVERSITY

There are more than 300,000 indigenous people from 26 ethnic groups in Venezuela. About one third of these live to the south of the Orinoco River (OCEI, 1992). Most of the people are strongly dependent upon forest resources as they practice shifting cultivation, hunting, fishing and gathering. The organisation and political activity of the indigenous population has increased significantly in the last few years. Their most pressing demand is the recognition of their land rights. Recently, an indigenous group from the State of Bolívar demanded that the Congress of the Republic intervene to stop the Forest Service giving a management concession that was in its territory to a timber company.

Among the Amazonas ethnic groups the Yanomami (13,000), Piaroa (2500) and Yekuana (1500) are the most numerous and least affected by acculturization. When national parks and (national) biosphere reserves have been created, the rights of the ethnic groups to continue their way of life and normal activities (shifting cultivation, hunting, etc.) have been taken into account and, at the same time, colonisation by non-indigenous people has been forbidden.

Forest conservation in the Southern Orinoco region of

Venezuela is very important for the conservation of indigenous cultures. The recent creation of the Alto Orinoco-Casiquiare Biosphere Reserve (83,000 sq. km) by the Venezuelan Government forms a good basis for the establishment of a special programme concerned with the conservation of both the natural resources and local cultures. The Permanent Committee for this national biosphere reserve includes representatives of the local indigenous communities. SADA-AMAZONAS, IUCN and AMA-Andalucia have prepared a five year project for the reserve (Franco *et al.*, 1992), which has been submitted to international sponsors for support.

Increasing sedentarization and acculturation of the indigenous population has increased their ecological impact on some areas, particularly in Guayana and Amazonas. In these areas, the soils and general ecological conditions are very poor for agricultural production and it is necessary to develop new agroecological systems to guarantee food production without major ecological disturbance. CAIAH is attempting to achieve this through research in Amazonas in cooperation with Venezuelan and foreign universities.

Gallery and other riparian forests are common in the central and southern parts of the country; they are frequently flooded. The canopy, at 20 m, is dominated by *Pterocarpus* spp., *Pithecellobium saman*, *Guazuma ulmifolia*, *Lecythis ollaria*, *Ceiba pentandra* and *Vochysia* spp. In the lower canopy are found *Capparis coccolobifolia*, *Acacia glomerosa* and *Casearia hirsuta* amongst others (FAO/UNEP, 1981).

The seasonal evergreen and deciduous forests in the northwest and, to a lesser degree, in the northeast of the country contain species such as *Astronium graveolens*, *Bombacopsis quinata*, *Bourreria cumanensis*, *Bursera*, *Cedrela mexicana*, *Swietenia macrophylla* and *Tabebuia* spp., as well as species of the palm genera *Attalea*, *Bactris* and *Acrocomia* (Franco, 1979; FAO/UNEP, 1981).

Mangroves

The coastal ecosystems of the Caribbean sea and the Atlantic ocean are rich in mangroves. They are estimated by several authors to cover about 6500 sq. km (MARNR, 1989; Pannier and Pannier (1989); Saenger *et al.*, 1983; Taylor, 1988), but Conde and Alarcón (1993) think this is *probably an overestimation, as a result of the inclusion of* Symphonia globulifera, *a plant whose light spectrum and shape makes it prone to be confused with mangroves in photointerpretation.* They regard the figure of 2500 sq. km, reported in MARNR (1986), to be more realistic; an earlier report by MARNR (1983) gives the figure of 3233 sq. km. The area of mangroves indicated on Map 33.1 is 6206 sq. km. Those in the Orinoco Delta are the most extensive; they make up around 68 per cent of the country's total mangrove area (MARNR, 1989). The common species are *Rhizophora mangle*, *Laguncularia racemosa*, *Avicennia tomentosa*, *A. officinalis* and *Conocarpus erecta* (FAO/UNEP, 1981).

During the 1970s the tall (30 m) *Rhizophora mangle* forest in the Guarapiche forest reserve (near the Orinoco Delta) was exploited for timber, but economic problems of the company and pressure from ecologists stopped this exploitation.

Forest Resources and Management

There are various different estimates given below for the extent of forest in Venezuela. The variation appears to be mainly due to the different years in which the measurements were taken, though the definition of forest varies between publications as well. A 1983 publication by MARNR *Mapa de la Vegetacion Actual de Venezuela* gives figures for different forest types as shown in Table 33.1. Though this map was published at a scale of 1:250,000, the interpretation work was done on aerial photographs at a scale of 1:50,000 and 1:100,000.

A later report by Centeno (1990) indicated that there were 455,600 sq. km of forest remaining in the country in 1988. Dense forest made up 416,000 sq. km of this, open forest covered a further 36,000 sq. km and pine plantations covered the remaining 3600 sq. km. The dense forests are made up of 243,400 sq. km of production forests, 114,000 sq. km of protection forests, 52,300 sq. km of gallery forests and 6300 sq. km of mangroves. Two years later, in 1990, FAO's estimate (FAO, 1993) was that there were 454,570 sq. km of moist forest (i.e. the tropical rain, moist deciduous and hill and montane categories of FAO's classification) remaining in Venezuela. FAO also gives figures of 2200 sq. km of of forest in the dry deciduous zone and 120 sq. km of forest in the very dry zone. Both these formations are drier than any shown on Map 33.1 or given in Table 33.2 and they have not been included in the statistics at

Table 33.1 Estimates of forest extent in Venezuela

Forest type	Altitude	Area (sq. km)
Tropical*	under 500 m asl	304,197
Transitional	500-800 m asl	189,313
Premontane	800-1,500 m asl	27,061
Lower montane	1,500-2,500 m asl	5,463
Montane	2,500-3,300 m asl	3,038
Subandean	>3,300 m asl	184
Total forest		529,059[+]

* includes 6,967 sq. km of dry deciduous forest — a drier formation than the dry forests shown on Map 33.1.

[+] excludes gallery forest and mangroves, figures for these in Table 4.1 of MARNR (1983) are 36,103 sq. km and 3,232 sq km respectively. All forest types in this table, except the Subandean, include areas of semi-deciduous and evergreen forest. The total figure, therefore, includes 82,007 sq km of semi-deciduous, 440,086 sq. km of evergreen and 6,967 sq. km of deciduous forest.

Source: Table 4.2 in MARNR (1983), with author's interpretation for altitudinal limits.

the head of the chapter. The area of closed broadleaved forest was considered to be 405,730 sq. km (FAO, 1993).

Forest cover in Venezuela, as measured from Map 33.1 and given in Table 33.2, is 542,682 sq. km. This is a somewhat higher figure for forest cover than in any of the other sources given above. This is almost certainly because though Map 33.1 is based on one prepared by Huber and Alarcon published in 1988 (see Map Legend), the data used for the source map reflect the status of Venezuela's vegetation in 1982 and there has been heavy deforestation throughout the country, except south of the Orinoco, since that time (O. Huber, pers. comm.). The forests shown as dry forests on Map 33.1 are the areas mapped as *deciduos* by Huber and Alarcon. These are not the much drier formations that FAO (1993) appears to be classifying as dry deciduous forest.

In Table 33.1, the author regards forests between 0 m and 800 m as lowland, those between 800 m and 1500 m as submontane and those over 1500 m as montane. The difference in the areas of the various forest types between Tables 33.1 and 33.2 is almost certainly because in the Huber and Alarcon map, physiognomy of the forest rather than altitude is used to differentiate the types.

To the north of the Orinoco River, in the mountain and Llanos region, the forests have been severely depleted. Since the beginning of the last century, when the colonial epoch ended, a kind of feudal land tenure structure has been in existence in the areas most suitable for agriculture. The forest land, mainly belonging to the State, is considered "public and avail-

Table 33.2 Estimates of forest extent in Venezuela

Forest type	Area (sq. km)	% of land area
Lowland moist	319,821	36.3
Submontane	139,655	15.8
Montane	25,188	2.9
Dry	29,269	3.3
Swamp	22,543	2.6
Mangrove	6,206	0.7
Total	542,682	61.5

Based on analysis of Map 33.1. See Map Legend on p. 321 for details.

able" for everyone who wants to develop a farm. The Agrarian Reform Law (1960) even recognizes deforestation as "land improvement", which has to be paid for by the State if it wants to recover the land. It is, therefore, good business to invade public forest land and deforest it.

In contrast, to the south of the Orinoco, the States of Bolívar and especially Amazonas, have been comparatively undisturbed. Until recently, only areas along major roads were deforested. However, increasing economic activity in Bolívar State means that the forest resources are being depleted there. The State of Amazonas has remained free from forest destruction caused by either cattle ranching or timber exploitation. Overall, therefore, the southern half of Venezuela still retains a major area of tropical rain forest.

The Department of Renewable Natural Resources, which was converted in 1976 to the Ministry of Environment and Renewable Natural Resources (MARNR), has promoted the creation of national parks, forest reserves and other areas to conserve Venezuela's natural resources. Both the National Institute of Parks (INPARQUES — Instituto Nacional de Parques) and the Forest Service (SEFORVEN — Servico Forestal Venezolano) are part of MARNR. MARNR was the first ministry for the environment to be set up in Latin America.

At present, SEFORVEN gives 30 year concessions to timber companies so that the companies will have a long term interest in the forest. The most important obligations of the timber companies are to defend the forest against shifting cultivators and to regenerate the production potential of the forest through silviculture. The system has been relatively successful in some areas in the Western Llanos (Ticoporo), but it has failed in others (Caparo). The rapid establishment of a forest plantation barrier at the forest frontier and construction of a timber factory, both giving employment to the local people, seem to be the decisive factors in the success of these schemes.

By 1992, about 31,000 sq. km of forest had been given out in concessions for forest management by SEFORVEN (Table 33.3). However, the timber companies are currently working at reduced capacity due to the economic recession. MARNR-SEFORVEN (1991) estimated that industrial roundwood production was 697,300 cu. m in that year, a somewhat lower figure than the estimate in FAO (1994) for 1991, which is the same as that for 1992 given at the head of the chapter. If demand increases, the timber companies will be able to step up timber production very rapidly. The Forest Service still has about 85,000 sq. km of reserve available for new concessions.

In the State of Amazonas, Venezuela is promoting a truly integrated and ambitious conservation programme as part of its membership of the Amazon Cooperation Treaty. Other member countries are Bolivia, Brazil, Colombia, Ecuador, Guyana, Peru and Surinam. Venezuela has banned both mining and timber exploitation in the State and, in enforcing this, the Venezuelan army has, several times, expelled Brazilian garimpeiros (goldminers) who have invaded territory in the upper Orinoco (Yanomami) region. In addition, 50 per cent of the area has been protected through the gazettement of four national parks, a dozen natural monuments (all tepuis are protected by law as natural monuments) and the 83,000 sq. km Alta Orinoco-Casiquiare (national) Biosphere Reserve. These protected areas contribute to the preservation of both the tropical rain forest and the culture of twelve indigenous groups including the Yanomami, Yekuana, Goahibo and Piaroa (see Box). To implement its Amazonas conservation policy, Venezuela has created the Autonomous Service for Environmental Development in

Table 33.3 Areas under forest management for timber production

Forest Reserve	State	Companies	Area (sq. km)
Caparo	Barinas	5	1,745
Ticoporo	Barinas	2	1,011
San Camilo	Barinas	1	800
Río Tocuyo	Yaracuy	1	270
Guarapiche	Monagas	2	292
Imataca	Bolívar	12	19,032
Forest Lot			
Delta Amacuro	Delta Amacuro	2	709*
San Pedro	Bolívar	4	7,200
Total		29	31,059

* palmheart

Amazonas (SADA-AMAZONAS) and the Amazonas Centre for Environmental Research "Alexander von Humboldt" (CAIAH). The country's initiatives in protecting its Amazonian forest have received worldwide approval.

Large plantations of *Pinus caribaea* have been established in the savanna of the Eastern Llanos. Nearly 200,000 cu. m of timber were harvested from these plantations in 1991 and a major expansion of the plantation forests is going ahead.

Deforestation

It is estimated that over the last forty years, approximately 60,000 sq. km of Venezuela's forest have been cleared (Catalán, 1993). The 60,000 sq. km of forest lost includes 30,000 sq. km of lowland evergreen and semi-deciduous forest in the flood plains of the western Llanos and south and west of Lake Maracaibo; 10,000 sq. km of lowland dry deciduous forest in the central and eastern Llanos; 10,000 sq. km of cloud forest in the Andes and Coastal Cordillera; and 10,000 sq. km of lowland evergreen forest in Guayana to the south of the Orinoco River (Veillon, 1976; Catalán, 1993). MARNR-SEFORVEN (1991) estimates the annual deforestation rate to be 1650 sq. km. FAO's estimate for annual deforestation in Venezuela between the years of 1981 and 1990 is considerably higher than that of MARNR-SEFORVEN (1991). Excluding the areas of dry deciduous and very dry forests, FAO estimates that 5881 sq. km of forest are cleared each year, a rate of 1.2 per cent per year (FAO, 1993).

A large proportion of the remaining cloud forest is protected in national parks or hydraulic reserves. However, in some areas, particularly in the Andes, cloud forest is being destroyed very rapidly for highly profitable farming of dairy cattle. Most of the watersheds covered by cloud forest are very important for water supply to big cities, hydroelectric power stations and irrigation projects (Franco, 1990).

The major factor promoting deforestation has been the construction of roads through virgin areas. In areas where logging has occurred, and consequently access has been improved, the fact that the forest is now "impoverished" is often used as a justification for the devastation of the remaining forest. There has also been considerable conversion of forest land to cattle pasture for extensive production of beef. Mining, for both gold and bauxite, is also contributing to forest destruction in Guayana and Amazonas (Franco, 1990). Gold-mining, by the estimated 60,000 *garimpeiros* in the State of Bolívar, is an economic

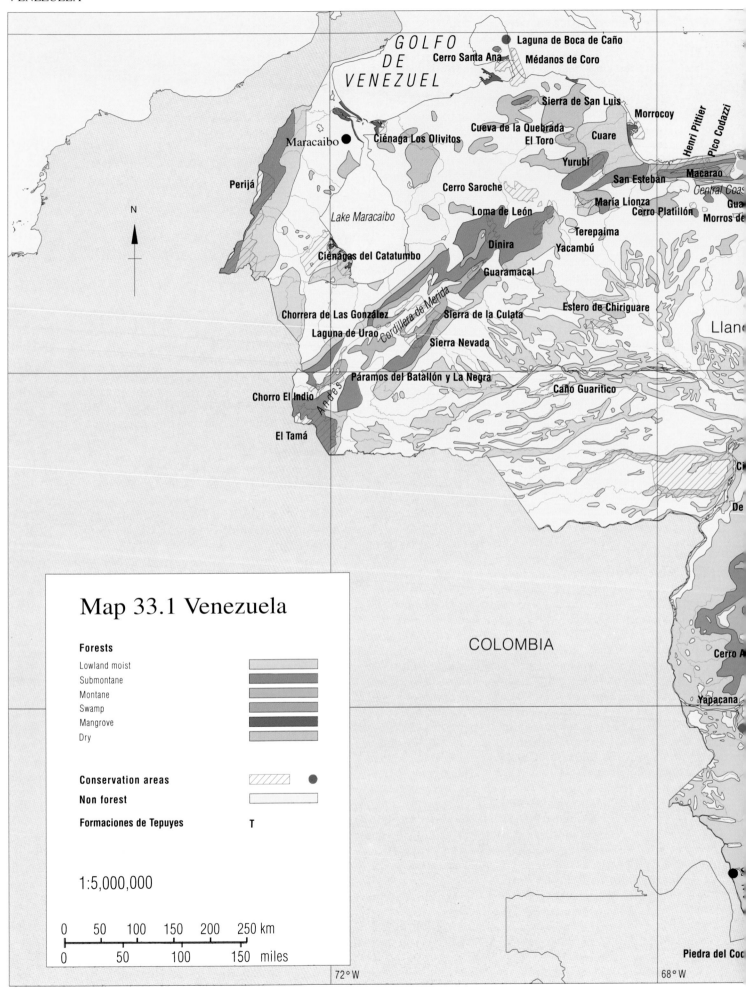

GOLFO
DE
VENEZUEL

Laguna de Boca de Caño
Cerro Santa Ana
Médanos de Coro

Sierra de San Luis
Morrocoy

Cueva de la Quebrada
El Toro
Cuare

Ciénaga Los Olivitos
Maracaibo

Yurubí

Henri Pittier
Pico Codazzi

Perijá

Cerro Saroche

San Esteban
Macarao
Central Coas

María Lionza
Gua

Loma de León
Cerro Platillón
Morros de

Lake Maracaibo

N

Terepaima

Dinira
Yacambú

Ciénagas del Catatumbo

Guaramacal

Estero de Chiriguare

Chorrera de Las González
Cordillera de Mérida
Sierra de la Culata

Llano

Laguna de Urao
Andes
Sierra Nevada

Páramos del Batallón y La Negra
Caño Guaritico

Chorro El Indio

El Tamá

Ci

De

Map 33.1 Venezuela

Forests

Lowland moist	
Submontane	
Montane	
Swamp	
Mangrove	
Dry	

Conservation areas

Non forest

Formaciones de Tepuyes   T

COLOMBIA

Cerro A

Yapacana

1:5,000,000

0	50	100	150	200	250 km

0	50	100	150	miles

72° W

68° W

Piedra del Coc

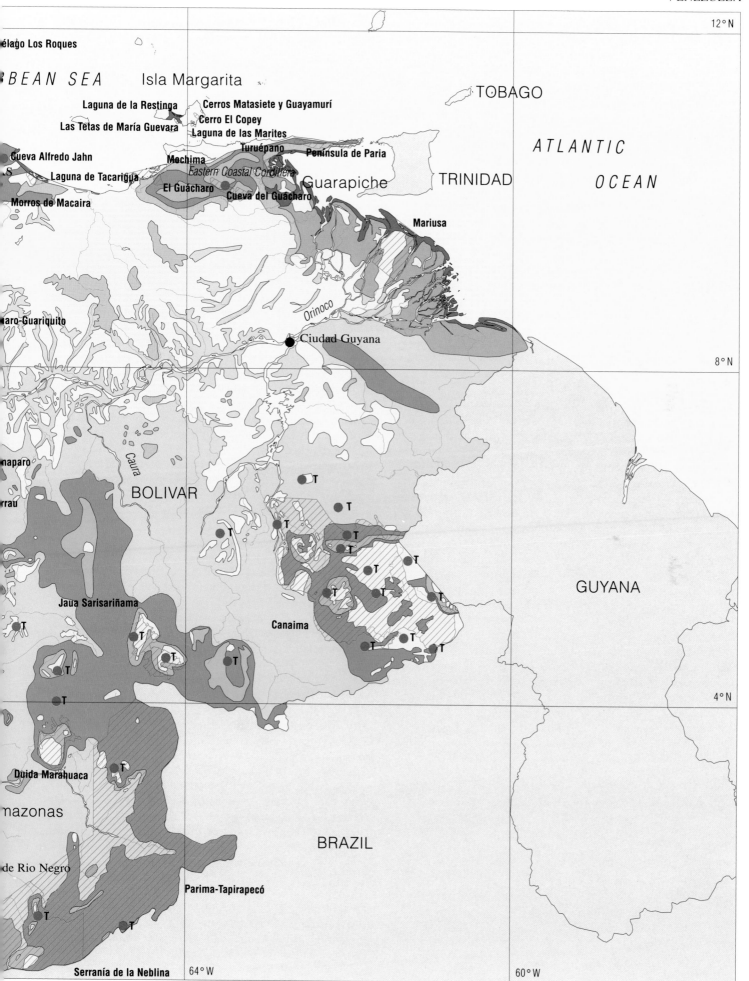

12° N

élago Los Roques

BEAN SEA   Isla Margarita

Laguna de la Restinga   Cerros Matasiete y Guayamurí
Cerro El Copey
Las Tetas de María Guevara   Laguna de las Marites

Cueva Alfredo Jahn   Mochima   Turuépano   Península de Paria

Laguna de Tacarigua   Eastern Coastal Cordillera   Guarapiche

Morros de Macaira   El Guácharo   Cueva del Guácharo

TOBAGO

ATLANTIC

OCEAN

TRINIDAD

Mariusa

aro-Guariquito

Orinoco

Ciudad Guyana

8° N

naparo

Caura

rrau

BOLIVAR

GUYANA

Jaua Sarisariñama

T

Canaima

Duida Marahuaca

mazonas

BRAZIL

4° N

de Rio Negro

Parima-Tapirapecó

Serranía de la Neblina   64° W   60° W

activity which gains local political support. Fuelwood and charcoal is not used to a great extent in Venezuela, the 776,000 cu. m estimated by FAO (1994) is less than that used in most of the other South and Central American countries. MARNR-SEFOR-VEN (1991) estimated that only 41,250 tons (about 46,700 cu m) were used in a year.

The high rate of forest destruction will almost certainly continue in coming years. The socio-economic crisis present in most Latin American countries, promoted by international debt and the reduced price paid for exports, has recently caused political instability in Venezuela. The application by the government of a neoliberal and "open market" economic policy has significantly increased inflation and the gap between rich and poor. As a consequence, pressure on the environment and natural resources has increased and the prospects for successful environmental protection programmes has worsened.

The government is promoting exports of Venezuelan products and the agro-industrial sector is already responding to the better facilities they have been offered. For instance, in the flood plain of Lake Maracaibo, banana plantations and beef cattle production are expanding with a consequent increase in pollution and deforestation in the area. Similarly, oil palm plantations have been expanding into areas of natural vegetation in the eastern Llanos.

Biodiversity

Five important South American biogeographical regions (Andean, Caribbean, Guianan, Amazonian and the Orinoco Llanos) are represented in Venezuela. The flora and fauna are accordingly rich. The country has been estimated to have more than 20,000 species of flowering plant, including 1500 species of orchids. Despite the fact that only about 20 per cent of the Venezuelan Amazonas region has been explored, more than 5000 plant species have already been described from there. About 20 per cent of the plants in the country are endemic. There are 323 mammal species (15 endemic), 1325 birds (51 endemic), 246 reptiles (55 endemic) and 183 amphibians (76 endemic), as well as more than 1000 fish species in the Orinoco region alone (MARNR-POA, 1984; Eisenberg and Redford, 1979; Eisenberg, 1989; Phelps and Meyer, 1979). Table 33.4 shows the international importance of the wildlife from the Venezuelan Amazon region.

Threatened mammals include the spectacled bear *Tremarctos ornatus*, the giant otter *Pteronura brasiliensis*, the margay *Leopardus wiedii*, the black-headed uakari *Cacajao melanocephalus* and the bat *Leptonycteris curasoae* (Groombridge, 1993). None of these species is endemic.

Twenty bird species are listed as threatened by Collar *et al.* (1992), 11 of them are endemic and most inhabit forest, particu-

larly montane forest. Endangered forest species include the táchira emerald *Amazilia distans*, the Paria redstart *Myioborus pariae*, both of which are endemic, and the northern helmeted curassow *Pauxi pauxi*. Areas with the highest degree of endemism are the Paria Peninsula, the Andes, the Coastal Cordillera and the Pantepui Region.

Threatened reptile species include the giant South American river turtle *Podocnemis expansa*, the red-headed Amazon turtle *P. erythrocephala*, the zulia toad-headed turtle *Phrynops zuliae* and the American and Orinoco crocodiles, *Crocodylus acutus* and *C. intermedius* respectively. The turtles are mostly hunted for food, while the crocodiles are killed for their skins. The spectacled caiman *Caiman crocodilus* is very abundant and there has been an attempt to exploit it commercially under the official technical supervision of PROFAUNA (the Venezuelan Wildlife Service).

There are ten amphibians in the country which are considered to be in danger, though none is listed as globally threatened by IUCN. These are two endemic *Bolitoglossa* salamanders and eight frogs from the genera *Atelopus*, *Minyobates* and *Dendrobates*. On top of the table mountains, frogs from the genus *Tepuihyla* have been discovered, a different endemic species on each tepui (Ayarzaguena, 1984; Ayarzaguena *et al.*, 1992; Donnelly and Myers, 1991; Gorzula, 1992).

Information on fish and invertebrates is generally lacking. However, one of the world's largest butterflies, *Thysania agripina*, is found in Venezuela and one endemic species, *Parides klagesi*, is considered threatened (Groombridge, 1993).

More details on the threatened animals in the country will be established with the production of the Red Data Book for the animals of Venezuela, a collaboration between several hundred national scientists and approved by PROFAUNA, which was published in late 1994.

Conservation Areas

Venezuela's first protected area was created in 1937; this was the Henri Pittier National Park ("Rancho Grande") which protects more than 1000 sq. km of cloud forest and coastal forest in the Coastal Cordillera. However, it was not until MARNR was set up in 1976 that a coherent protected areas management system was put into place (IUCN, 1992). The National Institute of Parks has been relatively successful in creating an extensive nationwide national parks system so that currently there are 42 national parks and 20 natural monuments administered by INPARQUES (Table 33.5), they cover an area of around 142200 sq. km or 16.1 per cent of the country's land area. This is more than in any other Latin American country. Faunal Refuges, administered by MARNR, are also shown in Table 33.5 as these are in IUCN's category IV. Exploitation of the animals is not allowed in these refuges, whereas it is allowed in the faunal reserves.

These areas are strongly protected by law and there are, on paper, very severe restrictions on their use. However, political will and economic resources are often lacking and the majority of protected areas are not adequately managed, which leaves them open to illegal exploitation. In addition, INPARQUES frequently has to compete with other government departments for its funding, particularly SEFORVEN and the Ministry of Energy and Mines, and in some instances industrial projects take precedence over protection of the conservation areas. Well known examples illustrating the lack of protection include the degradation of the Caracas Protection Zone, the threat to the Cuare Faunal Refuge and Ramsar Site from pollution and urban expansion, gold-mining in Canaima, Yapacana and Serranía de

Table 33.4 Total number of species and those listed by CITES and IUCN from the Amazon region of Venezuela.

Taxon	Total Species	CITES*	IUCN**
Mammals	180	15	15
Birds	650	8	3
Reptiles	84	10	11
Amphibians	53	–	0
Fish	320	–	0

*   On Appendix 1
**   On 1990 IUCN Red List

Source: Franco et al. (1992)

la Neblina National Parks and the gas pipeline planned for the Península de Paria National Park. The strategy has been one of creating a large number of protected areas irrespective of the government's ability to manage them (Gondelles, 1992).

In 1983, the Organic Law for Territorial Planning defined 25 categories of areas that required special administration owing to their particular production, recreation or protection potential (IUCN, 1992). These form the system of Areas under Special Administrative Regime (Areas Bajo Régimen de Administrative Especial — ABRAE). The main categories and the area they cover are shown in Table 33.6. Hunting is allowed in wildlife reserves, sustainable exploitation is allowed in the protective zones. It is illegal for forest reserves and forest lots to be converted into agricultural land, but they may be used for timber production. Various restrictions apply to the other categories shown in Table 33.6; their use is under the official supervision of MARNR.

In 1991, MARNR and INPARQUES formulated a proposal for a new and comprehensive Protected Natural Areas Law and this will supersede the present system of conservation areas (IUCN, 1992).

Venezuelans respect their national parks; this is manifest in the continuous fight by conservation groups defending El Avila National Park, which has become a symbol of the city of Caracas, as well as by the growth in the activities of NGOs working in national parks. However, there is little public support for protection of other forest land which has no apparent use. This is the case with the forest reserves and other protected areas in flat lands. As a result, SEFORVEN finds it more difficult to fulfil its function than does INPARQUES.

A law passed in 1992, the Penal Law of the Environment, imposes fines and imprisonment on anybody hunting wildlife or destroying its habitat in national parks. It also makes environmental impact assessments a legal requirement for industrial development. Although the Chamber of Commerce and Industry

Table 33.5 Conservation areas of Venezuela

Existing protected areas in IUCN's categories I–IV are shown below. For information on Ramsar sites and Biosphere reserves see Chapter 8.

National Park

Aguaro-Guariquito*	5,858
Archipiélago Los Roques	2,211
Canaima*	30,000
Cerro El Copey	71
Cerro Saroche	323
Chorro El Indio*	108
Ciénagas del Catatumbo*	2,694
Cinaruco-Capanaparo*	5,844
Cueva de la Quebrada El Toro*	85
Delta del Orinoco+	3,310
Dinira*	420
Duida Marahuaca*	2,100
El Avila*	852
El Guache+	122
El Guácharo*	627
El Tamá*	1,390
Guaramacal*	210
Guatopo*	1,225
Henri Pittier*	1,070
Jaua Sarisariñama*	3,300
Laguna de la Restinga*	189
Laguna de Tacarigua*	391
Macarao*	150
Mariusa*	3,310
Médanos de Coro*	913
Mochima*	949
Morrocoy*	321
Páramos del Batallón y La Negra*	952
Parima-Tapirapecó*	34,200
Península de Paria*	375
Perijá*	2,953
San Esteban*	435
Serranía de la Neblina*	13,600
Sierra de la Culata*	2,004
Sierra de San Luis*	200
Sierra Nevada*	2,764
Terepaima*	187
Tirgua+	910
Turuépano*	726
Yacambú*	146
Yapacana*	3,200
Yurubí*	237

Natural Monument

Cerro Autana*	0.3
Cerro Platillón	80
Cerro Santa Ana*	19
Cerros Matasiete y Guayamurí	17
Chorrera de Las González	1
Cueva Alfredo Jahn*	0.6
Cueva del Guácharo*	2
Formaciones de Tepuyes*°	10,698
Laguna de las Marites	37
Laguna de Urao*	0.3
Las Tetas de María Guevara*	17
Loma de León	73
María Lionza*	117
Meseta La Galera+	nd
Morros de Macaira*	1
Morros de San Juan	28
Pico Codazzi*	119
Piedra del Cocuy*	0.2
Piedra La Tortuga+	5
Piedra Pintada+	14

Faunal Refuge

Caño Guaritico*	93
Ciénaga Los Olivitos*	257
Cuare*	118
De la Tortuga Arrau*	174
Estero de Chiriguare*	322
Isla de Aves+	0.5
Laguna de Boca de Caño*	5

Total	143,131

*   Area with forest (including moist, dry and mangrove) within its boundaries as shown on Map 33.1
+   Not mapped — data not available to this project.
°   marked by a 'T' on Map 33.1

Source: WCMC (unpublished data)

Table 33.6 Numbers and areas of other Conservation Areas in Venezuela, excluding those listed in Table 33.5.

	No.	Area (sq. km)
Wildife Reserve	2	878
Hydraulic Reserve	9	17,196
Protective Zone	48	120,134
Forest Reserve	10	113,471
Forest Lot	8	10,529
Biosphere Reserve (National)	2	92,765
Total	79	354,973

(FEDECAMARAS) has expressed its concern about this law and its negative effects on the growth of the economy, MARNR is committed to it and intends to create a body of Environmental Police in 1993 to enforce the law.

Conservation Initiatives

In Venezuela, the people's concern about the environment and natural resources is growing steadily. MARNR, employing more than 2000 people, has assumed leadership of the conservation initiatives in the country. Many projects have been established for watershed management, soil conservation, protection of wildlife and development of national parks, forest reserves and forestry plantations. MARNR and the State and City governments are working together to control waste and sewage disposal, as these still cause considerable pollution in the country. In addition, MARNR and the military are trying to keep illegal gold-mining in Amazonas under control. There have been a large number of NGOs formed since the mid-seventies, with as many as 80 of these concerned with environmental matters (EcoNatura, 1993). In addition, there are some 9000 registered Neighbours' Associations, many of which deal with local environmental problems.

At the World Parks Congress in Caracas in 1992, major additions to the protected areas system of Venezuela were announced. Much of the expansion of the system has occurred in the south, with the creation of the huge Alto Orinoco-Casiquiare Biosphere Reserve. The EC has provided around US$1 million to support a project to strengthen Venezuela's parks. This project involves training, research and resource monitoring and is run by INPARQUES-WCS-EcoNatura. The World Bank intends to provide additional funds for the parks system in mid-1994.

PDVSA, the State Venezuelan Oil Company which produces nearly three million barrels of oil daily, recently signed an agreement for environmental protection proposed by MARNR. The company has to invest more than US$600 million a year in environmental protection.

Near San Carlos de Río Negro an ecological research project has been maintained by national and foreign scientists for more than 10 years, producing important information about the tropical rain forest in Amazonas (Medina and Cuevas, 1989). Three years ago, Nichare Research Station was set up in Caura watershed in what is probably the largest block of absolutely pristine forest in South America. No activity other than subsistence hunting/agriculture by the Ye'kuana is allowed. CONICIT (National Council for Science and Technology) is also promoting more research on biodiversity and the environment.

The national IUCN Committee is working towards the production of a National Programme Document which will set out conservation priorities in the country.

The next few years will be historically decisive for Venezuela. Although some important goals have already been achieved, including environmental legislation, an institutional basis and a wide system of protected areas, the country must find alternative methods of political and socio-economic development. The success of the current environmental policies will depend strongly upon doing so.

References

Ayarzaguena, J. (1984). Una nueva especie de *Dischydodactylus* en la cumbre del tepui Marahuaca. *Memorias Sociedad de Ciencias Naturales La Salle* 120: 215–220.

Ayarzaguena, J., Señaris, J.C. and Gorzula, S. (1992). El grupo *Osteocephalus rodriguezi* de las tierras altas de la Guayana venezolana. *Memorias Sociedad de Ciencias Naturales La Salle* 137: 111–139.

Catalán, A. (1993). *Estimación de la Deforestación en Venezuela a través de Imagenes de Satélite.* Dirección de Vegetación–DGSIIA, MARNR, Caracas, Venezuela. Pp. 68.

Centeno, J.C. (1990). *El Desarrollo Forestal de Venezuela.* Instituto Forestal Latinoamericano, Mérida, Venezuela. Pp. 59.

Collar, N.J., Gonzaga, L.P., Krabbe, N., Madroño Nieto, A., Naranjo, L.G., Parker III, T.A. and Wege, D.C. (1992). *Threatened Birds of the Americas. The ICBP/IUCN Red Data Book.* ICBP, Cambridge, U.K.

Conde, J.E. and Alarcón, C. (1993) Mangroves of Venezuela. In: *Conservation and Sustainable Utilization of Mangrove Forests in Latin America and Africa Regions. Part 1: Latin America.* ITTO/ISME Project PD114/90(F). Pp. 211–243.

Donnelly, M.A. and Myers, Ch. (1991). Herpetological results of the 1990 Venezuelan Expedition to the summit of Cerro Guaiquinima, with new tepui reptiles. *American Museum Novitates* 3017: 1–54.

EcoNatura (1993). *Directorio de Organizaciones Ambientales No Gubernamentales de Venezuela 1993.* EcoNatura, Caracas. Pp. 93.

Eisenberg, J.F. (1989). *Mammals of the Neotropics: The Northen Tropics. Vol 1.* University of Chicago Press, Ltd, Chicago, U.S.A.. Pp. 449.

Eisenberg, J.F. and Redford, K.H. (1979). A biogeographic analysis of the mammalian fauna of Venezuela. In: *Vertebrate Ecology in the Northen Neotropics.* J.F. Eisenberg (Ed.). Smithsonian Institution Press, Washington, D.C., U.S.A.

FAO (1993). *Forest resource assessment 1990: Tropical countries.* FAO Forestry Paper 112. FAO, Rome, Italy.

FAO (1994). *FAO Yearbook: Forest Products 1981–1992.* FAO Forestry series No. 27, FAO Statistics Series No. 116. FAO, Rome, Italy.

FAO/UNEP (1981). *Proyecto de Evaluacion de los Recursos Forestales Tropicales. Los Recursos Forestales De La America Tropical.* FAO, Rome, Italy.

Finol, H. (1992). *Planificación Silvicultural de los Bosques ricos en Palma Manaca* (Euterpe oleracea) *en el Delta del río Orinoco.* Instituto de Silvicultura, Universidad de Los Andes. Ministerio del Ambiente y de los Recursos Naturales Renovables, SEFORVEN, Caracas, Venezuela.

Franco, W. (1979). *Die Wasserdynamik einiger Waldstandorte de West-LlanosVenezuelas und ihre Beziehungen zur Saisonalität des Laubfalls.* Unpublished doctoral thesis, Göttingen University, Germany.

Franco, W. (1988). *Suelos del Lote Boscoso San Pedro y las Reservas Forestales de Imataca, Guarapiche y Ticoporo.* Universidad de Los Andes, Merida, Venezuela. Pp. 201.

Franco, W. (1990). Consideraciones sobre el bosque humedo tropical en Venezuela: problematica y soluciones. *Revista Forestal Venezolana* XXII (32): 123–132.

Franco, W. and Dezzeo, N. (1992). Soils and soil water regime in the terra firme — caatinga forest complex near San Carlos de Río Negro, Amazon Territory, Venezuela. In: *Proceedings of the 2nd International Symposium of Forest Soils (ISSS).* Held in Ciudad Guayana, Venezuela, November 1992.

Franco, W., Clavero, J. and Plonczak, M. (1992). *Proyecto de Conservacion Ambiental y Preservacion de las Comunidades y Culturas Indigenas en la Reserva de Biosfera Alto Orinoco — Casiquiare (Venezuela).* SADA-AMAZONAS, IUCN and AMA-Andalucía. Caracas. (Documents A, B and C of a project — sent to the EC in Brussels).

Gondelles, R. (1992). *El Régimen de áreas Protegidas en Venezuela.* Banco Consolidado Caracas. Pp. 68.

Gorzula, S. (1992). La herpetofauna del macizo Chimantá. In: *El Macizo de Chimantá.* Huber, O. (Ed.). Todmann, Caracas. Pp. 490.

Groombridge, B. (Ed.) (1993). *1994 IUCN Red List of Threatened Animals.* IUCN, Gland, Switzerland and Cambridge, U.K. 286 pp.

Huber, O. (1982). *Esbozo de las formaciones vegetales del Territorio Federal Amazonas.* MARNR, Caracas.

Huber, O. and Alarcón, C. (1988). *Mapa de la Vegetación de Venezuela.* MARNR & The Nature Conservancy, Caracas, Venezuela.

Huber, O. and Frame, D. (1989). Venezuela. In: *Floristic Inventory of Tropical Countries. The Status of Plant Systematics, Collections, and Vegetation, plus Recommendations for the Future.* Campbell, D.G. and Hammond, H.D. (Eds.) Pp. 362–374. The New York Botanical Garden, New York.

IUCN (1990). *1990 IUCN Red List of Threatened Animals.* IUCN, Gland, Switzerland and Cambridge, U.K.

IUCN (1992). *Protected Areas of the World: A review of national systems. Volume 4: Nearctic and Neotropical.* IUCN, Gland, Switzerland and Cambridge, U.K.

MARNR (1983). *Mapa de la Vegetacion Actual de Venezuela: sintesis.* Ministerio del Ambiente y de los Recursos Naturales Renovables, Caracas, Venezuela.

MARNR (1986). *Conservación y Manejo de los Manglares Costeros en Venezuela y Trinidad Tobago.* (Síntesis). (PT) Serie Informes Técnicos DGIIA/IT/259, Caracas.

MARNR (1989). *Manglares de Venezuela. Distibución geográfica de los manglares en Venezuela.* Cuadernos Lagoven, Caracas.

MARNR-POA. (1984). *Sistemas Ambientales Venezolanos.* Dirección General Sectorial de Planificación y Ordenamiento del Ambiente, MARNR. Caracas.

MARNR-SEFORVEN (1991). *Anuario Estadístico.* Caracas, República de Venezuela.

Medina, E. and Cuevas, E. (1989). Patterns of nutrient accumulation and release in Amazonian forest of the upper Río Negro basin. In: *Mineral Nutrients in Tropical Forest and Savanna Ecosystems.* Proctor, J. (Ed.). Blackwell Scientific Publications, Oxford. Pp. 217–240.

OCEI. (1992). *Resultados Preliminares del Censo Indígena.* Oficina Central de Informática y Estadística (OCEI). Caracas.

Pannier, F. and Pannier, R.F. (1989). *Manglares de Venezuela.* Cuadernos LAGOVEN, PDVSA, Caracas. Pp. 68.

Phelps, W. and Meyer, R. (1979). *Una Guía de las Aves de Venezuela.* Gráficas Altamirano, C.A. Caracas. 484 pp.

Saenger, P., Hegerl, E.J. and Davie, J.D.S. (1983). (Eds). *Global Status of Mangrove Ecosystems.* Commission on Ecology Papers No. 3. IUCN, Gland, Switzerland.

Taylor, J.G. (1988) (Ed.) *Manglares. La importancia económica de los manglares en la política, planeamiento y manejo de los recursos naturales costeros.* FUDENA, Caracas.

Veillon, J.P. (1976). La deforestación en los Altos Llanos Occidentales de Venezuela entre 1950 y 1975. In: *Conservación de los Bosques Húmedo de Venezuela.* Sierra Club & Consejo de Bienestar Rural de Venezuela, Caracas, Venezuela.

Authors: Wilfredo Franco, Director, Centro Amazónico de Investigaciones Ambientales Alexander von Humboldt, SADA-AMAZONAS, Caracas, Venezuela and Chris Sharpe, WCMC, Cambridge, U.K., with contributions from Otto Huber, Caracas, Venezuela.

Map 33.1   Venezuela

Mapped forest information has been derived from the *Mapa de Vegetacion de Venezuela*, prepared by Otto Huber and Clara Alarcon. The map was published by The Ministerio del Ambiente y los Recursos Naturales Renovables and The Nature Conservancy in 1988 at a scale of 1:2 million, but reflects the status of the vegetation cover in Venezuela for approximately 1982 (O. Huber, pers. comm., October 1991). Since then, heavy deforestation has occurred north of the Orinoco, especially in the Andes. A digital version of this map was kindly made available to WCMC by BIOMA. In addition, the booklet, *Manglares de Venezuela* (MARNR, 1989) was used to map the mangrove areas more accurately.

The forest cover and forest types shown in this Atlas are an amalgamation of Huber & Alarcon's forest classes. Huber & Alarcon's map is classified into four distinct regions, based on relief: *Region A — Insular y litoral; Region B — Llanuras bajas; Region C — Colinas* and *Region D — Montañas.* These regions are segregated further into smaller geographical sub-regions and then categorised by vegetation/land use type. From these finer vegetation categories, those listed as *bosques* (including mangroves) are shown as forest on Map 33.1. All other categories have been amalgamated into non-forest; e.g. savanna, scrub and grassland are included in non-forest.

From Huber & Alarcon's 150 vegetation classes, 74 have been combined into the broad forest categories shown on Map 33.1. To formulate these broad categories, some assumptions during data harmonization have been made: 1. the evergreen, semi-evergreen, riverine, cloud forest and semi-deciduous forest categories have been combined to form the moist forest classes shown in this atlas; 2. the dry forests include all forests which have been classified as deciduous on the Huber & Alarcon map; 3. the type of forest, i.e. lowland and montane rain forest, has been determined by the finer classification on the source map. Those forest categories of the Huber & Alarcon map defined as 'basimontanos' are included in lowland rain forest, forests classified as 'submontanas' are included in submontane forests and those defined as 'montanas' have been included in the montane forest cover. Where the source category shows two types of forest, implying transitional formations (i.e. submontanos/montanas, or semi-deciduous/deciduous), then the former forest type has been selected (unless the colour coding on the map suggests otherwise) and harmonised accordingly.

The source forest categories have been harmonised in the following manner: lowland moist forests, including riverine forests — classes 9, 10, 14, 15, 21, 24, 33, 35, 41, 48, 49, 50, 51, 59, 64, 65, 71, 72, 73, 75, 80, 81, 85, 86, 110, 122; submontane forests — 66, 74, 82, 87, 88, 94, 95, 97, 99, 97, 103, 106, 109, 111, 116, 127, 130, 131, 135, 139, 144, 148; montane forests — 89, 98, 107, 108, 113, 114, 123, 132, 136, 140, 149 (these include the Tepuyana <u>forest</u> vegetation classes: i.e. 114, 123, 132, 140, 149); dry deciduous forests — 8, 16, 34, 105, 39, 60, 70, 93, 96, 143; swamp forests — 42, 43, 53 and mangroves — 4,6 and 44.

Protected areas have been digitised from a published map *Republica de Venezuela — Areas Bajo Regimen de Administracion Especial* at a scale of c. 1:2.5 million, compiled by the Ministerio del Ambiente y de los Recursos Naturales Renovables and Servicio Autonomo Forestal Venezolano and published in 1991.

ACRONYMS

AMI	Integral Management Area
ANCON	Asociación National para la Conservación
APN	Administración de Parques Nacionales
AT	Alianzas Tripartitas
BAS	Belize Audubon Society
CARE	Cooperative for Foreign Remittances
CATIE	Centro Agronómico Tropical de Investigación y Enseñanza
CCC	Caribbean Conservation Corporation
CCE	Comisión de las Comunidades Europeas
CCT	Centro Científico Tropical
CDC	Conservation Data Centre
CDF	Centro de Desarrollo Forestal
CEAP	Centre for Environmental Studies and Policies
CECON	Centro de Estudios Conservacionistas
CEDI	Centro Ecunêmico de Documentação Informação
CELOS	Centre for Agricultural Research in Surinam
CFCA	Caribbean Forest Conservation Association
CI	Conservation International
CIDA	Canadian International Development Agency
CIFOR	Center for International Forestry Research
CIIFE	Caribbean International Institute for Forestry and the Environment
CITES	Convention on International Trade in Endangered Species of Wild Fauna and Flora
CLIRSEN	Centro de Levantamientos Integrados de Recursos Naturales por Sensores Remotos
CNF	Cámara Nacional Forestal
CNRS	Centre d'Etudes de Géographie Tropicale
COHDEFOR	Corporación Hondureña de Desarrollo Forestal
CONAI	Comisión Nacional de Asuntos Indígenas
CONAMA	Comisíon Nacional del Medio Ambiente
CONAP	Consejo Nacional de Areas Protegidas
CONATEF	Comisión Nacional Forestal
CONIF	Corporación Nacional de Investigación y Fomento Forestal
CONTACTYT	Consejo Nacional de Ciencia y Tecnología
CORDES	Regional Development Corporations
CPD	Centres of Plant Diversity
CUMAT	Centro de Investigaciones y Estudio de la Capacidad de Uso Mayor de la Tierra de Bolivia
DAF	Ministère de l'Agriculture et de la Forêt
DDE	Direction Departementale de l'Equipement
DED	Servicio Alemán de Cooperación Social-Técnica
DIGEBOS	Dirección General de Bosques
DINAF	Dirección Nacional Forestal
DIREN	Regional Environment Office
DNP	Dirección Nacional de Parques
DNR	División of National Resources
DPN	División de Parques Nacionales
DPNVS	Dirección de Parques Nacionales y Vida Silvestre
DVS	Departamento de Vida Silvestre
EBA	Endemic Bird Area
ECCO	Asociación de Ecología y Conservación
ENSO	El Niño Southern Oscillation
EUNED	Editorial Universidad Estatal a Distancia
FAO	Food and Agriculture Organization of the United Nations
FONAMA	Fondo Nacional para el Medio Ambiente
FPCN	Fundación Peruana para la Conservación de la Naturaleza
FPN	Fundación de Parques Nacionales
FSCD	Forestry and Soils Conservation Department
FUCSA	Fundación Cuero y Salado
FUDENA	Fundación para la Defensa de la Naturaleza
FUNAI	National Indian Foundation

FYDEP	Empressa Nacional de Fomento y Desarrollo Económico de El Petén
GAHEF	Guyana Agency for Health Sciences Education, Environment and Food Policy
GDP	Gross Domestic Product
GEF	Global Environment Facility
GFC	Guyana Forestry Commission
GIS	Geographic Information System
GNP	Gross National Product
GNRA	Guyana National Resources Agency
GTZ	Deutsche Gesellschaft für Technische Zusammenarbeit (German Aid Agency)
IBAMA	Instituto Brasileiro de Meio Ambiente e dos Recursos Naturais Renováveis
IBGE	Fundación Instituto Brasileira de Geografia e Estatística
ICBP	International Council for Bird Preservation (now BirdLife International)
ICDP	Integrated Conservation-Development Project
IDAEH	Institute of Anthropology and History
IDB	Interamerican Development Bank
IGAC	Instituto Geografico "Augustin Codazzi"
IICA	Instituto Interamericano de Cooperación para la Agricultura
IIED	International Institute for Environment and Development
INAFOR	Instituto Nacional Forestal, Guatemala
INBio	Instituto Nacional de Biodiversidad
IMP	Iguana Management Project
INC	Instituto Nacional de Colonización
INDERENA	Instituto Nacional de los Recursos Naturales Renovables y del Medio Ambiente
INE	Instituto Nacional de Estadistica
INEFAN	Instituto Ecuatoriano Forestal y de Areas Naturales y de Vida Silvestre
INEGI	National Institute of Statistics, Geography and Information
INPA	Instituto Nacional de Pesquisas na Amazônia
INPE	Instituto Nacional de Investigaciones Espaciales del Brazil
INRENARE	Instituto Nacional de Recursos Naturales Renovables
IPGH	Instituto Panamericano de Geografía e Historia
IRA	Instituto de Reforma Agraria
ISPAN	Institut de Sauvegarde du Patrimoine National
ISPN	Institute for the Study of Society, Population and Nature
ITTO	International Tropical Timber Organization
IUCN	World Conservation Union
IWRB	International Waterfowl and Wetlands Research Bureau
JCDT	Jamaica Conservation and Development Trust
KfW	Kreditonstalt für Wiederaufbau
LANDSAT-TM	LANDSAT-Thematic Mapper
LBL	Lawrence Berkeley Laboratory
MACA	Ministerio de Asuntos Campesinos y Agropecuarios
MAG	Ministerio de Agricultura y Ganadería
MAGA	Ministerio de Agricultura, Ganadería y Alimentacíon
MARNR	Ministerio del Ambiente y de los Recursos Naturales Renovables
MIRENEM	Ministerio de Recursos Naturales, Energía y Minas
MMOM	Metodo Mexicano de Ordenamiento de Montes
NAFTA	North America Free Trade Association
NFAP	National Forestry Action Plan
NGO	Non Governmental Organisation
NPAS	National Protected Areas System

NRCD	National Resources Conservation Department
NRED	National Report on Environment and Development
NYZS	New York Zoological Society
OAS	Organization of American States
ODA	Overseas Development Agency
ONF	Office National des Fôrets
ORCA	Oficina Regional para Centro América
ORSTOM	Office de la Recherce Scientifique et Technique Outre Mer
OTS	Organization for Tropical Studies
PAFC	Plan de Acción Forestal de Colombia
PAFCR	Plan de Acción Forestal de Costa Rica
PAFE	Plan de Acción Forestal de Ecuador
PAFG	Plan de Acción Forestal para Guatemala
PARC	Protected Areas Resources Conservation Project
PEA	Programa de Educación Ambiental
PFA	Permanent Forest Areas
PIN	National Integration Programme
PPF	Plan Piloto Forestal
PRB	Population Reference Bureau
PROAFT	Programa de Acción Forestal Tropical
PRONAREG	Programa Nacional de Regionalización
SADA-AMAZONAS	Servico Autónomo para el Desarrollo Ambiental del Estado Amazonas
SARH	Secretariat of Agriculture and Water Resources
SEA	Secretaría de Estado de Agricultura
SENMA	Secretaría Nacional del Medio Ambiente
SI-A-PAZ	Sistema de Areas Protegidas para la Paz
SINAP	National System of Protected Areas
SPI	Servicio de Protección Indigena
SPN	Servicio de Parques Nacionales
STINASU	Stichting Natuurbehoud Surinam
SUBIR	Sustainable Use of Biological Resources
SUFOREN	Subsecretaría Forestal y de Recursos Naturales Renovables
SURENA	Subsecretaría de Estado de Recursos Naturales
TFAP	Tropical Forest Action Plan
TNC	The Nature Conservancy
TTFNC	Trinidad and Tobago Field Naturalists Club
UC	University of California
UCEFO	Association of Forestry Communities and Ejidos of Oaxaca
UN	United Nations
UICN	Union Mundial para la Natureleza
UNCED	United Nations Conference on Environment and Development
UNDP	United Nations Development Programme
UNEP	United Nations Environment Programme
UNESCO	United Nations Educational, Scientific and Cultural Organization
USAID	United States Agency for International Development
USDA	United States Department of Agriculture
UWI	University of West Indies
WCED	World Commission on Environment and Development
WCI	Wildlife Conservation International
WCMC	World Conservation Monitoring Centre
WRI	World Resources Institute
WWF	World Wide Fund for Nature

GLOSSARY

Alluvial Related to material deposited by running water.

Altiplano High plateau or plain; tableland.

Angiosperm Flowering plant (class Angiospermae).

Anthropogenic Created by man.

Anuran Amphibian of the order Anura.

Avifauna The birdlife of a region or a period of time.

Backswamp Swamp in a backland.

Barrier reef Coral reef parallel to shore, separated from it by a lagoon (qv).

Biodiversity Richness of genes, species, and ecosystems.

Biogeography Definition of an area by its fauna and flora.

Biomass The amount of living matter in a defined area.

Biome Large natural community of flora and fauna adapted to conditions in which it is found.

Biosphere The part of the planet containing living organisms.

Biota The flora and fauna of an area.

Biotope An area or habitat of a particular type, defined by the organisms that typically inhabit it.

Black-water Refers to water containing biologically active matter.

Brake Rough or marshy land, usually overgrown with one kind of plant.

Broadleaved Refers to any tree of the subclass Dicotyledonae of the class Angiospermae.

Buffer zone An area peripheral to a national park or reserve which has restrictions placed on its use to give an added layer of protection to the conservation area itself.

Caatinga Scrubby, xerophytic scrubland in areas of alternating flood and drought.

Campesino Latin American Indian farmer/labourer.

Campina Open forest on white sand.

Canopy The cover formed by the branches and leaves of trees in a wood or forest, usually refers to the top forest layer.

Catchment A river basin; sometimes only its upper portion.

Cay A low, insular bank or reef of coral, sand, etc.

Cerrado Scrubland with savanna-like vegetation.

Clearfelling Complete clearance of a forest.

Climax Final stage in natural succession of a community of organisms, in equilibrium with environmental conditions.

Closed forest Effectively complete forest with canopy cover of 40% or more (as defined by FAO).

Cloud forest Wet tropical montane and submontane forest (500-3500m); clouds are present even in dry season.

Colluvial Relating to rock and soil accumulated at the foot of a slope.

Cordillera Chain of mountain peaks.

Cretaceous Geological epoch covering 144 million years B.P. to 65 million years B.P.

Cryptogam Plant that reproduces by means of spores; has no flowers or seeds.

Deciduous Refers to tree that sheds its leaves annually

Ecofloristic Refers to the flora of a geographical region or habitat.

Ecosystem A natural unit consisting of organisms and their environment.

Ecotone Transition area between two adjacent ecological communities.

Edaphic Produced or influenced by the soil.

Elfin woodland Forest with canopy about 5 m, gnarled growth; the highest of the montane formations.

Emergent Refers to trees with crowns conspicuously taller than the surrounding canopy.

Endemic Confined to a particular area.

Eocene Geological epoch from 58 million years B.P. to 37 million years B.P.

Epiphyte Plant that uses another plant for support, not for nutrients.

Estuarine Found or living in an estuary.

Ethnobiology Study of plant and animal life in relation to a race or people.

Fluvial Refers to a stream or river.

Floodplain The floor of a valley over which a river may flood.

Gallery forest Forest along a river.

Geomorphology Study of the physical features of the earth's surface and their relation to geological structures.

Greenhouse gases Gases which cause infra-red radiation to be retained in the atmosphere (e.g. methane and carbon dioxide), so warming the Earth's surface and the lower part of the atmosphere.

Herb Any seed-producing plant with non-woody green stems.

Herbaceous Adjective from herb.

Herpetofauna Reptile fauna.

Holocene Present geological epoch; began 10,000 years B.P.

Hydromorphic Having an affinity for water.

Igapó Forest flooded by black waters.

Isthmus Narrow strip of land connecting two larger land areas.

Karst Cavernous, deeply eroded limestone.

Lagoon Shallow coastal backwater separated from the ocean by a physical barrier such as a sand bar.

Lateritic Refers to hard, impermeable soil unsuitable for cultivation (laterite).

Leach To remove a substance from the soil through percolation.

Lepidoptera Butterflies and moths.

Liane/liana Climbing/twining plant in tropical forests.

Lithological Refers to the study of rocks.

Littoral Area between the low and high tide levels.

Llanos Very flat alluvial region, northern Venezuela.

Loma Small hill or slope.

Mangrove Salt-adapted evergreen tree found in the intertidal zone of tropical/subtropical latitudes.

Massif A principal mountain mass.

Meander A turn or winding of a river.

Miocene Geological epoch from 26 million years B.P. to 5 million years B.P.

Monoculture Cultivation of a single crop.

Monospecific Having a single species.

Montane Growing or living in mountainous areas.

Nearctic Refers to biogeographical subregion including Greenland and North America north of tropical Mexico.

Neotropical Refers to biogeographical subregion, including tropical and subtropical regions of America.

Niño, El Flow of unusually warm surface water on west coast of South America that produces climatic fluctuations.

Open forest Areas dominated by trees with crowns not touching; less than 40% crown cover (as defined by FAO).

Oxbow Crescent-shaped lake formed when a river breaches the neck of a pronounced river meander (qv).

Paleoclimate Climate of geologically past times.

Palynological Refers to the study of pollen, spores, etc. to interpret past climates.

Páramo The vegetation of high tropical mountains in South America.

Passerine Refers to songbirds that perch.

Peneplain An ancient land surface shaped by erosion.

Perhumid Permanently humid; no dry season.

Phenology Science of the relations between climate and periodic biological phenomena, such leaf fall.

Physiography Study or description of natural phenomena.

Pleistocene Geological epoch from about 2 million years B.P. to about 10,000 years B.P.

Pliocene Geological epoch from 5 million years B.P. to 2 million years B.P.

Podsolize To form soil through leaching in upper layers and accumulation of matter in lower layers with specific horizons.

Point-bar Sand or gravel deposit on the inner curve of a meander (qv).

Precambrian Geological era from about 4600 million years B.P. to about 600 million years B.P.

Pulpwood Wood used for making paper.

Puna High Andean grasslands.

Quaternary Present geological age; began about 2 million years B.P.

Rain forest Perhumid forest in either tropical or temperate latitudes.

Refugium Region where biological communities have remained relatively undisturbed over long periods. Plural: refugia.

Resguardo Lands communally owned by indigenous peoples through legal title.

Riparian Frequenting, growing on, or living on the banks of streams or rivers.

Roundwood Wood in its natural state as felled or otherwise harvested.

Savanna Tropical or subtropical tall-grass plain with widely spaced trees.

Seringueiro Migrant labourer.

Silviculture Cultivation and management of forests and woodlands.

Soil profile Vertical section of the soil from surface to underlying unweathered material.

Stadial Refers to a stage.

Storey Layer or stratum of a forest.

Sustainable Capable of harvesting or using a resource so it is not permanently damaged or destroyed.

Sustainability Noun from sustainable.

Taxon Any of the groups into which an order is divided; contains one or more related genera. Plural: Taxa.

Taxonomic Relating to the principles of scientific classification.

Tectonic plate Plate involved in the deformation or movement of rock in the earth's crust.

Tepui Table mountain.

Terra firme Dry, unflooded land.

Tertiary Geological period from about 65 million years B.P. to about 2 million years B.P.

Topography The configuration of land, including relief and the positions of natural and man-made objects.

Trade winds Winds blowing from subtropical high pressure to the equatorial zone of low pressure.

Transpire To give off water vapour (refers to plants).

Trophic Relates to nutrition.

Understorey A layer of vegetation beneath the canopy of a forest.

Ungulate A hoofed mammal.

Várzea Forest on sedimentary soil; subject to annual flooding by white water.

Vascular Refers to channels carrying fluids (in plants).

Volant Flying or capable of flying.

Watershed Line separating two river basins.

Xerophytic Adapted to live and grow with limited water.

Zonation Distribution of organisms in biogeographical zones.

INDEX OF SPECIES: FAUNA

INDEX

INDEX OF SPECIES: FLORA

INDEX

GENERAL INDEX

INDEX